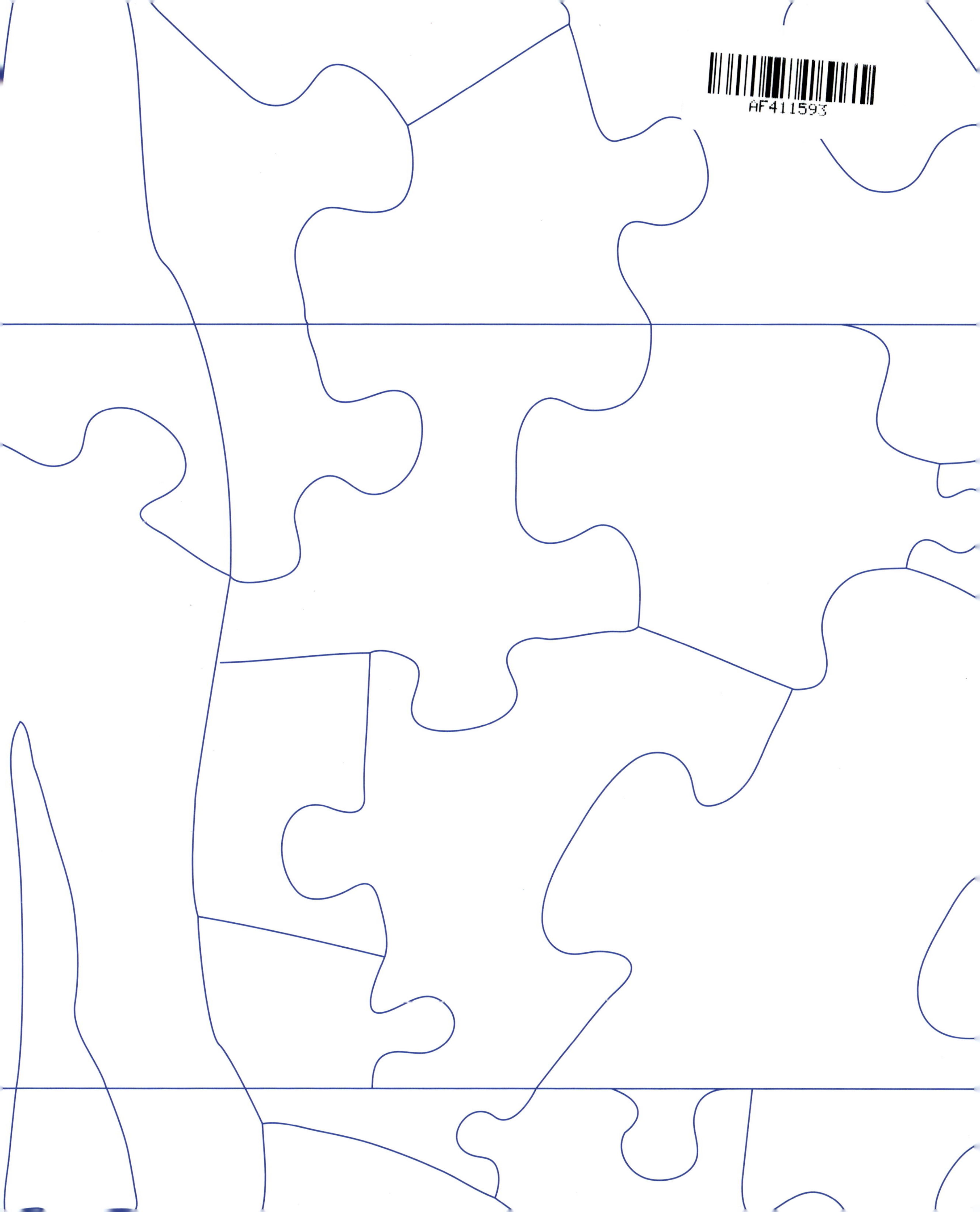
AF411593

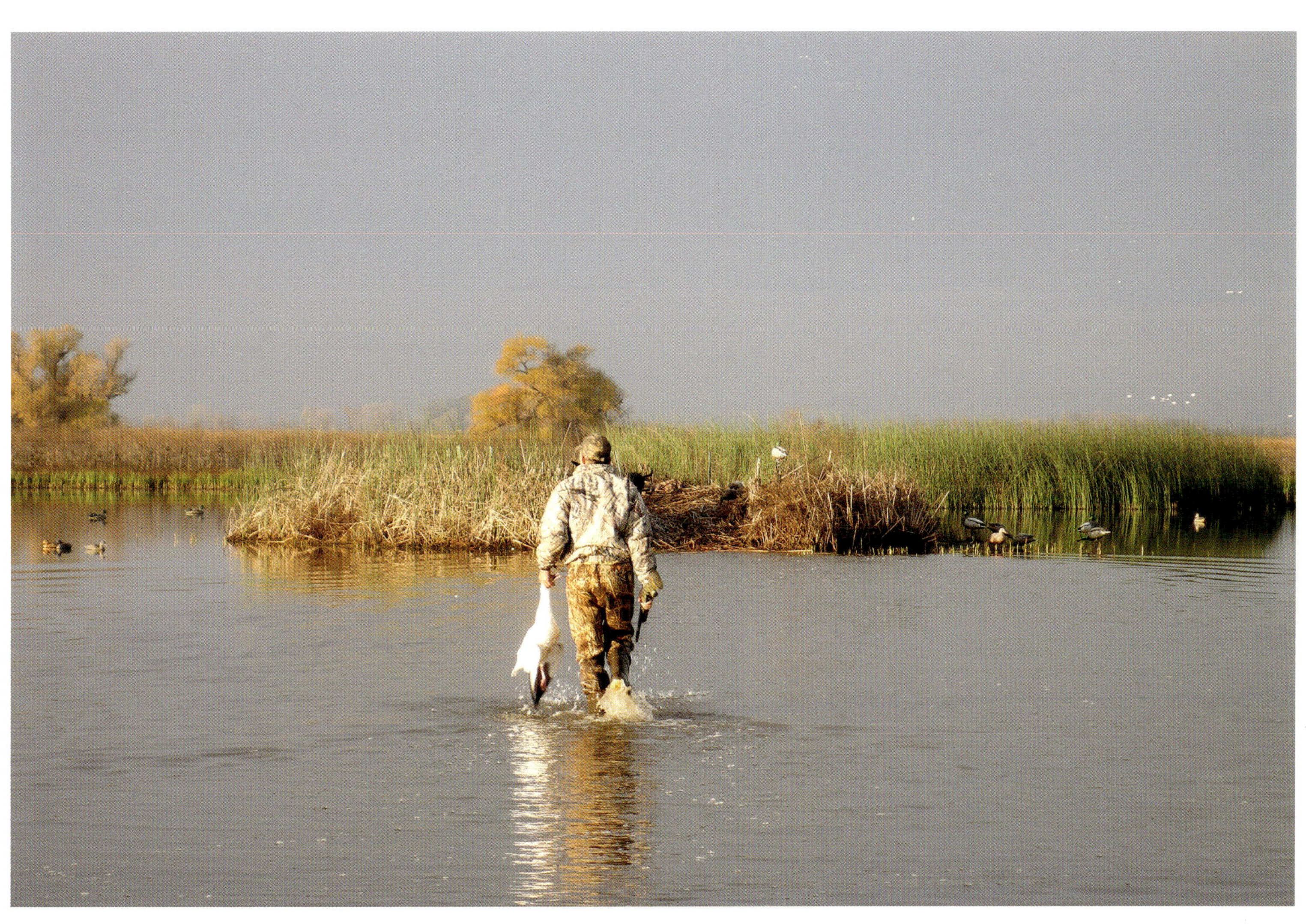

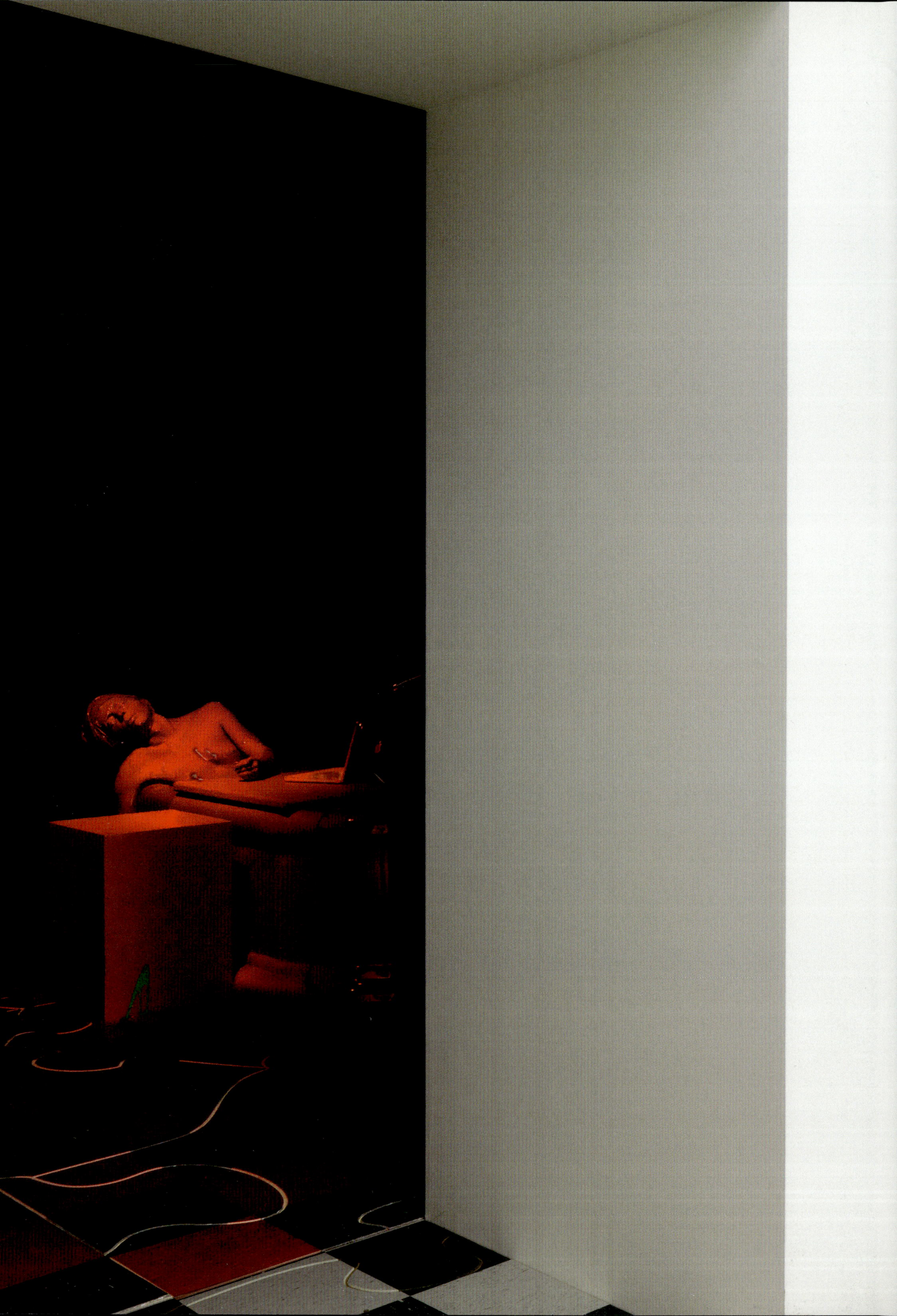

RICHARD JACKSON
Ain't Painting a Pain

DENNIS SZAKACS

With essays by
**Michael Darling, Jeffrey Weiss,
John C. Welchman,** and
Dennis Szakacs

With contributions by
**Hans Ulrich Obrist,
Philippe Van Cauteren,** and
Fatima Manalili

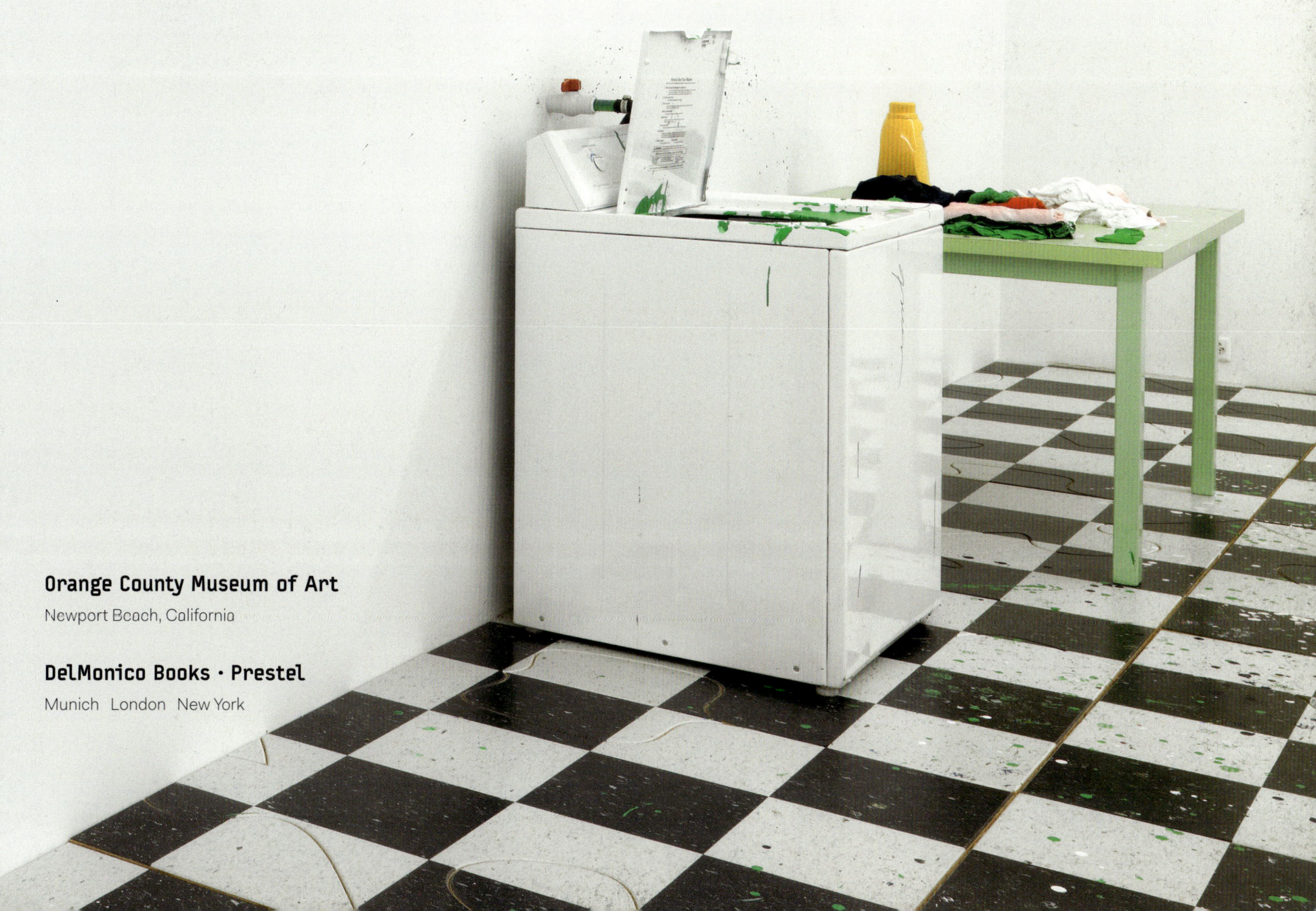

Orange County Museum of Art
Newport Beach, California

DelMonico Books · Prestel
Munich London New York

This catalog was published in conjunction with the exhibition **Richard Jackson: Ain't Painting a Pain**, organized and presented by the Orange County Museum of Art, Newport Beach, California.

Exhibition Itinerary
Orange County Museum of Art
February 17–May 5, 2013

Museum Villa Stuck, Munich
July 25–October 13, 2013

S.M.A.K. Municipal Museum of Contemporary Art, Ghent
February 28–June 29, 2014

Richard Jackson: Ain't Painting a Pain is made possible by The Andy Warhol Foundation for the Visual Arts, Jean and Tim Weiss, Rennie Collection, Vancouver, and Hauser & Wirth.

The catalog is underwritten by Lenore and Bernard Greenberg.

Additional support is provided by David Kordansky Gallery.

Publications Manager: Stephanie Emerson
Copyeditor: Karen Jacobson
Designer: Beverly Joel, pulp, ink.
Color separations: Echelon Color, Venice, California
Printer: Ninodruck GmbH, Neustadt, Germany

Front cover: *The Laundry Room (Death of Marat)*, 2009. Installation view, Hauser & Wirth, Zurich, 2009
Endpapers: Richard Jackson, drawing for *The Blue Room* (detail), 2011
Frontispiece: Richard Jackson duck hunting at Refuge Gun Club, Colusa County, CA, December 14, 2006; pp. 2–3: Richard Jackson, *The Laundry Room* (detail), 2009. Installation view, Hauser & Wirth, Zurich, 2009; pg. 304: Richard Jackson deer hunting at Jackson Ranch, Colusa County, CA, August 2006
Back cover: *Bob's Pictures* (detail), 2006–10

© 2013 Orange County Museum of Art, Newport Beach, and Prestel Verlag.

Library of Congress Cataloging-in-Publication Data

Richard Jackson : ain't painting a pain / curated by Dennis Szakacs ; essays by Michael Darling, Jeffrey Weiss, John C. Welchman, and Dennis Szakacs ; with contributions by Fatima Manalili and Hans Ulrich Obrist.
   pages cm
This catalog was published in conjunction with the exhibition *Richard Jackson: Ain't Painting a Pain*, organized and presented by the Orange County Museum of Art, Newport Beach, California, February 17–May 5, 2013.
   Includes bibliographical references.
   ISBN 978-3-7913-5226-8
1. Jackson, Richard, 1939---Exhibitions. I. Szakacs, Dennis, 1962- II. Jackson, Richard, 1939- Works. Selections. 2013. III. Orange County Museum of Art (Calif.)
N6537.J313A4 2013
709.2--dc23

2012020047

Published by
Orange County Museum of Art
850 San Clemente Drive
Newport Beach, CA 92660
USA
Tel +1 949-759-1122
Fax +1 949-759-5623
www.ocma.net

In association with DelMonico Books, an imprint of Prestel
Prestel is a member of Verlagsgruppe Random House GmbH

Prestel Verlag
Neumarkter Strasse 28
81673 Munich
Germany
Tel 49 89 4136 0
Fax 49 89 4136 2335
prestel.de

Prestel Publishing Ltd.
4 Bloomsbury Place
London WC1A 2QA
United Kingdom
Tel 44 20 7323 5004
Fax 44 20 7636 8004

Prestel Publishing
900 Broadway, Suite 603
New York, NY 10003
Tel 212 995 2720
Fax 212 995 2733
sales@prestel-usa.com
prestel.com

ISBN: 978-3-7913-5226-8

CONTENTS

FOREWORD AND ACKNOWLEDGMENTS

Richard Jackson: Ain't Painting a Pain is devoted to an American maverick who has redefined and expanded painting over a forty-year period. The exhibition is conceived as a series of eleven room-scale installations from 1970 to 2013, most never before shown in the United States, accompanied by over 150 of Jackson's related preparatory drawings, works on paper, and models—significant works in their own right that provide essential insights into his methodology and process. Foremost among these is *100 Drawings* (1978), each a different proposal for a painting project, presented now for the first time since its creation. To especially mark the occasion of this retrospective, Jackson has produced a major new outdoor piece, *Bad Dog* (2013), a twenty-eight-foot-high puppy establishing his territory on the side of the museum.

During the late 1960s and early 1970s Jackson exhibited at the legendary Eugenia Butler Gallery in Los Angeles, together with artists such as Bas Jan Ader, John Baldessari, Edward Kienholz, William Leavitt, Allan Ruppersberg, and Ger van Elk. Jackson's work was entirely site-specific—each piece was created within a museum or gallery space and destroyed when deinstalled. *Ain't Painting a Pain* includes recreations from the three main series that he developed over the first twenty years of his career: large-scale "wall paintings;" room-size "painted environments;" and monumental "stacked paintings." More than simply innovative formal experiments, these works helped set the tone for much of the most important art to emerge from Los Angeles over the next three decades, where unfettered ambition and irreverence toward cultural orthodoxies combined to unleash brash new forms under the Southern California sun. By the early 1990s, Jackson began to build all manner of elaborate "painting machines," which he activates prior to an exhibition opening, and which viewers experience as evidence of a performance rather than as a performance itself. These mechanized works employ pumps, motors, fans, propellers, air compressors, and spray hoses to deploy paint in increasingly inventive and outlandish ways. *Ain't Painting a Pain* includes seven of these room-scale works, six of them Jacksonian reinterpretations of cannonical works by Jacques-Louis David, Edgar Degas, Marcel Duchamp, Jasper Johns, Pablo Picasso, and Georges Seurat. In foregrounding this particular series from the second half of his career, the retrospective seeks to establish the framework for Jackson's ongoing struggle with painting's past and future.

For much of the 1990s through the present, Jackson was exhibited far more frequently in Europe than in the United States. His relationship to Bruce Nauman and Paul McCarthy, who were both embraced there long before achieving renown here, helped introduce Jackson's work to curators more open to its exuberance and iconoclasism. Jackson's rethinking of the forms and structures of painting also found a far warmer reception in Europe, which arguably has a deeper tradition of artists who up-end its conventions while still embracing the activity (Alberto Burri, Lucio Fontana, Yves Klein, Niki de Saint Phalle, Daniel Spoerri, and Günther Uecker among many others). While teaching at UCLA in the early 1990s, Jackson was also an influential mentor to Jason Rhoades and a new generation of artists who emerged from Los Angeles.

In the United States, Jackson is the heir to Jasper Johns, Jackson Pollock, and Robert Rauschenberg. Their breakthroughs, however, took successive generations of American artists away from the further expansion of painting and toward the new genres that their work anticipated, which left Jackson outside of the prevailing narratives of post-1960s American art. We are delighted to offer this reassessment, which continues our longstanding commitment to championing essential yet under-recognized artists.

Firstly, and most importantly, thanks to Richard Jackson, whose humility and humor make his work all the more bold, and who gave me extraordinary amounts of time and freedom to interpret a career that is one of the most radical in American art. His example of quiet perseverance is one that other artists, and all museums, would do well to follow more frequently, and has inspired me every day during the four years that we have worked on this project together. Alberta Mayo, Jackson's longtime partner, helped us locate and secure important archival material, carefully and patiently assisted with numerous fact-checking and proofing duties, and served as our final authority on all things Jackson. This exhibition would not have been possible without their trust and affection.

Guided by an exemplary board of trustees, OCMA is fortunate to have the freedom, flexibility, and funding to pursue an exhibition program that takes risks and is acknowledged internationally for its innovation, independent spirit, and original scholarship in modern and contemporary art. Our major donors and supporters value these qualities and provide the resources that enable us to dream, experiment, and act. Many thanks to the Rennie Collection, Vancouver, for their substantial commitment to Richard Jackson, and for providing the resources to construct the *5050 Stacked Paintings*, an ambitious installation that Jackson conceived in 1980, and that is presented for the first time in this exhibition. The initial encouragement and enthusiasm of Bob Rennie and Carey Fouks helped build momentum for this retrospective, as did the assistance provided by Wendy Chang, director of the Rennie Collection.

Hauser & Wirth has served as Richard Jackson's primary gallery since 1998, and their devotion to his work was evident in every phase of this project. We are especially grateful for their outstanding support, technical assistance, help in locating important early works in European collections, photography, and providing the production costs for the extraordinary *Bad Dog*. Iwan Wirth, Marc Payot, Florian Berktold, and Karin Seinsoth, have each extended themselves in myriad ways to help realize this exhibition. Special thanks to the Andy Warhol Foundation for the Visual Arts, especially President Joel Wachs, former Program Director Pamela Clapp, and Program Director Rachel Bers for their substantial investment in this exhibition and in our exhibition program over the years. Trustee Tim Weiss and his wife Jean have been among the most generous donors to the museum and their ongoing commitment to artistic excellence gives us the confidence to pursue projects that only the brave dare attempt. Lenore and Bernard Greenberg also provided early and essential support, specifically for the exceptional exhibition catalogue you now hold in your hands, the first scholarly publication ever devoted to Jackson's career. We also thank David Kordansky Gallery and Galerie Georges-Philippe & Nathalie Vallois for their support of Jackson's work and of this project.

We are extremely pleased that the exhibition will travel to Europe and thank in particular our colleagues Michael Buhrs, Director, Museum Villa Stuck, Munich, and Philippe Van Cauteren, Artistic Director, and Philippe Vandenweghe, Managing Director, S.M.A.K. Municipal Museum of Contemporary Art, Ghent. Their participation and partnership is a major factor in the exhibition's resounding success.

The generosity of numerous lenders made this show possible, including the Corcoran Gallery of Art, Washington, D.C.; Beth Rudin DeWoody; Friedrich Christian Flick Collection, Hamburger Bahnhof; Galerie Georges-Philippe & Nathalie Vallois; Galerie Lelong Zurich; Elizabeth A. Greenberg; Lenore and Bernard Greenberg; Barbara Haskell; Hauser & Wirth; Hauser & Wirth Collection, Switzerland; Moira and Fred Kamgar; Jeff Kerns Collection; Nancy Reddin Kienholz; David Kordansky Gallery; Los Angeles County Museum of Art; The Menil Collection, Houston; Alison Terbell Nikitopoulos and Dimitris E. Nikitopoulos; Rennie Collection, Vancouver; Rubell Family Collection, Miami; Robert and Susy Rufli, Zurich; Robert and Shaké Sarkis; Manny and Jackie Silverman; Martin Seol Family Foundation; Kathryn Wortz; and private collectors who wish to remain anonymous.

Richard Jackson: Ain't Painting a Pain will be the definitive publication on the artist's work for years to come, due in large part to the contributions of a stellar group of essayists, who for the first time have located Jackson's work within broader art historical and theoretical concerns. John C. Welchman, Jeffery Weiss, and Michael Darling each embraced this mission with great enthusiasm, intelligence, and insight, as readers of their work will already know. Hans Ulrich Obrist's in-depth interview with Jackson reveals much new information about the artist's interests. Fatima Manalili led a group of collaborators, including David Mather, Andrew Berardini, and Alberta Mayo to create the extensive chronology in this volume, an indispensable account of Jackson's history.

The catalogue owes its existence to a talented team led with great skill by Publications Manager Stephanie Emerson. Editor Karen Jacobson offered many valuable insights and greatly enhanced the text. Beverly Joel's brilliant design is the perfect complement to Jackson's work. Tony Manzella, Echelon Color, Venice, and Klaus Prokop, Ninodruck, also provided important contributions to the book's beautiful color and printing. In addition, we thank proofreader Dianne Woo and OCMA intern Sarah Waldorf, who ably assisted on the bibliography. We thank the many lenders and photographers for supplying images and permission to reproduce in this volume, in particular Chris Bliss, who so beautifully photographed the series *100 Drawings* as well as other works; Corinne Isabelle Rinaldis at Hauser & Wirth; and Rosamund Felsen. Our publishing partner, Mary DelMonico at DelMonico Books/Prestel, has ensured that Jackson's publication will reach the broader audience it deserves.

The entire OCMA staff has reached new levels of accomplishment with this exhibition. After this, it's clear that we can do anything. I'm especially indebted to Deputy Director Glenn Peters for overseeing all financial, legal, and contractual requirements, and who took on increased organizational responsibilities so I could focus on this project, one that has given me great personal and professional satisfaction. Curatorial Associate Fatima Manalili has risen to the occasion in every way imaginable and become an essential member of our curatorial team. Exhibitions and Collections Manager Anna-Marie Sanchez, and Director of Operations Albert Lopez have expertly produced the largest and most complex exhibition and tour ever organized by this museum, each finding new and ingenious ways of realizing our ambitions by overcoming the persistent constraints of time and resources. Director of Marketing and Communications Kirsten Schmidt has worked tirelessly to promote the exhibition, both locally and internationally, and has ensured that Jackson's art will be seen and experienced by as many people as possible. Our Education Department, led by Lisa Silagyi, has developed innovative ways to introduce Jackson's work to the public, and deepen and expand involvement with his art. Associate Development Director Donna Hosterman has ably and cheerfully managed fundraising duties and special events related to the exhibition's completion.

Given Jackson's accomplishments and his increasing relevance to younger artists, a retrospective of his work is long overdue and essential to the ongoing recovery of art history in Los Angeles, as well as to the larger re-evaluation of post-1960s American art. Richard Jackson may well be the "hardest working man in the art world," and if the results of our labor, in the service of his art, contribute to greater appreciation and understanding of his singular vision, then we will have done something of merit.

Dennis Szakacs
Director
Orange County Museum of Art

I am from a country that has had a painting tradition since the first half of the fifteenth century, a country that was home to Vincent van Gogh for a couple of years, and where Jacques-Louis David's *Marat assassiné* has been permanently housed in the Royal Museum of Fine Arts (in Brussels) since 1893. I am from a country where, in 1994, Jason Rhoades created his marvellous work entitled *PIG (Piece in Ghent)*, a complex installation that makes direct reference to *Adoration of the Mystic Lamb* (1432) by the van Eyck brothers, and where, in the seventies, an artist proposed blowing up the Royal Museum of Fine Arts in Antwerp in the name of art. So this country's mental-cultural geography includes a number of elements that cannot leave you indifferent: the history of a genre (Hans Memling, Peter Paul Rubens, James Ensor, René Magritte, Luc Tuymans etc.), the presence of the work by Jacques-Louis David, and the link with your friend and pupil Jason Rhoades. You are from a country where the myth of Hollywood is a reality, where endless landscapes dictate a tendency and appetite for monumentality to its artists, and where art history is shaped by the grand gesture. Not the intimate smallness of Jean Fautrier, but by the explosive directness of James Rosenquist. It is probably a country that always approaches history like current events—or perhaps the reverse—and which acts on the basis of a faith in the possibility of repeatedly reinventing everything again. And it is this that you do over and over, but from a critical distance, remote from the logic and mechanisms of the art business, acting within the defining perimeter and laws of your studio and personal experiences. I think I read somewhere that, in your view, today's artists too often start out from a similar education and experiences when creating their oeuvre. May I thus presume that you are saying that artists are defined more by elements external to their work? In your case the studio is a refuge, a safe haven and a control room where your fascination with painting and your playful admiration for a number of masters and/or their work (Marcel Duchamp, Georges Seurat, Pablo Picasso, Barnett Newman, to name just a few) leads to an absurdist and intelligent iconoclasm fuelled by your own life story. How else would you have arrived at a work in which Edgar Degas's *petite danseuse* is subjected to a remake? Images interest you when they form a problem so the process only becomes interesting when it is unpredictable. A small aesthetic temptation is enough to make short work of it. As an artist, unlike many others, you soon dropped successful tried and tested artistic formulas. You see it as the artist's responsibility to shift the boundary, both mentally and spatially, on the basis of an analysis of a medium and an artistic practice. Each work, and the time-consuming business of creating it, reminds me of the steps of a scientific element, as if it were an experiment, a planned and calculated moment limited in time and space. With shrewdness and a tendency to irony you have appropriated several concepts that resided in the idiom of painting in the second half of the twentieth century: abstraction, gesturality, chance, the destructive gesture. At the same time, on the basis of your contacts with artists in the sixties and seventies, you also absorbed the no-nonsense logic of minimal and conceptual art. The result is not conceptual painting, but rather a radical and consistent

Ain't Painting a Pain, 2009. Neon, MDO
base, metal box. Edition 1 of 5. 55 ⅛ × 35 ⅜ ×
7 ⅛ in. (1140 × 89.8 × 18.1 cm). Rennie
Collection, Vancouver

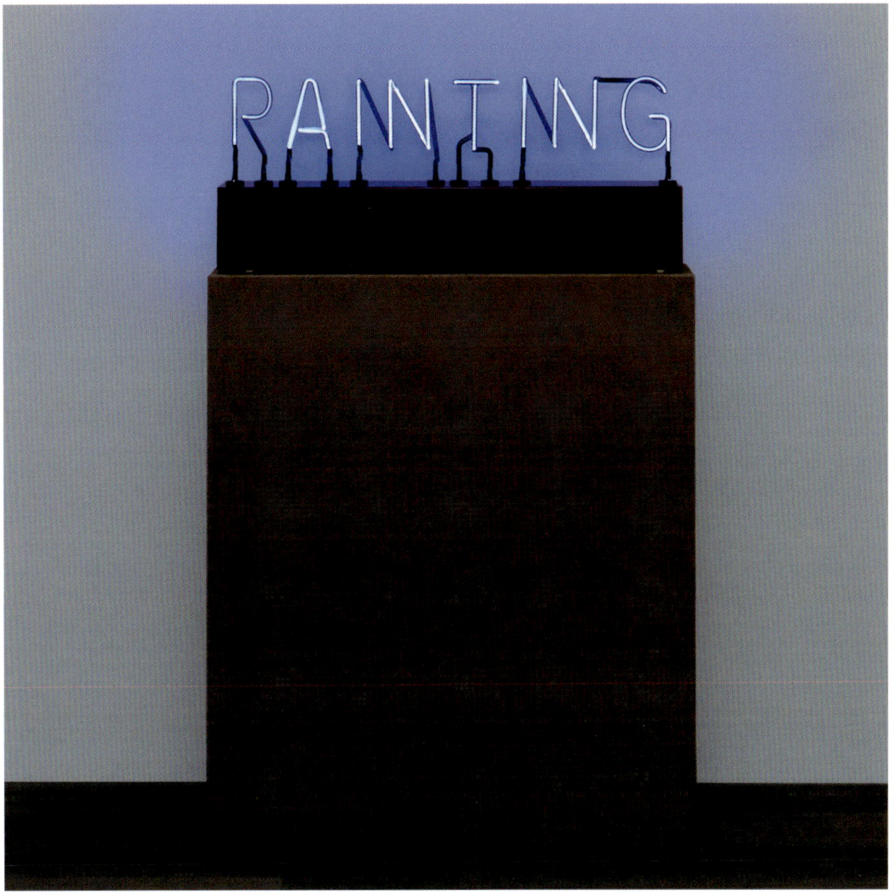

thinking through and methodical execution of a number of principles. The artwork's
importance as an object is here secondary to the viewer's experience of it and the
slow process of its production by the artist. The scale of your works and their
possibly unintended spectacular nature may mean your work might be described
as a form of elitist populism. Its immediate comprehensibility and accessibility give
it a broad appeal, while the remaking of several works from the art history canon
give it a hermetic aspect with a critical, ironic, and sometimes scabrous undertone.
One way or another, I am reminded of the 1928 "Manifesto Antropófago" by the
Brazilian poet Oswald de Andrade. You do not cannibalize any other culture, but you
do cannibalize the myth of the artist genius, the art history of the twentieth century,
and the machismo of the art world, using them to make a playful and critical
statement that combines the gesturality of Pollock, the indifference of Duchamp
and the mechanics of Jean Tinguely into a form of "conceptual baroque" in which
monumentality is measured on the scale of the artist and not on that of art history.

Philippe Van Cauteren

Artistic Director
S.M.A.K. Municipal Museum of Contemporary Art
Blainville, September 25, 2012

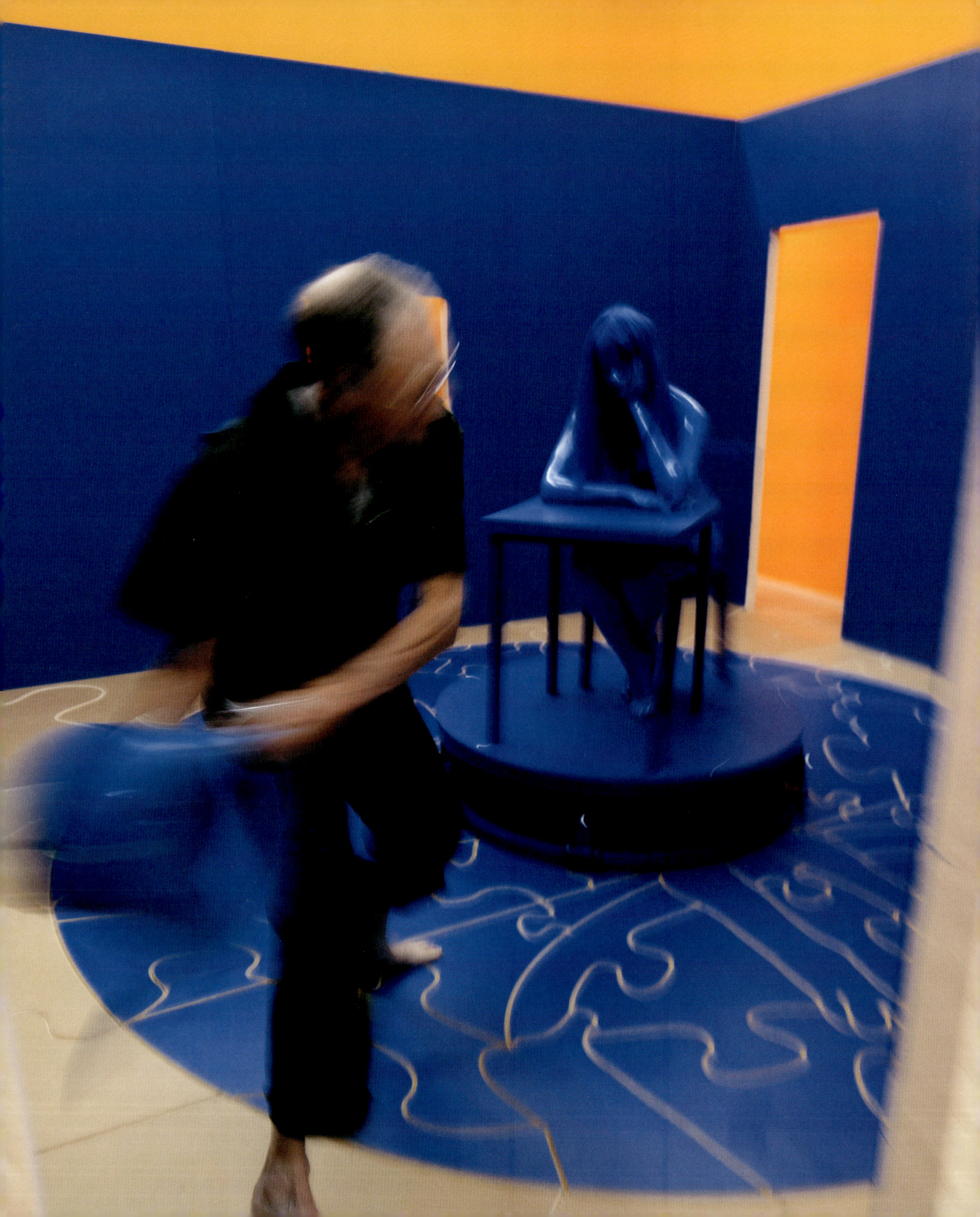

AIN'T PAINTING A PAIN

DENNIS SZAKACS

Since the early 1970s Richard Jackson has done more than any other contemporary figure to expand the possibilities of painting. Beginning with his large-scale, site-specific wall paintings and room-size painted environments, and continuing with his monumental stacked canvases and more recent anthropomorphic painting "machines," Jackson's wildly inventive, exuberant, and irreverent take on "action" painting has dramatically extended its performative dimensions, merged it with sculpture, and repositioned it as an art of everyday experience rather than one of heroic myth.

Born in Sacramento, California, in 1939, Jackson studied art and engineering at Sacramento State College. A restless personality with a boundless capacity for hard work and the physical gifts of an athlete, he spent his youth in the Coast Guard, mined for gold in the Sierra Nevada, cut Christmas trees in Northern California, and spent weeks at a time in the wilderness on deer- and duck-hunting trips, a rugged activity that he still relishes at age seventy-three. Jackson came to art later than most of his contemporaries, and with a background unusual for an artist. He moved to Los Angeles in 1968 and has lived there ever since.

Early in his career Jackson became friends with Edward Kienholz, a fellow hunter whose blunt, uncompromising, and democratic approach to art was a significant influence on the younger artist. Like Kienholz, Jackson knew how to make and fix things, and his ability to work with wood, metal, motors, and

Richard Jackson installing *The Blue Room*. 2011. Fiberglass, steel, wood, Formica, urethane paint, acrylic paint, canvas, wig, motor, rubber, and control panel. 175 × 175 × 108 in. (444.5 × 444.5 × 274.3 cm). Rubell Family Collection, Miami

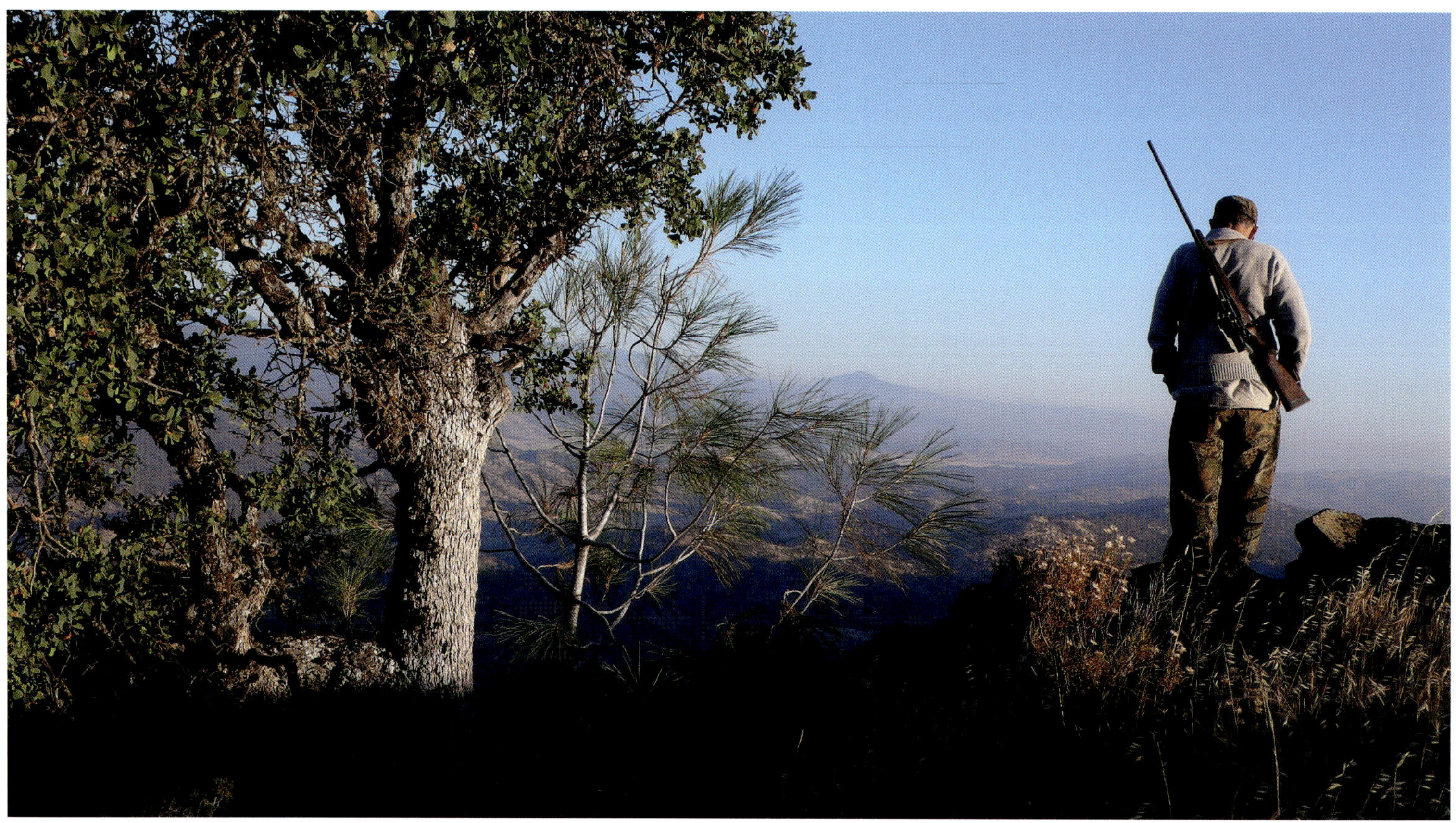

pumps has always been at the very center of his art. In Kienholz's posthumous retrospective exhibition catalog, edited by Walter Hopps for the Whitney Museum of American Art in 1996, Jackson writes: "First I liked Ed's art, but then I liked Ed, he was my hunting partner. I found an artist who likes to hunt, finally. Not easy in a politically correct time and atmosphere to find an artist who likes to hunt or would admit that they like to hunt. Ed and I hunted together for years at his place in Idaho and my place in California. Hunting camp. One of the greatest places in the world."[1]

Years earlier Hopps had become Jackson's most important curatorial advocate, organizing his first museum survey (and his only one until the present exhibition), *Richard Jackson: Installations, 1970–1988*, at the Menil Collection in Houston. Beginning in 1968, Jackson launched a series of ambitious painting projects unprecedented in post-1960s American art, and the exhibition summarized twenty years of astonishing activity. At the time of the opening, Hopps stated, "Richard Jackson is to conceptual painting what Bruce Nauman is to conceptual sculpture."[2] This was not hyperbole. The two artists had met in 1964, while Nauman was studying at the University of California, Davis, and Jackson was running the art gallery at California State University, Sacramento. They become friends and eventually lived together for five years in Hopps's

1. Richard Jackson, "A Few Words about Ed Kienholz," in *Kienholz: A Retrospective*, ed. Walter Hopps, exh. cat. (New York: Whitney Museum of American Art, 1996), 283.

2. Walter Hopps, quoted in Patricia C. Johnson, "The 'Object-Makers'/Art by Young Germans on Exhibit," *Houston Chronicle*, June 19, 1988.

house in Pasadena. Jackson introduced Nauman to deer hunting on his two-thousand-acre ranch in Colusa County, California, land that Jackson's family, descendants of Andrew Jackson, homesteaded in the 1800s and that Jackson still owns today (FIG. 1). The camaraderie of the Jackson clan during those trips made a lasting impression on Nauman, who recalls eating the heart and liver of a freshly killed deer and the vivid sight of deer carcasses hanging from trees.[3] Neither artist is particularly forthcoming about his influence on the other, yet during the 1960s and 1970s they shared an interest in the perceptual and psychological possibilities of mazes, corridors, and walls. During the 1980s and 1990s both began to motorize sculpture and employ animal motifs.

Jackson's early contact with Kienholz had an equally significant impact, and the uncontrolled interactions of paint and materials in Jackson's work may be linked to Kienholz's "broom paintings" from the 1950s, essentially wall reliefs made from bits of found wood and other objects. Kienholz would pour paint onto them and spread it over the surface with a broom. He explained that if he "could make something really ugly, it might help him understand beauty."[4] Jackson's inversion of the canvas in his wall paintings, using the front to apply paint onto the wall and exposing the back of the stretcher to the viewer, is related to Kienholz's *Art for Art's Sake* (1959; FIG. 2), in which "the viewer is confronted with the stretchers on the back of a painting that is so close to a large mirror as to make the front surface virtually unseeable."[5] Later, in the early 1990s, when Jackson's work turned figurative, Kienholz's use of a deer skull in *The Little Eagle Rock Incident* (1958) and a stuffed duck in *The U.S. Duck, or Home from the Summit* (1960) (FIG. 3) may have triggered Jackson's use of animal forms and hunting metaphors.

Painting has always been at the heart of Jackson's work, and at the outset of his career he was driven by a relentless desire to build on the

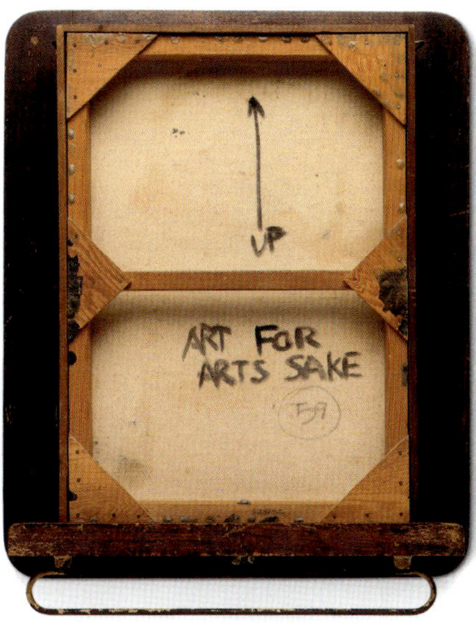
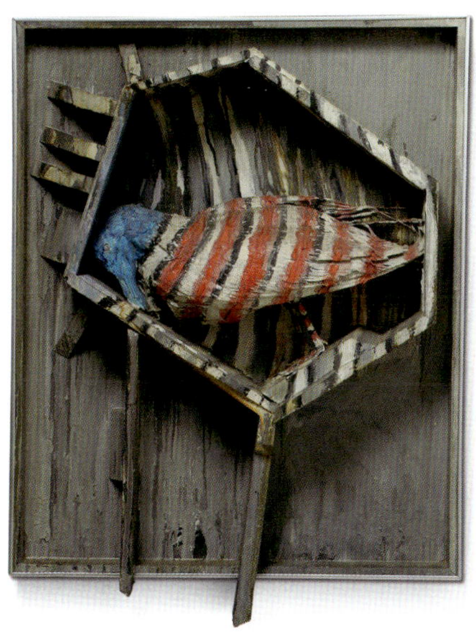

FIG. 2 (left)
Edward Kienholz, *Art for Art's Sake*, 1959. Oil and photomechanical reproductions on canvas, mirror, wood, and metal towel rack. 30 × 20 × 4 in. (76.2 × 50.8 × 10.2 cm). Collection of Ms. Lynn Susholtz

FIG. 3 (right)
Edward Kienholz, *The U.S. Duck, or Home from the Summit*, 1960. Construction, mixed media, assemblage, collage. 26 7/16 × 21 1/4 × 6 in. (67.1 × 54 × 15.2 cm). Los Angeles County Museum of Art, Michael and Dorothy Blankfort Bequest (AC1999.35.27)

3. Juliet Myers (assistant to Bruce Nauman), conversation with the author, May 18, 2011.

4. Edward Kienholz, in Rosetta Brooks, "Plates and Commentaries," in Hopps, *Kienholz*, 60.

5. Walter Hopps, "Plates and Commentaries," 77.

advances in the medium put forth by Jackson Pollock, Jasper Johns, and Robert Rauschenberg. Far more interested in the process of making his work than in how it eventually looked, Jackson devoted the first twenty years of his career exclusively to site-specific projects that were carefully planned in preparatory drawings and models, painstakingly executed by the artist, and then destroyed at the conclusion of each exhibition. The architectonics of his painting installations was a hallmark of the 1988 Menil exhibition, which presented his large-scale "wall paintings" created by sliding still-wet canvases across gallery walls to create abstract murals of impressive graphic power and formal variety (one measuring thirteen feet high by seventy-nine feet long); room-size "painted environments" (often mazes or other kinds of architectural interventions built with wood, canvas, and paint that viewers could enter and encounter); and "stacked paintings" (thousands of stretched canvases that were painted and stacked facedown to create monumental enclosures and sculptural works). Like Duchamp, who would come to be a major influence on him, Jackson believes

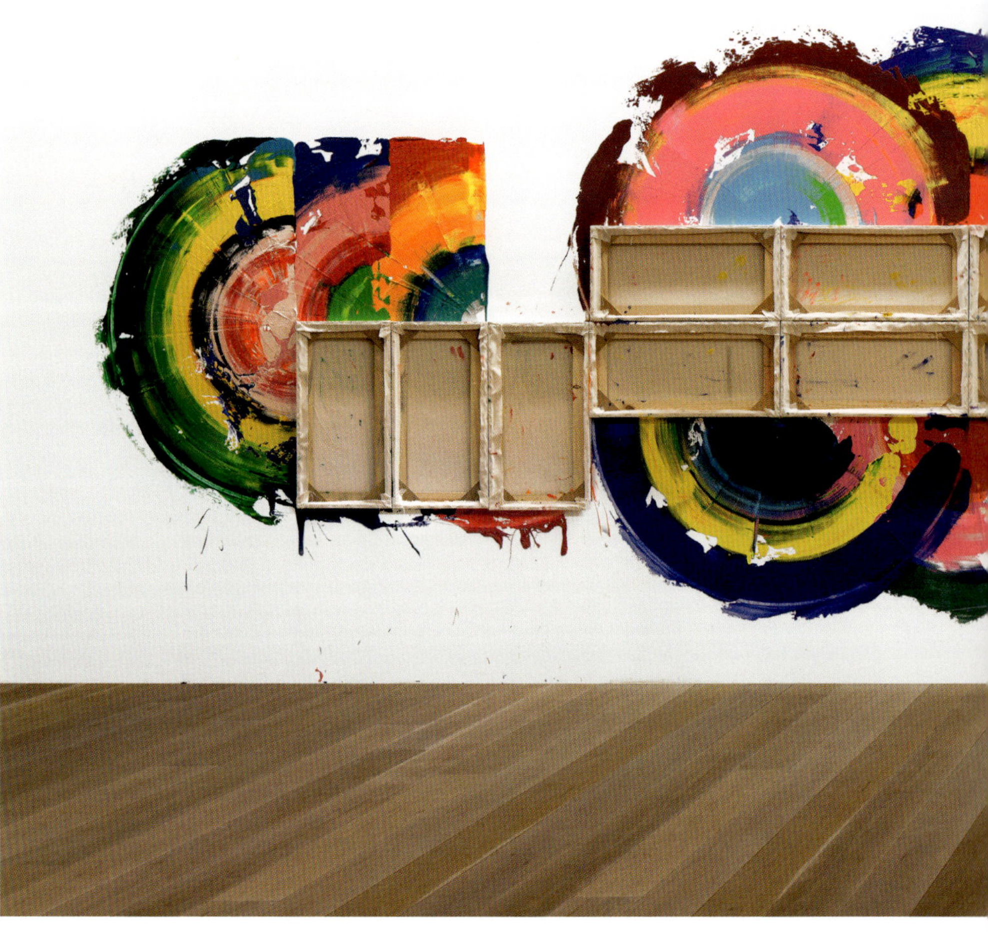

that the viewer completes the work of art, and he regards his installations less as objects than as experiences.

Much of Jackson's work of the 1970s and 1980s introduced a series of inventive inversions and concealments aimed directly at upending the technical and stylistic conventions of painting (FIG. 4). Canvas, paint, space, and even time were each reconfigured, often simultaneously in a single work. Stretched canvas was transformed from a surface to receive paint into a device for applying it, from a support for illusionistic space into sculpture, and from an object that is perceived whole into one that reveals itself only in parts. Paint was turned from a means of expression into a method of adhesion, and from a carefully applied substance into one that is indiscriminately poured, smeared, spattered, and thrown. Spatial and temporal dislocations abound. One painting was destroyed to create another. Backs of paintings became as important as fronts. Two or even four painted surfaces would interact and change as they were slid past, over, or under each other. Painted environments were perceived one way

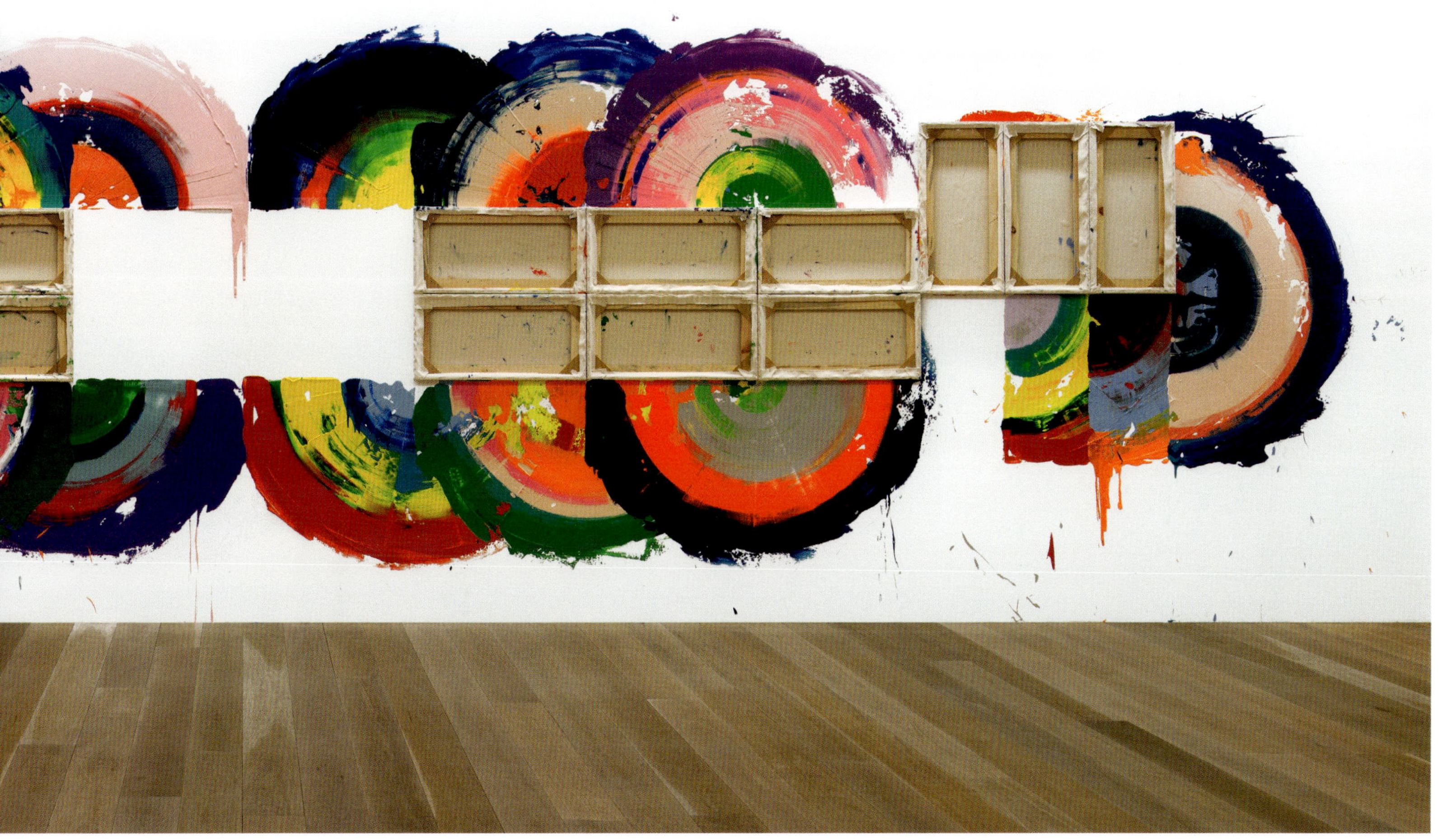

FIG. 4
Richard Jackson, *Rennie 101*, 2009–10.
Acrylic paint, wood, eighteen canvases.
120 × 396 in. (304.8 × 1005.8 cm).
Rennie Collection, Vancouver

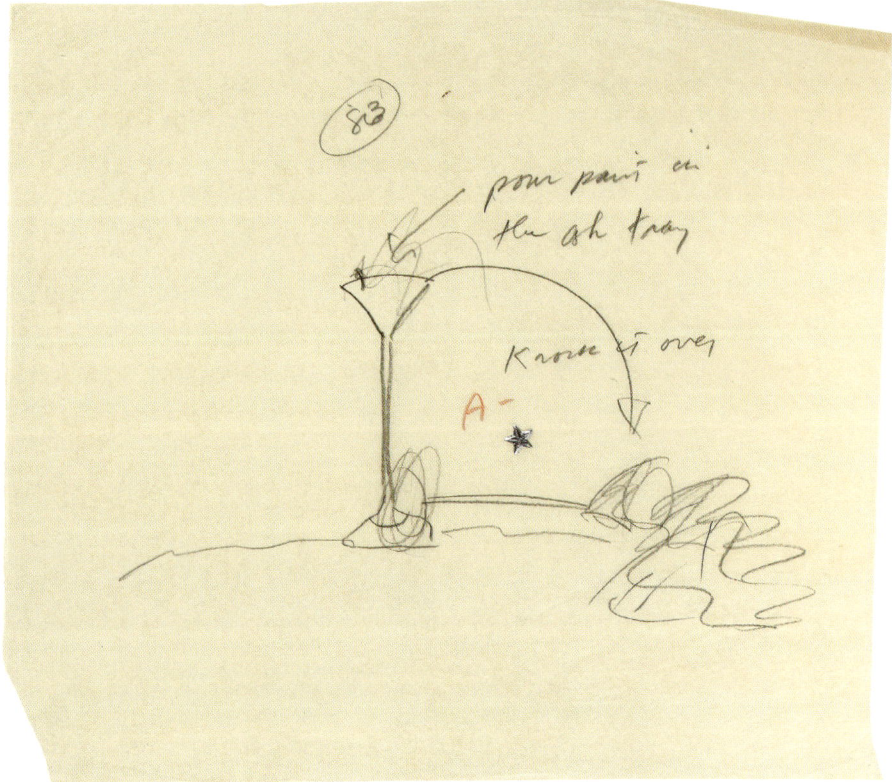

upon entering them and another upon exiting. Huge amounts of time and material were deployed for ephemeral constructions that ultimately live in viewers' minds.

Jackson's rethinking of the methods, spaces, and places for painting took him in a staggering number of directions, all conceived and presented with a combination of deadpan seriousness and irreverent wit. In 1978 Edward and Nancy Kienholz invited him to exhibit at their Faith and Charity in Hope Gallery in Hope, Idaho, and Jackson produced a series of one hundred drawings, each one a different proposal for a painting project (FIG. 5). The proposals, which are discussed in greater detail in Jeffrey Weiss's essay in this volume, include placing a bucket of paint on top of an open door that is then shut and filling a chest of drawers with paint. Each drawing included instructions on how to make the painting, written in the artist's hand, and was given a letter grade by Jackson. The more original the setup, the more absurd the action described in a drawing, the higher the grade. The project is similar to the movie stunts of Harold Lloyd (FIG. 6), which require the performer to carefully plan and choreograph a sequence of dangerous moves, a strategy that would become even more elaborate in Jackson's mechanized installations and clocks. As a sort of index to Jackson's working process, and an invaluable record of his protean output, the *100 Drawings* include proposals for works that he had already made and for works that he would realize years or even decades later, as well as ideas that were ultimately abandoned.

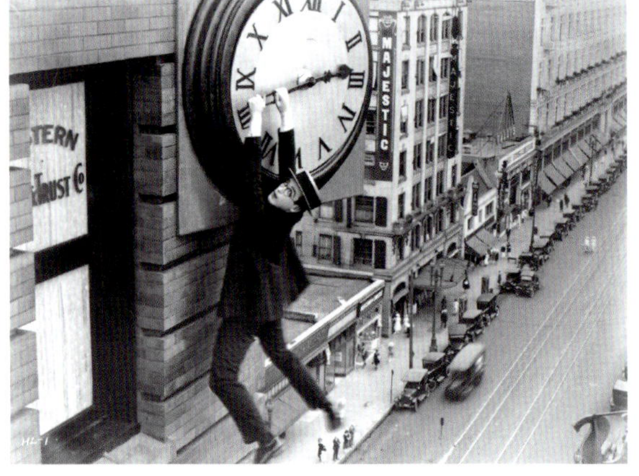

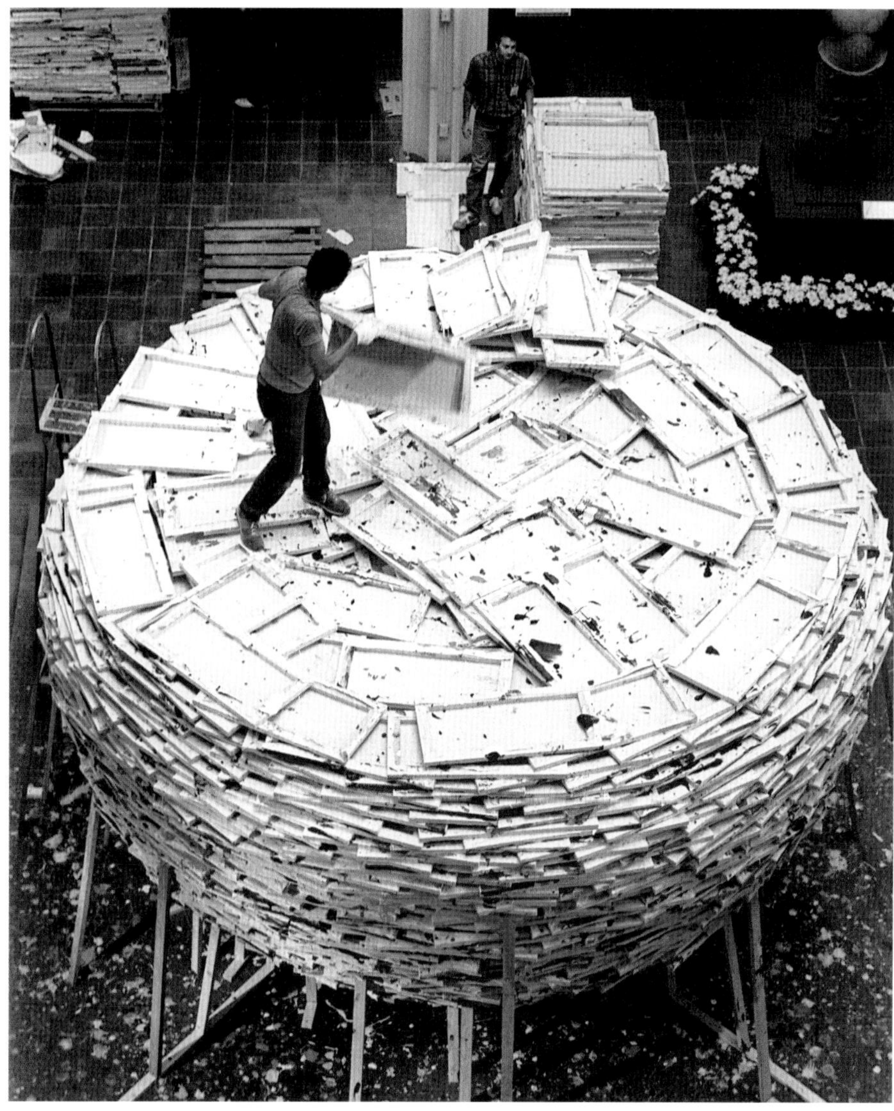

The opening of the Menil survey marked an important transitional point for Jackson. He was almost fifty years old, had participated in significant exhibitions organized by influential curators at major museums in the United States and Europe, and was shown by the most adventurous galleries in Los Angeles. Yet to earn a living, he toiled most days as a building contractor, an art handler, or a studio assistant for friends while making his art at night or on weekends. Jackson said then that he was "tired of looking at paintings,"[6] an odd statement from someone so obsessed with making them, yet understandable given his other interests and the herculean labor expended on his large-scale installations of the preceding two decades. In a remarkable series of photographs documenting his installation of *Big Ideas 2—3000 Pictures* in the atrium of the Ahmanson Building at the Los Angeles County Museum of Art in 1981,

6. Susan Chadwick, "For Richard Jackson,
the Point Is Painting," *Houston Post*, July
17, 1988.

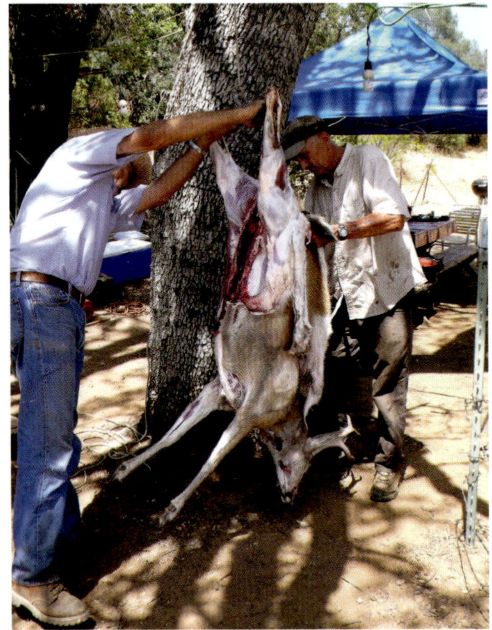

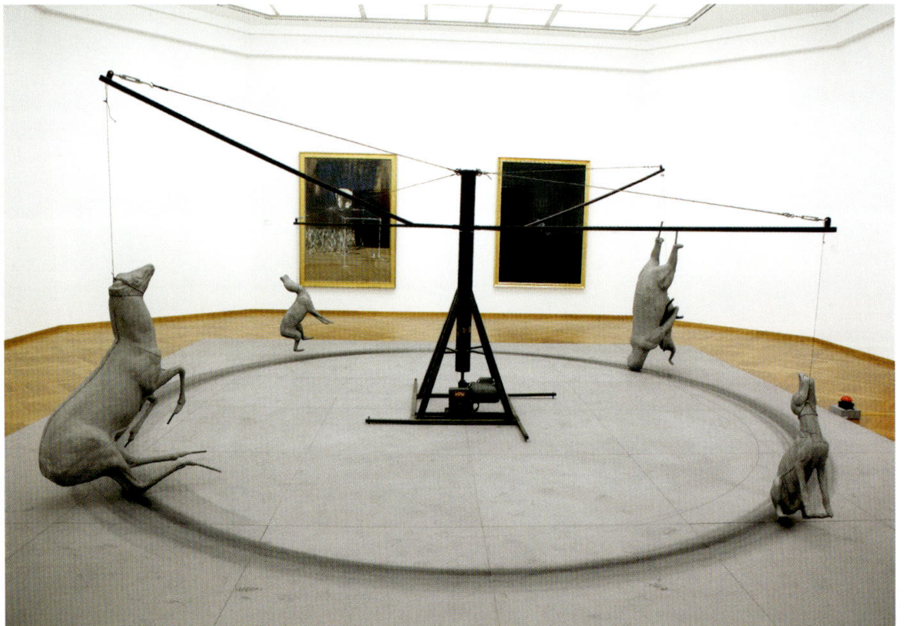

Jackson can be seen making each of the canvases in his studio and then assembling the work on-site, canvas by canvas, each one attached to the next only by the paint slathered between them, until the sixteen-foot-diameter sphere was completed (FIG. 7). "Scale is only important if accomplished by an individual," says Jackson. "If a company makes 100 canvases a day, no big deal, if an individual does 100 after working all day, it has a different scale."[7] The photographer Rolf Schroeter documented the construction of a wall painting and a stacked painting that Jackson made for a solo exhibition at Galerie Tschudi in Glarus, Switzerland, in 1989. The former required a large scaffold to execute and the dexterity and strength of a high-wire walker; a photograph of the latter shows Jackson perched precariously on a ladder extending his body to place a canvas on top of a tall stack.

The nature of work figures prominently in Jackson's thinking, yet he makes little distinction between artistic labor and any other kind, except to disparage lack of individual effort. "Now a lot of artists don't make anything themselves and the most useful tool in the studio is not the cordless drill, it's the cordless phone. They are on the phone all day begging for money or telling people what to do. That's not the way I choose to spend my time." More working-class hero—Robert De Niro in *The Deer Hunter*—than Marxist academic (FIGS. 8, 9), Jackson in many ways fits the archetype of the western individualist. "It's about independence," he says. "It's an American thing, you know, 'This whole son-of-a-bitch is mine and I don't need any help.' And you're not going to get any help, which is also very American! The United States can go to the moon but what can an individual do? I'm more interested in the kind of person who wants to go to the moon on their own."[8]

7. Jackson, quoted in Iwan Wirth, ed., *Richard Jackson: Deer Beer*, exh. cat. (Cologne: Oktagon, 1998), 91.

8. Richard Jackson, in Dennis Szakacs, "The Circus Is in Town" (interview), *Mousse*, no. 25 (September 2010): 44.

Ambition and self-sufficiency are essential to the Jacksonian definition of labor, which he uses as a way to assert personal freedom over societal control, a struggle that is also central to his work. Jackson's labors, however, are often repetitive, rote actions. His tedious construction of thousands of canvases for his stacked paintings is related to Walter De Maria's concept of "meaningless work," an oppositional strategy that advocated "work that does not make you money or accomplish a conventional purpose."[9] And Jackson's investment of thousands of hours in making and stacking paintings that are then unstacked and thrown away is analogous to De Maria's example of digging a hole and then covering it or moving wooden blocks from one box to another, back and forth. "Meaningless work is potentially the most abstract, concrete, individual, foolish, indeterminate, exactly determined, varied, important art-action-experience that one can undertake today," according to De Maria. "This concept is not a joke. Try some meaningless work in the privacy of your own room. In fact, to be fully understood, meaningless work should be done alone or else it becomes entertainment for others and the reaction or lack of reaction of the art lover to the meaningless work cannot honestly be felt."[10] Alberta Mayo, Jackson's longtime partner, made a T-shirt for him with a clock face that says, "the man who proved that time isn't money" (FIG. 10). This decoupling of time from the hierarchies of a capitalist system of labor was immortalized in Jackson's installation *1000 Clocks* (1987–92) (FIG. 11), a work that he began to mark his fiftieth birthday, in which an entire room was built to hold one thousand clocks, each

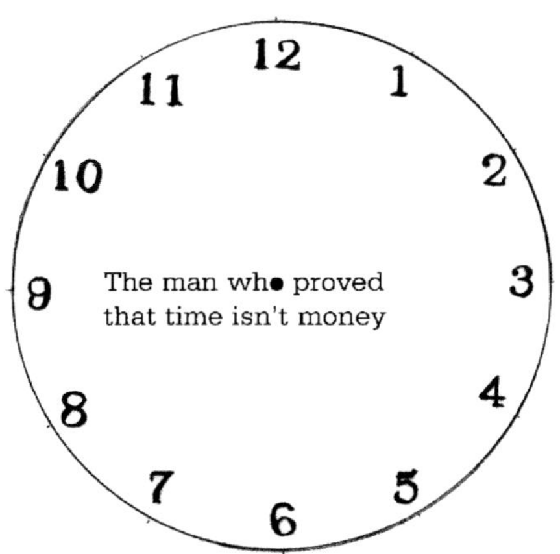

FIG. 10 (below)
Graphic design by Alberta Mayo, 2002

FIG. 11 (right)
Richard Jackson, *1000 Clocks* (detail), 1987–92. Steel aluminum, electronic parts, fluorescent lights, oil paint, plastic. 141 ¾ × 432 ¼ × 360 ¼ in. (360 × 1098 × 915 cm). Hauser & Wirth Collection, Switzerland. Installation view, Staatliche Kunsthalle Baden-Baden, Germany

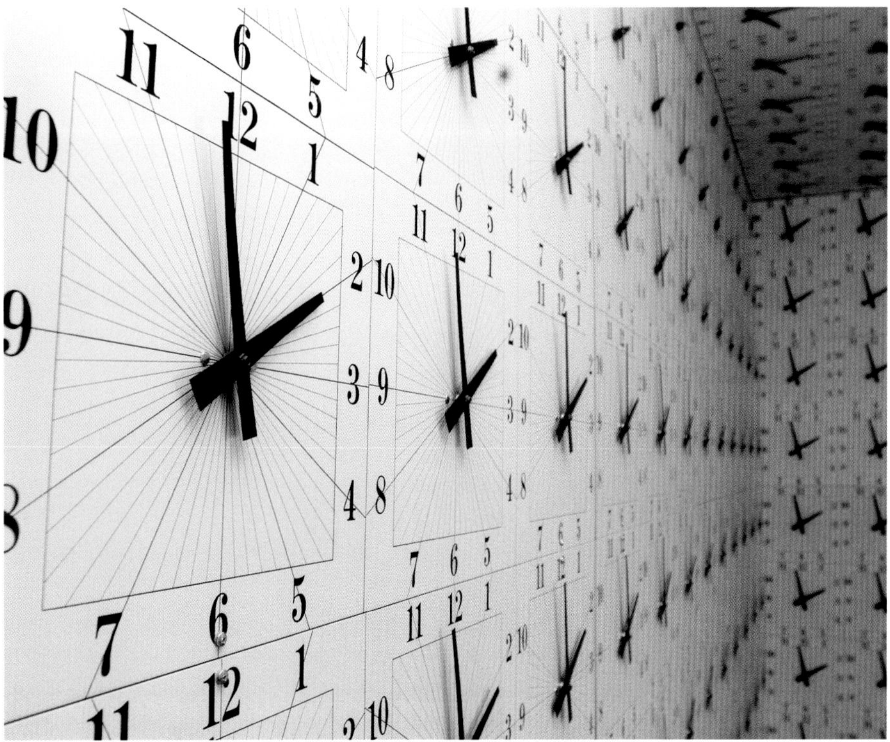

9. Walter De Maria, "Meaningless Work" (March 1960), in *An Anthology*, ed. La Monte Young (ca. 1962; reprint, Cologne: Heiner Friedrich, 1970).

10. Ibid.

handmade by the artist, arranged in rows on all four walls and across the entire ceiling, with each clock synchronized to the same time. The comparison to De Maria gains even more credence given Jackson's desire to construct and activate his works alone, away from the viewer, so that they are, in his words, "evidence of a performance" rather than performances.[11]

The Menil survey finally brought Jackson to the point at which he had perfected his means of production and exhausted his ability to push the concepts any further. He was "tired" of paintings. The success of the very experiments that created some of the most radical conceptual paintings in the history of American art was leading to their failure in his mind, and he needed to find a way out of his mazes, corridors, walls, and stacks. "With the wall painting, the more I did them, the more familiar I became with the materials, the nicer they came out. That's why I lost interest in them," he says. "When you take part in an activity or are involved in a process, something can go wrong, and that's when it gets interesting. It's not interesting if everything is going well. It's only interesting when problems are presented to you and then you have to creatively solve them."[12] He needed a new set of problems to work on, ones that would move him past the pure architectonics of canvas and paint.

After *1000 Clocks*, Jackson's next step in this new direction was an installation at the Santa Monica Museum of Art in 1992 titled *Big Confusing Ideas* (FIG. 12), in his words "a transitional piece using objects and painting together. The piece is confusing, or confused."[13] Jackson built a fifty-by-fifty-foot room, surrounded on four sides by a corridor made from steel bars. Visitors could enter the corridor and view the interior of the room, which was filled with an elaborate series of armatures containing twenty-two identical life-size male figures made from fiberglass, arms rigidly at their sides and legs together. All the figures were painted white with black stripes and motorized so that they spun around their central axis. With motors whirring, figures spinning at all angles, and myriad stripe patterns intersecting everywhere, viewers experienced a sense of entrapment and vertigo induced by the optical, spatial, and sonic effects of the installation. Susan Kandel, writing in the *Los Angeles Times*, said of the piece, "the power of this installation—and Jackson's work in general— is that it forces us to see that in 'real' life, the way out is far less clearly marked."[14]

Although *Big Confusing Ideas* may have been a metaphor for the prison of painting that Jackson was trying to escape at that time, it nevertheless provided some of the keys that he would later use to unlock the door. A startling break from the conceptual abstraction that had defined his career, it pointed the way to a conceptual realism (recalling his *Bedroom* of 1976–82) that came at painting from the opposite direction. Rather than pulling painting apart and inverting its structural components to expand its spatial and temporal possibilities, Jackson began to employ the figure to investigate the problems of picture making, moving from an essentially deconstructive approach to one that was more generative, that was about remaking rather than disassembling.

11. Jackson, in Szakacs, "Circus Is in Town," 44.

12. Ibid., 46.

13. Jackson, quoted in Wirth, *Deer Beer*, 114.

14. Susan Kandel, "Trapped behind Bars: Richard Jackson at the Santa Monica Museum of Art," *Los Angeles Times*, May 23, 1992.

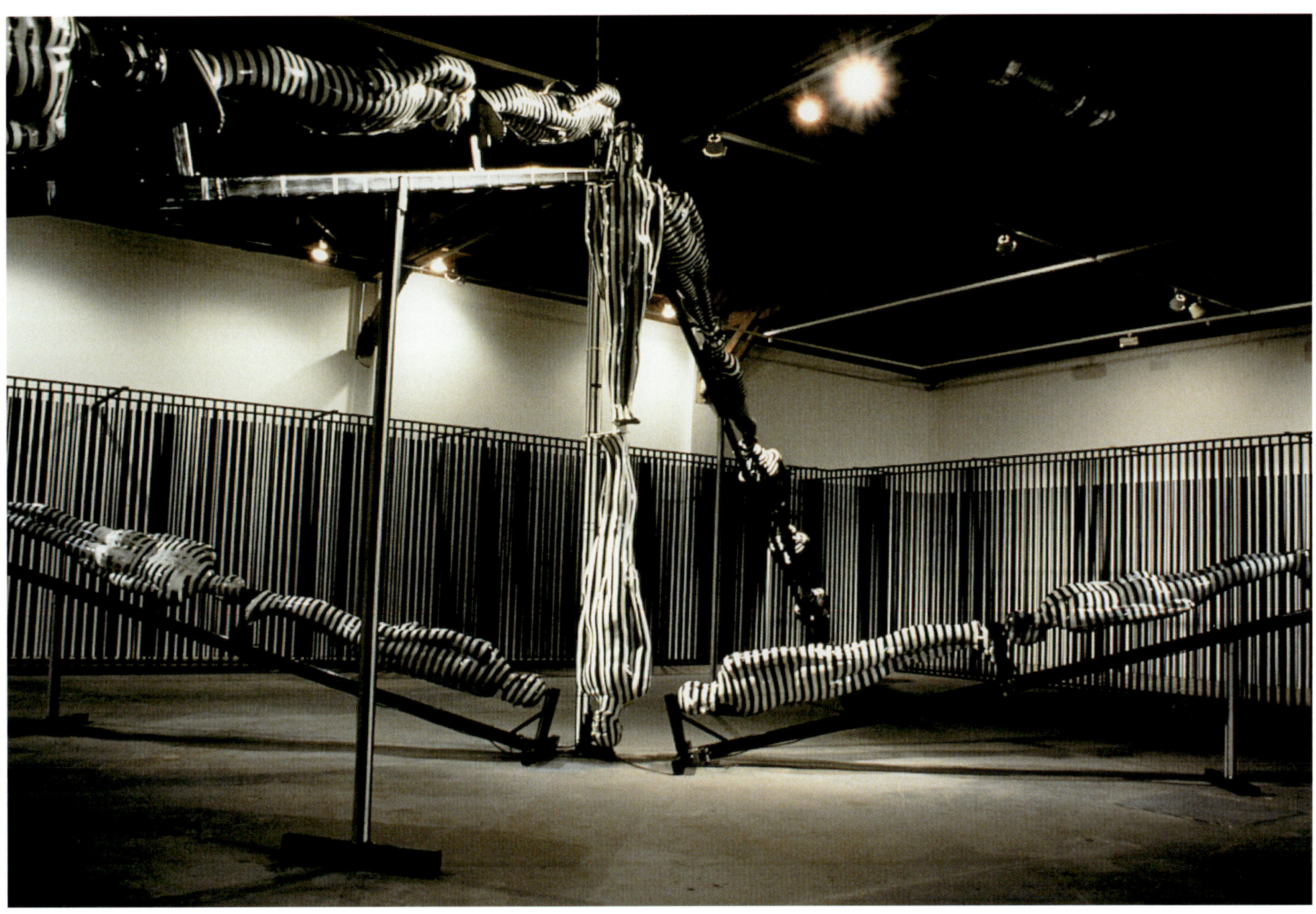

As Jackson states in the interview with Hans Ulrich Obrist in this volume: "My favorite kind of painting is realistic painting where you can introduce content. I think abstract painting is kind of devoid of anything. It's hard to conceptualize something that doesn't have any [content]." Jackson's transition into figurative or realistic machines that deliver or deploy paint in increasingly demonstrative ways also led him to a sustained engagement with canonical works from art history, works that he would reimagine and through which he would continue his ongoing struggle with painting's past and future. An example that neatly summarizes both the physical labor and the conceptual rigor that he applies to the medium is *Ain't Painting a Pain* (2009). The piece, which furnished the title for this retrospective, is a neon sign of the word Painting, within which the words ain't, Painting, a, and Pain flash in succession. For Jackson, the pain in painting encompasses the full spectrum of its production, history, critical reception, museological status, and market distribution, all of which his work challenges in one way or another.

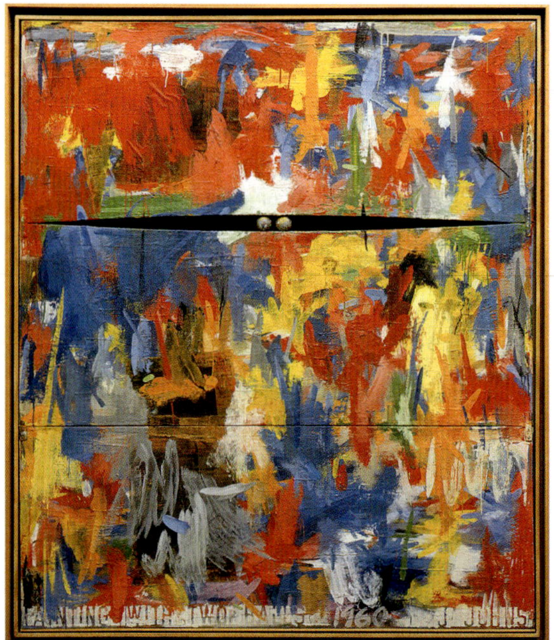

FIG. 13
Jasper Johns, *Painting with Two Balls*,
1960. Encaustic and collage on canvas with
objects. 66 × 54 in. (167.6 × 137.2 cm).
Collection of the artist. Art © Jasper Johns/
Licensed by VAGA, New York, NY

Four years prior to *Big Confusing Ideas* and just before the Menil survey, Jackson made his first version of *Painting with Two Balls* (1987–88), a work inspired by Johns's 1960 painting of the same name (FIGS. 13, 14). The installation consisted of two large aluminum spheres, painted in stripes and targets, suspended vertically between the floor and ceiling and placed in front of a steel cage that enclosed a wall painting of unfolded, two-dimensional projections of the spheres. An exercise in how reality can be modeled in ways that communicate spatial and physical information and, like *Big Confusing Ideas* and *1000 Clocks*, a play on perceptual entrapment, the installation was Jackson's first attempt to directly address a work that was essential to his formative years as an artist. Recalling a 1960 visit to New York City, Jackson said: "I saw Jasper Johns's paintings at the Guggenheim and thought his *Painting with Two Balls* was the greatest painting I had ever seen. I thought it was so strange, and I still do."[15] Clearly, "strangeness" and an iconoclastic challenge to predecessors—in this case Johns's castration of abstract expressionism and conflation of sculptural and pictorial space—are attributes that would draw Jackson to each of the works that he would come to remake over the next twenty-five years: Georges Seurat's *A Sunday on La Grande Jatte—1884* (1884–86) in 1992, a second version of Johns's *Painting with Two Balls* (1960) in 1997, Marcel Duchamp's *Étant donnés* (1946–66) in 2006, Edgar Degas's *Little Dancer, Aged Fourteen* (ca. 1878–81) and Jacques-Louis David's *Death of Marat* (1793) in 2009, and Pablo Picasso's *Blue Room* (1901) in 2011. The enigmatic and sometimes controversial nature of these works, their status as touchstones in the development of modern art, the biographical details and working methods of the artists themselves (particularly as related to Jackson's own history and artistic interests), and the web of connections that they establish between past and present come together in this series to establish one of the most sustained and rigorous investigations of art history in all of contemporary art.

Beginning with French neoclassical painting and moving through impressionism, postimpressionism, Picasso's blue period, and surrealism, Jackson's series of remakes focuses almost entirely on Paris during its period of artistic preeminence, from the late eighteenth century to the early twentieth. New York figures into the series only from 1946 to 1966, when Duchamp secretly produced *Étant donnés* in a Greenwich Village studio and Johns was making his first formal breakthroughs. The works that have gained Jackson's attention were made between the French Revolution and the American social revolutions of the 1960s, and he essentially skips modernism's most fertile period in Paris between the wars. Pollock is his only true modernist hero, perhaps because he brought the movement to its formal conclusion, and is the artist who continually reverberates throughout Jackson's work, as a sort of meta-influence. There seems to be a clear antimodernist bent to Jackson's project, with his embrace of Dada and rejection of the conventional modernist narrative of abstraction from Kandinsky to Brancusi to Mondrian. Here is Jackson on Rothko: "I read an article

---

15. Jackson, in Szakacs, "Circus Is in Town," 44.

about Mark Rothko, how he killed himself in the studio and they found 750 paintings in the racks. Shit, when I read that I wanted to kill myself because they were all the same! There's no doubt in my mind. It's one idea and you keep making it, and making it, and making it, and pretty soon you just come to the end of the line. That's the problem with minimalism. You take away everything and then you don't have anything. You don't have anything to do."[16]

When asked in the interview in this volume about his connection to Paris, Jackson did not mention any of the artists he has copied, instead saying: "One of my favorite paintings in the world is there. Monet's *Water Lilies*. It's a room again, and it's a painting that you can visit only if you go to that place. So it's a place. Or it's an experience or an event." He added, "My favorite French painter is Monet for sure." Finally, when asked if he had copied Monet, Jackson's response was: "No. Too hard."

Yet it is difficult to imagine anything harder than the process Jackson invented to remake Seurat's *La Grande Jatte* (FIG. 15), one that upped the

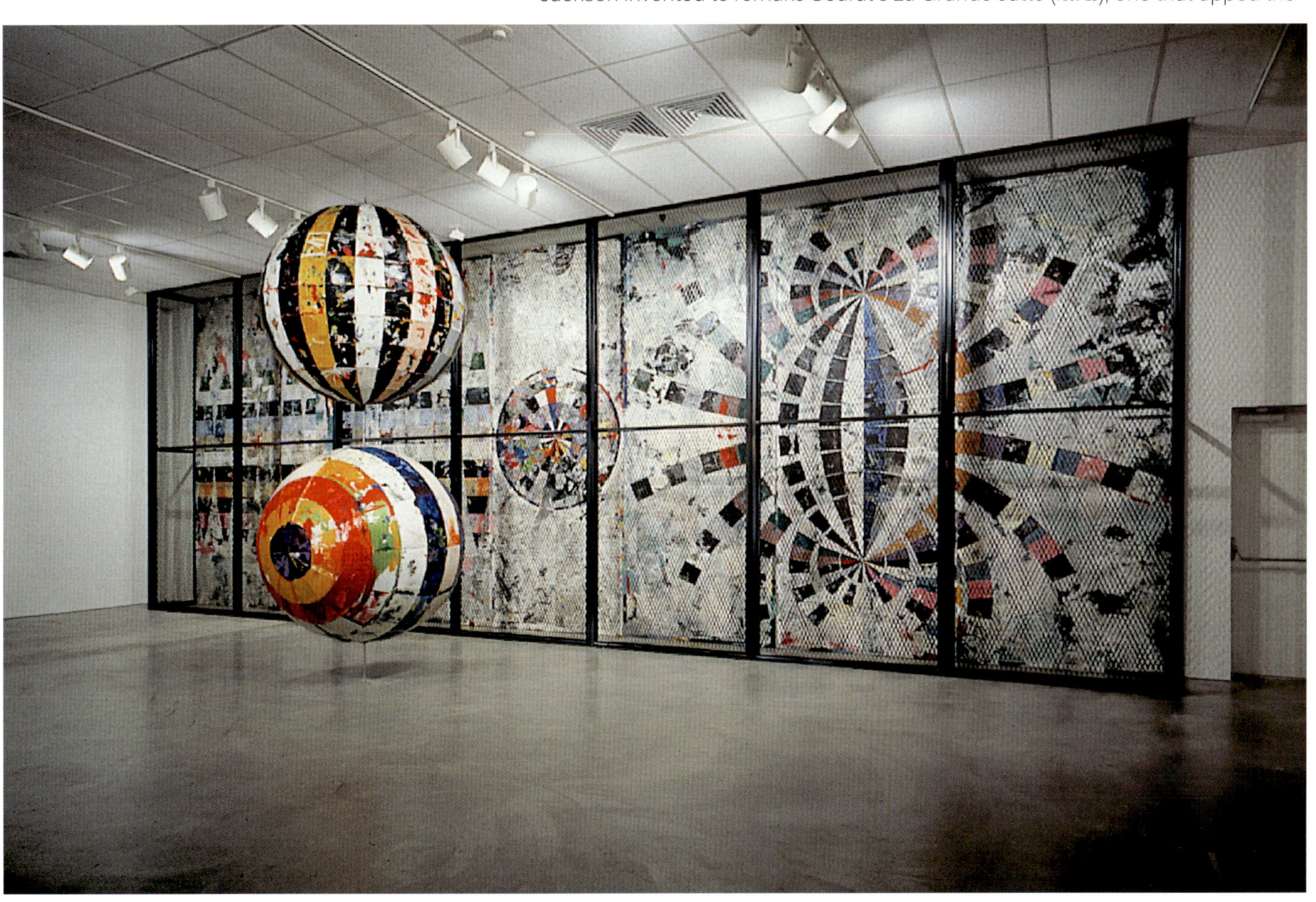

16. Ibid., 46.

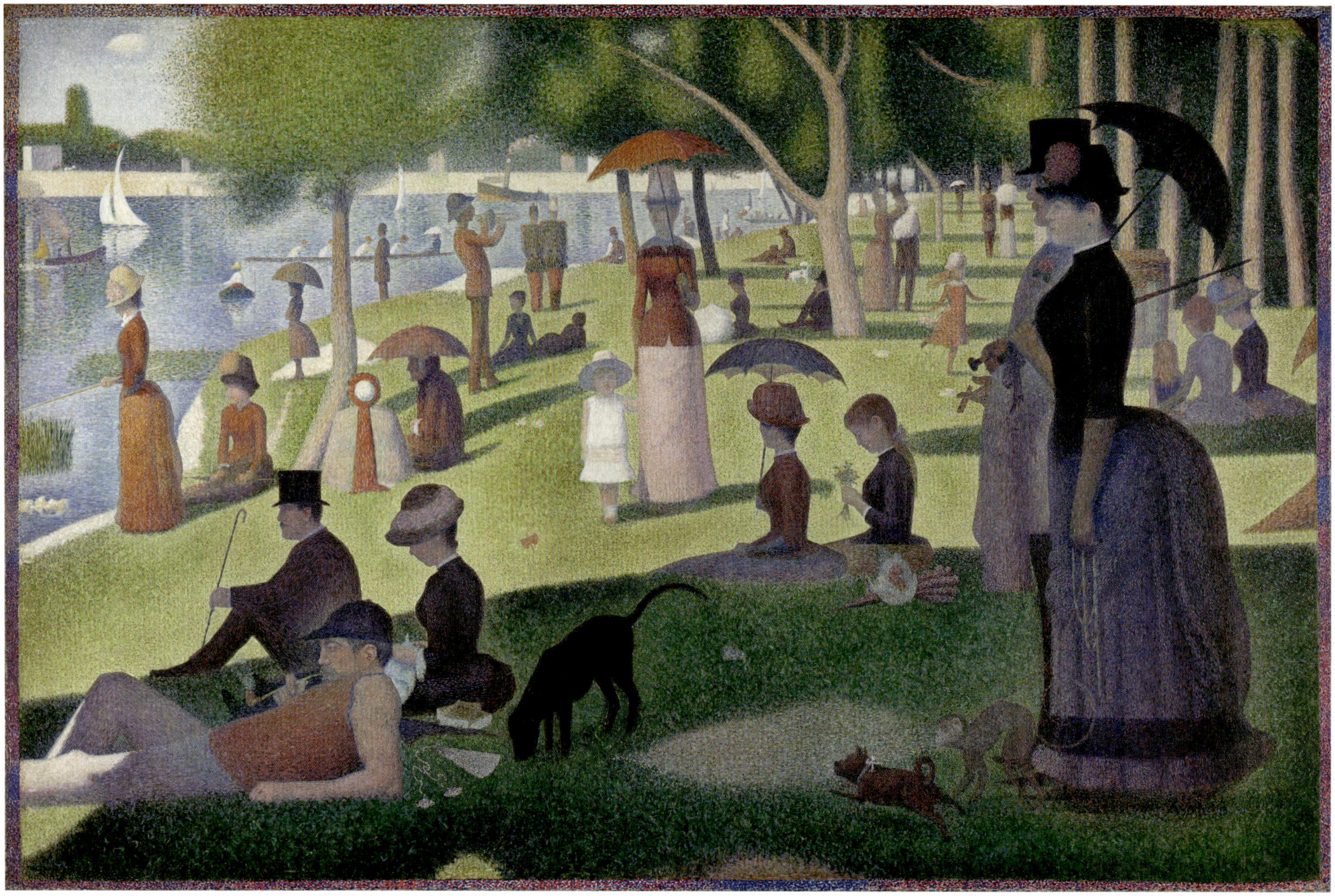

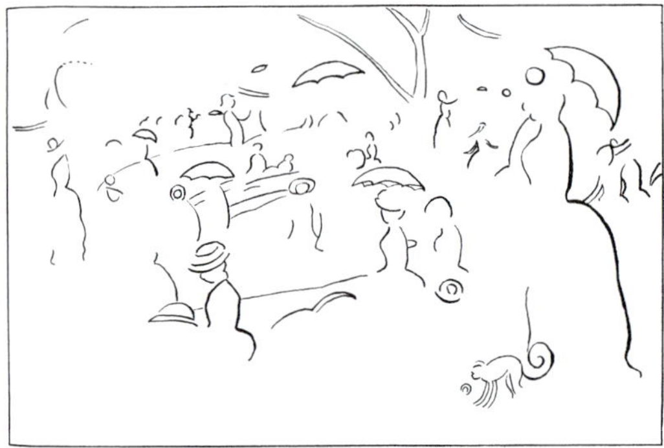

FIG. 16
*The Curved-Line Organization of "La Grande
Jatte,"* in Daniel Catton Rich, *Seurat and
the Evolution of "La Grande Jatte,"* University
of Chicago Press, 1935

ante on Seurat's labor-intensive pointillist technique. *La Grande Jatte* is in many ways the odd work out in Jackson's series of remakes. The painting depicts respectable members of the French middle class enjoying a relaxing day at the park, as opposed to the implied violence in *Death of Marat*, the disembodiment of *Étant donnés*, the deformations of *Little Dancer, Aged Fourteen*, the poverty of the *Blue Room*, or the symbolic castration of *Painting with Two Balls*. Yet despite the painting's pleasant, bourgeois subject matter, Seurat was a loner who led a largely anonymous life, died at the age of thirty-two, and was for the most part neglected and unknown. According to Daniel Catton Rich, the official French attitude to his work was hostile, and only one major Seurat, *The Circus*, remains in France, willed to the Musée du Louvre by an American collector, John Quinn.[17] The circumstances of Seurat's life and critical reception share certain parallels with Jackson's, such as his own largely withdrawn position from the Los Angeles art world, greater recognition abroad than at home, and his intense concentration on art rather than on the social scene.

17. Daniel Catton Rich, *Seurat and the Evolution of "La Grande Jatte"* (Chicago: University of Chicago Press, 1935), 2.

Seurat's masterpiece took two years to make and measures 81¾ by 121¼ inches. In *Seurat and the Evolution of "La Grande Jatte,"* Rich states that the painting is the "most complex in organization of Seurat's seven major paintings and is unique among the work of all modern artists for the thoroughness with which each part was studied before finding a place in the finished canvas."[18] This laborious planning is similar to the long, methodical development and construction of many of Jackson's installations, most notably the five-year period required for *1,000 Clocks*—its regimented ticks perhaps the sonic equivalent of pointillism or punching the time clock at work—and may also be seen in the detailed studies Jackson produced for his major painting projects of the 1970s and 1980s, which often resemble engineering drawings or architectural plans.

Jackson began *La Grande Jatte (after Georges Seurat)* in 1992, and the painting will never be completed. It measures 132 by 198 inches, significantly larger than the original, and the entire canvas is divided into nearly five hundred equal-size grids that Jackson used as reference points to draw by hand the outline of all the main compositional elements in the picture. Both the straight-line and curved-line organization of Seurat's composition, as presented in the Rich study of the painting (FIG. 16), are found in Jackson's effort to faithfully reproduce its spatial complexity. Jackson's painting process involves dipping a lead pellet into the desired color, loading it into a pellet gun, and firing it at the canvas from approximately twenty-five feet away. Each pellet leaves a small colored indentation on the canvas and then falls to the floor (FIG. 17). Jackson estimates that he has taken ninety thousand shots at the painting, yet it is barely 10 percent done. While Seurat slowly assembled his composition piece by

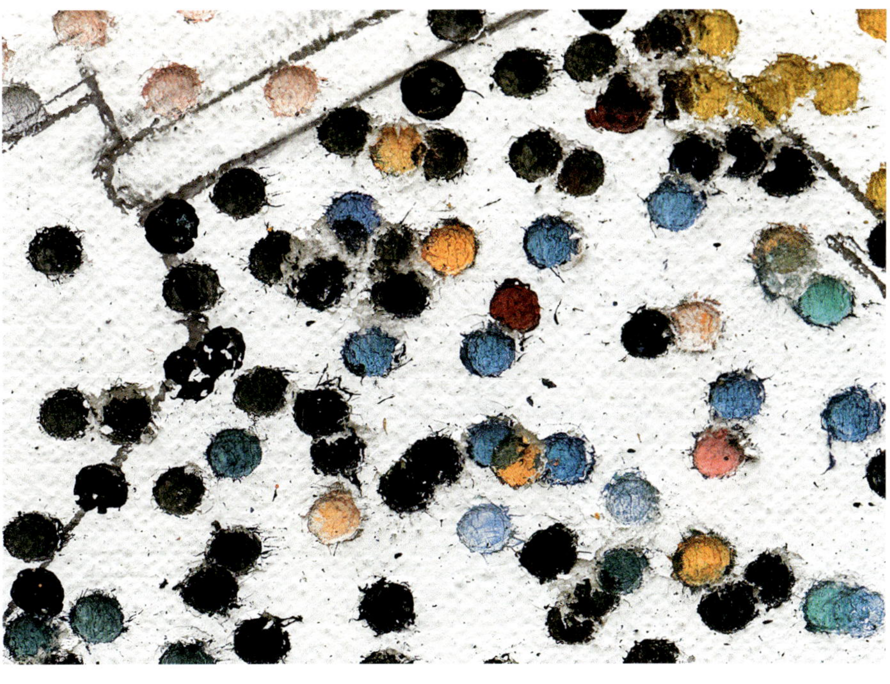

FIG. 17
Richard Jackson, *La Grande Jatte (after Georges Seurat)* (detail from 2006), 1992–. Oil and graphite on canvas. 132 × 198 in. (335.3 × 502.9 cm). Rennie Collection, Vancouver

18. Ibid., 3

piece—producing seventy preliminary drawings, painted sketches, and studies—Jackson works even harder to bring the image into existence by shooting it to life, a paradoxical act essential to understanding his art. Jackson is an artist who obsessively measures both his labor and his time, and with *La Grande Jatte (after Georges Seurat)*, he found a way to make an infinity painting, one that he cannot finish no matter how much effort he applies to its production.

La Grande Jatte (after Georges Seurat) establishes Jackson's project of remaking art history as a way to restore iconoclastic acts of creation, not for his own aggrandizement but to recall the rebellious attitudes largely absent in a highly institutionalized art world. He often states that "most artists now come from similar backgrounds and training,"[19] which he equates with a homogenization of current artistic practice. He is not interested in appropriation as a means to question the meaning of images in a media-saturated culture, the nature of authorship, or even a critique of master narratives. In the case of Seurat's painting, he has focused on an essential work in the transition from impressionism to cubism, one that the cubists admired for its structure and sense of space and that reintroduced a certain classical order at a time when paintings were often done quickly and with a flurry of brushstrokes. Seurat's prismatic spectrum and the organization of his palette may also relate to Jackson's use of color in his wall and stacked paintings and certainly can be linked to his use of complementary colors in works such as *Pump Pee Doo* (2004–5) and *Five Glass Heads* (2006). Seurat once said, "while certain critics see some poetry in my work, I paint by my method with no other consideration,"[20] words that could easily apply to Jackson.

Seurat's picture is known and recognized by millions around the world and has entered into the popular consciousness in ways that must appeal

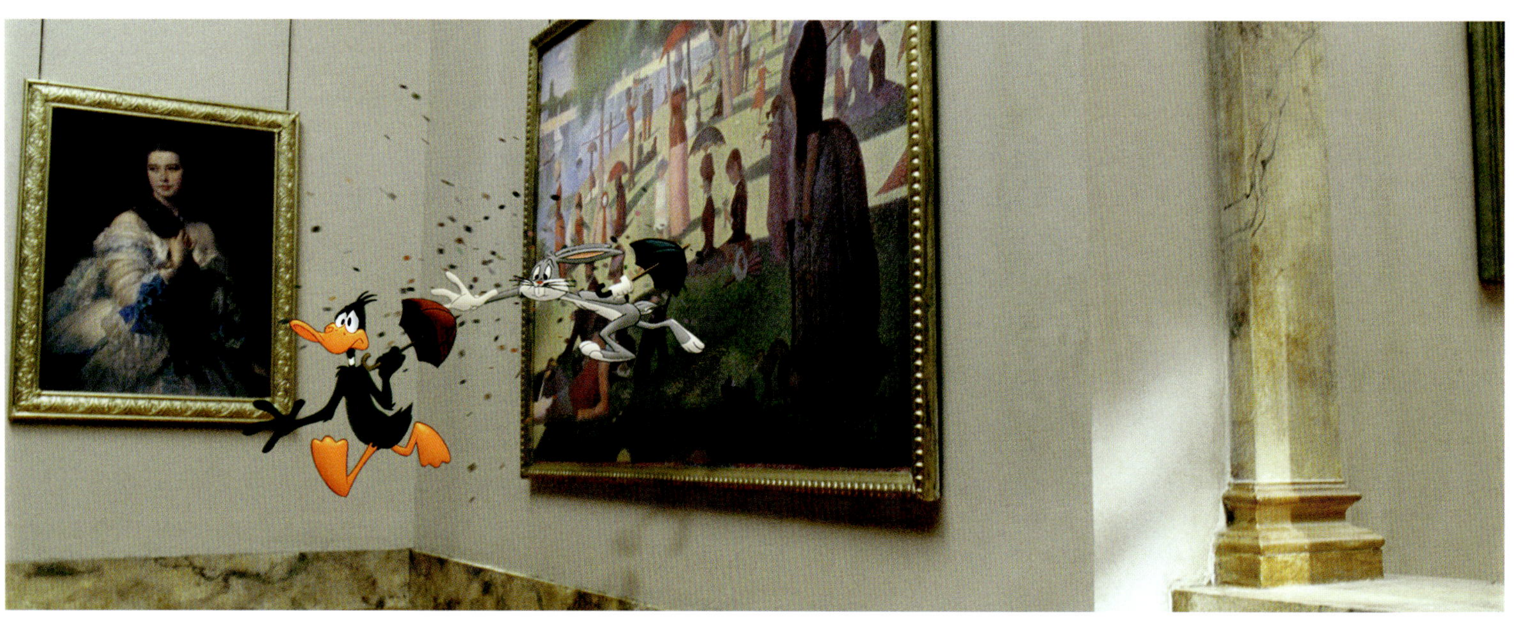

19. Jackson, in Szakacs, "Circus Is in Town," 46.

20. Georges Seurat, quoted in Rich, *Evolution of "La Grande Jatte,"* 6.

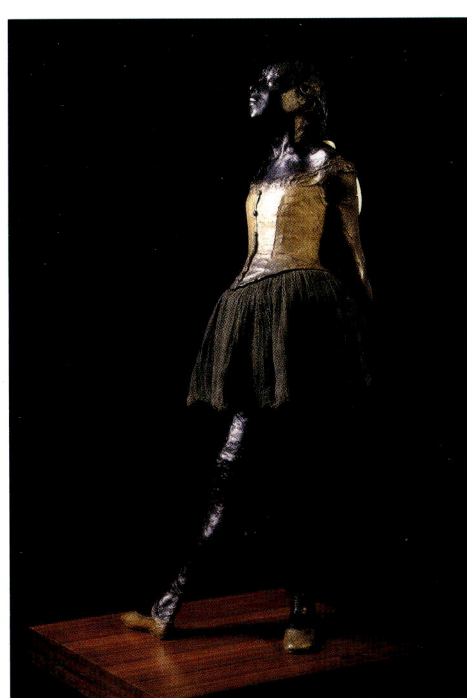

to Jackson's subversive sense of humor and populist bent. In addition to inspiring Stephen Sondheim's 1984 musical *Sunday in the Park with George*, the painting plays a prominent role in the movie *Ferris Bueller's Day Off* (1986), when the teenage protagonists skip school and visit the Art Institute of Chicago. One of them becomes transfixed by the little girl holding her mother's hand in the painting, and the camera flashes from his eyes to the girl and back again, in increasing close-ups, until only the dots of color from which she is made and the boy's eyes fill the frame. The act of looking and the act of making come together, all through an act of transgression played out in a temple of art. Best of all, however, is an episode from *Looney Tunes: Back in Action* (2003), in which Elmer Fudd, gun in hand, chases Bugs Bunny and Daffy Duck through an art museum and into the painting. Fudd's errant shots scatter the painting's dots, in the exact reverse of how Jackson makes his version, and when they all jump out of the painting and back into the museum, Bugs recites a definition of pointillism and then aims a fan at Fudd, who dissipates in a flurry of color (FIG. 18). The cartoon inserts a sense of chaos, violence, and satire of high culture into Seurat's otherwise tranquil afternoon, much in the same way that Jackson's working-class hunter invades the bourgeois scene at gunpoint. The gun and the fan, two of Jackson's signature painting tools, are here used to upend both the propriety of painting and the solemnity of the museum.

Like Seurat's *La Grande Jatte*, Degas's *Little Dancer, Aged Fourteen* (FIG. 19) is one of the best-known and most discussed works in the history of modern art, an object of great public affection and curiosity. When it was first presented in 1881 at the sixth impressionist exhibition, critics were sharply divided. Many called it horrible, repugnant, and ugly, while the novelist Joris-Karl Huysmans declared it the "first truly modern attempt at sculpture."[21] Following Degas's death, his wife and daughter authorized the Hébrard foundry in Paris to produce bronze casts from the original wax figurine, and twenty-seven casts were produced between 1920 and the 1950s. Jackson first encountered the work at the Norton Simon Museum in Pasadena, which owns one of the bronze casts: "I built crates for a company that stored a lot of art work for the Norton Simon Museum and the Hammer. I actually handled the Degas ballerina. I thought it was the weirdest, kinkiest thing I'd ever seen. This little shrunken girl and you could lift up her skirt. The ballerina was all dressed-up, with a bow, but deformed. I have to say, I never liked Degas' work."[22] Jackson made his *Ballerina* in 2009 by taking numerous measurements of the Norton Simon piece. Working from photographs, he sculpted the figure from Plasticine and then had it cast in bronze at a foundry in Santa Ana, California. It is dressed, just like the Norton Simon bronze, but the ballerina is turned upside down, her head and shoulder resting uncomfortably on a plain wooden pedestal, her legs splayed in the air, with a tray attached to one foot and the other on a bronze tree branch that helps support the sculpture. Jackson poured paint into the tray, and it flowed through the sculpture and out the dancer's head onto the top of the pedestal, down its sides,

---

21. Joris-Karl Huysmans, quoted in Richard Kendall, *Degas and the Little Dancer* (New Haven, CT: Yale University Press, 1998), 45.

22. Jackson, in Szakacs, "Circus Is in Town," 46.

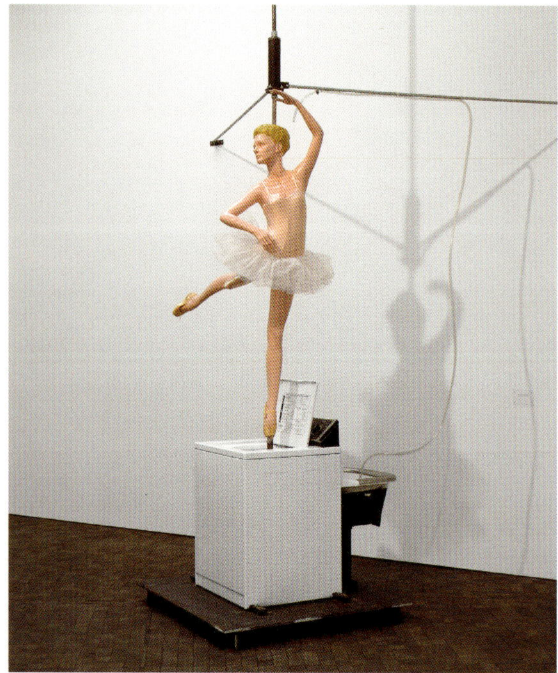

and onto the floor. *Ballerina* was made in an edition of five, in red, yellow, blue, black, and white versions.

The dancer first appeared in Jackson's work twelve years earlier, in 1997, in a piece titled *Ballerina in a Whirlpool* (FIG. 20). Inspired by his daughter's ballet lessons, the work consists of a dancer standing on top of an open washing machine that spins her around to deploy paint. *Ballerina in a Whirlpool* brought together two of Degas's primary subjects, the ballerina and the laundress, and is important as a precursor to Jackson's *Ballerina* and his *Laundry Room* (FIG. 21), a large-scale installation at Hauser & Wirth gallery in 2009. In that work Jackson employed several washing machines to "wash" clothes in paint, which he then hung on racks to dry. The culmination of *The Laundry Room* installation was the *Marat* mise-en-scène.

Although Jackson says that *Ballerina* is more spoof of Degas than homage, the two artists nevertheless have much in common. Degas was an ardent copyist, spending hours in the Louvre, and, like Jackson, was shy and fiercely private. Degas's dancers, laundresses, and singers were all workwomen, bent and distorted from labor, poor, and often the victims of sexual predators. "Their gestures were those of work, bodies deformed by labor," writes Carol Armstrong in *Odd Man Out: Readings of the Work and Reputation of Edgar Degas*.[23] Jackson's attraction to the Degas figure is related to his own labor, the repetitive motions of the dancer similar to those required to make and stack his canvases and clocks. Moreover, the repetition of Degas's imagery is analogous to the seriality of Jackson's wall paintings and stacked paintings, and Degas's fragmented views of dancers, "disjointed parts touching other disjointed parts,"[24] correspond to the

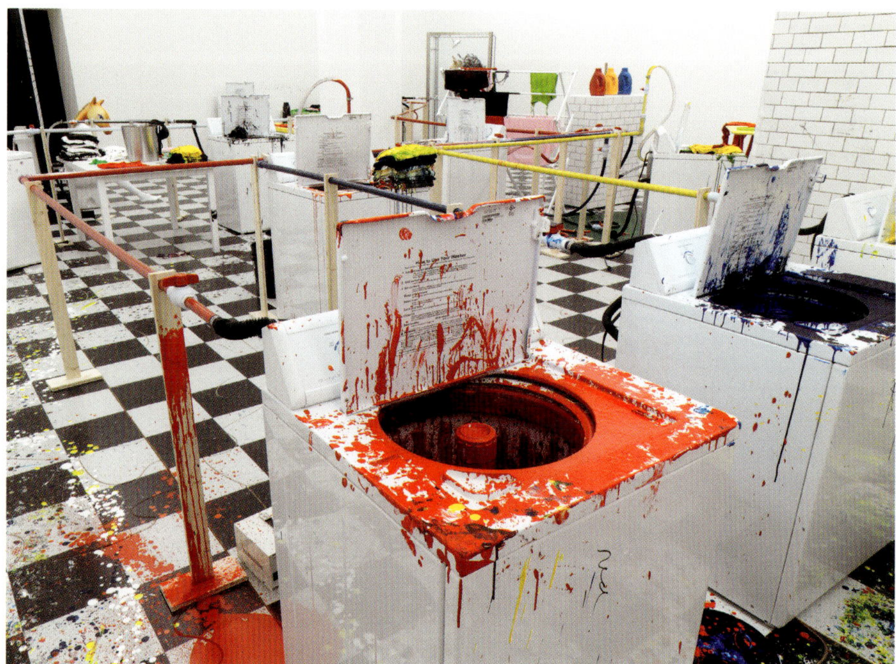

23. Carol Armstrong, *Odd Man Out: Readings of the Work and Reputation of Edgar Degas* (Los Angeles: Getty Research Institute, 2003), 50.

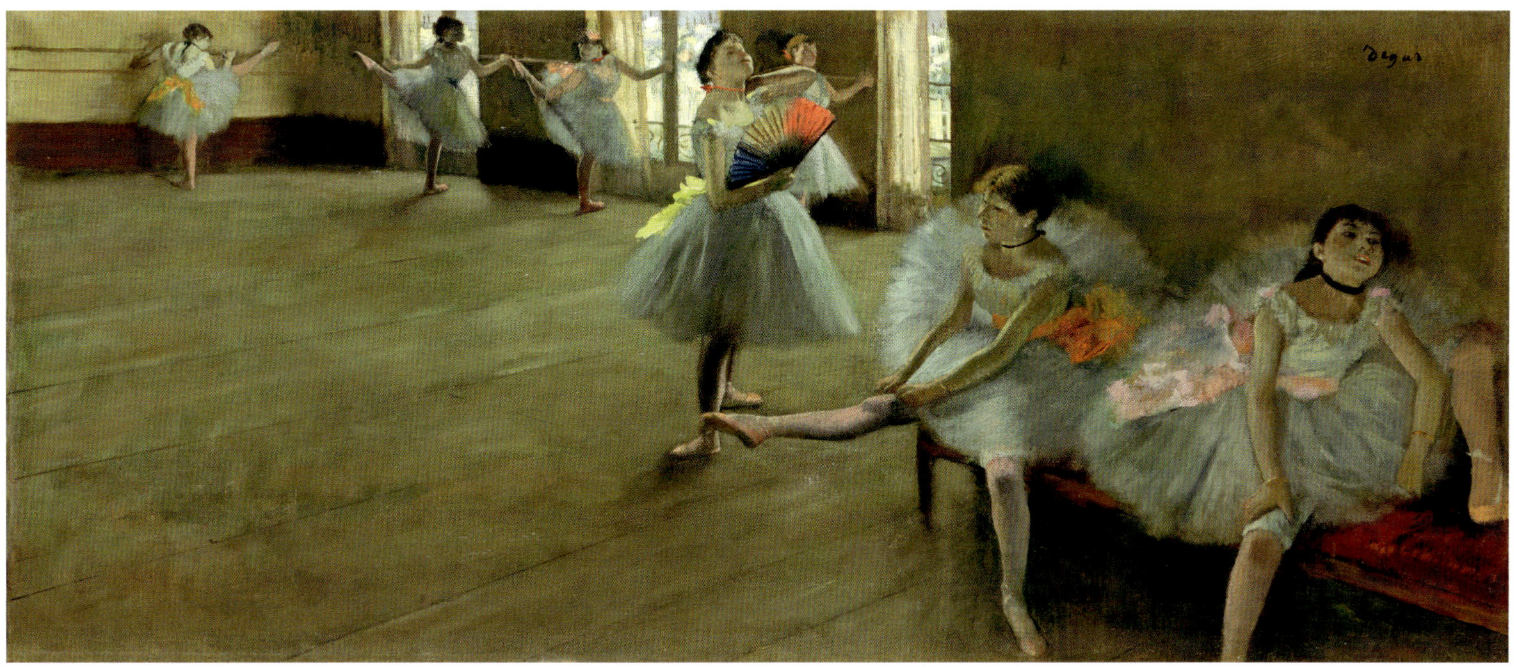

FIG. 22
Edgar Degas, *The Dancing Lesson*, ca. 1880.
Oil on canvas. 15 ½ × 34 ¹³⁄₁₆ in. (39.4 ×
88.4 cm). Sterling and Francine Clark Art
Institute, Williamstown, MA

shifting sense of space in Jackson's mazes, rooms, and painted environments (FIG. 22). Degas made the armature for the original wax figurine of *Little Dancer, Aged Fourteen* from broken wooden paintbrushes,[25] an almost too perfect transposition of painting into sculpture that Jackson turns around by producing sculptures that make paintings. The critic Edmond Duranty wrote in 1886 that Degas's painting *Madame Camus in Red* was indicative of the artist's "systematic preoccupation with strangeness,"[26] a comment that could describe Jackson's entire career.

While *La Grande Jatte* and *Little Dancer, Aged Fourteen* are among the most famous works of the nineteenth century, Marcel Duchamp's *Étant donnés* is undoubtedly one of the most enigmatic of the twentieth and is considered the artist's final masterpiece (FIGS. 23, 24). Created in secret in a small studio from 1946 to 1966, after Duchamp had publicly renounced art making for chess, *Étant donnés* was not discovered until after the artist's death in 1968 and was unknown even to his closest friends. Anne d'Harnoncourt, then a young curator at the Philadelphia Museum of Art, worked with Paul Matisse, the son of Duchamp's widow, to transfer the work from New York to the museum in 1969. Almost forty years later, d'Harnoncourt recalled, "the appearance of *Étant donnés*, you can't say it was the conclusion of Duchamp's work, because what Walter Hopps and I both felt was that Duchamp's work is more like a picture puzzle that you are putting together, it's a network, there are many strands and many pieces and you can make as many themes, you can make as many connections. . . . I thought of it as a really important and fascinating piece that had infinite numbers of connections with a lot of other things in Duchamp's work and a lot of other work by other artists, like Kienholz, for example."[27]

24. Ibid., 58

25. Kendall, *Degas and the Little Dancer*, 100.

26. Edmond Duranty, quoted ibid., 54.

27. Anne d'Harnoncourt, interview by Hans Ulrich Obrist, in *A Brief History of Curating* (Zurich: JRP | Ringier, 2011), 178.

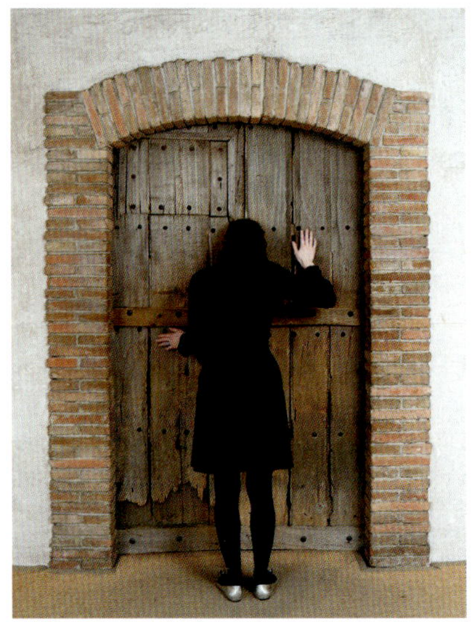

Marcel Duchamp, *Étant donnés: 1° la chute d'eau, 2° le gaz d'éclairage . . . (Given: 1. The Waterfall, 2. The Illuminating Gas . . .)* (exterior and interior), 1946–66. Mixed media assemblage: (exterior) wooden door, iron nails, bricks, and stucco; (interior) bricks, velvet, wood, parchment over an armature of lead, steel, brass, synthetic putties and adhesives, aluminum sheet, welded steel-wire screen, and wood; Peg-Boa. 95 ½ × 70 × 49 in. (242.6 × 177.8 × 124.5 cm). Philadelphia Museum of Art: Gift of the Cassandra Foundation, 1969

Jackson would certainly have discussed Duchamp's work with his friends Kienholz, Nauman, and Hopps. The latter had organized Duchamp's first museum retrospective in the United States at the Pasadena Art Museum in 1963, an exhibition that had a profound effect on the artistic community in Southern California. Jackson's remake of *Étant donnés*, titled *The Maid's Room*, was produced in 2006 for an exhibition at the Galerie Georges-Philippe & Nathalie Vallois in Paris (FIGS. 25, 26). Unlike Seurat and Degas, who are largely absent from the critical discourse around contemporary art, Duchamp is a defining figure, and *Étant donnés* has been the subject of several re-creations, including a major installation by the Canadian artist Marcel Dzama titled *Even the Ghost of the Past* (2008), and the work has been quoted by many other contemporary artists, including Robert Gober, Jeff Wall, Hannah Wilke, and Ray Johnson.[28] Duchamp's anonymous—some have even argued androgynous—female nude is transformed by Jackson into a French maid, an icon of male heterosexual fantasy. *Étant*

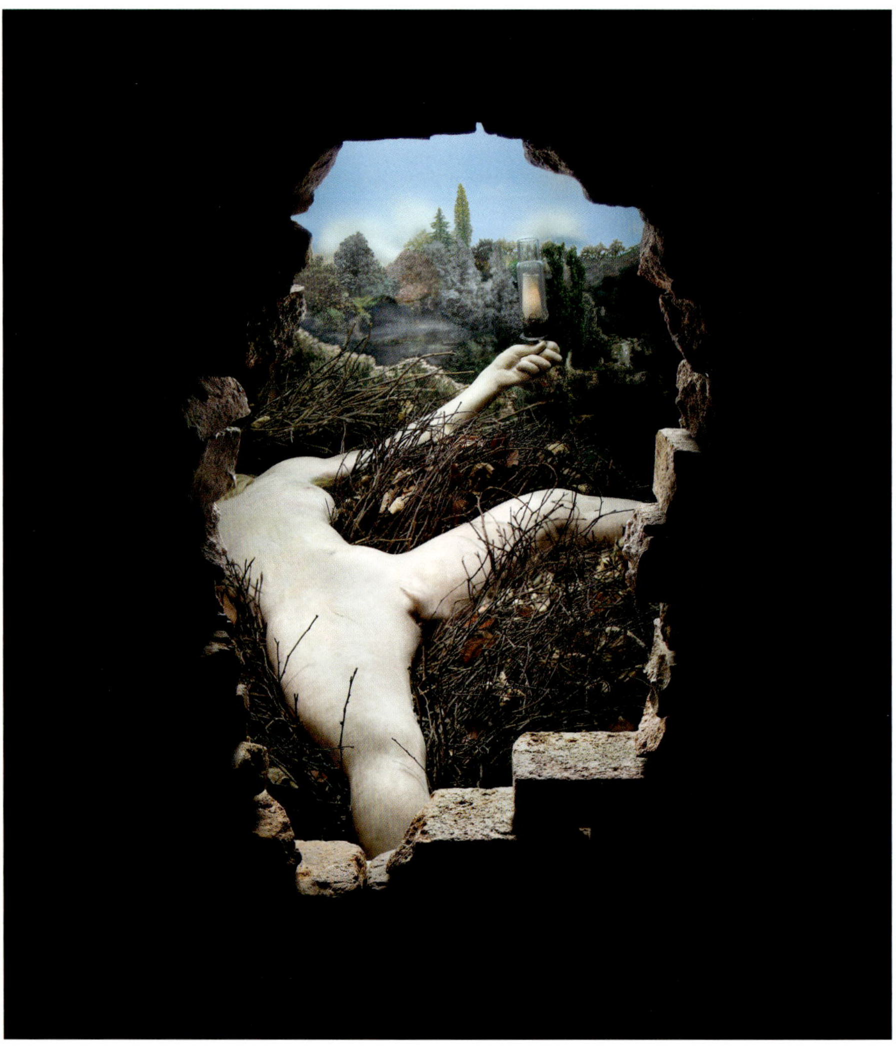

28. See Michael R. Taylor, "Legacy," in *Marcel Duchamp: Étant donnés*, exh. cat. (Philadelphia: Philadelphia Museum of Art; New Haven, CT: Yale University Press, 2009), 198–222.

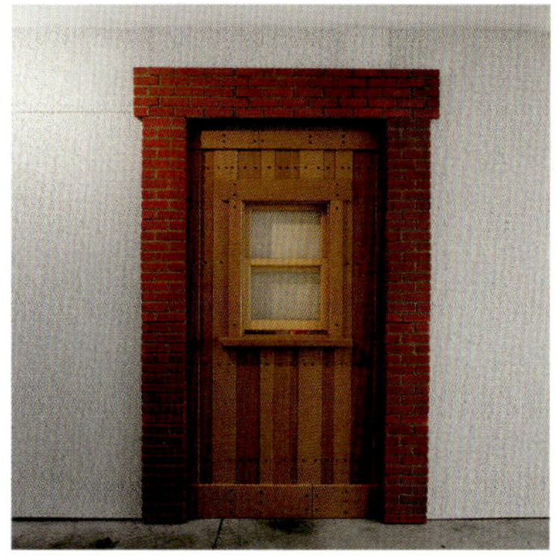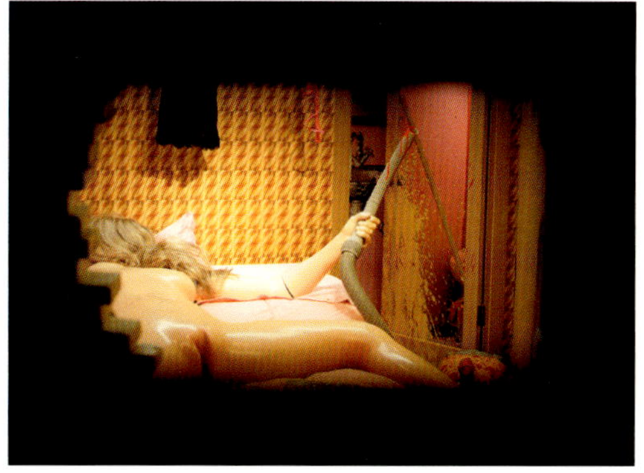

donnés' power to shock derives in part from its ambiguity and artifice, its sexual references often embedded in the hermetic codes of Duchamp's artistic language. The gas lamp held by the figure in the original, for example, is discussed by Michael Taylor in his extensive study of the work as an "erotic charge" that recalls both the electric light source in the transvestite mannequin Rrose Sélavy from 1938 and the light above Duchamp's boyhood bed, which later became a symbol of sexual energy for the artist. Likewise, the grotto that Duchamp created for the *Exposition internationale du surréalisme* in 1938, which informs the landscape of *Étant donnés*, is a secret site of erotic activity, hidden from the outside world but accessible to voyeurs.[29]

In his remake, Jackson takes these implicit sexual references from *Étant donnés* and makes them lurid. The woman lies on a bed with a pink cover instead of in a mysterious forest grotto; the gas lamp is replaced with a vacuum cleaner hose, which has discharged red paint all over the yellow bedroom walls; the waterfall is transformed into a running sink and a bidet, which has sprayed yellow paint onto the red bathroom walls; and the mannequin is smooth and shiny, her black negligee hanging above the bed, more like a cheap sex doll than the hyperrealistic figure of the original. The only nod to the elusive nature of Duchamp's work is a view of a forest outside the bathroom window, a photograph taken at the Jackson ranch. *The Maid's Room* is an *Étant donnés* for the Internet porn generation, a bawdy romp of riotous color that reinvents a work that, as one critic wrote, "calls into question the whole nature of art."[30] The installation also reflects the more prominent role played by sexuality and gender in Jackson's art after he began working with the figure in the early 1990s. Men and women alike are generally bent, contorted, spun, folded over, twisted, and turned, their bodies used as vessels to hold and throw paint and the paint itself a symbol for bodily fluids, particularly in works such as *The Dining Room* and *The Delivery Room*.

While Jackson exposes the latent sexual desire within *Étant donnés*, he is also intrigued by the work's perceptual dimensions; Duchamp's methods of construction; and the long, secret production of the work. As Taylor explains, "the grotto can also be connected to [Duchamp's] interest in going 'underground' and living a secluded life equivalent to that of a cave-dwelling

29. Taylor, *Étant donnés*, 34–35.

30. Richard Roud, quoted in Taylor, *Étant donnés*, 175.

hermit."[31] Jackson often speaks of himself as an "underground" artist, one who is uncomfortable with too much exposure; lives humbly in Sierra Madre, away from the center of the Los Angeles art world; and spends weeks at a time in the woods hunting deer. Here again is the desire for solitude, shared as well with Seurat and Degas, and the attraction to works with a long gestation that require extensive labor to solve both technical and perceptual problems. During the conception and production of *The Maid's Room*, Jackson closely studied Duchamp's *Manual of Instructions for Étant donnés*, first published by the Philadelphia Museum of Art in 1987, on the twentieth anniversary of the artist's death,[32] and published his own instruction manual for *The Maid's Room* in 2007. Jackson's manual is a nearly exact copy of the format and layout of the original. He recalls:

> I realized just how smart [Duchamp] was, the illusion, and the intelligent choices that he made. Anything that you can't see through the hole doesn't exist; which is pretty nice because you have to imagine it. What that piece does is what I'd like my paintings to do. They're all finished, nobody saw how you did them, so they have to imagine what the process was. *Étant donnés* is really just a pile of junk, about how this pile of junk turned into a beautiful environment. It's really crudely made and Duchamp invented the whole process. And instead of looking through holes in the door like in the original, you look through a window that is down low so you feel like a little kid peeking into the maid's room. It's kind of a joke.[33]

Jackson's use of a window rather than a peephole is a perceptual pun on top of a perceptual pun. In discussing the critical reception of *Étant donnés*, Taylor cites Jean-François Lyotard's 1977 study *Les transformateurs Duchamp*. Lyotard argues that the work "replicates the model of linear-perspective construction by presenting the female mannequin and her landscape environment through the jagged opening of a breached brick wall, which he understood to be a parody of Leon Battista Alberti's notion of the picture plane, metaphorically described as an open window in his 1435 treatise *On Painting*."[34] Jackson's equation of the work with the very origin of pictorial perspective—*The Maid's Room* is in fact positioned between two windows—recalls his early perspective drawings for the stacked-paintings projects and the two-dimensional projections of spheres in the first *Painting with Two Balls* installation.

Jackson made his *Death of Marat* in 2009, the same year as *Ballerina*. Jacques-Louis David's masterpiece was completed in 1793, in the months following Charlotte Corday's murder of his friend Jean-Paul Marat, the leading journalistic voice of the revolutionary left (FIG. 27). David's reputation as the most important painter in France had been secured a decade earlier, and his

---

31. Taylor, *Étant donnés*, 35.

32. Marcel Duchamp, *Manual of Instructions for Étant donnés: 1° la chute d'eau, 2° le gaz d'éclairage . . .* (Philadelphia: Philadelphia Museum of Art, 1987). An expanded edition was published in 2009.

33. Jackson, "Circus Is in Town," 46.

34. Jean-François Lyotard, cited in Taylor, *Étant donnés*, 191.

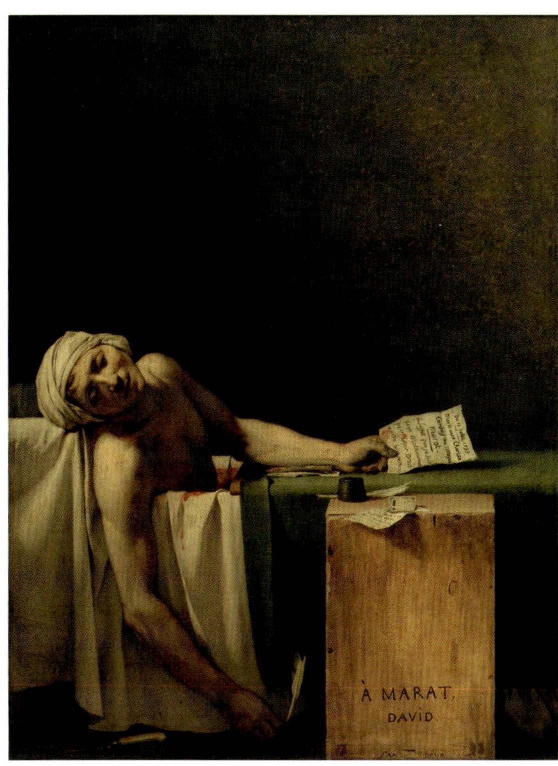

FIG. 27
Jacques-Louis David, *Marat assassiné*
(Death of Marat), 1793. Oil on canvas. 64 ×
50 in. (162 × 128 cm). Royal Museum of Fine
Arts, Brussels

austere brand of history painting marked a major shift away from rococo affectation. David also played a substantial role in the political events of his day, as Warren Roberts has noted: "Among the major artists of his or any other age his political role is unique. He signed the death order for Louis XVI and Marie Antoinette; he was elected to the National Convention, of which he served one term as president; he was a member of the Jacobin Club and served a term as president; and he held seats on the Committee of General Security and the Committee of Public Instruction. He signed warrants that resulted in the execution of enemies of the Revolution, and as a close ally of Robespierre he orchestrated civic pageants whose purpose was to solidify public support for the Revolution."[35]

David, like Marat, was an enemy of the royalist academies. And although Jackson taught in the art department at UCLA for five years, his aversion to traditional studio programs led him to cofound the Mountain School with the artists Piero Golia and Eric Wesley, a former student from UCLA. The school is a free series of seminars and lectures for graduate art students, held in a Los Angeles bar, that brings together a diverse group of scientists, philosophers, writers, and artists to discuss issues and ideas outside the standard academic setting.[36]

Jackson's *Death of Marat*, as mentioned earlier, was the culmination of his *Laundry Room* installation, which along with the *Painting with Two Balls* installations and *The Blue Room*, turns a painting into a sculpture that makes a painting. The transformation of two-dimensional works into three-dimensional room-scale installations is part of Jackson's way of coming to terms with the originals and of working through the spatial, perceptual, and technical challenges required to do so. Yet he also reaches across history, place, and genre to make his re-creations, establishing new contexts for both the originals and the remakes. In his essay "Painting beside Itself," David Joselit presents the idea of "transitive painting," looking at artists, including Jutta Koether and Stephen Prina, who have "developed practices in which painting sutures a virtual world of images onto an actual social network composed of human actors, allowing neither aspect to eclipse the other." Although these artists produce works that are markedly different in tone and character, they have a common project: "to visualize the transitive passage of action from a painting out to a social network (or body), and from this network back onto painting." (In one of Koether's works, according to Joselit, "painting function[s] as a cynosure of performance, installation, and painted canvas," an observation that also pertains to much of Jackson's work.) Joselit argues that such practices disrupt the "stasis of reification," concluding: "Transitivity is a form of translation: when it enters into networks, the body of painting is submitted to infinite dislocations, fragmentations, and degradations."[37]

Jackson's entire series of remakes may be seen within the framework of Joselit's notion of transitive painting, but his *Death of Marat* provides a particularly compelling example. The installation presents Marat's bathroom,

35. Warren Roberts, *Jacques Louis David, Revolutionary Artist: Art, Politics, and the French Revolution* (Chapel Hill: University of North Carolina Press, 1989), 5.

36. See Thomas Crow, *Emulation: Making Artists for Revolutionary France* (New Haven, CT: Yale University Press, 1995), for an in-depth discussion of David's studio and the academies.

37. David Joselit, "Painting beside Itself," *October*, no. 130 (Fall 2009): 125, 130–31, 126, 134.

which the viewer may enter, dimly lit with a black-and-red tile floor and occupied by a human-scale realistic mannequin of Marat in a tub, posed exactly as in the painting. Jackson takes the complementary colors of red and green from David's painting and uses them as the predominant palette for the work: all its elements are bright red, except for the water in the tub and spatters of blood around it, which are bright green paint. The installation has the arresting visual presence and solemnity of the original, yet its bichromatic presentation makes it even more programmatic, a reminder that David's picture is a propaganda painting that transformed sordid political deeds into a vision of sacrifice. T. J. Clark called it the first modernist painting, for "the way it took the stuff of politics as its material, and did not transmute it."[38] Jackson brings the past into the present by replacing the letter from Charlotte Corday in Marat's hand with a laptop computer displaying an e-mail message from Corday, which reads:

> dear monsieur marat,
> i would like to introduce myself as one of your admirers. if you have time, i would like to stop by and relate to you some information that might be of interest concerning trouble in Caen. attached is my resume and photo.
>
> sincerely,
> marie-ann charlotte de corday d'armont

The photo is of porn star Jenna Jameson in period dress with large, artificial décolletage and smoky eye makeup. The résumé lists only her height, weight, measurements, and interests, which are "horseback riding and knife throwing." The notorious Corday, who believed in the ideals of the revolution and came to blame Marat for its increasing violence, is transformed into a contemporary femme fatale, and the Reign of Terror is conflated with the current American "war on terror." According to Roberts, Marat "lived in a world of categories, of antagonistic groups between which there could be no resolution of differences."[39] This same polarization of public debate has come to define post-9/11 American life, with competing liberal and conservative news sources that alternately celebrate and revile the Patriot Act, the rise of xenophobia and jingoism, the Tea Party, and "class warfare." *Death of Marat* is related to two other Jackson works that employ art history to address current economic and political realities: *The War Room* (2006–07) (FIG. 28) and *Accidents in Abstract Painting* (2012; an update of an earlier version first produced in 2002). *The War Room* installation revisits Jackson's interest in Johns through the latter's *Map of the World* (1969–71), which is printed on the outside of a large polyhedral structure that represents the entire globe. Buckminster Fuller's Dymaxion map is printed on the inside of the structure. Fuller created the map as a more realistic depiction of the size of and relationships between the continents, one

---

38. T. J. Clark, "Painting in the Year Two," *Representations* 47 (Summer 1994): 13–63.

39. Roberts, *Jacques-Louis David*, 64.

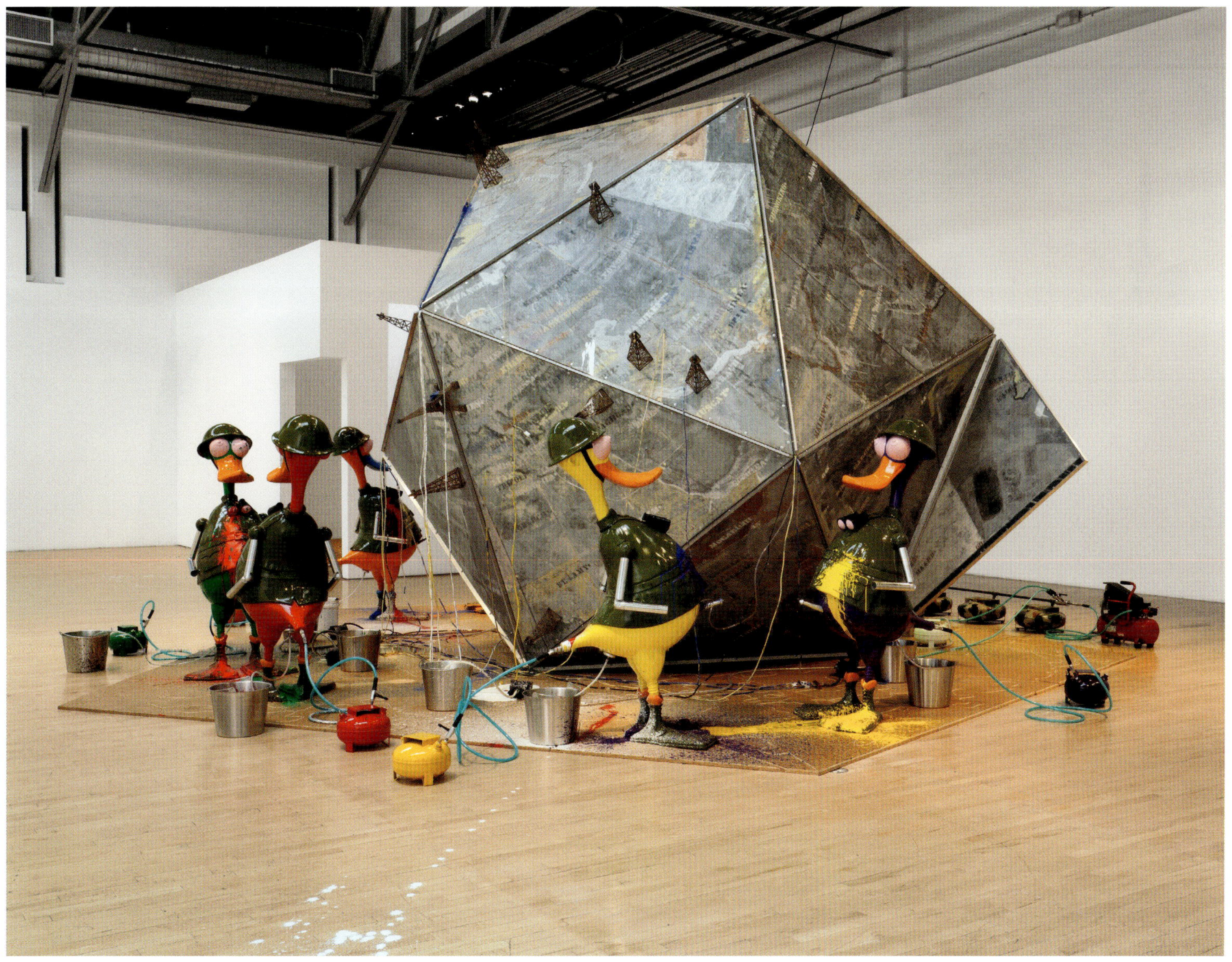

that eliminated the cultural biases of previous maps, which made the northern continents larger than the southern and distorted the scale of the oceans. Oil derricks mounted on the surface of the structure spray paint into the room, and sculptures of duck generals, placed inside and outside the structure, urinate paint onto one another and all around the installation. The connection to the first Gulf War and the invasion of Iraq in 2003 is unmistakable, linked to the use of the war on terror by the second Bush administration to attempt to gain control over the vast oil reserves required to fuel a ravenous consumer-driven economy that uses more oil per person than that of any other country. The Dymaxion map, which Fuller believed could be a powerful tool to promote

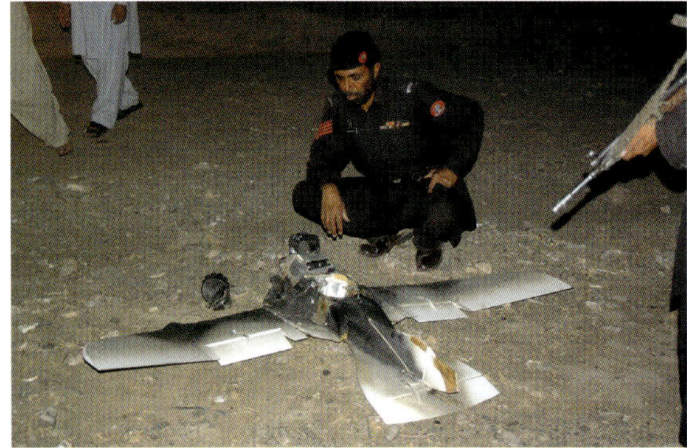

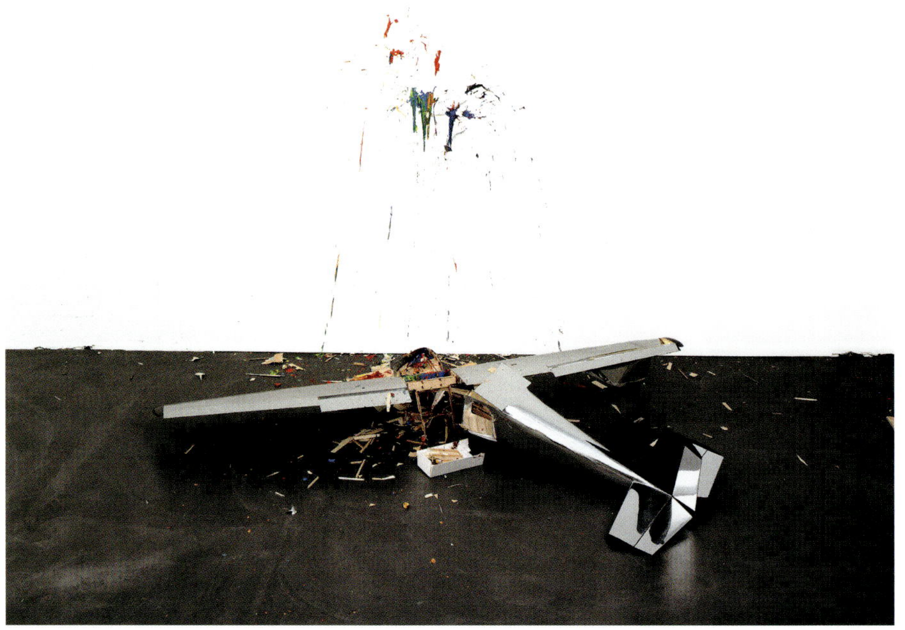

peace, is here turned inside out to depict the distortion in the allocation of natural resources between the United States and the rest of the world. Jackson has stated: "This is about the solution: B-52s, carpet bomb, condoms over the whole world, starting with California. It's about running out of resources."[40]

 Accidents in Abstract Painting (2012) was created for the Armory Center for the Arts in Pasadena as part of the Pacific Standard Time performance series. Remnants of the performance were exhibited together with *The War Room* at the Armory. Jackson commissioned the fabrication of a large radio-controlled model warplane with a fifteen-foot wingspan, loaded it with paint, and flew it into a temporary wall he built in a park adjacent to the Rose Bowl. His original idea, back in 2001, was to crash a real Cessna plane full of paint into the side of a building, but the plan was abandoned after 9/11. In 2003, he produced a small model of the Cessna and flew it into a wall inside Hauser & Wirth gallery in Zurich (FIG. 29), an installation that is reprised within the museum for the current retrospective. The 2012 version combines the send-up of abstract expressionism from the original with the military history of the Armory and brings to mind the current use of military drones to kill enemy combatants in Pakistan and Afghanistan (FIG. 30). In his review of the performance, the critic Christopher Knight wrote, "The work's raucous lampoon of Abstract Expressionist painting recalls the post–World War II era that saw America emerge as an international artistic powerhouse while Europe smoldered in ruins. In the 1950s the U.S. government's veiled promotion of dynamic, New York–based 'action painting' as a Cold War propaganda tool, symbol of a muscular cultural freedom that could contrast sharply with Communist control over individual expression, is unmistakable in an airplane elaborately painted in enemy-deceiving camouflage greens."[41]

40. Jackson, quoted in Robert Hobbs, "Richard Jackson: Expanding Painting's Limits," in *Richard Jackson: New Works, 2006–2007*, exh. cat. (New York: Galerie Yvon Lambert, 2007), 41.

41. Christopher Knight, "PST: Richard Jackson Makes a Painting with a Drone Airplane Crash," *Culture Monster* (blog), *Los Angeles Times*, January 23, 2012, http://latimesblogs.latimes.com/culturemonster/2012/01/richard-jackson-makes-a-painting-with-a-drone-airplane-crash.html#more.

FIG. 31 (top)
Pablo Picasso, *Woman with a Stiletto,
December 19–25*, 1931. Oil on canvas. 18 ¼ ×
24 ⅛ in. (46.5 × 61.5 cm). Musée Picasso, Paris

FIG. 32 (bottom)
Pablo Picasso, *The Blue Room (The Tub)*, 1901.
Oil on canvas. 19 ⅞ × 24 ¼ in. (50.5 × 61.6 cm).
The Phillips Collection, Washington, D.C.

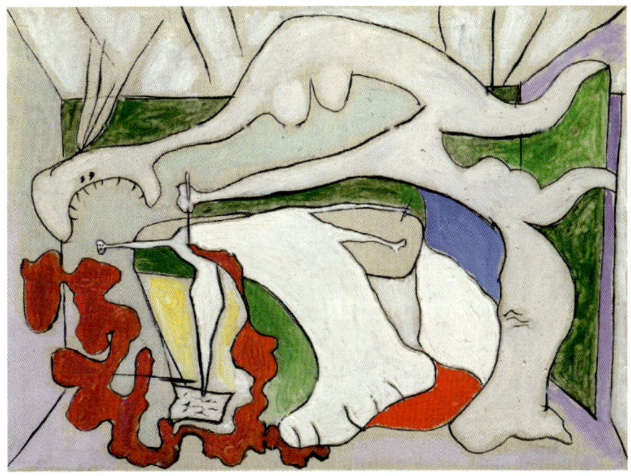

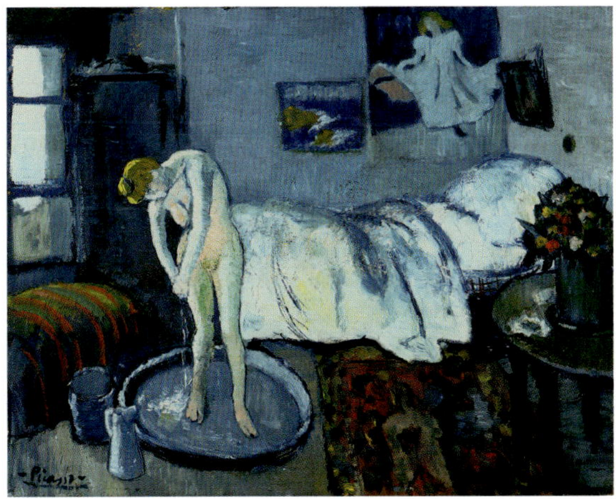

The use of drone aircraft to assassinate enemies of the American state marks what Andrew J. Bacevich, professor of history and international relations at Boston University, has called round three in the War on Terror: "Much as counterinsurgency supplanted 'shock and awe,' a broad-gauged program of targeted assassination has now displaced counterinsurgency as the prevailing expression of the American way of war."[42] In his trilogy of war works—focusing on the role of art in revolution, the pictorial representation of the power of nation-states, and Cold War–era cultural diplomacy morphing into the War on Terror—Jackson deploys a keen and acerbic use of art history while also channeling the creative-destructive impulses of his own artistic process. The milieus of David, Johns, and Pollock, and their iconoclastic responses to the cultural orthodoxies of their time, are for Jackson both the way into and the way out of the stylistic conventions that he believes are preordained in painting.

After nearly twenty-five years of engaging in remakes of the canon, it seems inevitable that Jackson would turn to Picasso, especially given the latter's own reworkings of his predecessors and his well-known statement that "sculpture is the best comment that a painter can make on painting."[43] In fact, Picasso is at the very hub of a network of associations with the artists that Jackson has copied, which must have brought him to finally address the titan of modernism. In a series of paintings Picasso made in 1917–18, following his viewing of a Seurat retrospective in Paris the previous summer, including *Harlequin with Violin* and *Return from the Baptism*, or *The Happy Family (after Le Nain)*, he incorporated pointillist surface into cubist space.[44] Picasso professed little interest in Degas's paintings, even though his first wife, Olga Khokhlova, was a former ballerina, yet he admired his sculptures and collected the monotypes of brothel scenes that Degas made late in life.[45] In 1917, when Picasso returned to classicism, he proclaimed himself a "new David," who would "rise up and sweep away all the 'mannerism' into which art had fallen."[46] And in 1931, just after his fiftieth birthday, Picasso painted a version of David's *Death of Marat*, which he knew and admired through reproductions, in response to a hemorrhage suffered by Olga. *Woman with a Stiletto* (FIG. 31) was finished on Christmas Day of that year and, as was often the case with Picasso, transformed the David work into a bloody psychosexual melodrama in which Olga became a murderous Charlotte Corday exacting revenge on him. Picasso made a second, "even more fiendish" drawing after *Marat* in 1934, following his divorce from Olga, in which she cuts the throat of Marie-Thérèse Walther, the young woman who had replaced her.[47] Finally, he saw Duchamp as a rival who potentially threatened his position as the leader of the avant-garde in the 1920s, in the end a prescient concern given that Duchamp now exerts far more influence on contemporary art than Picasso does.

In 2011, Jackson remade Picasso's *Blue Room* (1901), a seminal work in the Phillips Collection in Washington, D.C., which depicts Picasso's girlfriend Blanche bathing in his studio on Boulevard de Clichy (FIG. 32). John

42. Andrew J. Bacevich, "Slouching toward Persistent War," *Los Angeles Times*, February 19, 2012.

43. Picasso to Renato Guttoso, quoted in John Richardson, *A Life of Picasso: The Triumphant Years, 1917–1932* (New York: Knopf, 2007), 437.

44. Ibid., 14.

45. Ibid., 455.

46. John Richardson, *A Life of Picasso: The Painter of Modern Life, 1907–1917* (New York: Knopf, 2007), 433.

47. Richardson, *Triumphant Years*, 465.

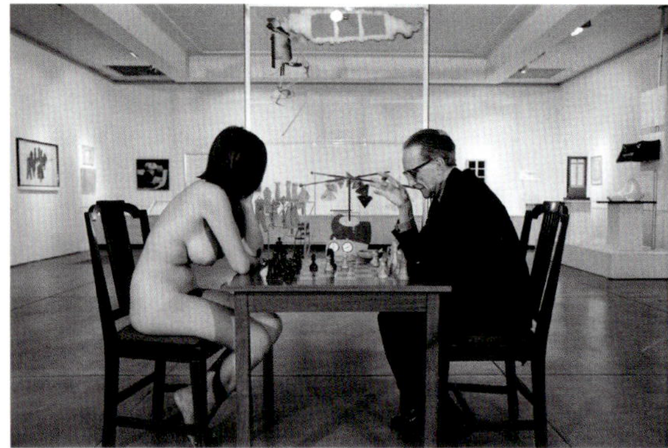

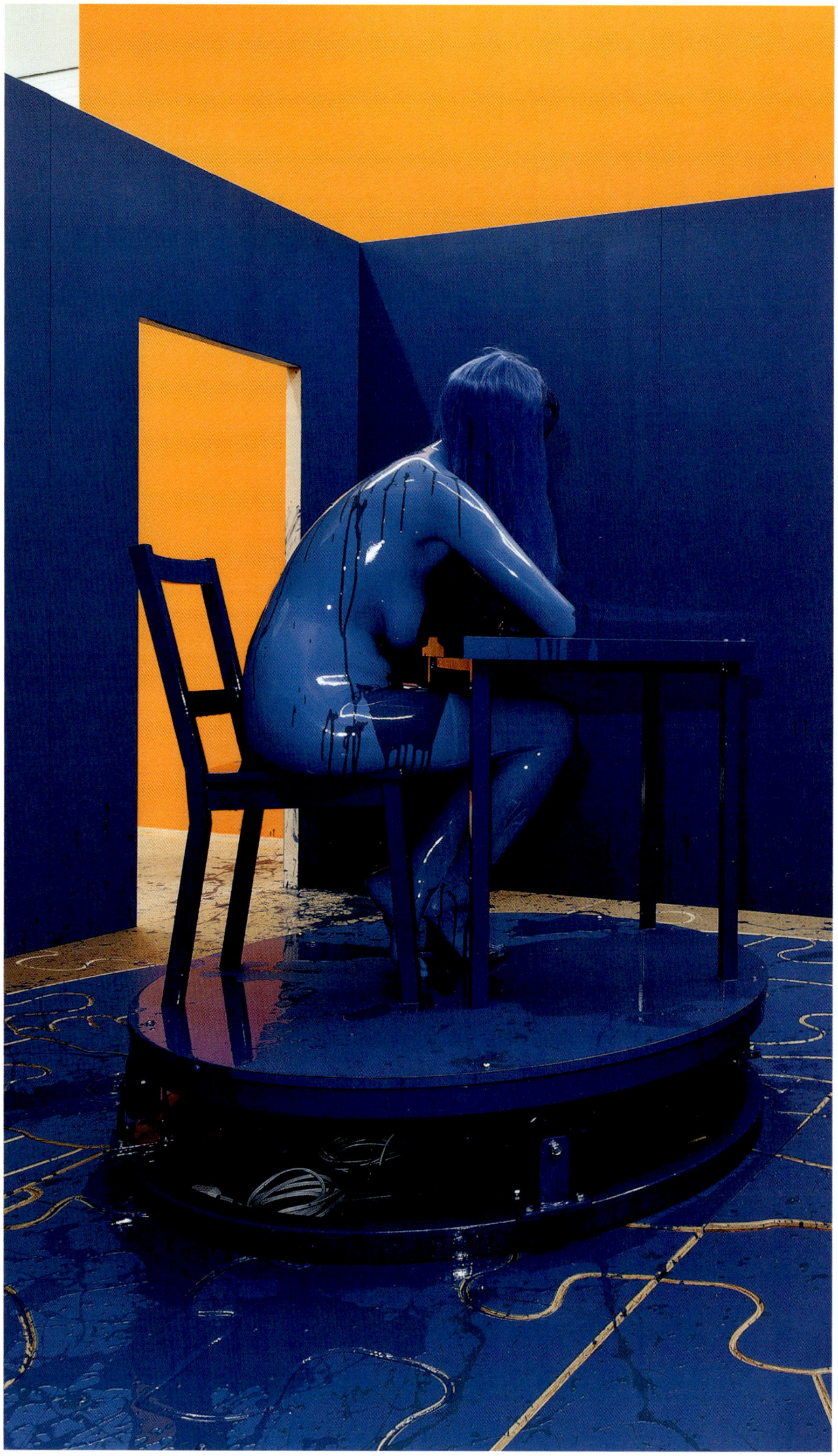

FIG. 33 (right)
Richard Jackson, *The Blue Room* (detail),
2011. Fiberglass, steel, wood, formica,
urethane paint, acrylic paint, canvas, wig,
motor, rubber, and control panel. 175 ×
175 × 108 in. (444.5 × 444.5 × 274.3 cm). Rubell
Family Collection, Miami

FIG. 34 (above)
Julian Wasser, *Marcel Duchamp playing
chess with Eve Babitz*, 1963. Vintage gelatin
silver print. 8 × 10 in. (20.3 × 25.4 cm).
Courtesy of the artist and Craig Krull
Gallery, Santa Monica

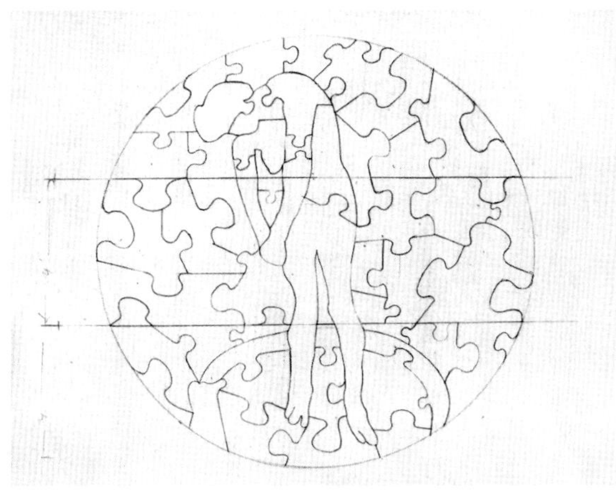

Richardson has noted the small scale of the nude in relation to the setting—"she looks like a piece of sculpture"—as well as the neatness of the room and the vase of flowers, which were uncharacteristic of Picasso.[48] In his 2009 Andrew W. Mellon Lectures on Picasso, T. J. Clark argues that *The Blue Room* is Picasso's "act of mourning for the century he was born in and his sense of the terrible century beginning." He describes the scene as "full of care and regret" and its sense of space as "belonging."[49] It is utterly different from the machinelike paintings that Picasso made ten years later, which were the first shattering look at what space would be in the twentieth century. As with *Painting with Two Balls* and *Death of Marat*, in *The Blue Room* (FIG. 33) Jackson turns the painting into a room-scale installation, replacing the furnishings from the Picasso painting with a nude life-size female mannequin, painted blue, seated at a small blue table in thoughtful repose with her chin resting in her hand. Jackson based the figure on the famous photograph of the nude Eve Babitz playing chess with Marcel Duchamp during his 1963 retrospective at the Pasadena Art Museum, a sly insertion of Picasso's rival into the setting (FIG. 34). The mannequin, the desk, and the chair sit on a motorized blue turntable, which spins as Jackson activates the installation by throwing bucketfuls of blue paint at the figure. The paint splashes onto the blue walls of the room and the puzzle-pattern floor, into which is cut the outline of the nude from the Picasso painting (FIG. 35). Jackson has used puzzle floors before in several of his installations, first in the autobiographical *Deer Beer* (1997–98), and later to cover the entire floor of a large gallery for an exhibition of his work at the Rennie Collection in Vancouver in 2010. The puzzles are indicative of Jackson's ongoing investigations into the process of perception, the way images are pieced together by both the artist and the viewer, and the network of interconnections within his work. (One is reminded of Anne d'Harnoncourt's description of Duchamp's work as "like a picture puzzle that you are putting together.")

 The turntable on which the figure in *The Blue Room* sits is a device that Jackson often uses in his painting machines to both deploy and catch paint. Here it is related to the function of the tray on the foot of his *Little Dancer*, and it refers to the tub in the Picasso original as well as to Degas's *Le Tub* from 1886. The entire room is perhaps what Clark described as "the worst that the new age can do," the very state of emptiness that he believed Picasso was resisting in the original.[50] Alone and without tenderness, without the comfort of the objects that Picasso so carefully painted, instead dripping in paint, the woman contemplates her own sense of anxiety and alienation while her doppelgänger from a century earlier stares back at her from the floor. It is an astonishing reversal, similar to the shocking bursts into the present that take place in Jackson's *Death of Marat* and *The Maid's Room* and one that Jackson himself may share, the hunter from another time who still kills his food, maintains his ranch, measures his labor, and takes aim at a complacent art world that he mostly outworks, outwits, and outruns at every turn.

---

48. John Richardson, *A Life of Picasso: The Prodigy, 1881–1906* (New York: Knopf, 2007), 225–26.

49. T. J. Clark, Fifty-Eighth Andrew W. Mellon Lecture, National Gallery of Art, March 22, 2009.

50. Ibid.

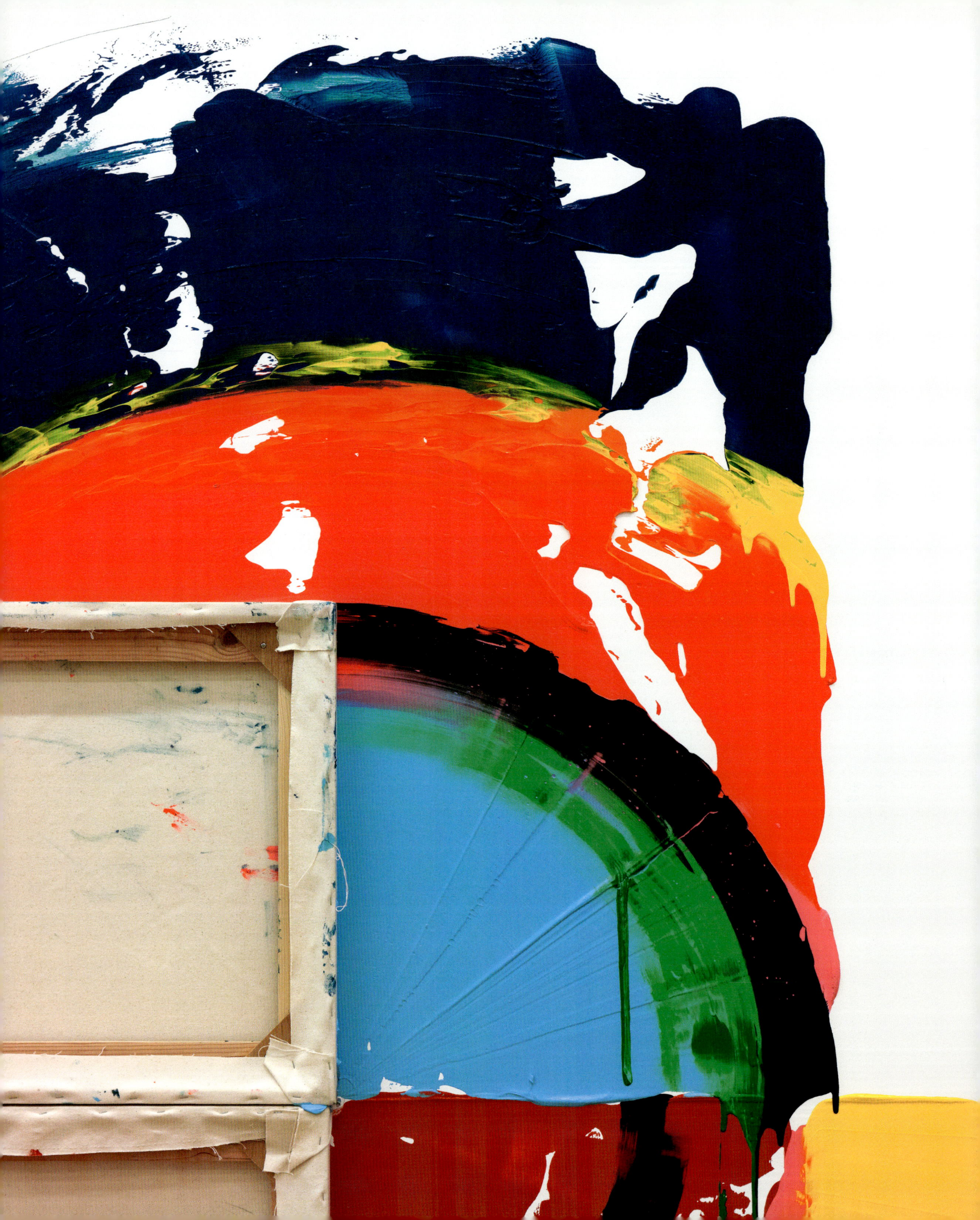

JOHN C. WELCHMAN

"BUT IT LOOKS LIKE ART"

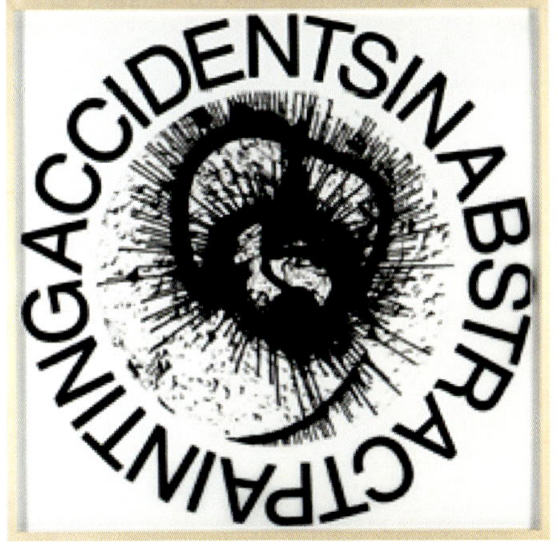

FIG. 1
Richard Jackson, *Accidents in Abstract Painting*, 2002. Oil and acrylic on mylar. 36 × 36 in. (91.5 × 91.5 cm). Courtesy the artist and Hauser & Wirth

(facing)
Richard Jackson, *Old Painting 70 Old Space 07* (detail), 2007. Acrylic paint, wood, eight canvases. 96 × 222 in. (243.8 × 563.9 cm). Rennie Collection, Vancouver

1 "I just need a place"

The places wanted, summoned, or dreamed of by Richard Jackson include somewhere to crash a 1:3 scale Cessna (modeled on his own) full of paint "into a wall that has the word 'Accidents' in abstract painting" (FIG. 1);[1] a place to activate a colossal, paint-flinging hybrid fan-cum-VW-Beetle; and another place to crash the real Cessna, full of yet more paint.[2] They include a series of pieces developed in and around domestic and institutional environments, such as the lost and largely unseen *The Bedroom* (1976–82), and at least one work dedicated to the art of displacement, the installation made in 1970 for Eugenia Butler Gallery in Los Angeles, confected from eight large paintings (a ninth was pulled through the structure as a paint spreader) arranged in a mazelike formation.[3] Jackson needed places to stack, walls to smear, and arenas to deluge; he even required a place to turn into a shooting range—with painting as his target.

The most tangible potential products of Jackson's ongoing dialogue with desire, need, and location, each of these places, once found, is a literal, physical space or situation but is subject at the same time to various processes of deferral. At the very beginning of his career, Jackson developed a working paradigm supplied by plans, annotated concepts, diagrams, and proposals, each drawing, note, or sketch standing in need of its own specific place of realization. Place, then, is the Jacksonian formulation for what others have referred to as *site* or situation. Yet the locative circumstances that he negotiates are less ineffably determined or rigorous than those defended in

The title of this essay cites a refrain often used by Jackson in lectures on his own work, most recently in a talk at Art Center College of Design, Pasadena, July 19, 2011. I would like to thank David Mather for his careful and creative research assistance.

1. "I just need a place" comes from Jackson's caption annotation to *Airplane (model)* (2000) in *Richard Jackson: Bank Job* (Vienna: BAWAG Foundation, 2002), 33: "This is a radio-controlled 1:3 scale model of my Cessna 150. There is a video camera on one wing that is used to make a DVD. I plan to crash it with paint inside. And I also plan to crash the real Cessna, radio-controlling it, into a wall that has the word 'Accidents' in abstract painting. Again, I just need a place."

2. Jackson found another place for this action. During the afternoon of Sunday, January 22, 2012, working with his collaborator Wyatt C. Sadler in Area H southeast of the Rose Bowl in Pasadena, he launched a radio-controlled military plane modeled at one-third scale into a nineteen-foot wall marked with a newly designed logo-cum-target. See my "Accidents in Abstract Painting," in *Richard Jackson: Accidents in Abstract Painting, the Armory* (Pasadena, CA: Armory Center for the Arts, 2012), 5–9.

3. Iwan Wirth, ed., *Richard Jackson: Deer Beer*, exh. cat. (Cologne: Oktagon, 1988), 36–37.

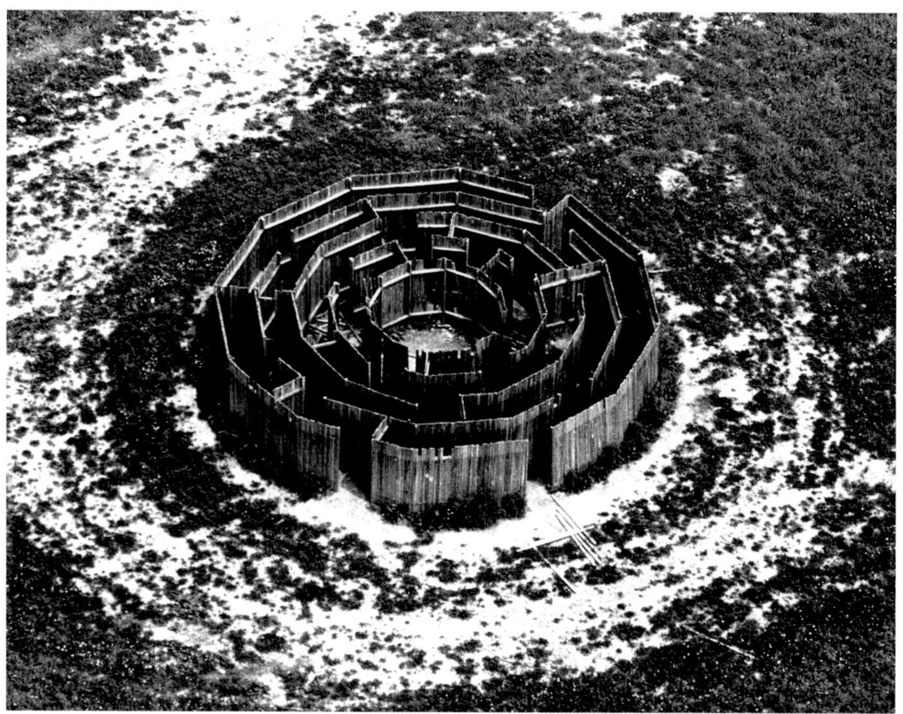

recent literature. In particular, the indefinite article that often precedes the artist's location-seeking projects releases several rounds of generalizing possibility: "a" place could be one of several or many as long as it serves the purpose of giving rise to a plan and hosting the resultant production. So while they should be particular enough to suit the needs of a given project—and are in this sense "specific"—Jackson's places are seldom *site-specific* in the self-consciously critical manner associated with current usage.

Jackson spoke of his commitment to a process-oriented denomination of place when he addressed the spectatorial itinerary engendered by *Untitled (Maze for Eugenia Butler Gallery, Los Angeles),* a work about getting to the point of working and perhaps the most metalocational piece he has made to date. "When you come to the middle of the maze," he suggested, "you don't see anything because you are looking at the back of the canvas." This observation gives rise to one of the foundational paradoxes of Jackson's oeuvre. For the very attempt to "broaden painting" by generating "a process that the viewer, going in and going through the work, must experience"[4] gives rise to a situation in which viewer-explorers are somehow expected to look without seeing as they arrive in the middle of the piece only to encounter the backside of a painting. Confronted by the normally invisible support structures of picture making, they are also brought face-to-rear with painting's mythic illusionism.

It is instructive to compare the Butler Gallery piece with another maze, made on the other side of the United States by Alice Aycock two years later, in July 1972, on the Gibney Farm in New Kingston, Pennsylvania (destroyed

4. Jackson's comments first appeared in print in German and have recently been retranslated into English and corrected by the artist; see Dieter Buchhart, "Richard Jackson: Ich bin ein Kunstterrorist" (interview), *Kunstforum International,* no. 165 (June–July 2003): 218.

in 1974) (FIG. 2). While Aycock's labyrinth, "a twelve-sided wooden structure of five dodecagonal rings approximately 32' in diameter and 6' high," appears to share a number of experiential qualities with Jackson's—including its "set up" of an "exploratory situation," a general interest in perception and the making of "psychophysical" space, and its involvement with "experimental time and memory"—the two projects are antithetical in almost every other dimension of reckoning, as well as in some of these. First and foremost, Jackson's rectilinear maze is emphatically designed for and committed to an interior space and built as an articulation of *painting*, just as Aycock's circular version, conversely, is specifically sited outdoors—reflecting, as the artist put it, "the notion that an organism both selects and is selected by the environment"—and consciously articulated in dialogue with *sculpture* and *architecture*.[5] Secondly, both the making of, and Aycock's later reflections on, her maze bristle with historical references, including "the American Indian stockade," "Zulu kraal," "an Egyptian labyrinth," and the Greek temple of Asclepius at Epidaurus.[6] His later works made in ironic dialogue with particular historical works notwithstanding, Jackson was, at this stage of his career, highly suspicious of external pretexts of any kind, preferring to concentrate on intensive personal investments of time and action in the conception and realization of his pieces. Finally, the promiscuous if abstract certainties of Aycock's maze, organized by what she described as "goal-directed situations" and (borrowing from Morse Peckham) "signs of orientative transition," could not be further removed from the oddball, inside-out disorientation solicited by Jackson.[7]

The subterfuge perpetrated by Jackson on the security of the site-specific has several other aspects. His critics and interlocutors, for example, have often been obliged—sometimes almost by accident, it would appear—to come up with formulas and descriptions that sidestep established terminology. Thus Harald Szeemann developed the phrase "place-related action" to account for the signature manner in which the artist takes up what he described as "the real element as stimulus."[8] In the same essay Szeemann returns twice more to variants of this formulation, offering a series of ready inflections tethered to the notion of place but evidently intended to think around it. One attends to the crucial articulation between what might be produced in the artist's studio and the location where a piece is subsequently realized: "It is not Richard Jackson's intention to be an artist who creates his oeuvre quietly for himself. . . . He is interested in the place-related demonstration of his work which is prepared in the studio."[9] Another iteration introduces a recalibrated version of the phrase "place-related installations" in the context of another, more forthright, aspect of the quizzical, negative dialectics that we encountered in *Untitled (Maze)*. For what is at stake here is not just the delivery of a spectator to the blind side of a relocated painting but the actual destruction of what was made in place. Noting that Jackson "has destroyed most of his painted place-related installations," Szeemann concludes, "Of course, failure is part of this extension of the concept of art, a risk

---

5. Alice Aycock, "Work" (1975), in *Post-Movement Art in America*, ed. Alan Sondheim (New York: E. P. Dutton, 1977), excerpted in Kristine Stiles and Peter Howard Selz, eds., *Theories and Documents of Contemporary Art: A Sourcebook of Artists' Writings* (Berkeley: University of California Press, 1996), 558.

6. Alice Aycock, "Maze" (1975), in Sondheim, *Post-Movement Art*, excerpted in Stiles and Selz, *Theories and Documents*, 558.

7. Alice Aycock, "Work," 558.

8. Harald Szeemann, "The Untiring Sparkle of the Hunter's Eye," in Wirth, *Deer Beer*, 12.

9. Ibid., 12.

which cannot be done away with."[10] One logic of Jackson's dissident commitment to place operates, then, as an antithesis to the fetishization of site through the unremitting desire to make it extra visible (socially, economically, institutionally) by permissively subtracting what passes as art from the necessity of its former location, without leaving any residue.

The idea of place as bookending an interval of "art" and being returned to itself thereafter opens up a related dimension of reckoning, to which Jackson himself points when he suggests that location operates as one half of a dialectical move activated by a relation to temporality. "The way the paintings are structured," he noted, "there's a place where it is located, a time where it exists. Everything has a time and a place, a life and a death like people! . . . The piece is designed for that space and the concepts are worked out."[11] The appositional coordination of place in time supplies an obvious set of material limits to Jackson's works, beyond which they cease to exist. It also points to what we can term a temporal specificity, which, as I discuss below (section 5, "Signs of Time: Activate/Automate"), organizes another key aspect of Jackson's work.

In addition to place relations and locative temporality, we can also come at Jackson's ideas of location through the notion of "making room." This process can be understood quite literally in the various rooms (*The Bedroom*, *The Dining Room*, *The Delivery Room*, *The Maid's Room*, *The War Room*; see section 4, "Rooms Service") that he has made or détourned in a loose series that, while present throughout his career, has been its dominant structuring principle in the twenty-first century. We can think of this turn as a more self-reflexive gesture of the kind referred to by Gottfried Boehm in 1988: "It is only when one is prepared to make room for Jackson, to free up the space for him, to give him the time, that one really gets to know him."[12] It is not accidental perhaps that the proposition to "make room" for Jackson is in Boehm's account articulated in another version of the dialectic of time and place that we have already encountered, as the act of "making space" for the artist is rearticulated as a call "to give him . . . time." Thus, the "very specific way" that Jackson "uses space and time," as Boehm put it, is associated with a certain kind of opening up or ceding of ground, that, while taken on by Jackson as he works, also needs to be given up by his viewers as they encounter what he makes.

But granting space as the result of an implicit, art-driven demand is quite different from making space gratuitously, as manifest in a commodity-driven culture that thrives on relentless accumulation. Jackson has pointed several times to the fact that "this society tends to produce and stockpile a lot of things that it doesn't need."[13] In his view, the need that underwrites the space-making activity of the artist is founded on an attempt to alter the whole regimen of viewers' thinking, not just to modulate their perceptions: "I think it's the artist's job to change the way other people think about art."[14] We can conclude that the art of "making space" is formulated by Jackson as a complex refraction of creative deliberation and making coupled with artistic self-

---

10. Ibid., 13.

11. Jackson, in Hans Ulrich Obrist and Alberta Mayo, "Unusual Behavior: Ping Pong" (interview with Jackson), in *Richard Jackson: Deer Beer*, ed. Iwan Wirth, exh. cat. (Cologne: Oktagon, 1998), 17–18.

12. Gottfried Boehm, in *Richard Jackson: Entstehung eines Wandbildes*, trans. Isabel Feder, exh. cat. (Zurich: Rolf Schroeter, 1988), unpaged.

13. Jackson, in Henry T. Hopkins, *California Painters: New Work* (San Francisco: Chronicle, 1989), 85.

14. Jackson, in Gregorio Salazar, "Richard Jackson's Museum of the Mind," *Public News*, no. 327 (July 20, 1988): 12.

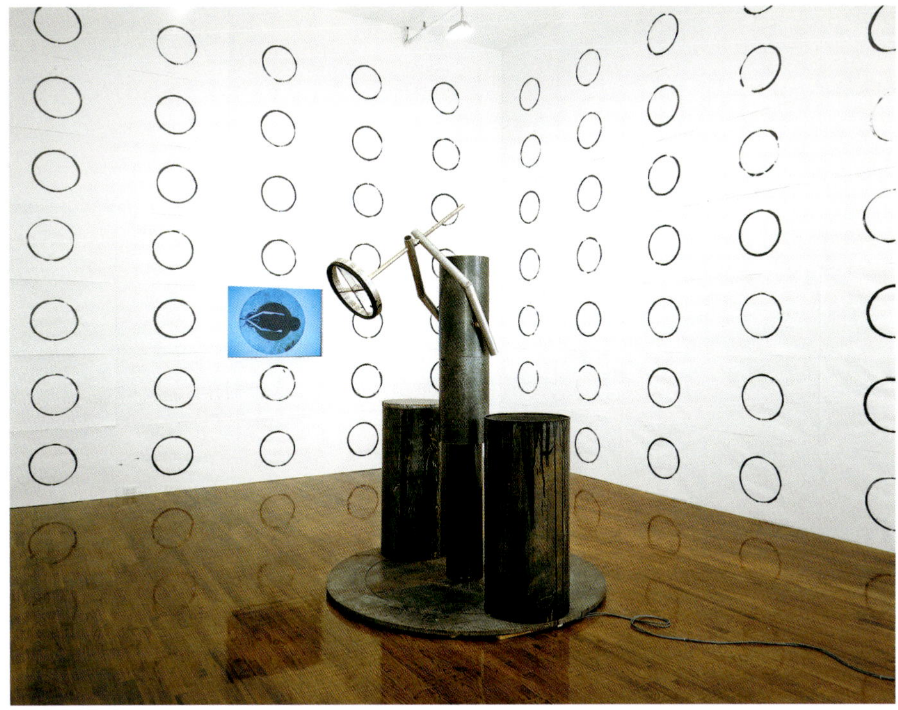

consciousness in the project of delivering to viewers a new capacity to "make room" for themselves.

For Jackson then, each eventual place is host to one or more processes—whether of an action kind—like piling, stacking, spraying, or crashing—or of a more generic type—such as painting, drawing, or sculpting—that inform and in part define it. The discussion that follows is organized around what seems to me the most significant of the places, processes, and renovated genres with which the artist has taken up in a career now spanning more than four decades. I argue that a crucial manifestation of Jackson's creative achievement is located in a signature, and often creatively unstable, negotiation between plan and event, process and product. In the end it might be the remorseless yet reflexive instability between these categories that paradoxically secures the originality of his contribution.

The route to this destination was not, however, an easy one, for it sometimes involved traveling backward with one's eyes shut. In an interview in what was the last significant monographic catalogue devoted to his work, published more than a decade ago, Jackson offers a number of predominantly, sometimes enigmatically negative definitions of his practice and ideas. Made allegorically transparent in *De Nada* (1997) (FIG. 3), a work in which zeros are stamped out by a cipher-issuing machine and then papered on the adjacent walls, the artist's serial disavowal seems to brook no limits. He refuses the notion of having or cultivating "a style"—something, he asserts, that he "hope[s] to never have";[15] he condemns as merely "silly" the need "to conserve painting in a

---

15. Jackson has also stated, "I don't have many good ideas and no exact style." In Buchhart, "Richard Jackson," 222.

nuclear age"; he undermines the compositional notion of painting based on touch, subtraction, and refinement ("the thing that is wrong with the painting process is that it is an editing process. . . . My work doesn't edit anything"); he argues against collaborative or group activities ("usually not my deal"); and despite his own apparent preference for process-based activity, carefully rejects those kinds of practices, notably associated with abstract expressionism and its legacies, that are "too much about process." Rounding out this litany of nonstandard deviations, Jackson also takes stock of the spectatorial situation noted above, in which "until recently the viewer could never witness the event [making a work], but could see that one occurred in a time period that they don't know anything about." And for good measure, he rails against critical overdetermination and art world chatter in general: "I am suspicious of people that talk too much about what I'm looking at." Even when he takes a stand against negativity itself and offers "an optimistic view of what [painting] could be," he does so in a negative formulation: "I felt then and I still feel that painting doesn't need to be an area of art described by the materials that are used."[16]

The negative spaces invested in by Jackson here and elsewhere offer us a model and a rationale for the time-inflected occupation and evacuation of place to which I am pointing. They are also a bulwark against the simplistic correlation of his work with *critique*: it is not that Jackson's work is not in some measure critical but rather that it occupies a different, possibly parallel, negative space—one that is constitutional rather than consumptive and that resists rather than exhausts itself in corrective allegorical realism. As emblematized most obviously by his signature occlusion of the canvas surfaces of the multiple "paintings" that make up his stack pieces, Jackson seems to have worked out his own material orientation to art practice as a series of refusals and deferrals of the aesthetic paradigms that were developed so vigorously as he shaped his own career in the 1970s.

His relationship to minimalism is key to Jackson's shadow semantic economy. While he resists the allure of new materials and smooth finish cultivated by most of the minimalist artists in the mid- and later 1960s, during an interview conducted in 1988, he referred to his overall painting project as having been premised on considerations drawn from the earlier movement: "Somehow," he declares, "this is based in minimalism."[17] If we examine what underwrites this assertion, it becomes clear that the derivation of Jackson's "allegiance" is actually channeled through an unsystematic negation of minimalist principles. First and foremost, while "minimalist" artists themselves complained about the reductive implications of the moniker, or brand name, visited on them,[18] Jackson's resistance to the mantra of reduction is almost absolute. For rather than offering to pare down his work to its essential elements, he offers a characteristically terse slogan—specifically directed as a reaction to minimalism—that turns this orientation upside down: "I never liked minimalism and still don't. I never thought that less was more because in my art more is more."[19] Rather that attempting

---

16. Jackson, in Obrist and Mayo, "Unusual Behavior," 17–23.

17. Jackson, in Salazar, "Museum of the Mind," 12.

18. James Meyer discusses the competing terms offered to describe the emerging movement in the 1960s—cool art, ABC, specific objects, primary structures, and minimalism itself—noting the sustained resistance to the latter designation by LeWitt, Carl Andre, Dan Flavin, Robert Morris, and Donald Judd. Meyer, *Minimalism: Art and Polemics in the Sixties* (New Haven, CT: Yale University Press, 2004), 47, 80–81.

19. Jackson, in Obrist and Mayo, "Unusual Behavior," 22.

some qualitative differentiation of the essential components of form and material—and separating these from humdrum, less privileged parts—he adds more volume and more material to processes that are often already excessive.

But in order to understand Jackson's relation to—and, perhaps, creative misunderstanding of—minimalism more thoroughly, we need to come at it from another side. While his systematic dissociation of the production of his artwork from any kind of subjective transformation appears to conform to some aspects, at least, of minimalist precept, Jackson not atypically pushes the matter beyond its apparent limits, as he virtually hectors a viewer weaned on models of aesthetic elevation: "Nothing is going to be revealed through painting . . . the material isn't going to tell you anything."[20] A parable he related in a recent interview underlines what is at stake in Jackson's negation of the essential and his constant drive to begin at the end: "I read an article about Mark Rothko, how he killed himself in the studio and they found 750 paintings in the racks. Shit, when I read that I wanted to kill myself because they were all the same! There's no doubt in my mind. It's one idea and you keep making it, and making it, and making it, and pretty soon you just come to the end of the line. That's the problem with minimalism."[21]

Given Jackson's premise that painting is rooted in an equality of moments (none privileged over the others), it is ironic that he conjures a vision of Rothko haunted by his own serial accumulation in the form of a pile of paintings engendered by a process of what Jackson takes for repetition. When Jackson sets out quite consciously to stack hundreds or thousands of paintings, each of which is literally unique (though their uniqueness is never flaunted), his process of aesthetic leveling confers equal attention on each element, setting them in a unitary system of production, which, in turn, conveys an overall effect. By imagining Rothko's paintings in a state of signifying redundancy—with all their purported sublimity and tragedy unseen and therefore unactivated— Jackson determines the presence of an *analogy* but not an *instantiation*. The analogy is double: first, Rothko's stash of one similar thing piled on another superficially resembles a gesture of minimalist repetition (even if by accident); secondly, the pile of paintings reminds the artist of his own stacks. But while as mere piles Rothko's works have their would-be transcendent referentiality suspended, they cannot be likened by any deeper comparative to Jackson's repurposed stacks. Instead Rothko's racked-up paintings are inadvertent monuments to the act of making, silent witnesses to the accumulation that besets all artists until their death puts an end to any more production. What this parable helps us to understand, above all, however, is how Jackson's thinking about art thrives in the unsettling, analogical space of the inadvertent.

The zones of contact between Jackson's work and other movements that played out around him, beginning in the later 1960s, are modeled on his diffident negotiation with minimalism. He makes work using actions and bodily gestures but keeps such "performance" largely out of sight, disavowing

20. Jackson, in interview by Christine Kintisch, in *Richard Jackson: Bank Job*, 5 (translation modified).

21. Jackson, in Dennis Szakacs, "The Circus Is in Town" (interview), *Mousse*, no. 25 (September 2010): 46.

any relation to "performance art"; he uses plans, labeled diagrams and concepts, and even plays with words but has no interest in sublimating the materiality of his processes or locations to the "conceptual" operations of ideas or language; and while engaged with specific sites, using and reformatting the walls and architectural constitution of gallery and exhibition spaces, and offering a profound investigation of the nature of the "room" (domestic, public, bureaucratic, etc.), rarely draws his work alongside the self-consciously critical operations of institutional critique or its more recent satellite discourses. In what follows, I will open out some of these points of noncontact and then mobilize them as the basis for a revisionary consideration of the somewhat aberrant locations of Jackson's practice when measured by the normative assumptions and movement structures of the post–World War II art world. But I will do so by following the inadvertent logic of Jackson's own orientations.

2 Stacking

Perhaps the closest anticipation of Jackson's signature stacking of canvases can be found in a series of works by Marcel Broodthaers each titled *Tableau-objet* (1967) . While the similarities are obvious—both artists piled stretched canvases one on top of the other, and the stack that results is the "work"—the differences between their enterprises are far more telling. For a start, Broodthaers used just a few canvases in three or more sizes, while Jackson employed hundreds or—in the most ambitious examples of the genre, such as *5050* (1998/2013; drawing, 1980; reconstructed in the current exhibition)—thousands, each of which is nearly identical in scale and format. In one of the *Tableau-objet* works, Broodthaers deployed four larger canvases, which became, de facto, a kind of base or podium supporting eight middle-size canvases, which are topped in turn by four smaller ones. In the example reproduced here (FIG. 4), four larger canvases rest on what appears to be a single, slightly larger one and support twelve medium-sized and three smaller canvases, the first of which is slightly larger in turn than the final two. Each constituent canvas is painted, somewhat irregularly, a different color: two are red, two dark blue, five light blue, two a slightly darker blue, three have a pinkish hue, two are light orange, while one is more purple and the bottom one is gray. What might have been a roomful of wall-hung paintings in five (or in other examples, three) "regular sizes" is made over as a graduated column. Among other forms and types, the appearance of the work is thus aligned with the tapered ethos of the monument or the stepped skyscraper, the incremental diminishments of which were mandated by safety and zoning laws.

Jackson's stacks, by contrast, give rise to a different range of formal configurations (FIG. 5). Some create a wall-like mass, as with *Big Ideas—1000*

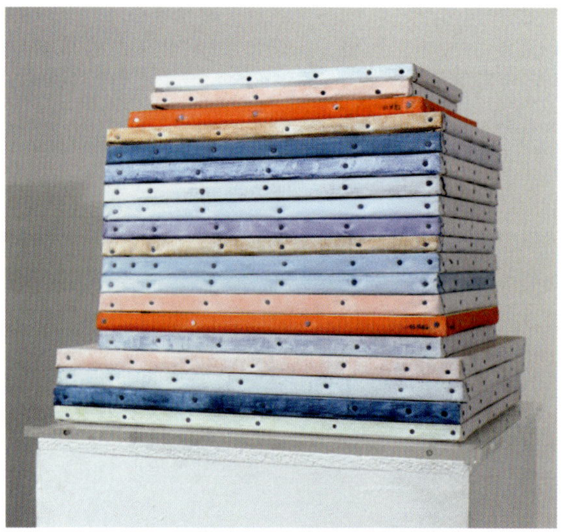

FIG. 5
Richard Jackson, *Bob's Pictures*, 2006–10.
Wood, canvas, acrylic paint. 234 × 246½ ×
17¼ in. (586.7 × 626.1 × 43.8 cm). Rennie
Collection, Vancouver

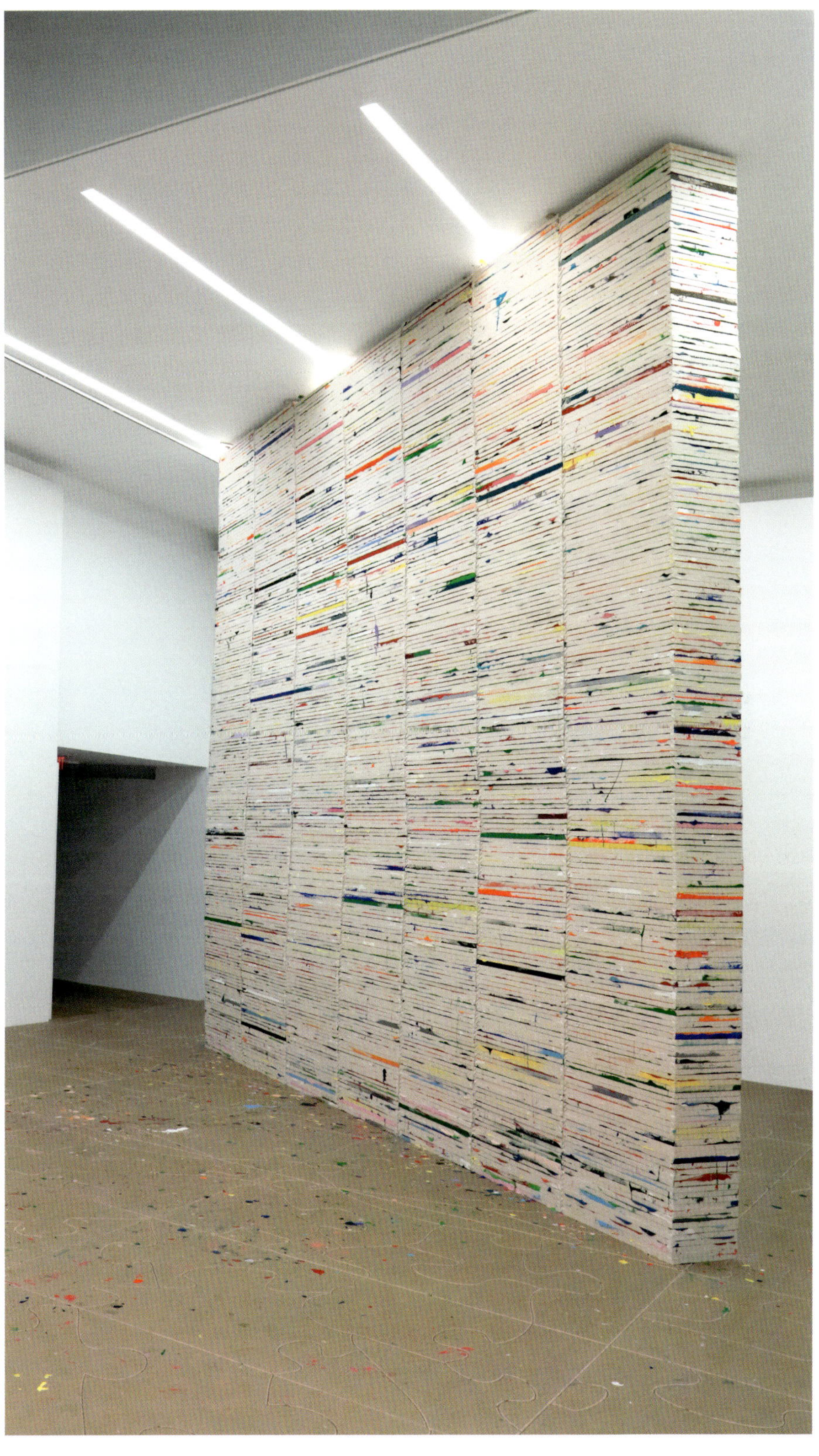

Pictures (1980) or *Bob's Pictures* (2006–10), which rises in a straight line from floor to ceiling with the thickness of one canvas. Following *Big Ideas—800 Pictures* (1981), Jackson's third exercise in the series, *Big Ideas 2—3000 Pictures* (1981) took the form of an approximate sphere sited in a ground-floor space at the Los Angeles County Museum of Art, which the artist was obliged to support with simple struts. Prompted by the need to produce curvature in all directions, the stacking method for *Big Ideas 2* was as unique as the resulting figure, in that the canvases on each "row" were separated by gaps, while those above and below were slightly indented or overhung.[22] Other installments entered into dialogue with the lineaments of columns or supports, as with *Big Ideas* (1988; Los Angeles Municipal Art Gallery),[23] or otherwise addressed the structural articulation of the exhibition space, while others were developed in more concentrated, "sculptural" forms or extended into larger enclosures, as with *Big Ideas—800 Pictures*. Some mixed the language of column and wall, as with the untitled stepped sequence of stacks shown at Galerie Tschudi in Glarus, Switzerland, in 1989. A few, including the gargantuan *5050*, also engage with incrementality, but instead of juxtaposing three or more size-oriented phases (as with Broodthaers's work), unravel themselves through a plurality of tiny steps that act in unison with the basic unit of articulation—the single canvas itself.

Several studies and models for *5050* bear witness to Jackson's experiments with serial additions and graduated effects. *Untitled (Model II for "5050 Stacked Paintings")* (1998) envisages a circular wall that starts one canvas-width high and then proceeds to form a complete circumference, with each subsequent stack adding a single canvas until the perimeter is closed (with a stack of one hundred paintings meeting the solitary initial piece). *Untitled (Model III for "5050 Stacked Paintings")*, made in the same year, proposes a very different solution to the stacked cohabitation of 5,050 paintings. Here Jackson thinks through a ziggurat-like gestalt as the paintings are assembled in a linear series, again in increments of one, that sweeps backward and forward ten times to create a progressively higher zigzag wall resembling an impossible set of tilted bleachers.

In his first notes for the Big Ideas series, jotted down in August 1979, Jackson estimated that he might need some six thousand smallish stretched canvases to fulfill his primary objective: to "make a painting that fills a room."[24] As we have seen, however, the first and third examples used one thousand and three thousand canvases, respectively, and ended up making first a wall-like and then a spherical intervention in the gallery spaces rather than completely displacing their volumes. Always alert to the social, durational, and symbolic signification of large, round numbers (*Big Ideas 2* was, quite literally, a big, round figure, and the artist's wall paintings were available for sale for a decade at $1,000 apiece), Jackson comes closest to his early estimate with *5050*. The title, of course, is freighted with delicious irony, for in addition to being a large number, fifty shy of six thousand, 5050 also connotes "fifty-fifty," the common expression

---

22. *Big Ideas 2—3000 Pictures* was realized for the exhibition *Museum as Site: Sixteen Projects* at the Los Angeles County Museum of Art in 1981.

23. *Big Ideas* (1988) is reproduced in Wirth, *Deer Beer*, 106, along with the note: "Painted and stacked canvases look like the structural columns in the exhibition space."

24. The August 1979 text is reprinted in Wirth, *Deer Beer*, 87.

for symmetrically split odds or something shared or borne equally. Read most directly, Jackson seems simply to be describing the heads-and-tails alternation of fifty-fifty, thus doubling up on the process of stacking. From another point of view, he might be suggesting that the work is 50 percent stacks and 50 percent paintings, or he could be proposing that the piece resists all the odds stacked against it, coming out as an epiphany of its own equilibrium.

Jackson's conceptualization of *5050* anticipates the art world's attention to similar matters, notably in the series of "equilibrium tanks" made by Jeff Koons in the mid-1980s, which includes *Three Ball 50/50 Tank (Two Dr. J Silver Series, Wilson Supershot)* (1985) (FIG. 6), the title of which is also aligned with the dispensation of fifty-fifty. The tanks were part of Koons's first exhibition at International with Monument Gallery, New York, *Equilibrium* (1985), which purported to investigate "the futile impossibility of balance in life and the inevitability of death."[25] While crossing paths numerically—and spherically—

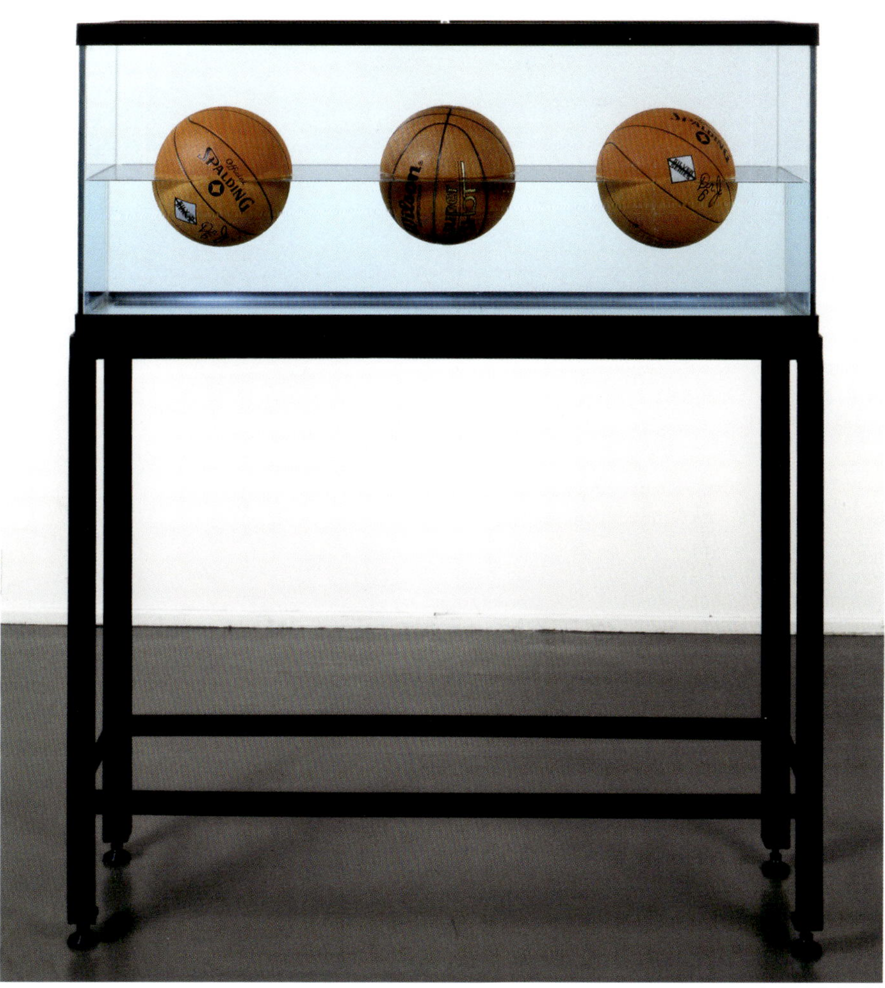

FIG. 6
Jeff Koons, *Three Ball 50/50 Tank (Two Dr. J Silver Series, Wilson Supershot)*, 1985. Glass, steel, distilled water, and three basketballs. 60 ½ × 48 ¾ × 13 ¼ in. (154 × 123.9 × 33.6 cm). The Broad Art Foundation, Santa Monica

25. Christies' Post War and Contemporary Evening Sale, Rockefeller Plaza, New York, May 9, 2006, http://www.christies.com/LotFinder/lot_details.aspx?intObject ID=4705675.

Koons and Jackson represent the heads and tails of the fifty-fifty. Koons deliberately embraced the advertising and media cultures of the corporatist 1980s,
farmed out most of his work to top-end fabricators, citing his own technical
incompetence, had a former day job as a stockbroker, and actively cultivated his
market success and art world celebrity. Jackson was never less than sardonic
about commercialism in all or most of its forms, cited the painstakingly
handmade (though never "precious") nature of his work as one of its defining
features, did blue-collar work in the building trade (even when he was already an
exhibiting artist), and debunked the careerist antics that he witnessed all around
him in the Reagan (and later) years.[26]

Jackson's fifty-fifty installations are an ambitious return to his
earlier proposal to "fill a room 'exactly' 1/2 full" of paintings. In a folio of drawings,
later self-published as a limited-edition book titled *1/2 full*,[27] the original concept
of stacking units volumetrically was extended through a series of configurations.
In a manner that recalls Sol LeWitt's permutations of "incomplete cubes,"
these two-point-perspective drawings allocate precisely half of a given space to
stacked paintings, and the resulting three-dimensional volumes create walls,
enclosures, checkerboard patterns, and sculptural forms according to the
straightforward application of geometric principles. The partial fullness that
results suggests a seemingly optimistic worldview, emblematizing a laborious
activity fronted by a curiously enthusiastic attitude. Even as Jackson claims to be
optimistic about extending the limits of painting, his work—through its strident
anti-illusionism—traffics in a flagrant critique of painting practices and the art
world more generally. So the half-full mentality is at once confirmed and denied
both by the physical ordeals of production (each individual work is handmade
by the artist) and by the artist's gruff demeanor and negative self-definition (see
section 6, "Give or Take: The 'Pain in Painting'").

Jackson and Broodthaers share a common interest in the
materiality of the constituents of painting and the work-like orders of its elemental
processes (canvas, stretchers and stretching, nails and tacking, etc.), but Jackson
takes all this one step further by involving himself, as Broodthaers deliberately
does not, in the crucial couplet of paint and painting. Not only does he do so in
the same matter-of-fact procedural terms that underwrote the stretching and
stacking, but he also obscures most of the results of his labor by burying it inside
the stacks. Both artists, then, have turned to the arena of the stretched canvas
only to turn their backs on its normative signification by formatting their paintings
back to front, or top to bottom. In Jackson's case, this move makes a pair with the
artist's guidance of the viewer to the blind side of painting in *Untitled (Maze)*.

The dozen or so years that separate *Tableau-objet* from Jackson's
first experiments with stacking in 1979 are, of course, coterminous with the
international rise of conceptual art.[28] One of the revisionist emphases of this
movement was a thoroughgoing dispute with the cultural ascendancy of painting
and the general assumptions vested in its expressive, formal, and other values.

26. Jackson was described by one critic
as "a construction worker who makes art."
Salazar, "Museum of the Mind," 12.

27. Richard Jackson, *1/2 full* (Privately
printed, 1983).

28. Jackson made his first written plan
and sketch for a stack in 1979.

We can identify two strands in which this resistance was played out. One—exemplified by John Baldessari's *Work with Only One Property* (1967–68) and Art & Language's *100% Abstract* (1968) or, rather differently, by Daniel Buren's deployment beginning in the mid-1960s of a compositionally minimal bifurcated field, or "stripe"—used the canvas itself in alliance with painted text (or, with Buren, took up with a residuum of appositional form) to point to the double articulation of any painted sign: its material constituencies, on the one hand, and its conceptual (and social) implications and assumptions, on the other. A second, possibly more radical strand rejected altogether the conventional formats of pictorial (or sculptural) articulation to take up with language, writing, performative gestures, reproductions, or documentation. Lawrence Weiner's wall pieces would seem to embrace aspects of both positions, using text inscribed not on canvas but on the wall, though in the process alluding to another location on which painting was traditionally made visible, the mural painting.

To put the matter briefly, I want to suggest that Broodthaers and Jackson provide bookends for the beginning and (possible) end of the conceptualist dispute with pictoriality. Both stage their articulations in the establishing materials of painting while resolutely undermining the marks on a canvas surface that had hitherto defined the very nature of pictorial space. While Broodthaers interleaved the scenes of visual and literary production, both artists refused to carry out their dispute with painting by converting the canvas into a page (or sign) in the manner of Baldessari and others, and in both language is defiantly absent so that the work is not declarative; nor does it attempt any kind of guaranteed "proposition." Both use humor and parody (which draws them closer to Baldessari, although he was not the only artist in the conceptual generation to make recourse to wit and irony),[29] so that the situational absurdity of presenting a mass of superficially contentless paintings is foundational to their different essays in counterpictorial practice. Both, then, produce a dispute with painting predicated on the material potency of its organizing structure (the stretched canvas), and for both this premise is simultaneously inalienable and redundant. The "pictorial" is superabundantly present as a sign yet gratuitously empty when read by a viewer equipped with the "language" of painting. Their work suggests that the end of painting was signaled neither by the advent of the perfect monochrome or the ultimate abstraction nor by the complete suspension of any intercourse with its predicates (as with much conceptual art). Instead they work in the space between the postmortem on painting's demise and its vicarious resurrection in the various neo-expressionisms that emerged following Broodthaers's early death and run parallel to Jackson's midcareer.

Another consequence of viewing the stacks of Broodthaers and Jackson as part of a continuum is that Broodthaers's now established location as an apostle of institutional critique becomes somewhat complicated. This is not because Jackson has nothing much to do with the premises or assumptions of institutional critique and Broodthaers is therefore freed from its spell by loose

29. See my essay "Don't Try for Laughs: John Baldessari and Conceptual Comedy," in *Black Sphinx: On the Comedic in Modern Art*, ed. John C. Welchman (Zurich: JRP | Ringier, 2009), 245–68.

association but because in both artists there is something stubbornly desanc-tifying, a strain of making that brings work into being without the stress or burdens of straining. Each artist has liberated himself from the necessity to believe—either in the operations of painting or in the crusading necessity somehow to best or defeat it.

---

3 Smearing and Swinging; or, The Whys and Wherefores of "Painting"

In the late 1960s—when Jackson began to think through the conditions of possibility for one of his most decisive interventions, the wall paintings—the very orientation of art to the wall that so often acted as its place and support structure had already been subject to profound reconsideration. One tendency—antici-pated by works such as William Anastasi's *Untitled (one gallon of industrial high-gloss enamel, poured)* (1966) but most visible, perhaps, in LeWitt's "wall drawings" and Weiner's wall-borne texts—offered to rejuvenate the wall itself as a site of inscription using direct application. In a lineage that runs somewhat indirectly from Weiner's removal of a three-foot-square section of plaster from a gallery wall in 1967 to Chris Burden's *Exposing the Foundation of the Museum* (1986), another tendency viewed walls as the paradigmatic arenas of the institutionality of art and so worked to invade, expose, disrupt, or collapse them. While Jackson's ideas for the wall seemed to align themselves, provisionally at least, with the first of these reconsiderations, the space engendered by the wall paintings is articulated by several commitments that, considered together, offer a wholly new orientation for the relations between art and wall, drawing them alongside the nomadic reanimation—even "explosion"—of the wall taken on by Le Corbusier and others in the mid-twentieth century.[30]

The linkages between Jackson's wall paintings and LeWitt's wall drawings have significance well beyond the fact that both started making process-based wall works in the same year (1968).[31] Obvious formal differences between their respective wall pieces belie conceptual similarities based on a shared reliance on planning. Further, Jackson's relinquishment of signature, personal, or expressive investments and his avoidance of progression from one stroke to the next or, equally, from one artwork to another, echoes one of LeWitt's prescriptions for conceptual art: "To work with a plan that is pre-set is one way of avoiding subjectivity. It also obviates the necessity of designing each work in turn. The plan would design the work. . . . This eliminates the arbitrary, the capricious, and the subjective as much as possible." LeWitt's commitment to "planning" and anterior decision making, and his concomitant relegation of "execution," which he termed "a perfunctory affair," gave rise to the striking proposition that the conceptually oriented artist strives to "make his work

30. See Romy Golan, *Muralnomad: The Paradox of Wall Painting, Europe 1927–1957* (New Haven, CT: Yale University Press, 2009), and the review by Michèle C. Cone, "If These Walls Could Walk," *Art in America* 99 (January 2011): 33–38. While Golan (like Le Corbusier) is concerned with the invention of mobile supplements to, or renovations of, the traditional wall-bound mural—tapestries, photomurals, mosaics—Jackson makes the wall itself a movable and temporary object.

31. "I started action-based painting in 1968. They were all wall paintings." Jackson, in interview with Marie de Brugerolle and Julien Bismuth, in *Ne pas jouer avec des choses mortes*, ed. Éric Mangion and Marie de Brugerolle (Dijon, France: Presses du réel; Nice, France: Villa Arson, 2009), 95. LeWitt's first wall drawing, *Drawing Series II 18 (A&B)*, was created at Paula Cooper Gallery in October 1968. See Patricia Norvell and Alexander Alberro, *Recording Conceptual Art* (Berkeley: University of California Press, 2001).

mentally interesting to the spectator," and finally that "the idea becomes a machine that makes the art."[32] For Jackson too, the plan defines the process: "It's part of the understanding of the process, to discover the system behind the work. I work out all the systems on paper. Some of the drawings look like the paintings in the way it functions: what comes first, what comes next, and what overlaps. That's all planned beforehand and must be planned exactly before going in, otherwise it might not work. I accept anything that happens during the painting process. What happens happens. When something fails, that is part of the work."[33] Following the conceptualization of an appropriate plan, painting is deployed simply as a physical act, no more invested with meaning than other, more mundane activities. Its value as a cultural activity depends more on the quality of the conception behind it than on any qualities associated with execution or construction.

But while taking off from similar conceptual premises, the wall installations made by these artists envision very different relationships between planning and execution. LeWitt, for example, created plans the parameters of which are sufficiently well defined that others are able to create the works, alongside or even in the absence of the artist.[34] Less stringent perhaps in their requirements, the works to which Jackson's drawings give rise, by contrast, are made—at his own insistence—by the artist himself without any assistance.[35] If Jackson concurs with LeWitt's overall prescription to follow a plan as closely as possible (within reason), his execution is beset by a host of uncontrollable elements, not generally encountered by LeWitt or his surrogate makers. LeWitt, of course, warned that an emphasis on the materiality of a work can overwhelm the idea that governs it: "The danger is, I think, in making the physicality of the materials so important that it becomes the idea of the work." Yet materiality, in his view, should not be spurned altogether but redirected or *converted*: "The conceptual artist would want to ameliorate this emphasis on materiality as much as possible or to use it in a paradoxical way. (To convert it into an idea.)"[36] Jackson can be said to take up with his own variant of the "paradoxical" method, posing it as a specific challenge or conceptual problem: how does the artist plan for—or simply imagine or anticipate—unplanned results? The physicality of his projects underscores a dominant strain in Jackson's thinking as the artist's conceptual bent and action-based procedures are fixated on the idea of material abundance. The flaunting of excess and the exhausting provision of "more" underwrite the artist's abiding "need" "to expand painting physically."[37] It is not just by virtue of his crusade against touch and compositional increment, therefore, that Jackson's plans often get out of hand.

In contrast to LeWitt's meticulous preparatory studies, with their sparely precise instructions for the physical implementation of his ideas, Jackson's rapid sketches capture the moment at which his techniques of inscription try and sometimes fail to keep up with his conceptual ambition. Jackson's often cartoonishly simple diagrams might contain altered or scratched-out elements,

---

32. Sol LeWitt, "Paragraphs on Conceptual Art" (1967), in *Sol LeWitt: A Retrospective*, ed. Gary Garrels (San Francisco: San Francisco Museum of Modern Art, 2000), 369–70. This text was originally published in *Artforum* 5 (June 1967): 79–83.

33. Jackson, in Duchhart, "Richard Jackson," 219.

34. LeWitt maintained: "The artist conceives and plans the wall drawing. It is realized by draftsmen . . . . The wall drawing is the artist's art, as long as the plan is not violated"; LeWitt, "Doing Wall Drawings," *Art Now: New York* 3 (June 1971): unpaged.

35. Jackson, in Obrist and Mayo, "Unusual Behavior," 19.

36. LeWitt, "Paragraphs on Conceptual Art," 371.

37. Jackson, in Szakacs, "Circus Is in Town," 43.

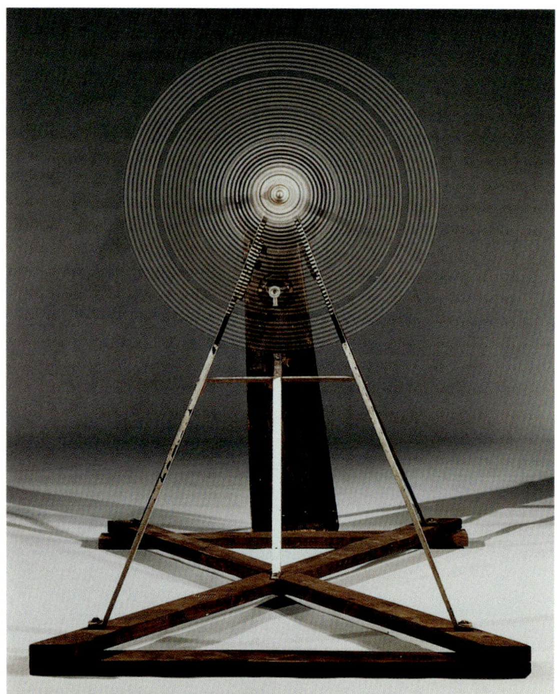

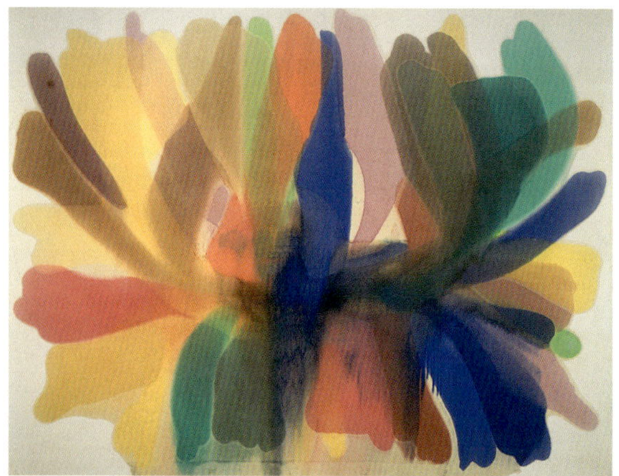

rehearsing his effusive processes in the safe confines of the white page—and often using wide margins as if to buffer the idea. One of the vital sources of his humor and exuberance is the assertion that while painting can resist conceptualization the artist is able to conceptualize how this resistance transpires. While the various forms of physical, material profusion (precipitated by paint and its applications) adopted by Jackson counteract the rigid process of planning, it might also be said that his *idea* of painting is actually animated by the production of unplanned activities and material excess. Jackson's attempt to conceptualize what cannot be fully conceptualized is a paradox in which he readily indulges.[38] For at some point his material processes overtake his ideas, which is part of the idea.

The relative weight that they accord to color and line marks another difference between the two artists. While LeWitt's wall works are organized by the provision of lines, even when color is overlaid onto the linear structure, the function and effects of color in Jackson's work are both more palpable and more deliberate: a viscous medium is spread and pushed beyond delimited boundaries, and when geometric lines or grids do appear, they tend to reinforce the qualities of color as amalgam and overlay. So while they share a number of conceptual premises, Jackson and LeWitt diverge profoundly in the types of rules that they apply to the execution of their work—only to return to a shared attitude toward the permanence, or lack of it, in the completed wall works, since their different formal and procedural principles both resist the indefinite preservation of "fine art."[39]

In spite of an obvious reluctance to reproduce the conventions of pictorial arrangement, Jackson's wall works also reinstate and preserve—at least in the form of "commentary"—one of the qualities most deeply entrenched in modernist painting: the gesture. Maurice Tuchman and Jane Livingston were among the first to point to "the broad comments on abstract gestural painting implicit in Richard Jackson's constructs."[40] In one dimension, Jackson's painting-by-smearing mirrors the gestural movement of expressionist application, but the idea of the stroke, or *tâche*, has been redirected through a diagrammatic plan of expressive motion. In certain respects, Jackson's insouciant gesture is suffused with the kind of irony invested by Roy Lichtenstein in his Brushstroke paintings from the mid-1960s, though Jackson refuses pop art's collusion with the mass-produced image by insisting, even if mutely, on his provision of an unrepeatable, individual act.

Jackson paints (perhaps we should say, "lays paint out") on the surface of a stretched canvas, which is positioned facing the wall, pinned in place, and then rotated so that the wet pigment is impressed onto the supporting surface. Using the canvas as an applicator, he produces a painting "negative" in the sense that what is remaindered on the wall is an inverse trace of the paint formation on the canvas itself, which, having been swung around in an arc, is left on the wall in a preordained position. The negative image thus generated also has

38. LeWitt alludes to a related paradox inherent in planning a wall drawing or, rather, in making a drawing on paper in anticipation of a wall drawing: "Ideas of wall drawings alone are contradictions of the idea of wall drawings." LeWitt, "Doing Wall Drawings," unpaged.

39. Acknowledging the limited temporality of many of his works, LeWitt stated: "The wall drawing is a permanent installation, until destroyed. Once something is done, it cannot be undone." Sol LeWitt, "Wall Drawings," in *Sol LeWitt*, exh. cat. (New York: Museum of Modern Art, 1978), 169.

40. Maurice Tuchman and Jane Livingston, introduction to *Los Angeles '72: Exhibition of Young Los Angeles Artists*, exh. cat. (New York: Sidney Janis Gallery, 1972), unpaged.

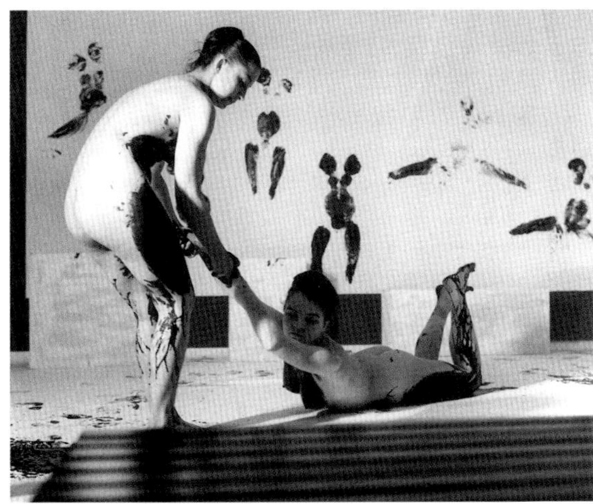

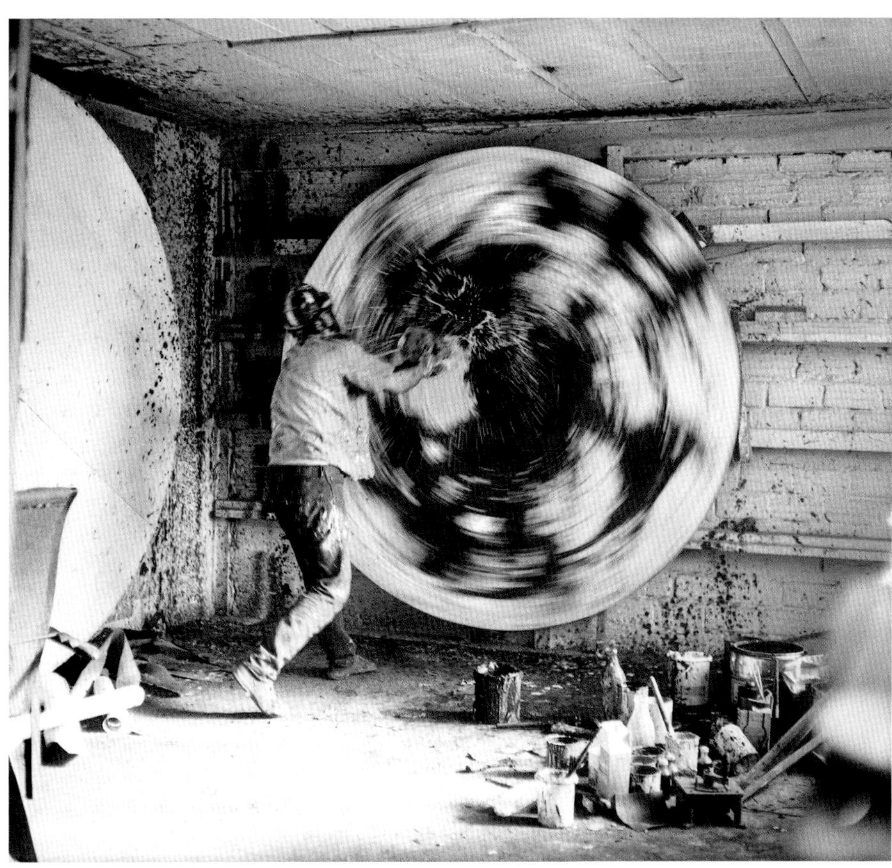

a filmic quality as the canvas is not just applied but turned so that the resultant marks on the wall are kinetic imprints produced by a looping or spooling action.

Drawing on an avant-garde formation that we can trace from Marcel Duchamp's rotary disks (FIG. 7) to Morris Louis's manhandling of unstretched canvases (in the cramped dining room of his Baltimore residence) to make his Floral series (FIG. 8) and other works in the late 1950s, the turning of the canvas is the defining operation of Jackson's application. As with some of its forebears, it is also a retort to the accumulated pictorial tradition of touching (by hand), dripping (with a stick), and pouring or staining. The activity of *pressing* relates Jackson's method, in turn, to other genealogies of touching, such as frottage and decalcomania, used by Max Ernst, Oscar Dominguez, and other surrealists. Only for Jackson, the image that results is not the product of a rubbing action that exports the textures and unevenness of a foreign surface; instead, paint is a kind of lubricant situated between canvas and wall that is smeared into place by the double moves of pressing and rotating. Closer parallels might be found with Yves Klein's Anthropometries, begun in 1960, in which paint-smeared female bodies were impressed onto paper or canvas on the floor or wall (FIG. 9); with the rotational disk paintings of Alfons Schilling, commenced in 1961 (FIG. 10);[41] or later with David Deutsch's rotating wall piece,

41. On the early development of Alfons Schilling's work, including his rotated paintings, see Hubert Klocker, "Die ersten Jahre / Vienna, Paris, 1956–1962," http://www.alfons-schilling.com/text1.html.

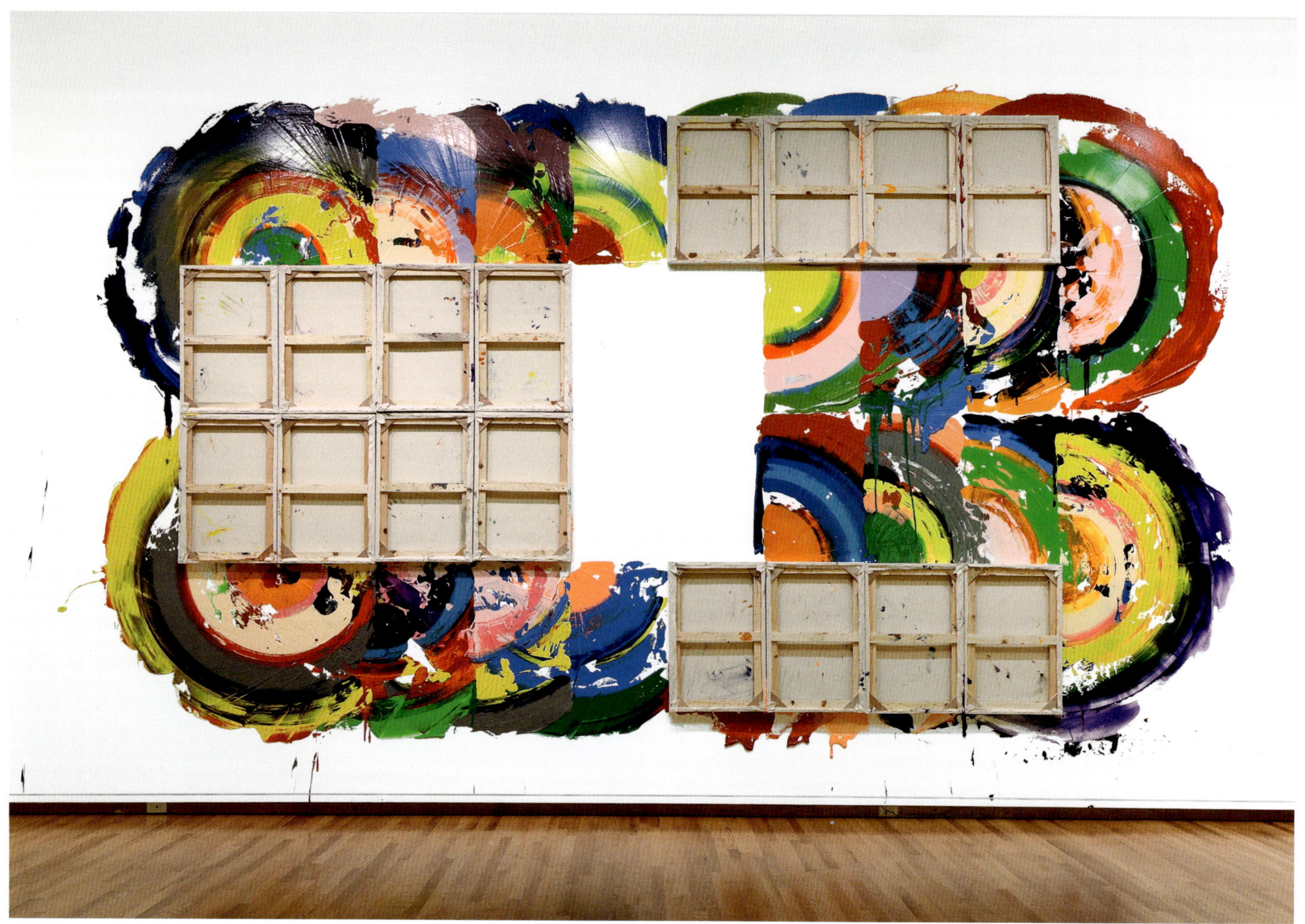

which appeared next to Jackson's work in an exhibition of art from Los Angeles at the Sidney Janis Gallery in New York in 1972.[42]

In Jackson's dispensation the canvas becomes its own brush—or palette knife—which acts as a backhanded delivery system for the as yet unsettled materials deposited on its surface, and in a sense he remains uninterested in—"un-impressed by" might be more accurate—the publicity and spectacle courted by Klein or the intimations of speed, force, and "infinity" solicited by Schilling. Like much in Jackson's work, his actions are clearly covert operations, as what funds the whole process of application—the initial supply of paint to the imprinting canvas—is neither witnessed by the viewer nor visible in the final state of the work. Instead the backs of the "spent" canvases are made over into the frontal aspect of the "image," obscuring parts of it (which must be apprehended by implication) and creating a defiant quasi-geometric material

42. See *Los Angeles '72.*

bulkhead at the center of the composition. The pattern on the wall appears to have emanated from "behind" the canvases, cartwheeling exuberantly out of their rough perimeters (FIG. 11). The physical act of smearing thus becomes the defining operation for Jackson's de-definition of painting, for not only does it dismantle the illusionistic practice of pictorial representation and negate both the geometric and gestural signing that replaced it, but the smear is also a defamation that bears down on every form of painted mark. As in the practice of stacking, the very idea of pictoriality has again been negated, this time by an act of smearing that tantalizes with its suggestion of an unrecoverable ideal or would-be pristine image while skewering the very need for such a distracting ruse. When Jackson went so far as to smear his own signature for the cover of an exhibition catalog published in 1978, he closed the circle on his rotational practice by turning defamation on himself.[43]

Another figure for this closure can be found in Jackson's awareness of the reach and limits of paint's material qualities. Working with smeared and stretched layers furnished by an arbitrary distribution system, he clearly gestures toward the physical limitations of the medium—especially as its capacity to cover reaches a point of exhaustion or no return. This might be Jackson's unexorbitant take on the vaunted "death of painting"—a piece of wound-down vaudeville as a colorful medium is spread around a surface, sputters, temporarily recovers, and then finally peters out. But there is a darker side to the diminuendo of spreading that signaled for one early commentator in 1975 "a rather disconcerting, even violent means of expression."[44] Jackson's work with paint simultaneously performs its malleability and uncovers the lack of solidity or permanence that takes refuge behind the inherent assertiveness, even aggressivity, of paint's ostentatious liquid form. Conjured now as a sort of monstrous presence or eerie materialization oozing from the spaces between solid structures, the paint evidences a determinate force applied in a seemingly arbitrary manner—masquerading as the globular, suppurating stuff of B-movie horror.

The de-facement of painting that Jackson instigates by obscuring the traditional pictorial surface and undermining normative viewing expectations might be described as a voluntaristic act of neo-iconoclasm. More specifically, he revisits the desire to expose the backside of painting, in dialogue with a historical genre—launched by Cornelis Norbertus Gysbrechts with *Trompe l'oeil, The Reverse of a Framed Painting* (ca. 1668–72) (FIG. 12) and *Easel with Still Life* (ca. 1670),[45] and revisited by Jasper Johns, Giulio Paolini, Roy Lichtenstein, and others in the 1950s and 1960s.[46] Jackson usually makes his work in publicly accessible spaces, precisely "where it belongs," he maintains, "instead of locked up in somebody's home where they're speculating on art like they speculate on gold."[47] But his version of the visual reversal of painting is transacted in a manner that subverts the preservation and collection of his works, seeming literally to reverse the conditions by which a collector associates an image with its monetary (or face) value. Jackson inverts the speculative value of images by

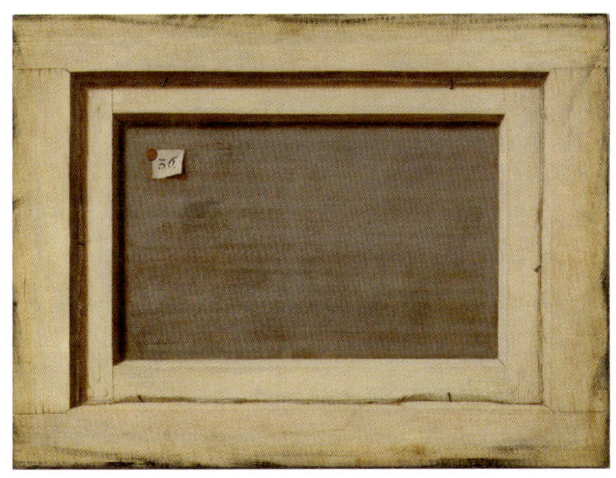

FIG. 12
Cornelis Norbertus Gysbrechts, *Trompe l'oeil, The Reverse of a Framed Painting*, ca. 1668–72. Oil on canvas. 87 × 66 in. (221 × 167.6 cm). Statens Museum for Kunst/National Gallery of Denmark, Copenhagen, Denmark

43. See *Richard Jackson*, exh. cat. (Hope, ID: Faith and Charity in Hope Gallery, 1978).

44. Judith Dunham, "'Both Kinds': Contemporary L.A. Art," *Artweek* 6 (May 3, 1975): 20.

45. If, as Amy Powell argues, the reversal of painting in Flemish art marked a historical relocation of painting from public spaces to private homes, it could be argued that Jackson's work frames painting's backside as a conceptual return to the public sphere. "Gijsbrechts' *Easel with Still Life* recalls the iconoclasm of the previous century, metaphorically re-enacting it by lowering the painting and turning it away. Turning a blank face towards the viewer, the reversed canvas recalls the origin of easel painting in the negation of the image." Powell, "Painting as Blur: Landscapes in Paintings of the Dutch Interior," *Oxford Art Journal* 33, no. 2 (2010): 149.

46. See Michael Darling, ed., *Target Practice: Painting under Attack, 1949–78*, exh. cat. (Seattle: Seattle Art Museum, 2009), 34–39.

47. Salazar, "Museum of the Mind," 12.

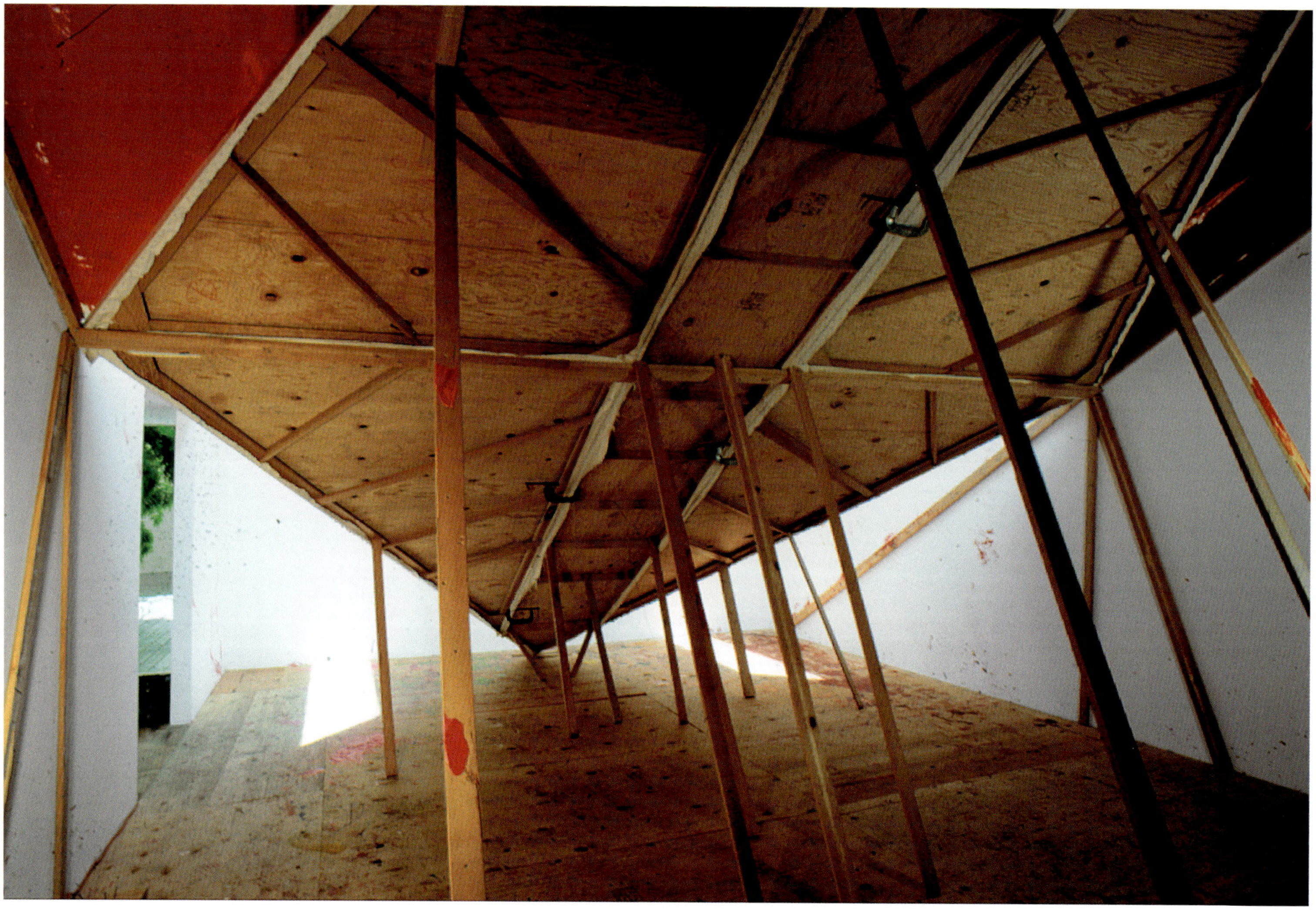

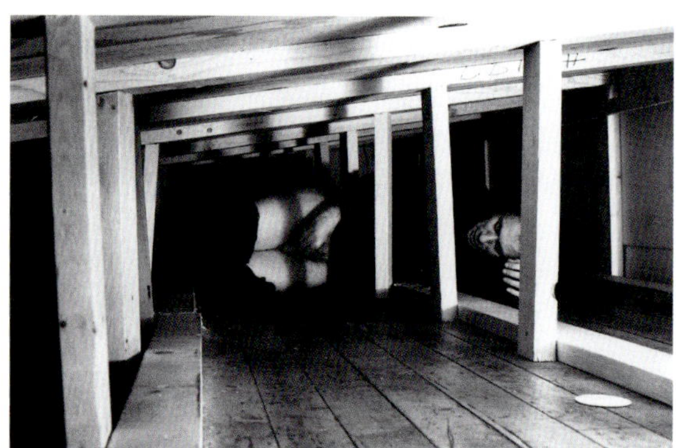

FIG. 13
Richard Jackson, *Untitled*, 1978. Canvas,
wood, acrylic paint. 192 × 321 × 229 in.
(487.7 × 815.3 × 581.7 cm). Installation view,
Rosamund Felsen Gallery, Los Angeles

FIG. 14
Vito Acconci, *SEEDBED*, Sonnabend Gallery,
New York, January 1972. Performance/
installation. Wood ramp: 2 ½ × 22 × 30 ft.;
9 days, 8 hours/day

metaphorically reorienting the viewer to the posterior of the work (FIG. 13). In *Untitled (Maze)*, we recall, the pictorial encounter is made over in the perverse form of a physical impediment coupled with a sort of predicament: because, once the failed encounter is staged, viewers must literally retrace their steps and reverse course, leaving behind what is already a reversal. To this scene in which painting is encountered but not viewed full-on—and then retreated from—Jackson adds another of those personal signatures that round out his pictorial deflection, noting in the late 1980s that he was, himself, "tired of looking at paintings."[48]

But there is yet another side in the matter of painting's defacement. For in addition to presenting us with an impossible array of hidden surfaces or fronts, Jackson also investigates the very conditions of the underneath. This concern arose in part from a kind of necessity, in that some of his works of the 1970s and 1980s required the construction of scaffolding,

48. Susan Chadwick, "For Richard
Jackson, the Point Is Painting," *Houston
Post*, July 17, 1988.

platforms, or temporary supports, which gave rise to a series of substructures or negative vantage points. In Jackson's untitled work of 1978, a sloping diamond-shaped canvas raised on props installed at the Rosamund Felsen Gallery,[49] his production of an underside takes its place in a lineage of more literal investigations of the underneath that reaches from Vito Acconci's iconoclastic *SEEDBED* (1972), staged under the Sonnabend Gallery in New York (FIG. 14), to Mike Kelley's inquiry into the social and formal constitution of caves, basements, and "sublevels" in *Sublevel: Dim Recollection Illuminated by Multicolored Swamp Gas* (1998), first presented at Jablonka Galerie in Cologne, and other works.[50] While Acconci interposes his own body and an engagement with one of its more private activities and Kelley takes up with the willfully faulty structures of memory, Jackson characteristically addresses what's behind the underneath by draining his substructure of any ostensible "content." Like his other "accidents" in abstract painting, Jackson's underspace not only is emptied of bodies or objects but also seeks no particular engagement with the qualities or effects of memory, formal organization, or the aesthetic, though he probably wouldn't shut them down if something cropped up. The view under the untitled work exists, then, only as an image and is an image only because it can be both seen and "taken"—unlike the closed faces of the stacked paintings or the fronts of the canvases remaindered in the wall pieces. What we witness here is nothing more and nothing less than Jackson taking us quite simply to the bottom of things.

These concerns, allied with the contention that painting is a predicament to be negotiated, emerged in an early work executed in Jackson's studio in 1970 consisting of a painted canvas nailed to the floor.[51] Here a faceless object, with its backside exposed, creates a sort of physical obstacle in that it becomes as much an impediment to movement through a space as an object to be "appreciated." At the same time, the insistent physicality of its placement in the middle of the floor engenders a sense of the impossible, inaccessible, and ultimately unavoidable image—in this case one step away from being walked all over. The preparatory sketch for the "floor painting" contains top and side views but is marked "no bottom view"—which is to say that it was specifically denied any frontal realization. Its consolidated facelessness marks it as a picture without a vantage point, an image that has utterly refused to give itself to vision. Grounded in thoroughgoing inaccessibility, this founding gesture of painting as impediment would manifest itself throughout Jackson's career in a combination of repetitions and revisions, eventually emerging as a surrogate condition that stood in for the very place of art. Yet in a scene marked by absence and aversion, the preeminent reconditioning to which Jackson subjects his frontless paintings is that of profusion. The mounting accumulation of material is an overweening accelerant that issues in an unseemly multiplication of the structures of painting well beyond the threshold of ordinary purpose in a bottomless orgy of pictorial abstinence.

49. See Wirth, *Deer Deer*, 76–77.

50. See also Mike Kelley, *Minor Histories*, ed. John C. Welchman (Cambridge, MA: MIT Press, 2002), 102–11.

51. For the associated drawing, subsequently destroyed, see Wirth, *Deer Beer*, 30.

Jackson once stated that his wall installations were "all worked out on paper like a blueprint for a house."[52] Aside from providing a ready metaphor for his process, architectural design and home building have broader ramifications for the artist's work. Jackson studied engineering in college and later worked for many years in the construction industry in the Los Angeles area. This calling was at times as important to the artist as his art—and sometimes more so.[53] But the two vocations were never really distinct. On the one hand, common construction practices are prominent among the techniques that he uses in and out of the studio and are regularly put to use in his interventions in exhibition space. On the other, both Jackson and some of his commentators have established important analogies (sometimes direct, sometimes more abstracted) between his mode of painting and the architectural interior. Embracing the artist's personal formation, his artistic methodology, the languages used to describe the making of his work (and later its naming), and a series of referential cues embedded in particular projects and their preparatory materials, the architectural discourse of domestic and other interiors organizes many of Jackson's physical and conceptual processes. Like Georges Braque, who delivered his hands-on experience with house painting and interior decoration (marbling, stenciling, texturing, and so on) to the radical project of early cubism,[54] and Frank Stella, who used "house painter's techniques and tools" to make his stripe paintings in the late 1950s,[55] Jackson brought the techniques of construction, and even its attendant work ethic, into profound articulation with his artistic practice.

That the reach of Jackson's thoroughgoing "constructionism" gave rise to more than metaphors, materials, and techniques is attested by an early in situ work, *Cut the Rug* (1973), which establishes, both formally and semantically, a pivotal tension that informs the artist's later practice: here the collision between linguistic proposition and material activation. In *Cut the Rug,* the preparation of the painted surface on the floor beneath the rug reemerges as a multicolored material flux never fully encountered even after the carefully incised letters were lifted out to reveal—in a misbegotten version of an Ernst decalcomania—the gooey pattern of chromatic adhesion beneath. The injunctive language of the title functions as a sort of schoolyard dare to peek beneath an apparently everyday domestic surface and discover a seething primary substance spreading out well beyond what can be taken in by a single glance. In addition to its intimation of the formless seepage excreted at the peripheries of Jackson's stacks, this dichotomy between language and paint would later assume a strongly libidinal character in the room installations and other works in which paint stands in for assorted bodily fluids. *Cut the Rug* also turns paint into a source of primordial adhesion, something that exists prior to its symbolic referential attribution to corporeal secretions and their sexual charges.

52. Salazar, "Museum of the Mind," 12.

53. In a letter to Donald Sultan from 1976, Jackson writes: "I have been working a big job in Topanga Canyon. . . . I have been working 12 hours a day and haven't had time to think up a bunch of art related esoteric horse shit to write about. Some times the job is more intresting [sic] and important than working in the studio." Reproduced in Wirth, *Deer Beer*, 140.

54. Following a meeting with Braque around 1905, Othon Friesz noted, "his father intended for him to be a decorator." Cited in Alex Danchev, *Georges Braque: A Life* (New York: Arcade, 2005), 37. Danchev makes several references to Braque's first vocation as a "painter-decorator" and its impact on his work as an artist; see, for example, 21–22, 131–32.

55. Frank Stella, lecture delivered at Pratt Institute, Brooklyn, in January or February 1960, reprinted in Brenda Richardson, *Frank Stella: The Black Paintings*, exh. cat. (Baltimore: Baltimore Museum of Art, 1976), 78; cited in Meyer, *Minimalism*, 81.

At the same time, the field of quietly scintillating, unseen substances stuck to the underbelly of the lettering opens up to another type of conceptually adroit aesthetic reversal. Jackson's visual experimentation is clearly informed by the provision of precise linguistic notations, which are used to dictate a plan, annotate a preparatory sketch, and (in this case and others) offer titular directives. As the preliminary drawing for the carpet work reveals, such linguistic and diagrammatic "clarity" can induce a flood of contingent activities, the uncontainable, messy execution of which threatens to overwhelm the plan. Jackson in fact breeds a chicken and lays its egg in a down-home variant of the ontological conundrum of priority: for the luminous fluid beneath the cut was laid down "first" and, but for the incision of the letters and their being lifted out, would have remained invisible. In *Cut the Rug,* the physical subtraction of language from material permits the visual substrate of the work to become visible: language constitutes both the injunctive first term of the work and is then traced on and taken out of the carpet as its physical declaration.

The complex two-step between language and visuality is one of the key relays in Jackson's career. His works often begin with preparatory drawings that articulate a clear set of propositions, sometimes in the form of worded commands that "insist" on the coproduction of the visual and tactile dimensions of a work. In the disguise of a simple domestic accoutrement, the carpet or rug represents a layer or covering placed on top of an architectural structure. The ideas of laying down and cutting out that activate *Cut the Rug,* as well as its equivocation with the visibility of an underneath, would be taken up and reformatted as Jackson turned to the structure of the wall as a place where paint is laid on, pressed down, and smeared round—once again by a woven surface, this time in the form of canvas.

While the more technical and conceptual aspects of Jackson's room service are omnipresent, they are often animated, and sometimes eclipsed, by an interest in what might be termed visceral contextualization. As evidenced in the drawings and plans for painting rooms shown at the Faith and Charity in Hope Gallery in Idaho in 1978, the most literal aspect of this contextualism envisages domestic spaces as so many sites—bed, bedroom, couch, living room, and so on—where a day-jobbing artist could make art; they stand for convenient places to "work" after a long day of work. As the Idaho exhibition was in large measure a product of Jackson's friendship with Edward and Nancy Kienholz, who had moved from Los Angeles to Hope, Idaho, in 1973, the difference it marked between Jackson's understanding of the domestic and theirs needs to be underlined.

The Kienholzes, of course, were often interested in "morbid" extra-domestic environments—including brothels, hospital rooms, automobiles, and bars—that "featured horrific social, sexual and medical practices and dramatized the psychic and social pain . . . attributed to the occupants of these spaces."[56] When domestic settings were used, as in *The Wait* (1964–65) or *Blue Boy and Pinkie* (1979), made shortly after Jackson's show, the inevitably ramshackle context is generally governed by a figurative presence and suffused with portent—the product

56. Cécile Whiting, *Pop L.A.: Art and the City in the 1960s* (Berkeley: University of California Press, 2006), 195.

of implied nostalgia, threat, decay, or violence. Like the combines of Robert Rauschenberg, the Kienholz interior was also sheathed or inflected with gestural run-offs in the form of drips, spatters, and smears of paint and other materials.

While borrowing certain aspects from the Kienholz legacy, most notably a hyperinflated retooling of its pictorial gesturalism, and returning much later to Kienholz-like scenes such as *The Delivery Room* (2007), Jackson rejected the older artist's crypto-narrative figuration, tableau frontality, and allegorical foreboding. Instead he rethinks domestic behaviors by creating a visceral sense of private routine and material accumulation to problematize the perceived limits of installing a public exhibition. As the leading indicator of his artistic activity, the paint in Jackson's pseudodomestic constructions also correlates with bodily excretions, expressing the processes of living while also standing in for the ceaseless flow of mostly private experience. While rounds of unstinting Jacksonian spatter seem to attest to a quality of violence that conforms to the myth of artistic "wildness," it is clear, as we will see, that this cliché is indulged and skewered in somewhat equal measure. If, by virtue of its institutional coordinates and manifest constraints, Jackson's paint does take on a vitalist quality that has been referred to as "libidinal," it is actually staged as the inevitable release of an instinctual force. Robert Hobbs suggests that Jackson's idea of paint is located in a "pre-semiotic" dimension, formed and exuded before the advent of social codification. As a "libidinal force" it thus resembles Jean-François Lyotard's deregulating and counterrationalist concept of the "figure."[57] In this view, paint symbolizes an erotic drive inaugurated by human, animal, or even mechanical activities, which erupts in and across the very locations that contain or, more literally, corral art.

Paint itself is subject to an epidemic of analogizing: not only is it something that can be flung, spun, pressed, and squeezed, but the viscous liquidity that defines it becomes a cipher for every conceivable bodily fluid or secretion. Blithely farted out or ejaculated by a squadron of pantomimic fauna (bears, dogs, ducks, and deer), it is also encoded in the visceral excreta of *The Delivery Room* as well as standing in for oil and other liquid deposits under the earth in *The War Room* (2006–07). In the process paint somehow gives onto life and death themselves. It symbolizes an emergence of private, everyday processes within the public sphere as well as supplying a host of bawdy references to bodily fluids. The aesthetic vitality attendant on Jackson's use of paint forces a doubly disruptive incursion into conventional display practices within what are usually sterile institutional environments. In particular, his works often turn into a series of containment problems, issuing never-ending spumes of uncontrolled, unstoppable liquid substances as if sourced from an overpowering, all-encompassing *Lebenswelt*. Until the barrel runs dry.

If, as Ernst Gombrich and others have shown, easel painting was born and then domesticated in the modern era as a function of the confined development of bourgeois taste,[58] Jackson proffers another set of domesticating drives, parallel and supplementary, in which the public sites of exhibition are

57. Robert Hobbs, "Richard Jackson: Expanding Painting's Limits," in *Richard Jackson: New Works, 2006–2007*, exh. cat. (Paris: Yvon Lambert, 2007), unpaged. Other critics make similar comparisons to the forces of the psychic unconscious, interpreting Jackson's spewing paint as "libidinal exercises in fluid mechanics." Vivian Rehberg, "Paris: Richard Jackson," *Modern Painters* 19 (October 2007): 99.

58. E. H. Gombrich, *The Uses of Images: Studies in the Social Function of Art and Visual Communication* (London: Phaidon, 1999), 108, cited in Powell, "Painting as Blur," 146.

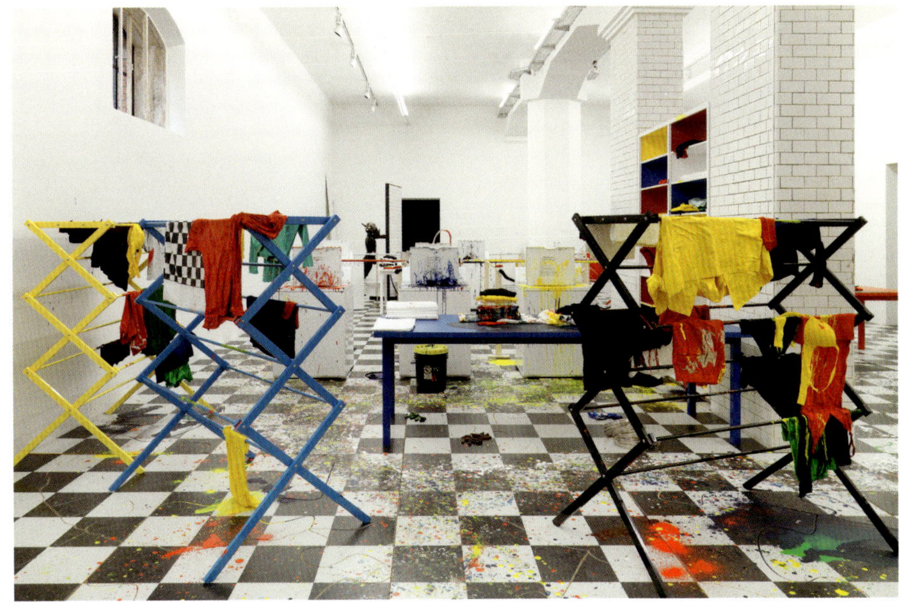

encroached upon by resolutely private acts. What had hitherto been hidden in
the studio—the unseemly labor of painting—is brought into the public sphere not
just as an integral part of visual experience but as the part that really matters
to Jackson: the physical articulation and material flow of the practice itself.
Of course, the making public of the seemingly private can only broker an ironic
return to painting's domestication—akin to an airing of the discipline's dirty
laundry (which Jackson hangs out quite literally in *The Laundry Room*, 2009)
(FIG. 15): for it offers to strip away painterly assumptions—and the attendant values
cloaking their public reception—to a visceral core. This reversal has a second
aspect, however, which should not be overlooked. As Jackson's paint torrents
are usually released in institutional settings, they may be said to emblematize
the return of festive, effusive potentiality to the public sphere, after centuries of
paranoid, privatizing repression. On the one side, perhaps, Daniel Buren's
resistance to the museum context through the manipulation of the primary
bifurcation of the stripe; on the other, Jackson's emissionary recasting of the
gallery through physical labor, a vision of painting as nonportable, inexorable,
and brought into being by the cheerful insouciance of the spurt.[59]

5 Signs of Time: Activate/Automate

Marks of time and general conditions of temporality are key concepts that
converge in Jackson's articulation of plan, process, and material. Despite the
arduous path often negotiated by the artist as he executes his most ambitious

59. Powell outlines what she takes to be a
conceptual turn by Daniel Buren from
painting as a private form: "For Buren, the
creation of the site-specific work is the
only way the artist can avoid having to
choose between the alienation of the
museum and the oblivion of the studio; it
is the only way, in short, to escape the
bind of the portable object." "Painting as
Blur," 145.

ideas, time might be said to start out for Jackson as something that simply bears witness to what he does: as he once noted of a particular piece, "it is evidence of how I spend my time."[60] The artist qualifies this association elsewhere, describing his artwork not simply as "evidence of a performance. But it's also about how you choose to spend your time. All we have is time."[61] The move here from an evidentiary quality to a volitional act is finally overtaken by the crushing inevitability of time, which becomes an experiential certainty that may be "all we have." Within this framework or temporal ascent, time is organized by Jackson in relation to physical accumulation (magnitudes of expenditure), symbolic impermanence (life span and death), and mechanized profusion. But the journey through such qualities is rarely as linear as that delivered by time in its most familiar condition as an additive system of intervals. Jackson's projects often derive from plans that, by being detoured through their execution, reveal recurring loops of potentiality that shuttle between the three conceptual axes of plan, process, and materiality that define this aspect of his work.

Perhaps the most common temporalized effect in Jackson's work is developed through the process of steady, relentless accumulation. As we have seen, the artist introduces various abundances of material into a space by actions that include stacking, spilling, and crashing. The sheer material excess precipitated in many of his productions triggers in the viewer a sudden awareness of the quantity of time spent. By manipulating the materials and signs of abundance, Jackson delivers an immediate challenge to his viewers. Leaving behind the aggregated remnants of methodical action, his works require an effort of mental reconstruction to understand the idea that inspired the sequence of events, similar to the way the nature and circumstances of a crime might be

FIG. 16
Richard Jackson, *1000 Clocks* (interior), 1987–92. Steel aluminum, electronic parts, fluorescent lights, oil paint. 141¾ × 432¼ × 360¼ in. (360 × 1098 × 915 cm). Hauser & Wirth Collection, Switzerland. Installation view, *Helter Skelter*, The Museum of Contemporary Art, Los Angeles

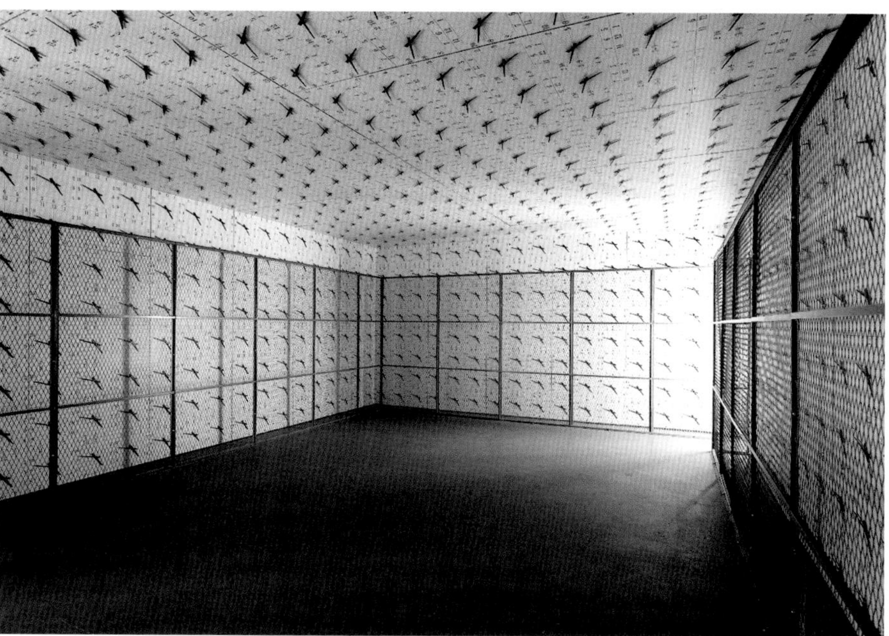

60. Jackson, in Obrist and Mayo, "Unusual Behavior," 20.

61. Jackson, in Szakacs, "Circus Is in Town," 44.

deduced from a survey of its place or scene. In direct conflict with the values connoted by stockpiled things—as with the hoard of artworks accumulated by a museum (or Rothko's stack of paintings)—the logic of irrational accumulation leverages the evidentiary effects of unusual and overextended behavior into perceptual triggers that register the immediacies of painterly effects. At the same time palpable shifts in magnitude—of number, scale, intensity, or duration—are conveyed as a kind of mental afterimage.

Jackson approaches the temporality of aesthetic experience from an altogether different angle when he introduces mechanical elements into his work. Instead of evidencing time through the accumulation of painting materials, he reorchestrates the artistic gesture as a conceptual plan—to fill a space and to fill his time as a working artist. Given that "all we have is time," Jackson's installation *1000 Clocks* (1987–92) (FIG. 16) becomes a maniacal, all-encompassing statement on its passage and transience. The other mechanical devices in his work—pumps, motors, fans, engines—operate in counterpoint to the disciplinary constraints of the replicated, measured time of the clock. Relieved of the artist's signature painterly effects, however, the clock installation is perhaps Jackson's most pessimistic work. It schematizes the same basic message of transience, then repeats it until it exceeds any reasonable measure of artistic—or other—propriety. As if they have taken a wrong turn—along a phantom limb of *Untitled (Maze)* perhaps—viewers are enclosed in a sonically stark room, in which they are forced to confront and then retreat from the inelegant truth of an endlessly stuttered sequence of seconds. The temporal wipeout of *1000 Clocks* is engendered by a scene of extreme *mechanicity* that might be the antithesis of the extreme *physicality* of painting so prominent in the majority of Jackson's works: for, like most of his pieces, it offers a commentary on expenditure and excess. The culmination of five years of single-minded construction, with every part "made or assembled by hand," *1000 Clocks* might have furnished one of the reasons why the artist offered the acerbic comment in a letter to Seth Siegelaub in August 1990 that while there was "more" "art, artists, recognition, money" two decades or so after it was commenced, there was also "less time"—and Jackson "liked it better when there was more time than money."[62]

Of course, the processes and materiality of paint are willfully asserted by the artist in his adoption of a wide variety of actions—pushing, spinning, whipping, spewing, stacking. The implications of this mélange of unruly painterly gestures was immediately apparent to Walter Hopps during a visit to Jackson's first *Bedroom* installation in Pasadena: "All this served for the most excessive drenching, splattering, and whiplashing of paint I've ever experienced."[63] As Hopps and others attest, seeing and experiencing Jackson's work as an encounter engenders the realization that its physically rambunctious qualities are derived from a kind of process-based painting in which nothing is held back, and the process itself, driven by the remorseless march of unseen time, has been fully externalized and revealed. Jackson's editorially unmitigated mode of making

---

62. Jackson, letter to Seth Siegelaub responding to a questionnaire titled "The Context of Art / The Art of Context; 1969–1990," a project for the Galerie Fricke in Düsseldorf, Germany; reproduced in *Bank Job*, 22.

63. Walter Hopps, "Richard Jackson and Action Painting," in Wirth, *Deer Beer*, 5.

and exhibiting refutes, in equal measure, the predicates of compositional adjustment, refinement, and revision, and the culling of works for public exhibition according to some undeclared principle of quality control: not only does his work not "edit anything," but "it's evidence of a work performed, of a process."[64] The place where evidence, process, and performance come together produces a moment when time itself is stacked—in a temporal inflection marked above all by its contagiously inevitable inevitability. So another of the compelling circles that surround the artist's work is that drawn by Jackson's timeline as he passes the baton of process from the artist to the viewer: "for me, it's important for the viewer to reflect on the process by which the work is created."[65] Lest we think that they were a mere mirage, conjured out of the fog of incrementality, Jackson orders room service for his viewers while they browse in his stacks of time.

In the question of Jackson's relation to time, two issues remain: the idea of the *temporary* and the concept of *activation*. Jackson's commitment to temporary constructions—which underscore both the fabrication process and the terminal condition of his projects—might be likened to the fleeting nature of performance art practices, in that their documentation constitutes the last remnant of an event that has finished and all but disappeared. But Jackson remains uninterested in the aesthetic suppositions of performance-based activity: "The wall paintings were never performances. They are evidences of performances. I like to activate a work in private. Viewers see how the work was performed; they take their ideas from the completed piece. People need to imagine how a work is made."[66] Despite making or permitting several videos documenting his more recent installations in particular, Jackson has remained consistent in this regard: in the process of executing predetermined plans he is careful to avoid assigning undue significance to the physical activity of making the works. He therefore assiduously disavows some of the key assumptions of performance art, including its relationship to theatricality, any belief or faith in the mythic presence of the artist-as-performer, and the practice of working in front of an audience.

Jackson recalibrates the notion of transience by posing it in a strategic alliance with innovation and accident. For innovation in painting involves a capacity to produce surprising or unpredictable results, which he aims to generate by harnessing the power of the accidental to unsettle expectations. This accounts for the "element of risk and failure" that Jackson determined was "an interesting part of the work"[67] (and about which Szeemann and others also commented). Jackson's distinct lack of concern with a final product leads to an unexpected canceling out of the art object by the art-making process. In one schematic note on his negotiation with these conditions, he writes, "Object/Of no interest," next to a parallel construction that reads, "Process/Art as a way of life."[68]

The accidental, even disastrous, profusion of paint in many of Jackson's later installations depends upon automated processes precipitated by both physical actions and technological components. Many of the works from the 1970s envision how physical acts that motivate the spreading of painting can

64. Jackson, in Obrist and Mayo, "Unusual Behavior," 18.

65. Jackson, in Buchhart, "Richard Jackson," 218.

66. Jackson, interview with Robert Hobbs, December 7, 2006; cited in Hobbs, "Expanding Painting's Limits," unpaged.

67. Jackson, in Obrist and Mayo, "Unusual Behavior," 18.

68. See Zeynep Rona, ed., *International Sculptors Symposium*, trans. Angela Roome (Bursa, Turkey: Uludağ University, 1995), 9.

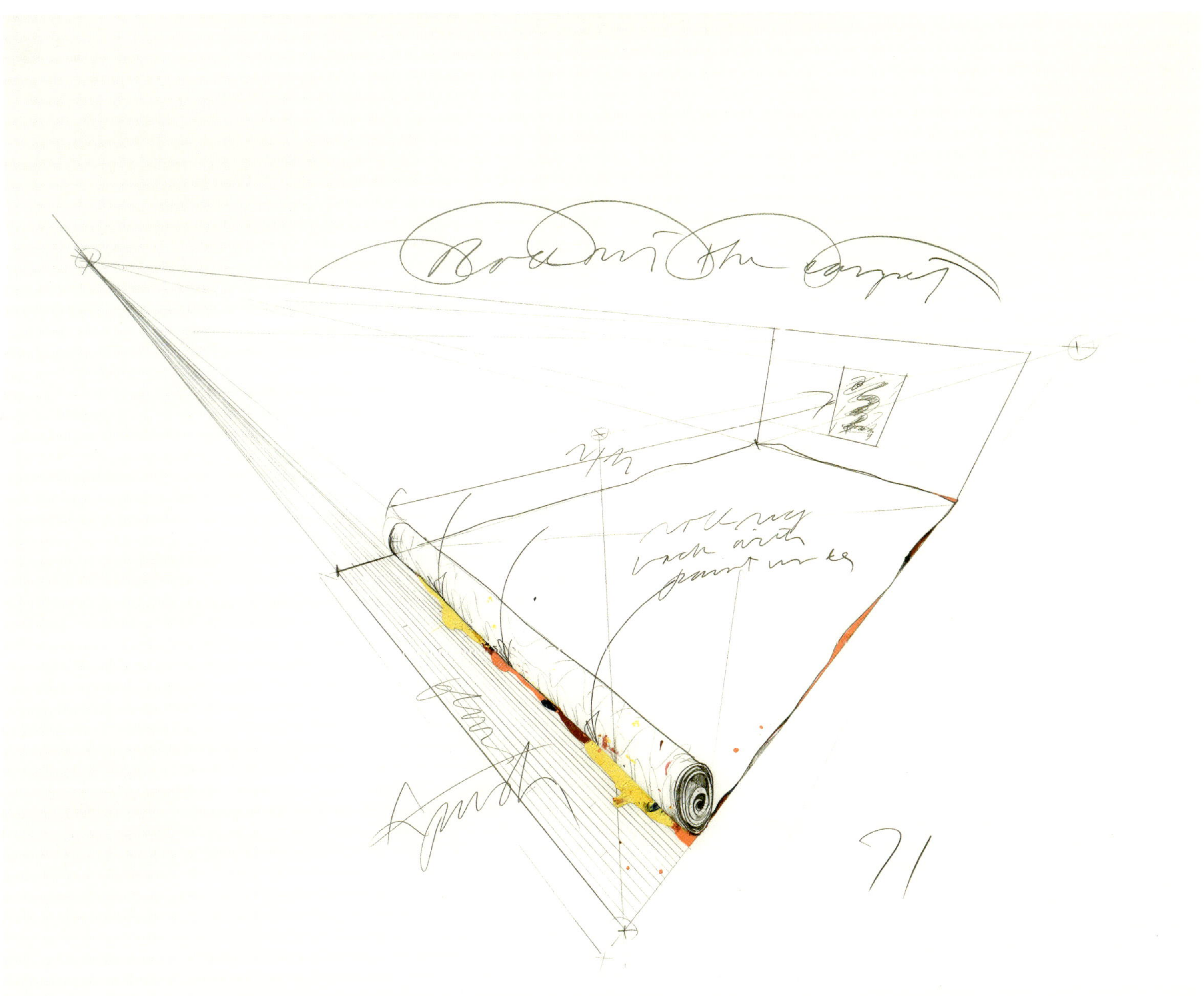

yield unexpected results, as in the opening or closing of a door explored in *Untitled ("Paint on the Rug")* (1970) and the unfurling of a carpet in Jackson's drawing for a painting made with a rug, *Roll Out the Carpet* (1971) (FIG. 17).[69] As such they relate to some of the processes—but not to the performative, video, or self-reflexive aspects—of Paul McCarthy's mock-actionist work with paint in the same years, such as *Face Painting—Floor, White Line* (1972) or *Whipping a Window and a Wall with Paint* (1974). Often framed within a domestic setting, Jackson's ideas for making artworks employing automatic gestures also allude

69. *Untitled ("Paint on the Rug")* (1970) was executed in 1981 for the group exhibition *California: A Sense of Individualism* at the L.A. Louver Gallery. The setup involved pouring wet paint behind a closed door. The text written on the drawing by Jackson reads: "The door opens, person goes in, turns on the light and discovers what he has done." Other works organized around the arbitrary spreading of paint occasioned by involuntary everyday actions include *Untitled (Car Windshield with Paint)* (1977). See Wirth, *Deer Beer*, 33, 40, 71.

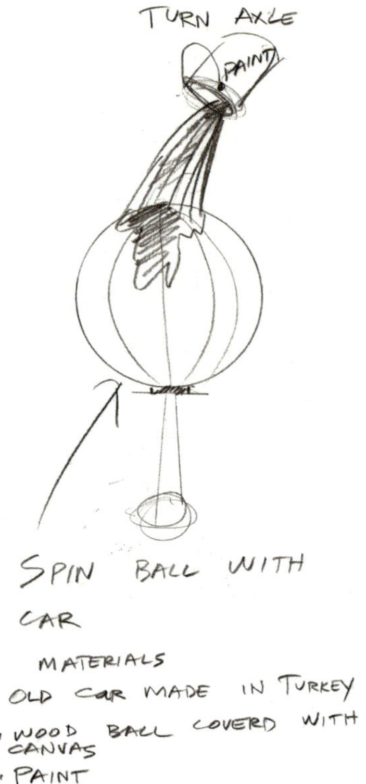

FIG. 18
Richard Jackson, Drawing for *Turkey Ball*
(detail), 1995. Pencil on paper. Approx. 30 ×
20 in. (76.2 × 50.8 cm)

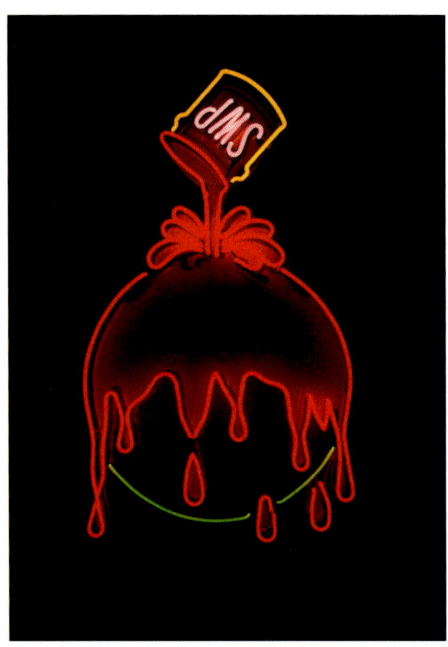

FIG. 19
Neon Sherwin-Williams company logo, n.d.
The Neon Museum of Philadelphia

to the stereotypical condition of the "struggling" artist who must take a day job to pay for art making after work. One drawing from the 1978 Idaho exhibition is inscribed: "painting for those to[o] tired to work on their art [be]cause they have to teach to earn a living. Stay in bed with the T.V. on and paint everything as far as you can reach."[70] Making humorous and caustic reference to the incapacity spawned by mental and physical exhaustion, these sketches for situational alternatives to studio practice also provide a reconceptualization of the nature of artistic investment. Painting, it would seem, does not require mental or emotional strain after all, and it can be performed automatically, amid one's daily activities—before bed, while sleeping, watching television, getting dressed. The wall paintings can also be read through the concept of automated work, since Jackson sets up the conditions by which paint is physically and kinetically introduced into a space.

Beginning in the late 1980s, Jackson's process shifted from engagement with various types of physical automatism to the inclusion of mechanical components—a move similar to the one made by McCarthy a few years earlier. With *Human Object* (1982), McCarthy replaced himself as a performer by using a humanoid surrogate; five years later he made his first fully mechanized sculpture, *Bavarian Kick* (1987), ushering in two decades of experimentation with automata, motile special effects, and animatronics, which culminated most recently with the animatronics pig made for (but little used in) *Caribbean Pirates* (2005–10).[71] Still dependent on the artist's presence and labor to design, assemble, and install, Jackson's plans became mechanized as he reframed automated, process-based art making into machinic activities. Like earlier projects that required automatic behaviors by the artist, the machine would supply a more literal vision of the conceptualist engineering of painting practice (recalling LeWitt's dictum of "the idea" becoming "a machine that makes art"). The distribution of viscous, chromatic material was now taken on by a battery of actual machines—guns, internal combustion engines, fans, and hydraulic pumps—underscoring Jackson's resistance to the presumption of artistic "struggle" and counteracting any lingering association of internal anxiety about the issuance and placement of pigment. For Jackson, a machine can execute the plan to make art every bit as effectively as a person.

When Jackson uses mechanical pumps and kinetic machines to fling, spew, and shower paint across various exhibition arenas, he releases the purest variant of a quality that has long been central to his work: *profusion*. *Turkey Ball* (1995) (FIG. 18), for example, employs a VW Beetle as the motor force to spin a white sphere onto which paint is poured from above. While the kinetic spinning of paint alludes to the faddish 1960s rotary art associated with Schilling and others, the planetary connotations of the pristine canvas sphere seem to refer more directly to the longtime logo of the paint company Sherwin-Williams (founded in 1866), which Jackson recalls seeing as a neon sign in the Bay Area (FIG. 19).[72] According to one recent account, the apocalyptic logo and the slogan "Cover

---

70. The drawing is reproduced in *Richard Jackson* (1978), unpaged.

71. See John C. Welchman, "Prop, Studio, Action: Paul McCarthy's Cuts," in *Sculpture and Film*, ed. Jon Wood and Ian Christie (Aldershot, UK: Ashgate, forthcoming).

72. Richard Jackson, conversation with the author, July 26, 2011.

the Earth," patented and first used by the company in 1906, were "doodled by an in-house wag in 1895, making fun of the Industrial Revolution's new global reach."[73] By today's marketing standards they seem, somewhat naively, to intimate the environmental destruction lurking within a not so subtly optimistic message about the contagious "spread" of commercial success. Jackson, however, reinterprets the logo and its imperative statement in an almost ridiculously literal manner in *Turkey Ball*. Once again, there is a menacing quality to the liquidity of paint: tipped onto the North Pole, it blankets the sphere, symbolizing a potentially unconscionable spillage of industrial product and a suffocating hazard for organic life.

But "the greatest spill on earth," as we might call it, suggests rather more than the careless delivery of a red toxic stew unleashed in the manner of a disaster flick. For in addition to its associations with pristine, "natural" conditions, the planetary sphere also represents an impossible distance or totality. It conveys the false sense that one can achieve an entirely objective view or, in the vein of humorously ironic literalism that so often plays through Jackson's work, the notion of the cosmic hand of God tipping the paint pot and "causing" the pour. At the same time, Jackson offers a tongue-in-cheek retort to Chris Burden's self-crucifixion on the back of a VW (FIG. 20). In a wider frame, one can't help seeing in all this an inadvertent nod to twentieth-century debates on the fraught relation between image and knowledge, interior and exterior points of view, and thought and action, in which the assumption that images, even vision itself, offered access to epistemological clarity was so often criticized.[74] In his own way, Jackson combats the ideology of illusionism and the qualities of aesthetic sensibility vested in easel painting. Fixated on the medium's tactile qualities, he reworks the supposedly critical distance of aesthetic perception, proposing instead an immersive experience in which painting, sculpture, and performance intersect. Indeed, his contestation of medium-specificity and his commitment to crossing genre and experimental intermediality figure in a drawing-diagram of artistic media that uses crude, hand-drawn arrows to connect the words *Sculpture*, *Performance*, and *Painting* in a closed loop—implying the ongoing displacement of each medium by other conditions or suppositions.[75] Another part of his plan is to let paint get out of control through spinning (*Turkey Ball*) (FIG. 21) or by pumping, spraying, launching, or drenching (*Painting with Two Balls*, 1997; *Do It Yourself Painting (Still Life)*, 1998; *Accidents in Abstract Painting*, 2002; *Cra-Z-Boy*, 2003). Unlike the effete individual strokes of the painter, often presumed to delineate experience, Jackson's paint comes flooding out of big-bore apertures, tanks, and vessels; invades the surrounding surfaces; and encircles and surprises the viewer, before settling seen and unseen into the nooks and crannies of a space. Here painting cascades, then seeps, beyond the scope of painting.

An elaborate response to the work made in 1960 by Jasper Johns of the same title, *Painting with Two Balls* (1987–88; see page 25) turns the stereo-

73. "Gloomy gus," post on the discussion thread "I Do Not Care for The Sherwin-Williams Logo," Stranger (Seattle), July 9, 2010, http://slog.thestranger.com/slog/archives/2010/07/09/i-did-not-care-for-the-sherwin-williams-logo-. The Sherwin-Williams website defends and rehistoricizes the logo as a "figurative emblem signifying quality, integrity and service" in the following terms: "Our historical logo is one of the most recognized company logos in existence. Created in the late 1800s, the logo's purpose was to represent the company's desire to help beautify and protect the buildings of the world." See http://www.sherwin-williams.com/property-facility-managers/specs-and-green-solutions/ecovision/green-initiatives/. The odd portentousness of the Sherwin-Williams logo has been recognized by other artists, including Mike Kelley, who reproduced it in *Plato's Cave, Rothko's Chapel, Lincoln's Profile* (Venice, CA: New City Editions; New York: Artists Space, 1986), 89.

74. Maurice Merleau-Ponty sums up a conceptual shift related to anti-illusionism in "The Eye and the Mind" (1960), the last text he completed before his death: "I do not see it [space] according to its exterior envelope; I live it from the inside; I am immersed in it. After all, the world is all around me, not in front of me." Merleau-Ponty, "The Eye and the Mind," in *The Primacy of Perception*, ed. James M. Edie, trans. Carleton Dallery (Evanston, IL: Northwestern University Press, 1964), 178.

75. The diagram is reproduced in *International Sculptors Symposium*, 9.

typical idea of testosterone-filled action painting even further on its head by retracing and exaggerating the "serious" formal displacement initiated in the original work. By interposing spherical elements into the process of painting, Jackson retains the original joke in which Johns aimed to complicate and comment on the formalist approach to flatness in painting. Retooling Johns's ball-assisted, counterformalist gaming into an action-based procedure of kinetic dispersal, Jackson explicitly reframed the original jest about masculine

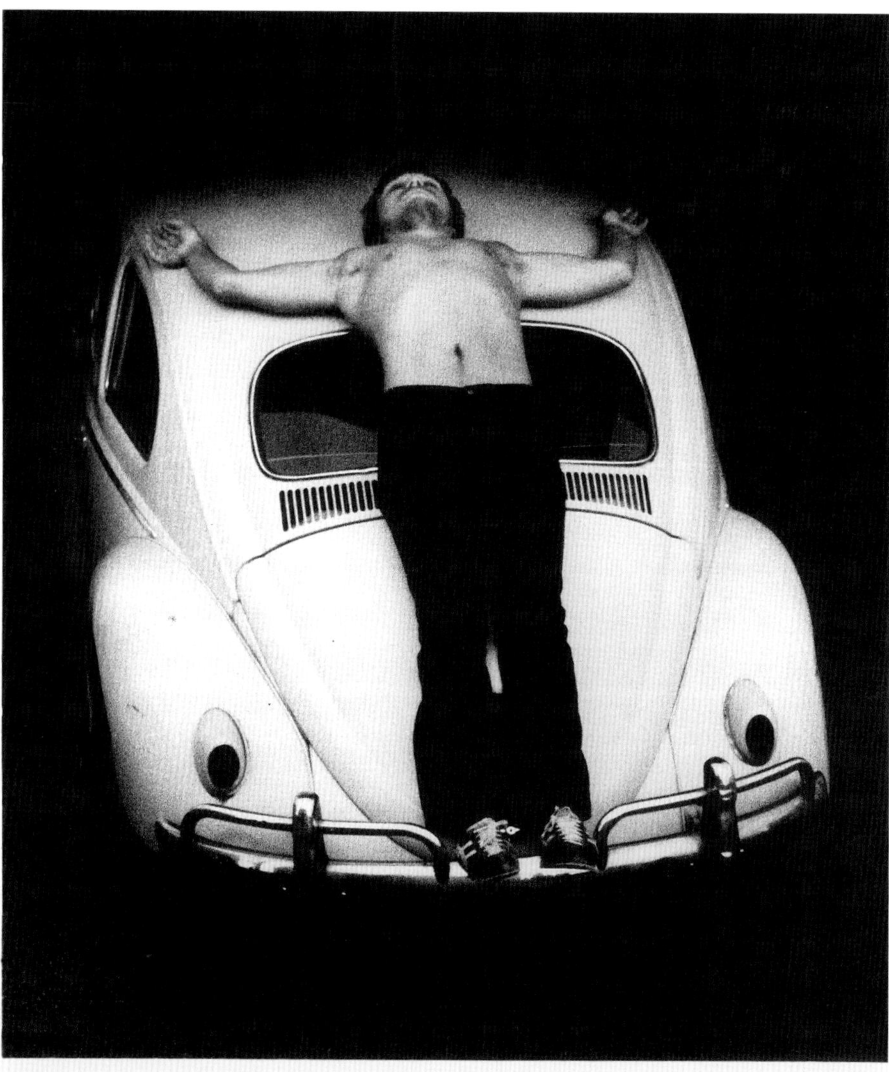

Trans-fixed
Venice, California: April 23, 1974

Inside a small garage on Speedway Avenue, I stood on the rear bumper of a Volkswagon. I lay on my back over the rear section of the car, stretching my arms onto the roof of the car. The garage door was opened and the car was pushed half-way out into the Speedway. Screaming for me, the engine was run at full speed for two minutes. After two minutes, the engine was turned off and the car pushed back into the garage. The door was closed.

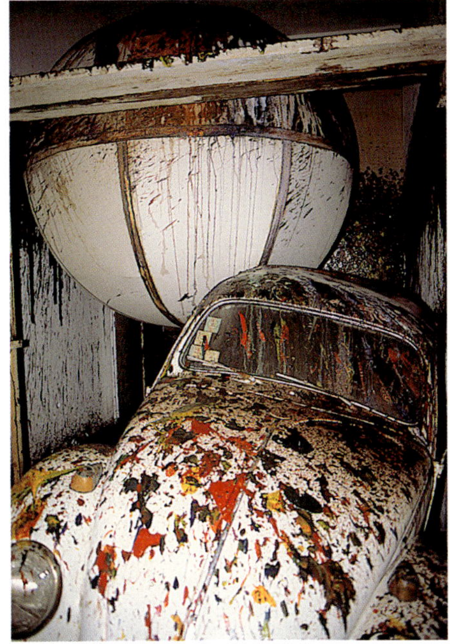

assertiveness in American painting. But he willingly risks taking his sense of humor too far by accelerating the force and redoubling the in-your-face liquidity of painterly investment. For *Painting with Two Balls* is also an inaugural work in another of the turns in Jackson's career during the last decade and half, which signals the advent of a new order in his reckoning with temporality and automation. In place of the unstable tangle of allusions and overlaps, aversions and dialogues that informed his relations to movements, issues, and individual artists in the 1970s and 1980s—to abstract expressionism or minimalism; to LeWitt, Bruce Nauman, or McCarthy—Jackson commenced a series of overt negotiations with specific historical works. One might say that the general ethos of "target painting" (by Johns, Kenneth Noland, etc.) gave way to "targeted practice"—literally in the case of *La Grande Jatte (after Georges Seurat)* (1992–), which is being fired into place with paint-tipped pellets. Just as the concepts of painting and critique worked out by Jackson in longs bouts of trial and error move in and out of focus with received wisdom, so too his reckoning with art history cannot be reduced to the referential modes to which we are most accustomed: the automatic borrowing of citation or appropriation and the generally uncritical demeanor of homage. Surely touched by aspects of each of these takes on the past, Jackson characteristically makes room for the play of his own obsessions (building, smearing, hunting) coupled with the surrender to a kind of technical oblivion as he recalibrates the temporalities and automation of modes of application and address; in the case of Seurat, outrageously speeding them up by ricocheting from dot to shot (and back).

6 Give or Take: The "Pain in Painting"

If the manifold ideas, techniques, actions, automations, and temporalities of Jackson's work don't find their resolution in either a singular or successive "style[s]," they are certainly strung along in what could be described as the "manner" of the artist, which is itself made up of several aspects. Chief among them is Jackson's humor—direct, even gruff, and singularly unrepentant. In its ironic forms it generally chafes at the gaps and impasses that have separated the artist from the politer confines of the art world, with its vernissages, collecting etiquettes, vainglorious ambition, and spurious morality. But Jackson is also the butt of his own jokes, or rather his laborious routines, unremitting work ethic, and star billing as a one-man band are ventilated by the kind of self-deprecation that tempers their reach and ambition with a double dose of reality checks and ready bathos. Even the vaunted ambition to "expand painting," a project that more than any other lies at the center of Jackson's four-decade-long project, is caught up in the artist's jocular skepticism: "I don't know if it's possible, but it amuses

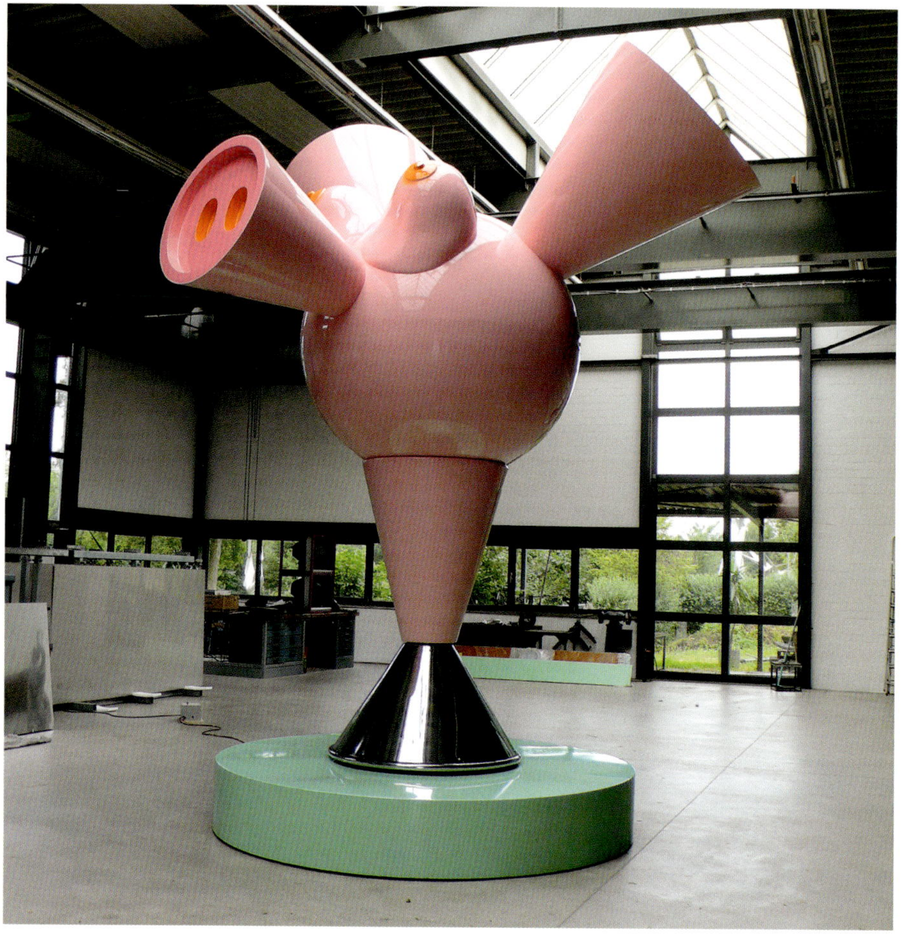

me (it's a good joke)."[76] While Jackson immediately adds a Samuel Beckett–like coda—"I'd like to keep on trying to broaden painting"—we get the sense that the manner behind the joke can be as important, sometimes more so, than painting itself. By its very nature this attitude is complex, evasive, and unpredictable.

Like several of his friends and colleagues who have worked in and around Pasadena, for example, Jackson dispatched various animals into art world locations to carry on a surrogate battle with the very idea of art. The monochrome fauna of his later work—including *Big Pig* (2009–10; FIG. 22)— are distant cousins of the slightly menacing and absurdist menagerie that comprises Nauman's cast cats, dogs, and unspecified "large animals"; McCarthy's libidinous pigs; and Mike Kelley's allegorical monkeys, frat-house horses, or crocheted dachshunds (FIG. 23).[77] While Jackson, of course, can bear down, pig out, or horse around with the best of them, his fauna—deer, bear, duck, wild boar, dogs (FIG. 24)—are also the literal targets or assistants of his hunting practice.

Now, "manner" can be figured in many dimensions, up to and including a general way of life. There has been much discussion (by Hobbs and others) about the radically antiexistentialist bent of Jackson's work (which, in

---

76. Jackson, in Buchhart, "Richard Jackson," 225.

77. Nauman began using taxidermists' molds to make cast sculpture in the late 1980s (see, for example, the cast aluminum *Untitled (Three Large Animals)* (1989); programmed by the Fondazione Nicola Trussardi, McCarthy's *Pig Island* was shown at Palazzo Citterio in Milan in 2010; on Kelley's menagerie, see "The Insect Connection" in my "The Mike Kelleys," in *Mike Kelley* (London: Phaidon, 1999), 78–82.

one sense, is clear).[78] Such a view is apparently confirmed by the artist's reiterated commitment to literalism and dehierarchization not only in relation to the institutionality of the art world but also in his conceptualization of the practices of art making. One result of this was that the straight-shooting, sometimes cantankerous Jackson plotted a middle way between two extremes in the manner according to which artists, by emerging necessity, negotiated during the later 1960s and 1970s with their galleries, reputations, and status in the commercial art world. These positions are epitomized by the activist careerism of Jackson's sometime stablemate in the Eugenia Butler Gallery, Joseph Kosuth, on the one hand, and the countercommercial "protocol of opposites" filtered through anonymous gestures of covert diffidence adopted by his near contemporary in the Sacramento area in the mid- and late 1960s, Stephen Kaltenbach, on the other.[79]

But Jackson was temperamentally unable to play duck and cover with the art world. He was constitutionally unsuited to patient self-camouflage while waiting out an uncertain role in its possible future (like Kaltenbach) or to aggressively embracing its possibilities and newly internationalized circuitry (like Kosuth and the constellation of celebrity artists who came of age in the wake of Jackson Pollock and Andy Warhol). In a letter to Donald Sultan in 1976, Jackson set it out with humorous sarcasm: "Christ I can't wait until we are all famous artists and don't have to put up with this crap anymore. We'll just be acholics [sic], hang out with only rich people and other artists. We can stay up all night having white on white conversations, and not worry about having to get [up] early to be on the job."[80] Jackson was utterly matter-of-fact about the resolute unmarketability of much of his own work during the 1970s and early 1980s (regarding his wall paintings, he commented, "Nobody bought one").[81] And he was both offended by and bitterly ironic about the personal and social consequences of the commercial "failure" of others around him. ("James Lee

FIG. 23
Mike Kelley, *Arena #10 (Dogs)*, 1990. Stuffed animals on afghan. 11 ½ × 123 × 32 in. (29.2 × 312.4 × 81.3 cm).

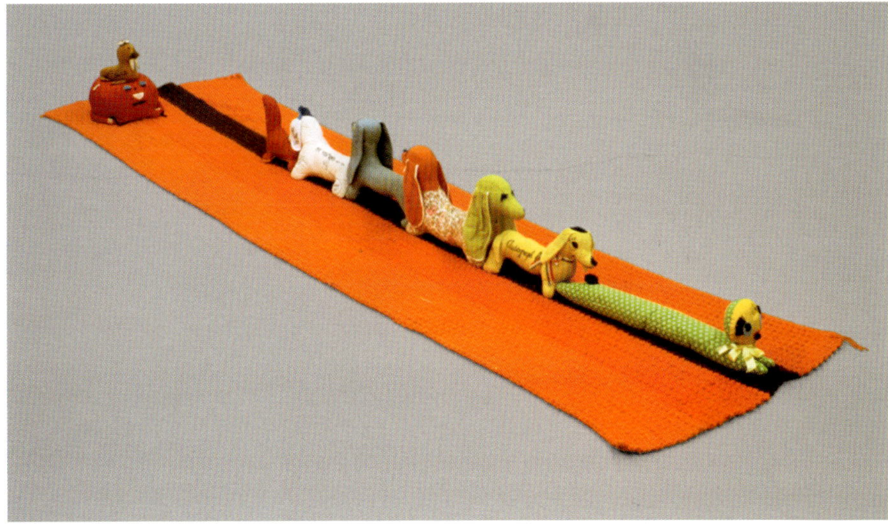

78. See Hobbs, "Expanding Painting's Limits."

79. Kosuth showed parts of his *First Investigation*, including definitions of the word *nothing*, at the Eugenia Butler Gallery in 1968, where Jackson exhibited in 1969 and again the following year, when he showed his maze constructed of canvases. For more on this context, see Alexander Alberro, *Conceptual Art and the Politics of Publicity* (Cambridge, MA: MIT Press, 2003), and my "Ideas Being Given: Joseph Kosuth's Media and Public Projects from the *Second*

Investigation (1969) to 2006" (lecture, "Die Aktualität der Conceptual Art," Bonner Kunstverein, Bonn, Germany, July 7, 2007). Kaltenbach moved from the Sacramento area in 1967, a year before Jackson left for Los Angeles. For a brief discussion of Kaltenbach's diffidently strategized "Kill My Career"-ism, see Sarah Lehrer-Graiwer, "Altered Ego," *Artforum* 49 (September 2010): 137: "Instead of possessively guarding his ideas out of competitive ambition like the young artists hustling around him, he became more and more interested in giving his ideas away, purposefully sharing information and spreading artistic possibilities as ways of exercising broad influence: what he called his Causal Art."

80. Jackson to Sultan, 1976, reproduced in Wirth, *Deer Beer*, 140.

81. Jackson, "Richard Jackson in Conversation with Christine Kintisch," in *Bank Job*, 4. This assertion of a complete absence of sales is modified elsewhere, as in Jackson's comment in relation to *Untitled (Maze)*: "Purchase price for the drawing and painting was $1,000. For ten years, the paintings and drawings sold for $1,000. Three works were realized for $1,000 in Los Angeles. One work was not destroyed." Wirth, *Deer Beer*, 36.

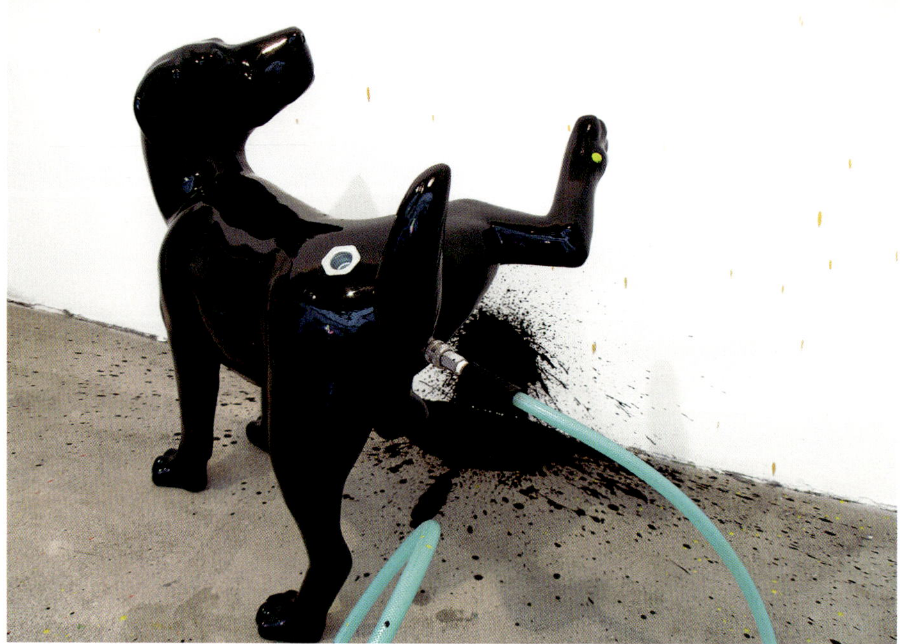

Byars, another good artist . . . never had anything. He died with nothing. Couldn't even afford to go to the doctor.")[82]

But even though Jackson drains the elements of prurient selfhood and mythologizing symbolism from his work with paint, he nevertheless poses it in a surprising set of ambitious, if deliquescent, alliances—with architecture and dwelling, with language and nullity, with the liquidity that defines life and flows through it, and with the burning sacrifice of dead carbons that simultaneously runs and ruins the planet. Paint is collateral for Jackson's vernacular sublime, the clearinghouse for the materiality of an art practice that strives for both emancipated irreverence and unauthorized relevance. To get to this oddball destination and at the same time make good on his belief that "an artist's job is to change people,"[83] he has stolen his way through art history, stopping at and occasionally cocreating way stations that include scattering, accumulation, linguistic materialization, ironic evaporation, transperformative painting . . . even, in his way, social amelioration. Always well aware that his commitment to profusion was at the same time an acknowledgment of inevitable limits—of description, of his own interventions, but also of the capacity, *caveat scriptor*, of art history or criticism to go after his achievement—he annotated an illustration of *Untitled (Model II for "5050 Stacked Paintings")*: "This work is excessive enough without a complete description of the piece . . . [it] puts the pain in painting."[84] The doubtful spaces between activity and product, time and place are joined here by another round of uncertainty that arises from any attempt to describe them. Here we encounter a final location about which Jackson is defiantly equivocal: his place in history. The artist makes no bones about it: "I hope that I am part of painting but not history."[85]

---

82. Ibid., 3, 4.

83. Ibid., 3.

84. See *Bank Job*, 26.

85. Jackson, interview in Mangion and Brugerolle, *Ne pas jouer*, 96.

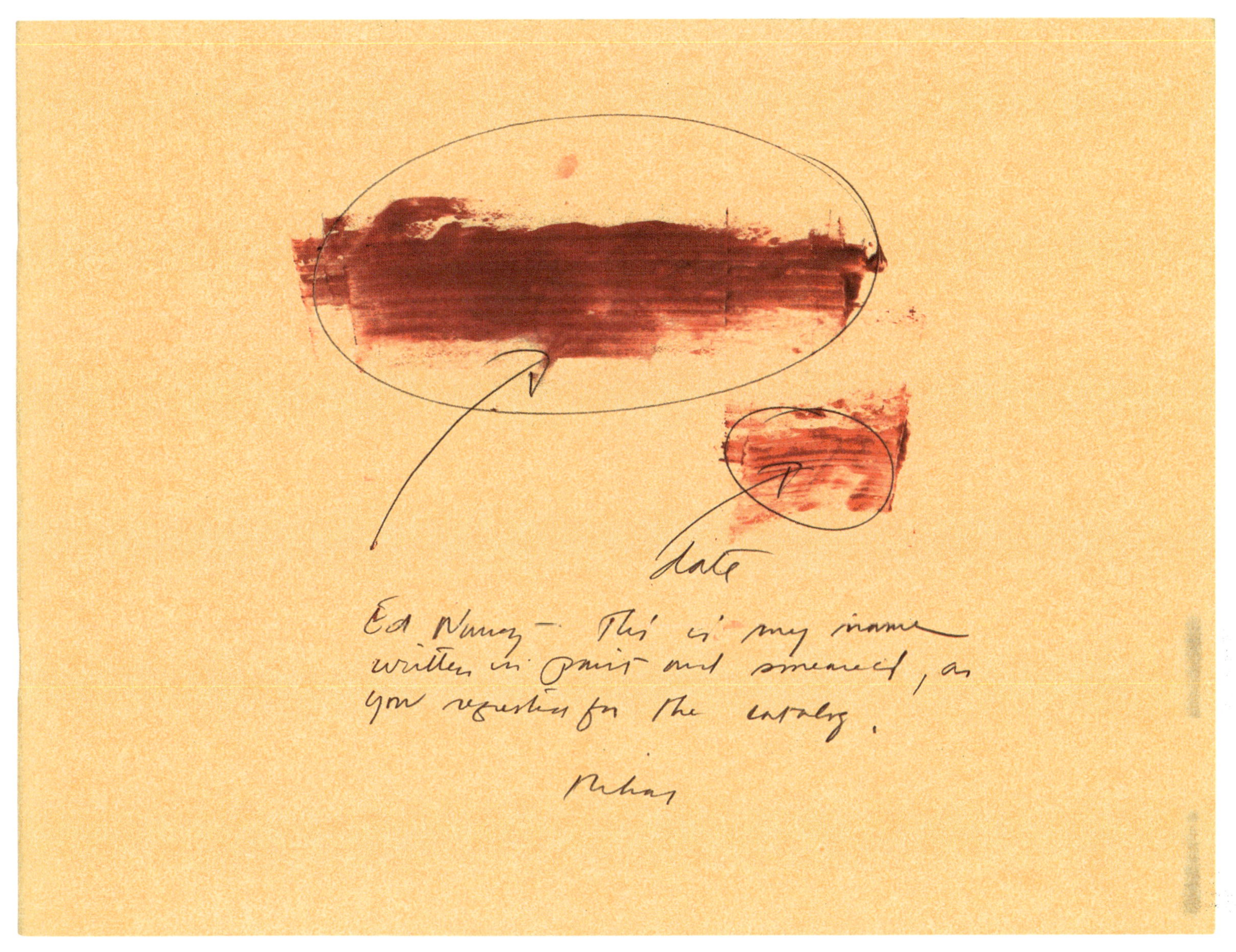

SELECTIONS FROM **100 DRAWINGS**

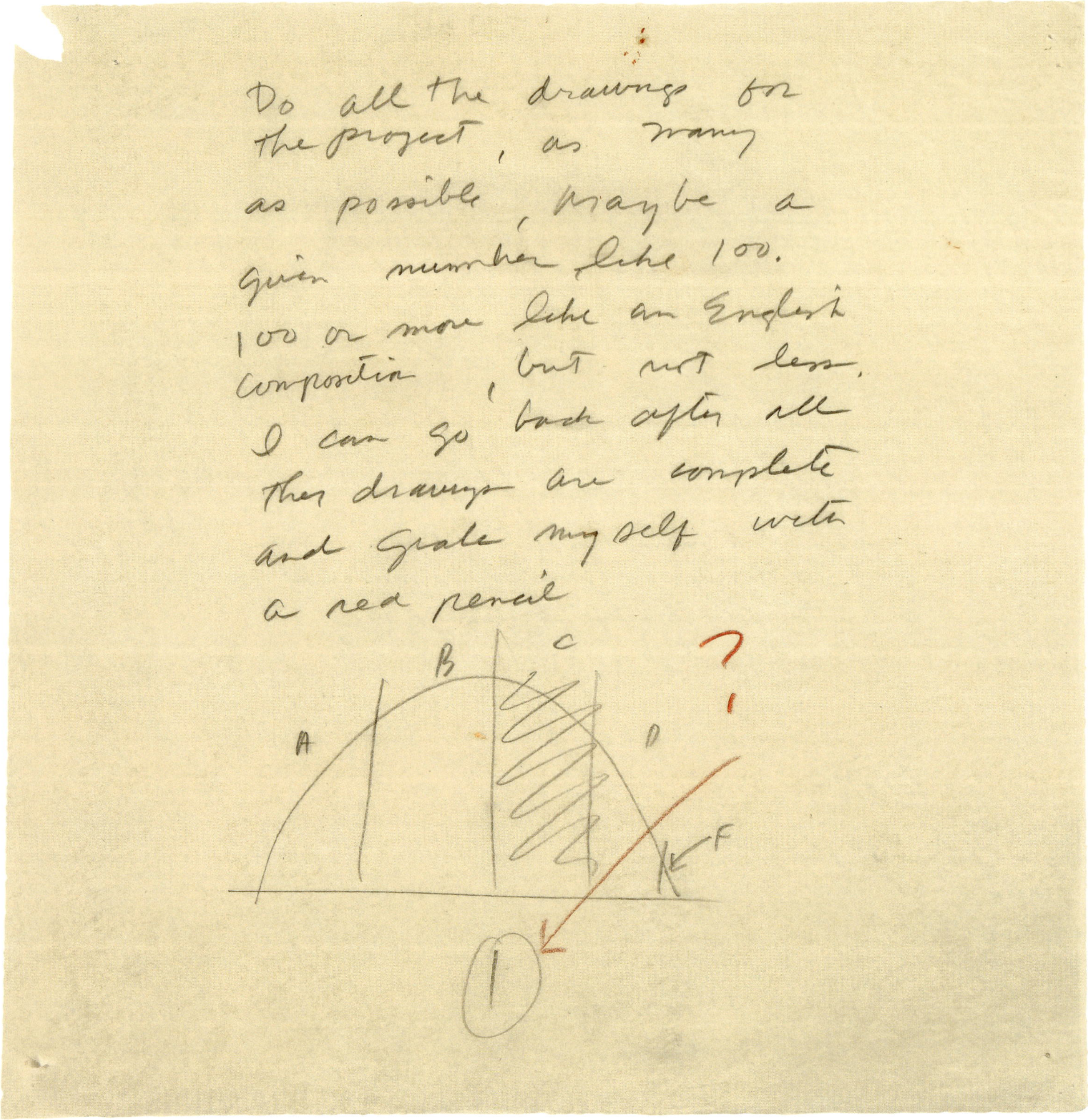

Do all the drawings for
the project, as many
as possible, maybe a
given number like 100.
100 or more like an English
composition, but not less.
I can go back after all
the drawings are complete
and grade myself with
a red pencil

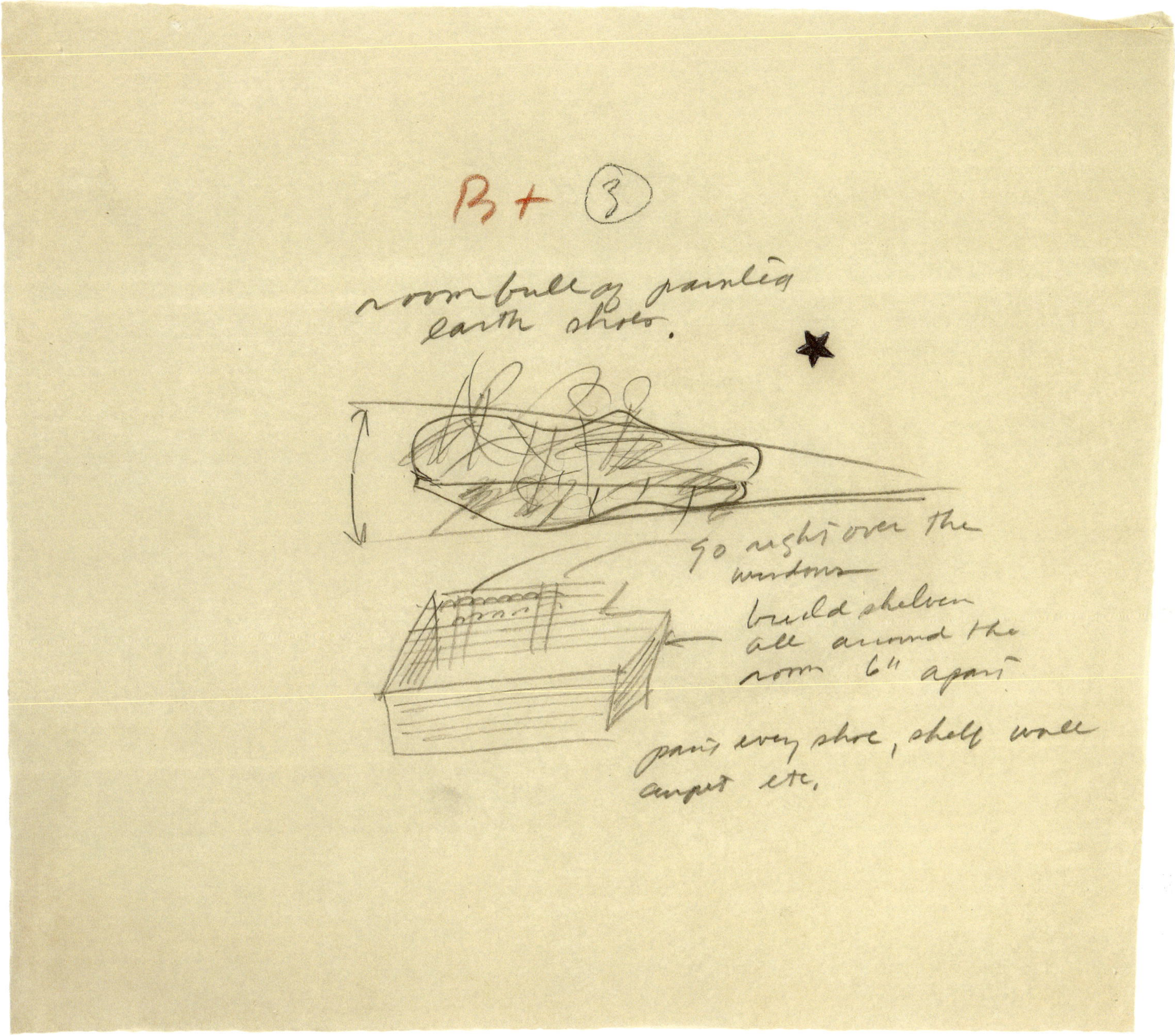

B₃ + ③

room full of painted
earth shoes.

go right over the
windows

build shelves
all around the
room 6" apart

paint every shoe, shelf wall
carpet etc.

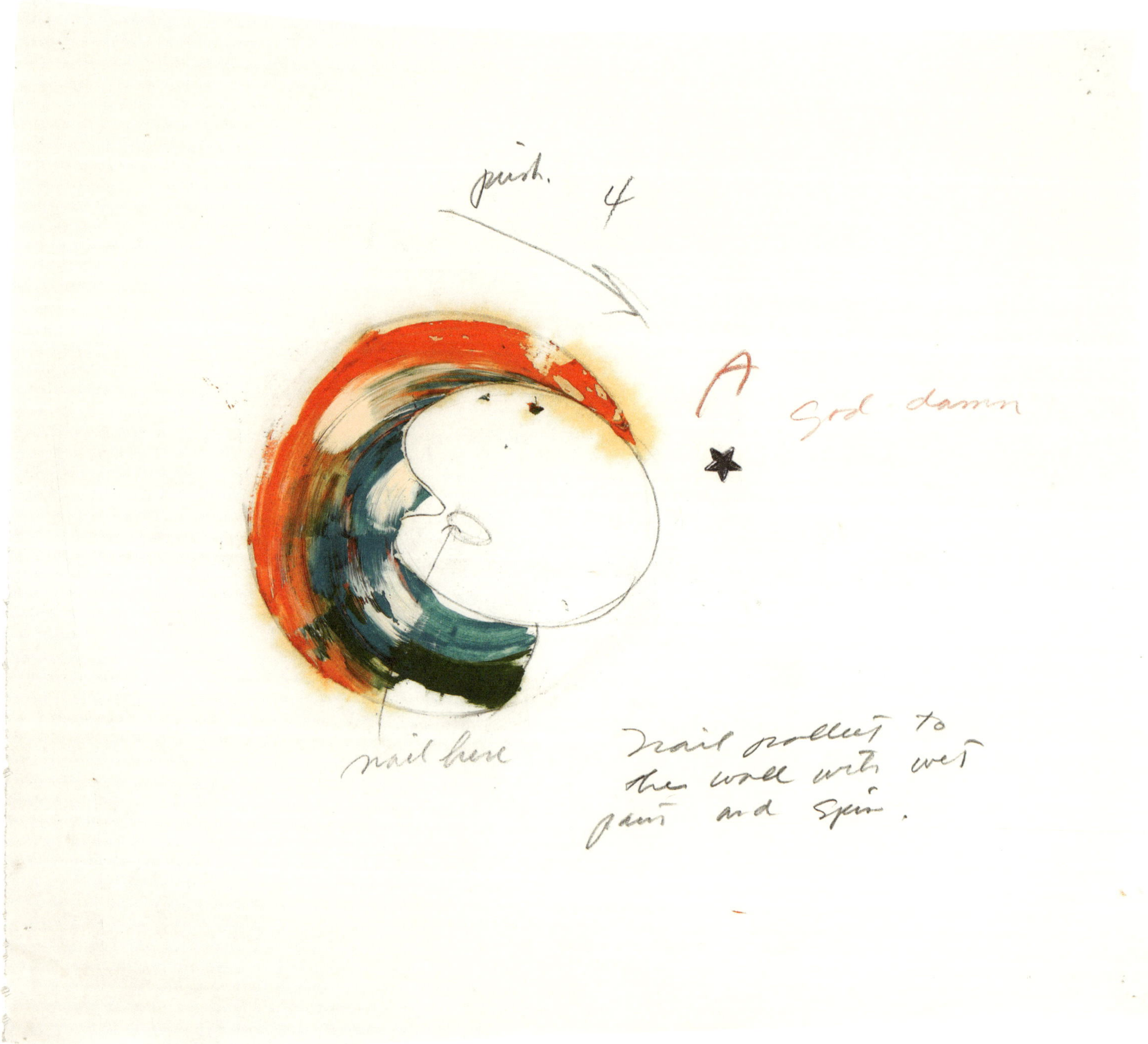

push. 4
A God damn
nail here
nail pollux to
the wall with wet
paint and spin.

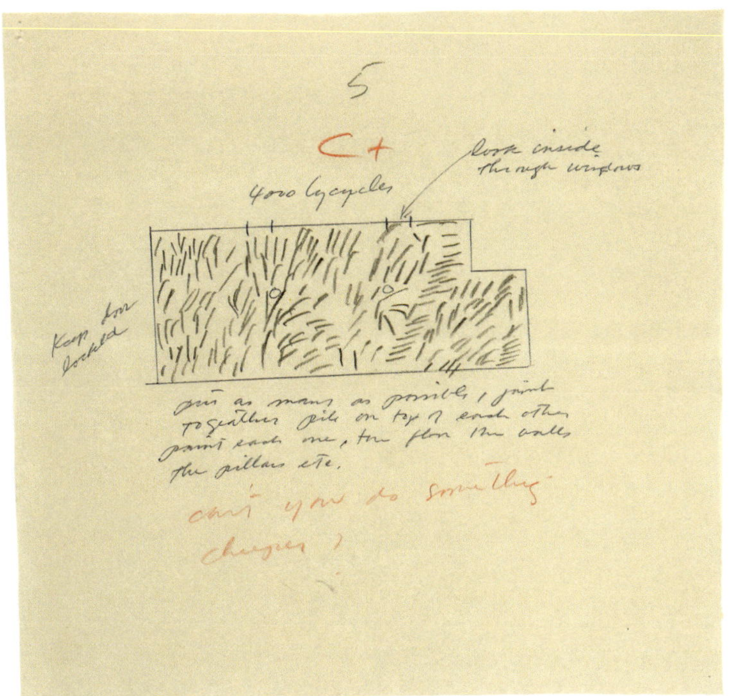

5
C+
4000 bicycles
look inside through windows
Keep door locked
put as many as possible, joint together pile on top of each other paint each one, the floor the walls the pillars etc.
can't you do something cheaper?

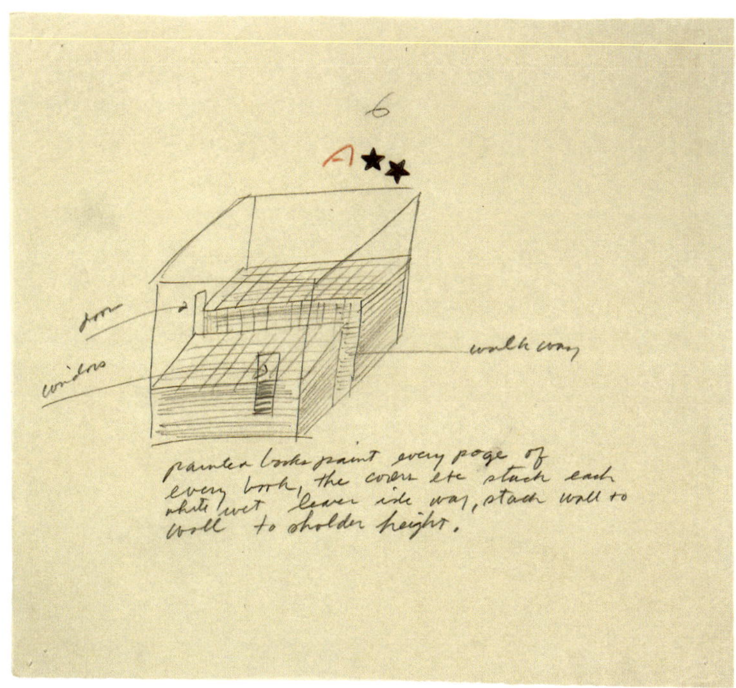

6
A ★★
door
windows
walk away
painted books paint every page of every book, the covers etc stack each while wet leave ink way, stack wall to wall to sholder height.

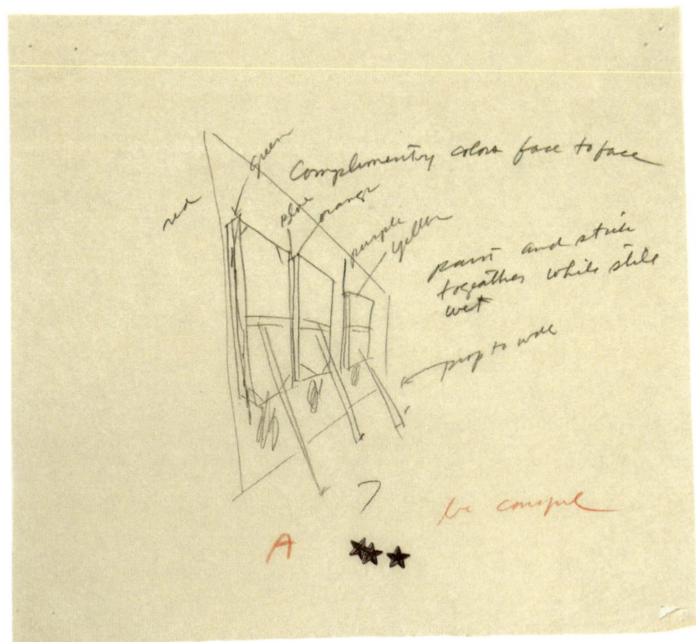

red
green
blue
orange
purple
yellow
Complementary colors face to face
paint and stick together while still wet
prop to wall
7
be cheaper
A ★★

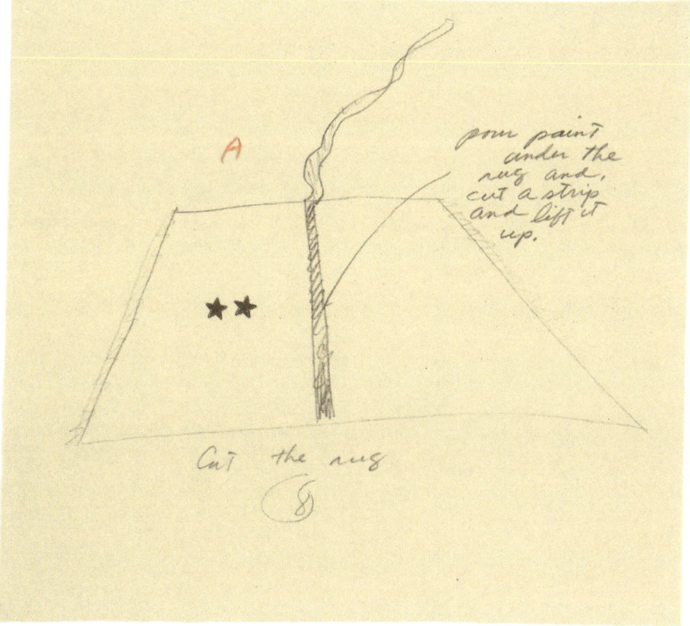

A
pour paint under the rug and, cut a strip and lift it up.
★★
Cut the rug
8

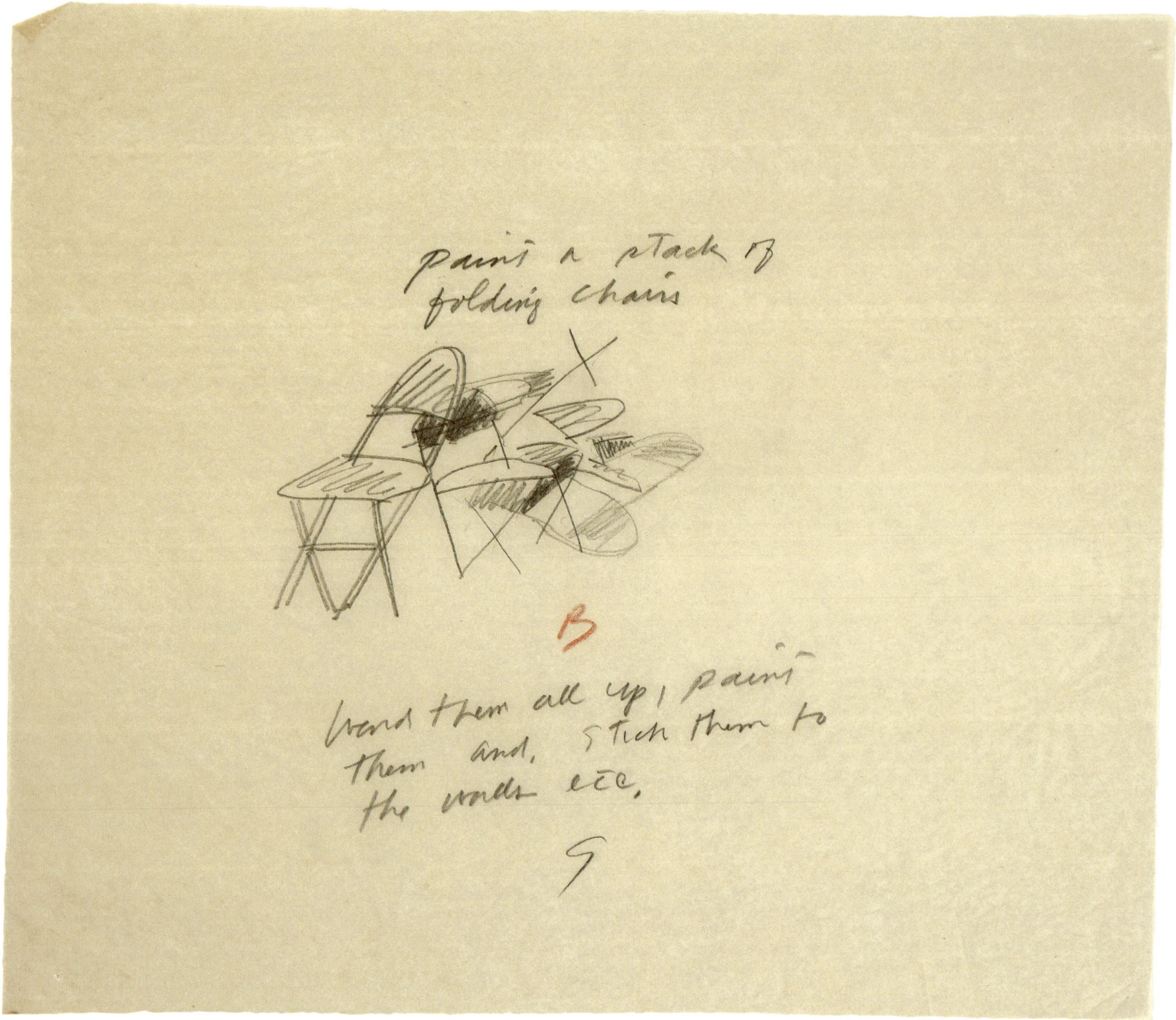

paint a stack of
folding chairs

B

bend them all up, paint
them and, stick them to
the walls etc.

G

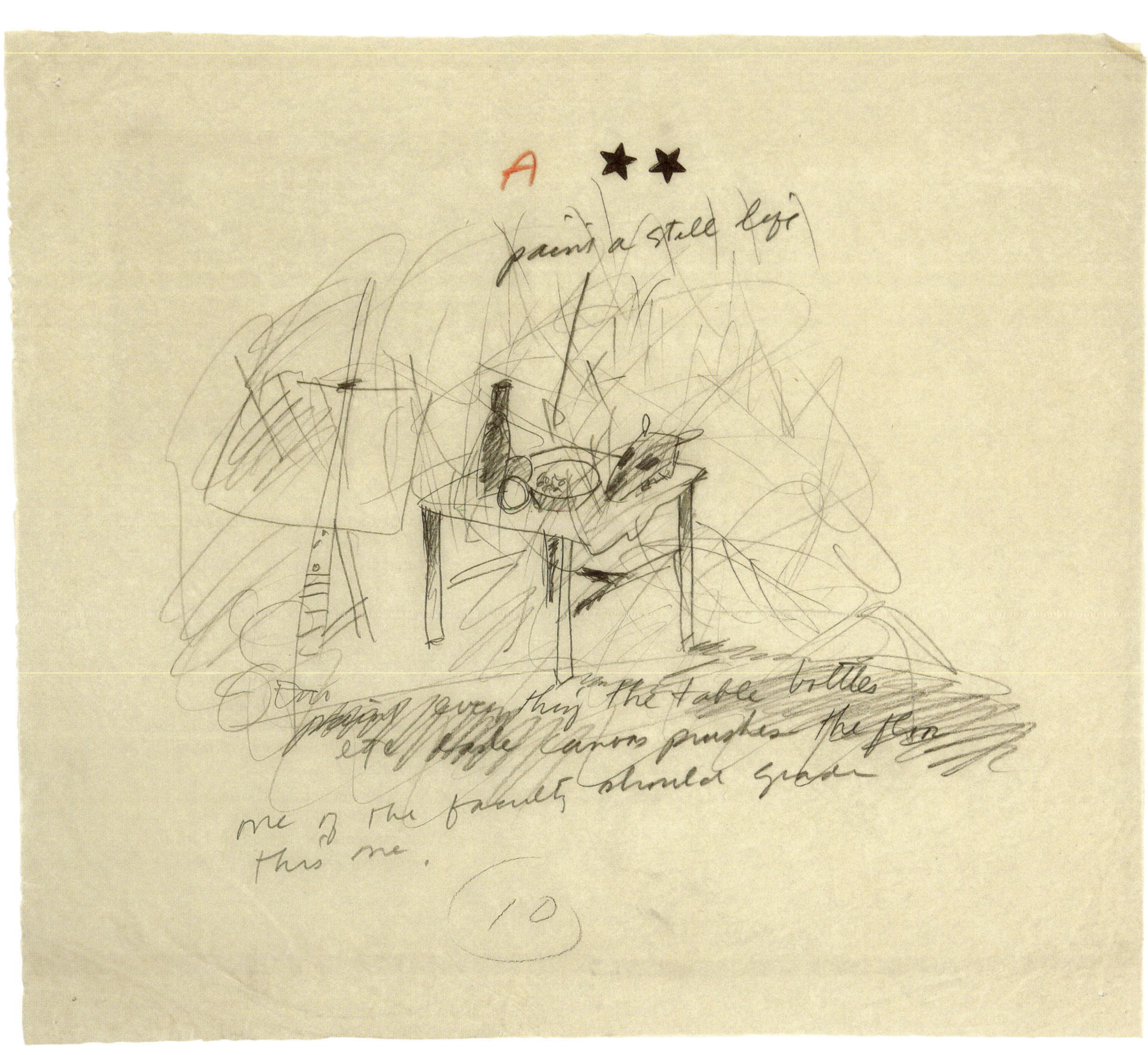
paint a still life?
painting everything the table bottles
etc canvas pushes the floor
one of the faculty should grade
this one.

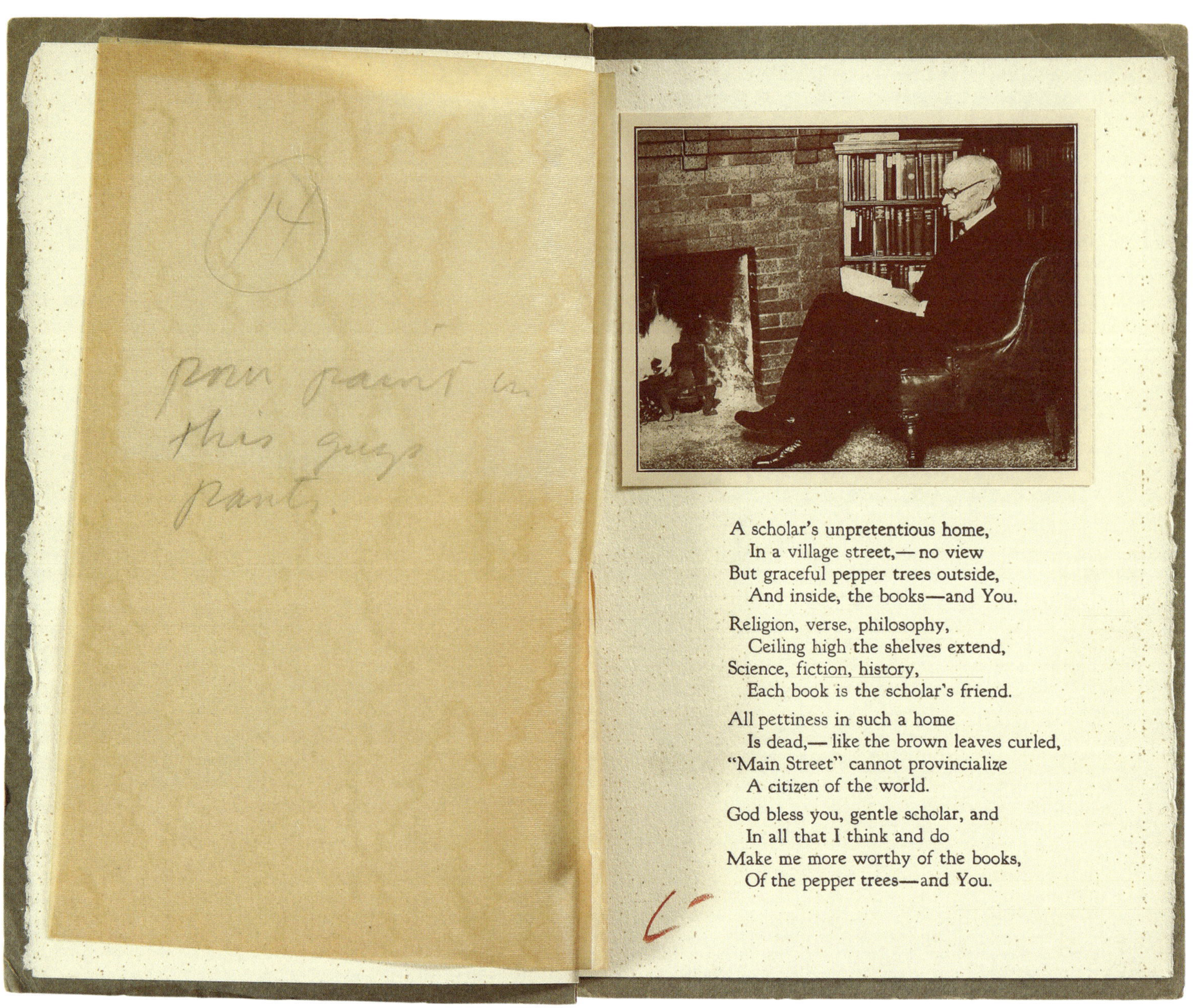

A scholar's unpretentious home,
   In a village street,— no view
But graceful pepper trees outside,
   And inside, the books—and You.

Religion, verse, philosophy,
   Ceiling high the shelves extend,
Science, fiction, history,
   Each book is the scholar's friend.

All pettiness in such a home
   Is dead,— like the brown leaves curled,
"Main Street" cannot provincialize
   A citizen of the world.

God bless you, gentle scholar, and
   In all that I think and do
Make me more worthy of the books,
   Of the pepper trees—and You.

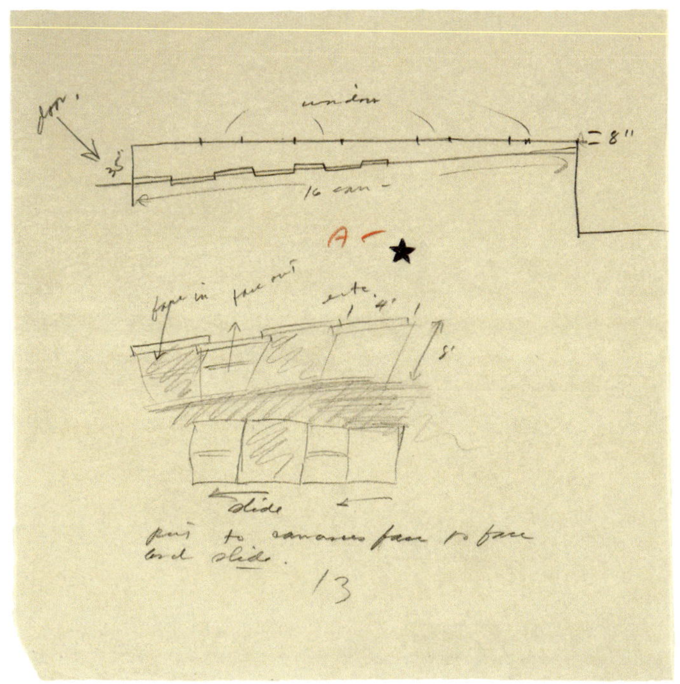

door
window
= 8"
2½'
16 cans
A
tape in face out
etc.
1' 4' 1'
5'
slide
pin to canvases face to face and slide.
13

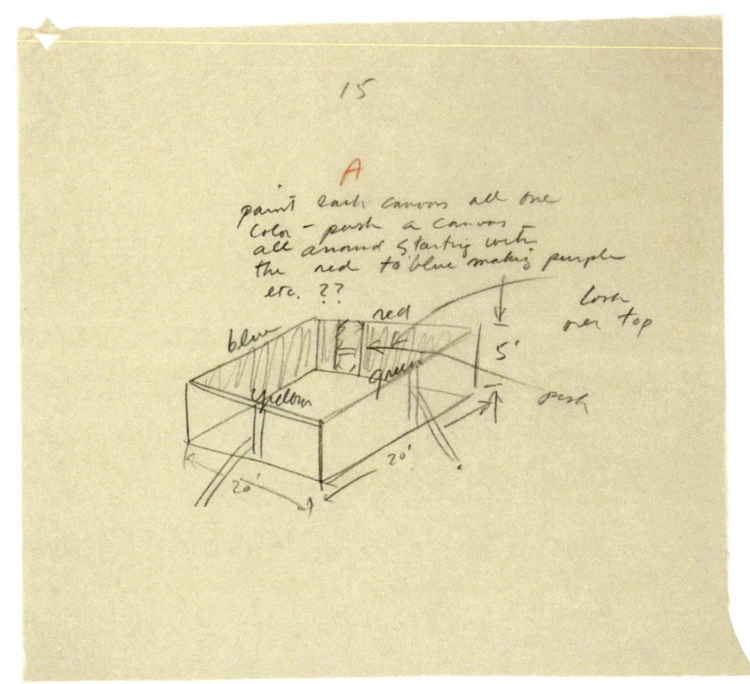

15
A
paint each canvas all one
color – push a canvas
all around starting with
the red to blue making purple
etc. ??
blue
red
green
yellow
5'
look over top
push
20'
20'

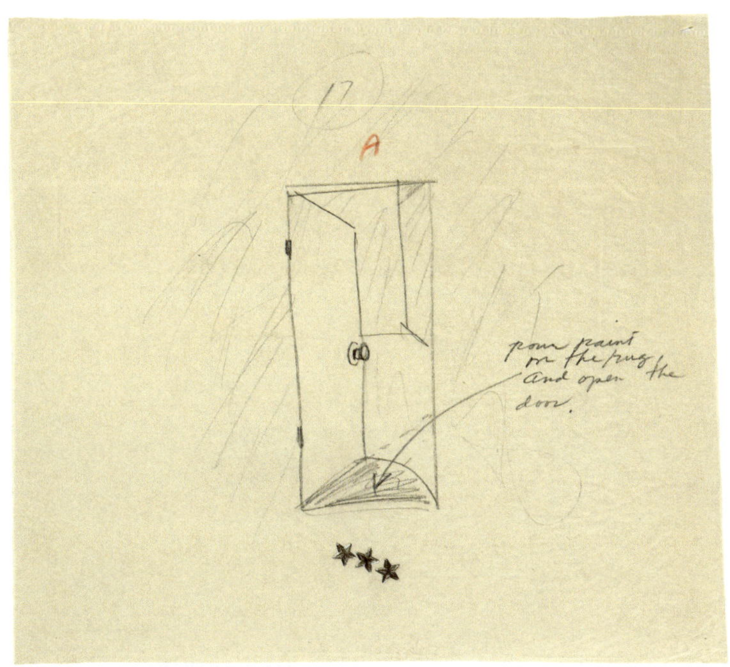

17
A
pour paint
on the rug
and open the
door.

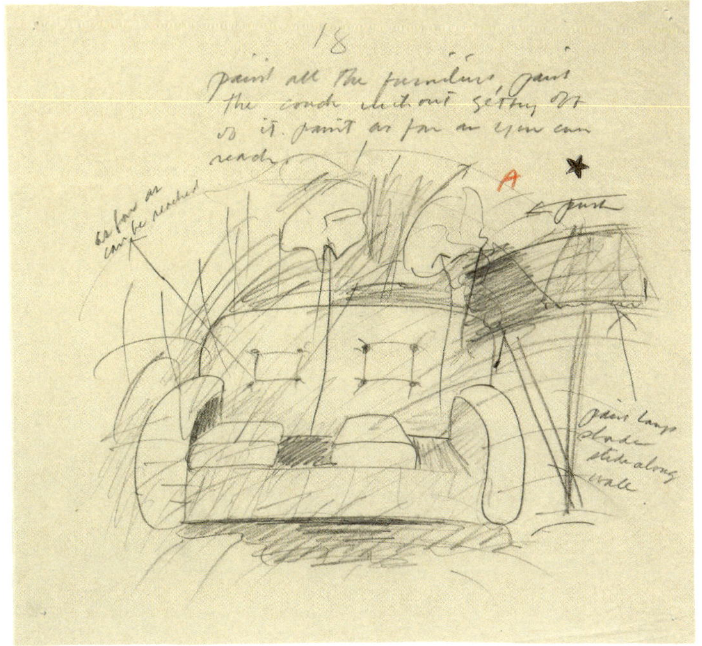

18
paint all the furniture, paint
the couch without getting off
of it. paint as far as you can
reach.
as far as can be reached
A
push
paint lamp
shade
slide along
wall

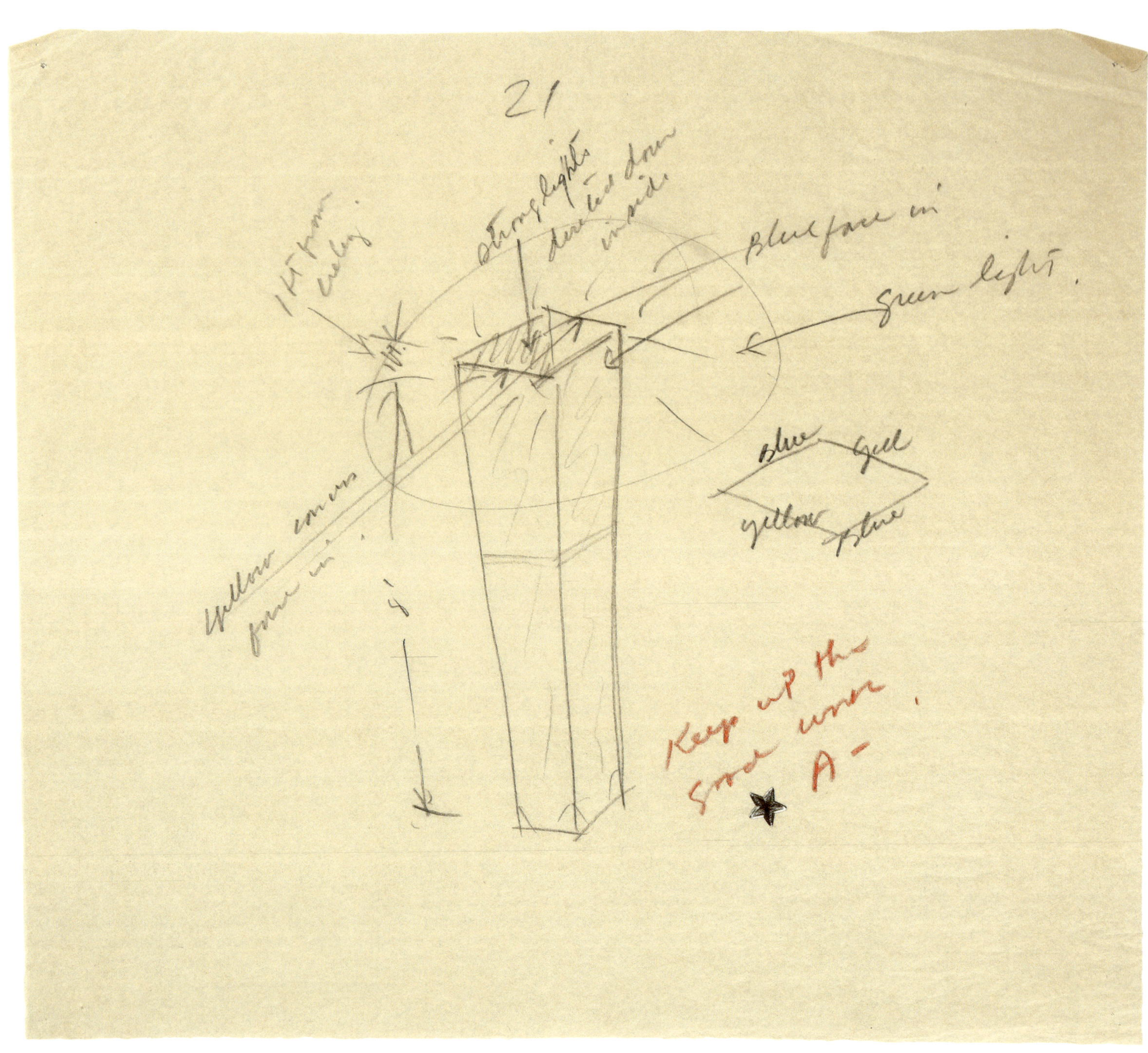
1 kw from
ceiling
strong lights
directed down
inside
Blue face in
green light
yellow comes
from in
blue   yell
yellow   blue
Keep up the
snow cover.
A —

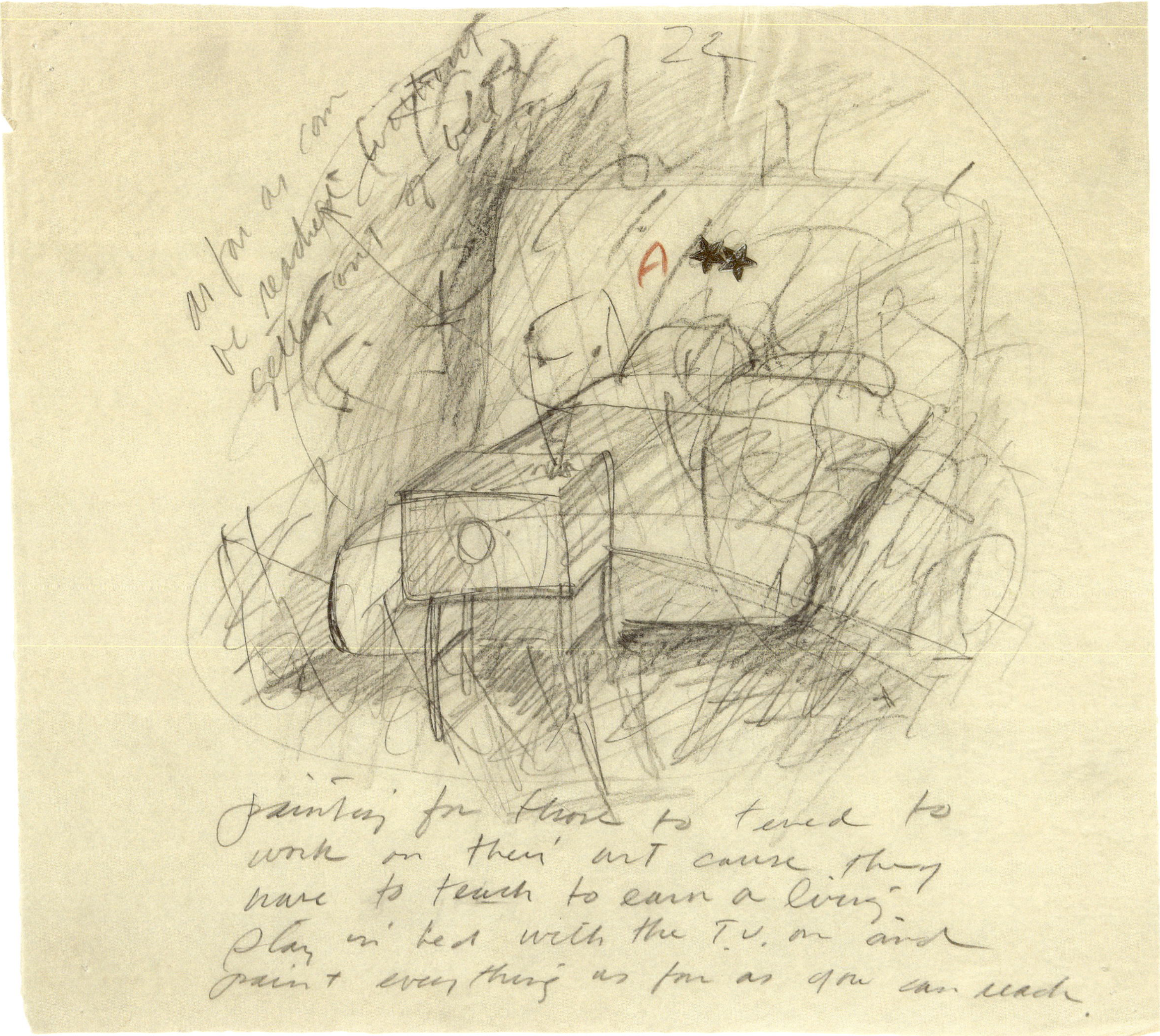

as far as you can
or perhaps without
getting out of bed

painting for those to tired to
work on their art cause they
have to teach to earn a living?
play in bed with the T.V. on and
paint everything as far as you can reach.

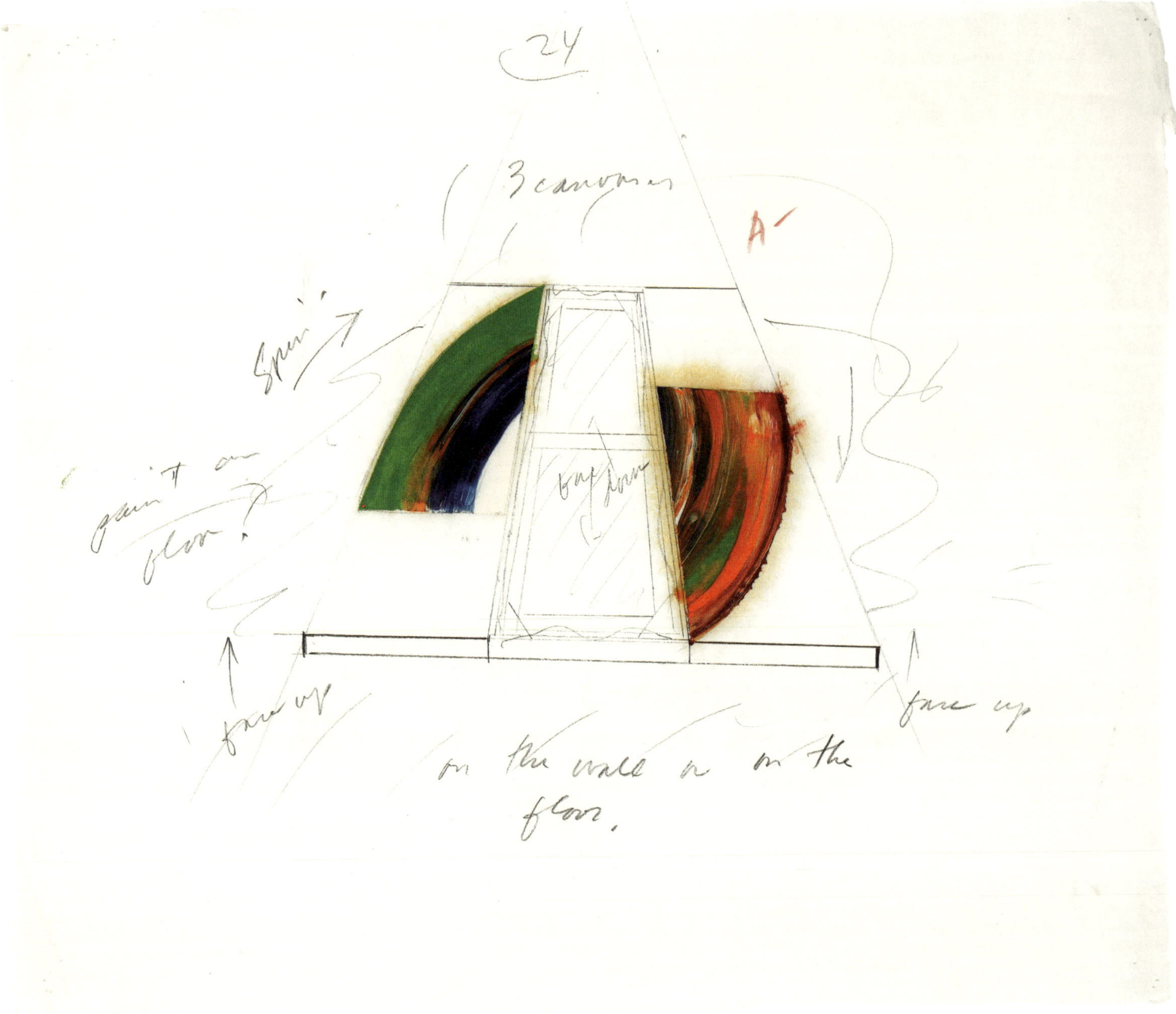

24
3 canvases
A
paint on floor?
face up
face up
on the wall or on the
floor.

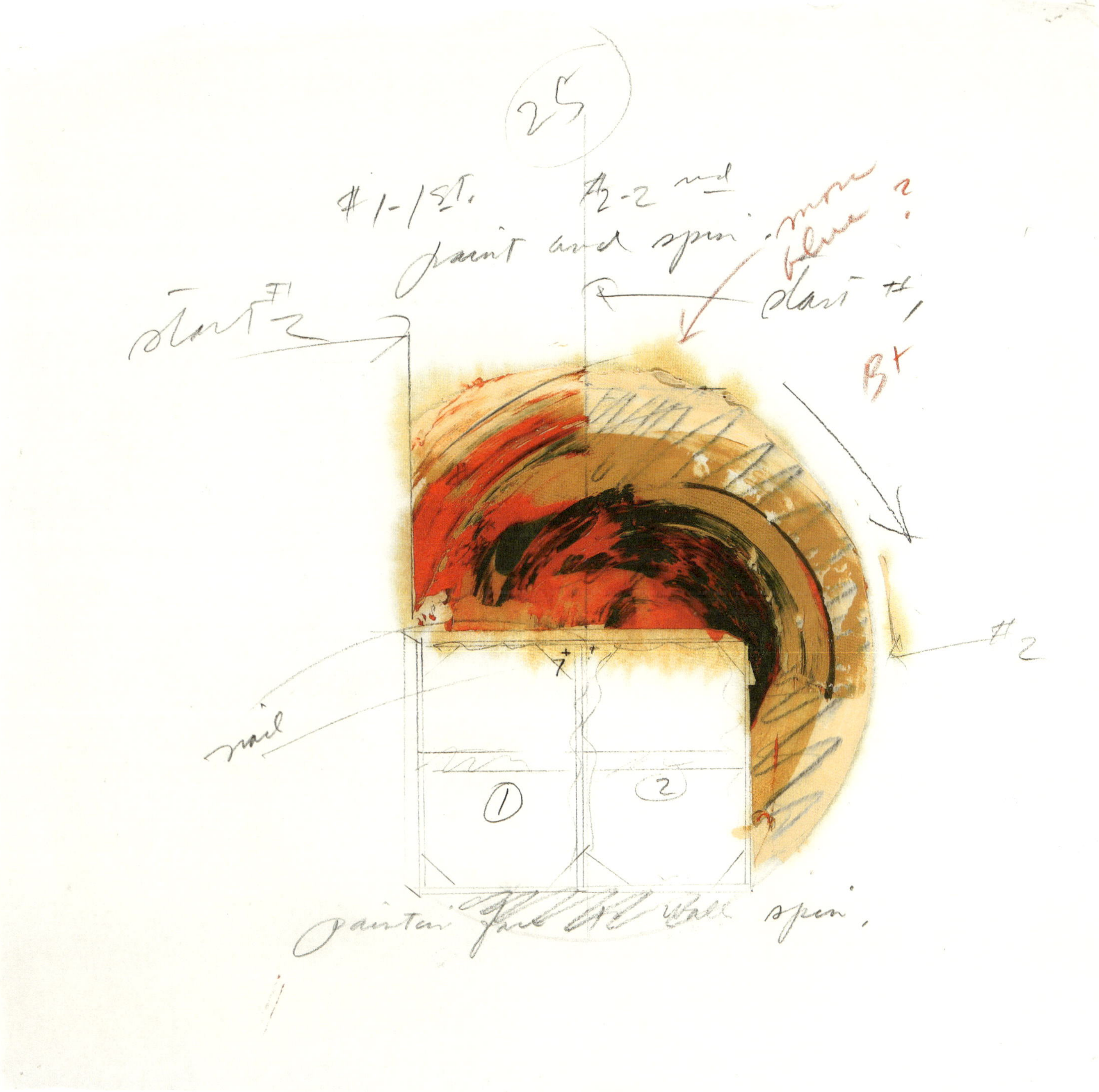

25

#1 - 1st.   #2 - 2nd.

paint and spin.   more blue ?

start #2   start #1

8°

nail

#2

① ②

painter full the wall spin.

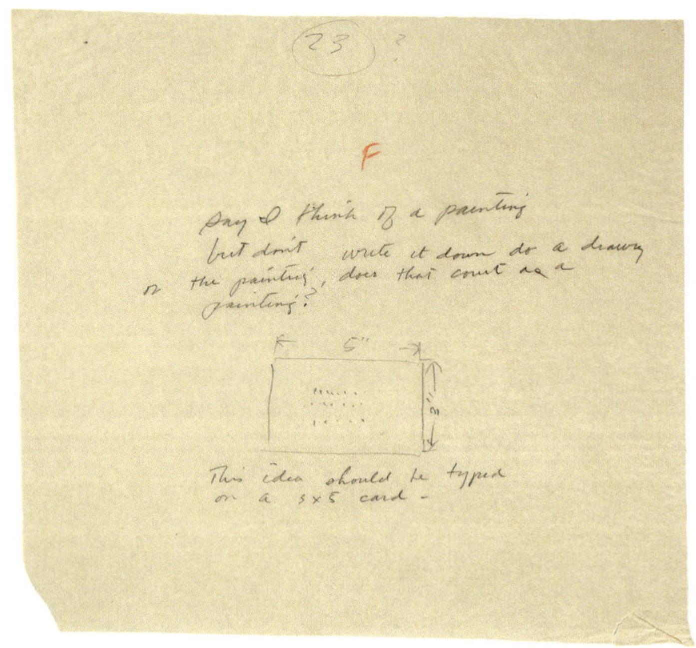

23 ?
F
Say I think of a painting
but don't write it down do a drawing
of the painting, does that count as a
painting?
5"
3"
This idea should be typed
on a 3 x 5 card –

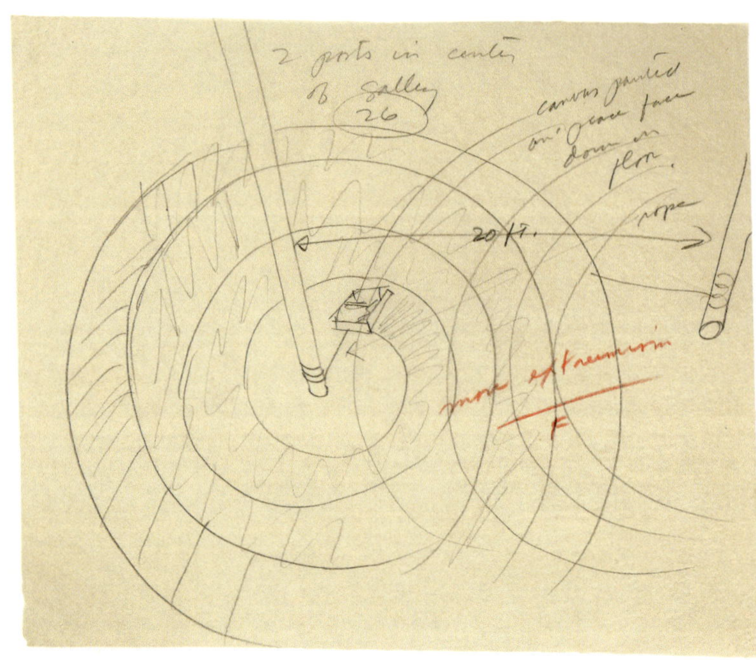

2 posts in center
B Galley
26
canvas painted
on grave face
down on floor.
20 ft.
rope
more extraneous
F

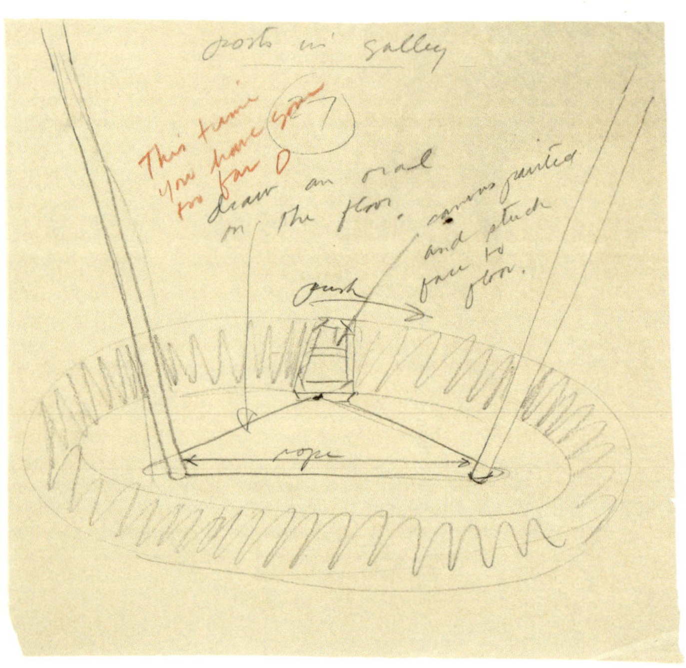

posts in galley
This time
you have space
too far D
1
draw an oval
on the floor. canvas painted
and stuck
face to
floor.
push
rope

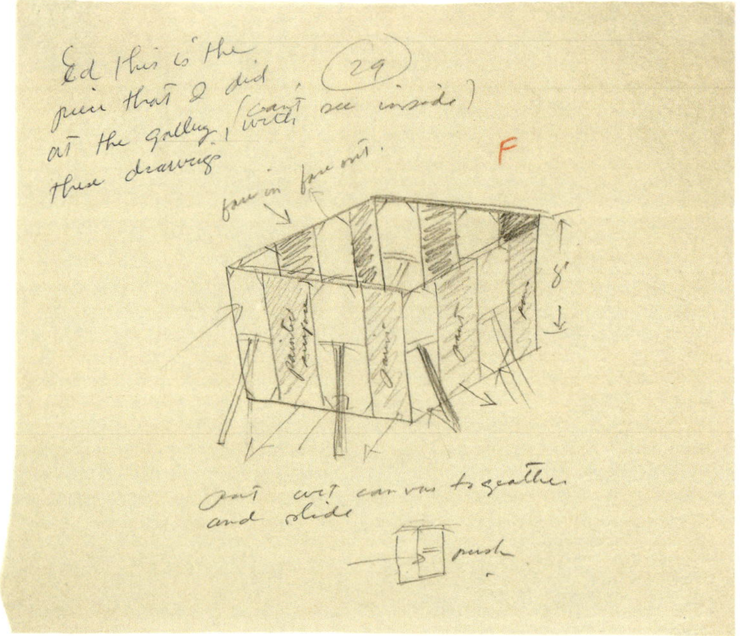

Ed this is the
piece that I did   29
at the galley. (can't see inside)
(with
these drawings
face in face out.
F
8'
can't cut canvas together
and slide
push

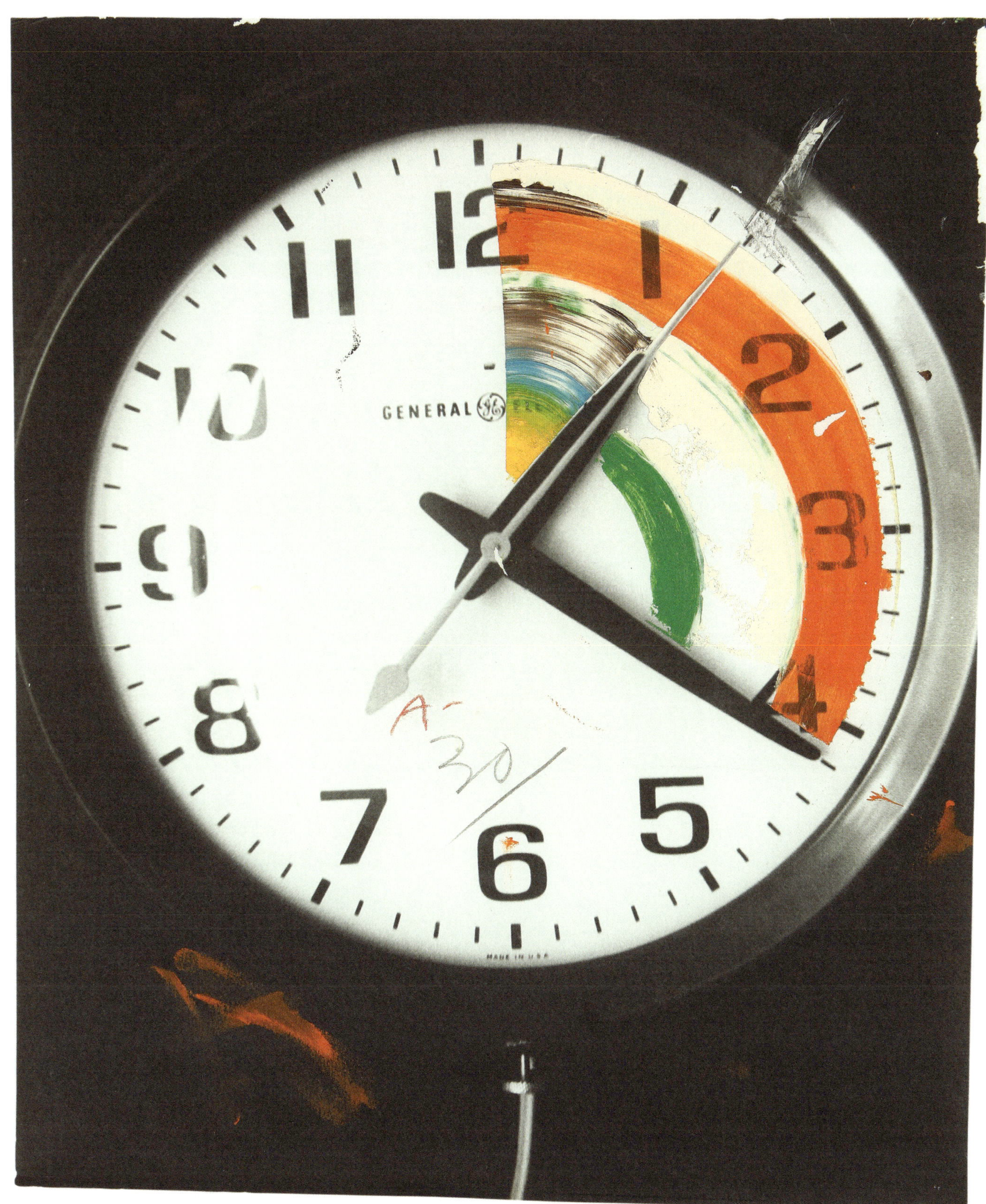

12
1
2
3
4
5
6
7
8
9
10
11
GENERAL
MADE IN U.S.A.

fill the pockets paint
all the inside outside
etch and sew them to-
gether.

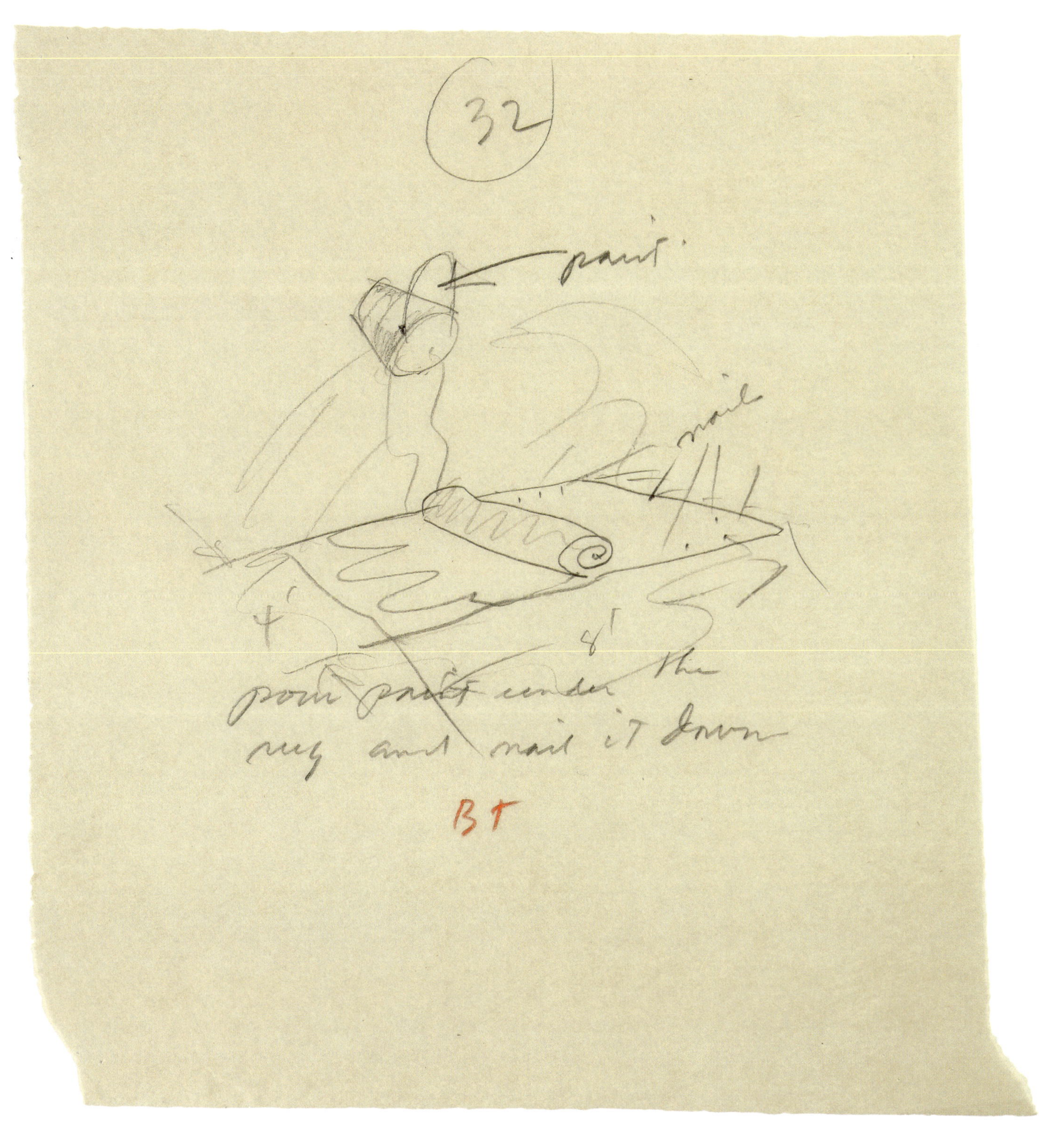
32
paint
nail
pour paint under the
rug and nail it down
BF

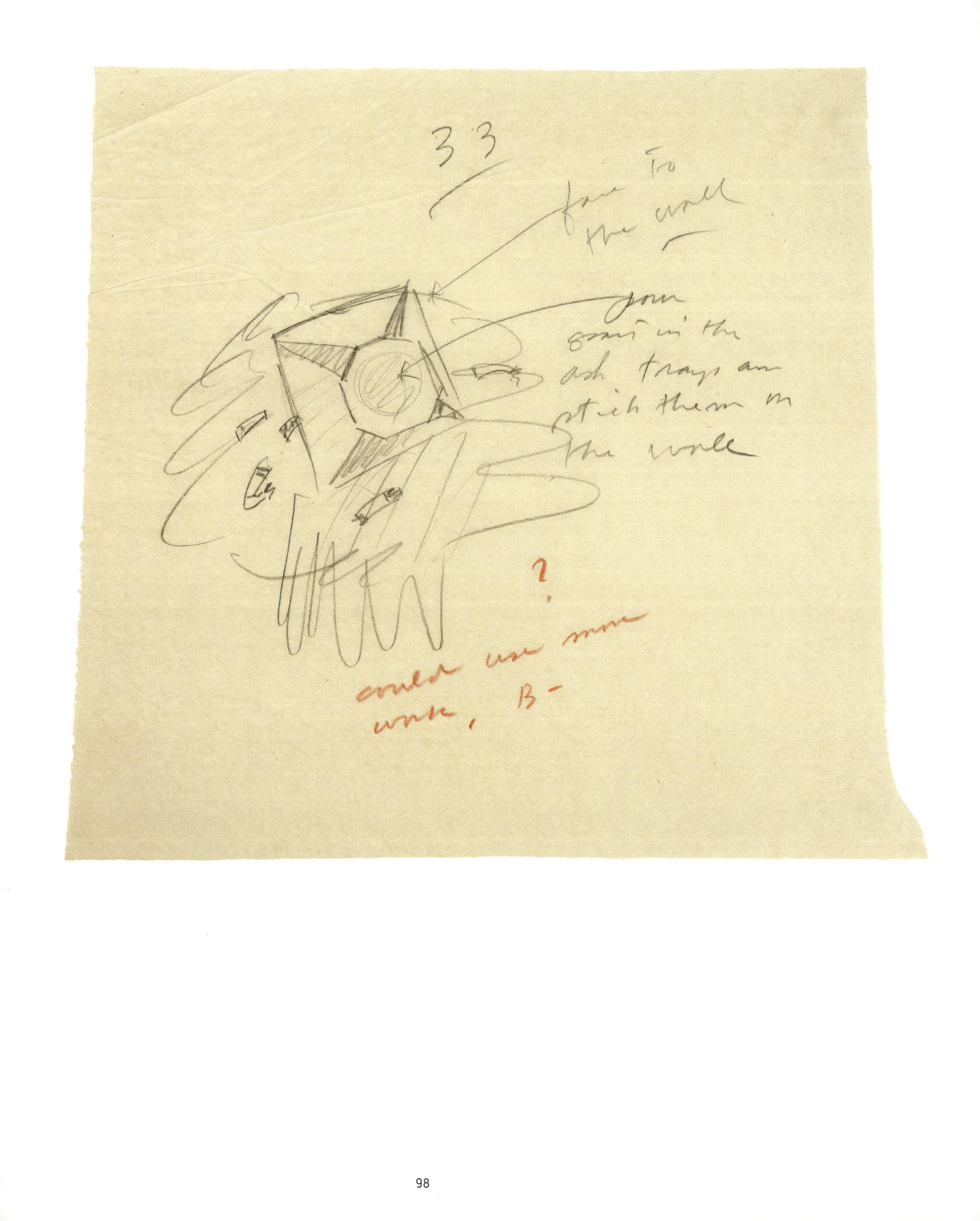

33

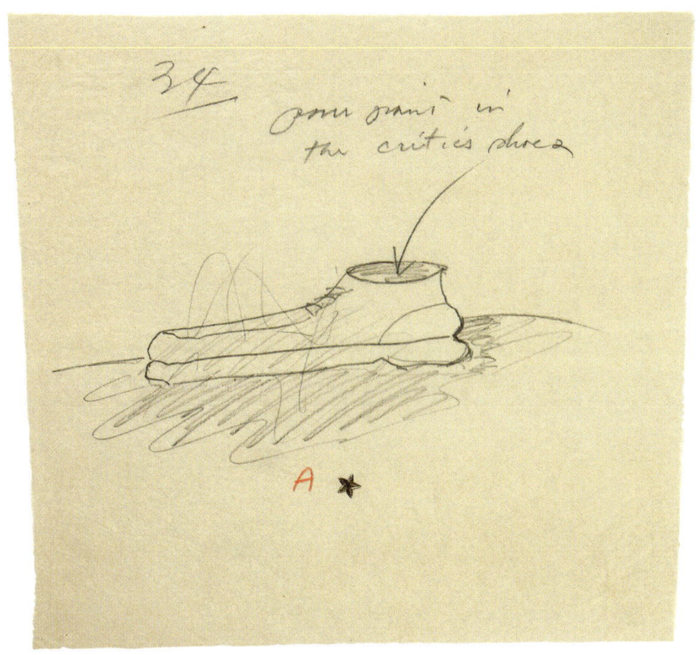

34
pour paint in
the critic's shoes
A

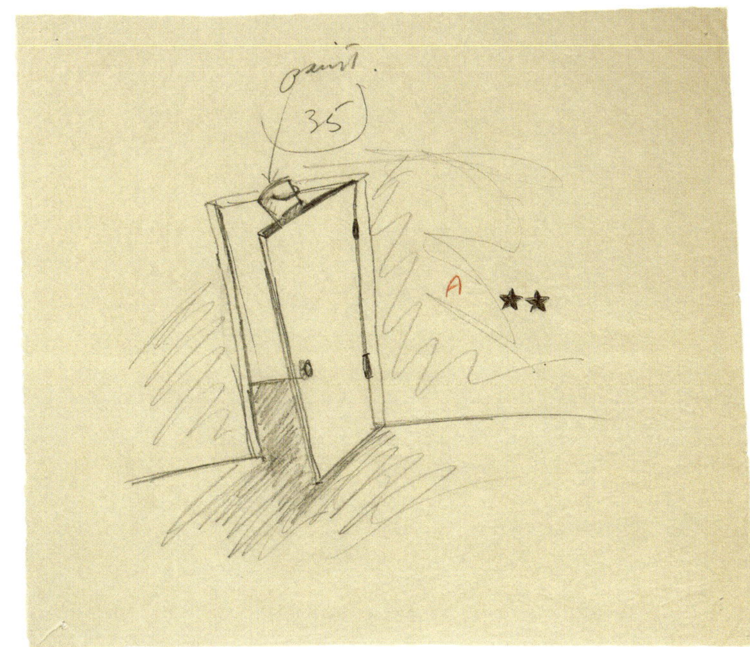

paint.
35
A

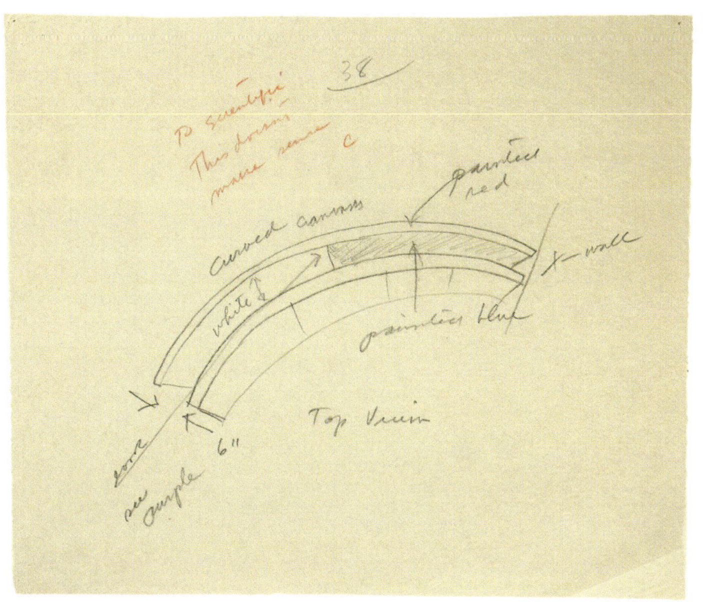

P sculpture
This drawing
makes sense
C
38
painted
red
curved canvas
X-wall
white
painted blue
Top View
door
see purple
6"

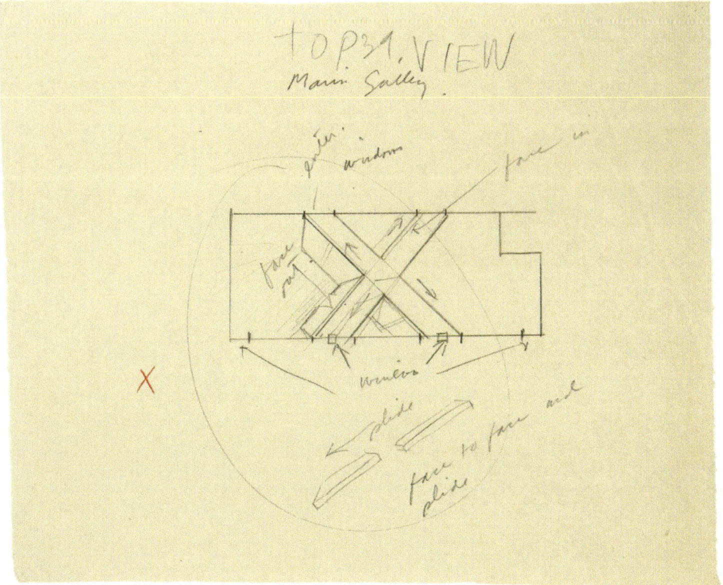

TOP 31. VIEW
Marin Gallery.
green
window
face in
face
out
window
slide
face to face and
slide
X

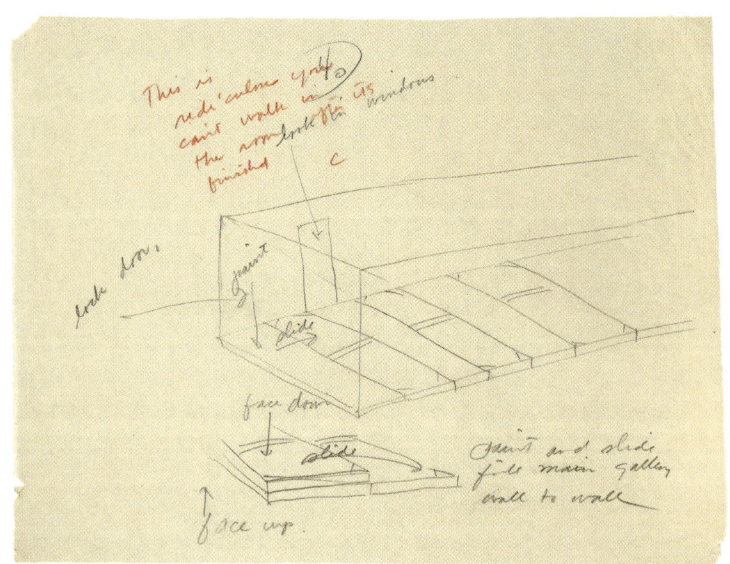
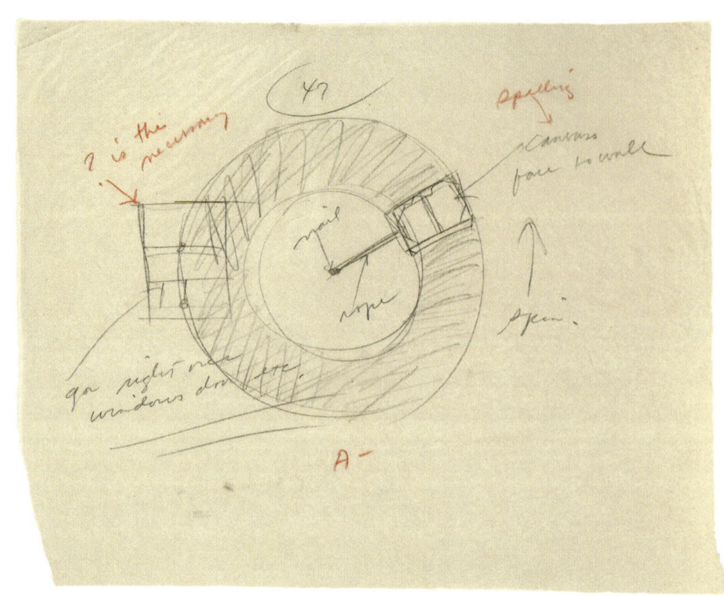
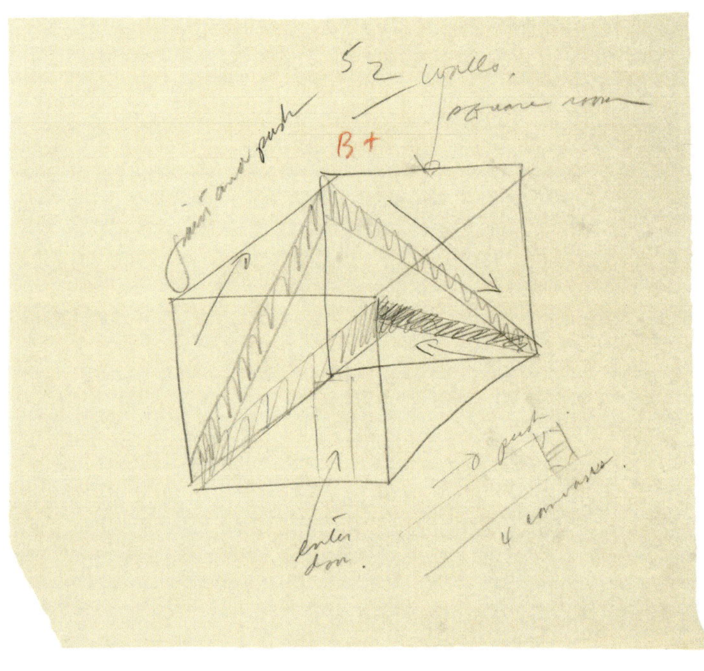
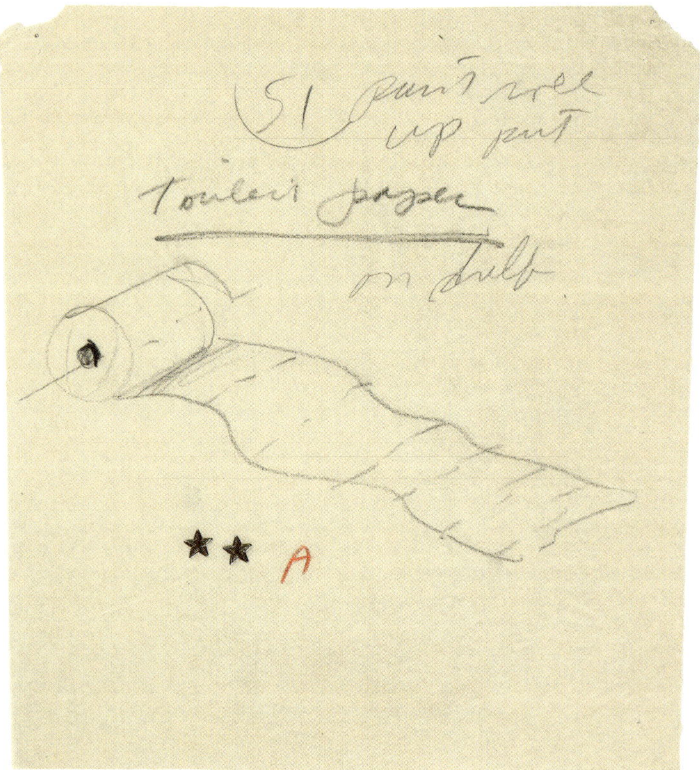

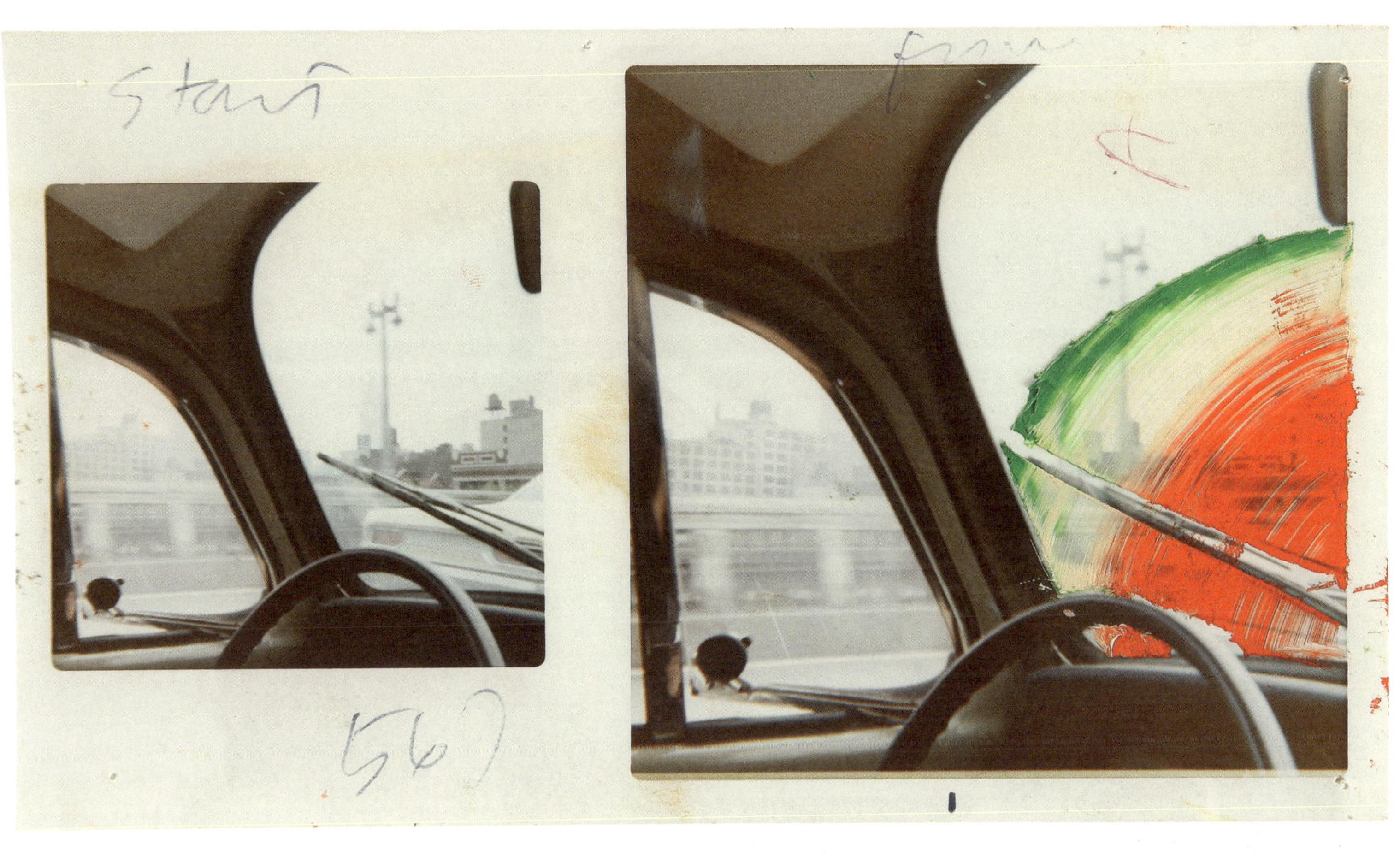

start
from
5607

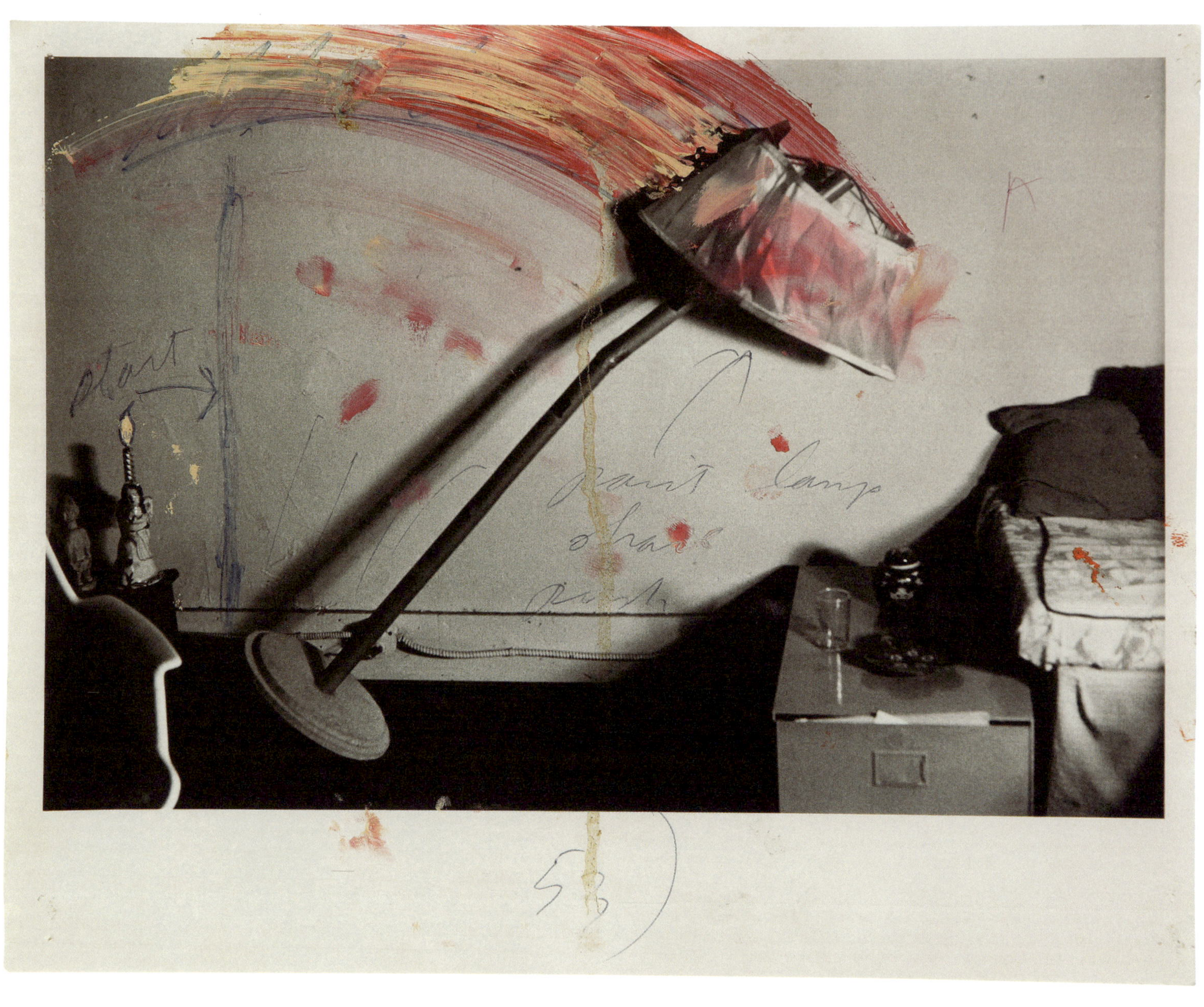

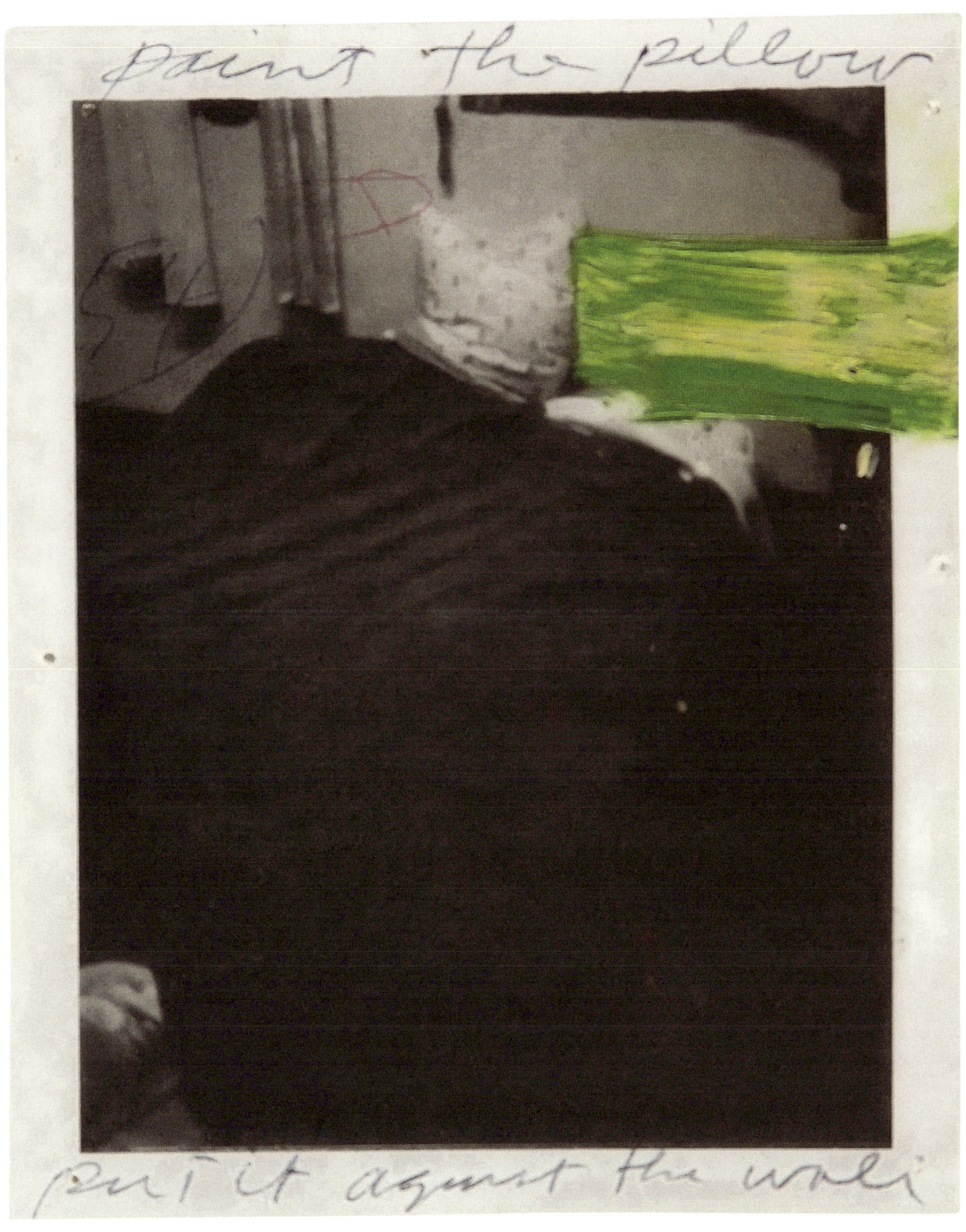

paint the pillow
put it against the wall

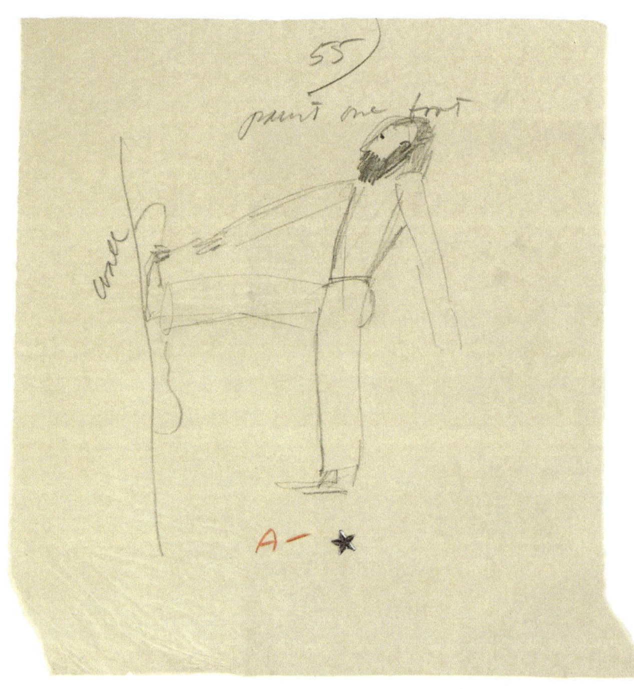
55
paint one foot
wall
A — ★

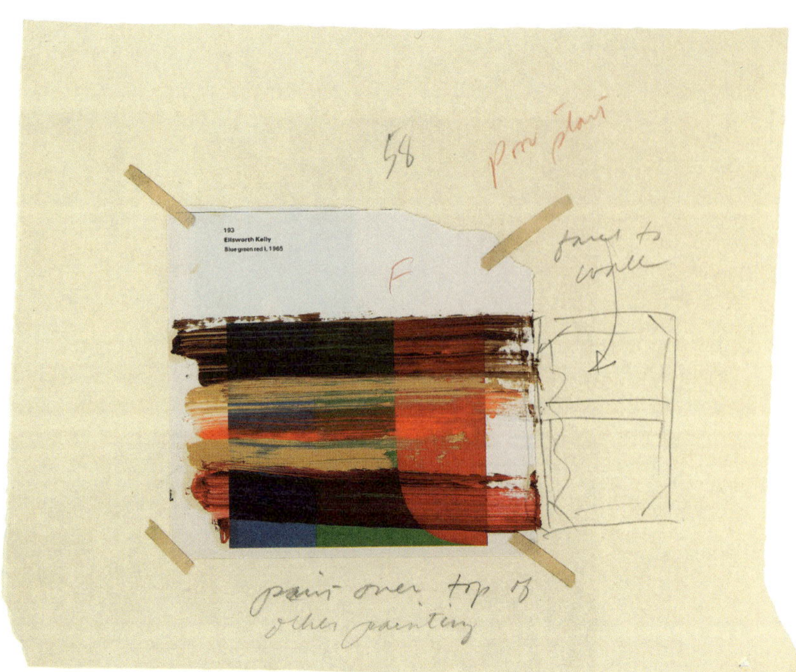
58
193
Ellsworth Kelly
Blue green red I, 1965
F
paint to wall
paint over top of
other painting

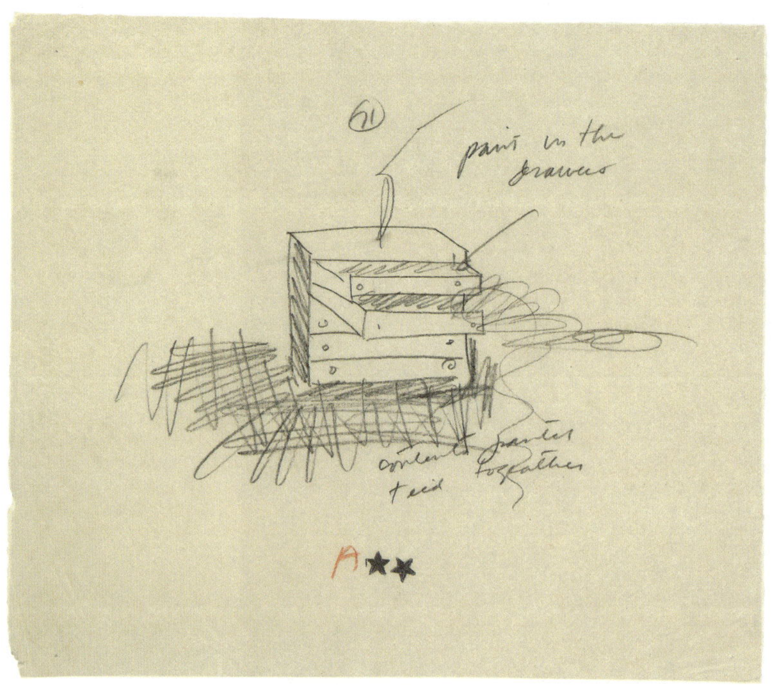
61
paint in the
drawers
contents glued
+ tied together
A ★★

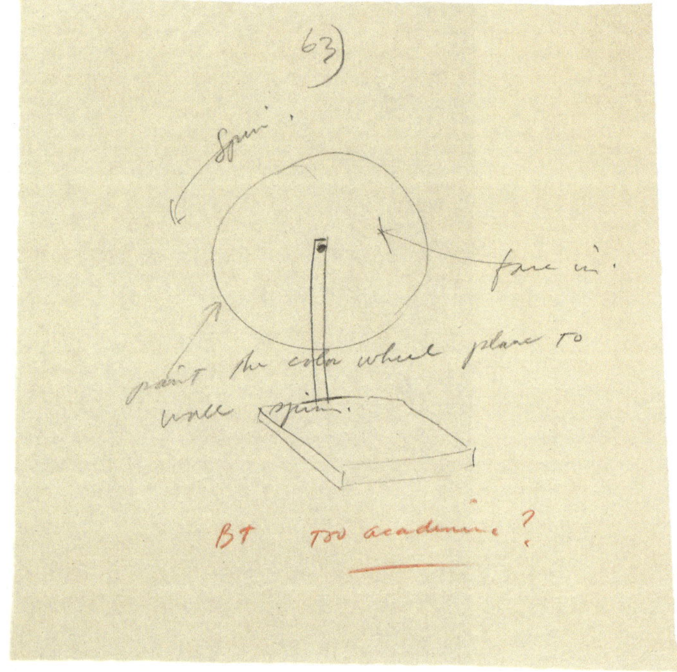
63)
spin
face in
paint the color wheel place to
wall spin
B+   too academic?

painting rolled tightly
at one end loose at the
other

rolled very tight.

F – don't bother
with those kinds
of people.
painted and
rolled wet.

18 inches

put on
floor to
dry.

painting for art critics to sit on
dedicated to William Wilson.

(4)

paint and stack all
the furniture in a
room —
living room
bed room
Kitchen etc.   room

TOP VIEW

stack
in center

B+

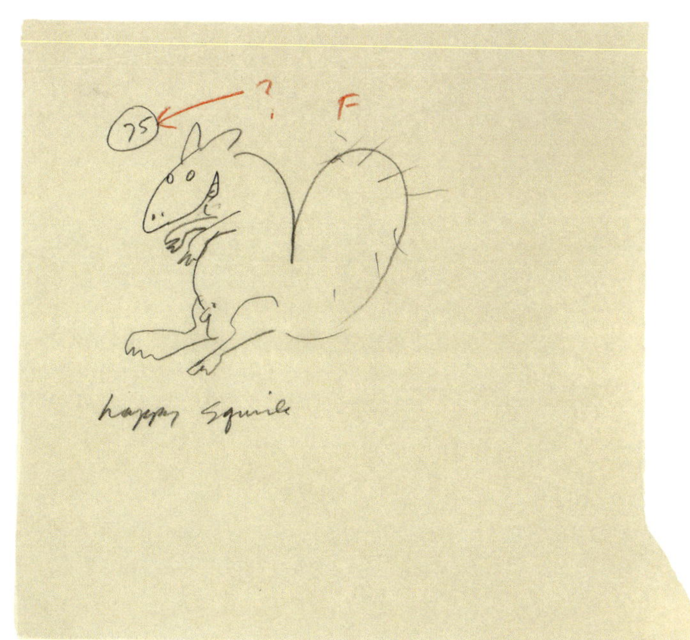
75
?
F
happy squirrel

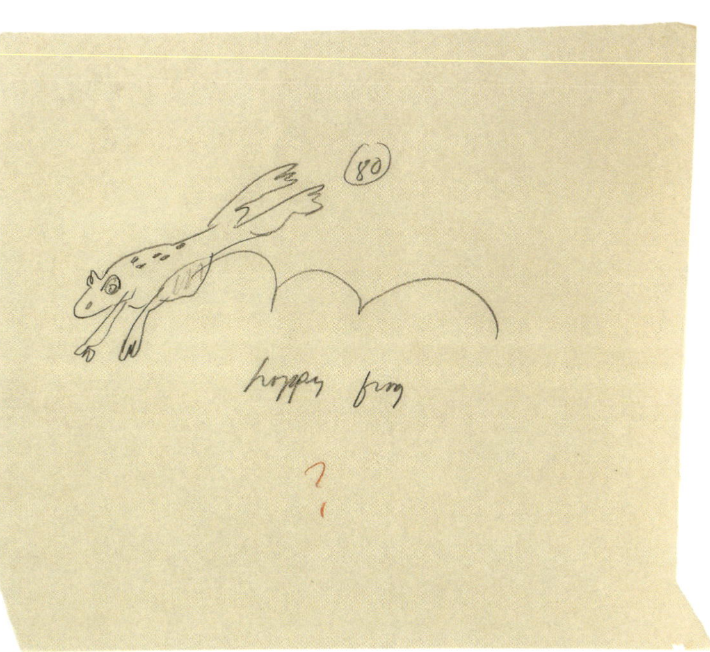
80
happy frog
?

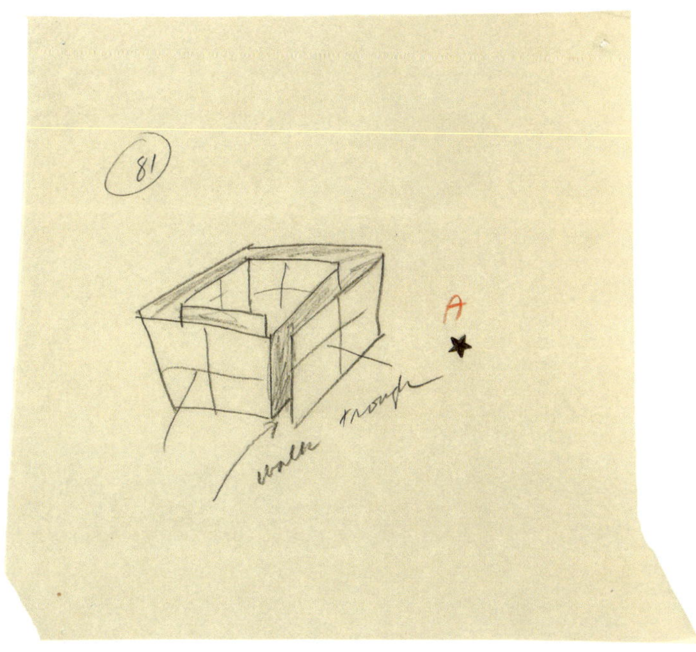
81
A
water trough

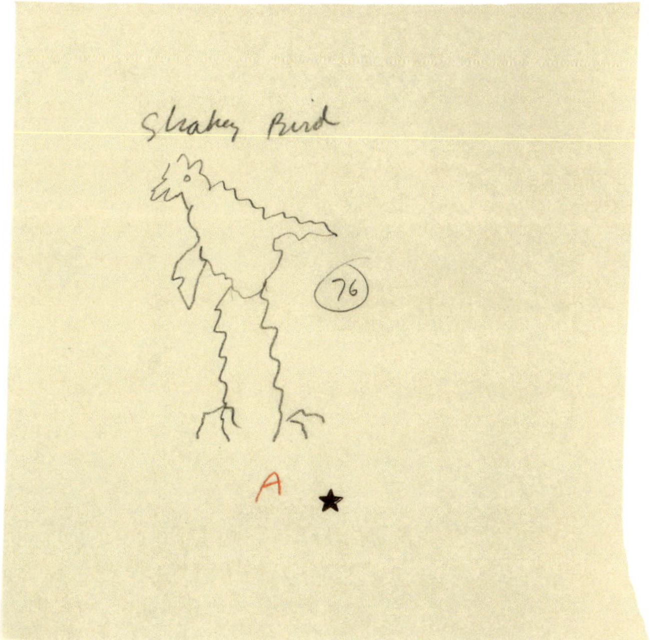
Shaky Bird
76
A

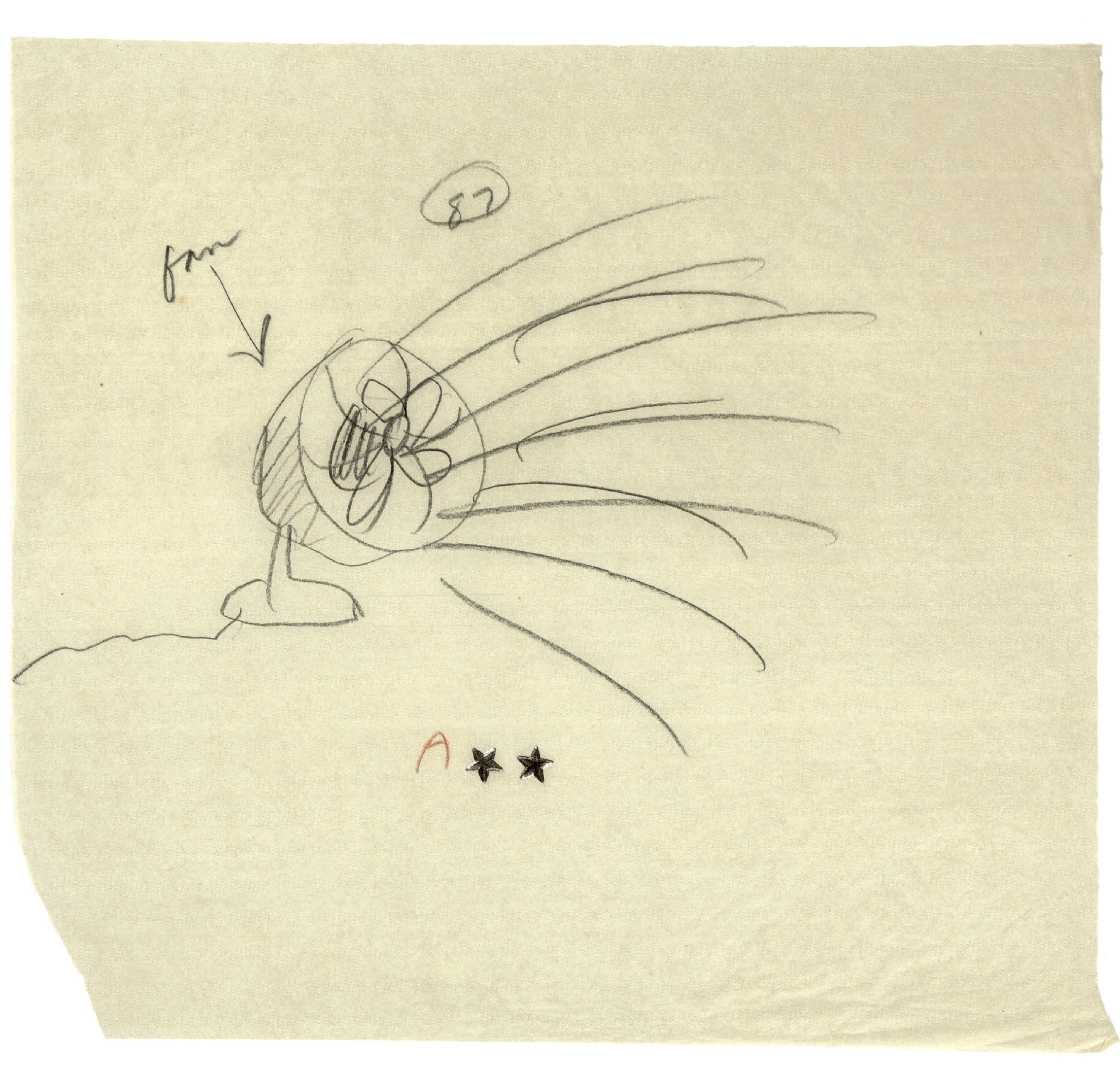

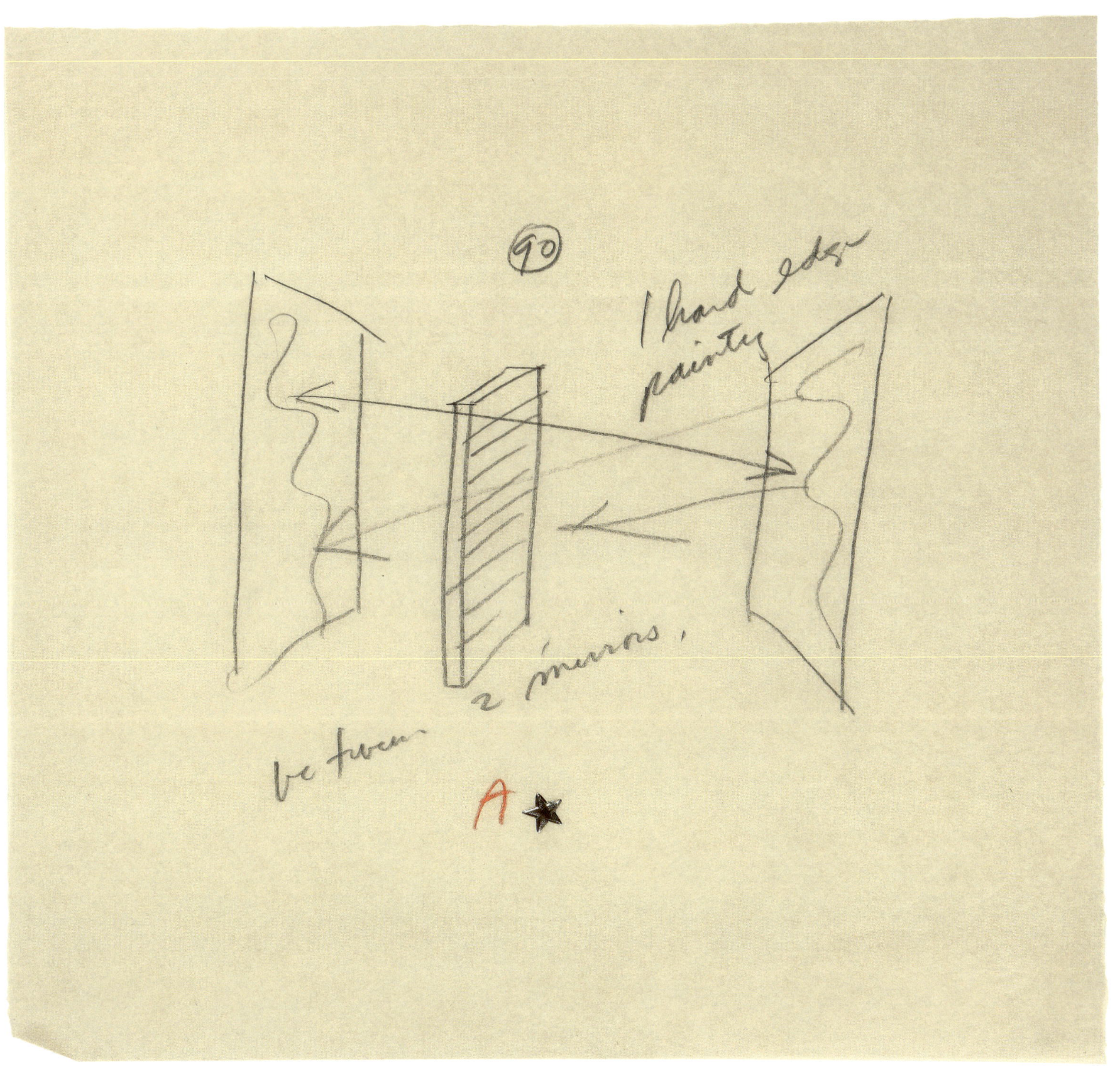

90
1 hard edge painting
between 2 mirrors.
A

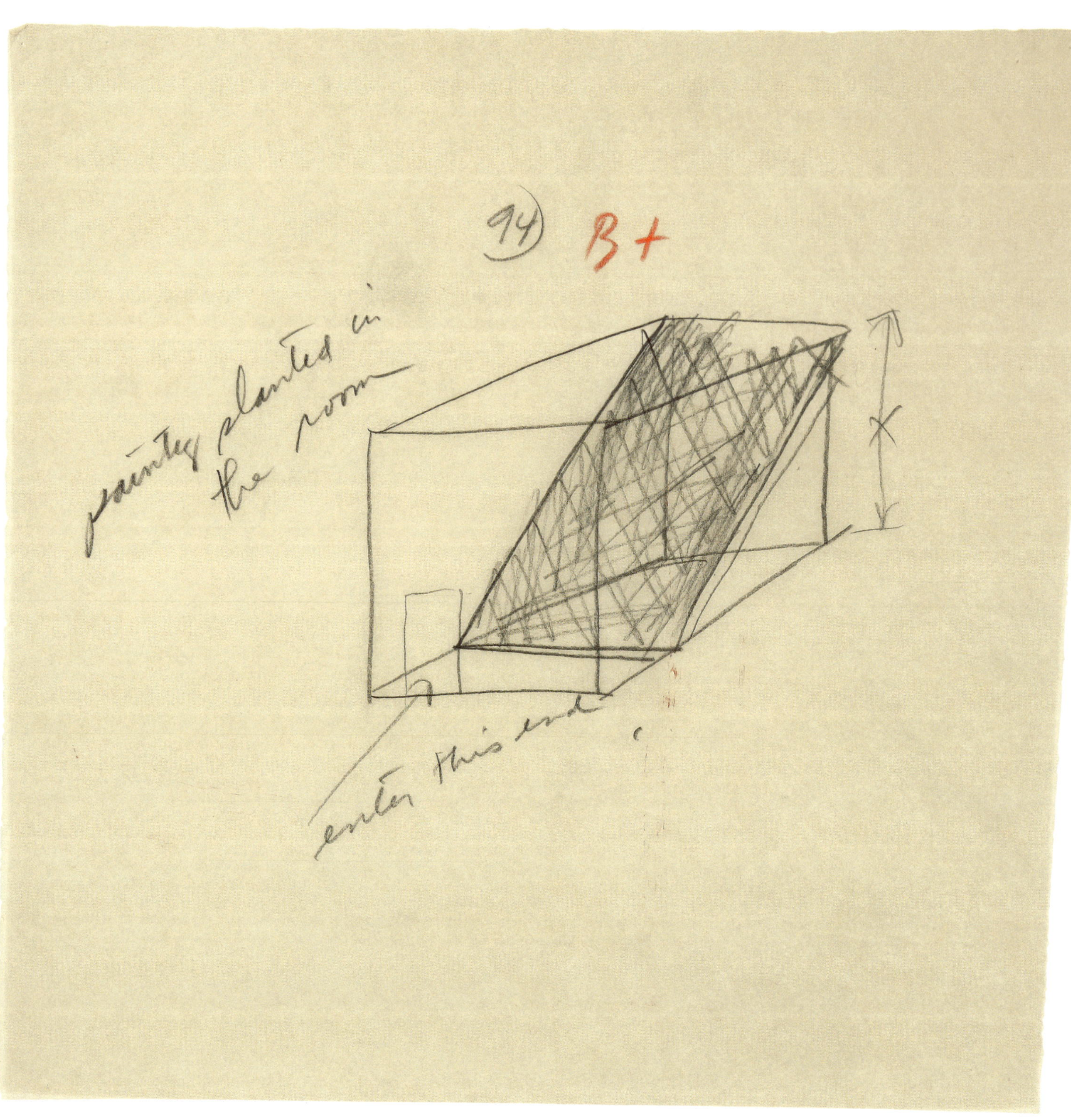
94)
B+
painting planted in
the room
enter this end

97

New York
New York
New York

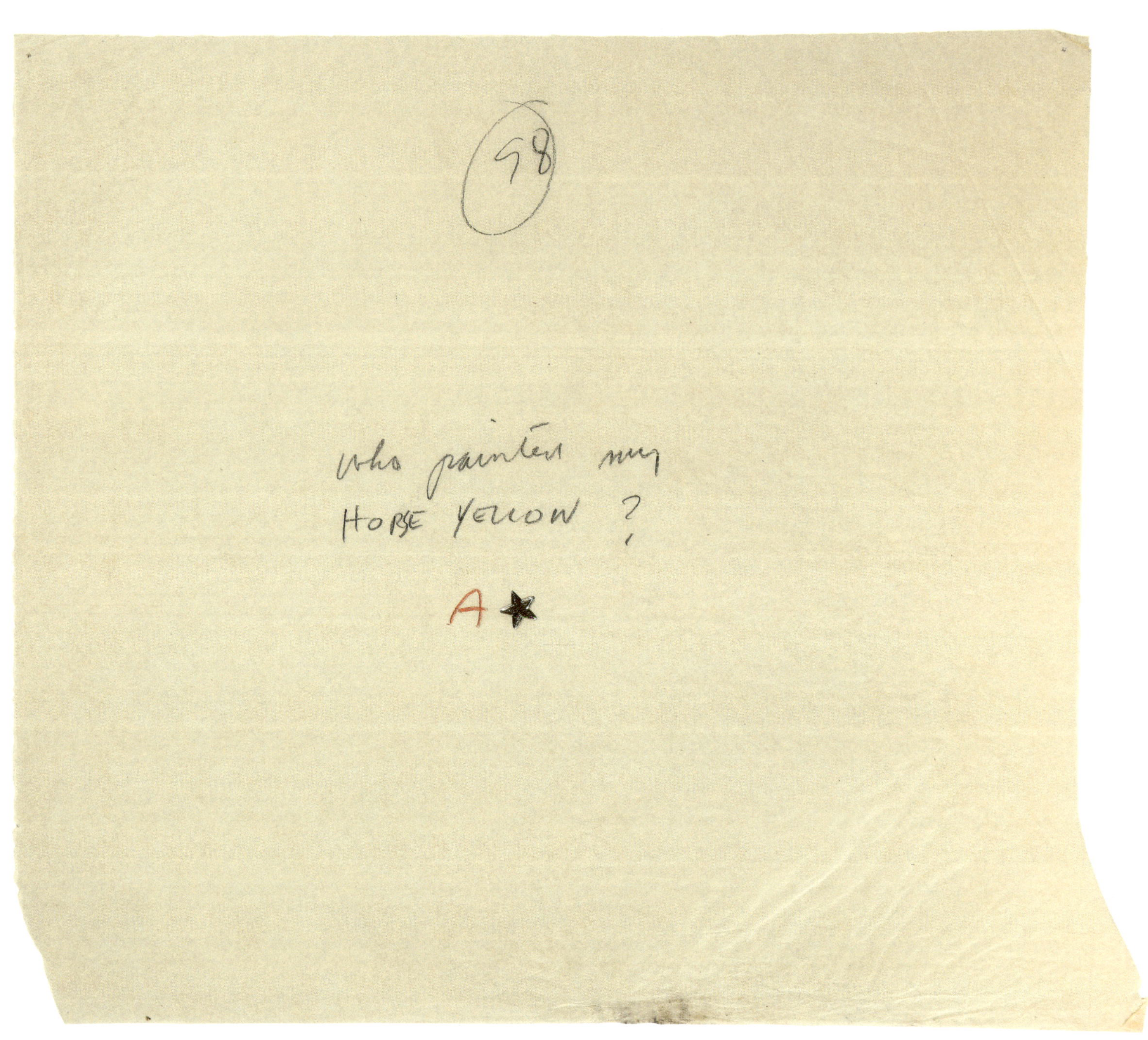
58

who painted my
HORSE YELLOW ?

A

F

Say I think of a painting
but don't   write it down do a drawing
the painting, does that count as a
painting?

5"   2"

This idea should be typed
on a 3 x 5 card —

PAINTING'S
PLAYBOOK

JEFFREY WEISS

"Right now, in the course of this conversation, ten thousand paintings have been made."[1] The remark, which was uttered by Richard Jackson during a recent interview, stopped me cold. We all bracket many things when we work; we must suspend our awareness of the world. This is certainly true of any artist, although there have been a few, such as Robert Rauschenberg, whose work sought to defy that limitation by letting most of the world back *in*. But Jackson wasn't speaking of the world; he was speaking of painting, and what he meant was that none of us, painters in particular, give much consideration to the sheer surfeit of activity and *things*. "Museums," he wryly continued, "are filling up." I had never thought of this. Is there such a thing as too much? It may finally be the wrong question to ask of art making, although it is usefully disorienting. And painting is a special case: having passed through a much-debated "crisis" after midcentury, the period during which Jackson came of age as an artist, the practice of painting was reimagined and reactivated many times, always as if the very idea of it now required a new rationale. Will the time come when we can simply say enough is enough? It sounds like an absurd proposition, but is it any more so than waking up and going back to the studio in the belief that one can contribute something even remotely original to that which has gone before?
And, either way, is it ever worth asking of art-making, "to what end?"

Jackson's irreverence expresses healthy skepticism rather than profound doubt. Nothing tells us that he ever really thought much about

Richard Jackson, no. 23 from *100 Drawings*, 1978. Pencil on tracing paper. 12 ⅛ × 13 in. (30.8 × 33 cm). Collection of Nancy Reddin Kienholz

1. Unless otherwise noted, all remarks by the artist in this essay come from an interview that I conducted with him on May 20, 2011.

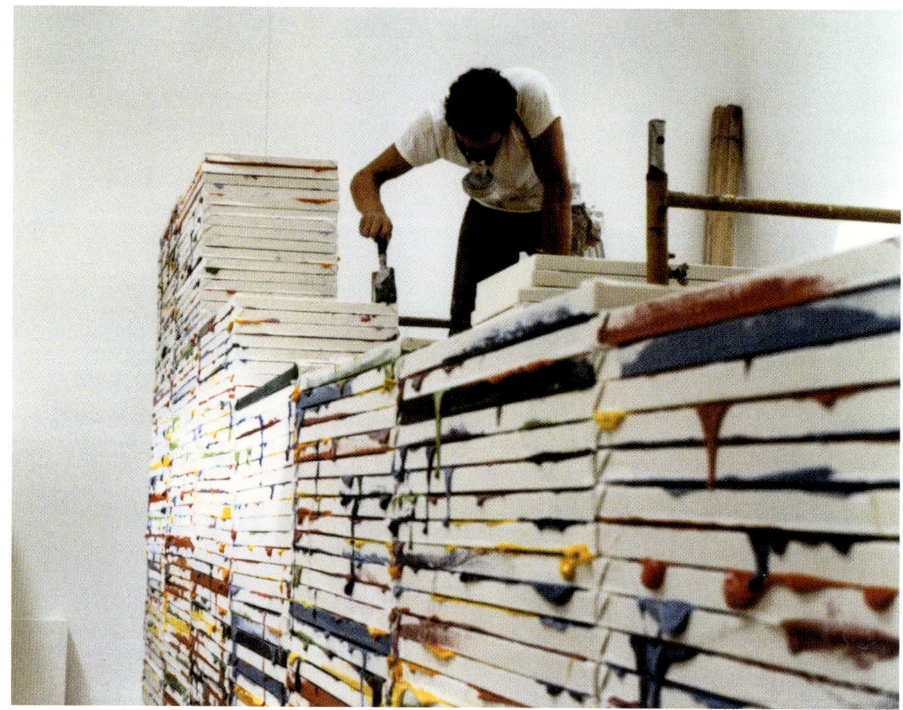

relinquishing a direct role in producing his own work. Indeed, while he emerged as an artist during the era of delegated fabrication in minimal art, Jackson never stopped making things himself and doing so through the kind of persistent labor that we associate with the ethic of a hard day's work. This is true of painting in particular: for *Big Ideas—1000 Pictures* (FIG. 1), a truly astonishing installation first produced in 1980 for the Rosamund Felsen Gallery in Los Angeles (and later re-created for the Menil Collection in Houston), Jackson stretched, primed, and painted one thousand canvases (each measuring 19 × 35 × 1¼ inches), which were then precisely stacked floor to ceiling to form a sixteen-foot-high monolithic wall, their paint surfaces permanently concealed (and defaced, since the stacking was executed while they were still wet).[2]

Our first and perhaps most lasting impression of *Big Ideas—1000 Pictures* is our sense of it as a kind of feat; sheer labor dominates every other quality that we normally associate with painting. Thinking of paintings as objects that exist in great number—one thousand paintings, ten thousand paintings— obviously corresponds to conceiving of painting practice as labor first. Together, effort and proliferation momentarily wrench us from conventional pictorial concerns—not to say the universalizing claims or values long associated with the aesthetic object—and require us to consider painting as an activity in the brute physical sense, and of the painted canvas as a thing among things. The strenuousness of producing *Big Ideas—1000 Pictures* is part of its content; in this way, the installation can be said to strike back (albeit with knowing futility) at the kind of repetition—or replication—associated with Andy Warhol: consumerism,

2. For information about *Big Ideas—1000 Pictures* and related works, see Iwan Wirth, ed., *Richard Jackson: Deer Beer*, exh. cat. (Cologne: Oktagon, 1998), and Jeffrey Browning, "An Architecture of Paint: Richard Jackson's Installations," *Arts and Architecture*, n.s., 3, no. 4 (1985): 44–49.

mechanical reproduction, and the standardization of industrial manufacture. Jackson has also said that, for a project like *Big Ideas—1000 Pictures*, the relentlessness of fabrication is strategic in that it keeps painting from avoiding the trap of style.

"Do all the drawings for the project, as many as possible, maybe a given number like 100. 100 or more like an English composition, but not less. I can go back after all the drawings are complete and grade myself with a red pencil."[3] This is Jackson's plan for a project in 1978 consisting of many small shorthand sketches: Jackson apparently made one hundred of them (on various kinds of paper), although fewer than that are now extant and numbering within the series is inconsistent. Most of the drawings concern painting. Specifically, the drawings record approaches to "painting" wherein the artist imagines applying paint, often from buckets, to everything in sight—floors, clothing, furniture, and other household objects, in addition to stretched canvases—or using an object (an electric fan, for example) as a tool for unleashing paint on the entire space of the room. The drawing project itself is, among other things, an exercise in persistence. But what the drawings often represent are one-off activities, many in the form of a spoof. Indeed, one sketch even concerns itself with art and labor. Proposal no. 22, a drawing of a bed, is accompanied by the following lines: "painting for those to[o] tired to / work on their art [be]cause they / have to teach to earn a living. Stay in bed with the T.V. on and paint everything as far as you can reach."

It is clear from the slapstick nature of the proceedings that Jackson was out for laughs, and, if the project is to be understood as homework, then his approach is a lark at the expense of schoolboy diligence—a long-running, gut-busting prank. Most of the sketches are indeed graded. At first it seems as if Jackson becomes his own instructor, the much-maligned substitute teacher whose seriousness qualifies him as an easy target—a well-meaning fool. But it quickly becomes clear that he remains the miscreant, appropriating the language of authority in order to bestow mock approval on his own outrageousness. No. 63: "Poor [sic] paint in the ash tray / Knock it over"; this note, accompanied by a quick sketch with arrows (just so there's no mistaking the intention), receives an A- and a star. Very good. But not quite *as* good as no. 18: "paint all the furniture, paint / the couch without getting off of it. Paint as far as you can reach." This qualifies for a solid A. No. 8—"pour paint / under the / rug and / cut a strip / and lift it / up"—is better still: nothing less than an A and two stars. Equally high marks are bestowed on simpler means, such as no. 87, the drawing with the fan (no text here—it's self-explanatory), and no. 35, a classic: "lodge an open bucket of paint atop a half-open door . . ."

Through it all, the seriousness of the enterprise is clear. Jackson is obviously deriving a lot of personal pleasure from behaving badly, but the object of his irreverence is monumental: the fate of painting itself at a time when its very viability was the subject of open debate within the international community of advanced art. I say this not to rob the hundred-proposals project of its hilarity

<hr>

3. The inscription occurs on proposal no. 1, which is reproduced along with a handful of others in *Richard Jackson*, exh. cat. (Hope, ID: Faith and Charity in Hope Gallery, 1978), unpaged.

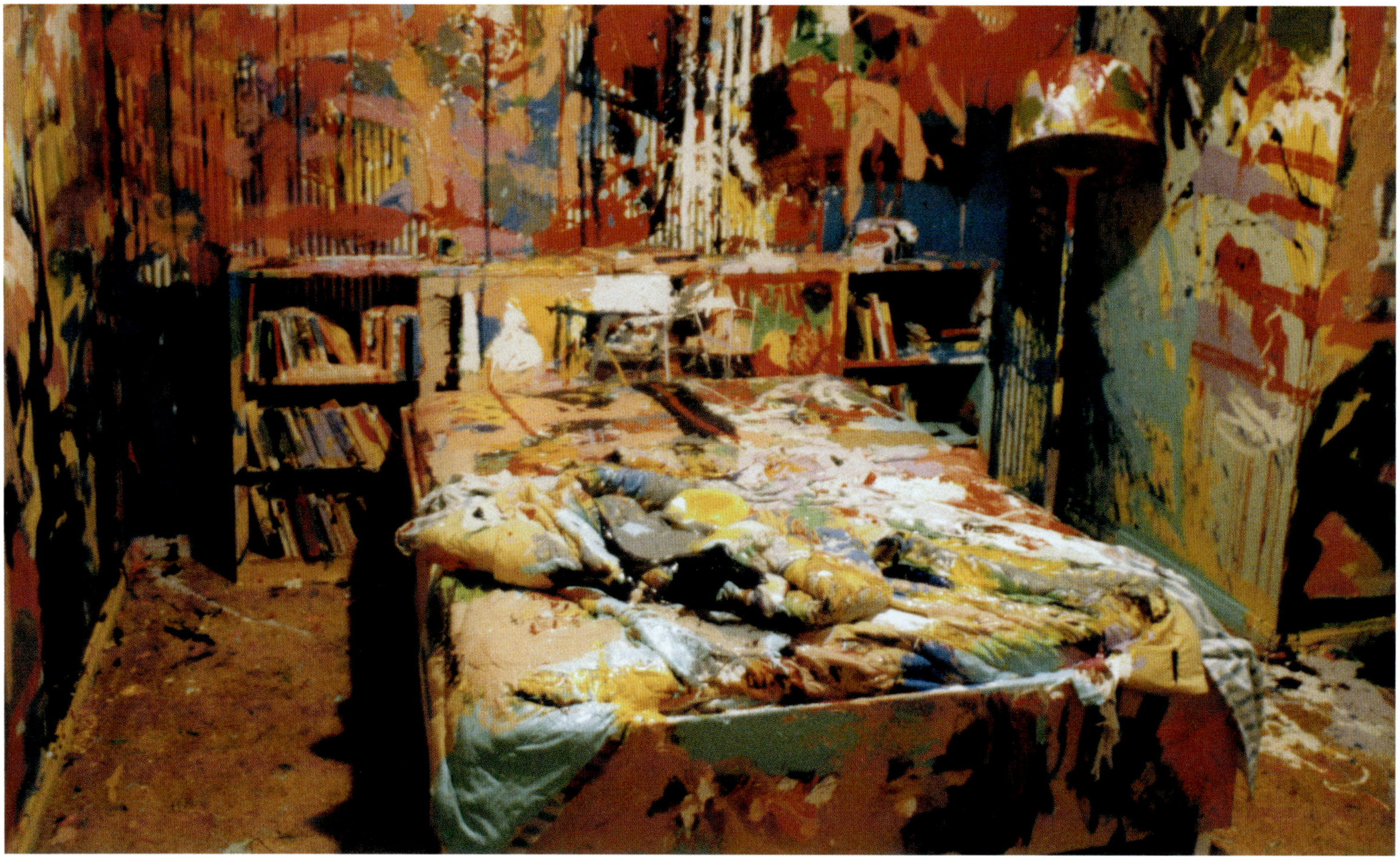

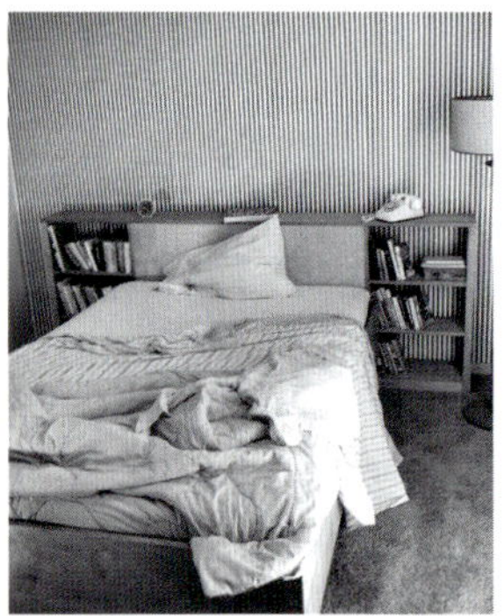

(just as I am loath to ruin the fun by embarking here on what amounts to the laborious explanation of a joke, although something of that is probably inevitable). I mean only to acknowledge that, during the 1970s, with regard to the ambition of Jackson's project, the stakes were high. It is probably the perceived pretentiousness of critical debates about the demise of painting that is being jabbed and prodded by his sketches (on which subject, see no. 34: "Pour paint in the critic's shoe"). Yet, reviewing the full run of proposals, it doesn't take us long to discover that Jackson was deeply devoted to seeking terms and coordinates according to which he could continue to paint and to make painting count. Judging from the evidence of the project, his approach sometimes takes the form of reckless disobedience, but it also represents a staunch refusal to overlook any action that might deliver practical results.

It should be acknowledged that by 1978 Jackson had already executed a number of the proposals contained among this group of sketches. Quite a few date back as far as 1970, when they were conceived and represented in much larger project drawings. These larger drawings, produced with a level of sophistication and finish that we associate with the sure proficiency of mechanical drafting (yet with evidence of an authorial hand), are precise two-point perspectival projections of outrageous objects—drawing exercises of exquisite technical control. In any case, the one hundred sketches constitute an inventory that looks both back and ahead. In that a number of the installations had also already been executed, the propositional nature of the project does not reflect anything like a conceptualist disavowal. (The closest Jackson comes to such a thing is proposal no. 23: "say I think of a painting / but don't write it down do a drawing / or the painting, does that count as a / painting? / This idea could be typed on a 3x5 card." The idea receives a resounding F.) Awash in running paint, Jackson's work of this period is instead nothing if not disgorgingly material, and the one hundred proposals represent a full catalog of ways and means.

We can begin to grasp this by compiling a list of procedures as they appear in the sketches: pouring, scraping, and sliding (or smearing) are the most common methods for working the paint (in addition to slathering it onto random objects with a brush or rag); stacking and rolling are things to be done to a canvas (either stretched or unstretched). Along with canvas, floor, and wall, flat supports include: curtains (no. 86); toilet paper (no. 51, which receives an A and two stars, as one would expect); rugs (nos. 8 and 32); and the pages of books: "paint every page of / every book, the covers etc stack each while wet leave isle [*sic*] way, stack wall to / wall to shoulder height." And then there is the application of household furniture: the falling lamp; the couch; a chest of drawers (no. 71: "paint in the drawers / contents painted / tied together," for which Jackson gave himself an A and two stars). Two unnumbered proposals, which take the form of photographs, show a paint-laden pillow scraping paint across the wall, both down and across. The images evoke a violent crime scene (and with respect to painting, that comparison is probably apt). It is important to note that these proposals are related to an installation called *The Bedroom* (1976–82) (FIGS. 2, 3), in which the room and its furniture were all fabricated by the artist himself and then splashed with paint. Even so, a referent for this group of proposals is surely Rauschenberg's astonishing *Bed* (1955; FIG. 4), which was exhibited widely throughout the 1960s and 1970s.

The proposals are derived from a genre of work that had already been developed within a circle of artists in Los Angeles, including Ed Kienholz and Paul McCarthy, to which Jackson belonged during the late 1960s and early 1970s. Such work, referred to as "instructional," was itself partly drawn from the activities of Fluxus and the Japanese Gutai group, and from Allan Kaprow's "happenings." It consists of works imagined and proposed in text form and only sometimes executed. As such, it can be understood as quite openly performance-based (which is to say that the text functions as a kind of event score). In the case of both McCarthy and Jackson painting takes the form of a crude mess. Some early videos by McCarthy demonstrate this: *Face Painting— Floor, White Line* (1972), for example, in which McCarthy drags his body across

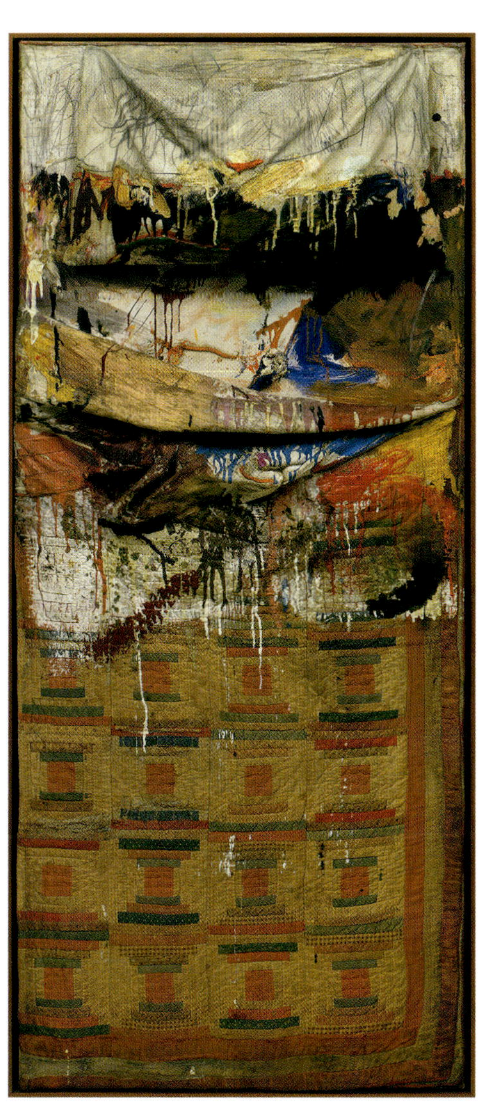

Robert Rauschenberg, *Bed*, 1955. Combine painting: oil and pencil on pillow, quilt and sheet on wood supports. 75 ¼ × 31 ½ × 8 in. (191.1 × 80 × 20.3 cm). The Museum of Modern Art, New York. Gift of Leo Castelli in honor of Alfred H. Barr, Jr. Art © Robert Rauschenberg Foundation/Licensed by VAGA, New York, NY

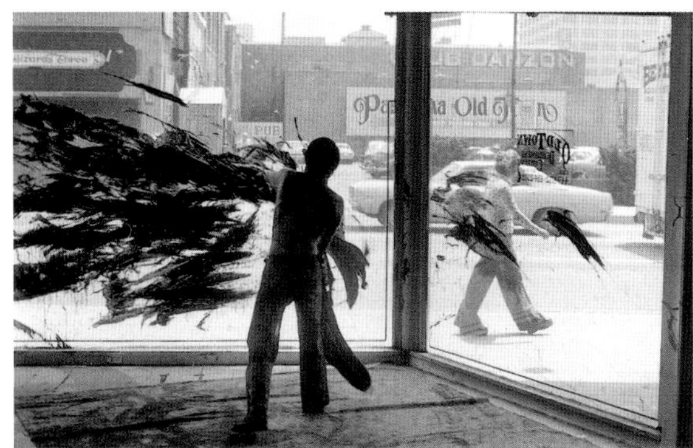

the floor through a continuous pour of white paint, and *Whipping a Window and a Wall with Paint* (1974; FIG. 5), which shows the artist smacking the walls of an abandoned storefront space with a paint-drenched drop cloth (using the canvas, so to speak, to paint the walls).[4]

The wild histrionics of *Whipping a Window and a Wall with Paint* is an absurd exaggeration of certain clichés that had long come to surround the legacy of abstract expressionism, with particular reference to Harold Rosenberg's concept of "action painting":[5] "At a certain moment," Rosenberg wrote, in a now indispensable (if sometimes derided) text of 1952, "the canvas began to appear to one American painter after another as an arena in which to act—rather than as a space in which to reproduce, re-design, analyze, or 'express' an object, actual or imagined. What was to go on the canvas was not a picture but an event." Rosenberg's characterization (it reads like a report from the front) is virtually a formula for the outrageous excesses of McCarthy and Jackson. For a generation of antiauthoritarians, his portentousness surely begged to be skewered; this could be accomplished by enacting his terms with such extreme literalness that they were made to appear absurd. "The painter no longer approached the easel with an image in his mind; he went up to it with material in his hand to do something to that other piece of material in front of him. The image would be the result of this encounter."[6] Cue the falling ashtray.

In fact, putting aside the question of parody for the moment, we might say that Rosenberg's text conditioned the transmission of abstract expressionist painting through the happening—that the line from Rosenberg to McCarthy and Jackson runs through Kaprow. The site for this transmission, a kind of hand-off, was the work of Jackson Pollock and even Pollock the man. "He created some magnificent paintings," Kaprow wrote in 1958. "But he also destroyed painting. . . . I am convinced that to grasp Pollock's impact properly, we must be acrobats, constantly shuttling between an identification with the hands and body that flung the paint and stood 'in' the canvas and submission to the objective markings, allowing them to entangle and assault us." That much is post-Rosenberg; then Kaprow turns a corner: "This instability is indeed far from the idea of a 'complete' painting. The artist, the spectator and the outer world are much too interchangeably involved here. . . . The crudeness of Jackson Pollock is not, therefore, uncouth; it is manifestly frank and uncultivated, unsullied by training, trade secrets, finesse." Kaprow's turn from painting to the world is completed by a pronouncement that will, with McCarthy and Jackson, take us back to painting: "Pollock as I see him left us at the point where we must become preoccupied with and even dazzled by the space and objects of our everyday life, either our bodies, clothes, rooms, or, if need be, the vastness of Forty Second Street." In 1966—in the text for his book *Assemblage, Environments, and Happenings,* a kind of instruction manual—Kaprow's release from painting is now complete: "The line between art and life should be kept as fluid, and perhaps indistinct, as possible. The reciprocity between the man-made and the ready-

---

4. For an account of McCarthy's work of this period and its broader context, see Magnus af Petersens, "Paul McCarthy's Forty Years of Hard Work—an Attempt at a Summary," in *Paul McCarthy: Head Shop/ Shop Head; Works, 1966–2006,* exh. cat. (Stockholm: Moderna Museet, 2006), 11–15.

5. The relevance of the term was first proposed in Walter Hopps, "Richard Jackson and Action Painting," in *Deer Beer,* 5–6.

6. Harold Rosenberg, "The American Action Painters," *Art News* 51 (December 1952); reprinted in David Shapiro and Cecile Shapiro, eds., *Abstract Expressionism: A Critical Record* (Cambridge: Cambridge University Press, 1990), 75–85.

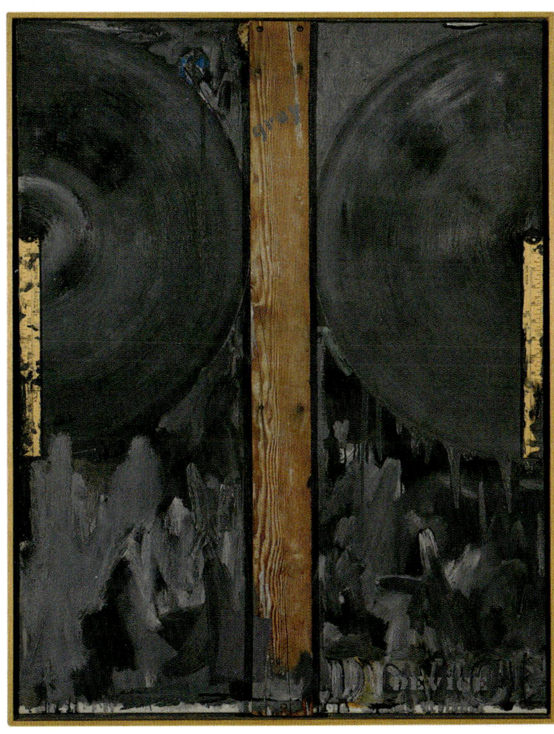

made will be at its maximum potential this way." With this comes a kind of art that suspends the conventions of quality and taste (or is oblivious to them): "Something will always happen at this juncture, which, if it is not revelatory, will not be merely bad art—for no one can easily compare it with this or that accepted masterpiece. I would judge this a foundation upon which may be built the specific criteria of the Happenings."[7]

Kaprow claims that there can be no painting after Pollock. But despite his apparent sympathy for Kaprow, Jackson refused to leave painting behind. The group of one hundred proposals is virtually a treatise on painting, even as it has very little to do with *producing* one per se. To further grasp this, we might do well to think of Kaprow's formula for the relation of art and life: the "reciprocity between the man-made and the ready-made." The man-made, in this construction, is the "art" side; the ready-made (and here Kaprow is drawing from Marcel Duchamp) belongs, we presume, to "life." But Jackson marshals both in order to implicate painting. Removing painting from the realm of sensibility and touch, he looks to *deploy* paint: to mechanize its means even as he, the artist, remains the key agent in any operation or procedure. Hence the use and abuse of extraneous objects—extraneous, that is, to painting, but otherwise close at hand. In this regard, in addition to Pollock, two artists loom large in the proposal series: Jasper Johns and Frank Stella. Each gave Jackson something to draw on and something against which to push back.

Returning to those pillows, we might want to say that Rauschenberg, whose combines and assemblages are loaded with common objects—a chair, a funnel, a ladder, stuffed animals, Coca-Cola bottles, a bound pillow—and saturated with streaks and discharges of thick paint, is an essential model for Jackson. There can be no question that his work represents an important precedent. (Indeed, Kaprow's notion of art and life may well have been adapted from the sort of remark that Rauschenberg was wont to make, although in truth the formulation, while attractive, is decidedly vague.) But the nature of assemblage, a chief medium for Rauschenberg, is largely foreign to the language of Jackson's work, being compositional rather than given. The streaks that Jackson's pillows make are instead dead ringers for the kind of mark—a trail of scraped paint—that occurs throughout Johns's works of the early to mid-1960s (FIG. 6), which were shown in multiple exhibitions and widely reproduced. Johns executed these scrapes with an object that he referred to as a "device": a stretcher bar, a ruler, or any other slat of wood. The device was generally attached to the painting with a screw at one end so that it was free to pivot, leaving arcs that course through the paint surface. This in fact is clearly the precise model for two of Jackson's proposals: no. 30, a photograph of a clock in which both the minute hand and the hour hand are shown to be scraping paint across the face; and no. 56, a pair of Polaroids that show Jackson having transformed a windshield wiper into a Johnsian device that smears paint across the glass. But the straight scrape was also practiced by Johns in various

7. Allan Kaprow, "Excerpts from 'Assemblage, Environments and Happenings,'" in *Happenings and Other Acts*, ed. Mariellen R. Sandford (London: Routledge, 1995), 235. For a discussion of Pollock and Kaprow in the context of postwar "new realism" in France and the United States, with an emphasis on the spectacularization of painting practice through happenings and related "events," see Julia Robinson, "Before Attitudes Became Form—New Realisms: 1957–1962," in *New Realisms, 1957–1962: Object Strategies between Readymade and Spectacle*, ed. Julia Robinson, exh. cat. (Madrid: Museo Nacional Centro de Arte Reina Sofía; Cambridge, MA: MIT Press, 2010), 23–40.

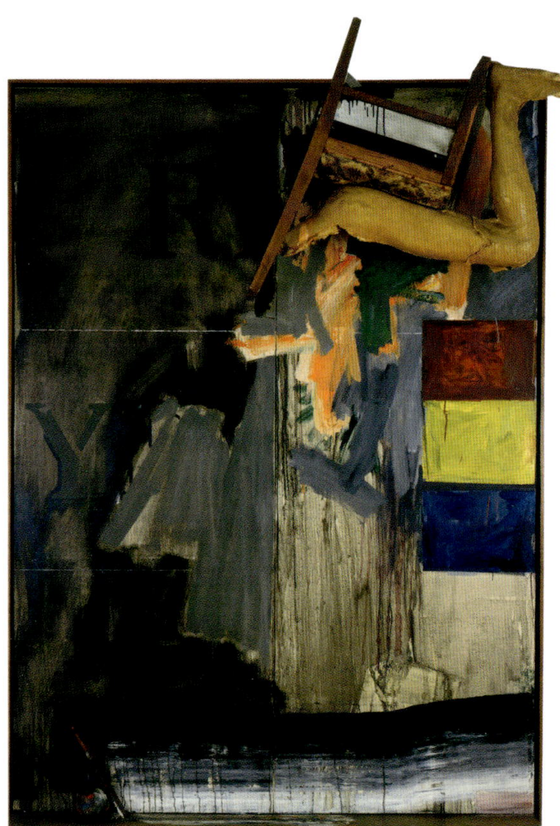

paintings, such as *Watchman* (1964; FIG. 7), in which a wooden slat has been used to draw a long smear of black, gray, and white paint along the bottom edge of the canvas (then, where it came to a halt, the device was fixed in place).

"Find a way to apply / make paint / with simple movements / of objects—the hand / a board, feather, string, / sponge, rag, shaped tools, comb / (and move the canvas against paint-smeared objects)."[8] This passage, from a Johns sketchbook of around 1963, reminds us that the example of Johns can be quite specific.[9] Jackson said that in Johns's work—in contrast to that of Rauschenberg—every small thing seems to possess meaning. Some objects also possess agency: "Put a lot of paint / & a wooden ball or / other object on a board. / Push to the other end of / the board. Use this in / a painting."[10] According to the logic of Johns's work, the "device" was an object that—following the conceptual implications of Duchamp's practice, which was of great interest to Johns— obviates certain conventions of aesthetic choice.[11] Since 1955, in paintings and drawings, Johns had solely enlisted preexisting images—a target, a flag, rows of numbers from 0 through 9—that were sign-like and flat and therefore coextensive with the canvas or sheet. Similarly, the device scrape was a way to move paint across a surface using quasi-mechanical means; here a certain loss of control complemented the readymade nature of the target or flag as image, as well as the stencils and other image-making tools that Johns also used. (Indeed, the rotating device was almost certainly derived from the motions of the compass with which he produced the concentric bands in one Target painting after another. Once he introduced the device, he abandoned the target.) Occasionally Johns would enlist a common object—a broom, for example, in *Fool's House* (1962)—to serve as a device, although the wooden slat was by far the most common implement.

In its way, the application of the device was a remarkable strategic move, and its consequences can be detected in minimal and postminimal art (in which the mechanical action of cutting into any resistant medium, for example, which often represented the sole means for producing a work, can be traced back to it).[12] In Jackson's work the function of the device—for which the hands of a clock and the windshield wiper are jokey surrogates, ordinary instruments that rotate over a flat surface for purely practical purposes—was obviously useful. At a time when painting practice was being abandoned by many of his contemporaries, the action of the device allowed Jackson to continue painting by transposing it, as a purely physical activity, from the canvas into the world at large (which, in a manner of speaking, became the support). It is according to these terms that Jackson might be said to have taken up Kaprow's prescription: that art—or something like it—lives with maximum intensity at the juncture of the man-made and the ready-made.

Anything can be a device. No. 17 is a drawing of a door; an arrow points to the floor, and the inscription reads: "poor [sic] paint on the rug and open the door." This was first proposed in a drawing of 1971, which bears the title *Paint on the Rug* and the inscription: "the door opens person / goes in, turns on the /

8. Kirk Varnedoe, ed., *Jasper Johns: Writings, Sketchbook Notes, Interviews* (New York: Museum of Modern Art, 1996), 52.

9. It should be noted that Jackson titled a major installation of 1987–88 after a painting by Johns: *Painting with Two Balls*.

10. Varnedoe, *Jasper Johns*, 54. The note is from a sketchbook that probably dates to 1964.

11. The Duchampian implications of the device were discussed in the art press of the 1960s. See, for example, Max Kozloff, "Johns and Duchamp," *Art International* 8 (March 20, 1964): 42–45.

12. This is a topic on which I have written previously. See Jeffrey Weiss, "Painting Bitten by a Man," in *Jasper Johns: An Allegory of Painting, 1955–1965*, exh. cat. (Washington, DC: National Gallery of Art, 2007), 2–56.

light and discovers / what he has done." In 1981 it was executed for an exhibition at the L.A. Louver Gallery (FIG. 8). But Jackson's device-objects are often extracted from the apparatus of painting itself. Proposal no. 4 is a sketch of an artist's palette tracing a smear of paint, with the inscription "nail pallet to the wall with wet paint and spin." It is further annotated (like some of Johns's device paintings)

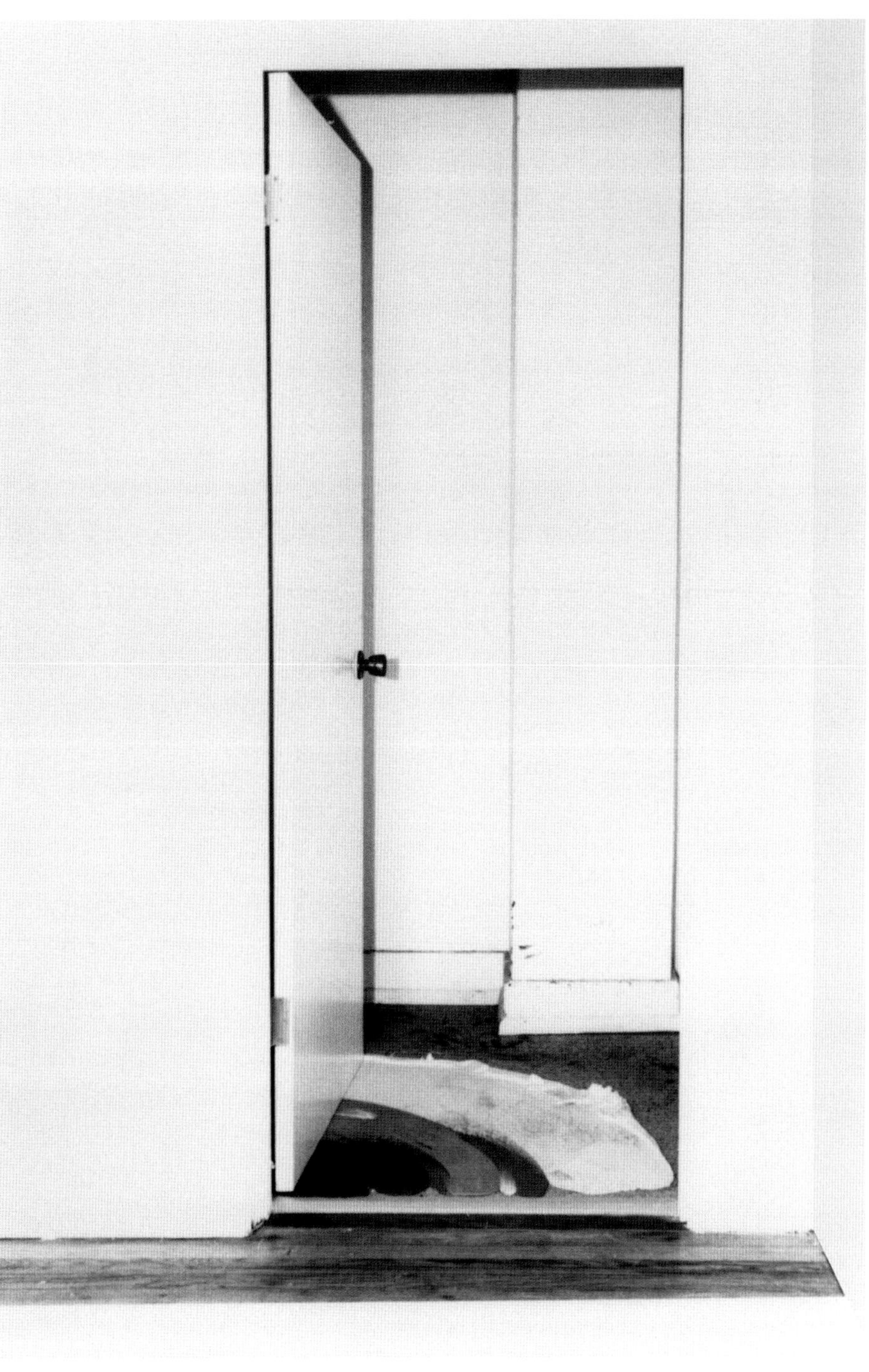

FIG. 8
Richard Jackson, *Untitled ("Paint on the Rug")*, 1970. Acrylic paint. 80 × 36 × 36 in. (203.2 × 91.4 × 91.4 cm). Installation view, *California: A Sense of Individualism*, L.A. Louver Gallery, Venice, CA

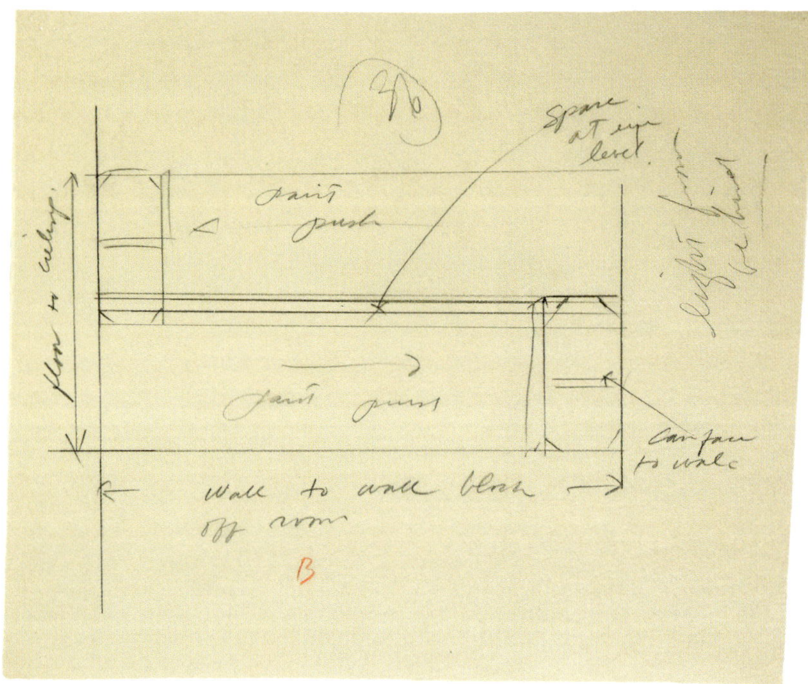

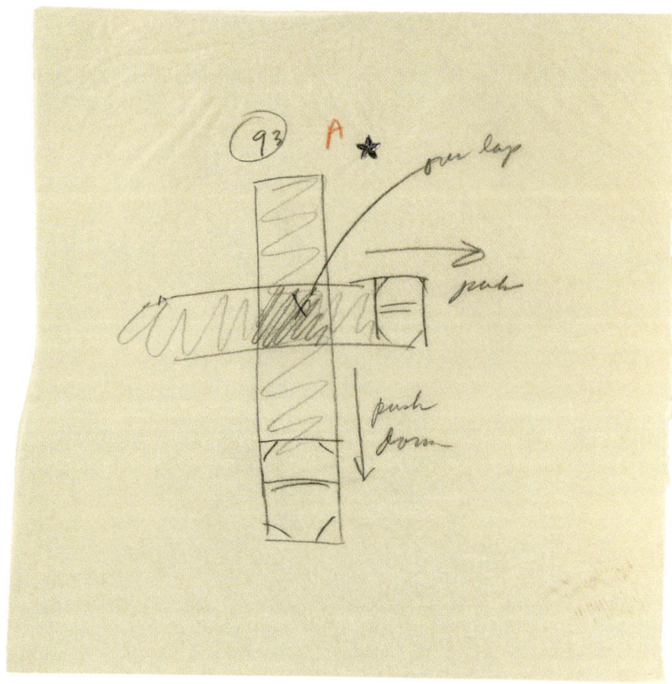

with a directional arrow and the word *push*. (Jackson gave the proposal an A, adding extra enthusiasm by remarking, "god damn.") The spinning palette is a variant of Jackson's most common device, the rotating canvas. Throughout the proposals—and occurring with some frequency in the earlier drawings (including one that appeared on the cover of *Art Gallery* magazine in December 1970)—we find the image of a stretched canvas. Seen from behind, its painted face is always pressed against a wall or other surface, with indications that it is to be nailed in place at one corner and otherwise left free to produce a paint-smeared arc. Such installations take many forms. Some are eccentric. Proposal no. 26 shows two poles standing in a room: one canvas is to be tethered to each; positioned facedown on the floor, they smear circular bands of paint, which gradually diminish, the tether growing shorter as it winds around the pole. Faulted by the artist for its "extremism," this proposal receives a failing grade. Jackson largely prefers putting the canvas device to work along the wall (in this way, he keeps it close to the conventional space of painting, heightening the transgression). In no. 25, two abutted canvases are pinned to the wall with nails driven through adjacent corners: "paint and spin / painting face to wall spin" (B+).

"He would load the surface of the canvas with raw pigment, squash it flat against a wall or ceiling or floor and then walk it, push it, slide it, swing it some other place on the wall where it was nailed in place and left." Kienholz's description of this technique—written on the occasion of an exhibition of the proposal sketches at the Faith and Charity in Hope Gallery in Hope, Idaho, in 1978—is succinct.[13] Throughout the group of one hundred proposals, wall

13. See Kienholz's statement in *Richard Jackson* (1978), unpaged.

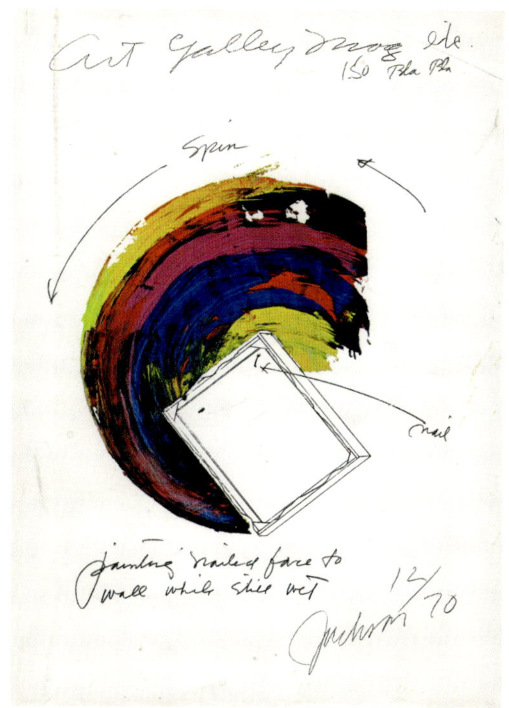

FIG. 11
Richard Jackson, *Untitled*, 1970. Oil and
pencil on paper. 30 × 24 in (76.2 × 61 cm)

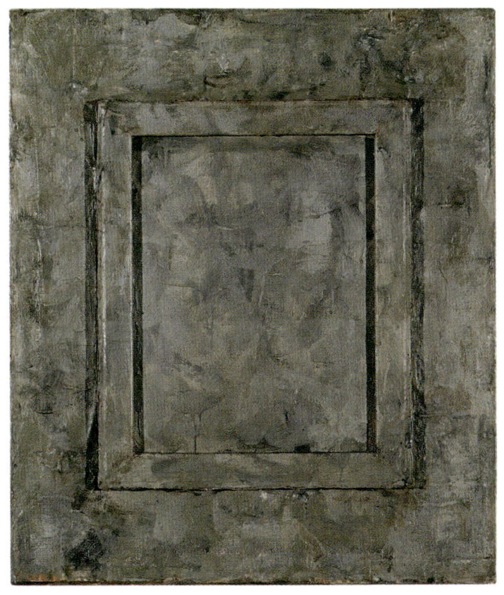

FIG. 12
Jasper Johns, *Canvas*, 1956. Encaustic
and collage on wood and canvas. 30 × 25 in.
(76.2 × 63.5 cm). Collection of the artist.
Art © Jasper Johns/Licensed by VAGA, New
York, NY

paintings of this kind are subjected to tireless iteration. In proposal no. 36 (FIG. 9), two stretched canvases, stacked vertically from floor to ceiling, smear paint in opposing directions across the upper and lower halves of a long wall. In no. 40, a series of canvases arranged facedown, with intervals between them that match their width, are pushed across the floor, smearing paint into the empty space. No. 46 shows the same principle at work, this time across a wall. Nos. 42 and 43 are variants of no. 25: two abutted canvases each nailed in place at one corner and rotated across a wall, together producing overlapping concentric trails of paint. In no. 52, a single painted canvas is pushed diagonally across each wall of a square room—up, down, up, down. No. 52 shows a canvas dragging paint along a wall and over a painting by Ellsworth Kelly: "paint over top of other painting" (thinking better of it, Jackson gave this proposal an F). For proposal no. 93 (FIG. 10), two canvases are pushed along a wall in horizontal and vertical smears such that the two trails intersect to form a cross.

Again, a number of these installation proposals, along with others that are not included in the group of one hundred (FIG. 11), had already been executed for various exhibitions, mostly on the West Coast. Together, however, the proposals form a kind of narrative, or better, a catalog in which Jackson's various approaches—from pratfall spillages to complicated investigations of geometric form—reflect on one another. In other words, the one hundred proposals represent Jackson's extended consideration of the methodology of his work: its implications—at the juncture of the man-made and the ready made—for a process-based form of abstract painting that circumvents the grand rhetoric that had subtended large-format painterly abstraction around midcentury, especially in the United States. Johns was helpful, and while he never "painted" with the face of a stretched canvas, facedown canvases appear in a handful of important works of the 1960s, such as *Fool's House* and *According to What*. The motif dates back to 1956, however, with *Canvas* (FIG. 12), which allows us to draw a key distinction: between Johns's radical negation (he has produced a monochromatic double refusal saturated in encaustic and gray paint) and Jackson's activation of the canvas device in the service of compositional risk.

Jackson's ambition for abstract painting places him far apart from contemporaries such as McCarthy and Bruce Nauman, with whom he otherwise shares the kind of deep skepticism that typifies his generation on both coasts. Instead, its closest complement occurs in Stella's work, in a sequence of paintings known as the Protractor series, produced during the late 1960s. The Protractor paintings were exhibited in Stella's early retrospective at the Museum of Modern Art in 1970, which was accompanied by a catalog written by William Rubin, the exhibition's curator.[14] Both the show and the catalog are landmarks in the history of a kind of painting that now seems to represent an apotheosis of "heroic" formalism, with a lineage that includes abstract expressionism and hard-edge color-field painting—from Barnett Newman through Morris Louis and Kenneth Noland. Stella's role is complex: the size and affect of his previous work,

---

14. William C. Rubin, *Frank Stella*, exh. cat. (New York: Museum of Modern Art, 1970).

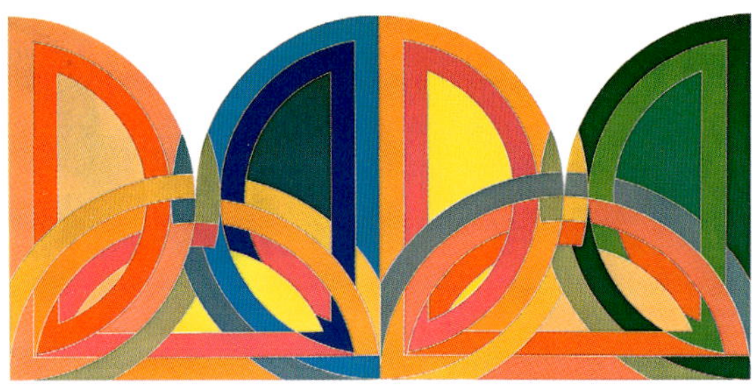

beginning in 1958 (with the so-called Black paintings), was clearly intended to compete with the work of Newman and Pollock, but the formal consideration he gave to graphic compositional elements that are responsive to—or even strictly derived from—the shape of the canvas has motivated critics to consider him a progenitor of minimal art. Names of movements and tendencies can be misleading; it is enough to say that, during the 1960s, Stella was one of the few artists devoted to the ongoing potential of the big canvas. The Protractor series (FIG. 13) actually represented a jump in size for his work, with some paintings reaching widths of twenty or twenty-five feet (they are generally ten feet high). Horizontal formats are based on three types of schematic design: "interlace," "rainbow," and "fan." The modular element from which Stella generated these

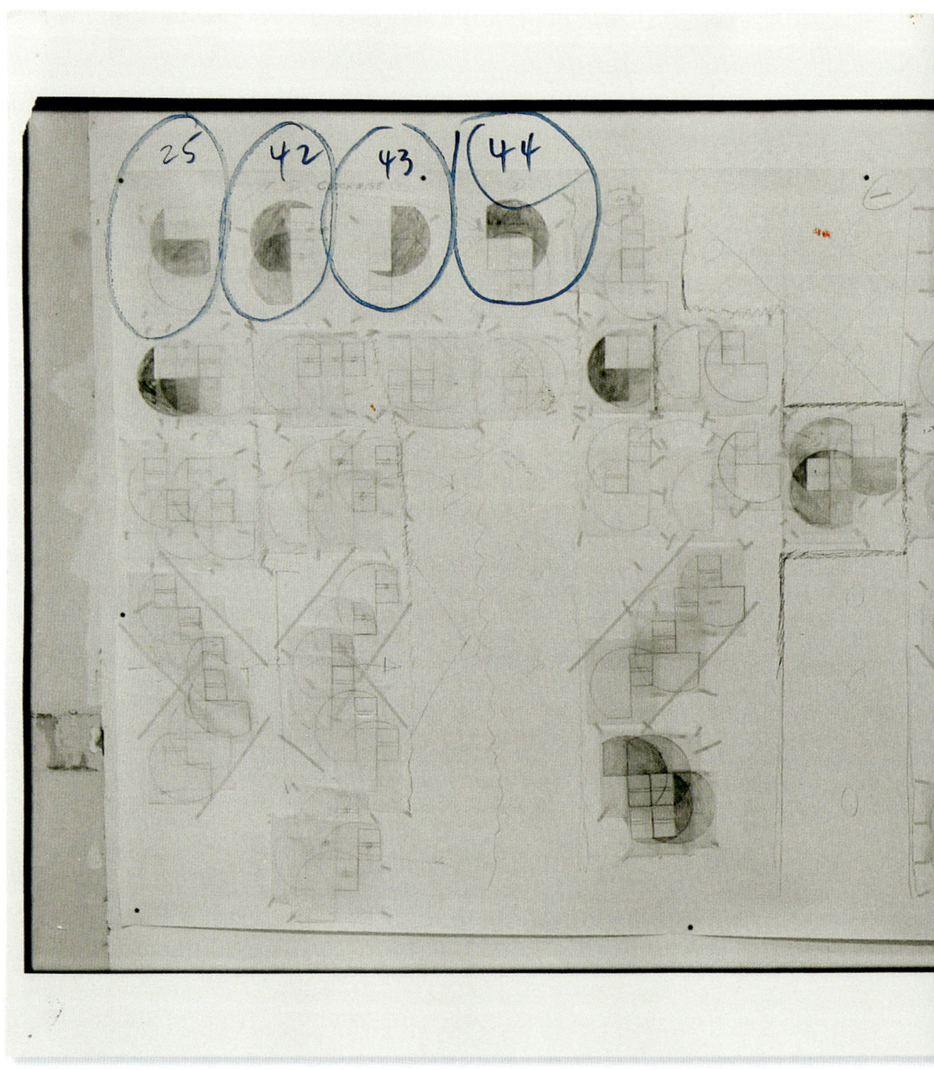

FIG. 14
Richard Jackson, no. 45 from *100 Drawings*, 1978. Two black-and-white photos taped together with pen. 8 × 19⅛ in. (20.3 × 48.8 cm). Collection Nancy Reddin Kienholz

compositions, a half circle (an arc attached to a straightedge), reflects the fact that the series began with drawings for which he rotated an ordinary protractor. Combinations within the three schematic types, however, attain surprising intricacy, with eccentric stretcher silhouettes yielding complicated internal configurations of bands. Rubin quotes Robert Rosenblum, who compared one of the paintings in the series to a complex system of architectural vaults.[15]

Jackson's proposal no. 45 (FIG. 14) actually consists of a photographic image of a large sequence of sketches for scrape paintings—for many works composed of various configurations of adjoining canvases that are used to smear paint on the surface of a wall. (The photograph is annotated with numbers, although sketches do not correspond to proposals bearing the

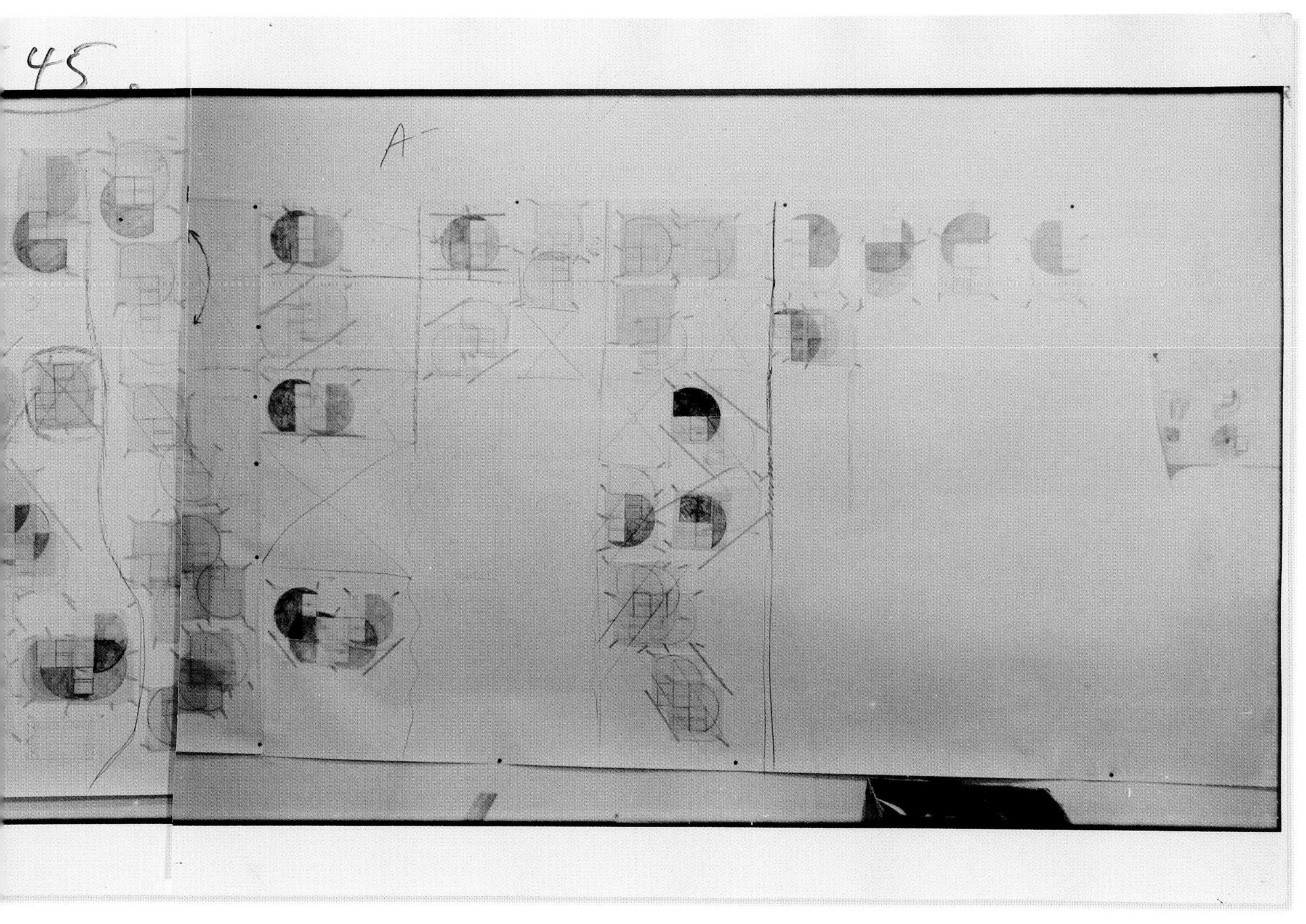

15. Ibid., 134. Many of Stella's titles are taken from the names of ancient circular cities in the Near and Middle East, and the formats of some are derived from the plan of the city in question or the city gate.

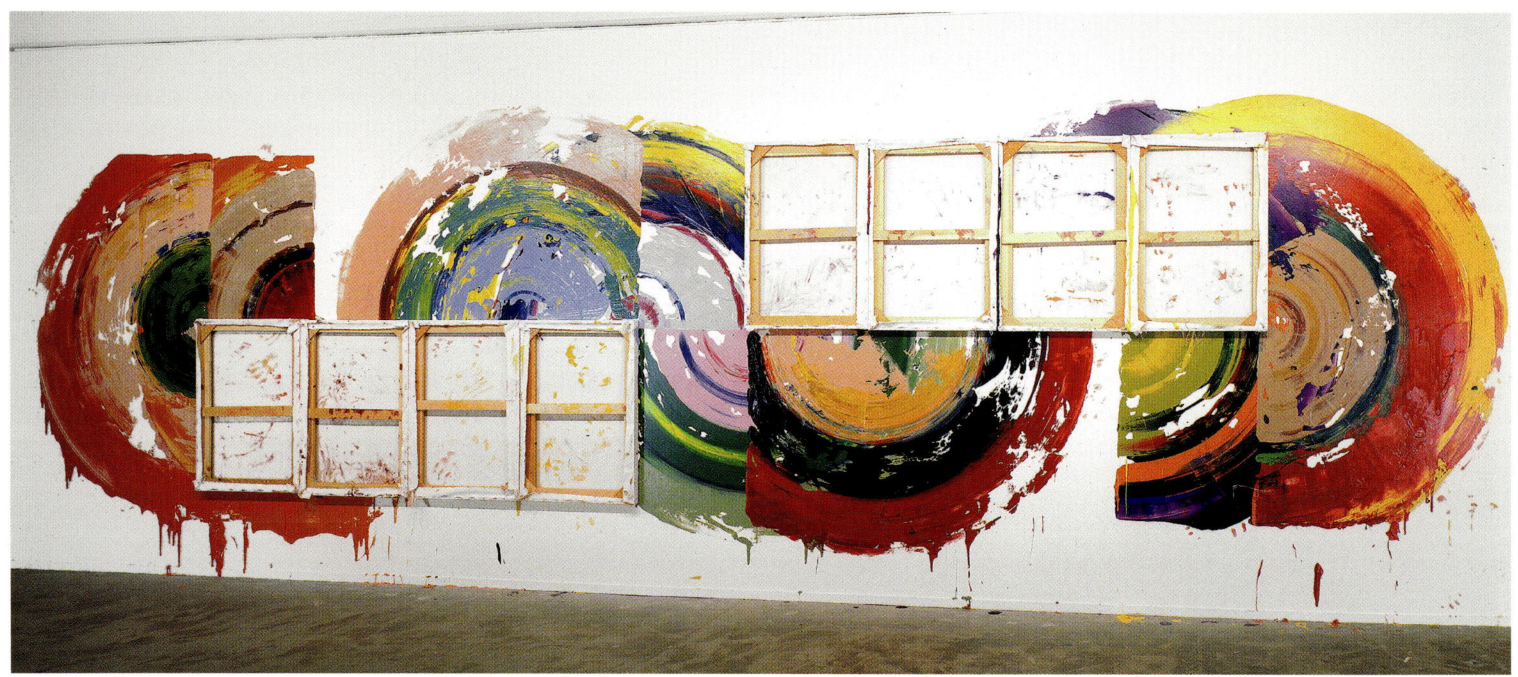

same number.) It is difficult to tell whether each effort stands for an individual work or, instead, if various rotations were to be combined to form works consisting of multiple parts, which was the case when Jackson executed some of these scrape paintings on gallery and museum walls during the early to mid-1970s (FIG. 15). Both the sketches and the works themselves—especially the more expansive ones—surely represent, in part, a series of extended riffs on certain principles demonstrated by Stella's paintings. It is the element of rotation itself, above all, that they share: the rotational nature of the design scheme, which, in many of Stella's Protractor paintings, is premised on concentricity (in Stella's case, the bands are precisely delineated, while Jackson's bands, produced by smearing a row of colors, are individuated through color—they resemble targets—but otherwise run together as a broad smear). And both employ rotation—shifting orientation—as a means of achieving permuting iterations of form. (With this in mind, it is instructive to compare a diagrammatic chart of the Protractor paintings that was published in Rubin's essay for the exhibition catalog to Jackson's iterative scheme as it is represented in proposal no. 45.) Their palettes differ: Stella often used commercial "fluorescent" colors, whereas Jackson's color scheme is high key but not as bright. (Moreover, Jackson's paint application is thicker than Stella's, lending his paint surface a material density that Stella avoids.) But color families do emerge in both bodies of work, even as the two artists try hard to diminish the impression—through color—of optical depth. Interlacing bands (Stella) and overlapping scrapes (Jackson) establish a certain sensation of shallow pictorial space, but the arrangement of colors largely manages to cancel that effect.[16]

---

16. Jackson would have ongoing recourse to Stella's Protractor paintings as a chief referent for his installations with painting; the most recent—and quite explicit— example is *The Little Girl's Room*, an installation produced in 2011 at the David Kordansky Gallery, Los Angeles.

Jackson's application of the canvas as a device would appear to have little real relation to the visual and conceptual strategies that we observe in Stella's work. Yet there is a device-like element in Stella's paintings in that the protractor is the tool that establishes the series' repertoire of configurations. In his early pursuit of the stripe or band (first rigorously applied in the Black paintings, in which patterns are partly determined by the rectilinearity of the stretched canvas), Stella adapted the deadpan structural nature of his work directly from Johns (from Johns's flags, as he has said). Both artists share a recourse to mechanical or a priori techniques that are quasi-"readymade." Jackson applied those techniques in his effort to save painting first by destroying it.

Needless to say, the key differences are clear: Jackson is not producing hard-edge geometric abstraction but marshaling it to investigate the life of painting in actual space. The stretched canvases that he uses to apply paint remain attached to the work's surface—to the wall. They finish by being a pictorial element, but their initial and primary function is that of a tool. Even as they occupy a material register that distinguishes itself from the paint surface, they pointedly influence our grasp of the significance of the paint. That is, they allow us to retrace the execution of the work; their presence, which is startling, flagrantly serves to expose the labor of making it. In this way, Jackson's wall paintings aggressively avoid what must have finally seemed, by 1970, like formalism's trap, the nagging implication of self-sufficient or transcendent aesthetic values.

Rubin identifies aspects of Stella's Protractor paintings, such as "interior patterning," that are "markedly decorative," and it is the decorative that he felt grew in significance over the course of the series, which comes to rely on relationships of figure to ground and the emergence of autonomous motifs that are not derived from the shape of the stretcher. He quotes Stella on this subject: "My main interest has been to make what is popularly called decorative painting truly viable in unequivocal abstract terms. Decorative, that is, in a good sense, in the sense that it is applied to Matisse. What I mean is that I would like to combine the abandon and indulgence of Matisse's *Dance* with the over-all strength and sheer formal inspiration of a picture like his *Moroccans*."[17] This is exactly what Jackson works so hard to resist. Speaking of this period, he now says that he pushed the permuting strategy of the wall paintings to the point of diminishing returns, becoming so proficient at working the changes that the technique ceased to test or surprise him. There was, he says, "no room for failure." Such a claim is deeply antidecorative, the kind of remark that you would expect more from a materialist than a formalist—more from Pollock, say, than Stella. Jackson navigates both sides, but his resistance to anything like the "decorative" (despite his obvious investment in refinements of form) is crucial. To further underscore this point, we need only recall the falling ashtray, the smearing door, and the painted bed.

Jackson's one hundred proposals constitute a scheme: they map the two sides of his work, its high formalism and its quotient of noise, which coexist in a state of perpetual collision that the artist clearly valued. The conflict returns

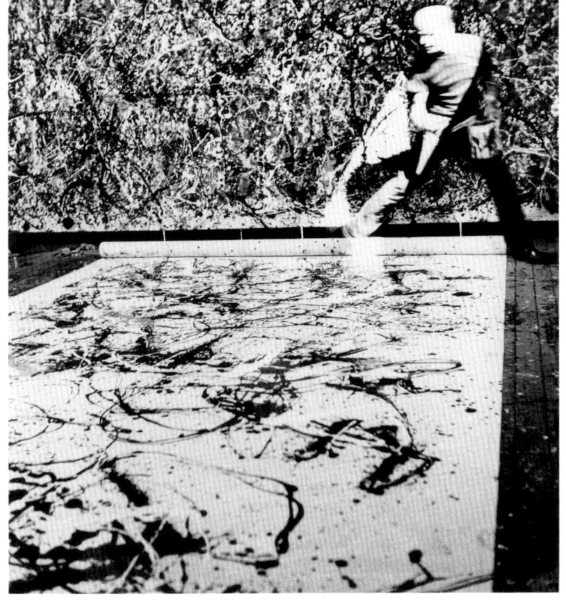

FIG. 16
Hans Namuth, *Jackson Pollock 1950*, 1980. Silver print. 31 ⅛ × 28 ¼ in. (79.2 × 71.8 cm). The Museum of Contemporary Art, Los Angeles

17. Frank Stella, quoted in Rubin, *Frank Stella*, 143, 149.

us to Pollock. Jackson remembers being moved as much by Hans Namuth's photographs and short film of Pollock at work (FIG. 16) as by the paintings themselves—or *more* so. He specifically recalls one passage from early in the film: Pollock changes his shoes before beginning to paint, and he pauses to shake something out of one of his paint-stained boots. The moment is almost comical, but it tells us a lot about Jackson's Pollock, an artist around whom things—strings of running paint as well as random bits and pieces of the artist's life—fall to the ground, sometimes indifferently and sometimes with purpose. For Richard Jackson, Pollock's practice seems to have signified an informal but intense cohabitation of the aesthetic and the real.

A contest between those two things was played out in various ways during the 1970s. The work of Philip Guston is surely relevant, almost allegorically so, in that Guston, who belonged to the generation of abstract expressionism, turned to a tough, fatly painted comic book manner of pictorial representation around the time that Jackson began developing his wall paintings and related work. Guston has credited this shift to his loss of faith in abstract painting during the 1960s, when it came to seem like an increasingly pointless refuge from social and political upheaval, although one-line explanations are inadequate to the larger circumstances of painting's collapsing imperatives. In a lecture of 1978 Guston quoted Franz Kline, who said that "creating" requires "the capacity to be embarrassed"—something, we might add, that formalism does not quite hold. "Painting," Kline said, "is like hands stuck in a mattress." After his exhibition at the Jewish Museum in 1966, Guston recalled: "I knew I wanted to go on and to deal with concrete objects. I got stuck on shoes, shoes on the floor. I must have done hundreds of paintings of shoes, books, hands, buildings and cars, just everyday objects. And the more I did the more mysterious these objects became."[18] Guston's objects, as they appear in his paintings, are sometimes abject and mistreated, and their caricatural identity means to make them as actual as actuality itself. Like all material things, they seek a state of rest: they fall onto tables and floors, where, we gather, they will remain.

Jackson's objects share their aggressive banality with Guston's, although, functioning as devices and supports themselves, they are less charged with personal meaning. Guston often depicted himself in his work, and it reminds us that Jackson is represented instead by things that happen. He sometimes implicates others ("the door opens person / goes in, turns on the / light and discovers / what he has done"), yet he is almost always the unseen protagonist of his work. The proposals, the project drawings, and the installations themselves together constitute a kind of playbook: a series of situations constructed in order to determine the short-term viability of certain moves. As such, his work makes the work of others—Johns or Pollock or Stella—look situational as well: the consequence of various gambits, actions, and circumstances. Without abandoning painting practice, or even displacing it, Jackson, for a time, turned painting into an event, one never less interesting than a bucket falling from the top of a door but sometimes, almost despite itself, a very good deal more.

---

18. Philip Guston, "Philip Guston Talking," in *Contemporary Art: A Sourcebook of Artists' Writings*, ed. Kristine Stiles and Peter Selz (Berkeley: University of California Press, 1996), 249–50.

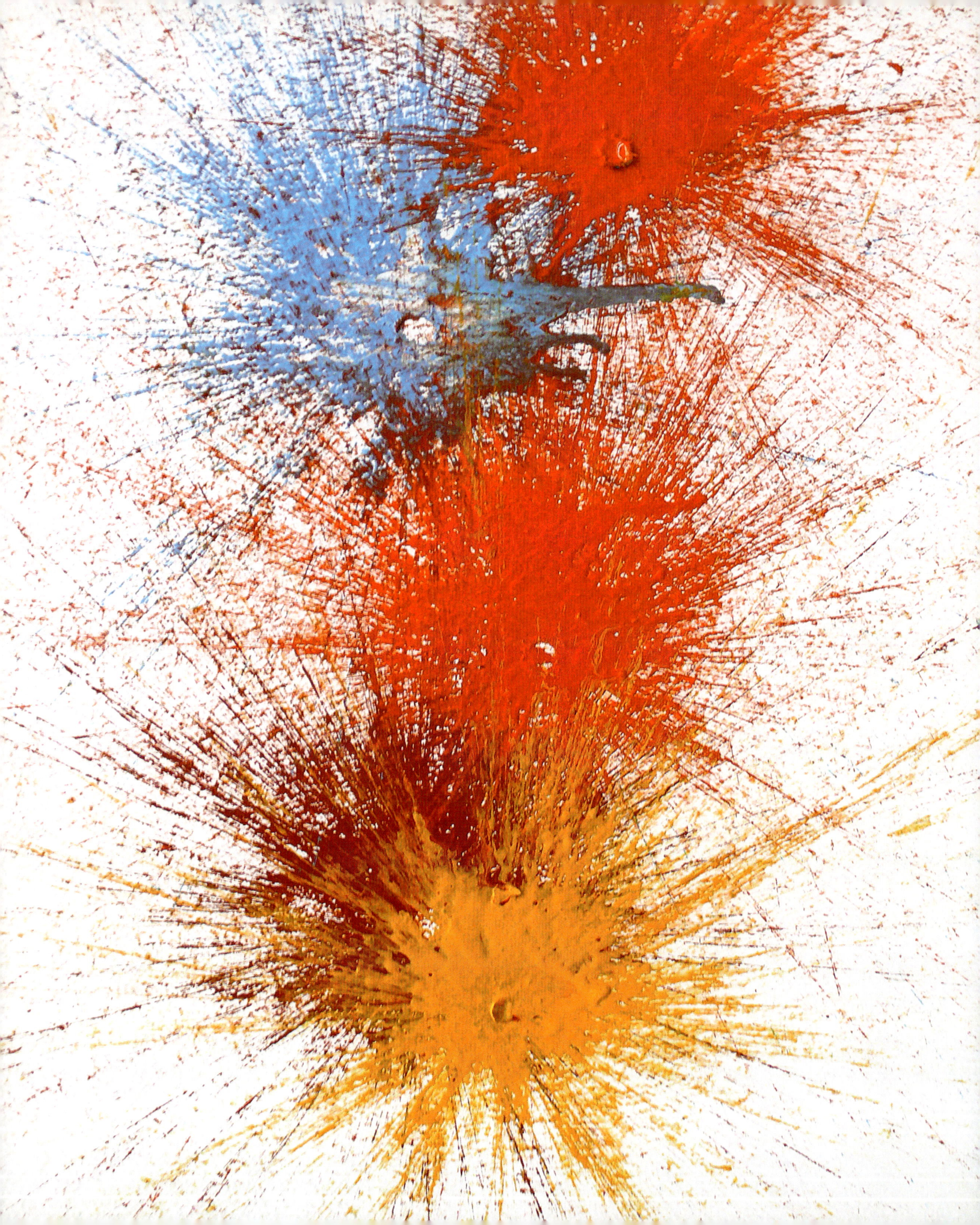

RICHARD JACKSON
IN THE LAST
OF THE MOHICANS

MICHAEL DARLING

Scene 1: Los Angeles basin, 1969.

Endless supplies of sun, asphalt, and palm trees tangled together in a sprawling knot. The broader counterculture taking hold across the country has started to take a darker turn, and L.A. has supplied some of the more searing images, with the Watts rebellion in 1965, Robert F. Kennedy's assassination at L.A.'s Ambassador Hotel in 1968, and the Manson murders in 1969 all carrying apocalyptic overtones (the 6.6 Sylmar earthquake in 1971 would be the icing on the cake). In this sun-kissed soup of movie stars, Black Panthers, hippies, surfers, and a rapidly diversifying immigrant population, a strip of La Cienega Boulevard in the middle of it all has already established itself as a hotbed of fine-art risk taking. It is there that Andy Warhol found his first audiences anywhere, that Ed Ruscha matched his painterly chops with Hollywood good looks (and the stunning women those looks attracted), and that Billy Al Bengston preened in a flashy Cadillac on his commute from the waves to the studio to the gallery.

To the east of this glamorous melting pot, up in the dry hills of Pasadena, which rarely caught the quenching ocean breezes of Venice, another scene was starting to form, fueled by Northern Californians and anchored by the Pasadena Art Museum and whip-smart curators like Walter Hopps and John Coplans. Finding his way there in 1969 from the goofier rebellions of the UC Davis funk-art scene was Bruce Nauman, who honed a brooding, body-oriented

Richard Jackson, *Deer Beer* (detail), 1998.
Mixed media. Dimensions variable.
Friedrich Christian Flick Collection,
Hamburger Bahnhof. Installation view,
Hamburger Bahnhof, 2008

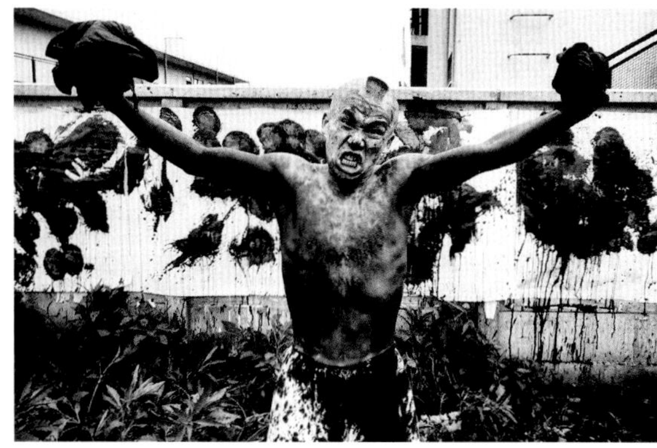

approach to sculpture that would soon be a lightning rod for new art. Another Sacramento refugee and a friend of Nauman's, Richard Jackson, our protagonist, would also find refuge in Pasadena in 1969 after arriving in L.A. one year earlier. Whereas Nauman's guiding reference was sculpture and the ways bodies and forms occupied and struggled against the coordinates of space and gravity, Jackson's path through art was guided by the pitfalls of painting. He was determined to capitalize on both its weaknesses and its strengths to open up new possibilities.

Flashback to 1949, postwar Italy and Japan: Jackson, only ten years old, was not yet aware of the changes afoot within the traditions of painting, beginning with the epochal gestures of Lucio Fontana and Shōzō Shimamoto, each of whom, in 1949, in war-torn countries on opposite sides of the globe, began cutting into and puncturing the surface of the canvas, ushering in a fecund period of experimentation, critique, doubt, and promise. This period of questioning caught up other artists in both countries, including Alberto Burri and Piero Manzoni in Italy and Ushio Shinohara, (FIG. 1) Kazuo Shiraga, and Yayoi Kusama in Japan. They were joined by Günther Uecker and Michael Buthe in Germany, Niki de Saint-Phalle in France, (FIG. 2) Otto Muehl and Günter Brus in Austria, Antoni Tàpies and Manolo Millares in Spain, John Latham in England, Mathias Goeritz in Mexico, Hélio Oiticica in Brazil, and of course Robert Rauschenberg and Jasper Johns in the United States, among many other artists in many other locales. All these artists rejected the sanctity of the wall-hung rectangular painting, corrupting and deconstructing the picture plane in an effort to find new life and

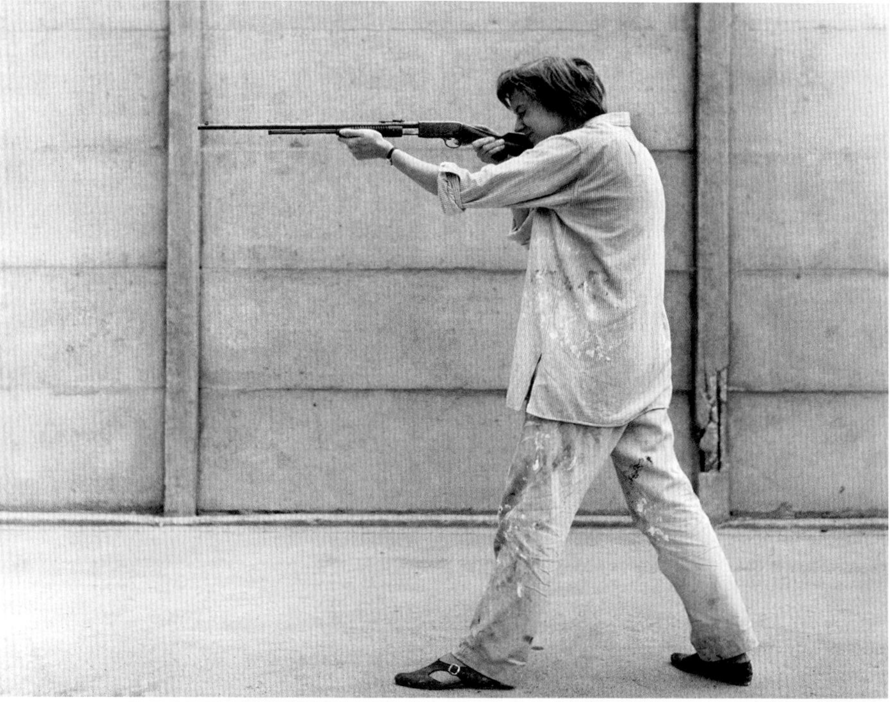

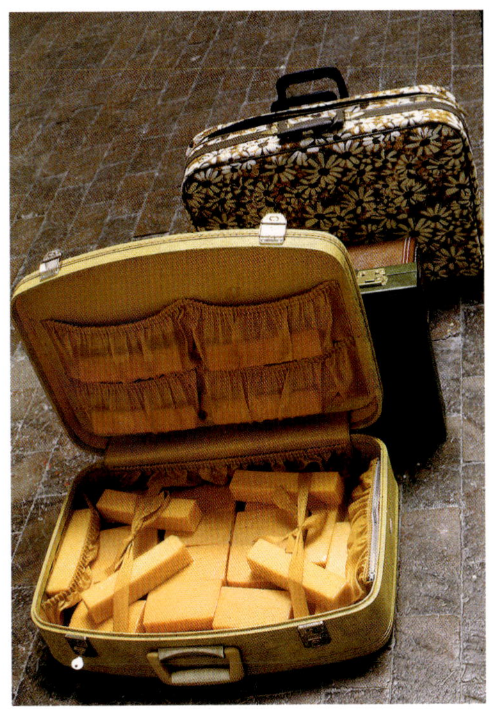

new meaning in this centuries-old pursuit. This is the tradition and the spirit that Jackson inherited, and as it turns out, in 1969, when he set up shop in Pasadena, a lot of the energy that had been dedicated to turning painting upside down was starting to be diverted elsewhere, was being dematerialized through the rhetoric of conceptualism, and within a handful of years was just plain abandoned by the mainstream art world in favor of a return to conventional figuration. The band of probing provocateurs with whom Jackson aligned himself—symbolized by Shinohara's antiauthoritarian haircut and physical assault on large stretched canvases—placed Jackson as a last-gasp hero in the struggle, already the "last of the Mohicans" in 1969. Some forty-plus years later, he would still occupy the role of a lonely rebel in a heroic battle with, against, and for painting.

Scene 2: Eugenia Butler Gallery, La Cienega Boulevard, Los Angeles, 1970.

One of the city's incubators of avant-garde ideas, the artist and gallerist Eugenia Butler would mount a groundbreaking show by Jackson in 1970 as well as a legendary show by Dieter Roth (FIG. 3). It was a watershed year for Jackson, establishing signature approaches for his painting practice that would guide him for years to come and earn him recognition worldwide. It started humbly in his studio with four experiments with paint and canvas, some of which were never shown in the outside world. One was a canvas painted and nailed facedown to the floor. A second consisted of two canvases, each painted with complementary colors and pressed together while still wet. A third featured a freestanding canvas in front of which a smaller canvas was dragged by a rope, leaving traces of the action. The fourth and final work utilized another freestanding canvas that served as a ground for a smaller painting to be pushed across it from top to bottom, dragging paint along as it went.[1] These test pieces simultaneously closed down and opened up painting, neutralizing it by obscuring or entombing the painted surface of the canvas, collapsing the distinctions between the art object and the wall, and using the stretched canvas itself as a painting tool. All these concerns would crop up in various forms for the next twenty-four years, providing a rich repertoire that could be adapted to many different situations and applications.

These four experiments reveal affinities with the work of Jasper Johns and Robert Rauschenberg, primarily with Johns's objectification of painting in works such as *Canvas* (1956) or in the group derived from *Device Circle* (1959), in which the means of leaving marks on canvas is both mechanized and made explicit. Rauschenberg's related heresies—such as *Bed* (1955; see page 119), which substituted bedsheets and a quilt for fine-art linens as the site of expressive activity (with all the sexual innuendo that carries)—were surely signposts for Jackson, as was Rauschenberg's decoupling of the painting and

1. These experiments were described by the artist in Iwan Wirth, ed., *Richard Jackson: Deer Beer*, exh. cat. (Cologne: Oktagon, 1998), 26.

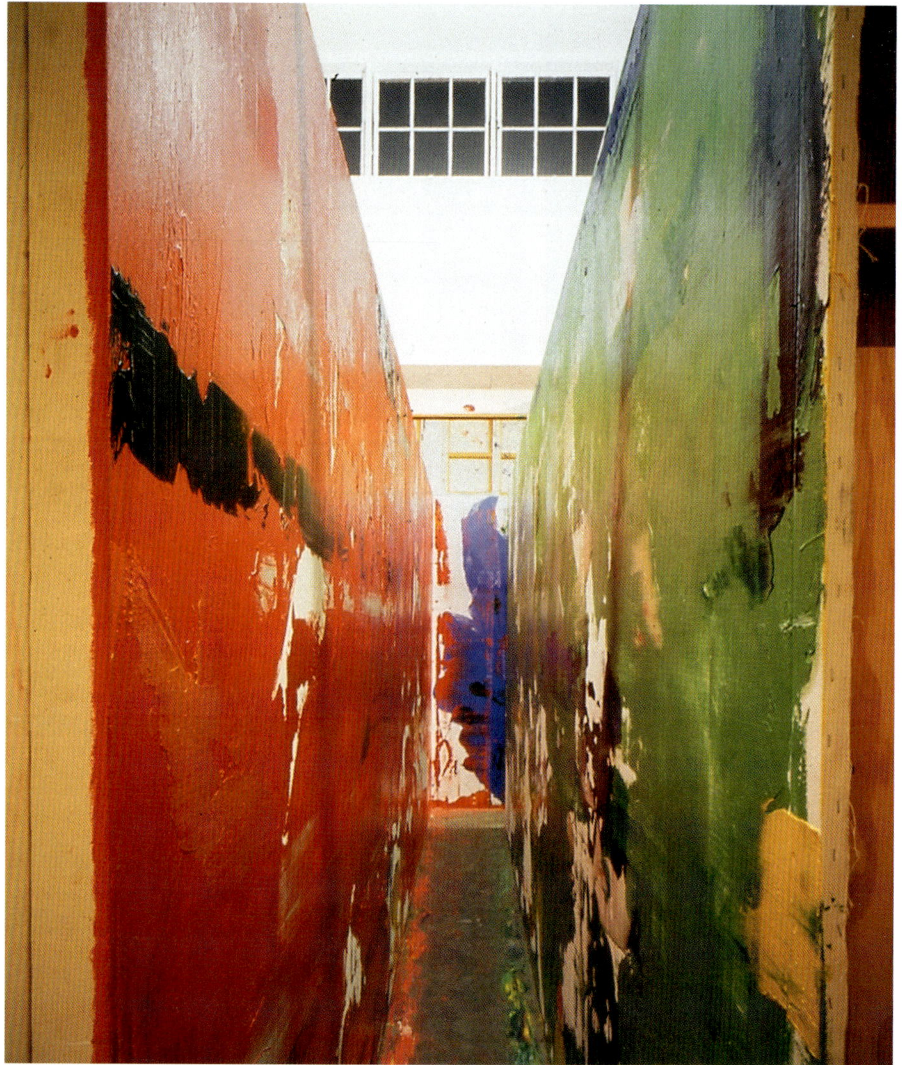

the wall in self-supporting works such as *Minutiae* (1954), *Untitled Combine (Man with White Shoes)* (1955), or *Gift for Apollo* (1959). The older artist's iconic *Monogram* (1955–59) would also prove prophetic when considering Jackson's push away from the canvas as the locus of his activity and toward three-dimensional objects, especially animals, as supports. Jackson's ironic send-ups of spatters, smears, and other signifiers of unbridled painterly bravado likewise found important precedents and sympathy in the work of Johns and Rauschenberg.

Even closer to hand for Jackson as a kindred artistic spirit, however, was Nauman, and this now famous sculptural innovator—as well as the milieu in which his work was shown, interpreted, and understood—clearly shaped Jackson's sculptural approach to painting. For the 1970 Eugenia Butler show, Jackson quickly extrapolated from the four experiments to an environmental scale, creating a walk-in labyrinth of stretched and painted canvases that drew viewers through a narrow corridor to a square center whose payoff is only the blank backs of the paintings (FIG. 4). Preceding the passage of visitors (one at a time) through this gauntlet was another canvas, the same height as the walls and the same width as the corridor, which was dragged against the interior surfaces as a tool of destruction (or at least defacement) and also creation. Haunting and psychologically charged, this untitled installation shares many similarities with Nauman's *Green Light Corridor* (FIG. 5) from the same year, as well as his *Four Corner Piece* (1971), which likewise induces self-consciousness and a palpable sense of menace in the sole participant. The neutrality with which Nauman constructed his pieces keeps the effect strictly within the realm of the body and the psyche while Jackson's installation plays on the same responses but complicates it further with a challenge to the orthodoxies of painting.

Other works from this period similarly participate in the burgeoning language of postminimalism but from Jackson's particularly painterly point of view. In 1970 he also started what is perhaps his most lasting and iconic series, in which a freshly painted canvas was smeared directly onto a waiting wall, again obscuring the difference between architecture and object, as well as conflating destruction with creation. These works acknowledge art's reliance on architecture and eliminate the separation between the studio and the public space in a way akin to Richard Serra's throwing of molten lead in Leo Castelli's New York warehouse just one year earlier, in 1969. The lead conformed to the corners of the gallery and thereby implicated the vertical and horizontal planes that organize three-dimensional space.

Roll Out the Carpet (1971; see page 71) is another seminal Jackson work that seems wholly of the period (at least in terms of sculptural practice) and

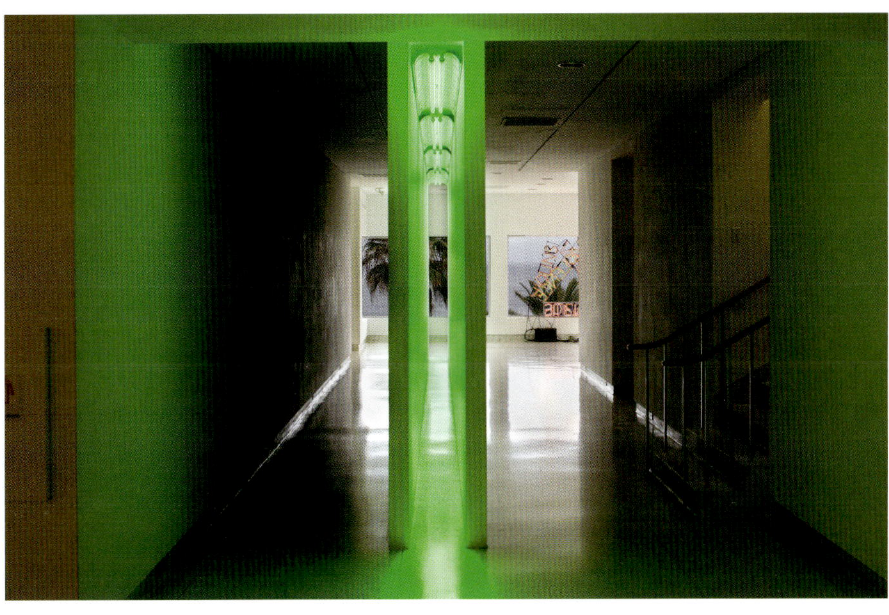

FIG. 5
Bruce Nauman, *Green Light Corridor*, 1970. Painted wallboard and fluorescent light fixtures with green lamps. Dimensions variable, approx. 10 × 40 × 1 feet (3 m × 12.2 m × 30.5 cm). Solomon R. Guggenheim Museum, New York. Panza Collection, Gift 92.4171. Installation view, Museum of Contemporary Art, San Diego

yet is practically unique within the discourse of painting. Here paint is applied to the floor of a room, edge to edge, and a carpet cut to the same dimensions is rolled onto it while the paint is still wet and then rolled back a certain amount to reveal the sticky, miscegenated mess. Only John Baldessari's filmed action *Six Colorful Inside Jobs* (1977); Lawrence Weiner's *An Amount of Paint Poured Directly upon the Floor and Allowed to Dry* (1968); or maybe Yayoi Kusama's theoretically boundless proliferations of polka dots, as documented in *Self-Obliteration* (1967), come to mind as similarly flexible, expansive, and environmental updates to painting, but none of these projects, save for perhaps Kusama's, would open up new directions within those artists' practices in the years to come. Daniel Buren would soon translate his striped canvases to a more environmental scale, but that too would come later and is fairly circumscribed in comparison. Jackson's dogged creation of an überpainting practice both critical and germinal was exceptional in the art world at this time and would remain so. *Roll Out the Carpet*, as well as the ever-expanding smeared canvases of the time, contains within it a sense of ambition matched with harrowing suffocation that can be seen as a metaphor for the historical burden that painting presents. The viscous pleasures of paint are held hostage, imprisoned, kept under wraps, and break through only in highly controlled ways, as when a canvas is dragged against the wall like a bloody body pulled from a crime scene.

Scene 3: Rosamund Felsen Gallery, La Cienega Boulevard, Los Angeles, 1980.

The sense of suffocation, horror, and beauty that had sustained multiple iterations of smeared canvases up to this point and would continue until 1994 reached a new level of sculptural ambition and pent-up aggression with Jackson's *The Big Idea* in 1979. Taking off from *Roll Out the Carpet* and increasingly space-intensive interim works like the untitled installations at Sacramento State University (1972); Rosamund Felsen Gallery, Los Angeles (1978); DAAD-Galerie, Berlin (1979); and Galerie Maeght, Zurich (1979), here Jackson again used the paint-smeared stretched canvas as a tool and a unit of construction. Again he denied the typical aesthetic appreciation and connoisseurship that a painted surface offers, burying it in stacks of canvases forming a wall. The first *Big Idea* proposed making a painting that fills a room, piling canvases one on top of the other from wall to wall and floor to ceiling, snuffing out subtlety and replacing it with sheer mass, volume, materiality, and presence. In the first iteration Jackson reckoned that it would require six thousand canvases and three hundred gallons of paint, a physical and financial challenge for any artist or gallerist, but slowly and surely he began to realize the dream.[2] At the Felsen Gallery a giant wall of dripping canvases was wedged

2. The artist notes that he covered the costs of the Los Angeles shows himself (ibid., 98).

between floor and ceiling to create *Big Ideas—800 Pictures* (1980). Another format was tried the following year at Betsy Rosenfield Gallery in Chicago, with an L-shaped enclosure for *Big Ideas—800 Pictures* (1981), and later that year *Big Ideas 2—3000 Pictures* (1981) (FIG. 6) appeared at the Los Angeles County Museum of Art in a giant globelike format that really started to send a message of messianic madness. Importantly, to emphasize the level of commitment and single-minded purpose, the artist himself made every stretcher bar, stretched every canvas, and primed and painted each painting. Like a human factory, he was able to produce one hundred per day.[3] The zeal of this project—the do-anything attitude and even gonzo (to borrow a notion from Hunter S. Thompson)

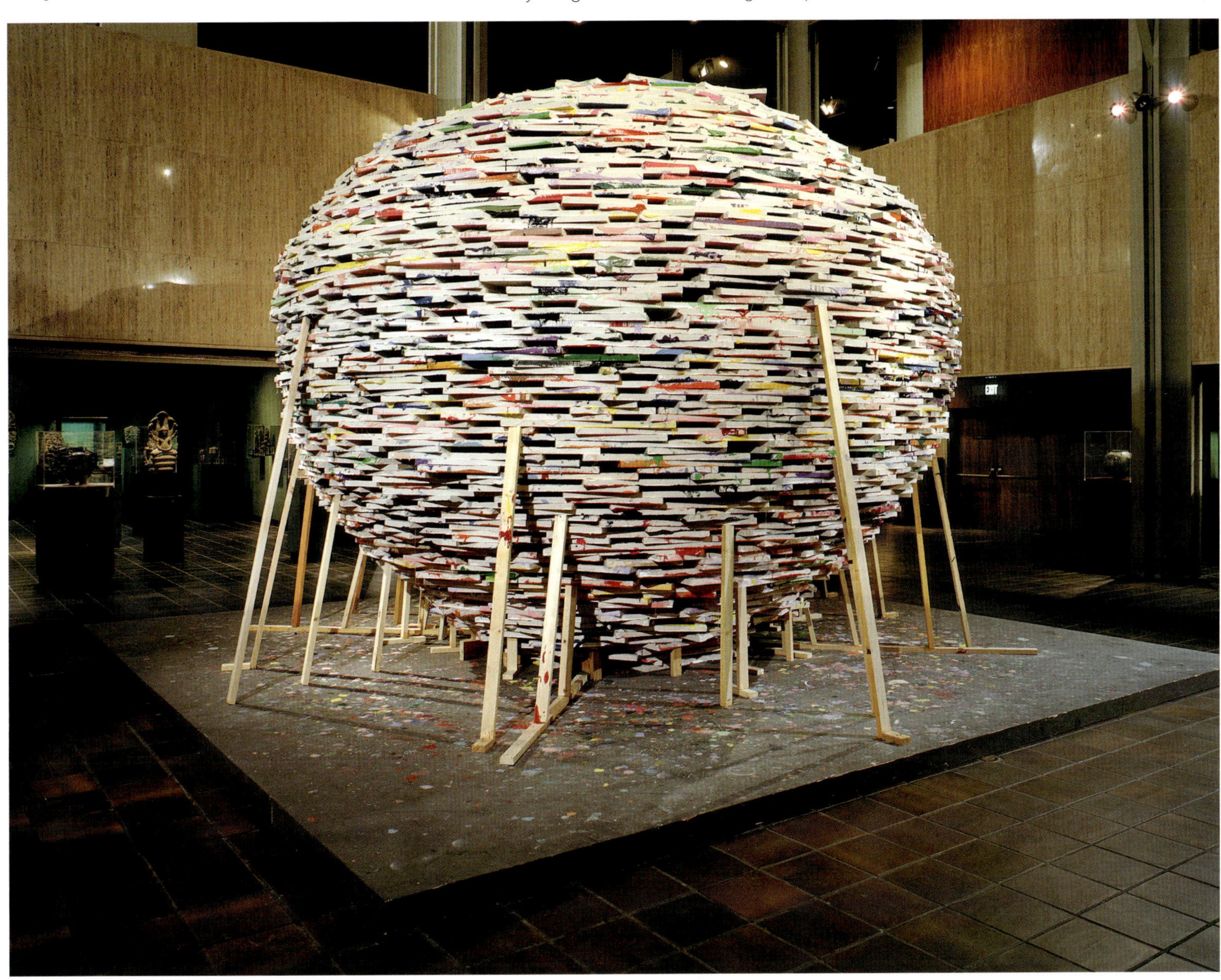

3. Ibid., 91.

spirit of the practice—not only opened the door for even more outlandish and outsize "paintings" to come but also, in retrospect, set an important tone for much of the most memorable and influential art that would be produced in Los Angeles over the next thirty years. Just this sort of fearless freedom and idealism characterized the later work of three other Felsen artists—Chris Burden, Paul McCarthy, and Mike Kelley—as well as that of Charles Ray and Nancy Rubins. Burden, Jackson, McCarthy, Ray, and Rubins would all go on to teach at UCLA, where students like Jason Rhoades, Toba Khedoori, Jennifer Pastor, Liz Craft, Pentti Monkkonen, Eric Wesley, and others would be encouraged to take similar risks and, in doing so, make Los Angeles the new capital for American art. Jackson's central role in the scene was acknowledged by his inclusion in the curator Paul Schimmel's seminal 1992 exhibition *Helter Skelter: L.A. Art in the 1990s* at the Museum of Contemporary Art in Los Angeles, which defined the major players in this renaissance.

Scene 4: Fourth Biennial of Contemporary Art, Lyon, France, 1997.

It is ironic that one of the next major breakthroughs in Jackson's work would take place in Europe. Just as he was about to take another protean leap into territory even more ambitious, aggressive, and innovative, the field of painting was taking a turn in exactly the opposite direction, leaving Jackson even more alone—a solitary, raging Mohican. The German school of post–World War II painting—which had been led by Gerhard Richter and Sigmar Polke down a path much different than Jackson's, one that was taken up by inheritors like Martin Kippenberger and Albert Oehlen—had just reached an impasse with Kippenberger's death at the age of forty-four. Former Kippenberger assistants Merlin Carpenter and Michael Krebber were starting to usher in a new phase of analytical painting, channeling the productive doubt of their forebears into practices characterized by a cool cynicism and detachment that took the questioning of painting to a highly intellectual and sometimes nihilistic level. Krebber's professorship at the Städelschule in Frankfurt exposed legions of students to his ideas, which included a notion of trying to do as little as possible and still operate in the realm of painting, a position that informs the predominant attitudes within the field today.

Jackson, in contrast, continued to pour as much effort and scale and energy and resources as was humanly possible into his project of making a contemporary painting. In Lyon, this took the form of perhaps his most spectacular work to date, his second version of *Painting with Two Balls* (1997), a Ford Pinto turned on its side atop a white pedestal so that two upward-facing wheels, turned by the car's motor, would in turn rotate two gigantic canvas-covered globes and a single stretched canvas. Paint of all colors was poured from above onto the globes, spattering all over the car, canvas, and surrounding room in an orgy of unbridled painterly expression. Jackson had tested this idea in slightly more modest form two years earlier in a work called *Turkey Ball* (1995), exhibited at the International Sculptors Symposium in Bursa, Turkey, in which a Volkswagen Beetle powered a turntable that rotated a single canvas globe to similar effect, but *Painting with Two Balls* was a stunning leap forward, taking the Jasper Johns work of the same name to a testosterone-fueled extreme. Whereas Johns was seeking to poke fun at the macho world of the abstract expressionists from the position of a young upstart in 1960, Jackson supersized and literalized the joke within the language of Los Angeles art of the 1990s, in which bigger and bolder was better, a form of diction that he played a great part in shaping. This work would initiate a long series of mechanized pieces as well as projects that took advantage of the viscosity of paint to wreak havoc on all manner of formerly pure surfaces, whether objects or rooms. Thus motors, propellers, and even turbojets found their way into Jackson's art while funnels, beer bottles, phalluses, air compressors, spray hoses, guns, and even a crashed airplane have been used to liberally distribute paint. The overt reference to a historical work would also be developed further, with Jackson taking on Jacques-Louis David, Edgar Degas, Marcel Duchamp, and Barnett Newman in variously extravagant scenarios and installations, compounding the evidence of his singular approach to painting.

Scene 5: The artist's studio, Sierra Madre, California, 2010.

Propped against a wall is a large canvas that is still mostly white but is nonetheless pocked with dots of color. Slowly emerging from the whiteness, perhaps never to be completed, is the image of another historical work, the French pointillist painter Georges Seurat's *A Sunday on La Grande Jatte—1884* (1884–86). Now as much cowboy as Indian, Jackson has been methodically dipping pellets in paint and shooting at the canvas with a rifle, using destruction and creation in equal measures to build up this composition. *La Grande Jatte (after Georges Seurat)* (1992–) is yet another icon of his repertoire, both a conceptually precise exercise and a wildly expansive gesture that, in the hands of a lesser artist, would become a big shtick involving armies of assistants. Jackson, true to form, must accomplish this task alone even if it means never finishing it, the extraordinary labor and effort integral to his personal investment in his "big idea." He knows the territory, having forged ahead long ago without the benefit of like-minded comrades to accompany him on this quixotic pursuit of a wider horizon for painting. It remains to be seen whether a new generation of artists will come around to his vision of the medium's future, but if they do, the trail will be well marked and won't take the easy route.

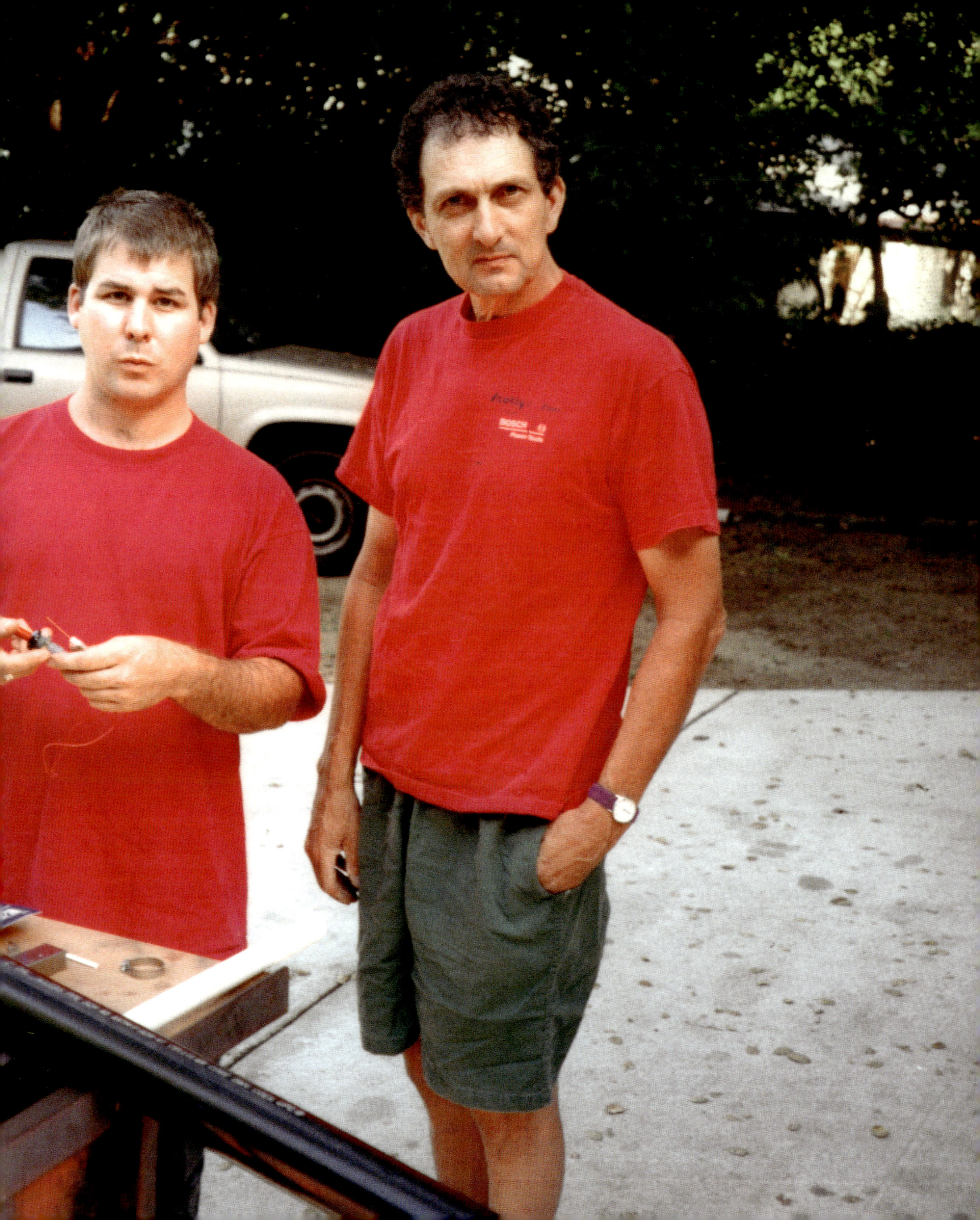

RICHARD JACKSON
IN CONVERSATION
WITH **HANS ULRICH OBRIST**

HUO I think we should dedicate this interview to the memory of Jason Rhoades (FIG. 1) because he introduced us. I'll never forget that he drove me to your studio when I came to L.A. for the first time. How did Jason get interested in your work? He always told me that you were his hero. When did you meet?

RJ Jason was a student of mine at UCLA. Right away I liked him. One time he went home at Christmas, and when he came back, he said: "I was looking at my mother's high school yearbook, and you went to high school with my mother. I saw your picture with a baseball uniform." It's true. (FIGS. 2, 3)

HUO Extraordinary.

RJ Yeah. And I didn't know her, because I think there were six or seven hundred people in the class. Because we came from the same area and a similar background, we became friends immediately. Then right away I realized that he was a great artist. You can tell, you know?

HUO It was instantly clear?

RJ Yeah, for me it was. Jason became my assistant, and because I never

FIG. 1
Richard Jackson (right) and Jason Rhoades,
ca. 1994

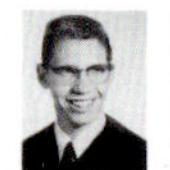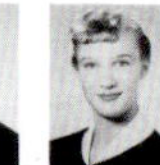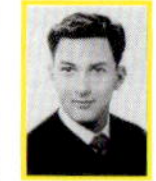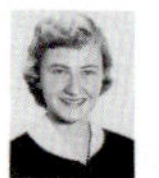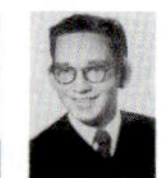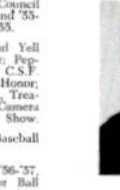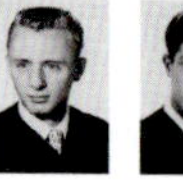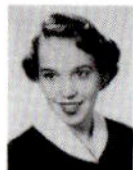

FIG. 2 (above)
Richard Jackson high school yearbook photo, 1957

FIG. 3 (above right)
Richard Jackson varsity baseball photo, 1957

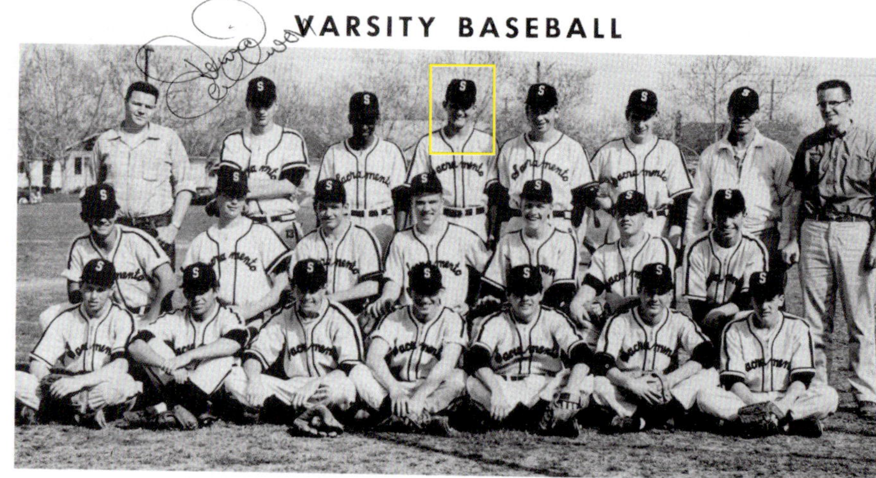

Top Row: Mgr. Bill Mugford, Dave Calhoun, Garland Gandy, Rich Jackson, Jack Schenk, Larry Walker, Coach Adams, Wayne Saunders.
Middle Row: Orlie Paine, Ron Williams, Mike Entz, O. J. Solander, Bill Gribben, Larry Johnson, Tom Brennan.
Bottom Row: Cork Werder, Manuel Mateo, Dave Gates, Jerry Taylor, Jerry Conway, Milt Champas, Dave Cooper.

finished school, I had a different theory about the way people learned. First you have to get the students to trust you, and then you set up an atmosphere that's conducive to them doing things. Instead of having small groups with this real intense theoretical thing going, you set up a big group, and then they learn from one another and push one another into projects. And all you do is sit back. Jason was good because he and I let the class get completely out of control. It was crazy: kids jumping off the building, throwing video cameras off the building. It really was pretty good. It worked for me.

HUO Talking about Jason as your student leads to your own beginnings. You grew up in Sacramento. How did you come to art? Or how did art come to you?

RJ I was studying to be an engineer. You had to take drawing because we did

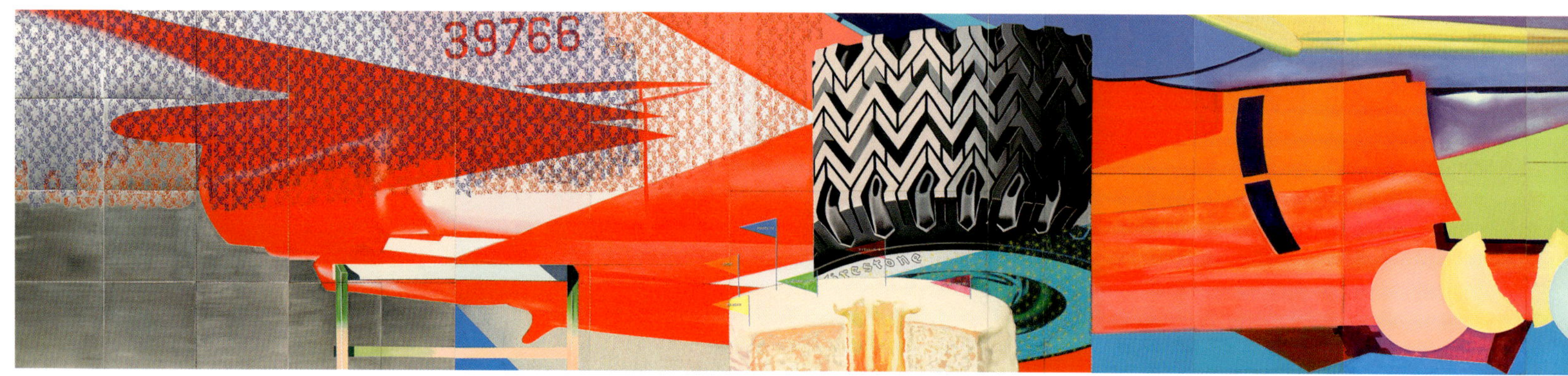

FIG. 4
James Rosenquist, *F-111*, 1964–65. Oil on canvas with aluminum, twenty-three sections. 10 × 86 ft. (304.8 × 2621.3 cm). The Museum of Modern Art, New York, Gift of Mr. and Mrs. Alex L. Hillman and Lillie P. Bliss Bequest (both by exchange). Art © James Rosenquist/Licensed by VAGA, New York, NY

engineering drawings, so I took a couple of art classes. One of the teachers at the school was Wayne Thiebaud, and he's a good artist and a very smart guy. That's what impressed me.

HUO So Wayne Thiebaud was a trigger of some sort?

RJ Yeah, because I realized that there's more to it. His favorite artist is Cézanne. It's very structured and academic in a way but really good painting, I think.

HUO So you started with Wayne Thiebaud, and that was before you moved to L.A., and that's obviously the sixties, and it's a time when the American art world is going from abstract expressionism into pop. Our last interview was in Paris in 1998. But thirteen years ago I really misunderstood because I thought that your background was a reaction against abstract expressionism.

RJ No.

HUO How did you situate yourself as a young artist within that tension between expressionism and pop art?

RJ I don't know. I really liked Rosenquist's work and still do. I liked the scale, like with *F-111* (FIG. 4). That was impressive work, but I also saw a Warhol exhibition at the Whitney that I thought was good. It's the real pop. I followed it, but I never got involved in it, never had any reaction against it. But abstract expressionism, I grew up with it. Pollock was very important for me (FIG. 5). I went to New York for the first time in 1960, and I saw a lot of abstract expressionism, and I saw a lot of Jasper Johns's work, which impressed me. I saw *Painting with Two Balls*, which I have remade since.

HUO So that was a kind of epiphany?

RJ I thought *Painting with Two Balls* was the strangest thing I've ever seen.

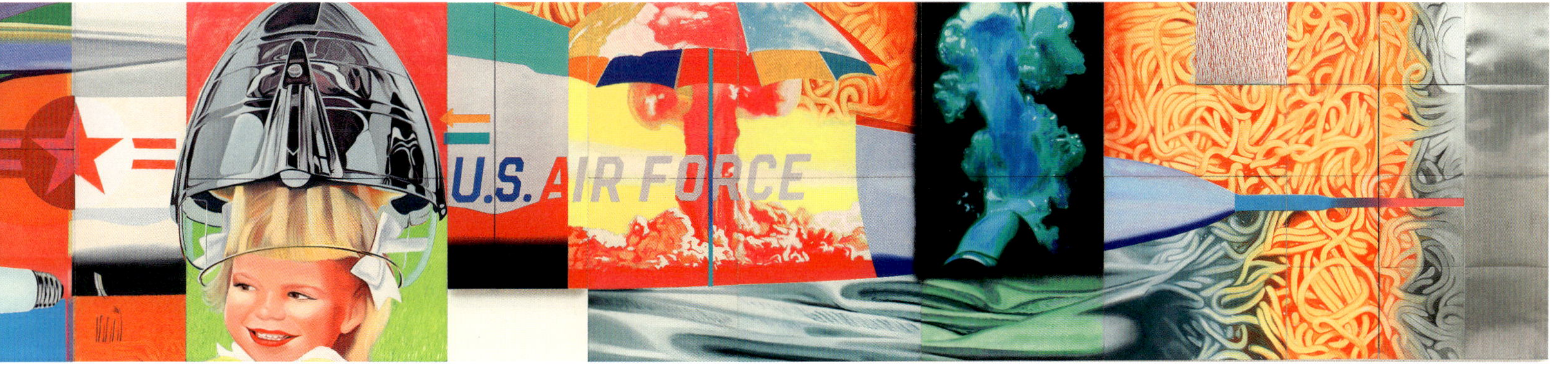

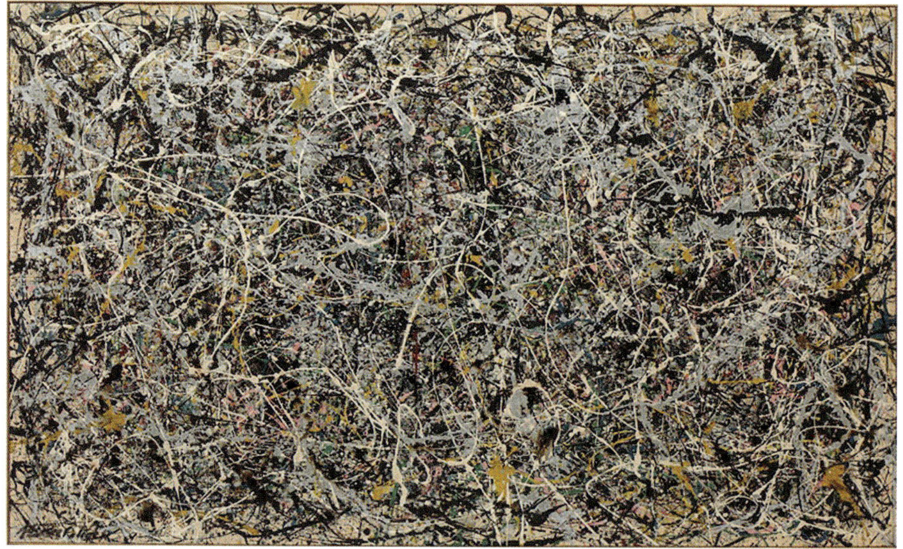

I was only twenty years old and living in Sacramento. Not so easy to be informed. So really, I think a lot of Jasper Johns, and the same with Bruce Nauman and Marcel Duchamp.

HUO When one thinks about a retrospective, it leads to the catalogue raisonné. What is the first entry in your catalogue raisonné? Where would you say the student work ends?

RJ I think pretty late for me, when I'm thirty. I had a hard time because there were a lot of other things I wanted to do, and they didn't involve art or artists, so I did those things for most of the 1960s, and looking back at it, I think that's what makes my art interesting.

HUO So you had this incubation time?

RJ Yeah. Now what I notice about artists is that their backgrounds are more alike than different. They stay in school until they're thirty, and they don't have to go into the military, which I did. They have a whole different freedom from responsibility in some sense. And also maybe their parents' generation made more money to give them that freedom. There are a lot of artists who don't have to work until they're out of school. We started a school— an ex-student of mine and another friend—the Mountain School. All the students there are thirty-something years old. They just can't get enough of school. That situation is more important than it used to be, and I think it's not a bad thing.

HUO For me, it was the same. When I was in my late teens, early twenties, I went on a grand tour, not producing anything, just looking. But you say you started at thirty—so the first pieces would be from 1970?

RJ 1969 to 1970.

HUO The floor paintings in the studio? How did you invent these floor experiments? It's basically nailing a canvas to the floor. It's really an instruction piece. How did that occur?

RJ I was trying to make painting more interesting. I think abstract expressionism got to this real high point, then it went backward. I just thought you could still work on it, make it interesting again. At least make the process interesting. I was always impressed with Pollock, his process. It seemed almost like a performance.

HUO There is this performative part. You used instructions, but at the same time you didn't leave painting behind; you applied them to painting. Can one say that?

RJ Absolutely. Even now, I struggle to keep painting. Sometimes I get sidetracked with objects. But I think the activity for me is the most important thing. More so than the result. When you do these things, you plan them out and then you take whatever comes along. I try not to make value judgments about which part's nice and which part's not. I think the activity is important, but it's also important that the performance part is not observed by the viewer (FIG. 6). These things need to be done in such a way that the viewer imagines the process rather than sees it. They re-create the activity and reconstruct how the painting is done. If they see the process, then they don't use their imaginations. They just come and look at it.

HUO So you'd agree with Duchamp that the viewer does half the work, at least.

RJ For sure, hopefully. Doesn't happen all the time, but it's an attempt.

HUO Another important moment in your work is the invention of the wall paintings. Albert Hofmann told me that one day he came to the lab and discovered LSD by chance. Penicillin was discovered completely by coincidence. When I interview scientists, they often say, "It was a rainy Wednesday and this and this happened." So how did you make this invention?

RJ Mostly I work them out in drawings. At that time, there was a lot of experimenting, trying things out. But all this work's been thrown away. There was absolutely no interest in it. And that didn't disturb me at all because I

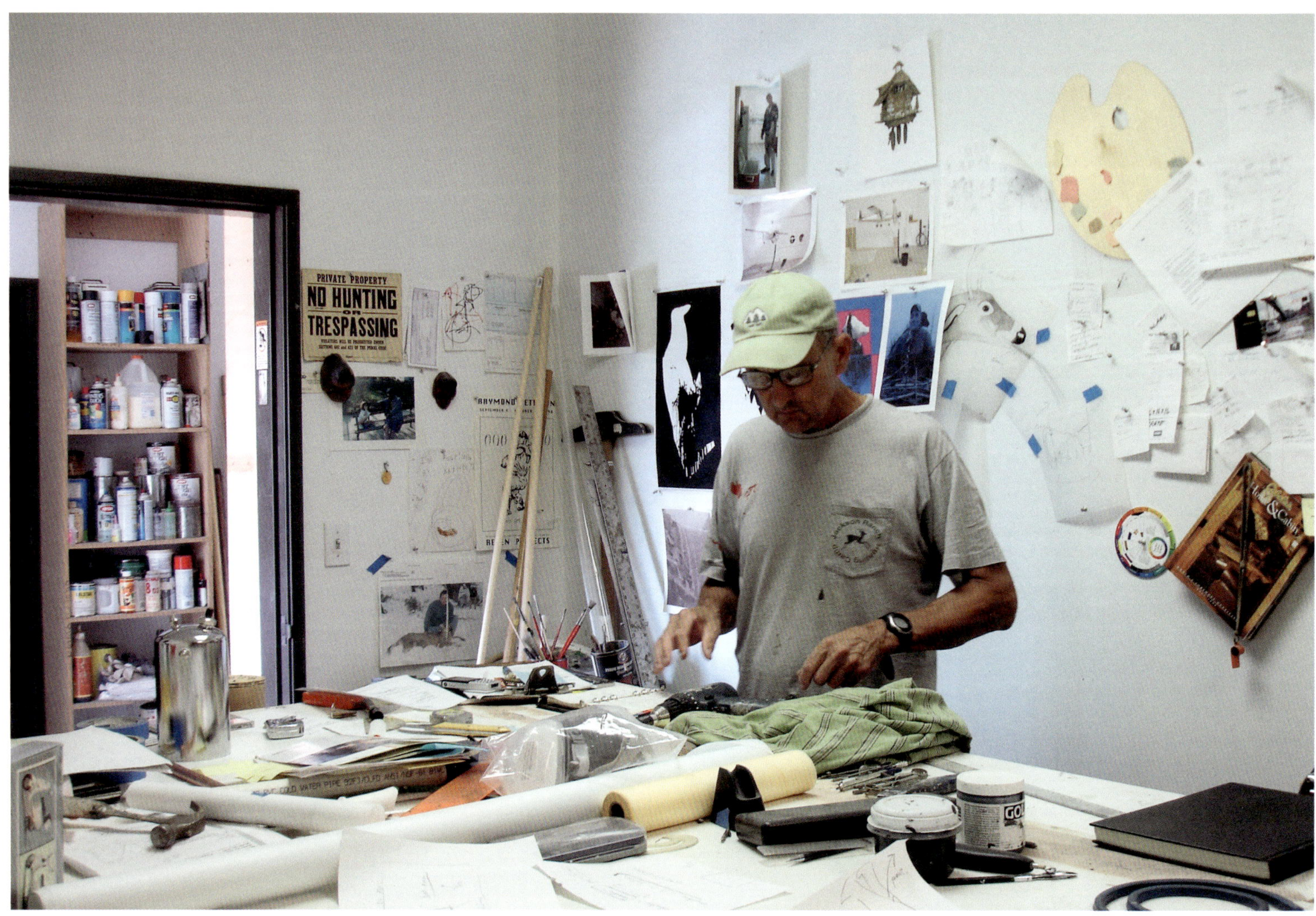

FIG. 6
Richard Jackson studio, Sierra Madre,
California, August 2005

always saw these things as events rather than objects. It was important that people see them. But they would live only in people's minds. Like word of mouth.

Because I'm interested in scale, the beauty of this is that each time people tell it, it gets distorted and changed. And in most cases it gets bigger. That was an important tool for me. I would do a three-thousand-painting piece and then people would say, "There must have been five thousand!" So the work not being around doesn't bother me at all. Modern art shouldn't be in institutions and preserved and fooled around with. Because it's created in a completely different spirit. It's made out of toilet paper and temporal materials. And conservators are so concerned with saving it.

HUO Paradox of now. Conservators spend years trying to conserve a decomposed yogurt or cheese.

RJ It is modern. It's like computers. In two years, you need another one. It's like Yoko Ono's book. It says, "When you're finished with the book, throw it away." Well, that's what I did. I can follow directions.

HUO You threw her book away?

RJ It said to, you know? They have this big Fluxus collection in Stuttgart, and it wasn't meant to be collected. It's crazy.

HUO The wall paintings are a sort of hybrid because, on the one hand, you see it's a wall painting, but on the other hand, it's also still a canvas on the wall. Can you talk a little bit more about this? You've done a lot of different variations of this.

RJ It's really hard for me to do these things now. They're not as interesting as when I was first making them. Just like any kind of painting, it gets better and better. But less interesting. It gets more refined or polished.

HUO You did one yesterday. How did that go?

RJ Oh, it's really easy. I mean, I did it in two days, and it's only four canvases.

HUO After the wall paintings, you went into the space. In 1970 you did a whole labyrinth for the Eugenia Butler Gallery. Can you tell me about this— when painting almost becomes architecture? I'm particularly interested in this labyrinth, which I think is a masterpiece.

RJ The idea with that painting is that you would pass through it and it would be an experience. You would be inside the painting. But you can't see the whole painting from any one place. You can't just back up and turn this thing into a rectangle. It's one of my favorite paintings because it really was successful.

HUO How would you say it's related to instructions? Throughout your books and literature, there are a lot of instructions. The labyrinth is a kind of instruction piece. Can you talk a little bit about the importance of instructions?

RJ You figure the work out, then you write down instructions on how to do it, and then you just do it, as a process. That's the evidence of the work. Usually in an exhibition I have the proposal, the instructions or plan for the piece, and then I have the piece. And they're two very different things. However, one is as important as the other. It was always my idea that you could own the instructions, the concept. And then we could do them later or whatever. I'm still interested in that. I'm interested in Duchamp's *Étant donnés* book. I reproduced the book because I reproduced the piece. I took the instruction manual and made a piece called *The Maid's Room*. I showed it in Paris because it was a French maid. From the instructions, and building the piece, you could see how he thought. How smart Duchamp really was. Because it's just made out of junk. It's incredible. It's about controlling the viewer. When you look through it, if you see it, it's there. But if you can't see it, it's not there. The legs aren't there on the figure. One arm is missing. You can't see it.

HUO Another important piece, besides the Butler maze, is *The Bedroom* from 1976–82. Can I say that *The Bedroom* is connected to *The Maid's Room*? Can you tell me about *The Bedroom*? You had filled rooms with paintings that you constructed. In other rooms paintings became walls, then labyrinths. All of a sudden, *The Bedroom* was different. It was a room as found. What triggered that?

RJ Just the experience of doing it, to see if it would lead anywhere, which it didn't necessarily. I worked on it for a long time, and only two or three people ever saw it. It was a piece in the studio for my own information because you couldn't move it. I never thought I'd redo it or anything. I guess I never really liked it in the end.

HUO So for you it's not one of your most important pieces.

RJ No. I think it goes back to what I was talking about earlier. It's more important because people never saw it. It just kind of exists. It has this thing about it. Walter Hopps loved this thing, and he never saw it.

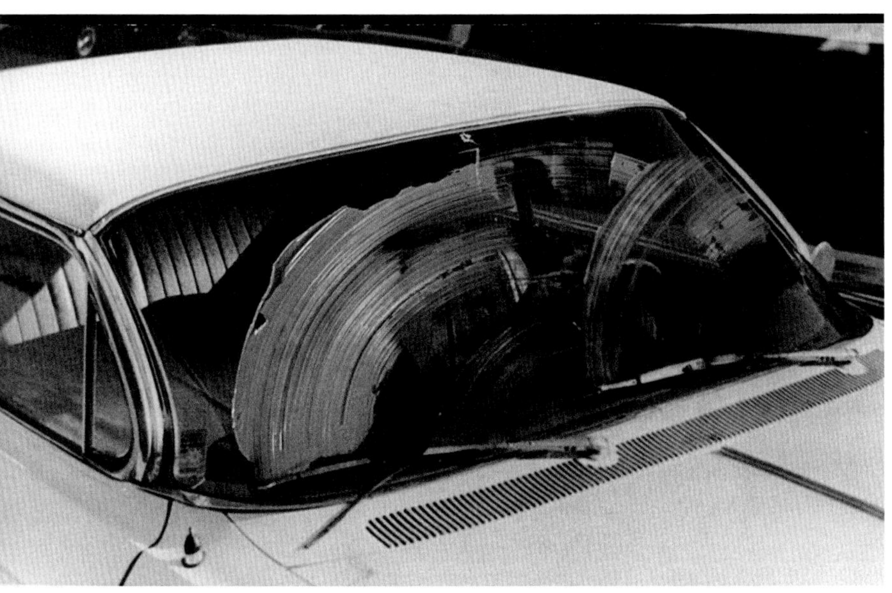

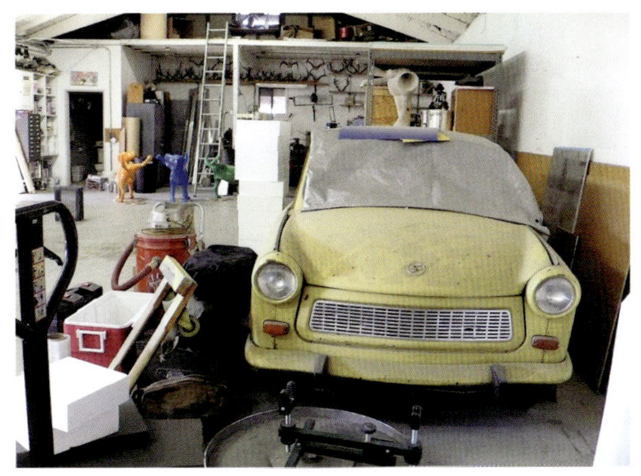

HUO Cars play a big role in a lot of your installations. When I interviewed Ed Ruscha, we spoke a lot about cars. When I came to see you for the first time with Jason Rhoades, I had never recorded an interview in the car, but Jason said, "Let's do it in the car." There seems to be—with Ruscha, with Rhoades, with you—this incredible car connection in relation to art and L.A. The first car piece of yours that I found was this car windshield (FIG. 7). Is that the first time a car entered into the work? And how did it happen? Was it a performance?

RJ It's fake. It's a photograph. And then I just put some paint on it.

HUO So basically you just added the color.

RJ On the photograph. And then rephotographed it.

HUO So that's the first time ever that you made a work with a car?

RJ Yeah. And there's still one more car I'm trying to do, but nobody will do it.

HUO Can you tell me about that?

RJ I want to radio control it and crash it full of paint. Porsche called me and said they wanted to do some sort of painting performance. They said, "We want the car to drive through the paint and then make a painting on the floor." I said, "Well, why don't you do it? What do you need me for?" I said to get the most expensive Porsche and fill it full of paint and smash it up. They said no.

HUO So that's your big unrealized project?

RJ Well, I'd like to crash it. I have a Trabant that I smuggled out of Eastern Europe (FIG. 8). I was going to use it to make a piece with Jason. I was going to have his body scanned and then reconstructed and put in the car. But that can't happen now. I could probably sculpt it, but I don't know. I have a sad feeling about the Jason thing because I went to high school with his mother and he could've been my son. He was that age. It was tragic.

HUO Do you have other unrealized projects besides that and the Porsche? Do you have any utopian sort of dreams?

RJ Because I've done clocks—I've done two different clocks—I want to do an upside-down cuckoo clock that's also inside out. You could walk inside, and it would be the largest cuckoo clock in the world. I went and measured the one now in the Black Forest.

HUO And you've got drawings for that?

RJ I have drawings, and I have a maquette.

HUO One can walk into immersive paintings; that would be an immersive clock.

RJ You walk in, and there's a bar inside so you can get cuckoo, and then all the animals come out of the wall.

HUO So the unrealized car, the unrealized clock. Do you have any unrealized landscapes, or houses, or buildings, or utopias, or your own city?

RJ No.

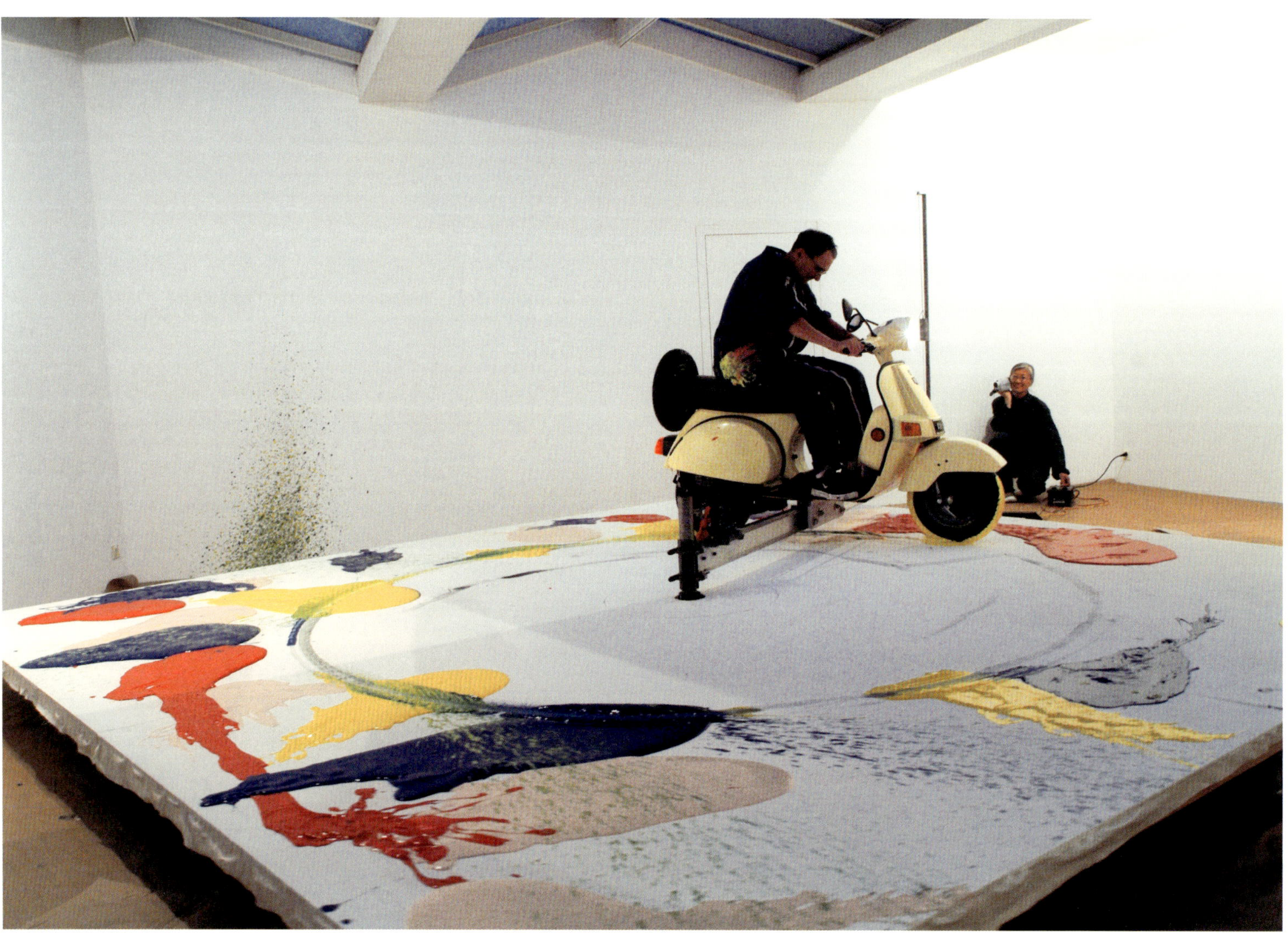

FIG. 9
Richard Jackson, *Cra-Z-Boy*, 2003–04. Vespa, mechanical elements, motor, remote control, canvas, acrylic paint. Approx. 85 × 226 ⅓ × 181 ⅖ in. (218 × 580 × 465 cm). Collection CNAP/FNAC, Paris

HUO Or dreams? What's your dream?

RJ Eventually to sell one of these things. Not easy to do.

HUO When we talked in 1998, you were doing lots of painting machines. When did you invent the idea of the painting machine?

RJ I think the first one was *Deer Beer*. That's kind of autobiographical, deer hunting and guns.

HUO What role does hunting play for you? For John Cage, it's the mushrooms, and for you it's the hunting. What's the importance of that?

RJ Well, I was born into it. My family homesteaded a plot of land that I still have. I've been going deer hunting since I was nine years old. I enjoy a lot of people who don't have any relationship to art. I don't always agree with their politics and attitudes. But I would rather know other people and what they're like instead of just artists and art people. Somehow that gives me information that's necessary for my work.
      My family goes back to Andrew Jackson, who was the first populist president. So I have this sort of populist thing, but I also have a reaction against it because in America now there's a populist movement in which all the stupid people think they can run the country better than the smart people. And that's a real problem.

HUO You've said the painting machines replace the body with machines to make paintings. And you've also said that when the activity starts hell breaks loose and it's completely out of your control. I'm curious about that out-of-control moment. The idea of not using your body anymore and the machine replacing it. Can you talk about this?

RJ I think with abstract expressionism there's a history of people trying to discover something that's an accident. You can only discover things with your mind. You can't discover things by just moving materials around. But in the painting process, there's this whole history of problem solving. You put one thing down here, and then you put one thing over there and then you have to solve this abstract problem in the process. When the machines get out of control, that's when the fun starts. That's when you're forced to be creative, to get back to the plan. One time I did a piece in Innsbruck. I drove a motorcycle on a circular platform full of paint (FIG. 9). And it wouldn't work. Everybody watching got really nervous.

HUO You got covered with paint at Innsbruck.

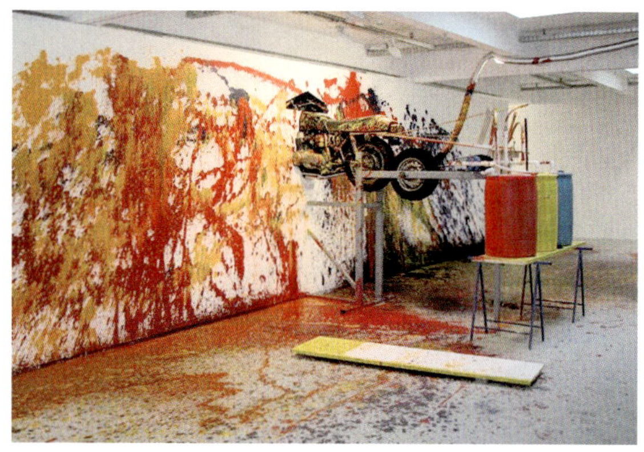

RJ Yeah, I was completely covered. There is a photograph of me. I'm red. I look like the devil. Just completely red. And I'm trying to make the yellow paint work. Like there's one hundred people who are nervous. Finally I figured it out. I got it going.

HUO Earlier you said that lots of your inspiration comes from outside the art world, hunting and all kinds of other worlds that inspire you. Yet there is also a moment in your work when you actually connect directly to art history: Jasper Johns's *Painting with Two Balls*. Also Barnett Newman's *Red, Yellow, and Blue* (FIG. 10). You've also re-created Jacques-Louis David's *Death of Marat* as a sculptural tableau. Edgar Degas's bronzed ballerinas.

RJ *The Maid's Room.*

HUO And Seurat, no?

RJ Yeah.

HUO *La Grande Jatte*. There's a whole aspect in your work that is more art about art. How do you choose these works? Why Seurat?

RJ Well, with Seurat, there's a whole theory that really doesn't hold. I think there are a lot of artists like that. They have these ideas and theories that somehow are supposed to relate to science that just don't work. Which is okay because then great works get made from that. I think Sol LeWitt is the same way. There's a ton of verbiage, but when you see the work, it's great. All the talk doesn't really hold true. I think that's the same as with Seurat. This idea about color. My Seurat painting is pretty amazing because it's been shot with a gun. Maybe 90,000 shots. It's not even close to finished.

HUO So it's an infinite painting.

RJ Yeah, I can go back and work on it anytime I want. And somebody bought it. And they're comfortable with the fact that it's not finished—and never will be, which is pretty good.

HUO Then there is *The Blue Room*—the whole Picasso connection and the blue period.

RJ Yeah, blue paint is poured over a blue figure that revolves. The image of *The Blue Room* is cut into the floor in blue. So it's just all blue. We had a house on our ranch, and it was all blue, and it was called the blue room by the family.

HUO Independently of Picasso.

RJ But probably about the same time. Turn of the century. There are certain works that are worth redoing. Or are inspiring.

HUO A lot of the works you revisit are connected to Paris—Seurat, Picasso, David, Duchamp. What's your connection to Paris?

RJ One of my favorite paintings in the world is there. Monet's *Water Lilies* (FIG. 11). It's a room again, and it's a painting that you can visit only if you go to that place. So it's a place. Or it's an experience or an event.

HUO Degas is another French connection for you. I just read his writings. He was very much into making copies.

FIG. 11
Claude Monet, Room 1 of *Nymphéas (Water Lillies)*, 1920–26. Musée de l'Orangerie, Paris

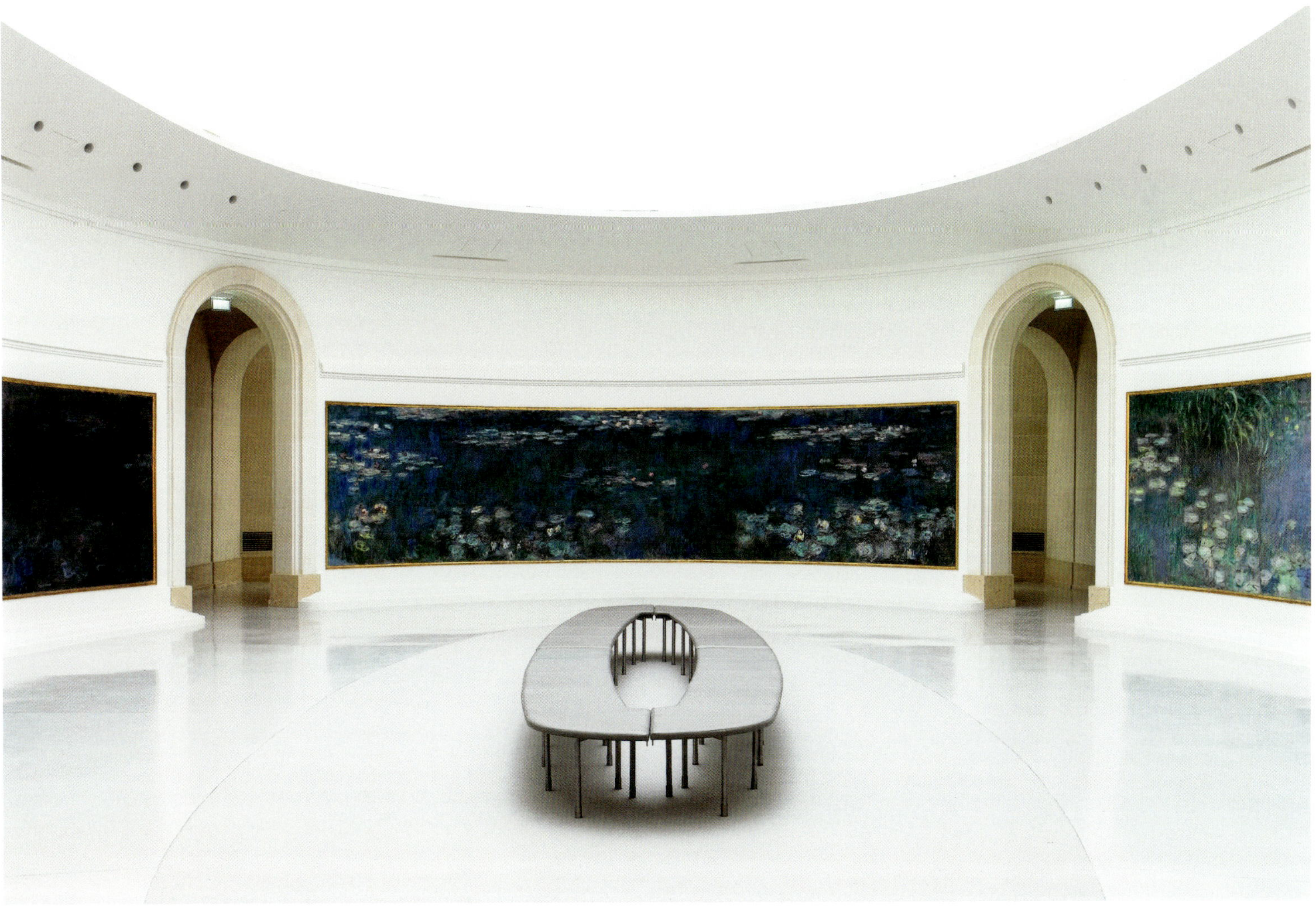

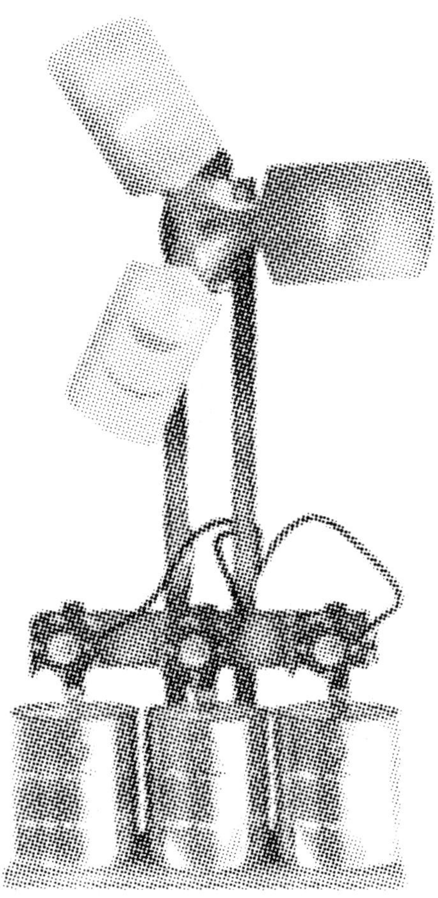

RJ I made a copy of the ballerina, and I smashed it and poured paint in it. I never really cared much for Degas. I saw a lot of it at the Norton Simon. Little sculptures, not so good. My favorite French painter is Monet for sure.

HUO But you've never copied him.

RJ No. Too hard.

HUO Would you talk a little bit about big productions? You've said that it's important to make them all by yourself because executing the idea is another way for you to think of the next project. The labor is another element of the work. The scale can be overwhelming. So is this still the case? That you do it all on your own?

RJ Well, not so much anymore. As much as I can. Some of the big projects I can't do. They involve toxic chemicals and need to be engineered.

HUO There was this whole idea that with instruction art in Fluxus anybody could do it, and so they usually send the assistants to do it. In your case it has to be you somehow who does it. Can't it be somebody else, really?

RJ Not really, no. Everybody thinks it can happen, but it can't because it's a fake. They did a Yoko Ono instruction piece in Seattle at an exhibition I was in, and people took liberties with it. One of the guards really took liberties with it. Changed the whole thing, got off the instructions. The museum people got really upset. But I think when you go out into the public anything's possible, and you have to be ready for that.

HUO But you do have do-it-yourself paintings (FIG. 12).

RJ Yeah. Nobody ever does those.

HUO Why?

RJ I don't know. There are a lot of my instructional pieces that are to be activated, and not one of them has been activated. Not one. Out of twenty-five or so sold. Nobody ever activates them. Isn't that strange?

HUO These are pieces that people could activate without you.

RJ Yeah, just push a button.

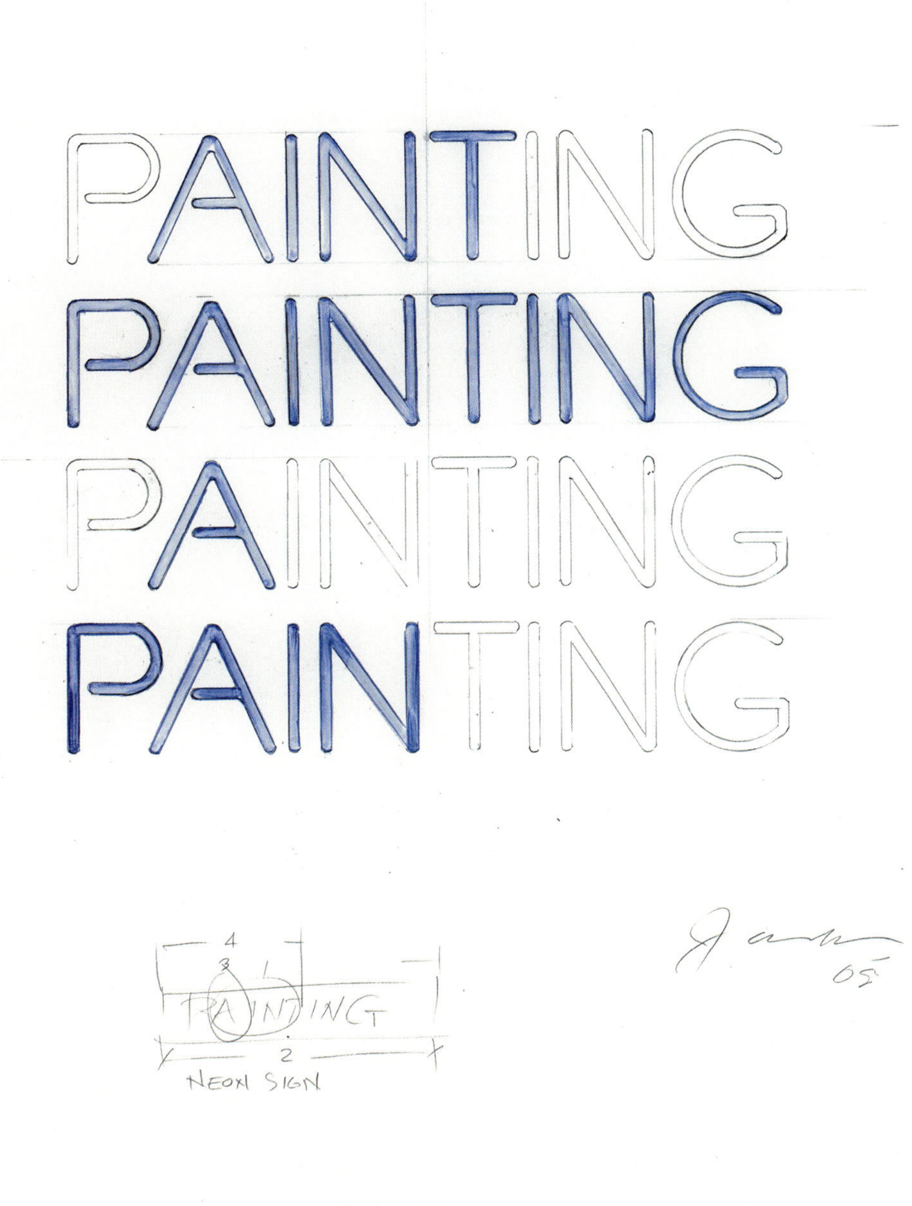

PAINTING
PAINTING
PAINTING
PAINTING
PAINTING
NEON SIGN

FIG. 13
Richard Jackson, *Ain't Painting a Pain*, 2008.
Pencil and oil on mylar. 42 1/8 × 48 7/8 in.
(107 × 124 cm). Rennie Collection, Vancouver

HUO But then they don't do it because they want to keep the object?

RJ With my wall painting, the idea that you can't move it doesn't appeal to anybody. They always pull me aside and say, "Don't you think we can figure out how to do this on a temporary wall that we could move around?"

And the answer is no. Of course we could do it, but no, it's not the same. There are plenty of people doing that, you know? It's called painting.

HUO What is the role of drawing in your practice? Is it a daily practice?

RJ No, unfortunately not. I talked to Paul McCarthy about this. We both like to draw, and everything's so complicated now that you don't have enough time to do it. But I try to do drawings to accompany each exhibition.

HUO In terms of extending or expanding abstract expressionism, I once had a long conversation about that with Allan Kaprow—that whole idea of expanding painting into installation into happenings. Have you ever been in contact with him?

RJ Yeah, we lived in Pasadena.

HUO Was he an important figure for you?

RJ He was friends with Bruce Nauman and myself. And we used to get together, but I never saw any of the happenings in Pasadena. Those things happened before I moved there. I've seen them reconstructed.

HUO For your show, you've got a great title, *Ain't Painting a Pain?* (FIG. 13). You have said: "The trap with painting is that people get addicted to the material. It almost becomes like craft. It becomes an area described by the material used. There are all these little sub-categories, but really it's just art. And that's the problem I have with painting."[1] Could you talk a little bit about the title?

RJ Well, I just think painting has become a pain for me. There's just a whole lot of people who are addicted to this process who don't have anything to add or don't even try. My favorite kind of painting is realistic painting where you can introduce content. I think abstract painting is kind of devoid of anything. It's hard to conceptualize something that doesn't have any . . .

1. Richard Jackson, in Dennis Szakacs,
"The Circus Is in Town" (interview),
Mousse, no. 25 (September 2010): 43.

HUO Content . . . That's the message of the title, somehow.

RJ Yeah.

HUO It's a manifesto against empty painting?

RJ It is.

HUO There's a little book by Rainier Maria Rilke, *Letters to a Young Poet*. What's your advice to a young painter or a young artist?

RJ Keep trying. There's an interesting artist in Vancouver, a painter, Andrew Dadson.

HUO I've seen his paintings in Turin. They are very thick.

RJ And then he scrapes them and puts the paint on top of the canvas. And then he painted his backyard (FIG. 14). He's young. So I'm pretty optimistic. I really like his work. I really like him. He's a nice guy.

HUO Well, nothing could be more wonderful than to end this interview on such an optimistic note.

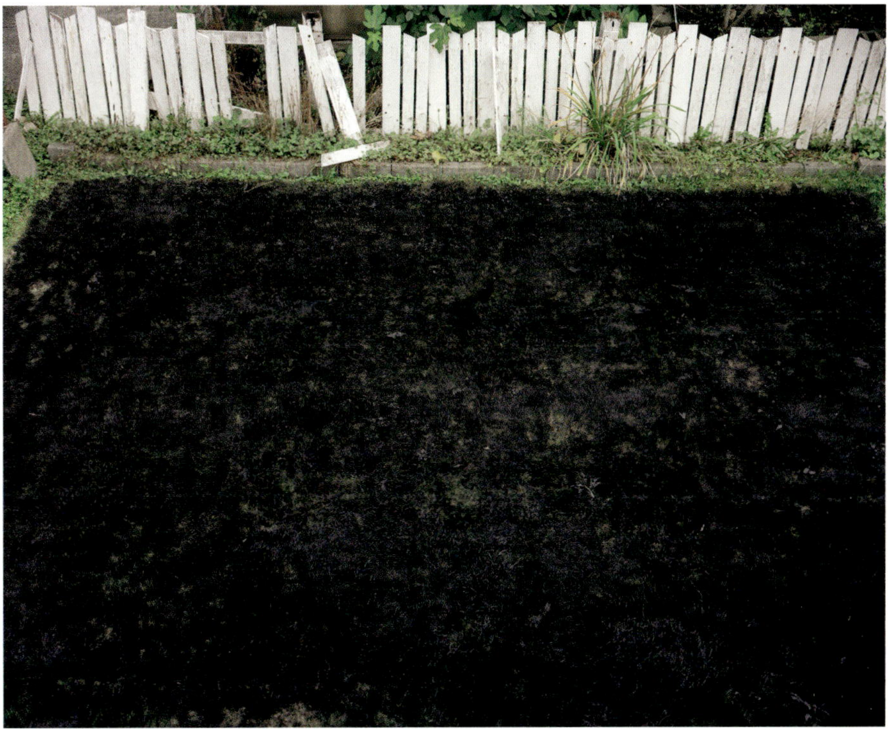

FIG. 14
Andrew Dadson, *Black Painted Lawn with White Fence*, 2006. Chromogenic print mounted on Plexiglas. 60 × 72 in. (152.4 × 182.9 cm). Rennie Collection, Vancouver

PAINTED ENVIRONMENTS AND WALL PAINTINGS

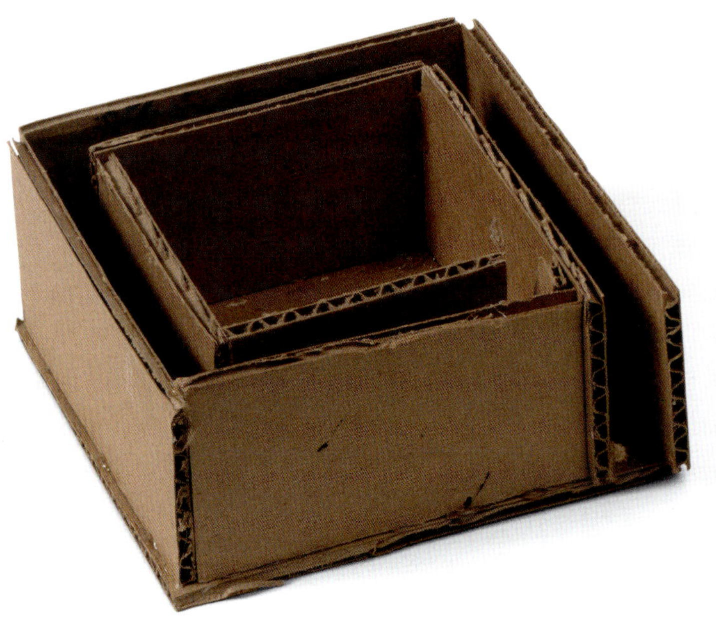

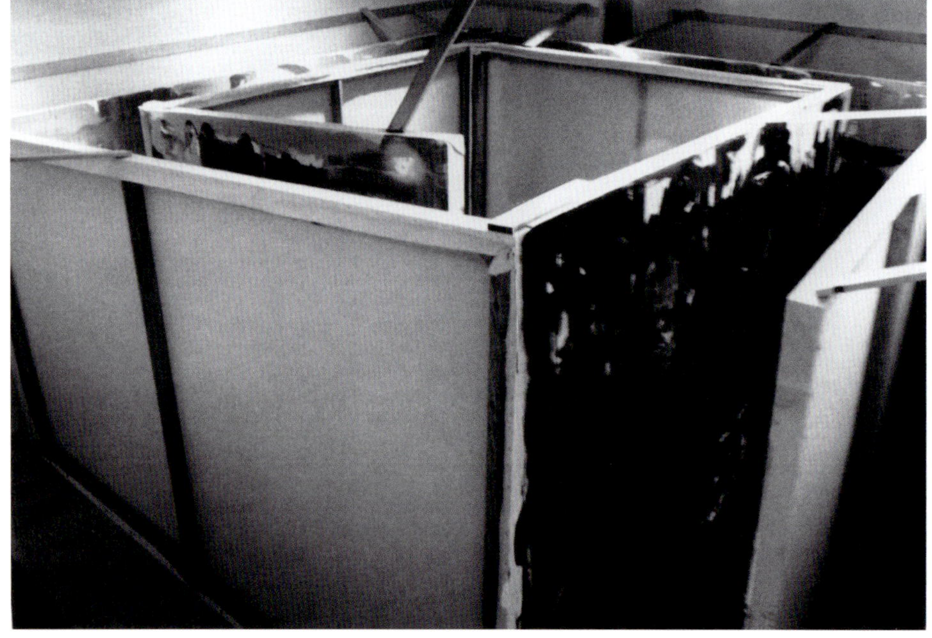

**Untitled (Model I Maze for Eugenia
Butler, Los Angeles)**, 1970
PLATE 1

(facing)
**Project Drawing (Maze for Eugenia
Butler Gallery, Los Angeles)**, 1970
PLATE 3

(bottom)
**Untitled (Maze for Eugenia Butler
Gallery, Los Angeles)**, 1970
PLATE 2

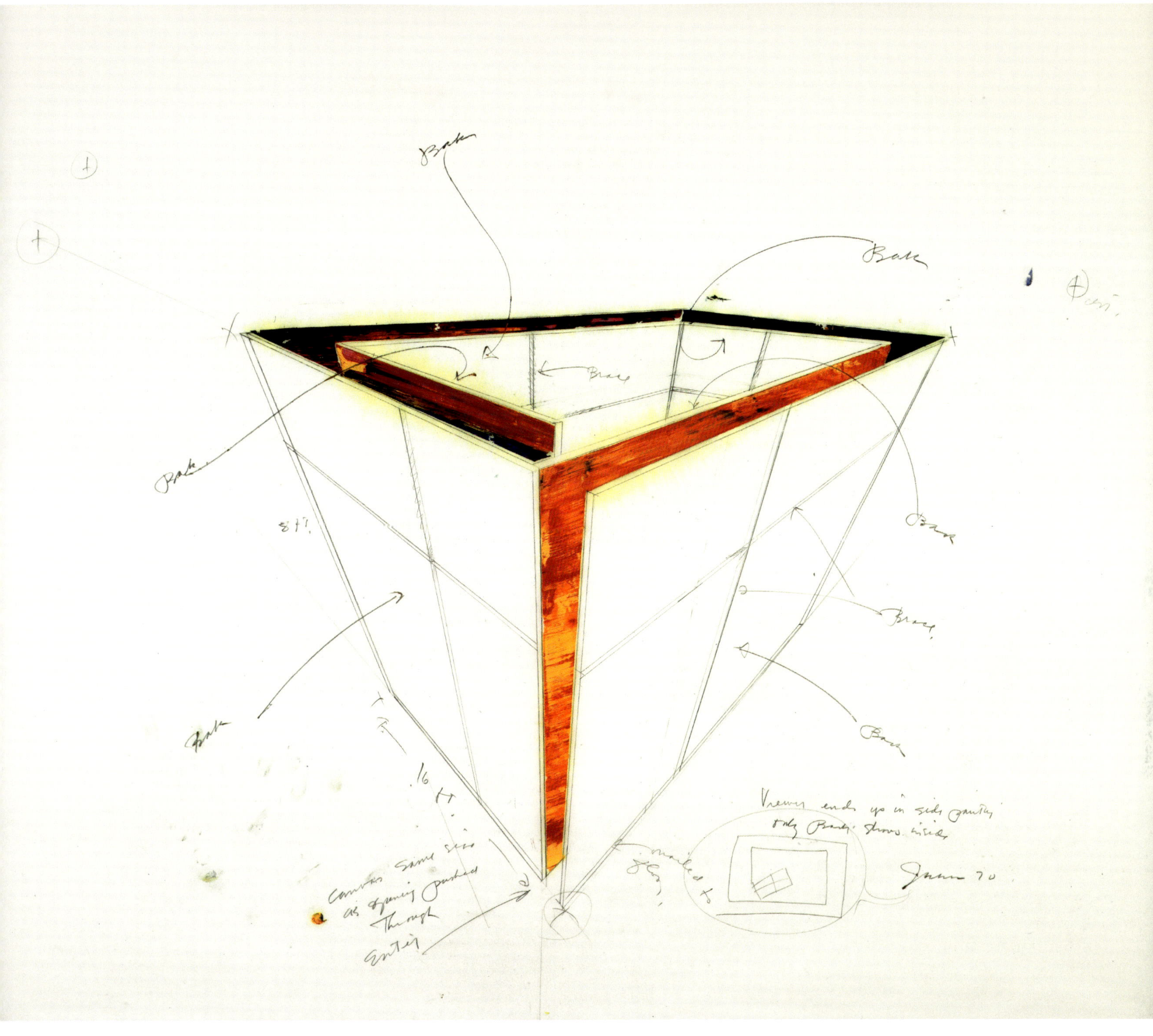

Back
Back
Back
Brace
Brace
Brace
Brace
Cross
8 ft.
16 ft.
Canvas same size
as opening pushed
through
Entry
nailed to
Viewer ends up in side gallery
only painting shows inside
Irwin 70

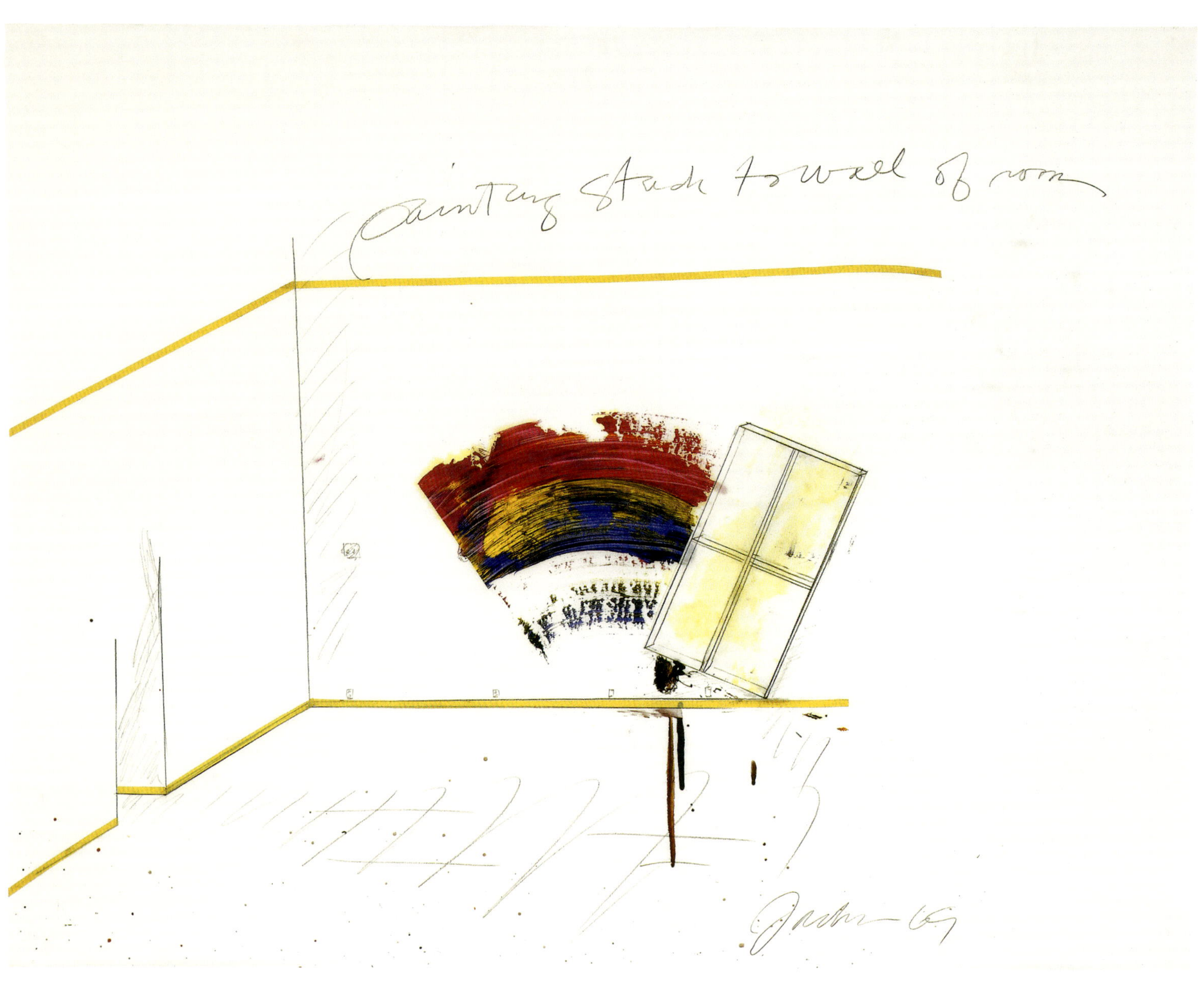

**Untitled (Drawing for)"Painting
Stuck to Wall of Room"),** 1969
PLATE 4

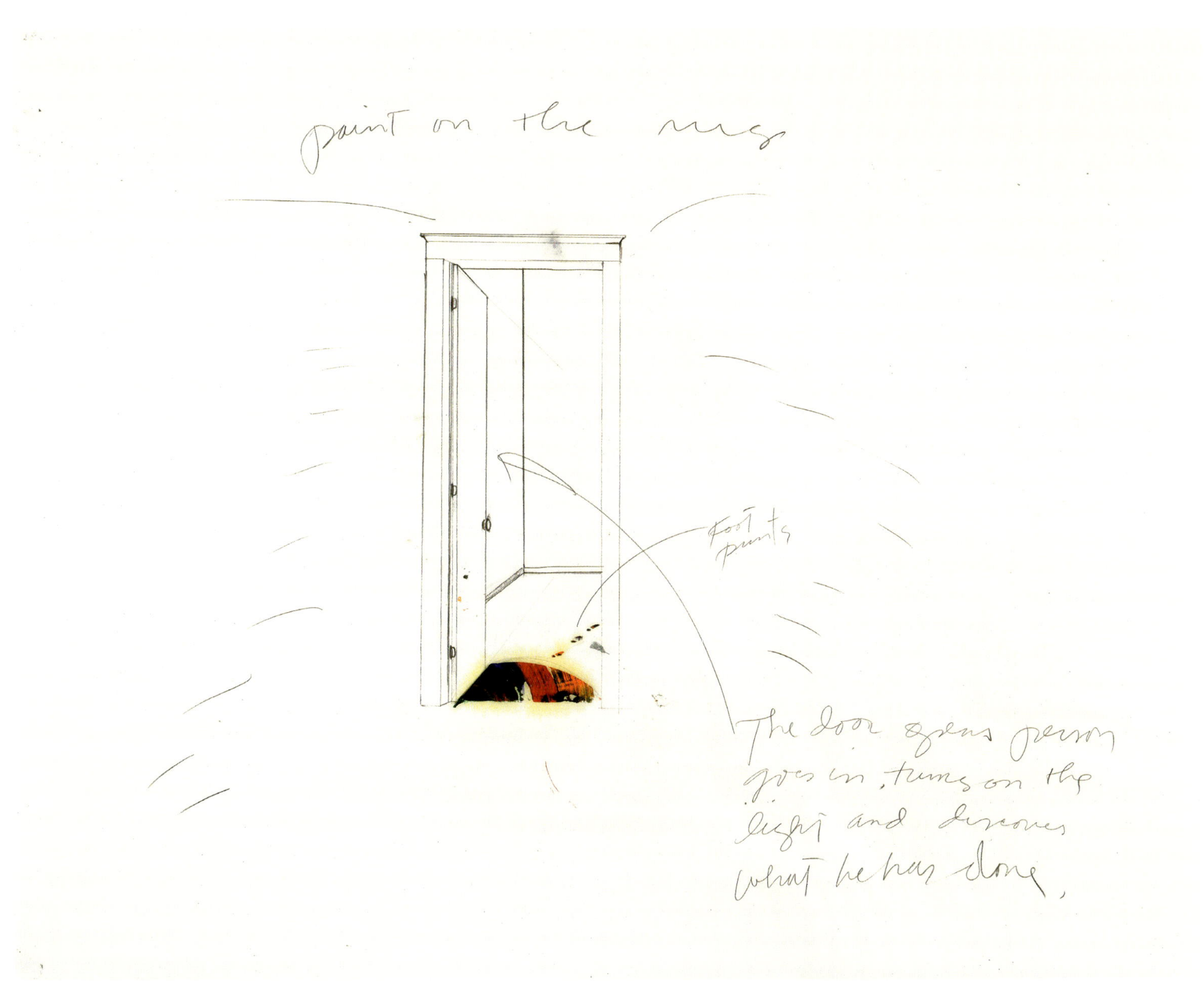

Untitled ("Paint on the Rug"), 1970
PLATE 5

Project Drawing, 1972
PLATE 6

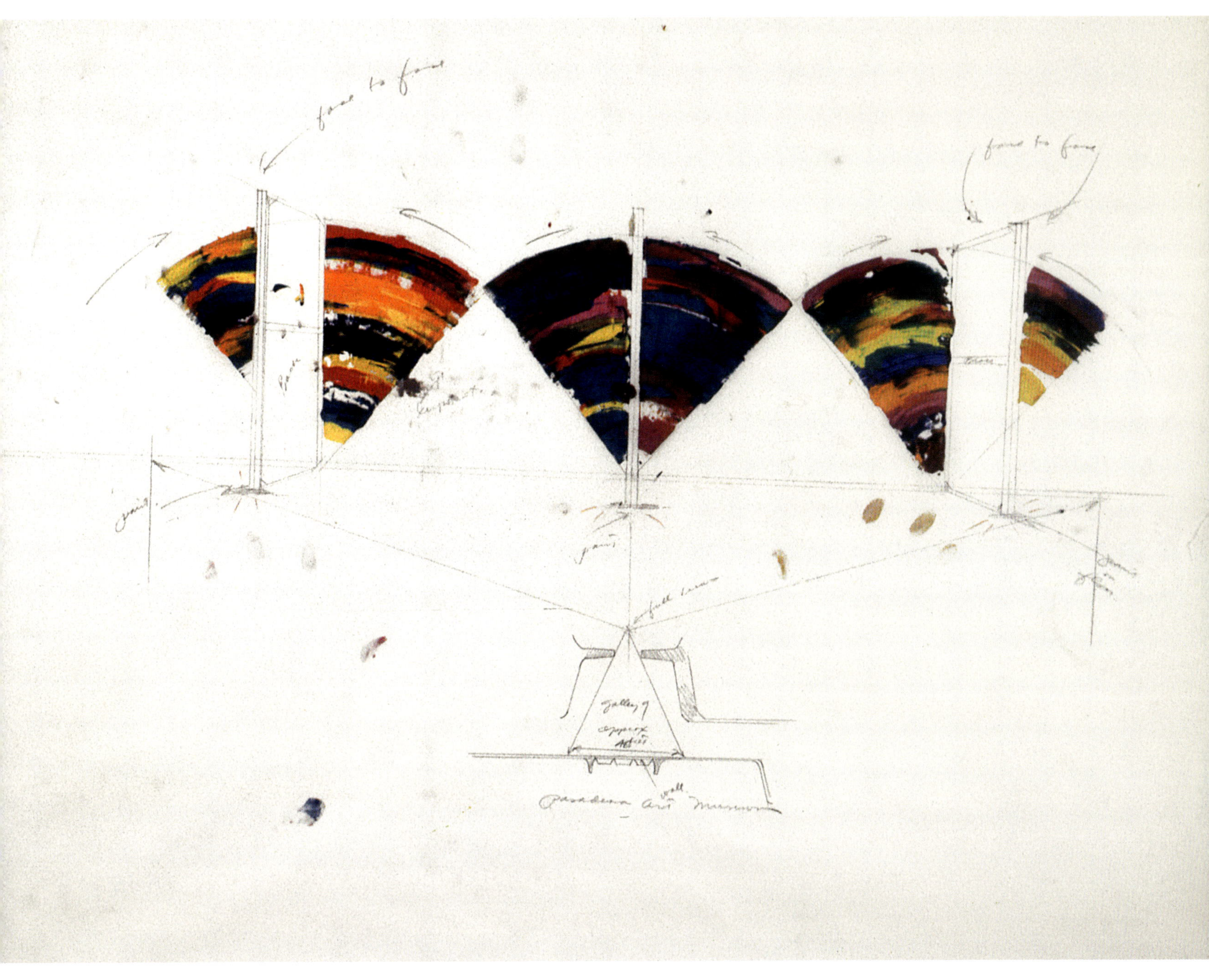

face to face
face to face
Gallery of
approx
Ab 33
Pasadena Art Museum
wall

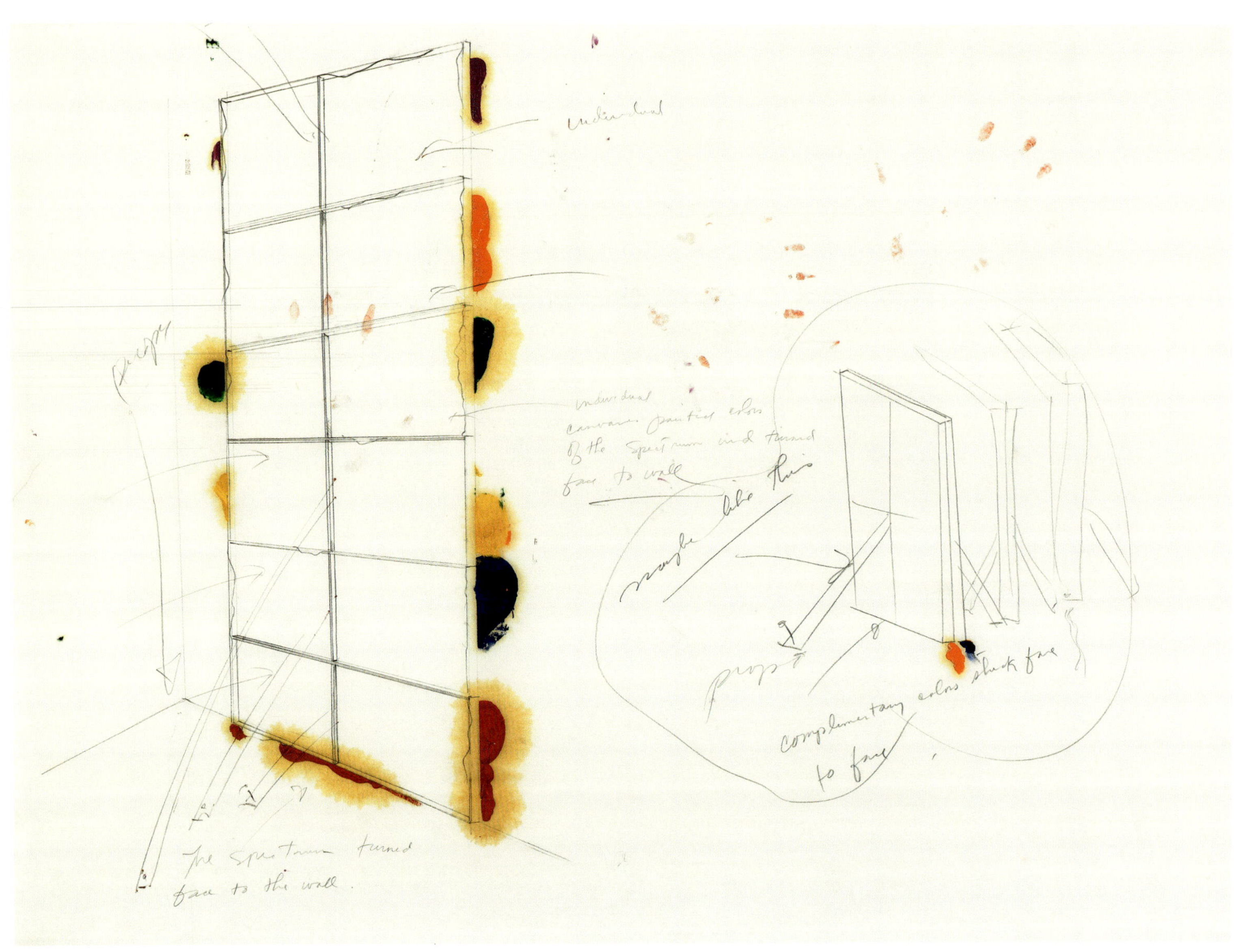

Untitled (plans for three-dimensional work), 1970

PLATE 7

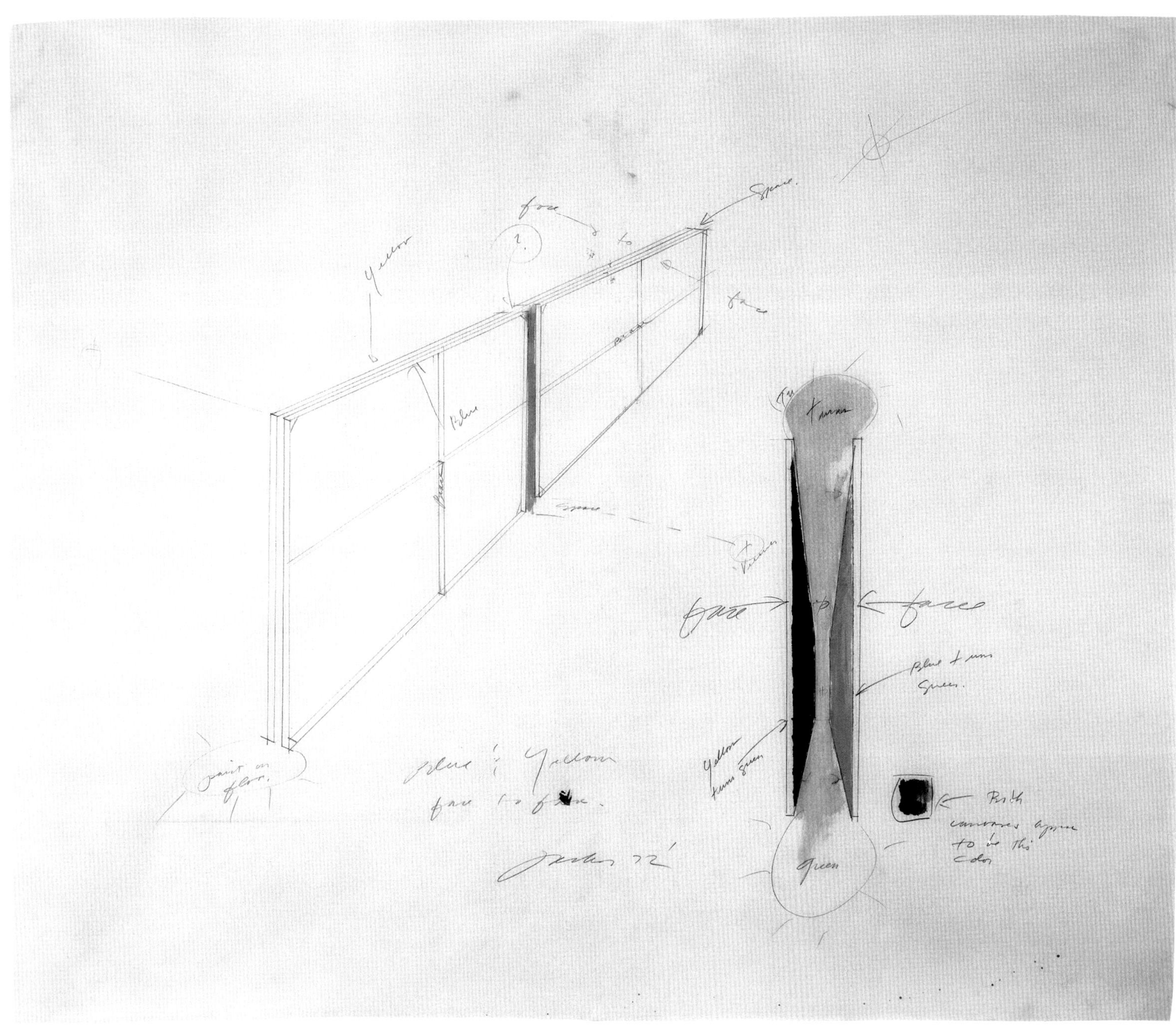

Untitled, 1972

PLATE 8

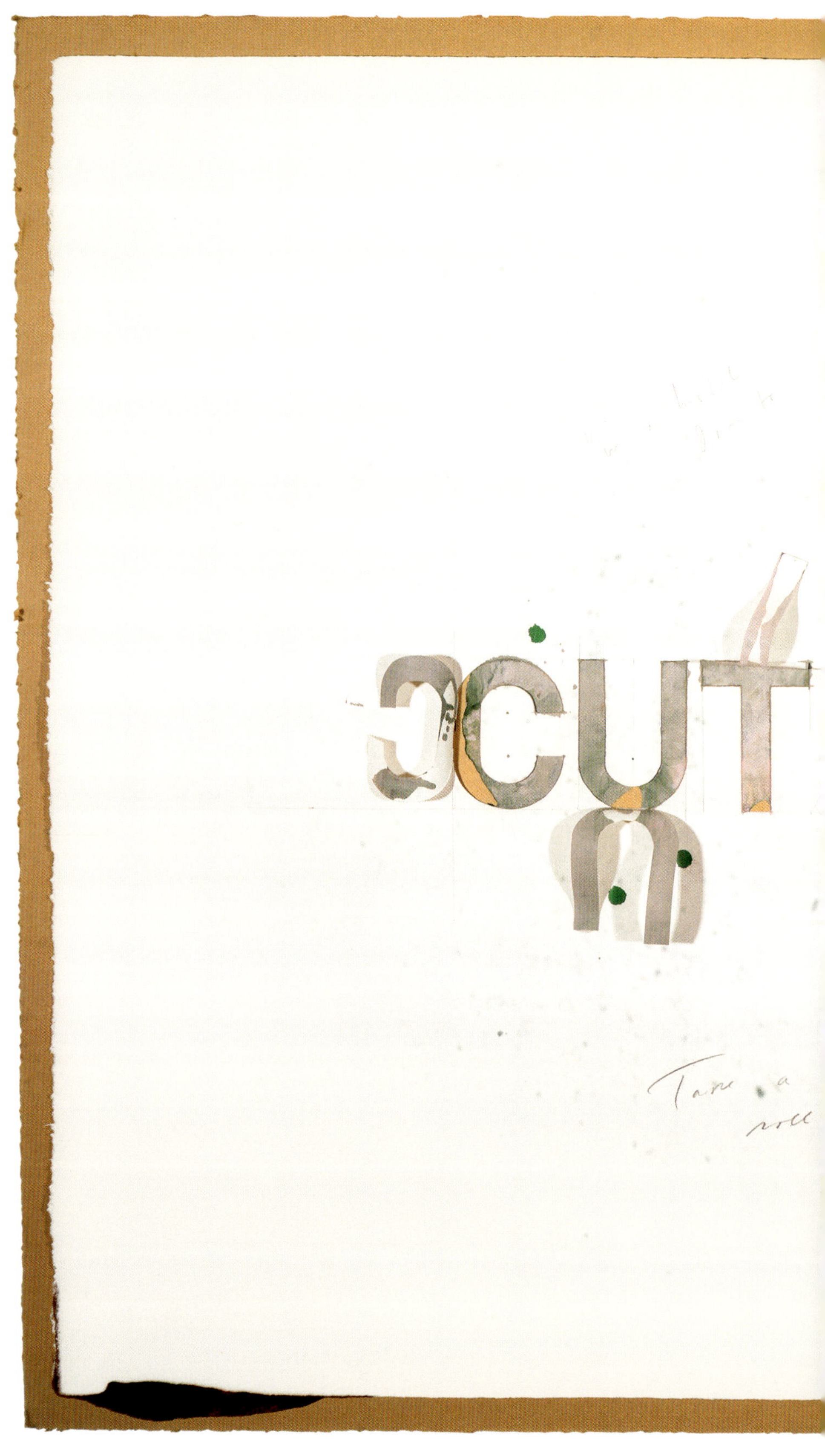

Cut the Rug, 1973
PLATE 9

THE RUG

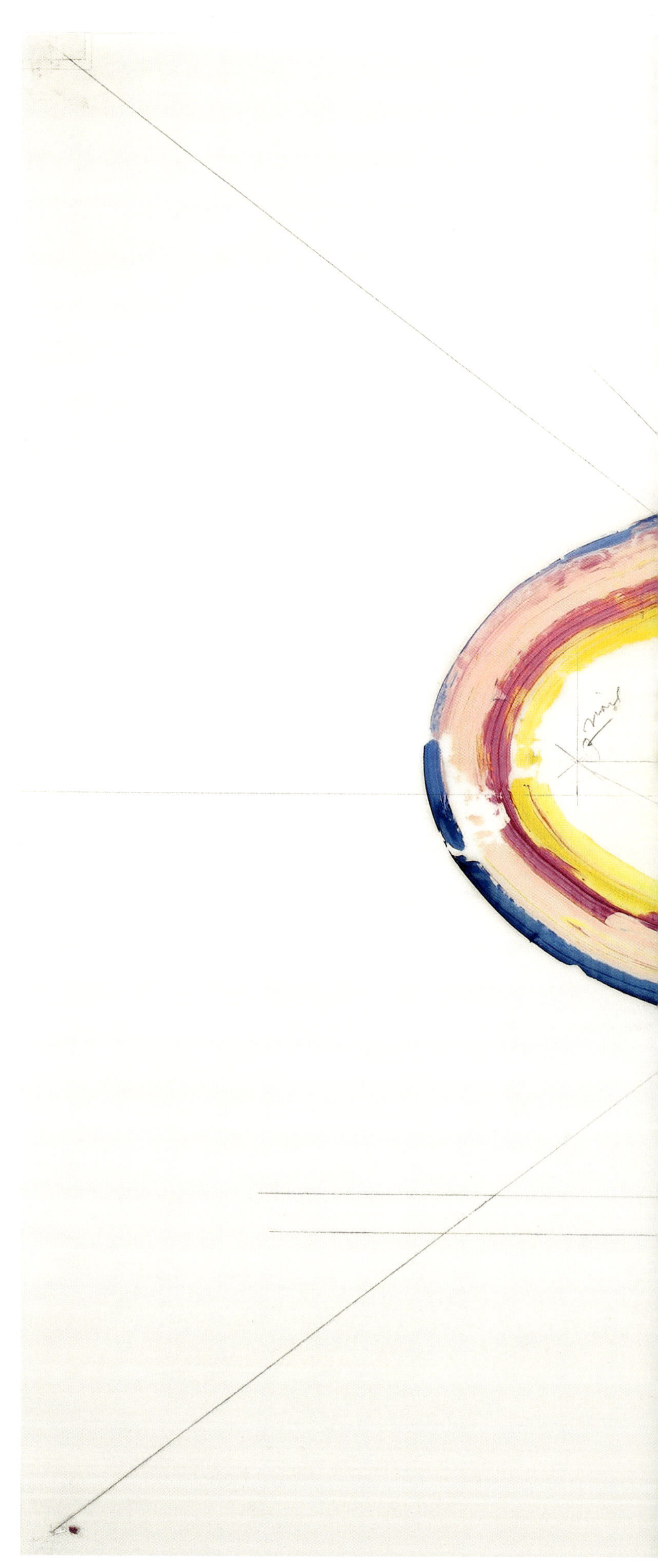

RIKOS, 1974
PLATE 10

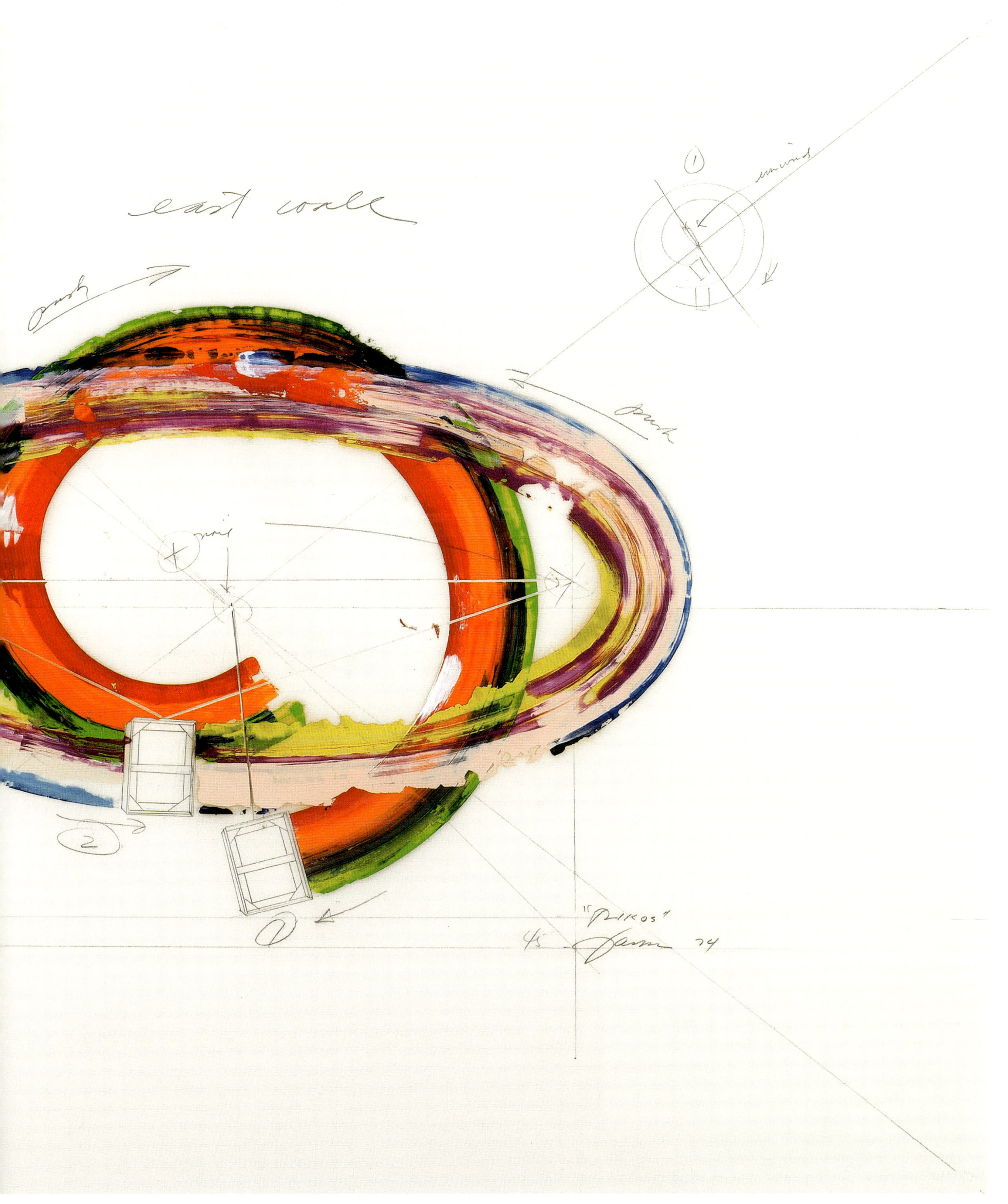

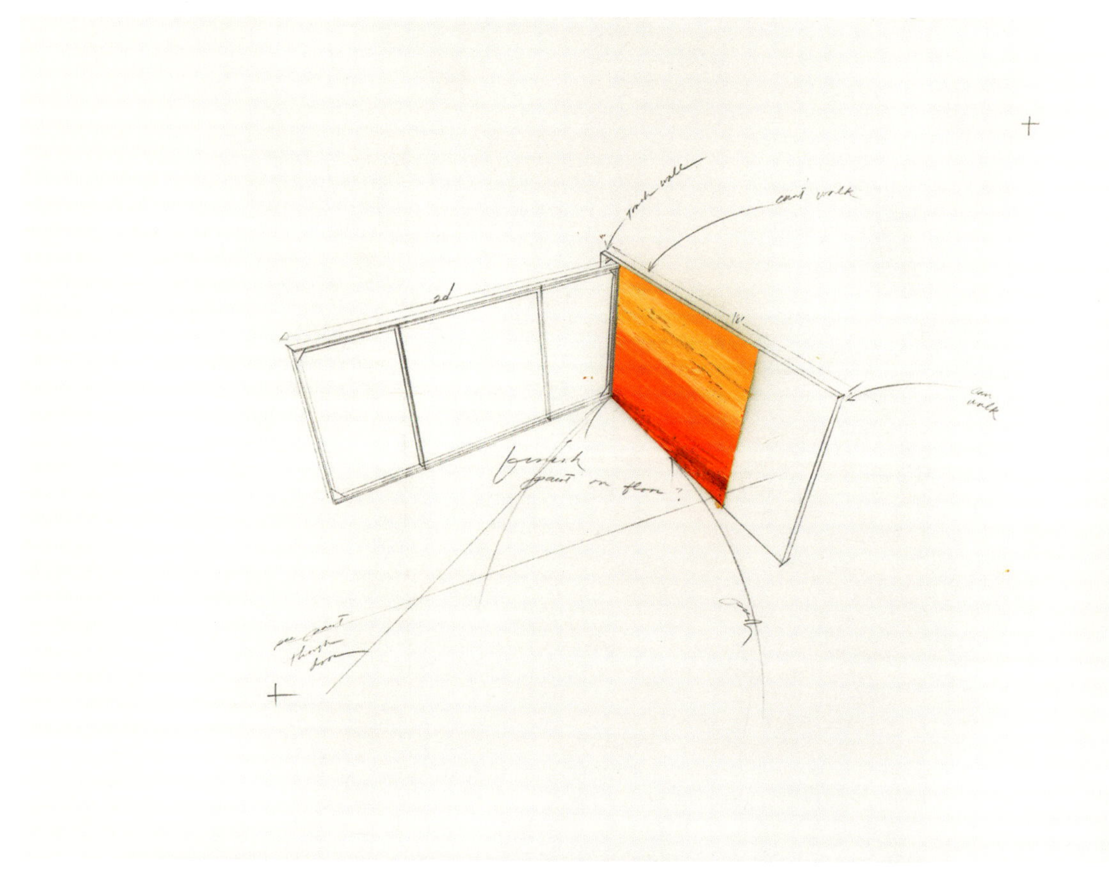

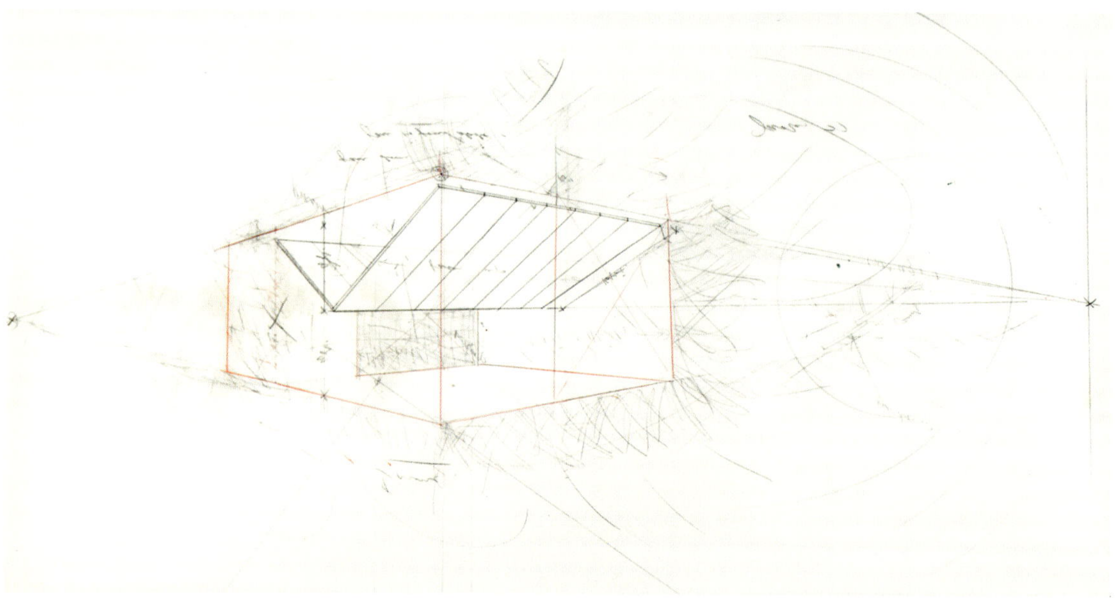

(top)
**Untitled (Drawing for a painting at
Bykert Gallery),** 1974

PLATE 11

(bottom)
**Untitled (Study for "Untitled
Free-standing Painting"),** 1977

PLATE 12

174

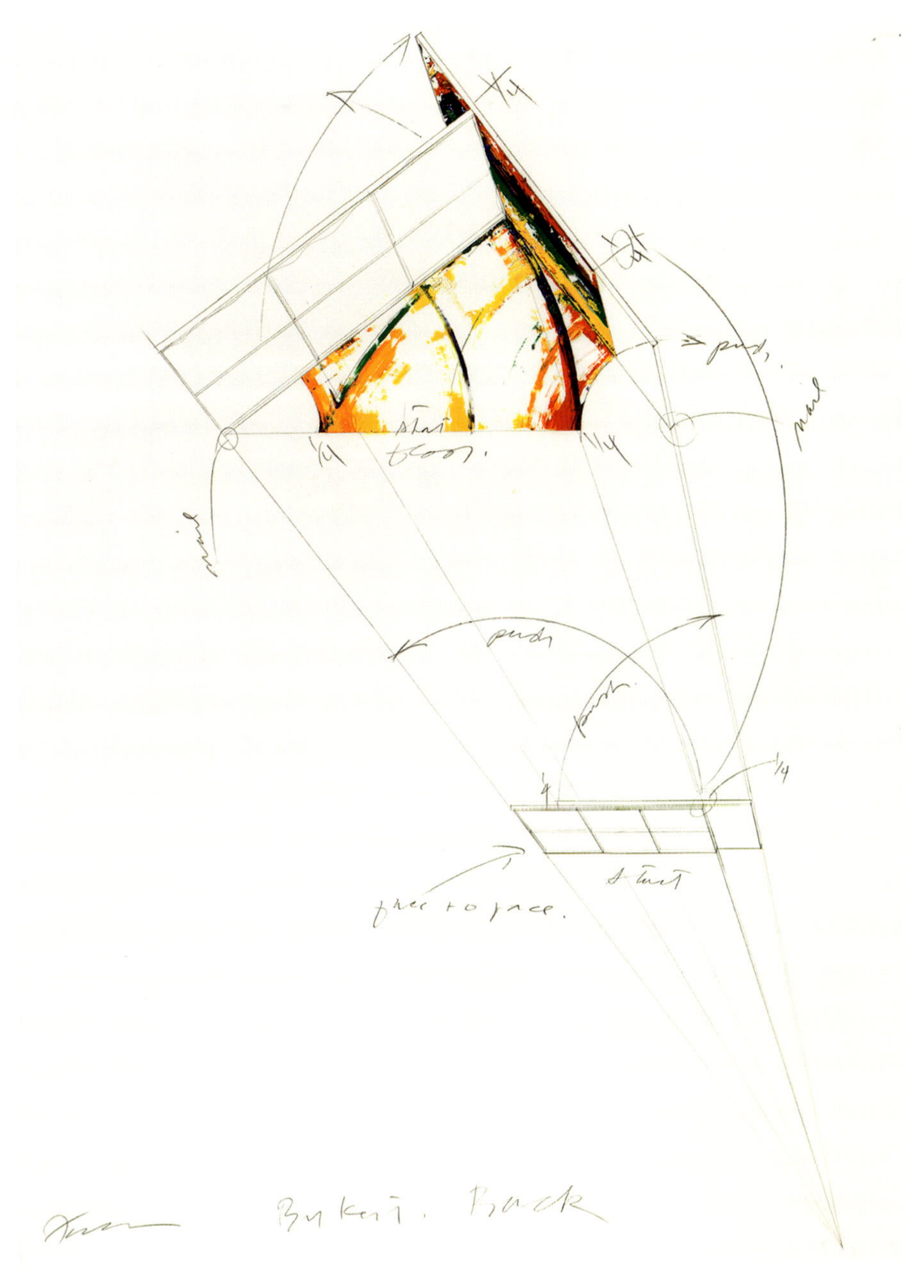

Project 1974, 1974
PLATE 13

Untitled, 1978
PLATE 14

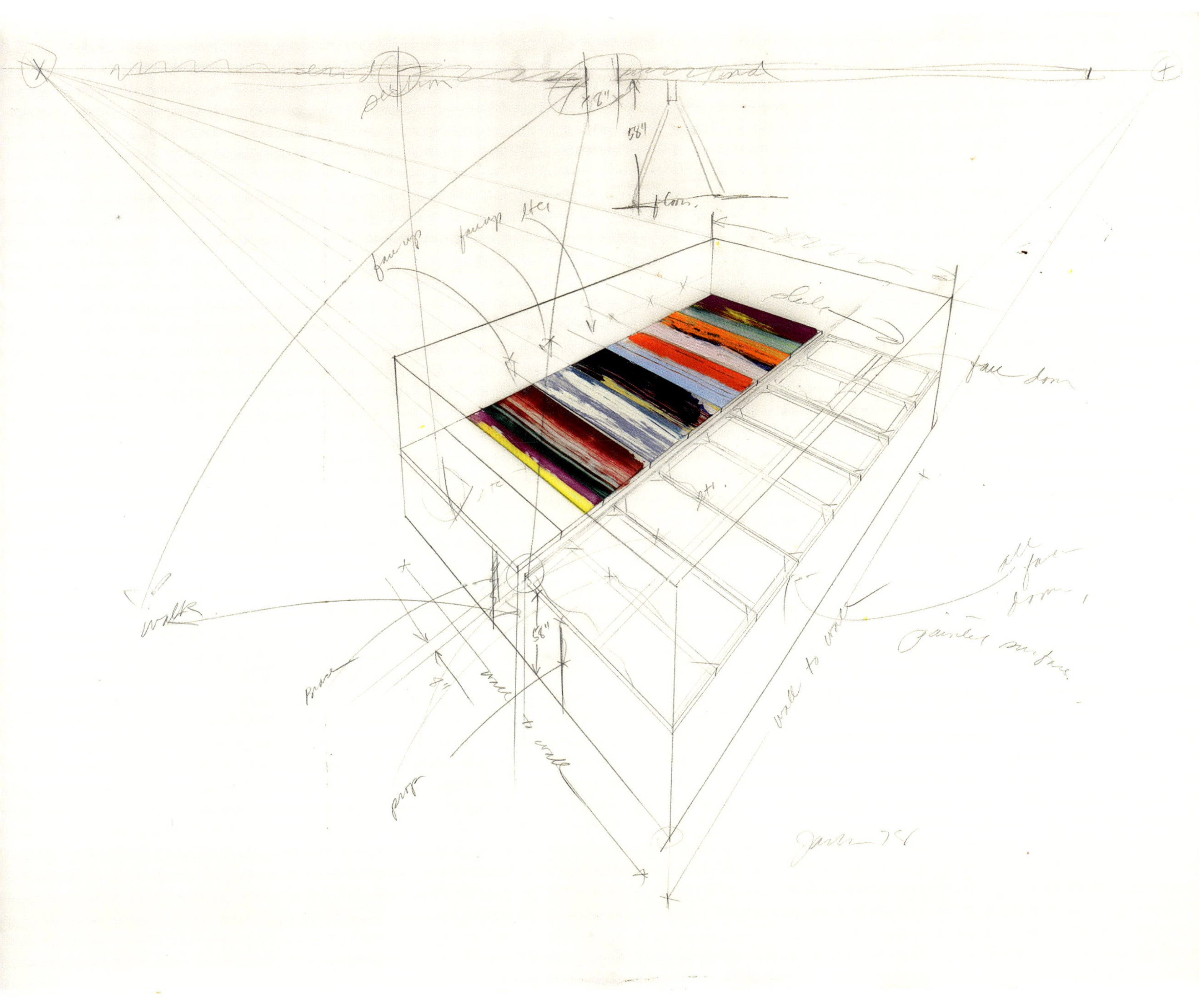

Untitled (Felsen Gallery), 1978
PLATE 15

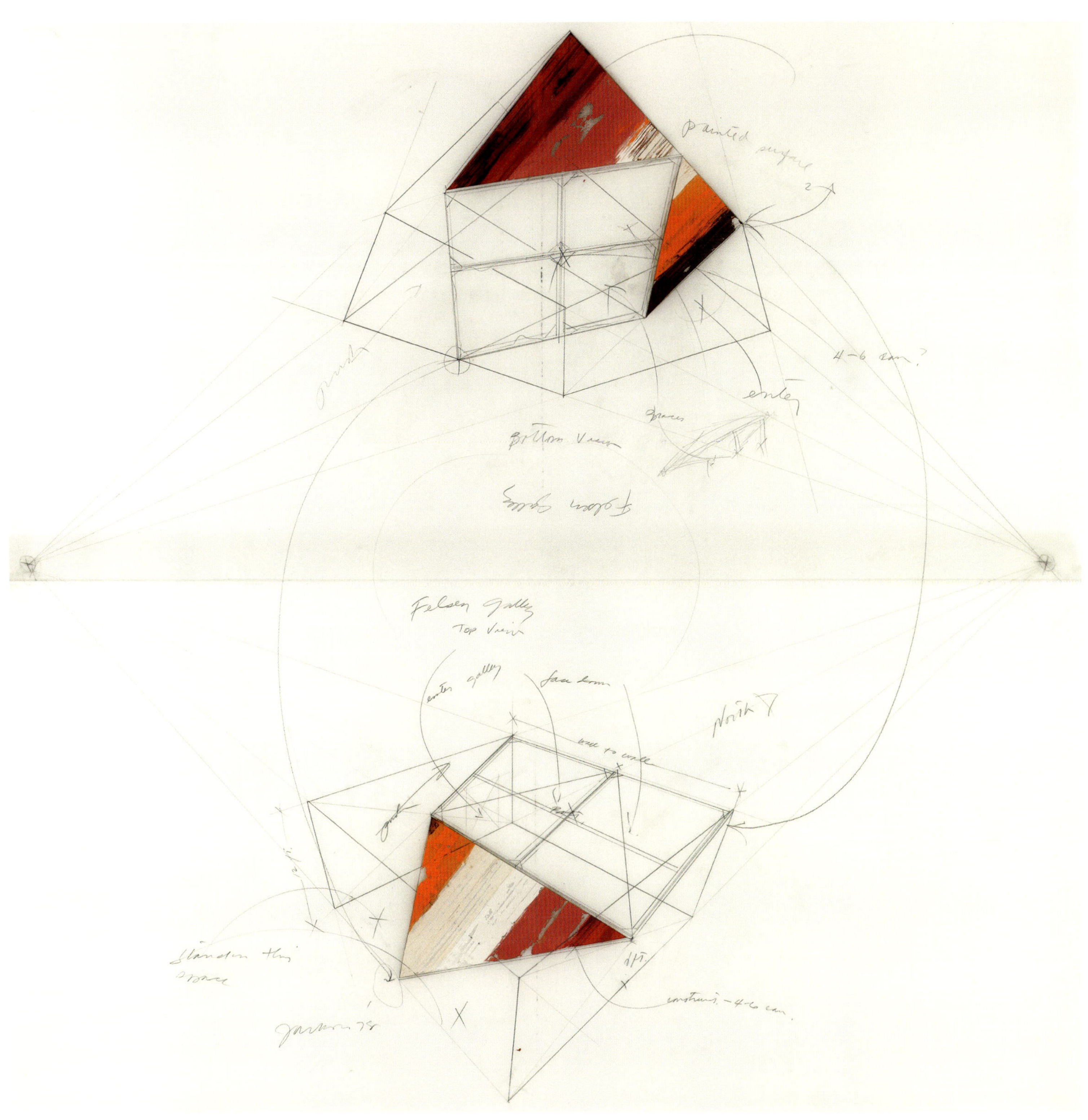
painted surface
4 - 6 cm ?
enter
Bottom View
Felsen Gallery
Felsen Gallery
Top View
enter gallery
face down
North
wall to wall
Slandered this
space
constant - 4-6 cm.

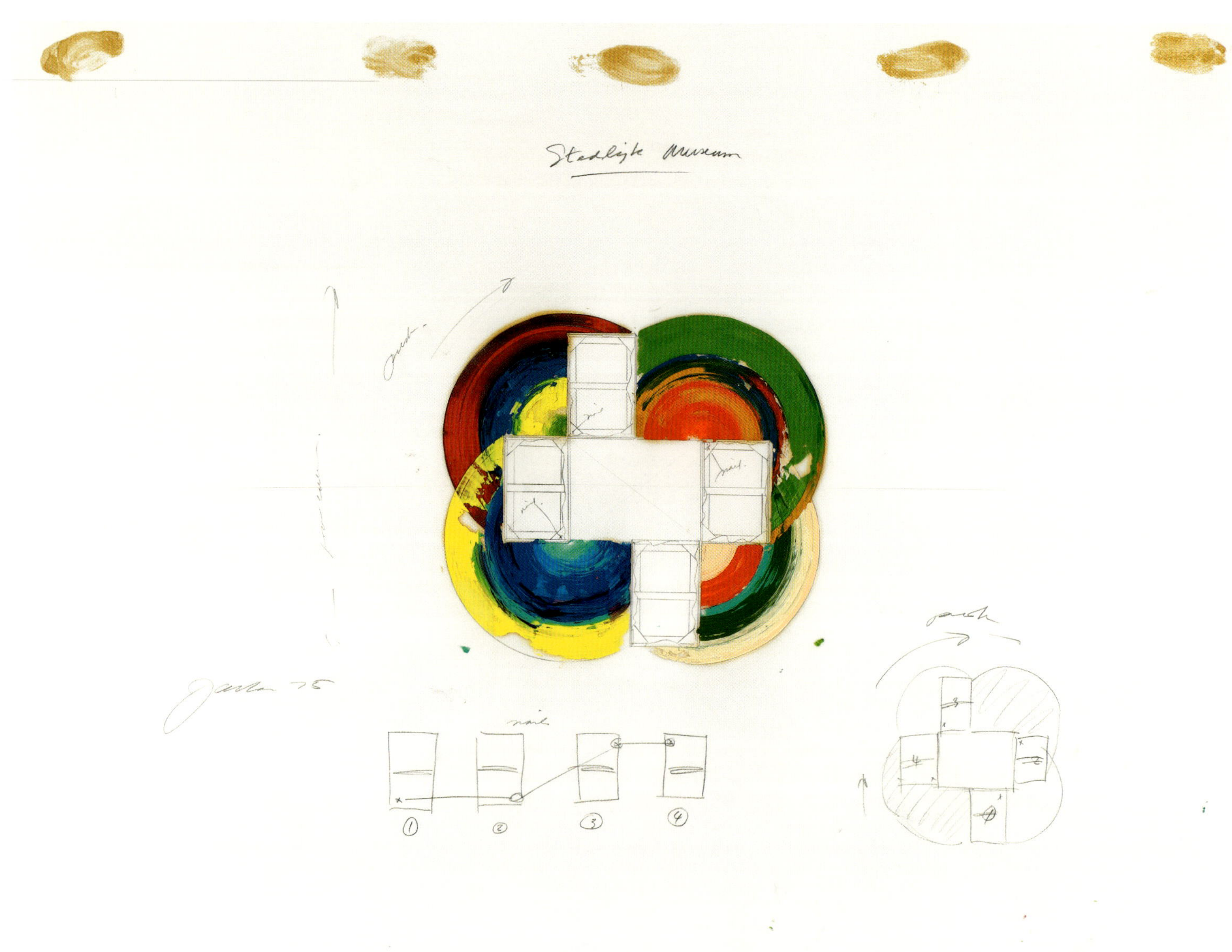

Stedlijk [sic] Museum, 1975

PLATE 16

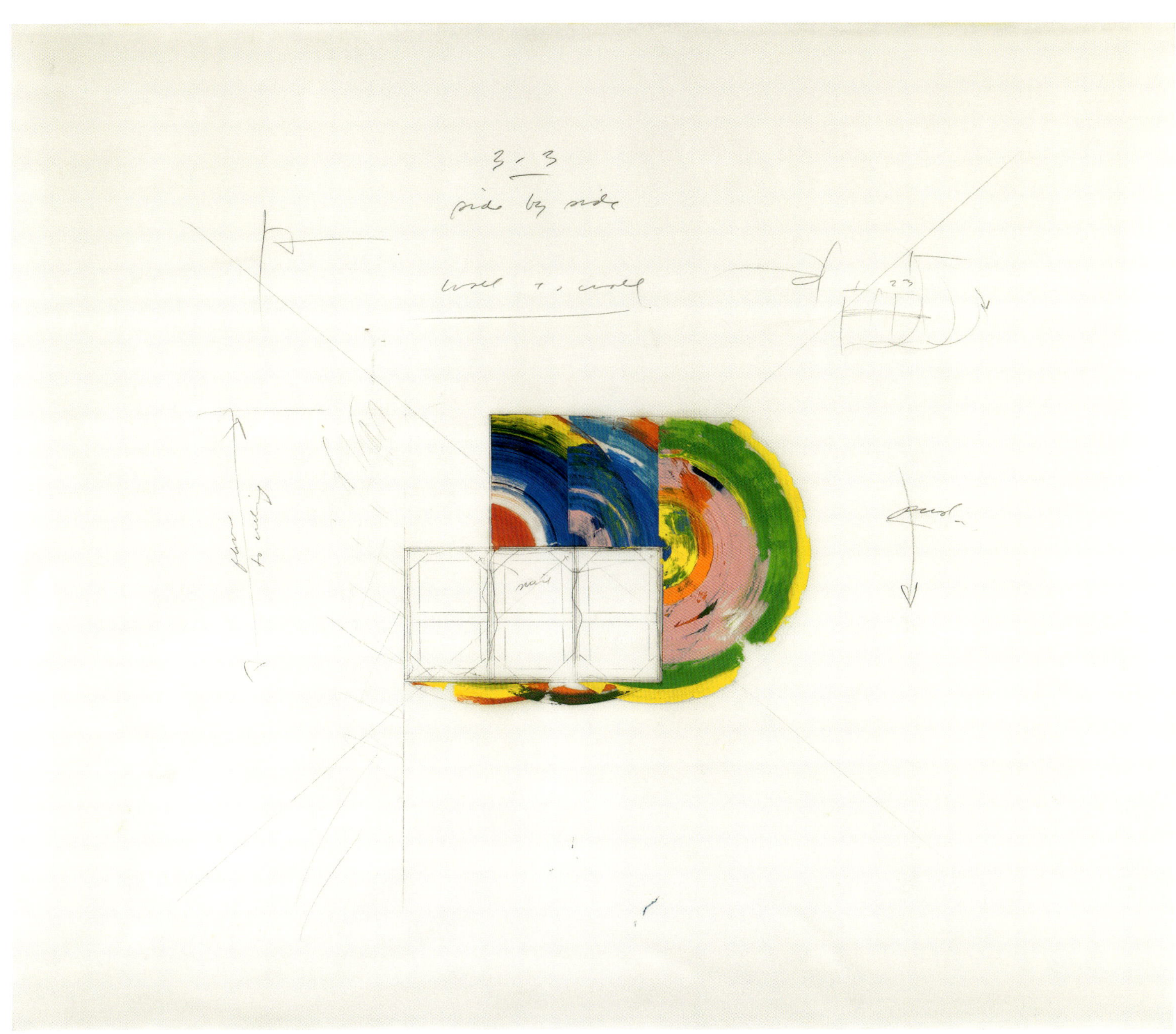

Untitled ("3-3 Side by Side"), 1975
PLATE 17

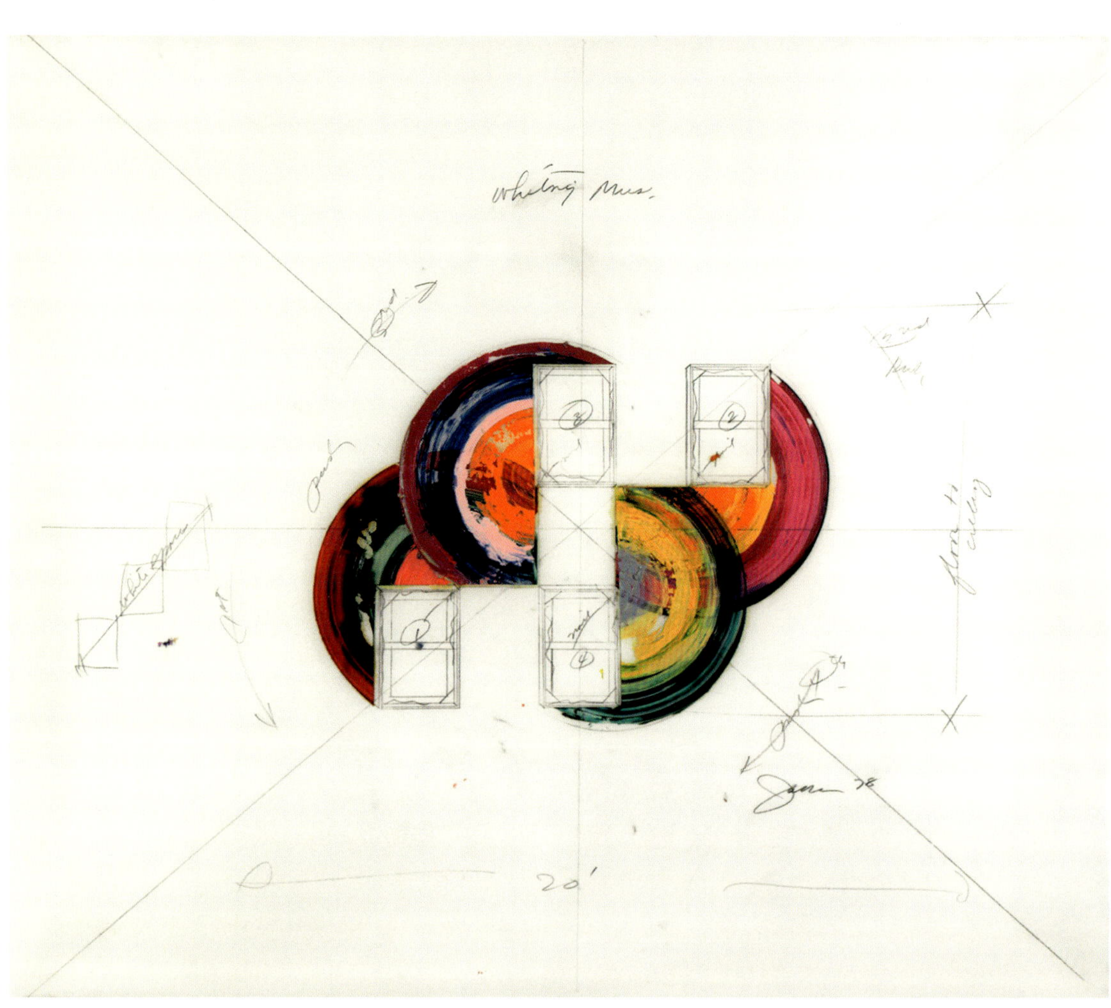

Untitled (Study for "Untitled Wall Painting"), 1978

(facing)
Big Ideals, 1979

Big Idea
wall to wall
floor to ceiling
Touching corner
of room.
paint walls floor ceiling etc.
[signature] 75

Planskizze für Installation
(Sketch for Installation), 1979
PLATE 20

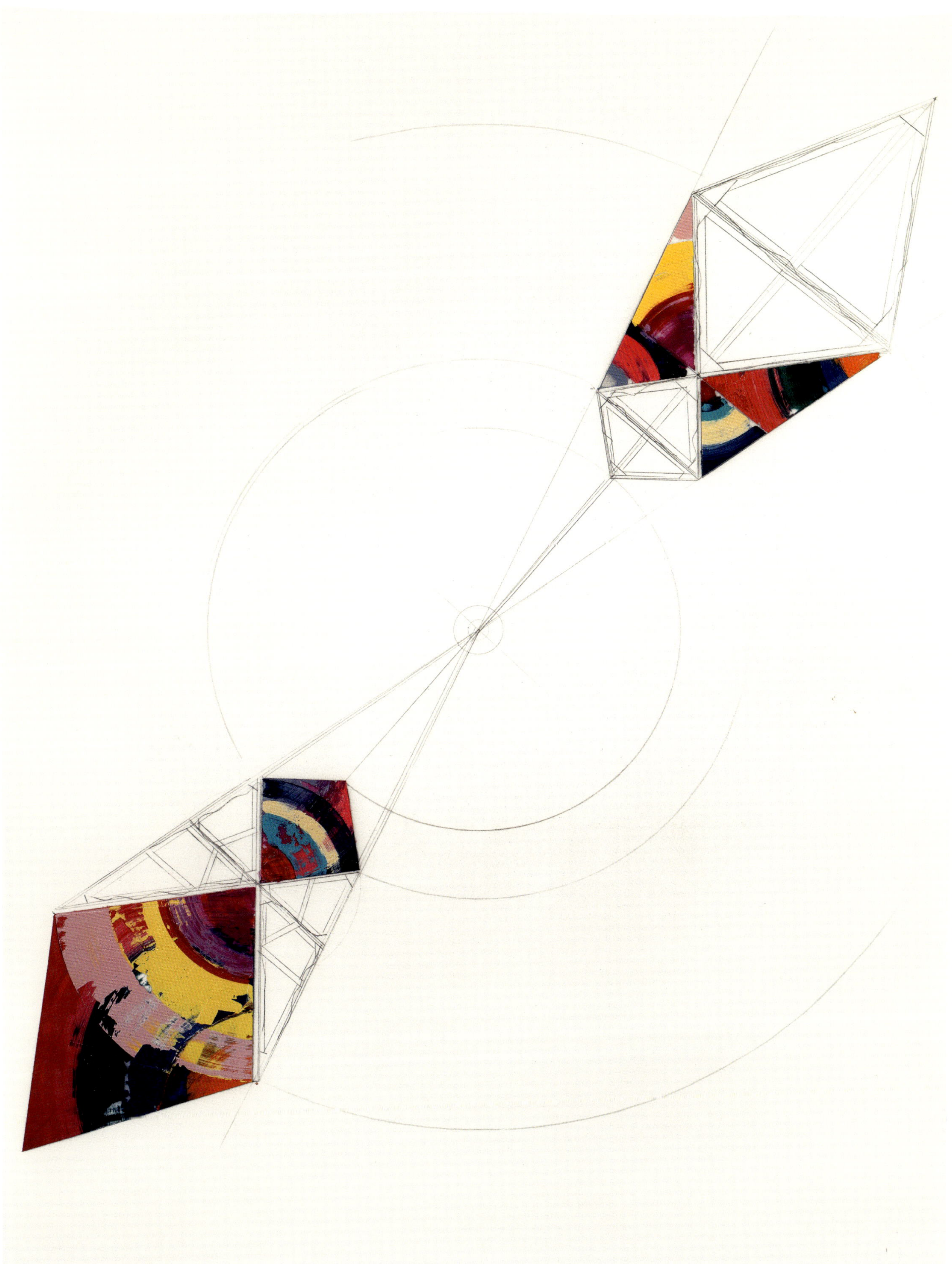

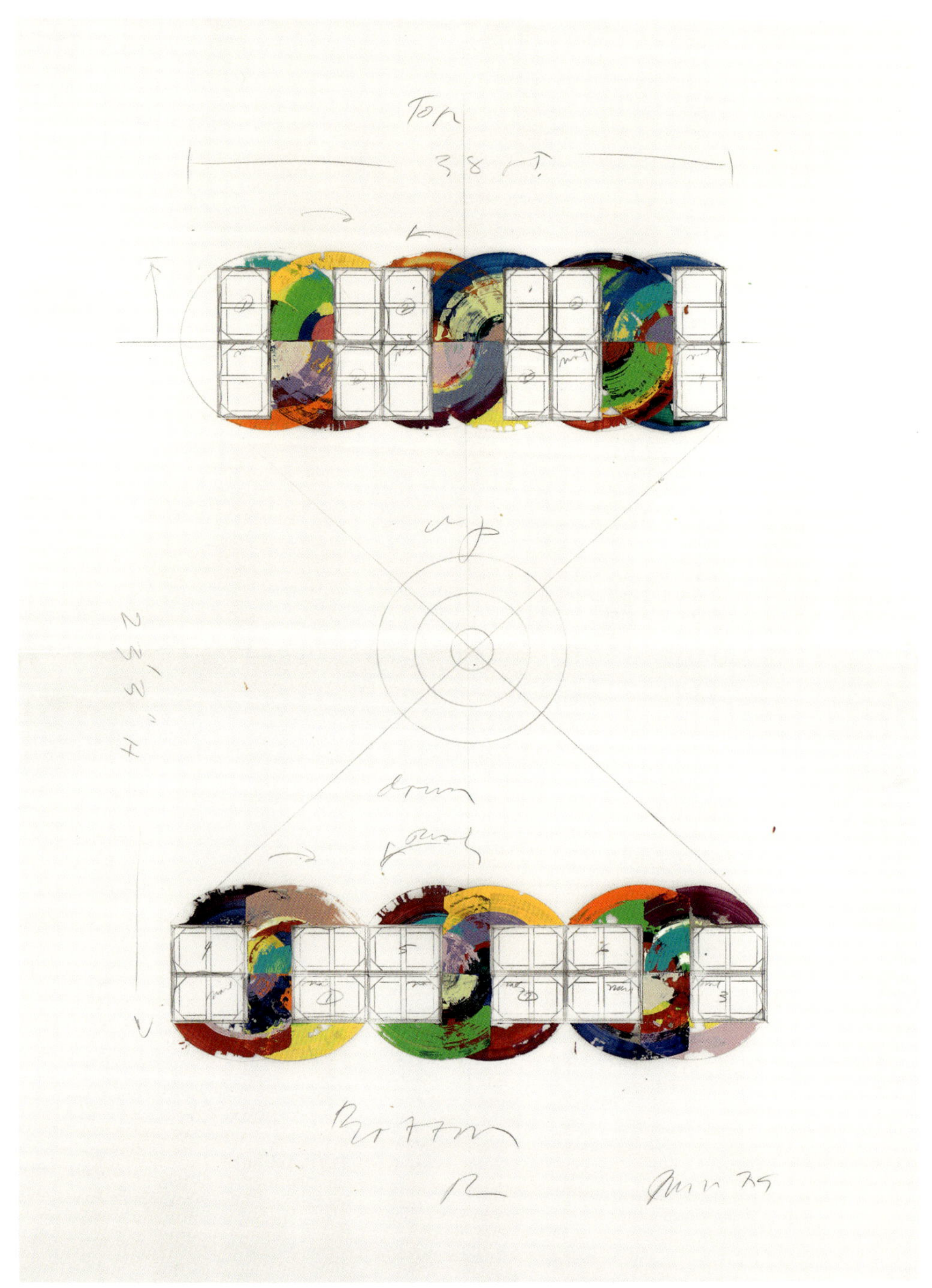

Untitled, 1979
PLATE 21

(facing)
P.S. 1.1.2., 1985
PLATE 22

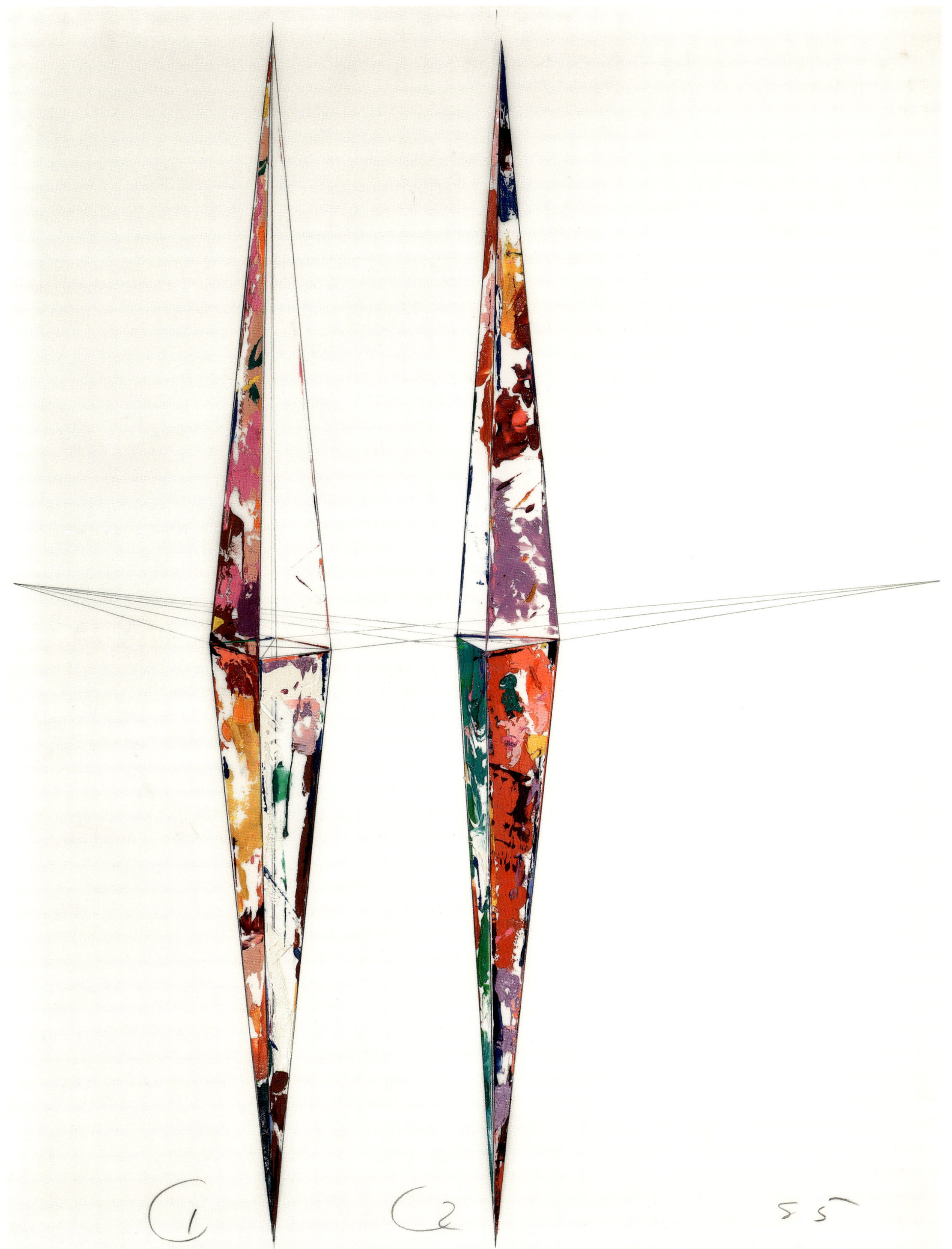
1
2
55

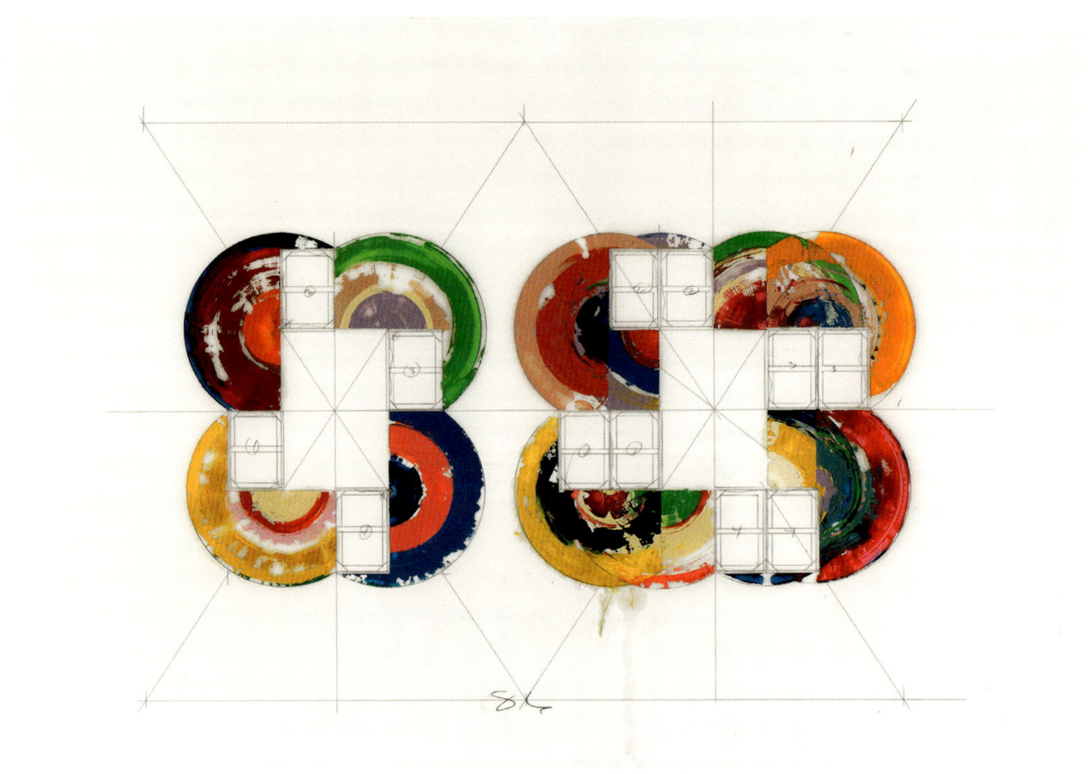

Untitled (Study for Wall Painting), 1986

(facing)
**Untitled (Study for "Painting with Two
Balls"),** 1986

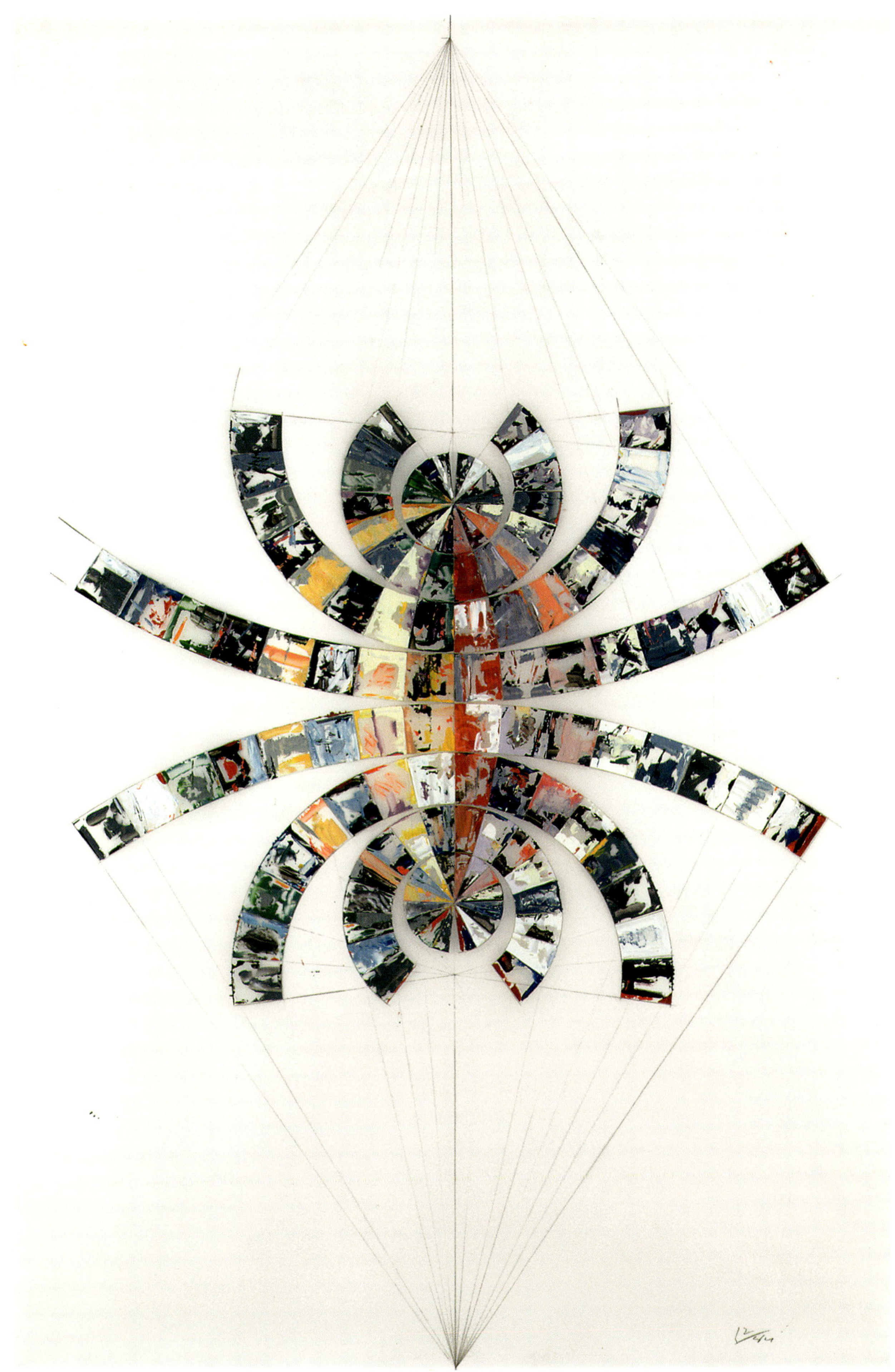

Big Ordeals (Project Drawing 2), 1986
PLATE 25

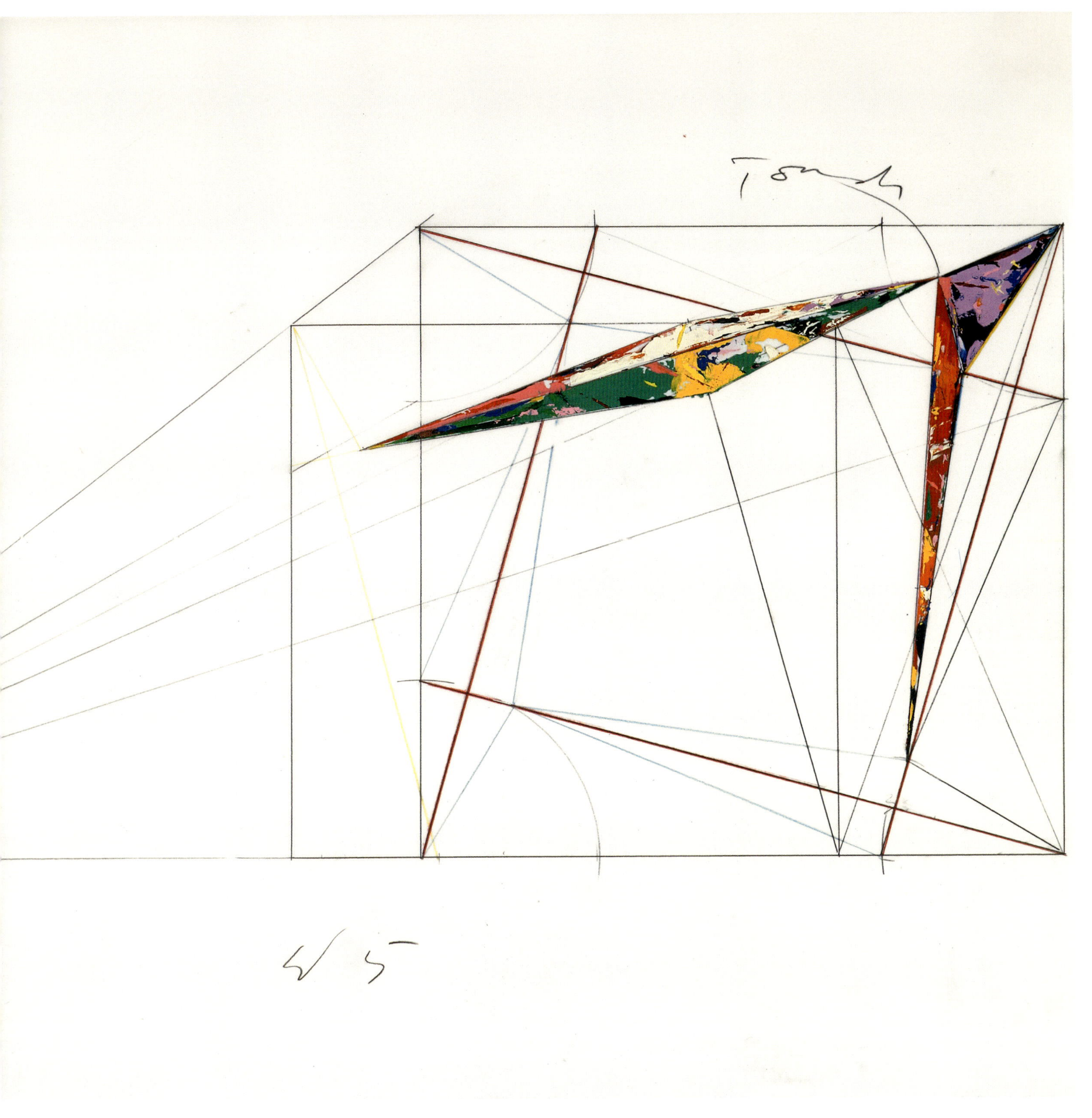

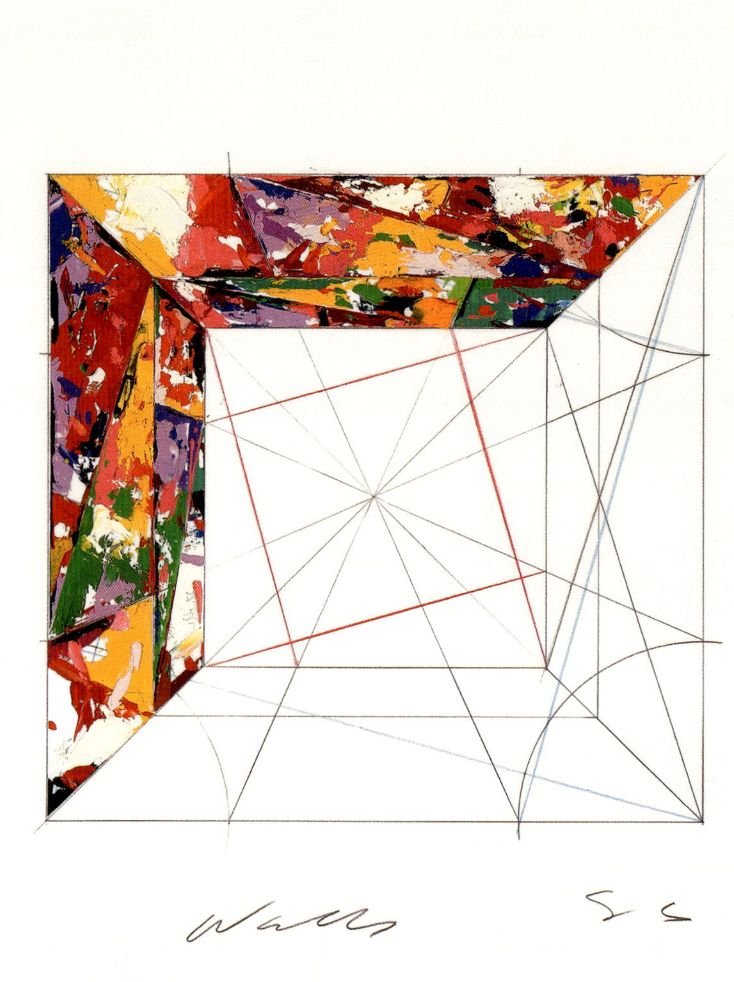

Big Ordeals (Project Drawing 3), 1986
PLATE 26

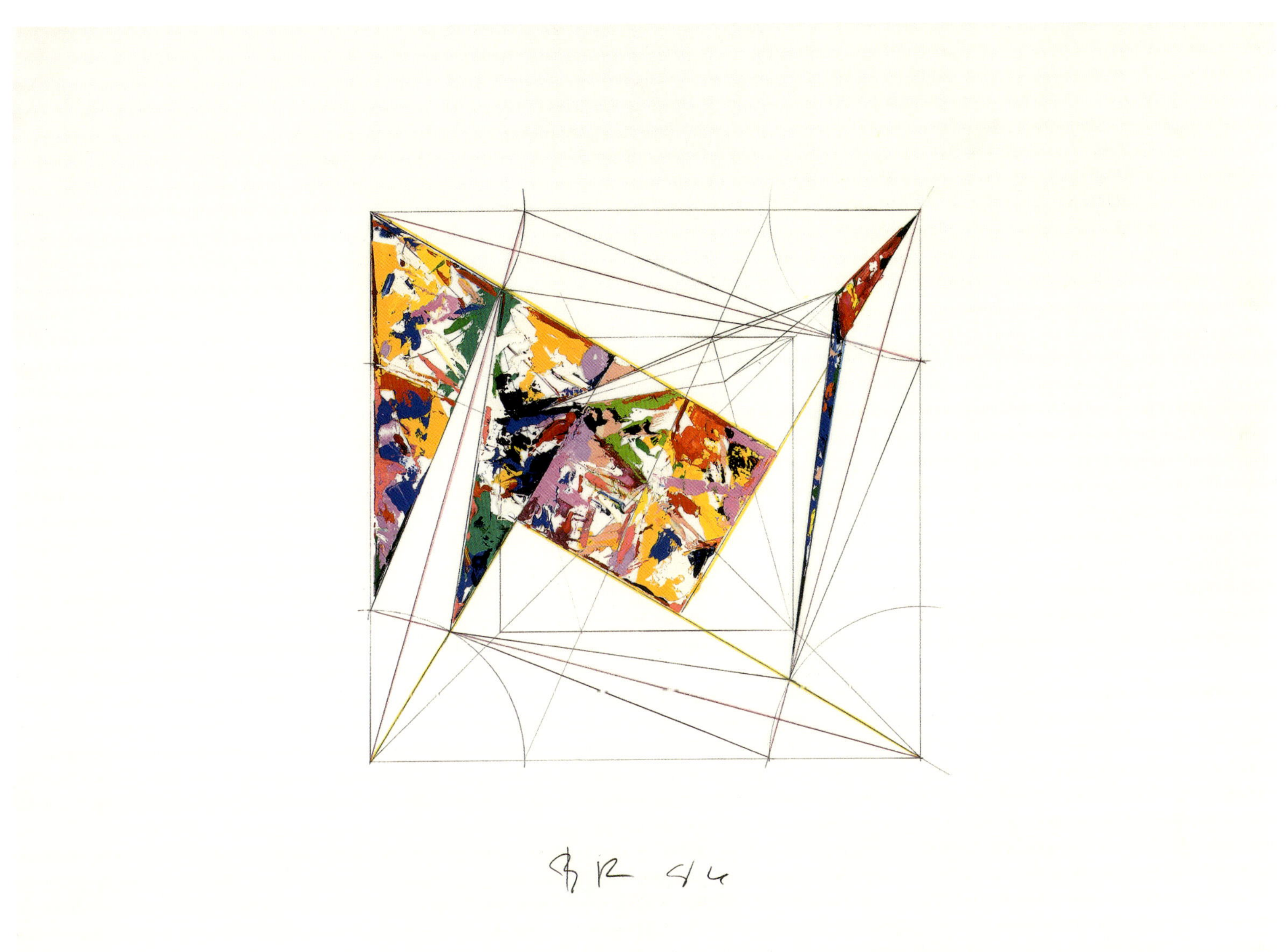

Big Ordeals (Project Drawing 4), 1986

PLATE 27

Untitled, 1987
PLATE 28

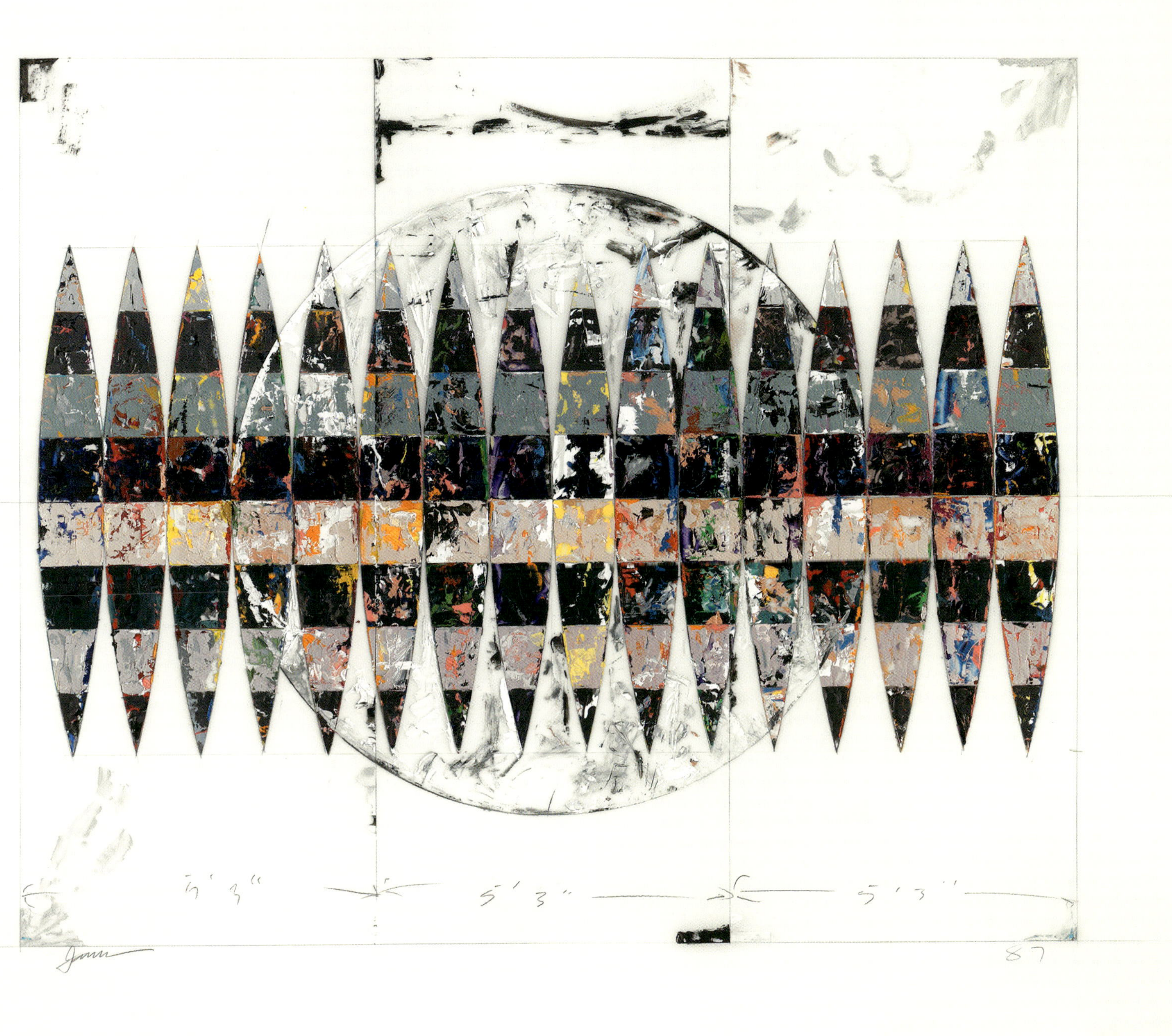

Wall Painting, 2012
PLATE 29

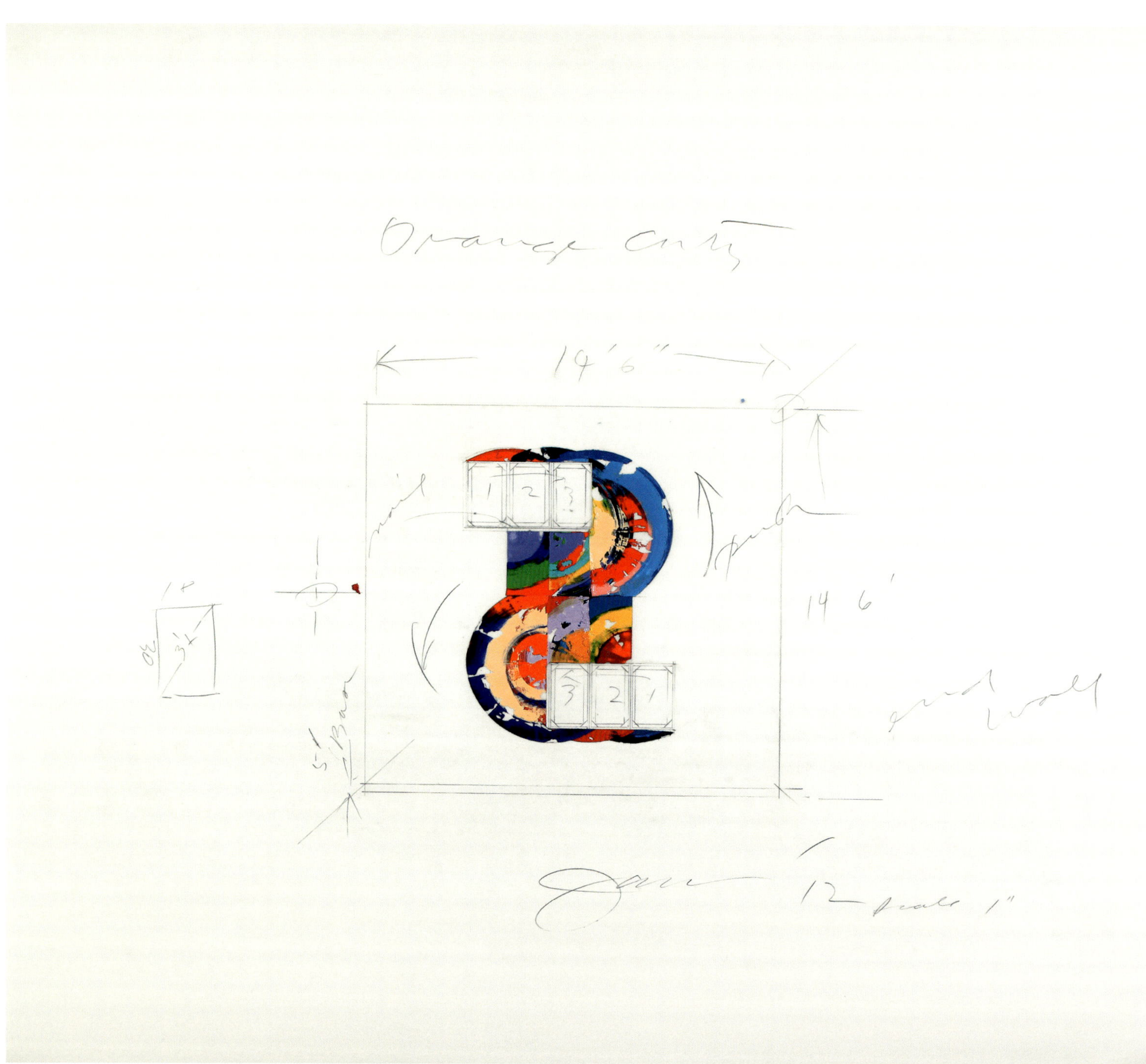

Untitled (Project for Orange County), 2012

PLATE 30

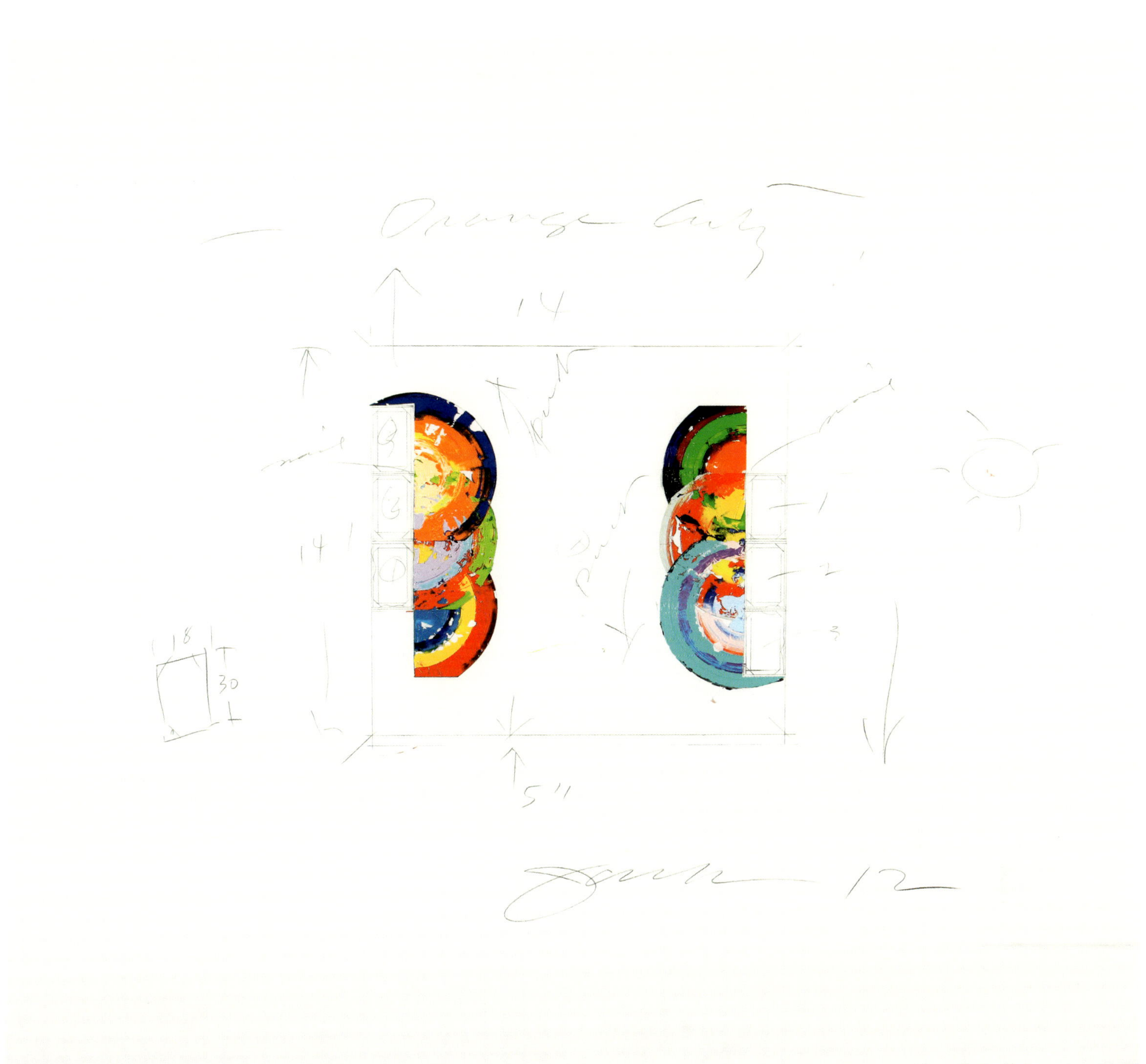

**Untitled (Project for Orange
County)**, 2012
PLATE 31

Untitled (Project for Orange
County), 2012
PLATE 32

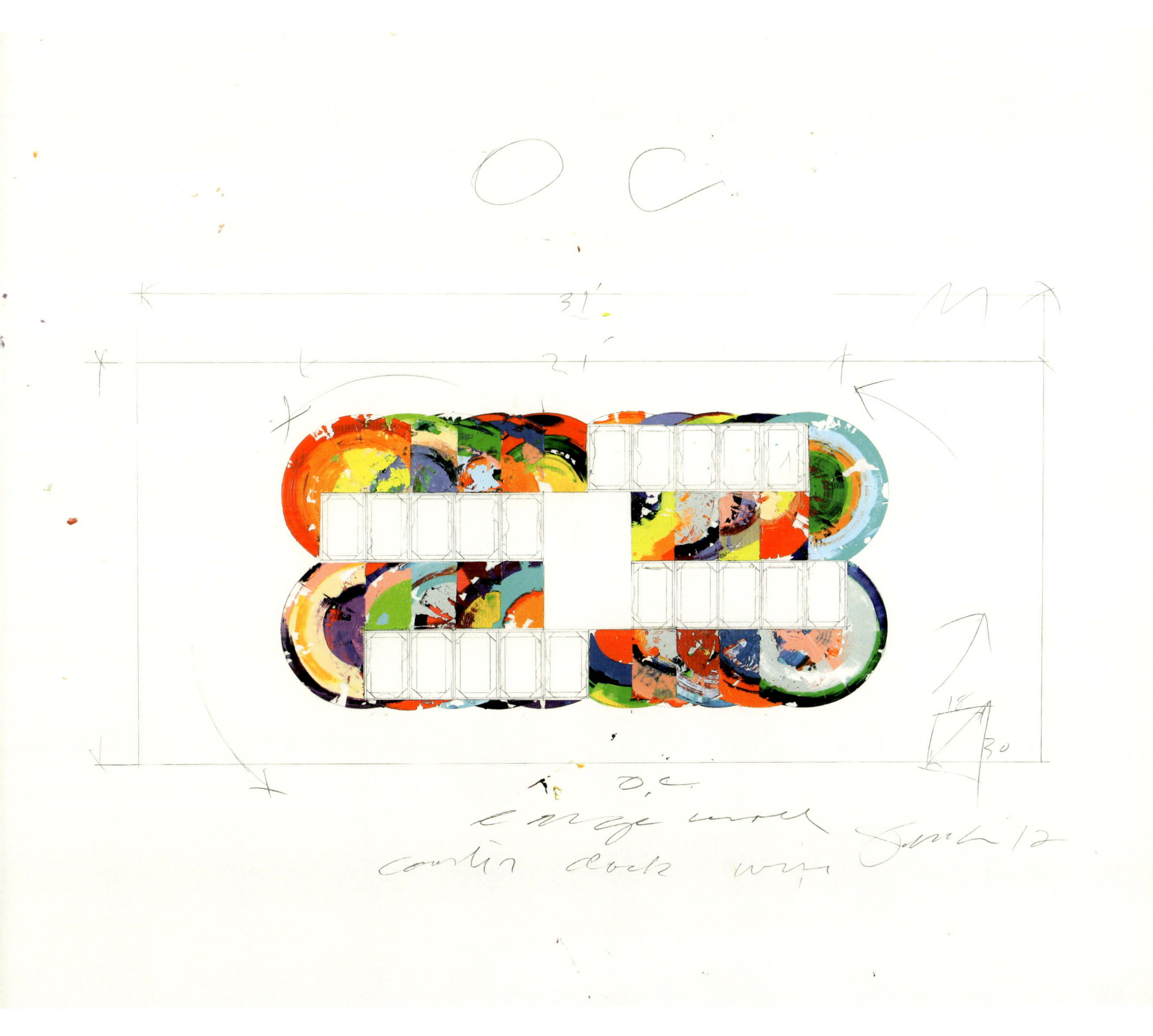

STACKED PAINTINGS

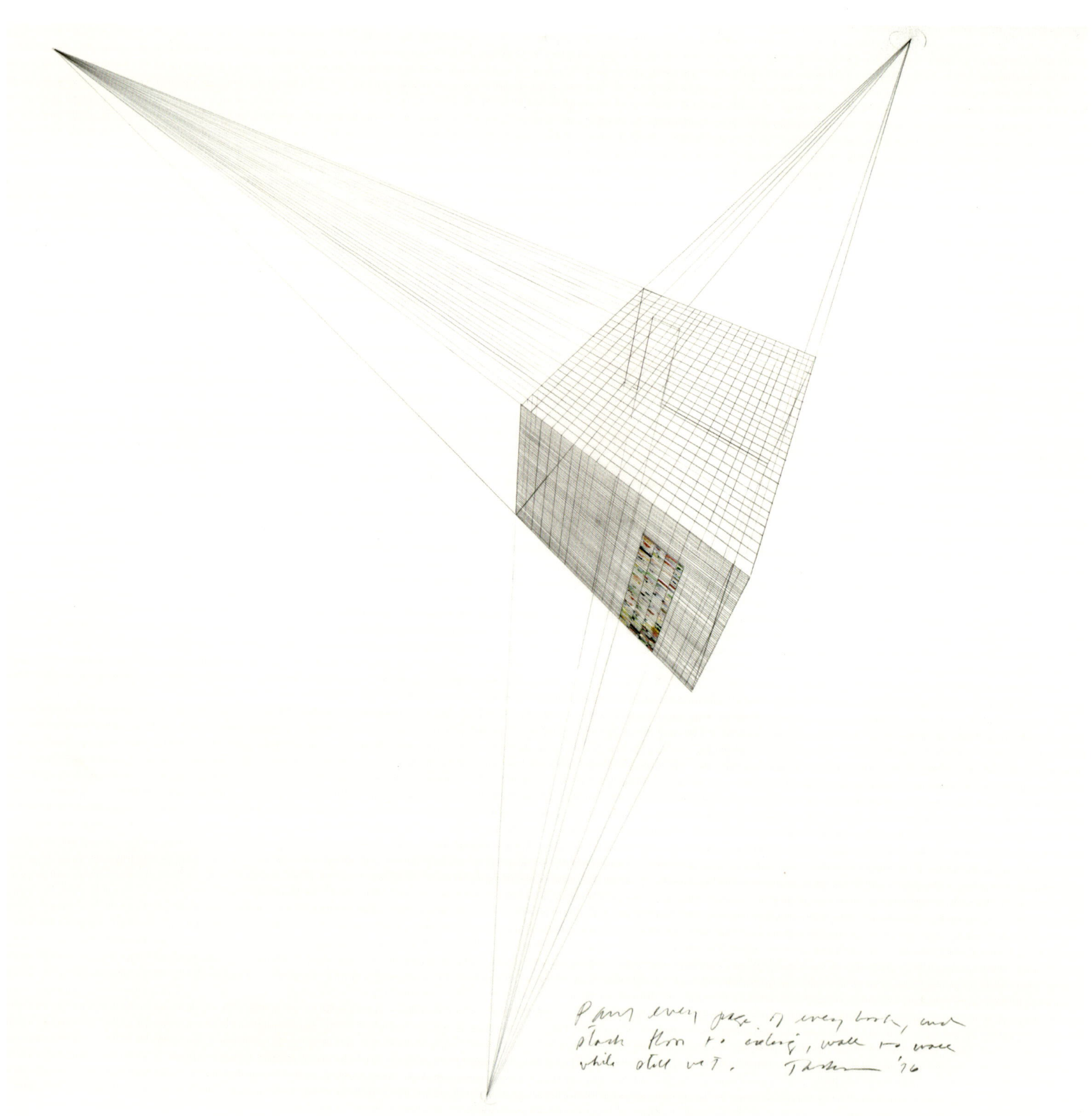

Untitled ("Paint every page..."), 1976

PLATE 33

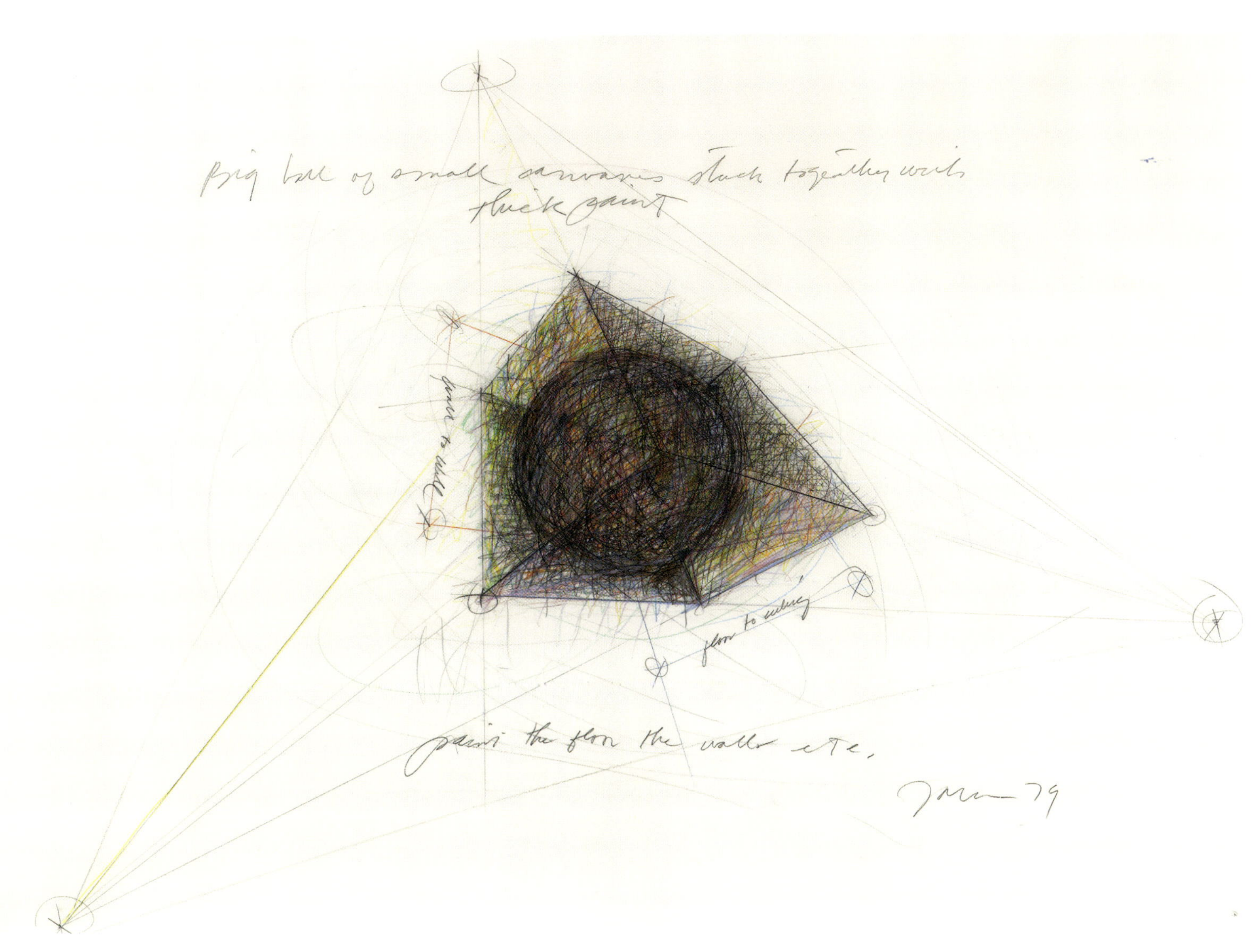

**Big ball of small canvases stuck
together with thick paint,** 1979

PLATE 34

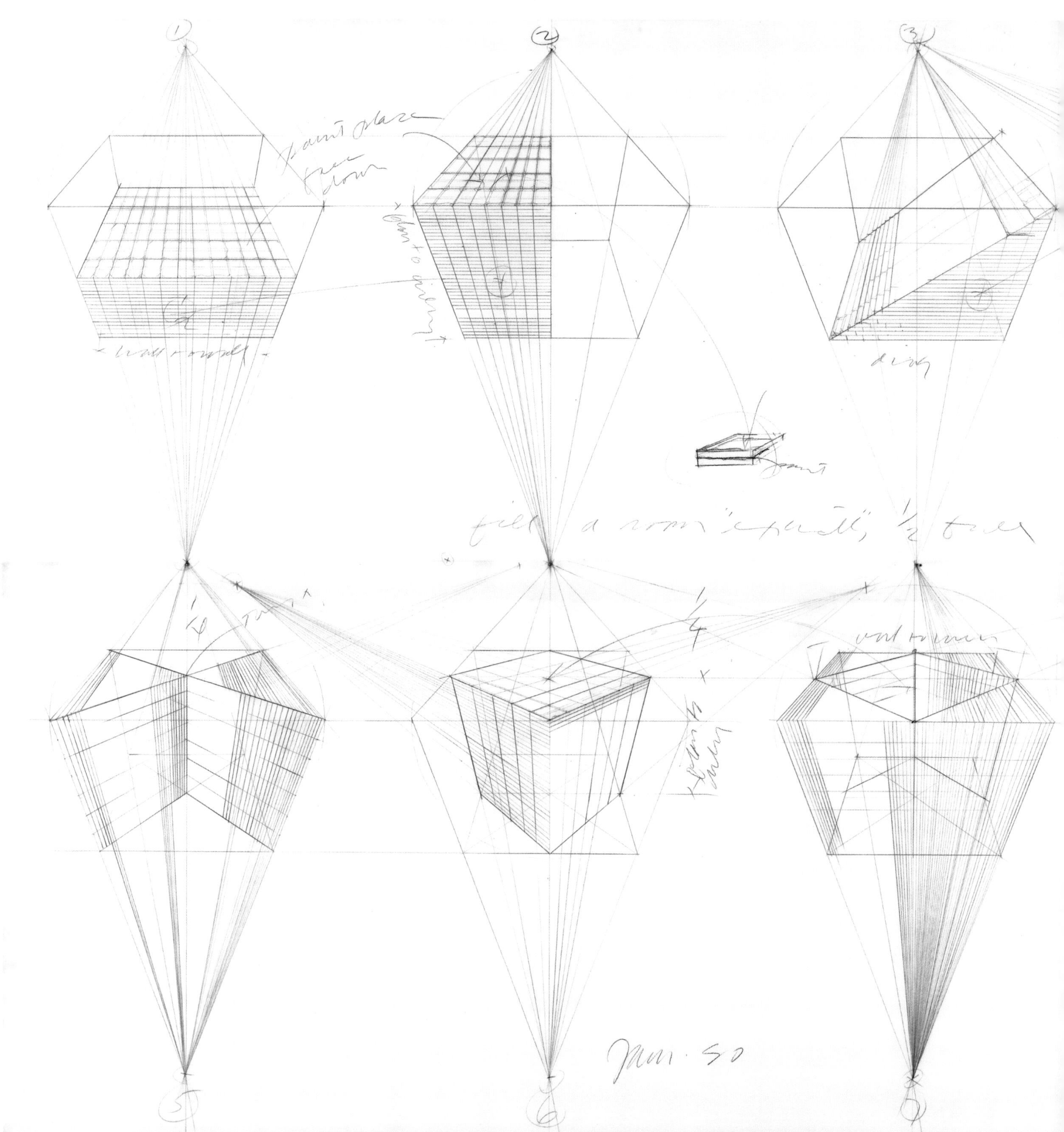

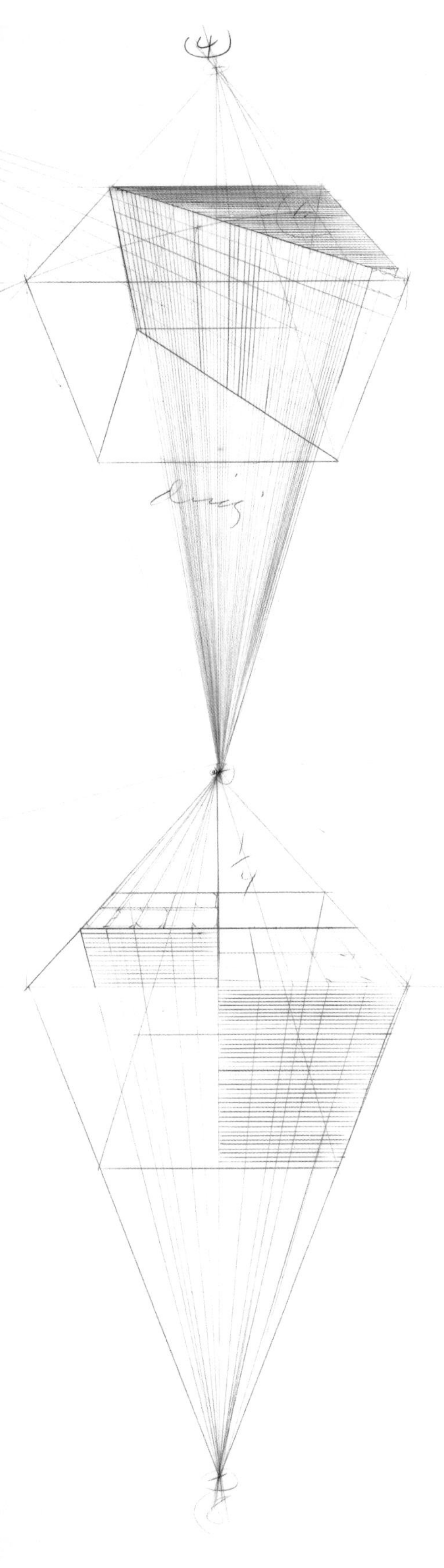

Eight Projects for Filling a
Room, ca. 1979
PLATE 35

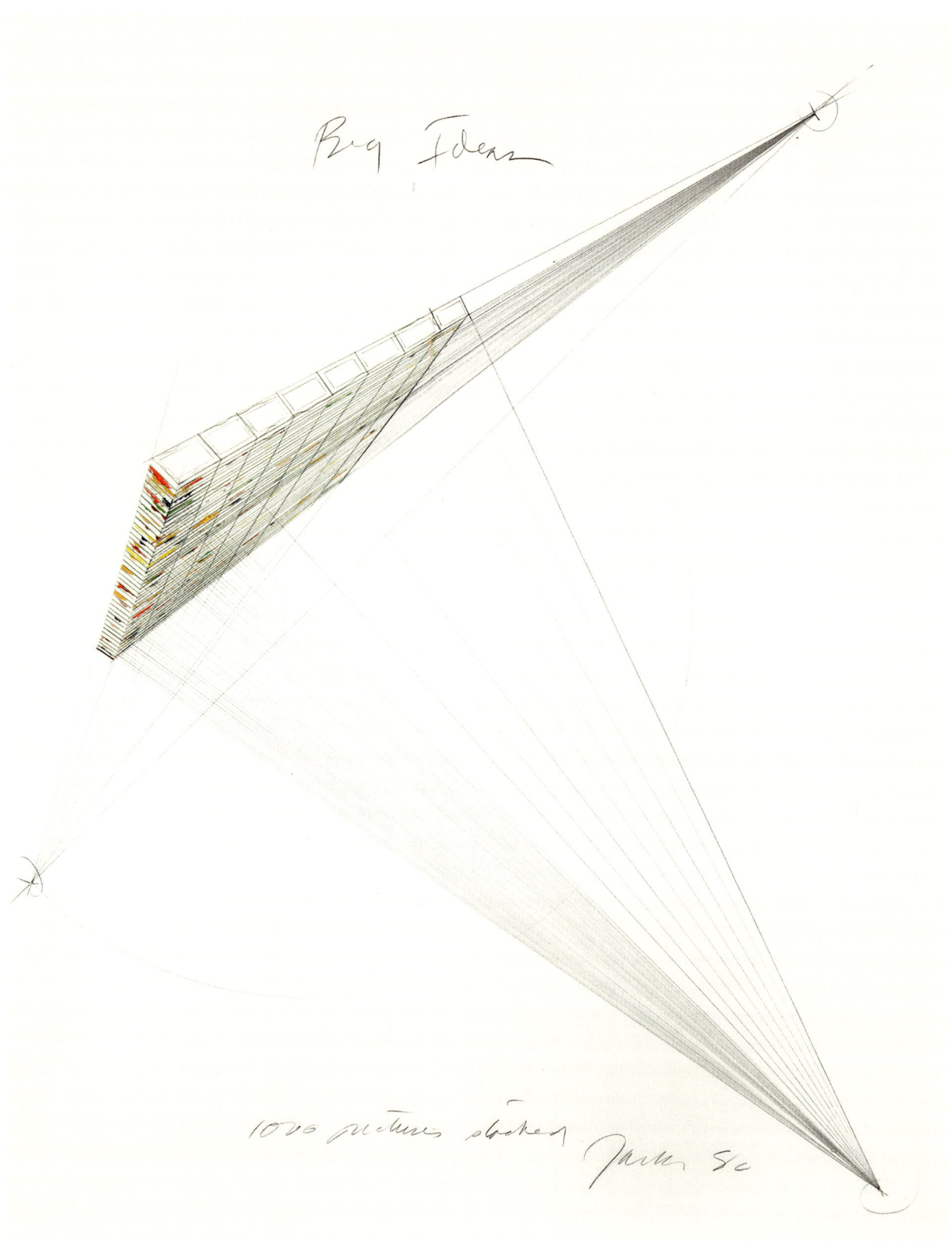

**Project Drawing for "Big Ideas—
1000 Pictures,"** 1980

PLATE 36

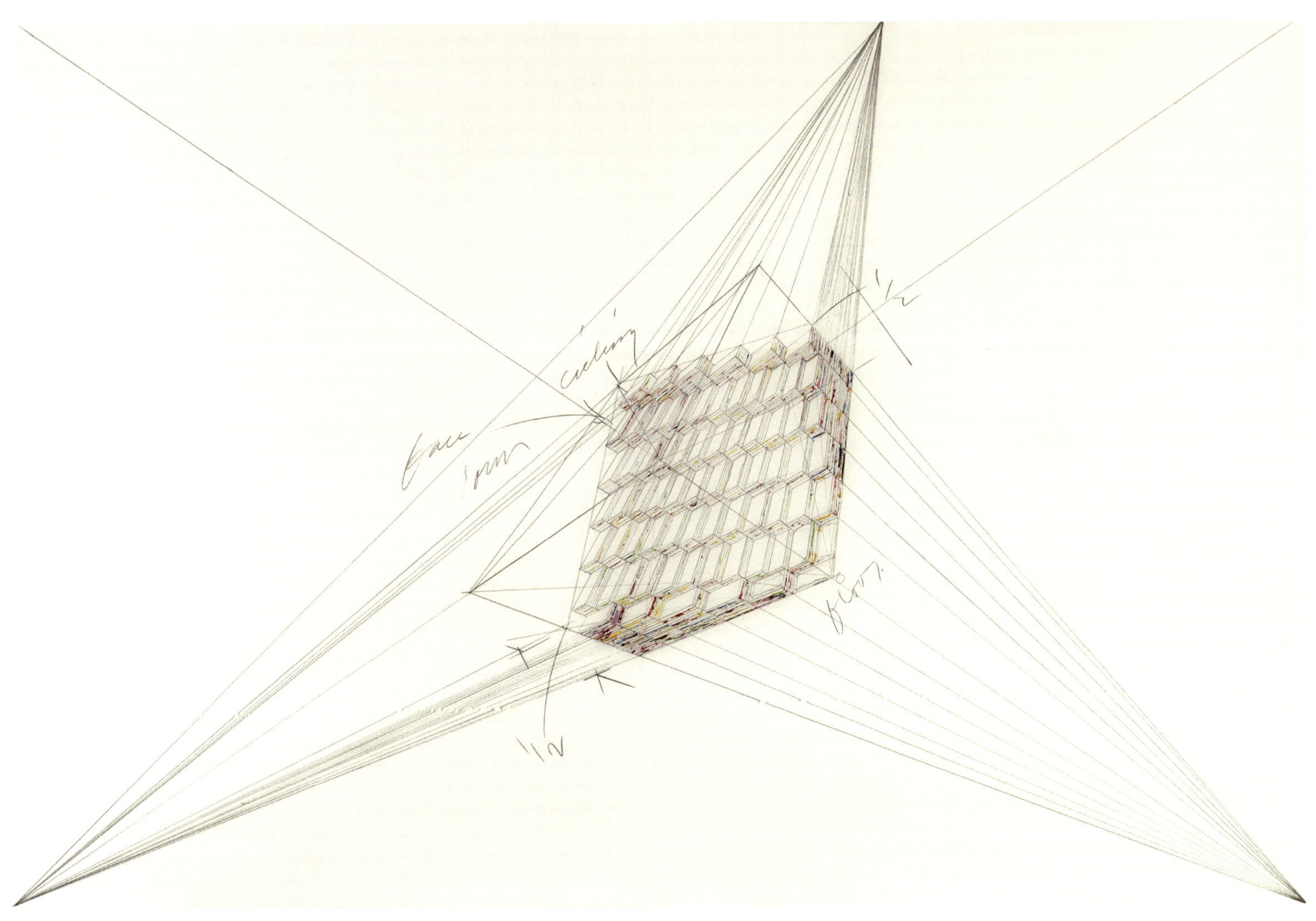

Untitled, ca. 1980
PLATE 37

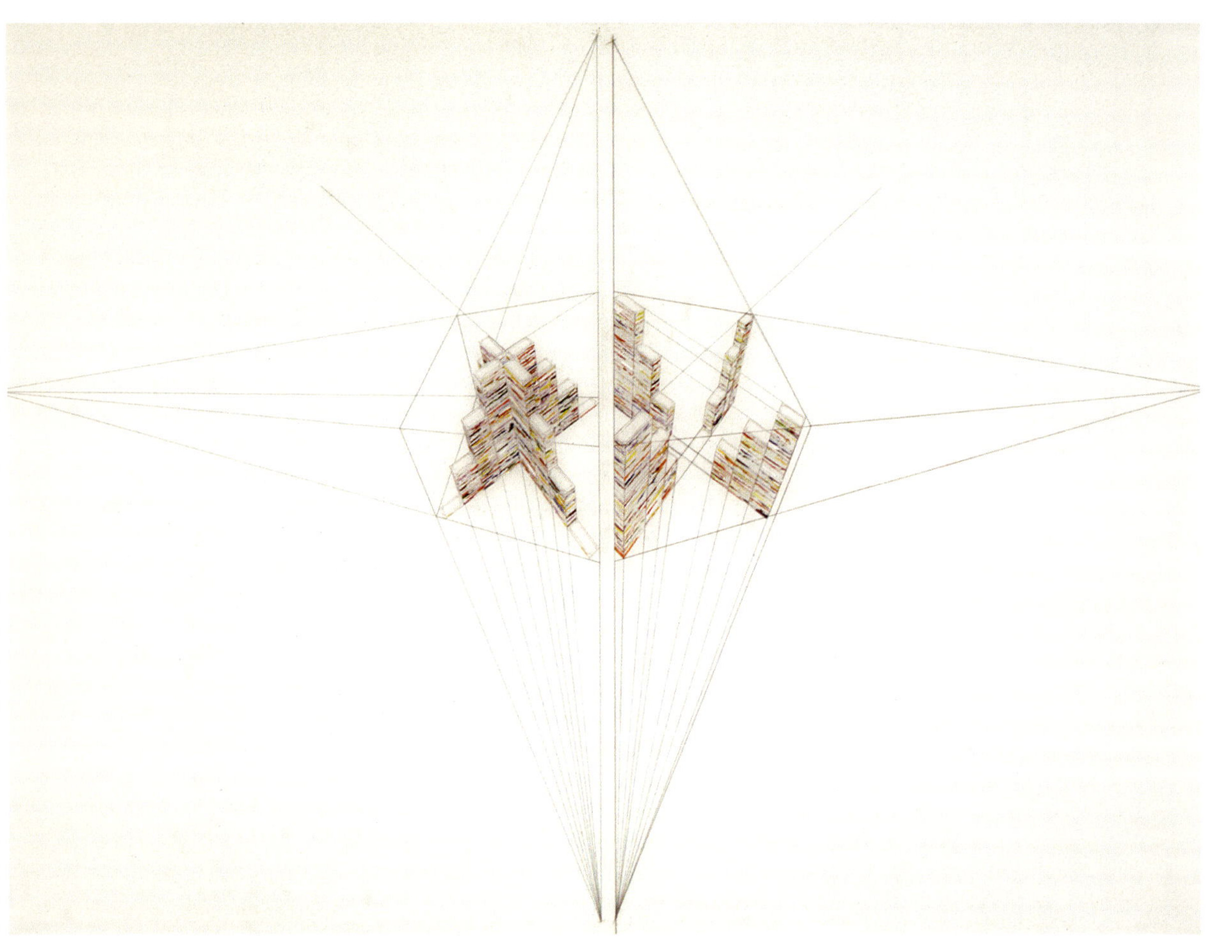

Untitled, ca. 1980
PLATE 38

(facing)
Untitled (Study I for "5050 Stacked Paintings"), ca. 1980–81
PLATE 39

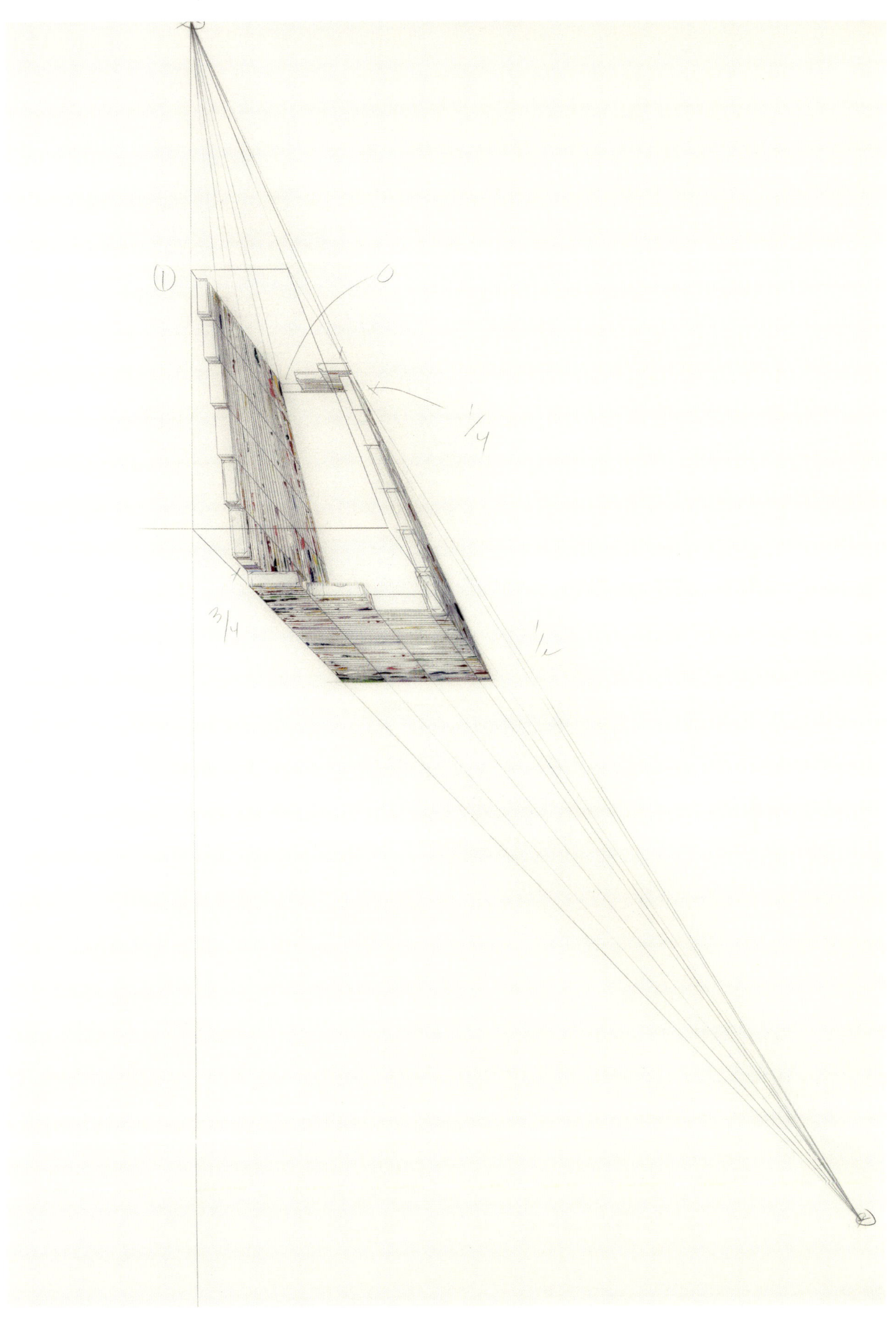

1
0
1/4
3/4
1/2

Fill a Room 1/2 Full III, 1981
PLATE 40

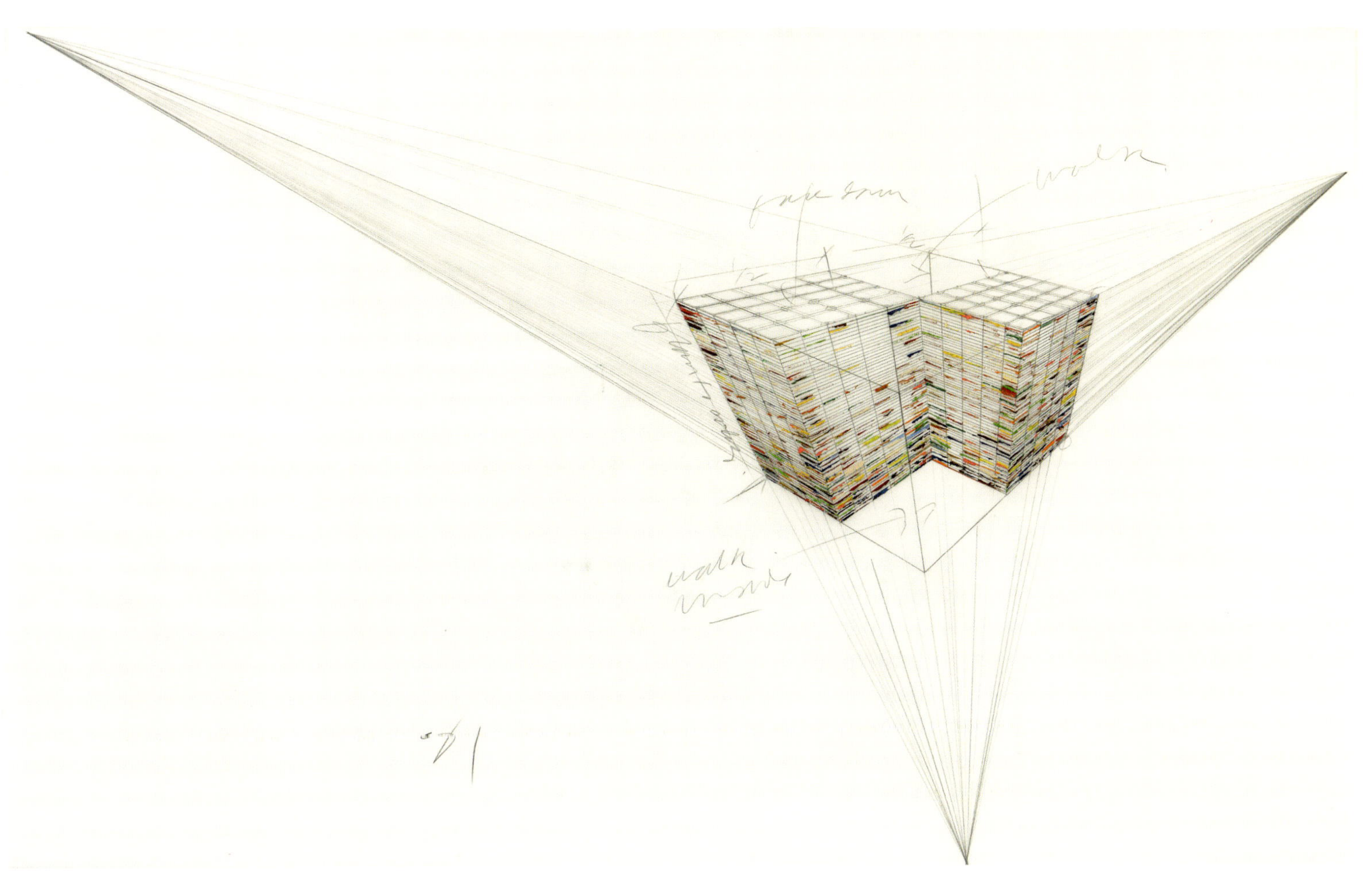

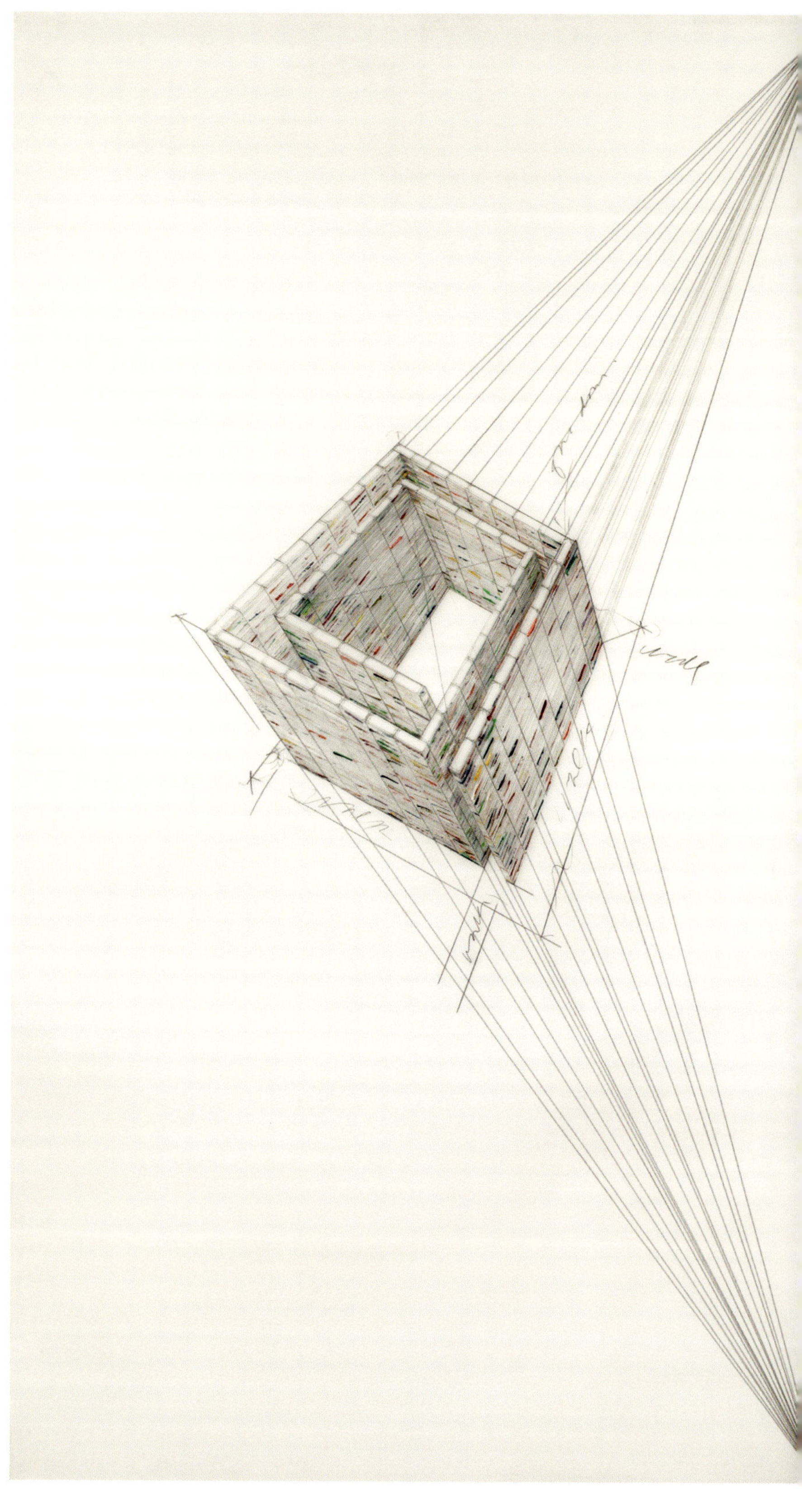

Untitled, 1983
PLATE 41

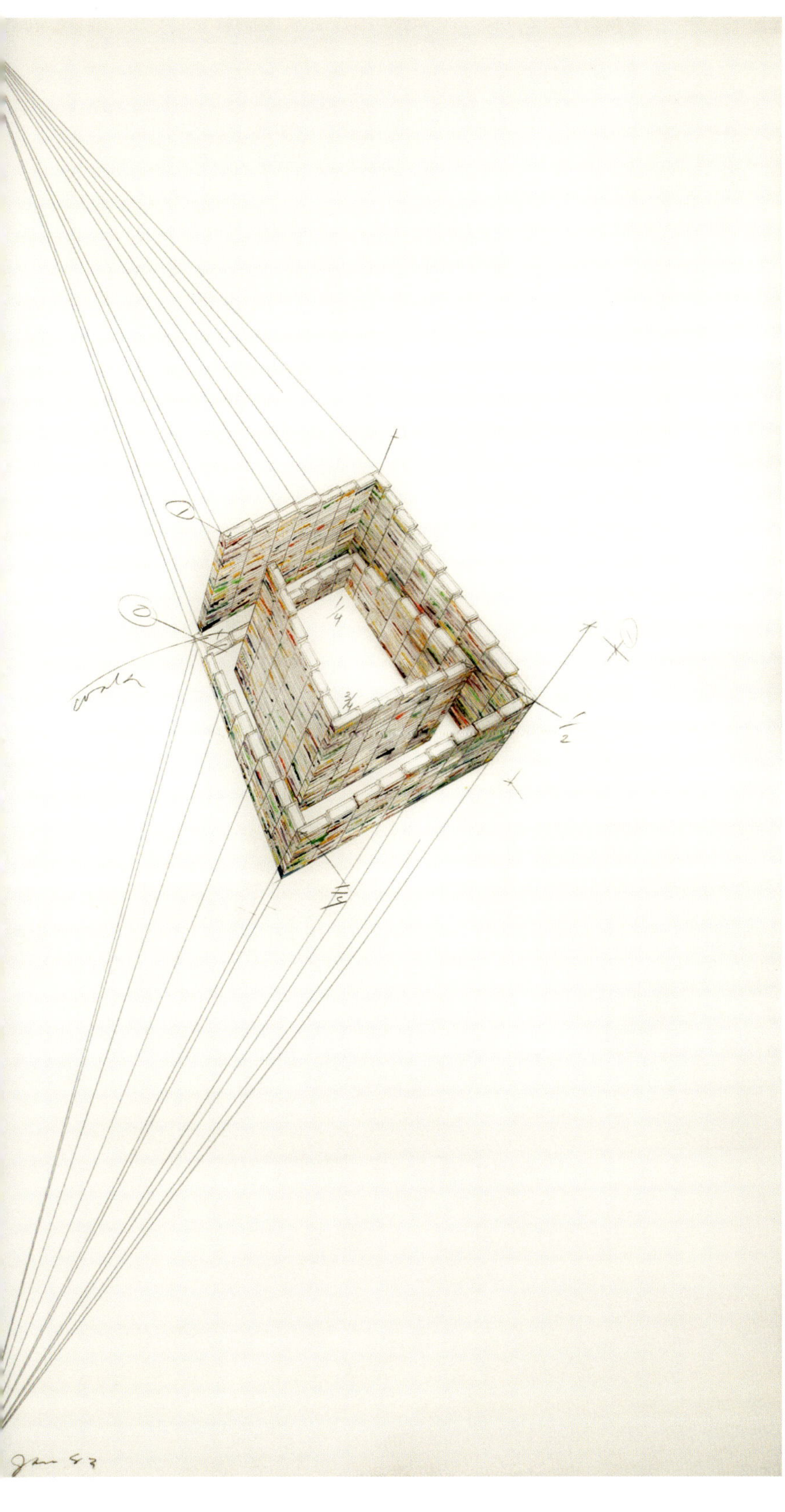

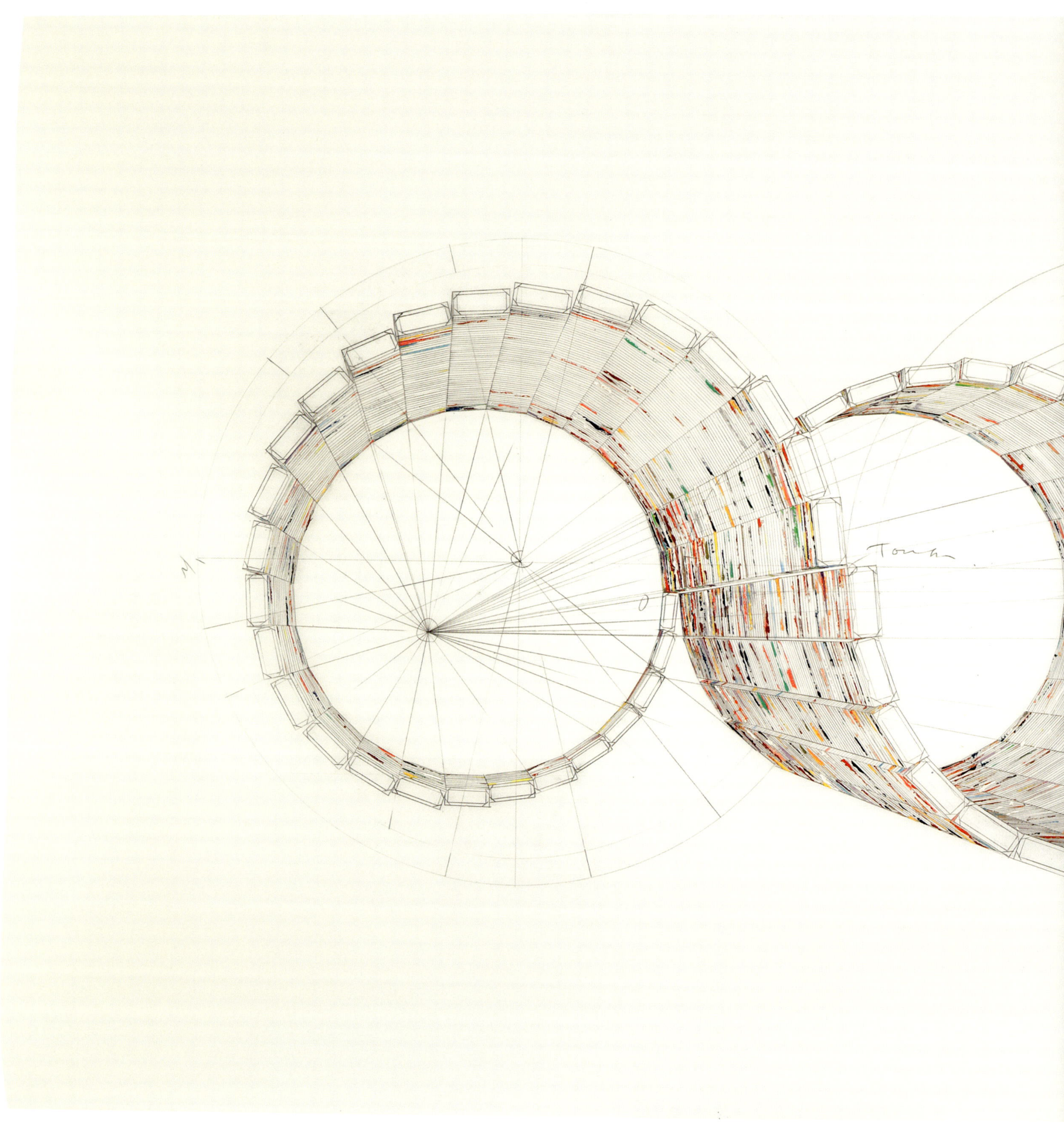

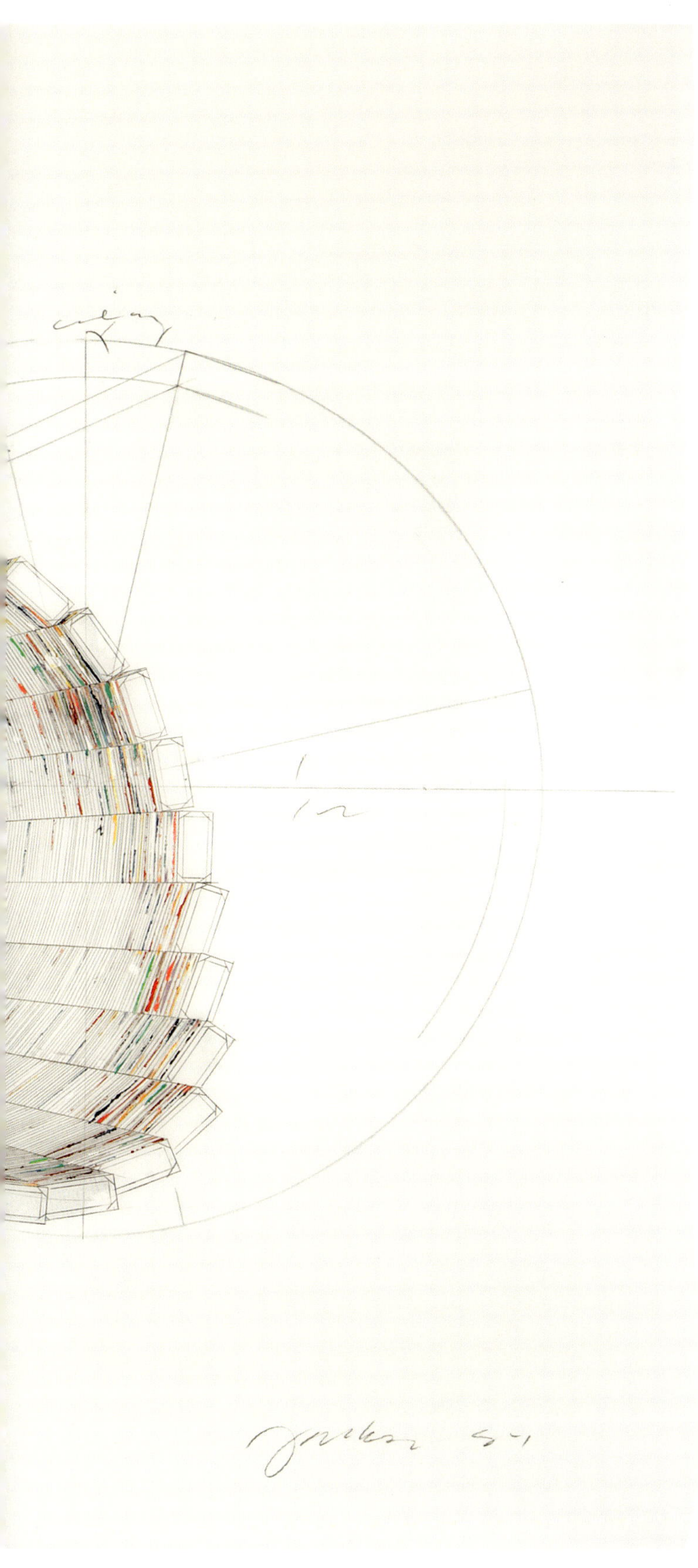

Untitled, 1984
PLATE 42

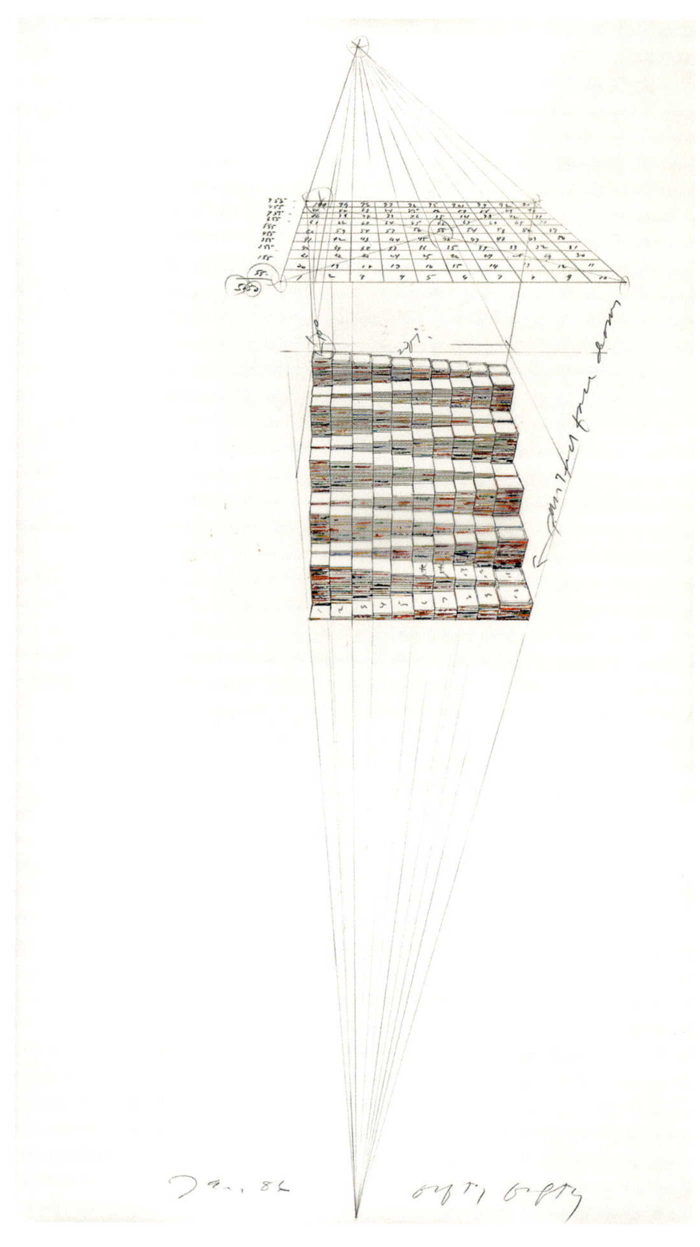

Schloss Solitude, projects und
plans, 1986
PLATE 43

(facing)
**Untitled (Study II for "5050
Stacked Paintings"),** 1999
PLATE 44

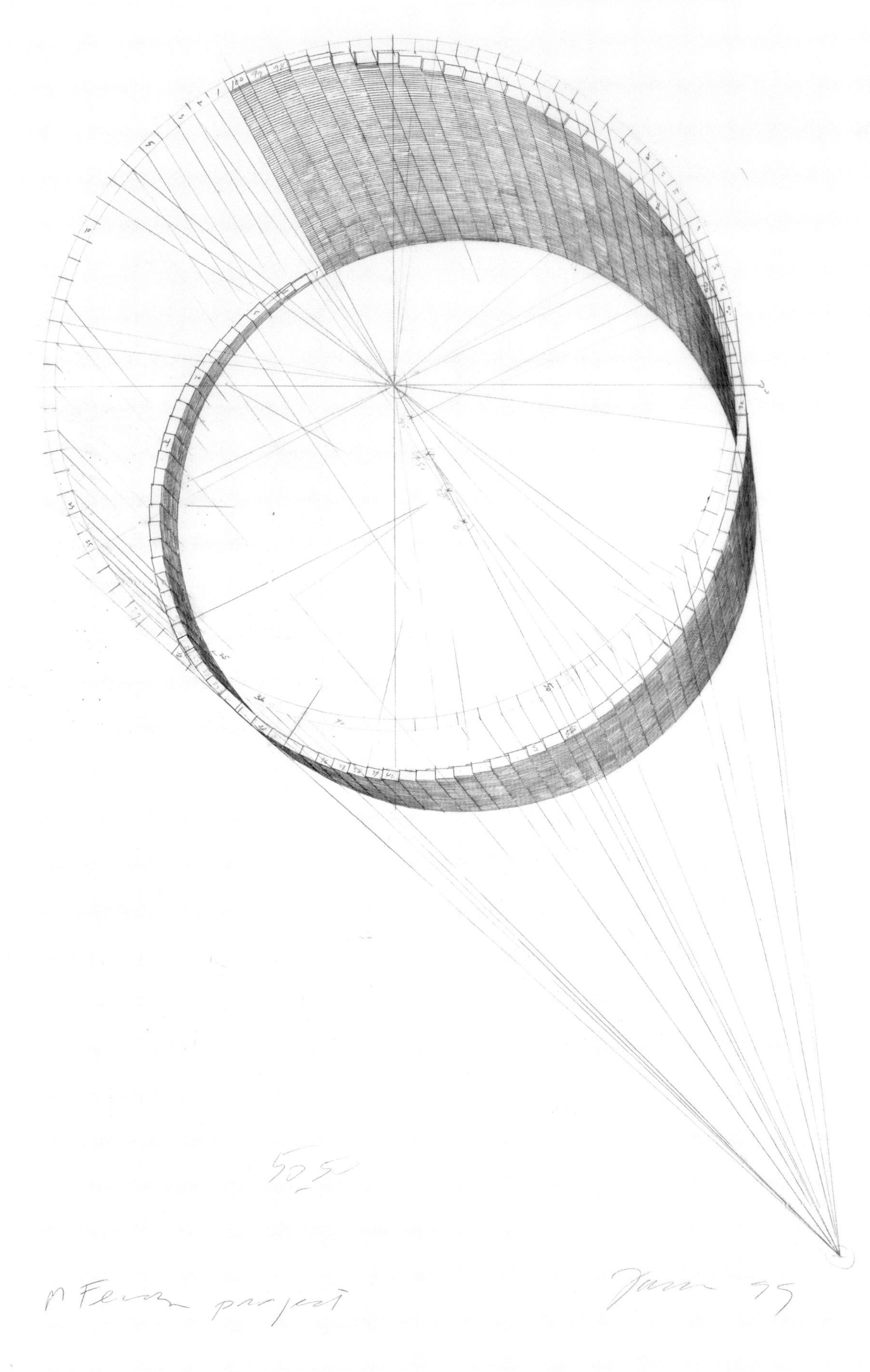

Feuer project
Jan 75

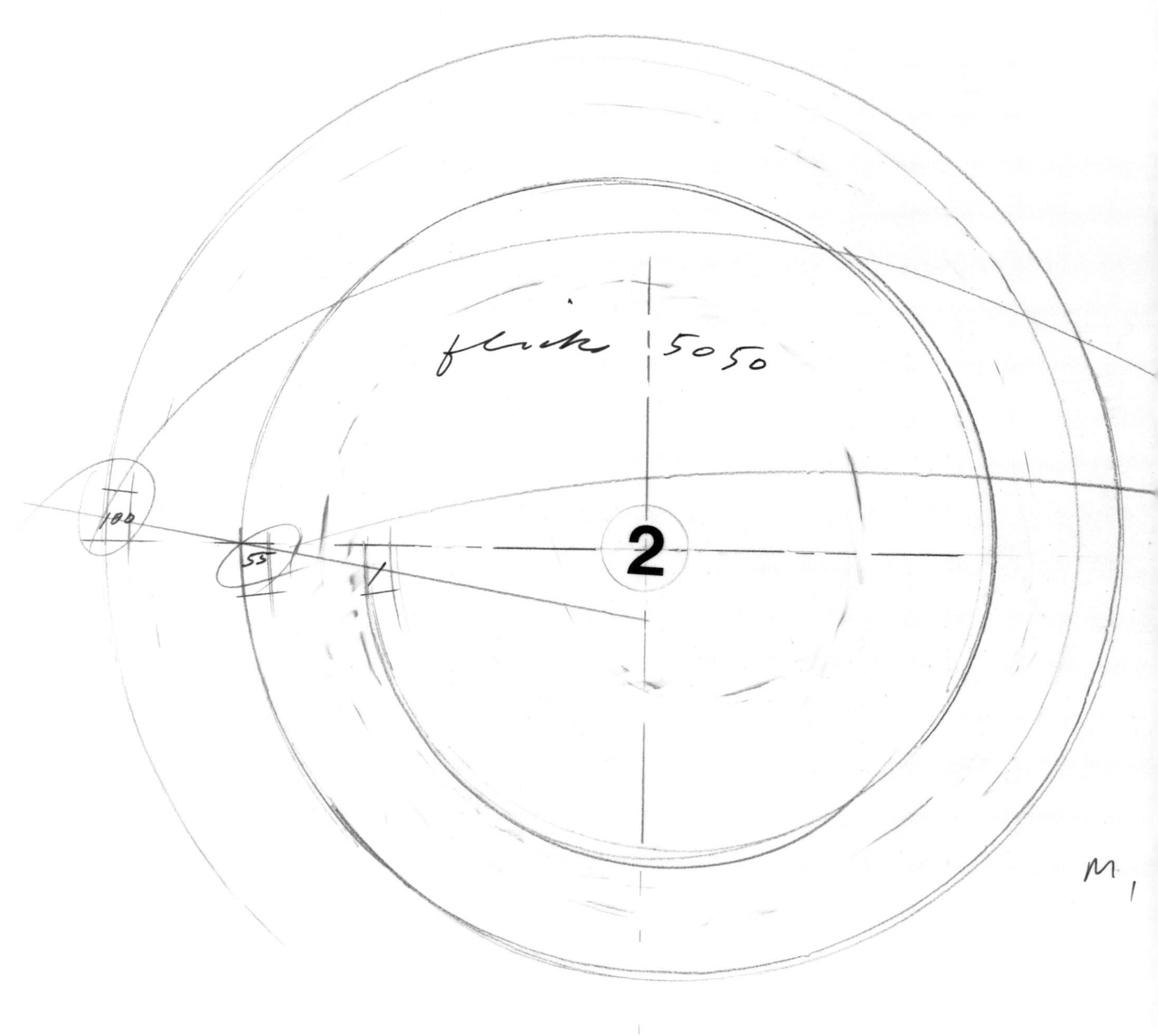

flick 5050
100
55
2
M

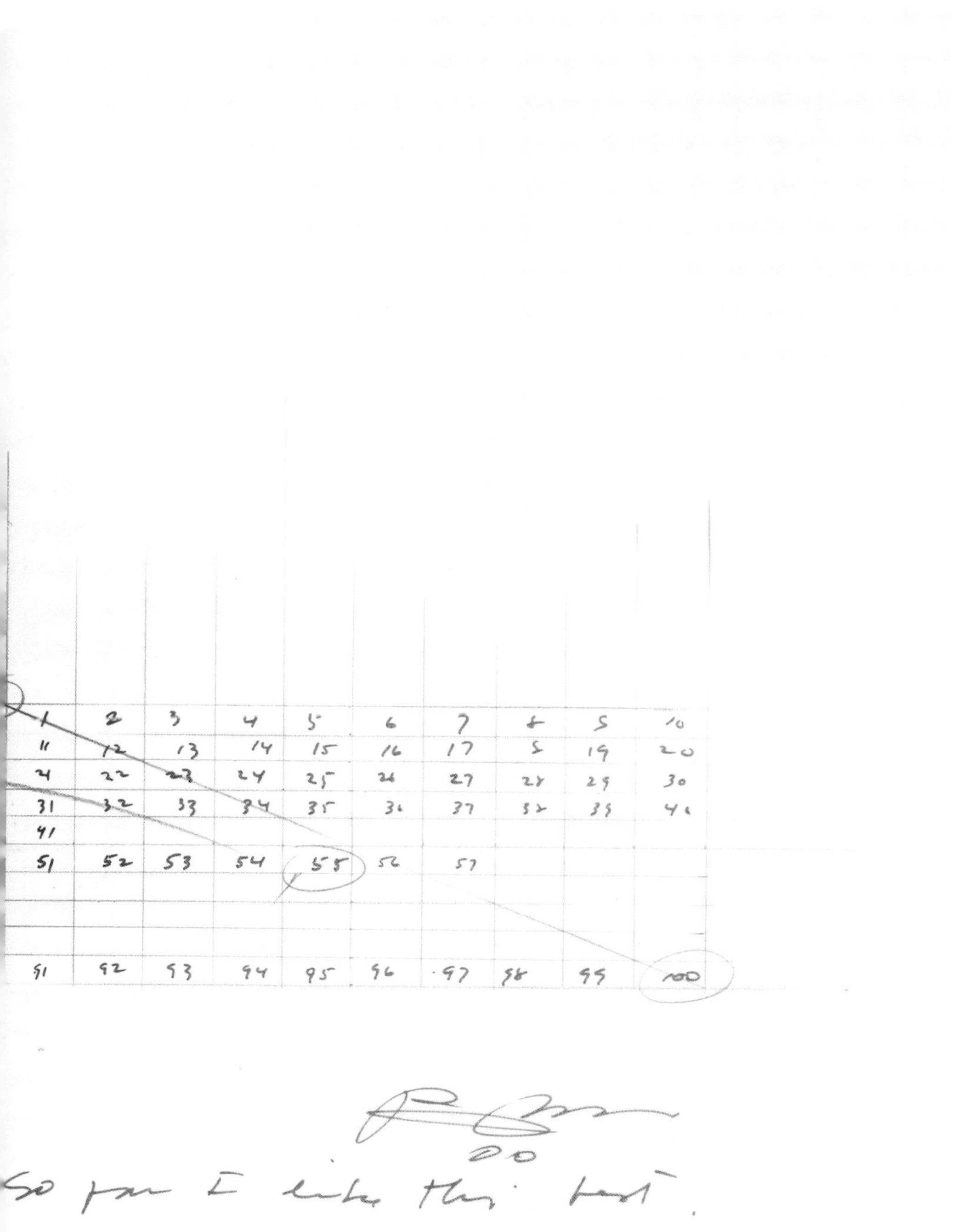

So far I like this best.

Untitled (Study III for "5050 Stacked Paintings"), 2000
PLATE 45

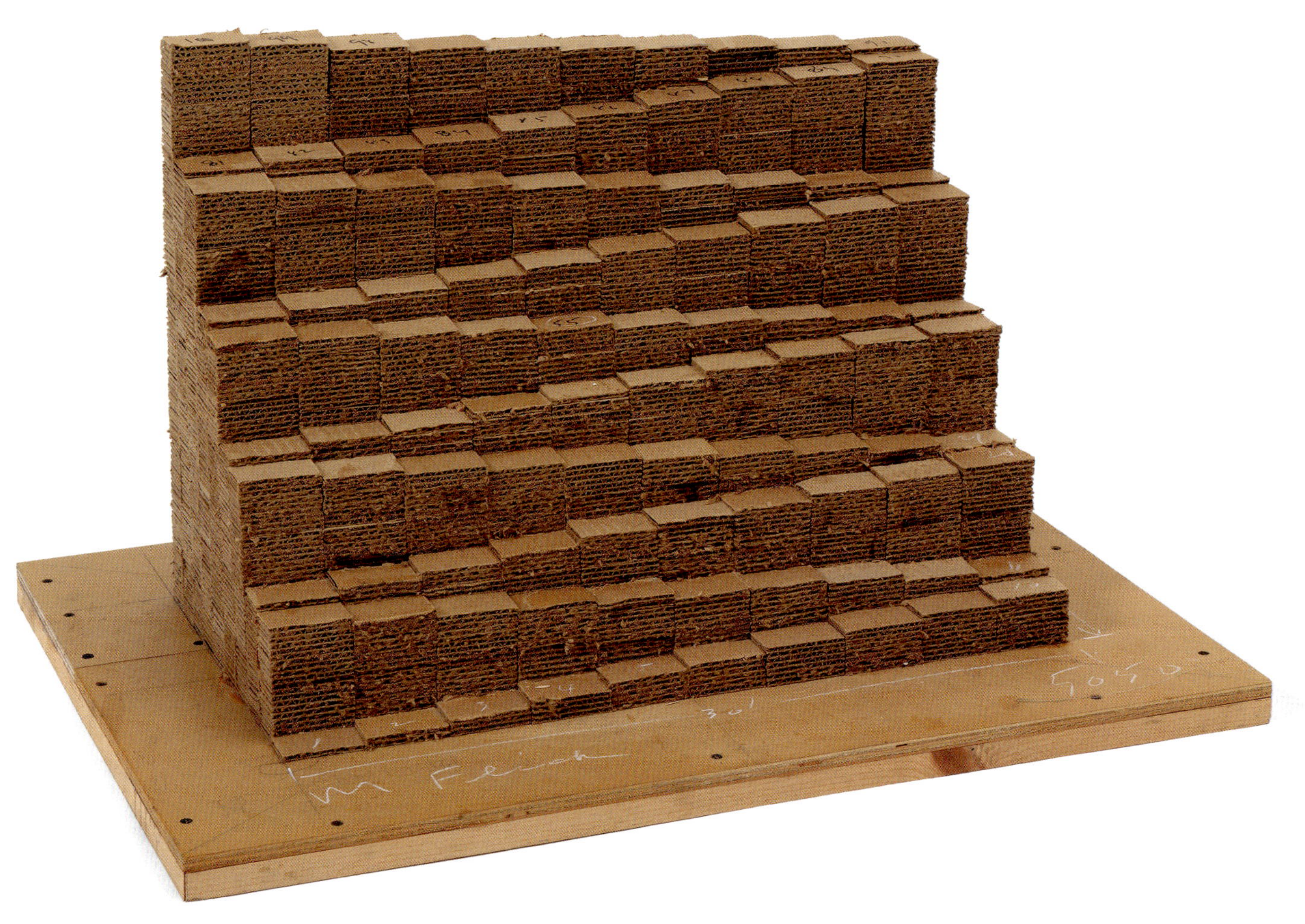

Untitled (Model II for "5050 Stacked Paintings"), 1998
PLATE 46

(facing)
Untitled (Model III for "5050 Stacked Paintings"), 1998
PLATE 47

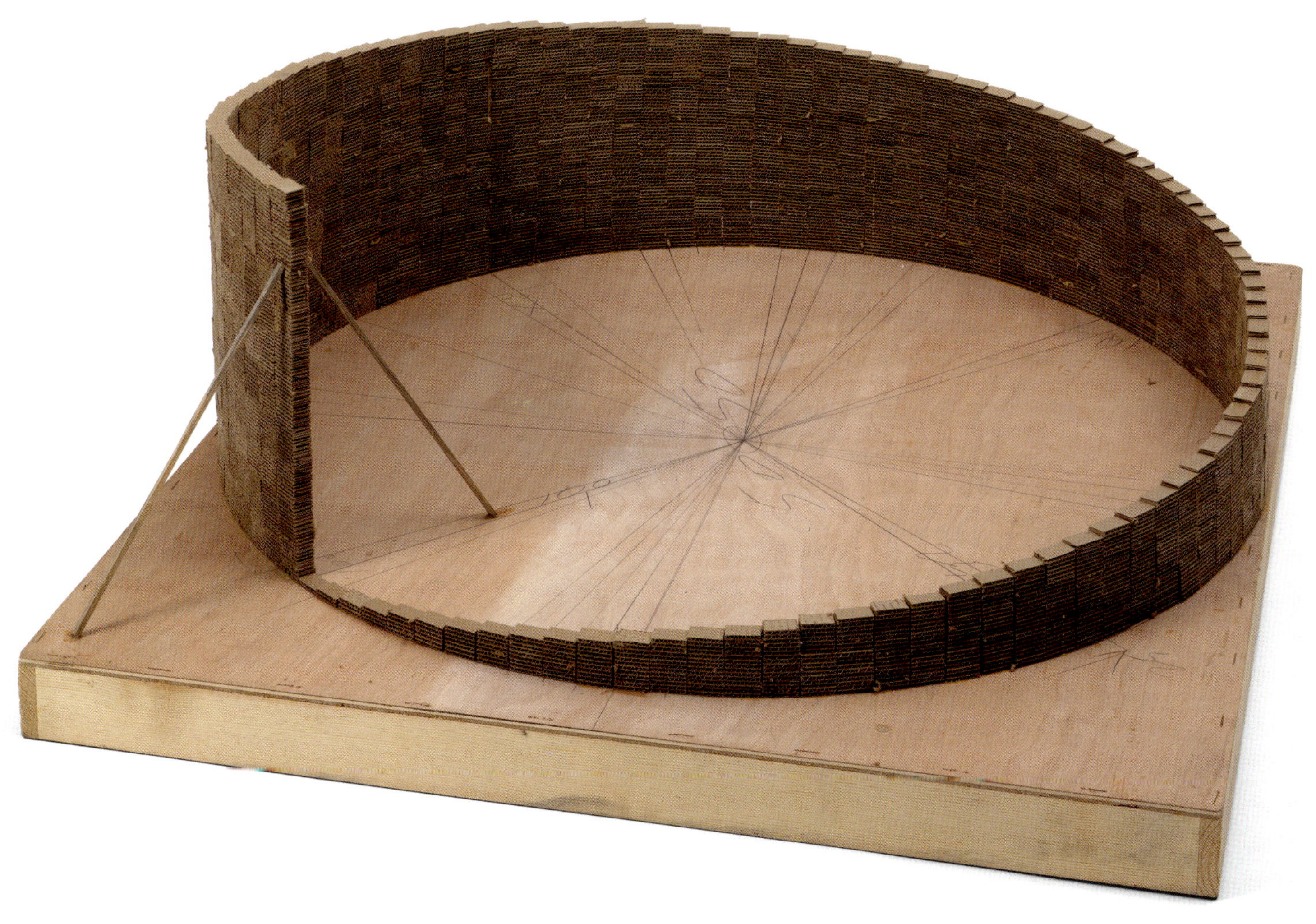

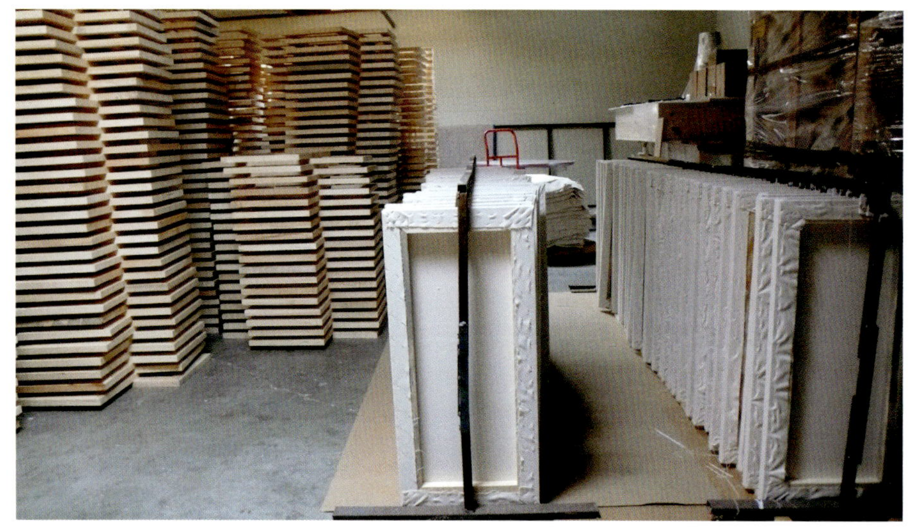

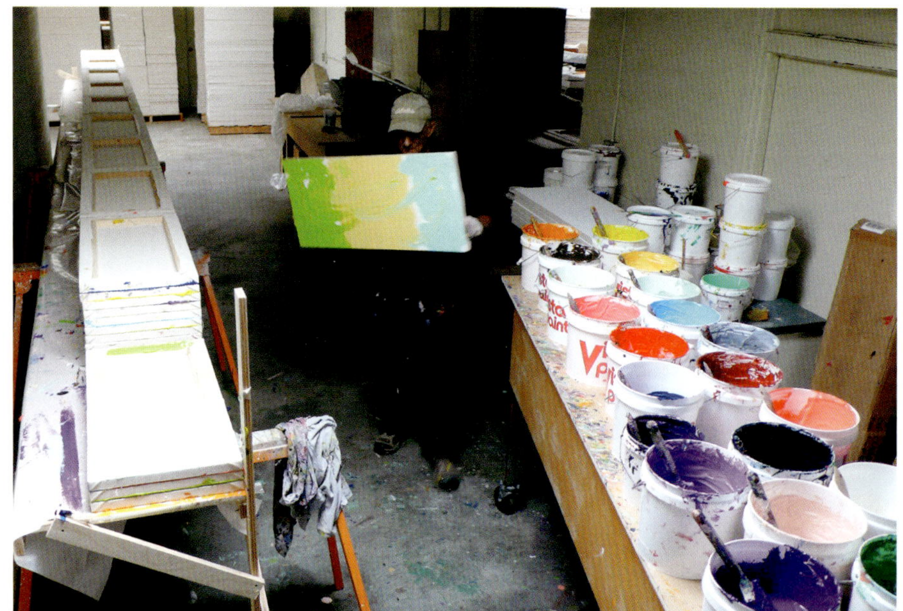

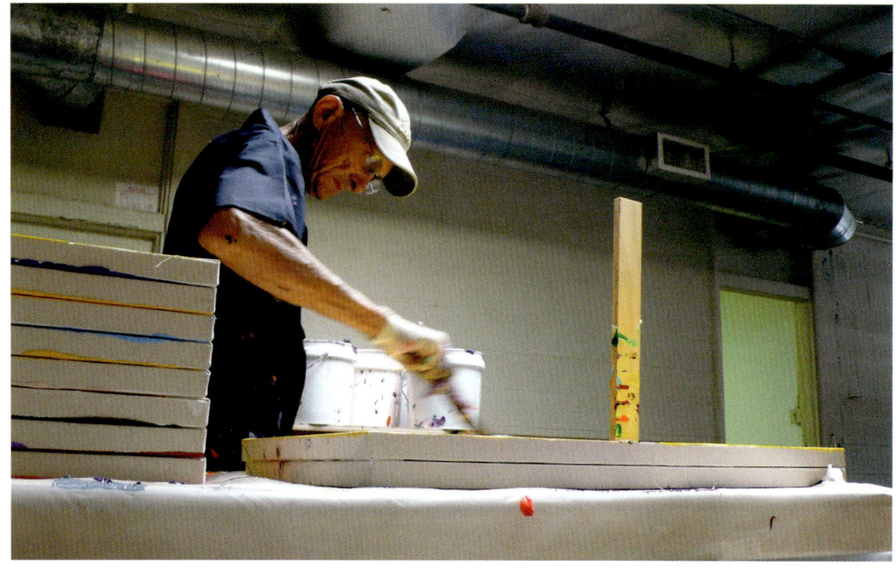

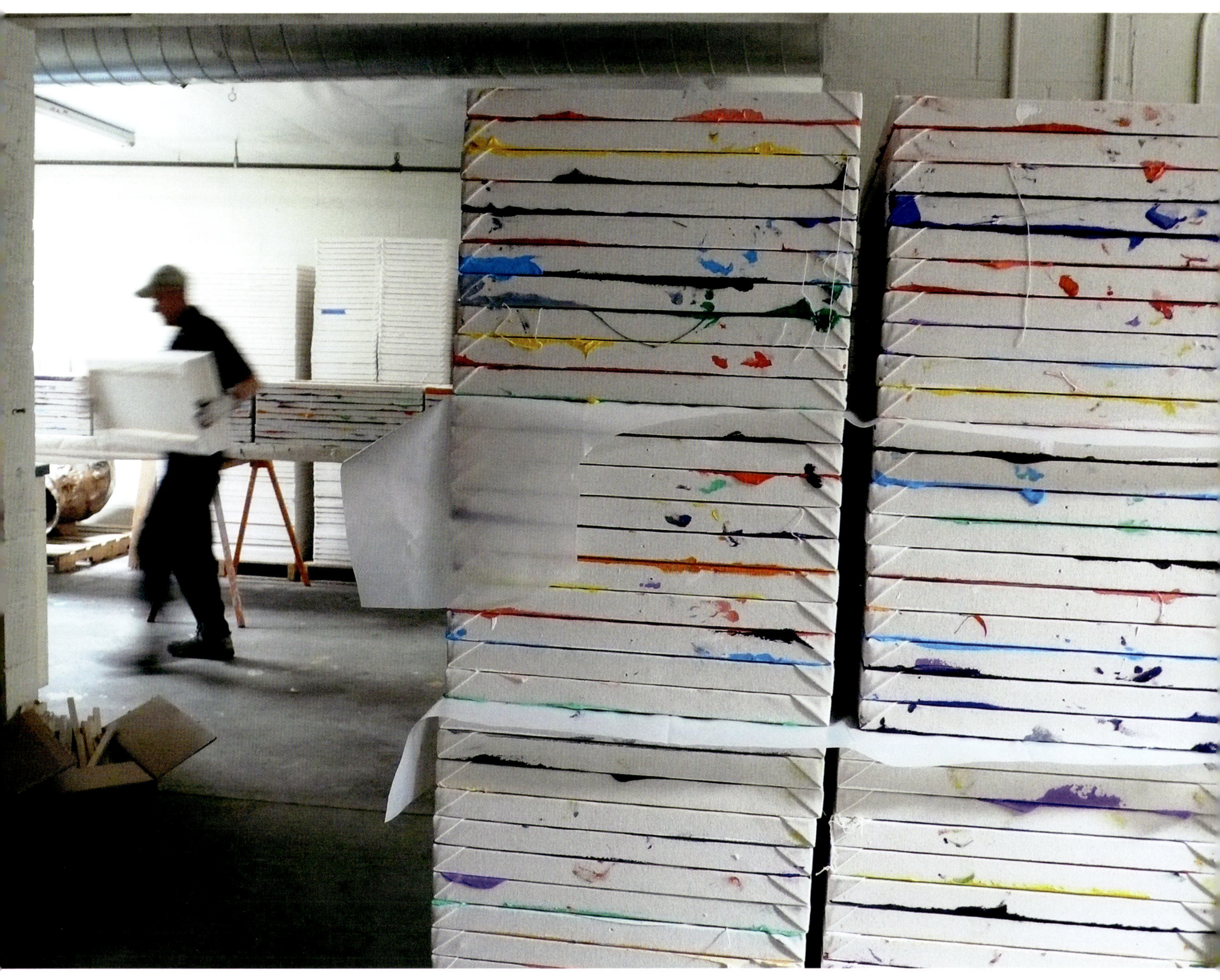

(all)
5050 Stacked Paintings
(in progress), 1980–2013
PLATE 48

INSTALLATIONS AND
PAINTING MACHINES

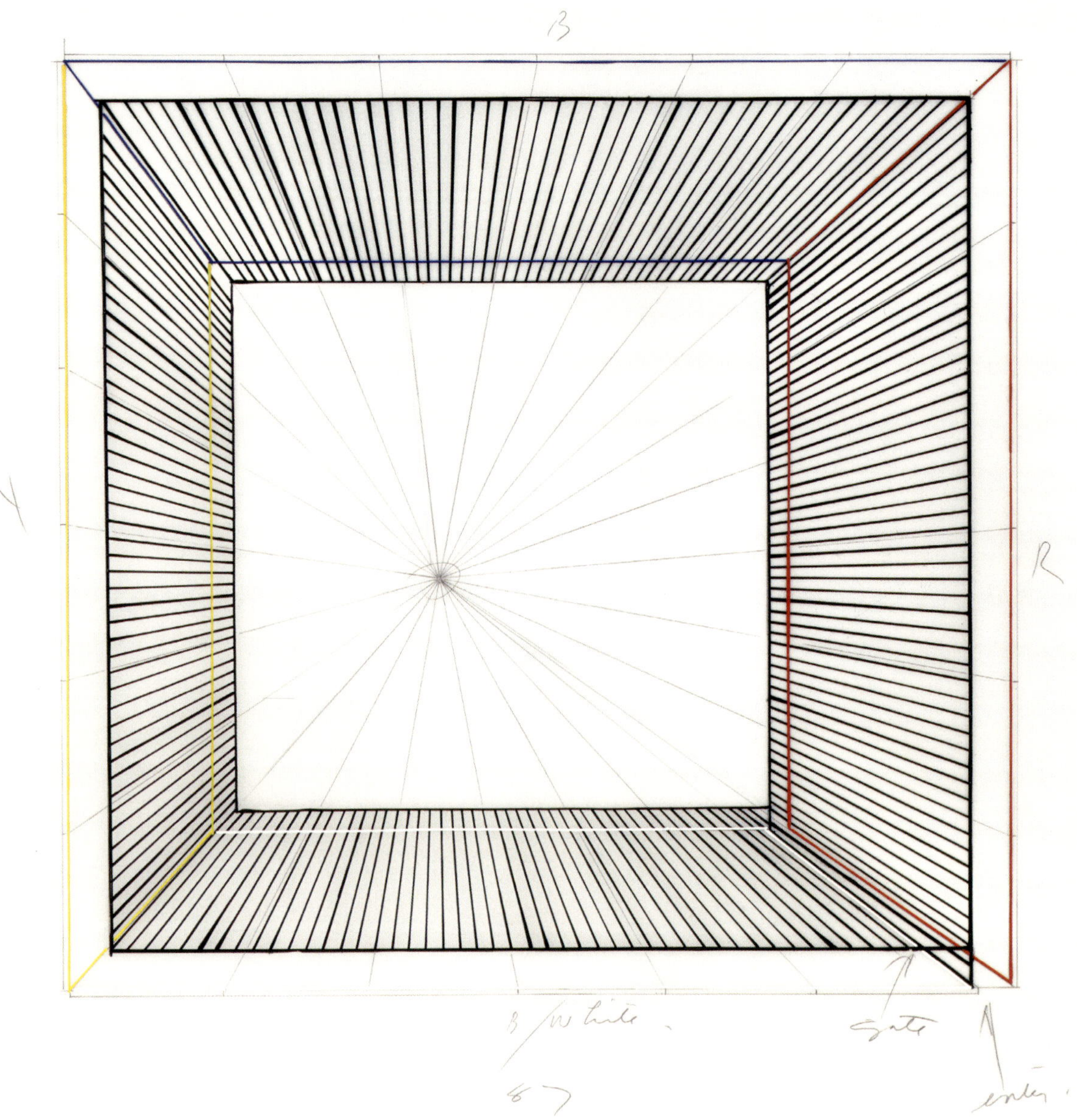

Untitled (Study I for "Good Deal"), 1987
PLATE 49

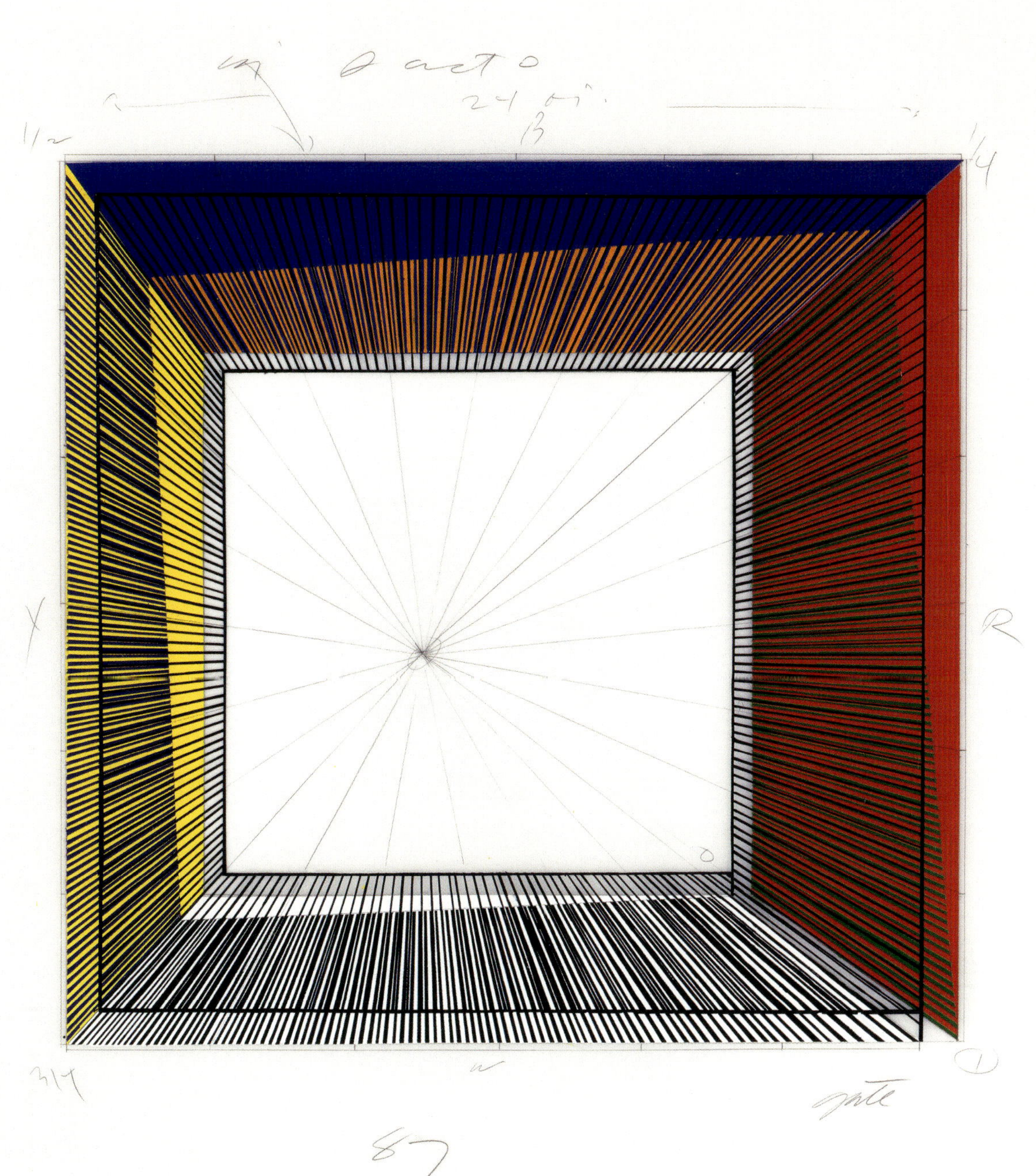

Untitled (Study II for "Good Deal"), 1987

PLATE 50

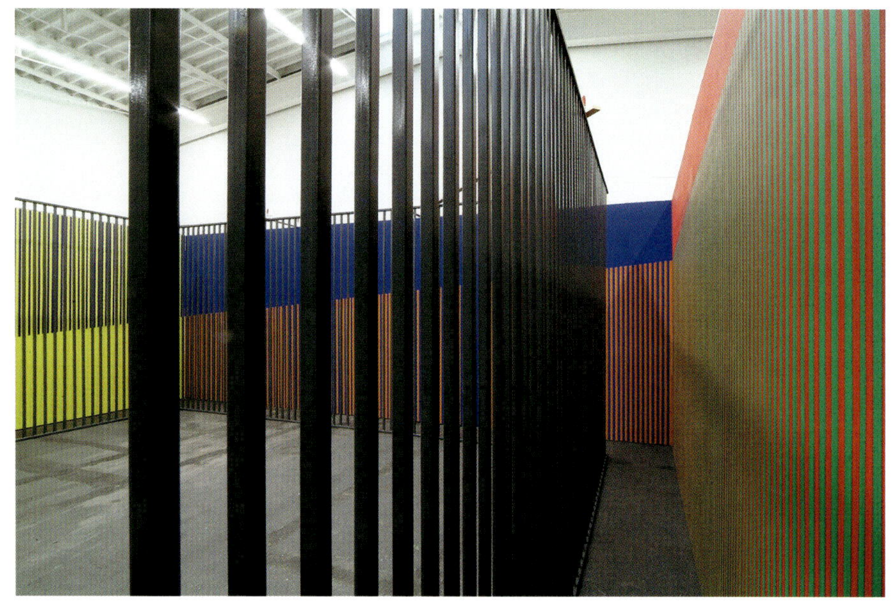

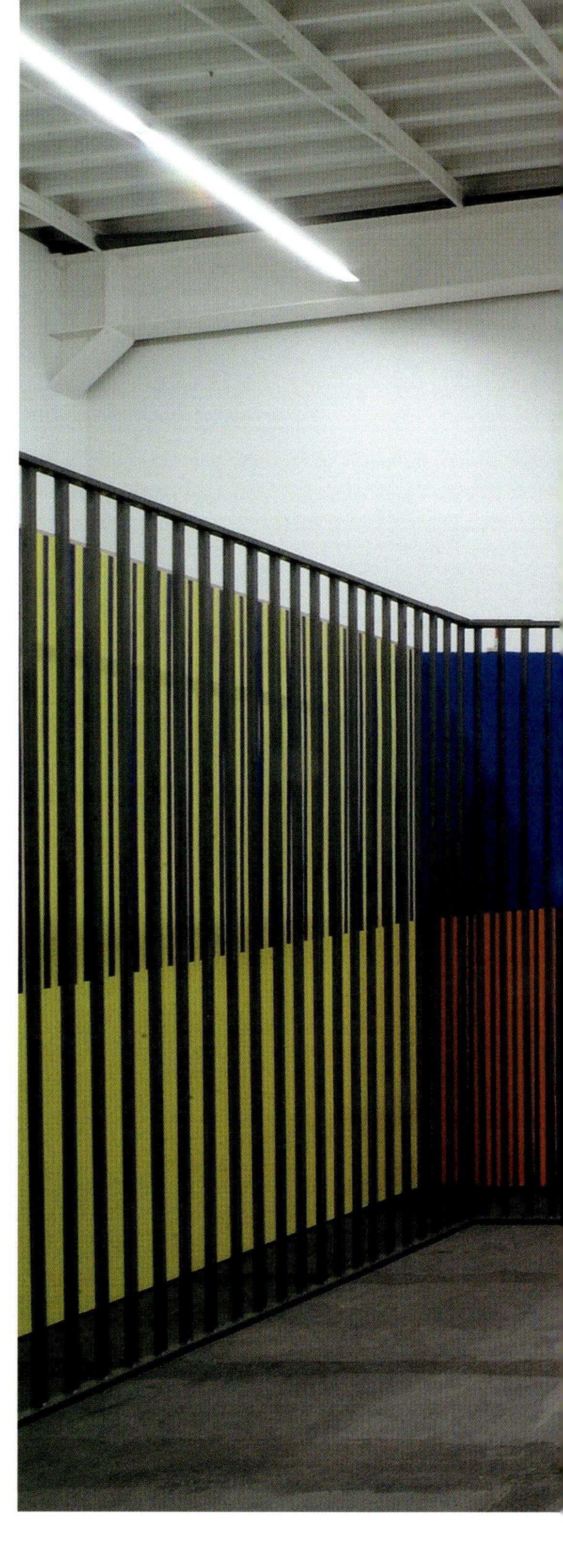

(above + facing)
Good Deal, 1987
PLATE 51

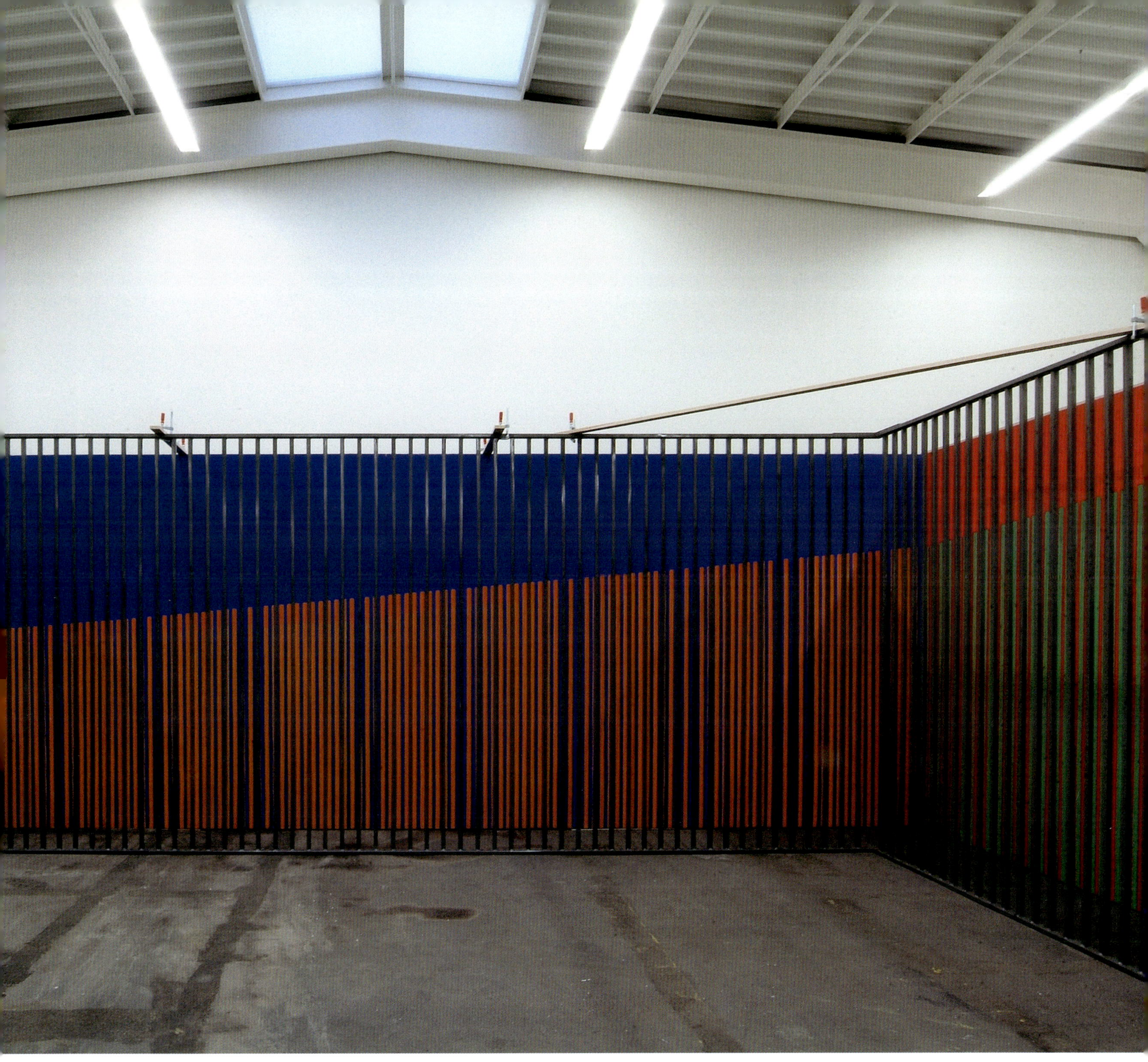

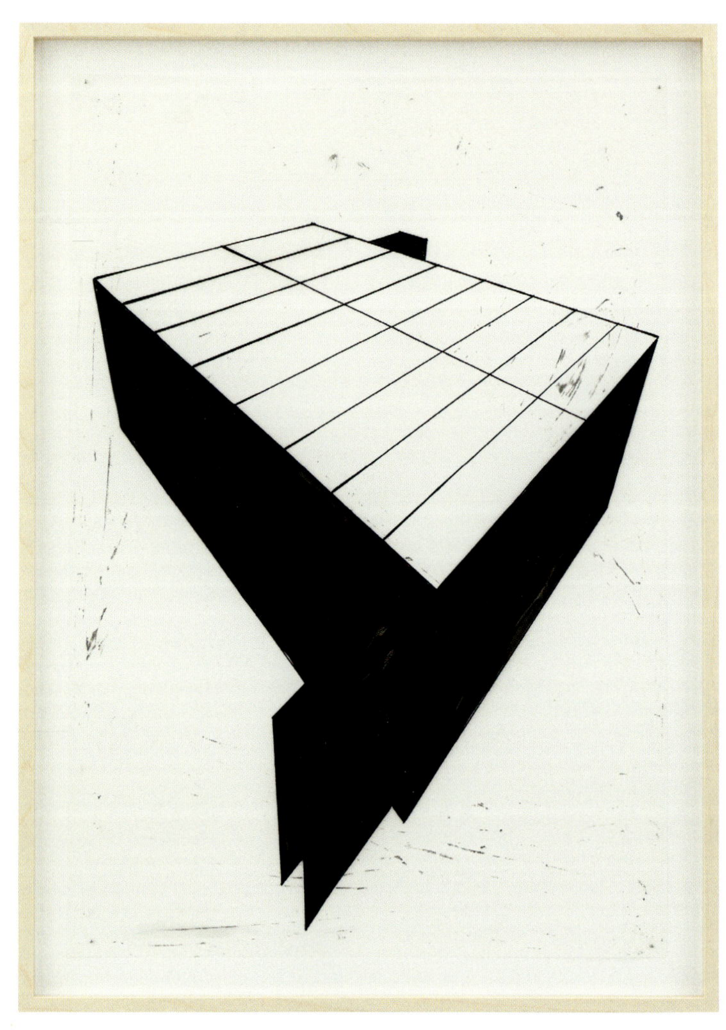

(all)
3 Drawings for "1000 Clocks,"
1987—92
PLATE 52

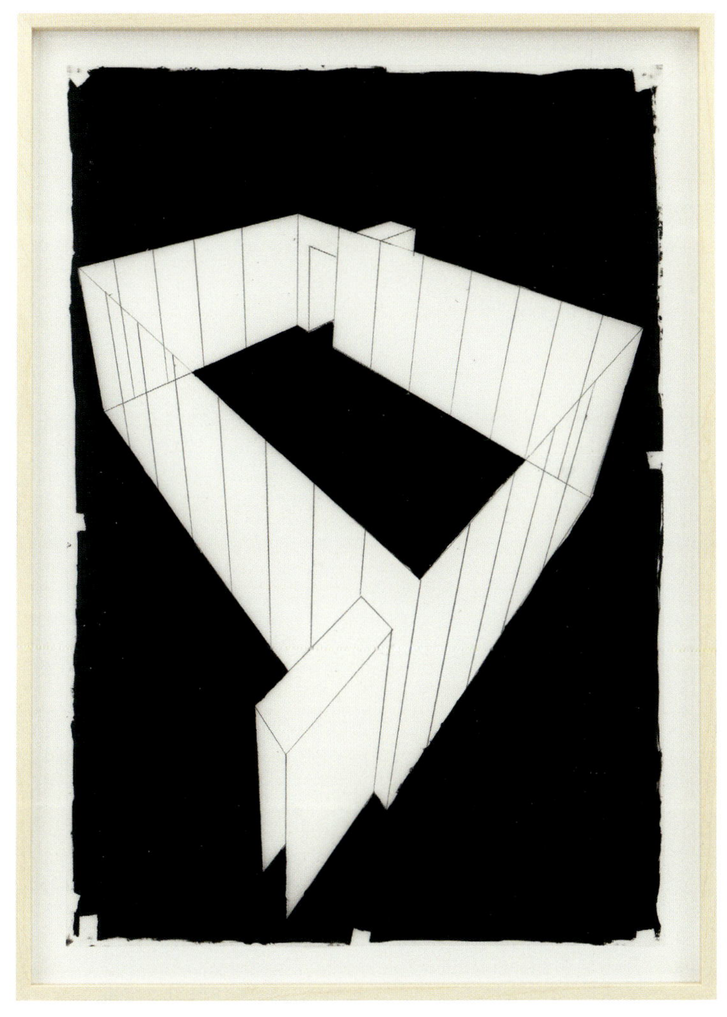 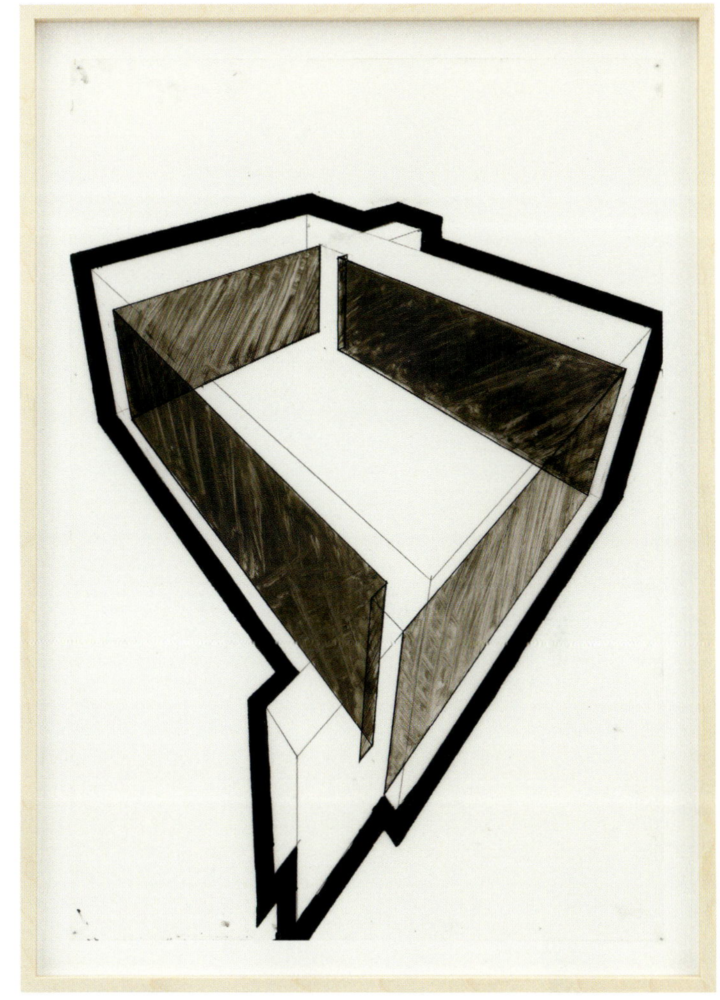

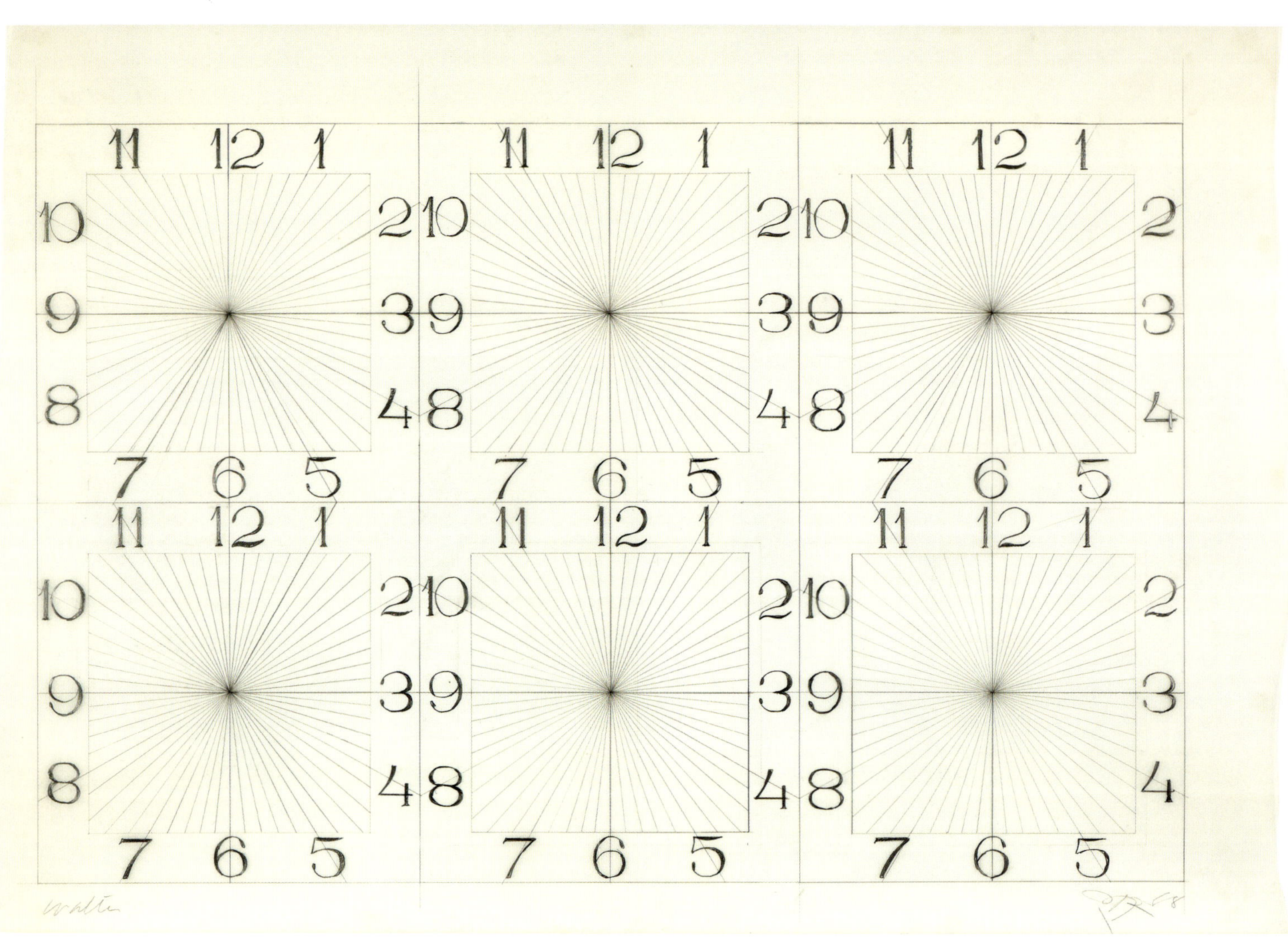

Clock Drawing, 1988

(facing, top + bottom)
1000 Clocks (exterior), 1987–92

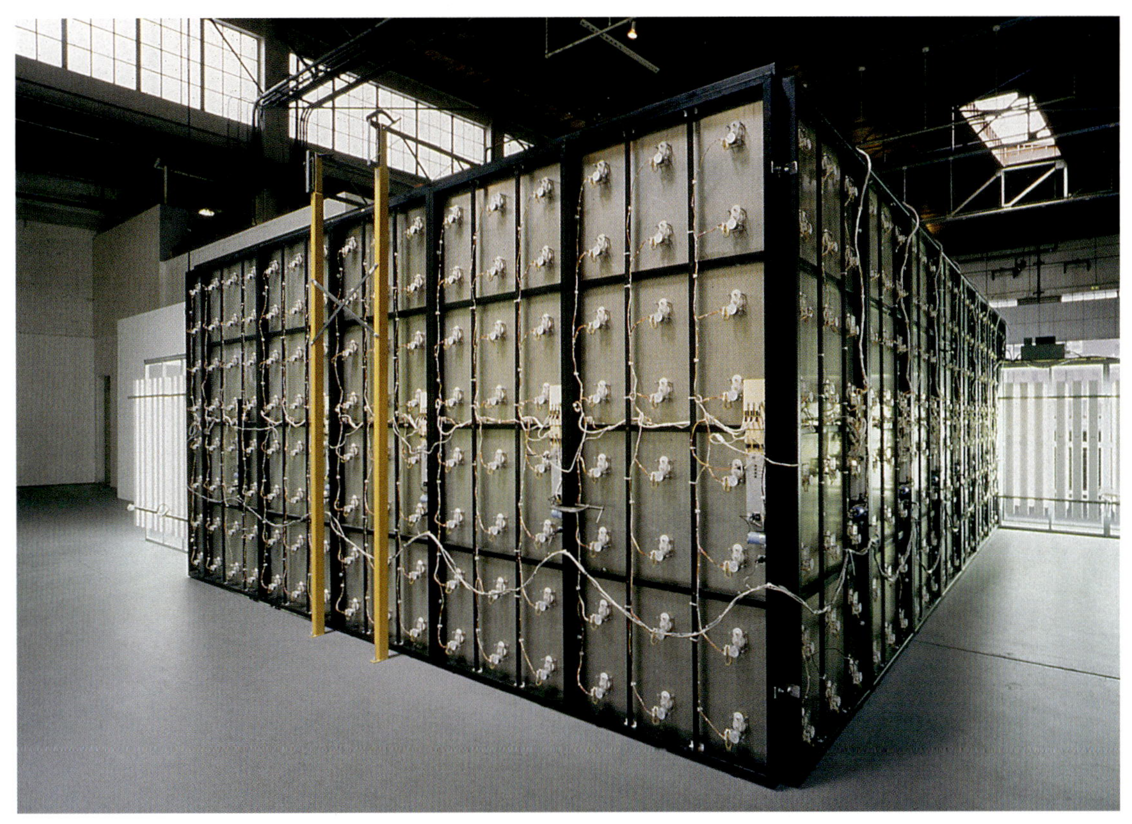

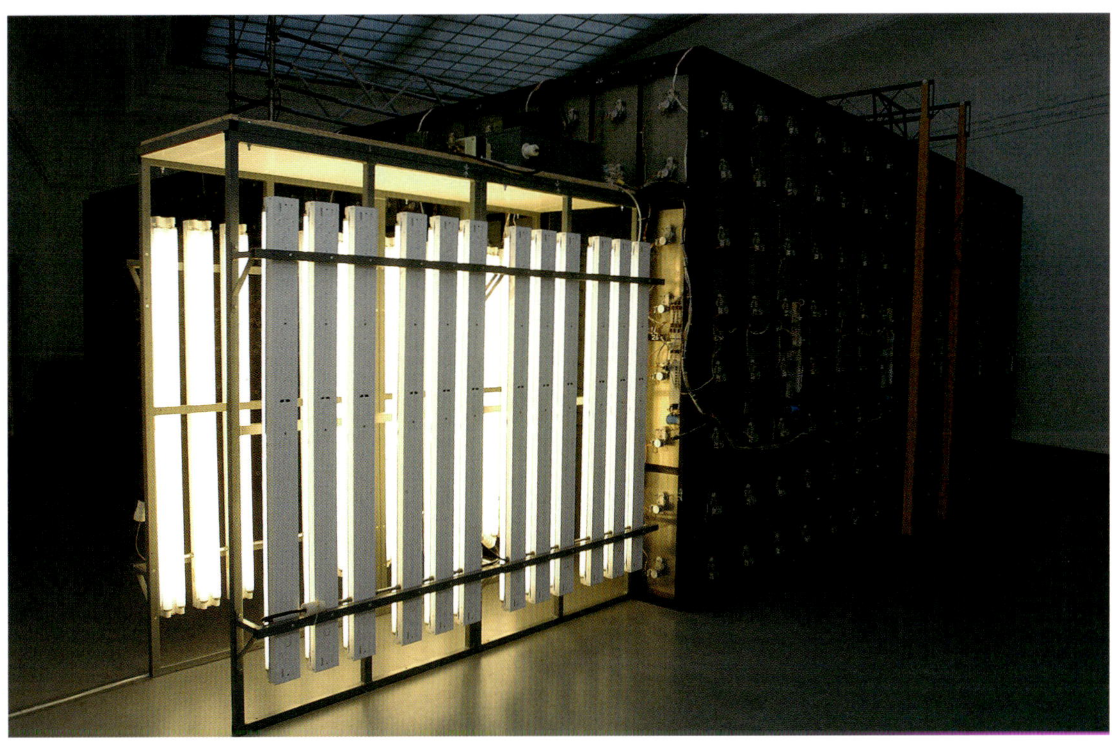

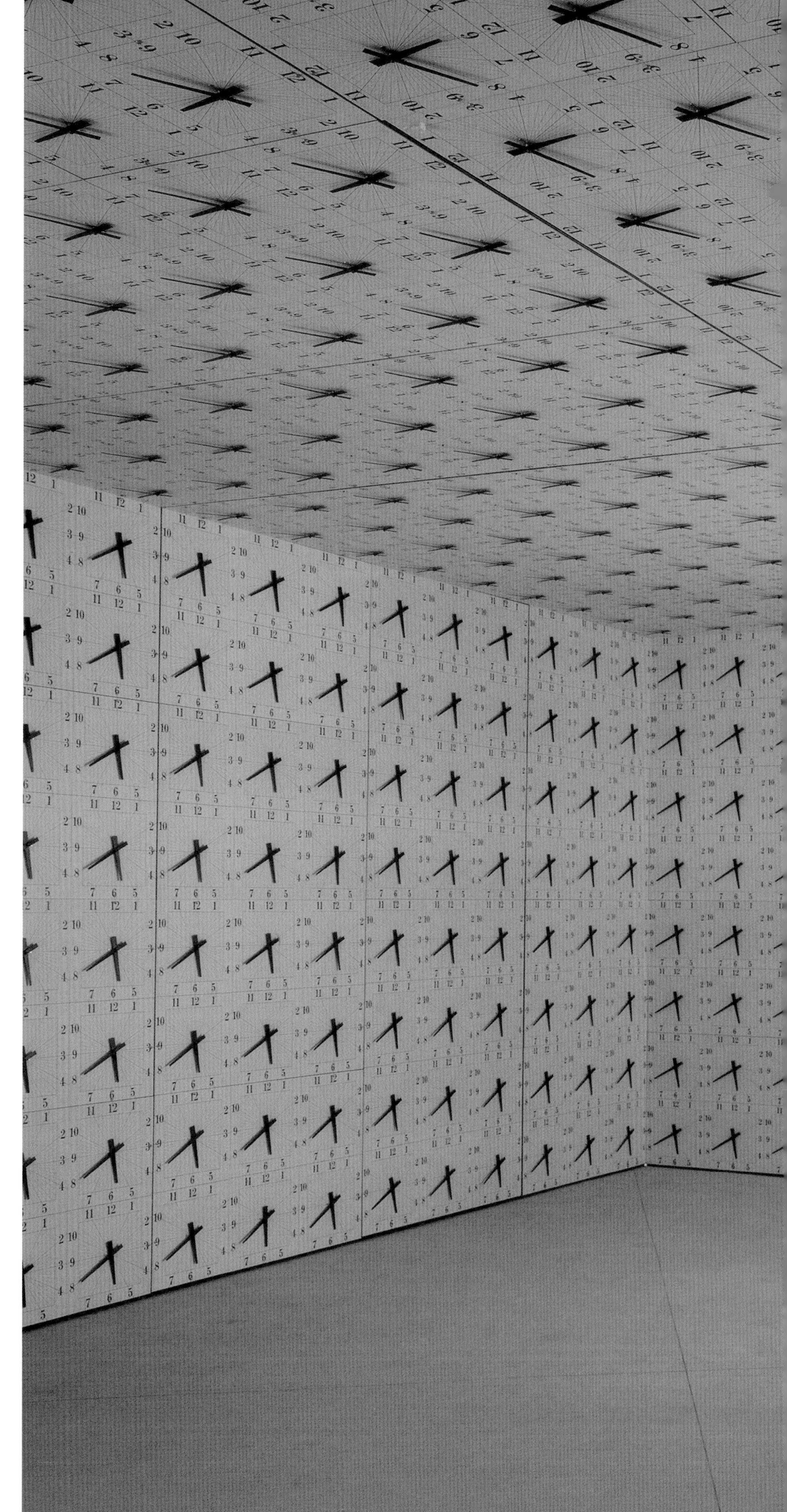

1000 Clocks (interior), 1987–92

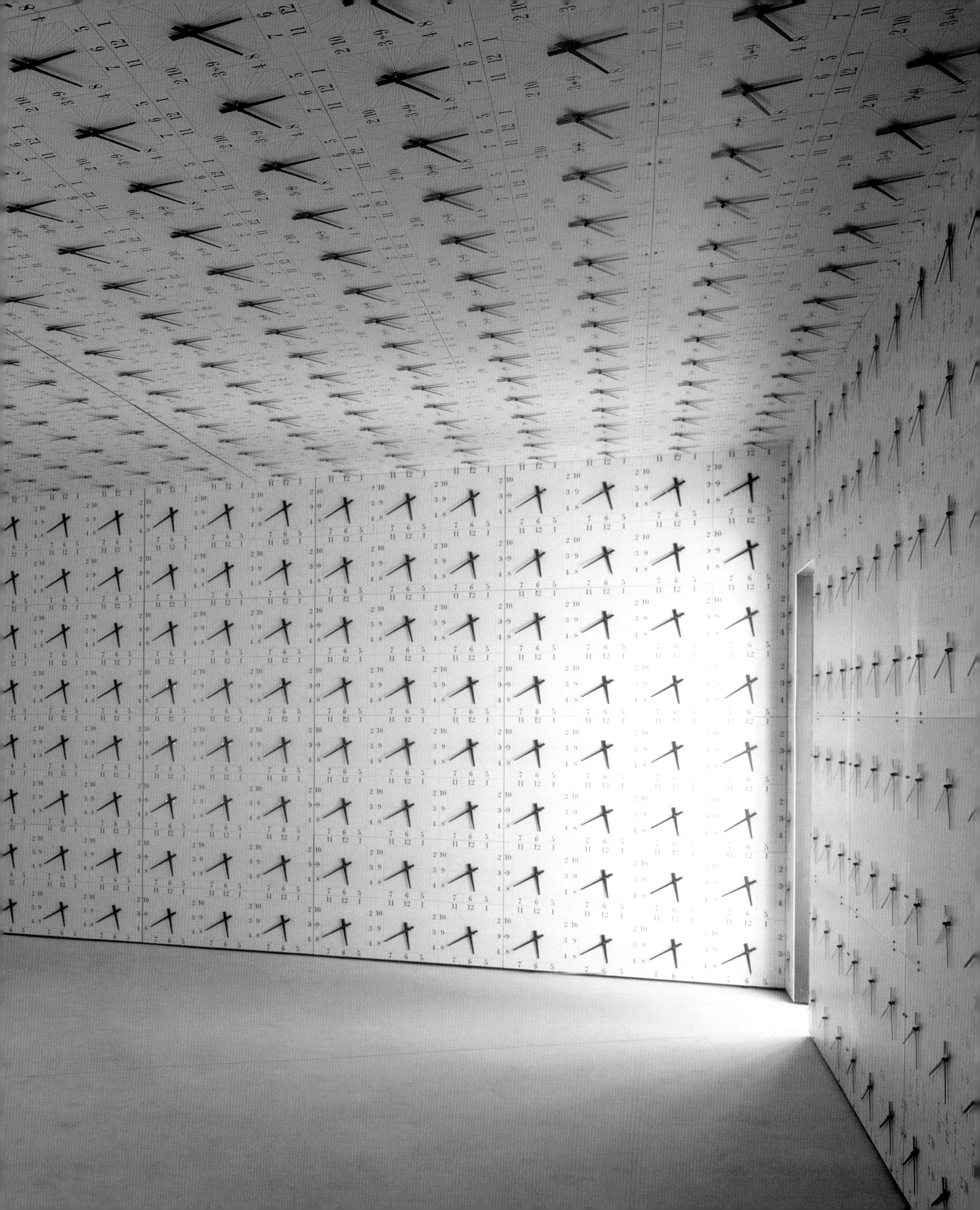

Painting with Two Balls, 1997
PLATE 55

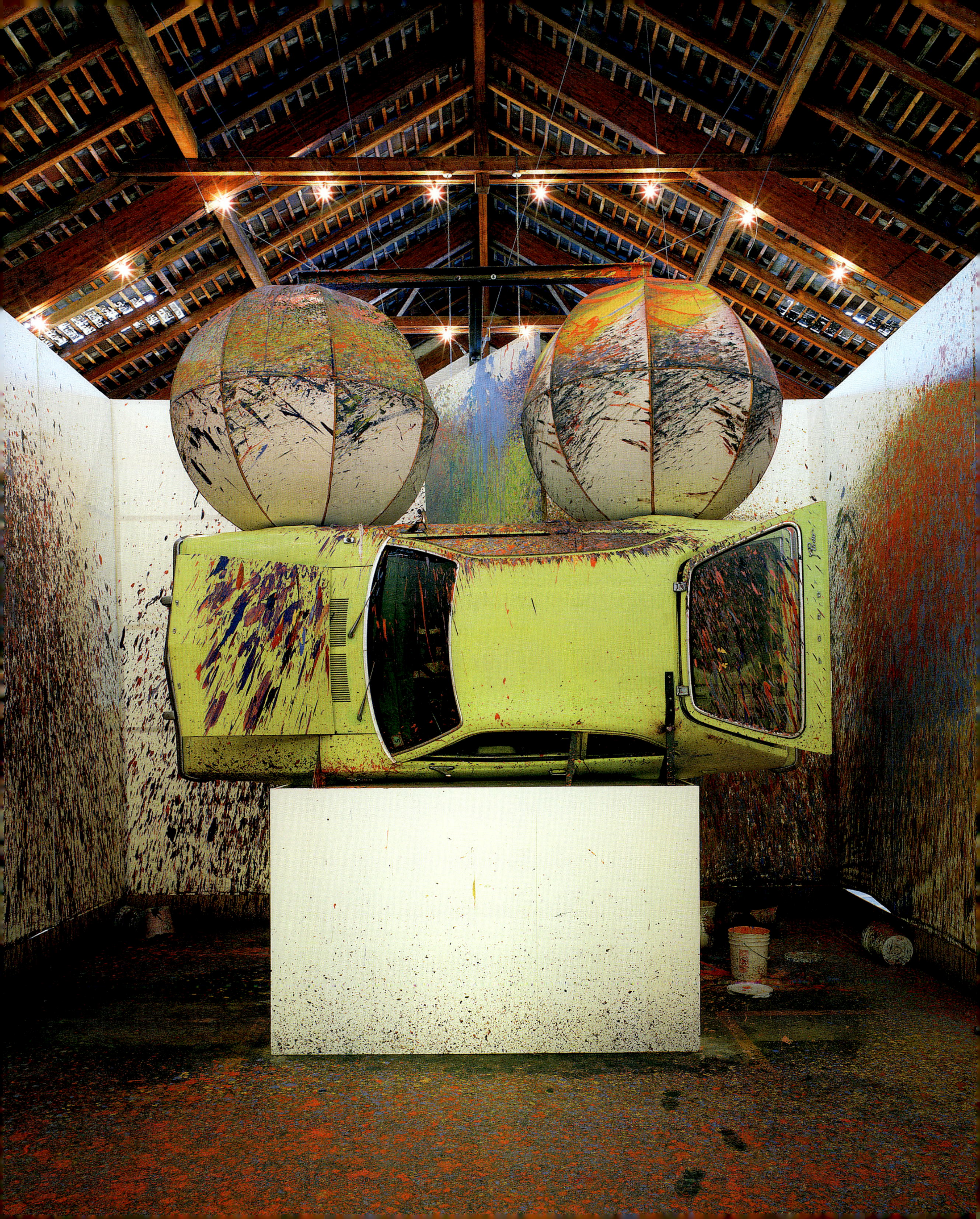

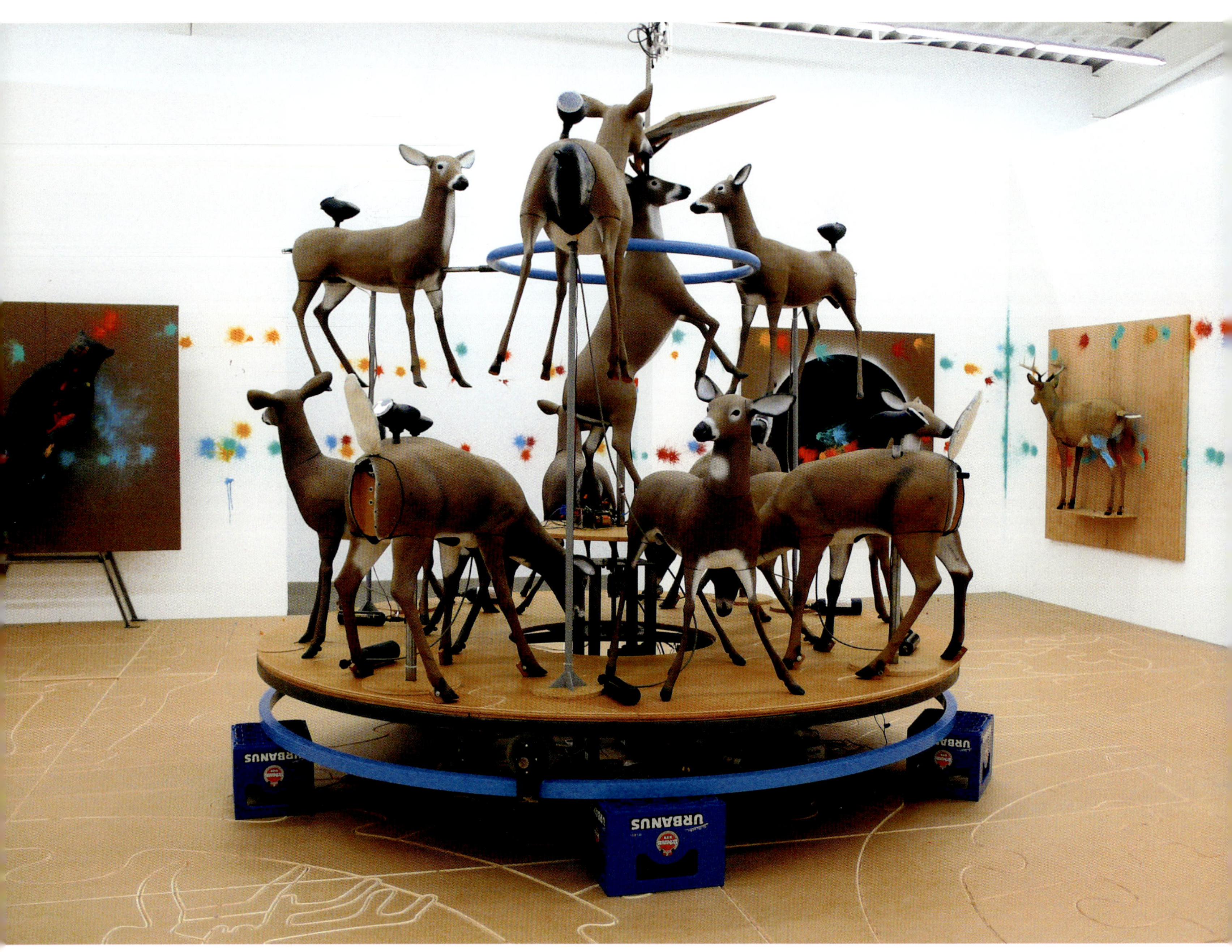

(all)
Deer Beer, 1998
PLATE 56

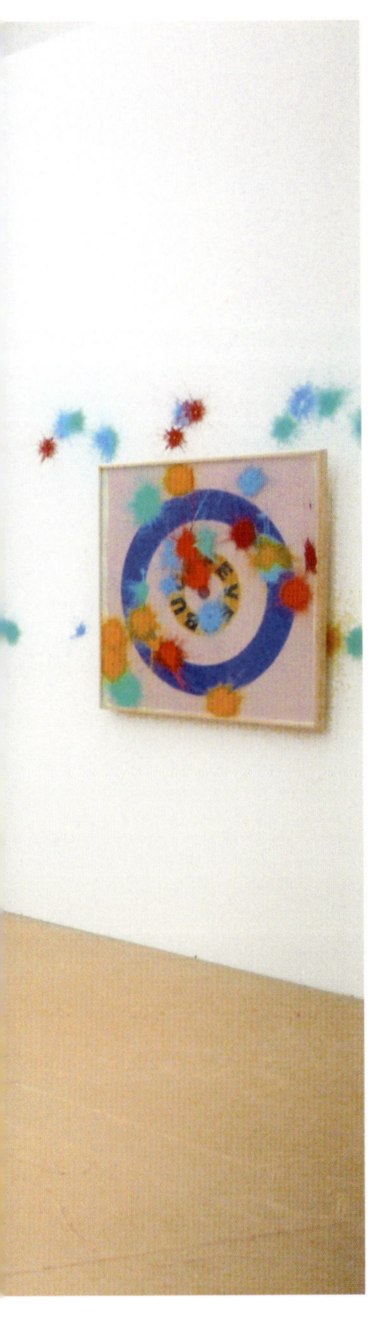

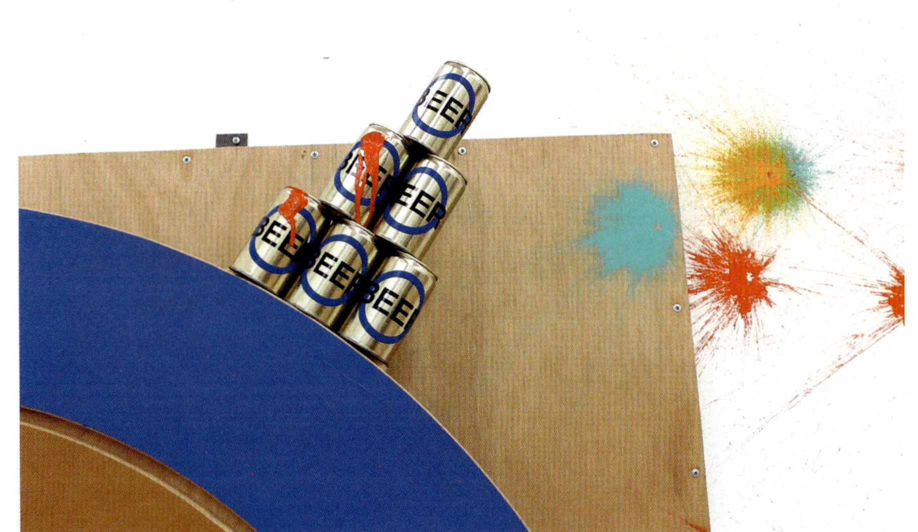
BEER
BEER
BEER
BEER
BEER
BEER

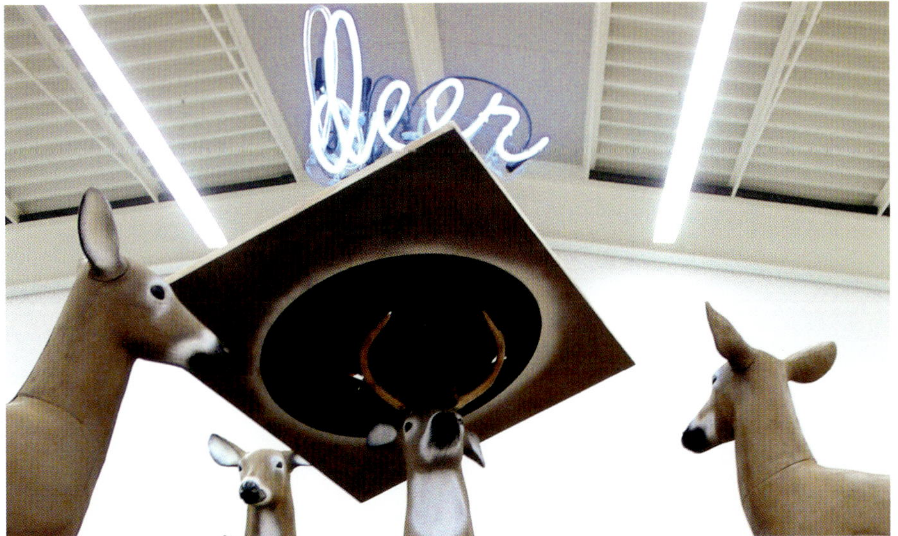
beer

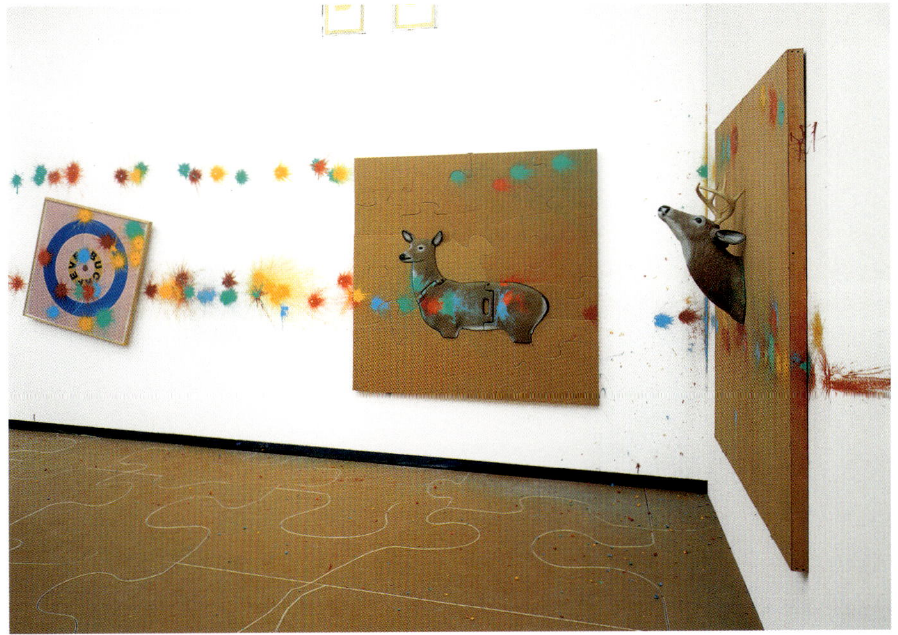

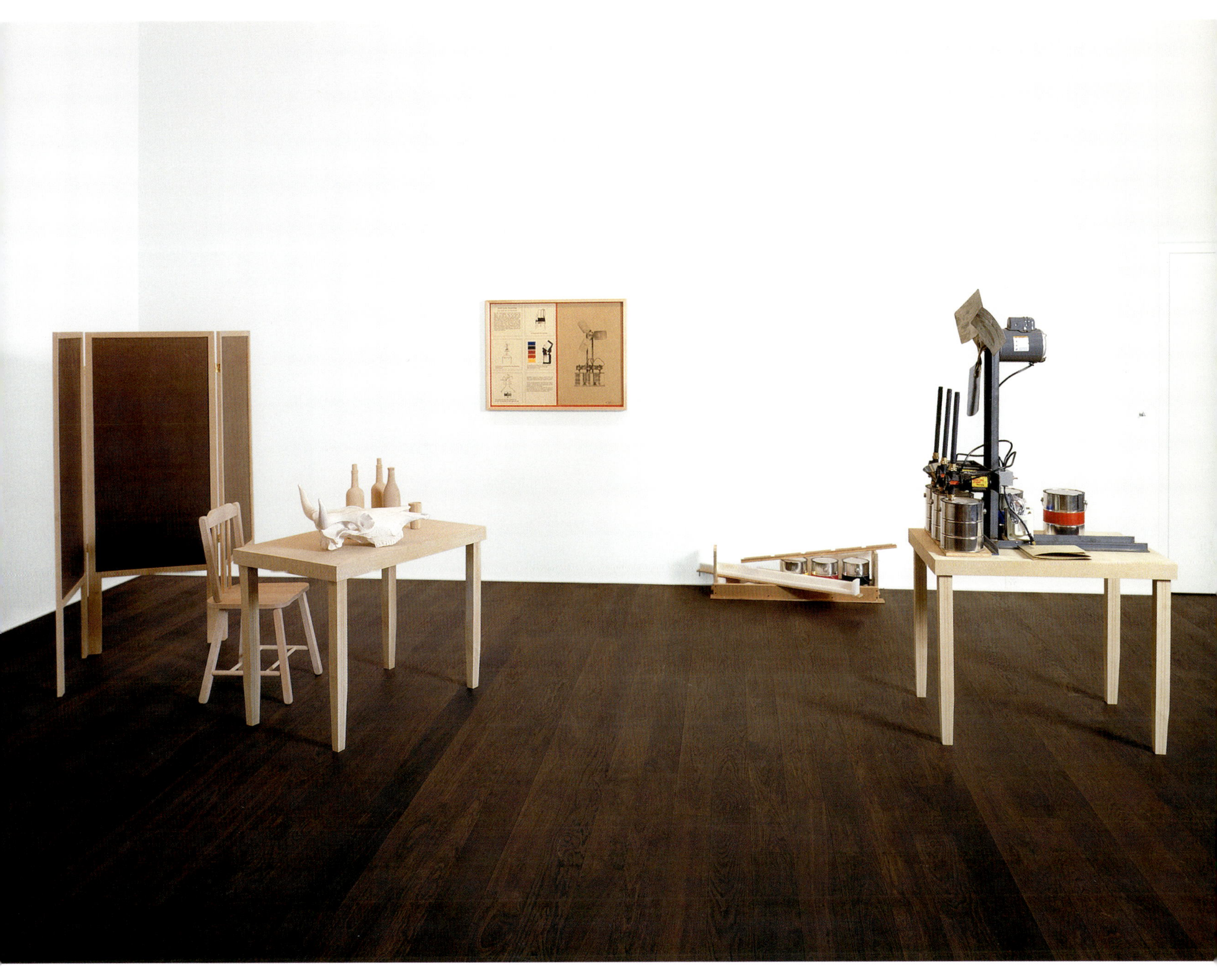

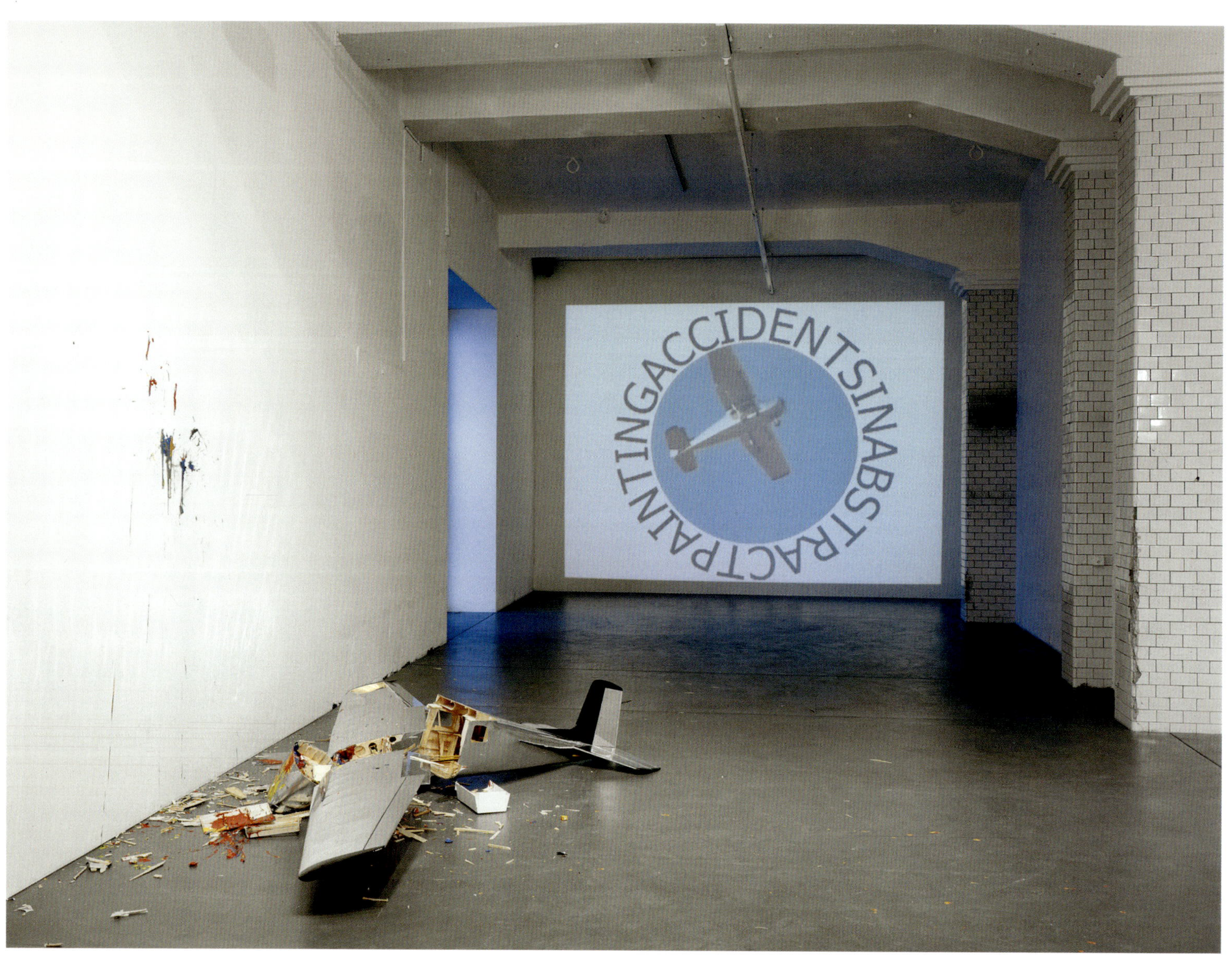

(all)
Accidents in Abstract Painting,
2002
PLATE 58

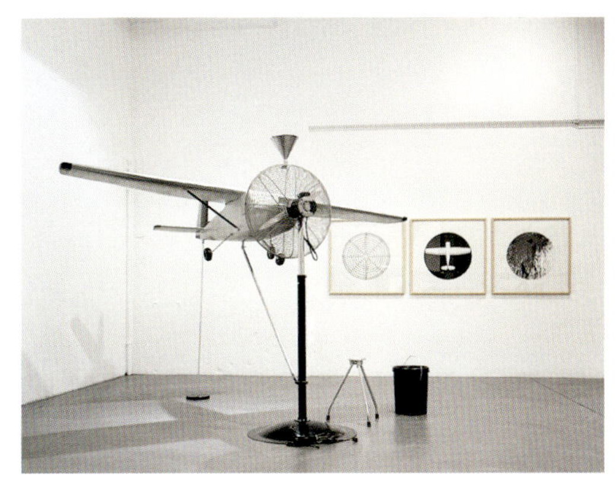

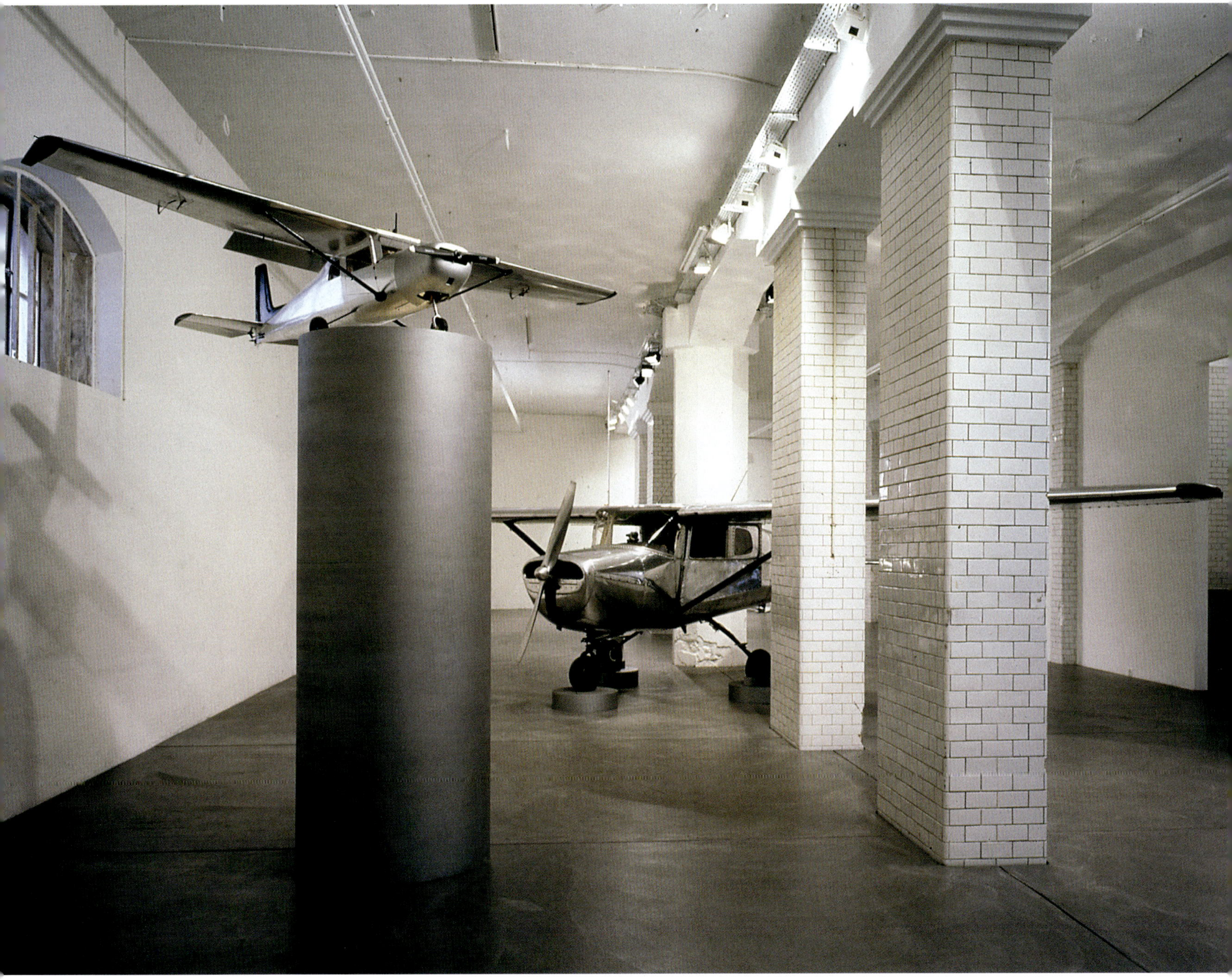

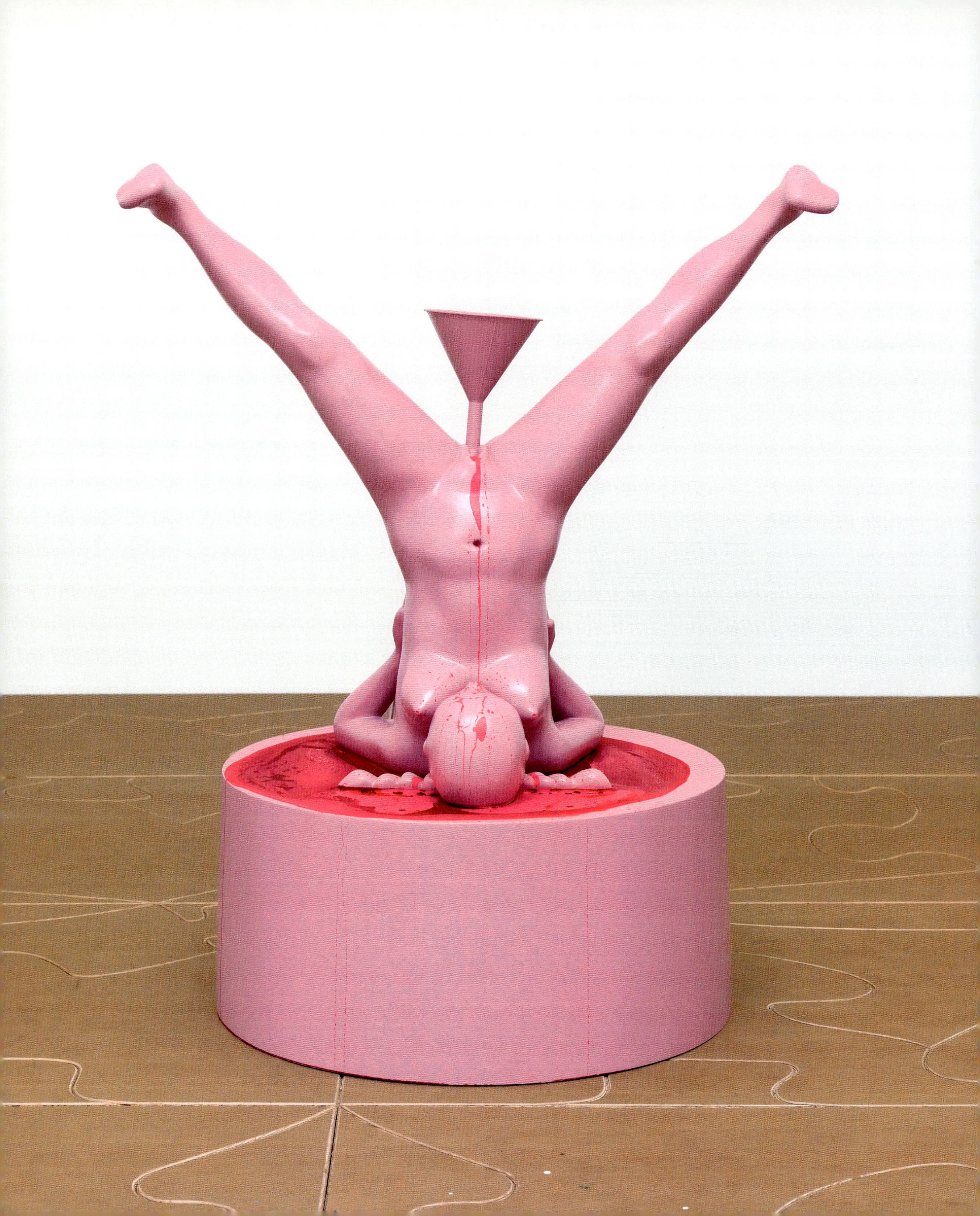

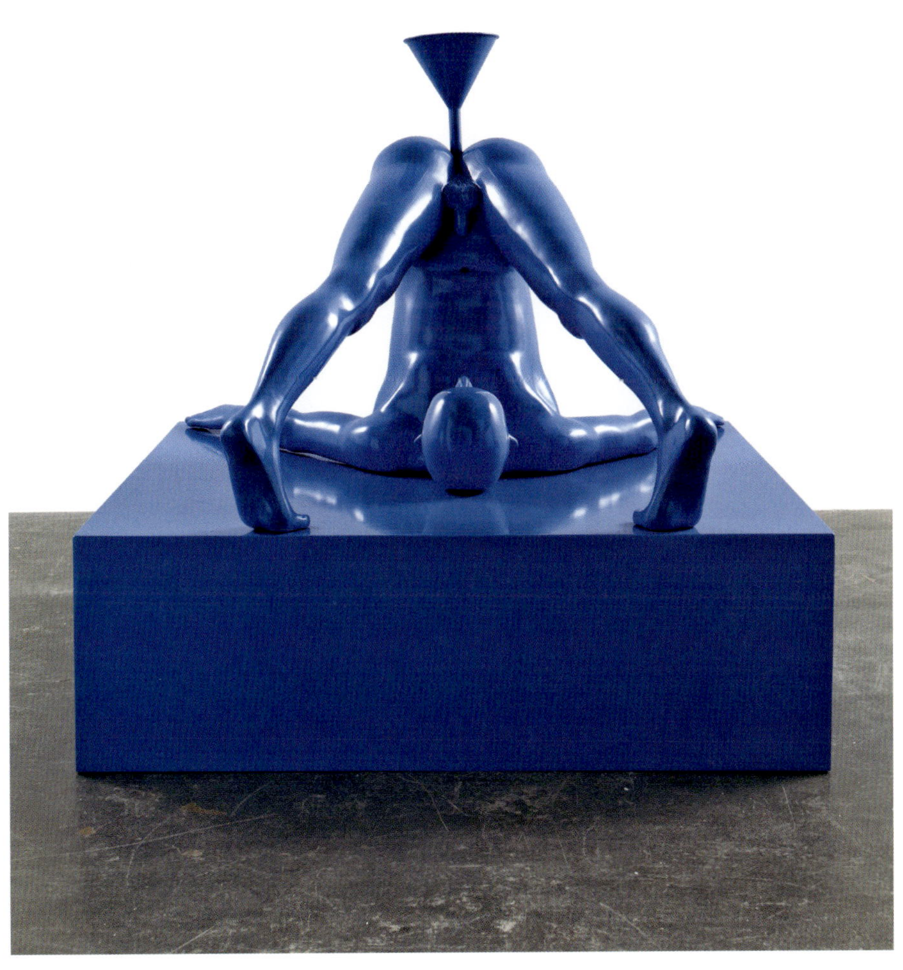

**La Grande Jatte (after Georges
Seurat)**, 1992–

(following spread)
**La Grande Jatte (after Georges
Seurat)** (detail from 2006), 1992–

PLATE 61

248

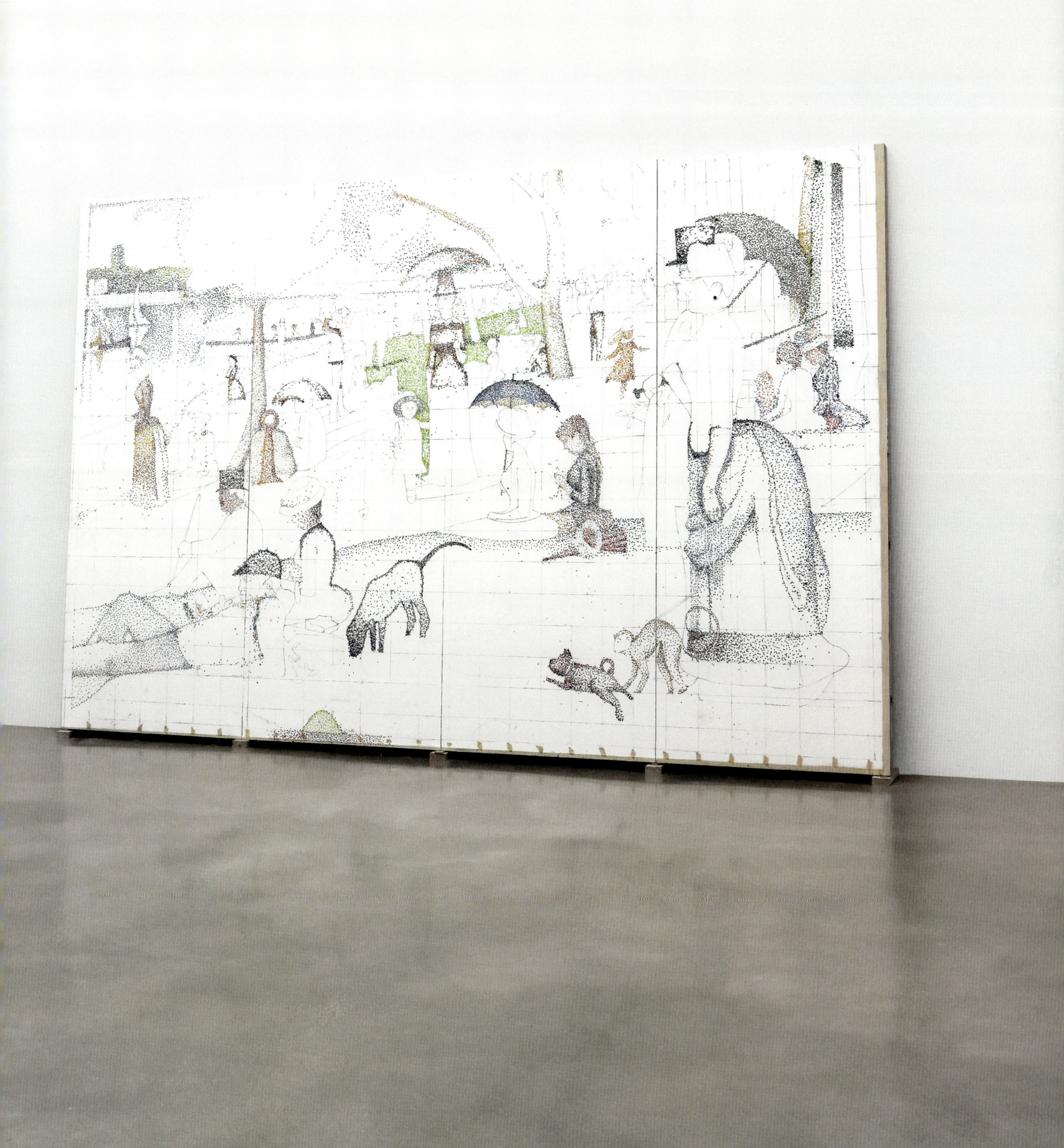

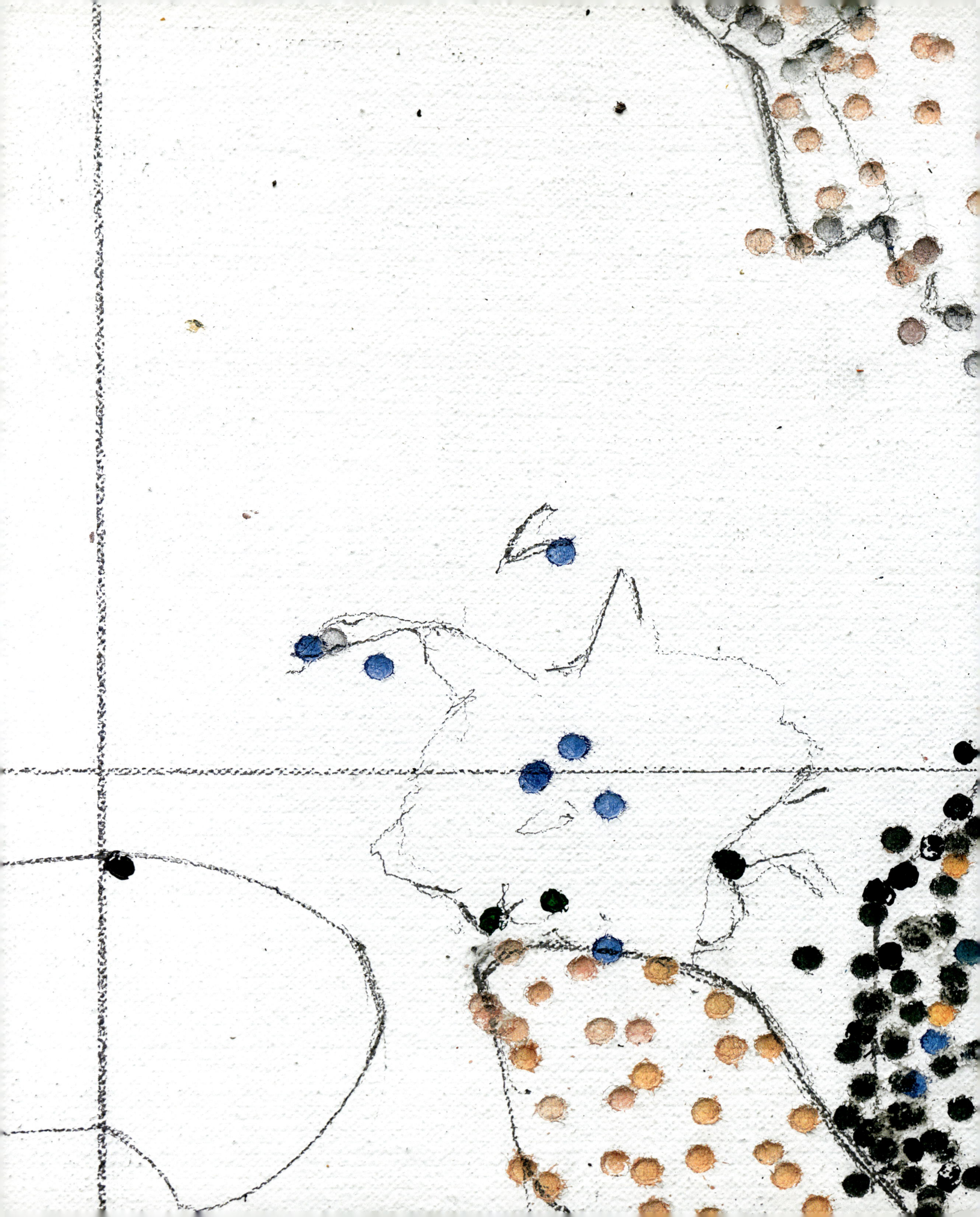

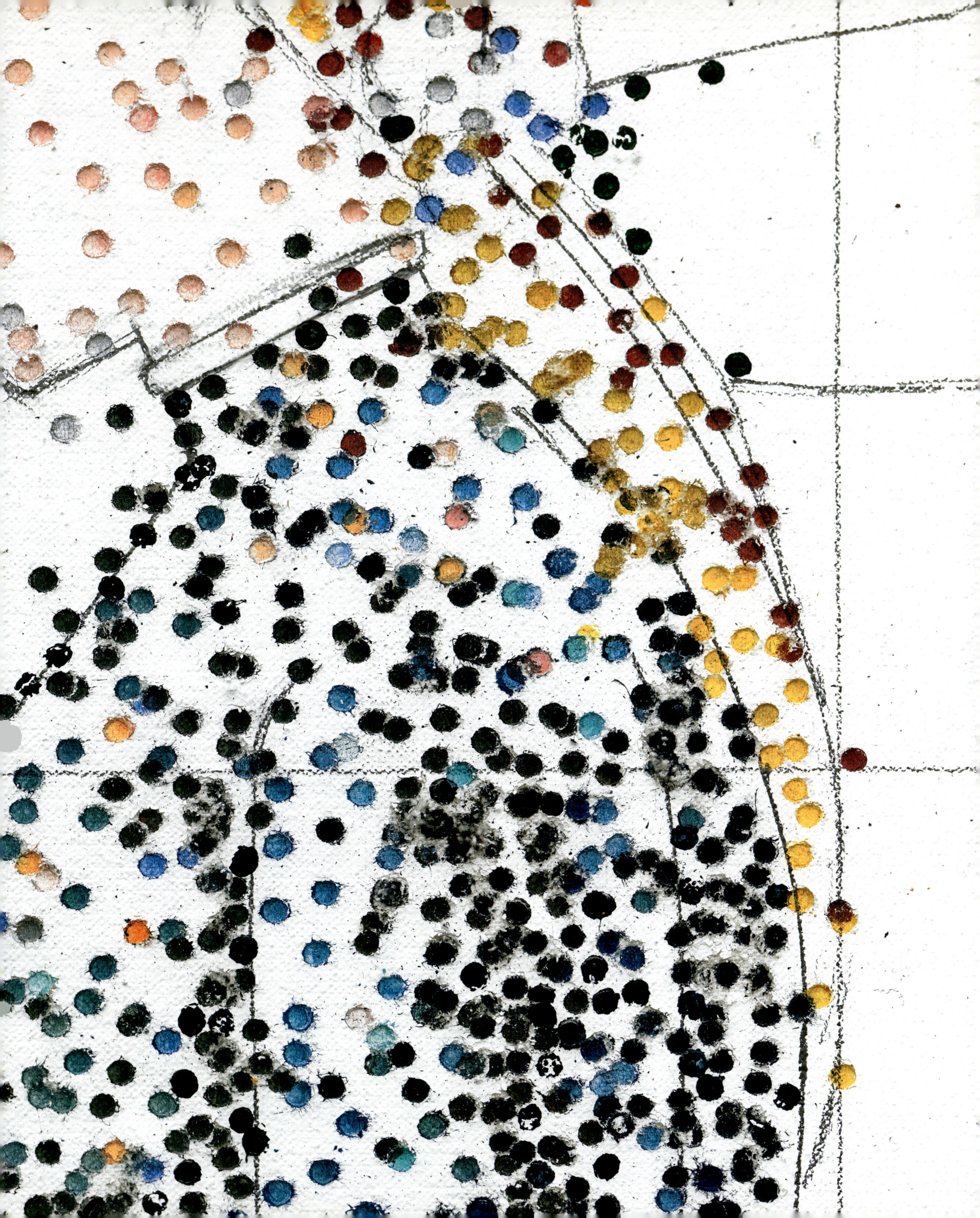

The Maid's Room (exterior), 2006–07

(following spread)
The Maid's Room (interior), 2006–07

PLATE 62

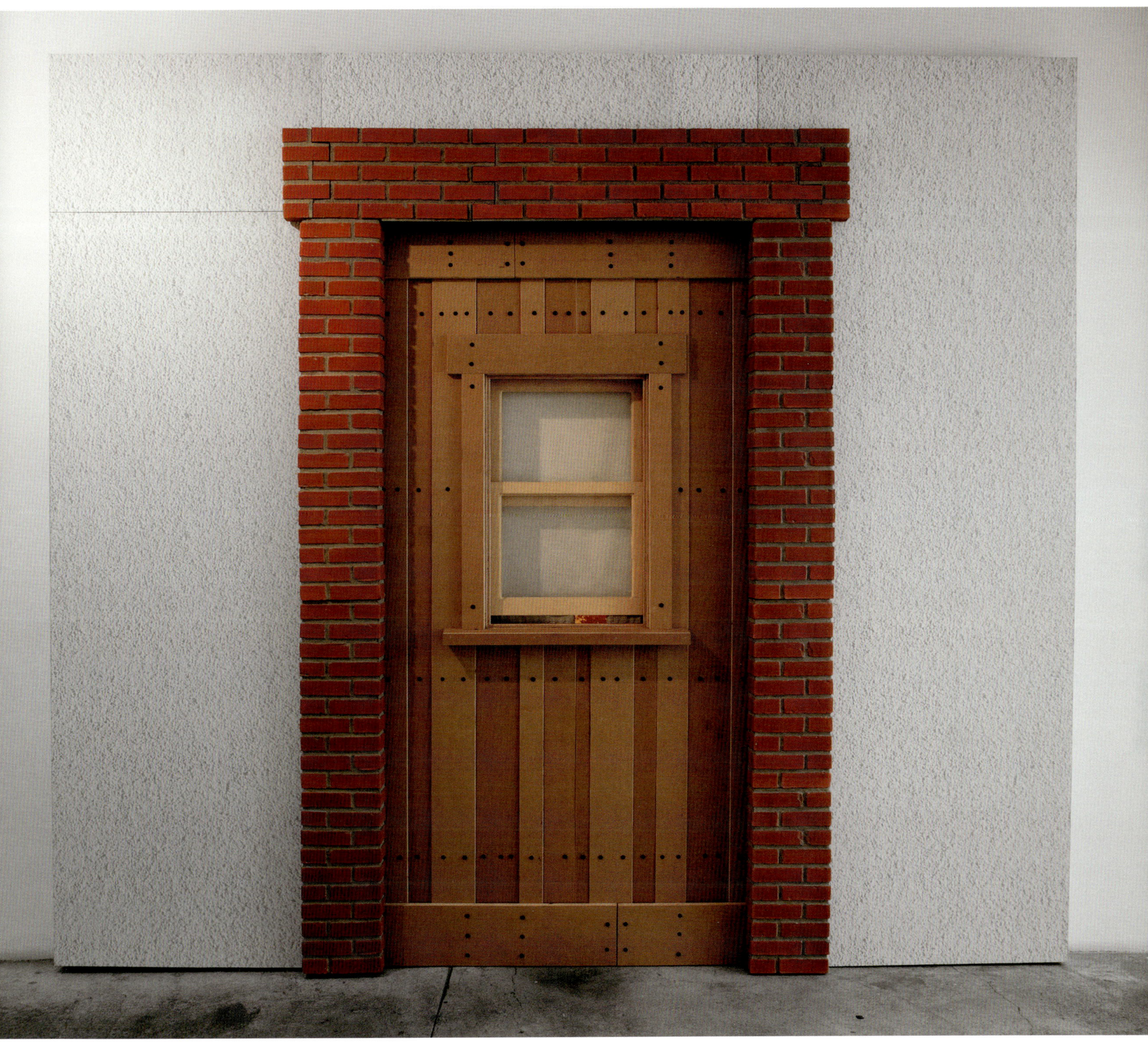

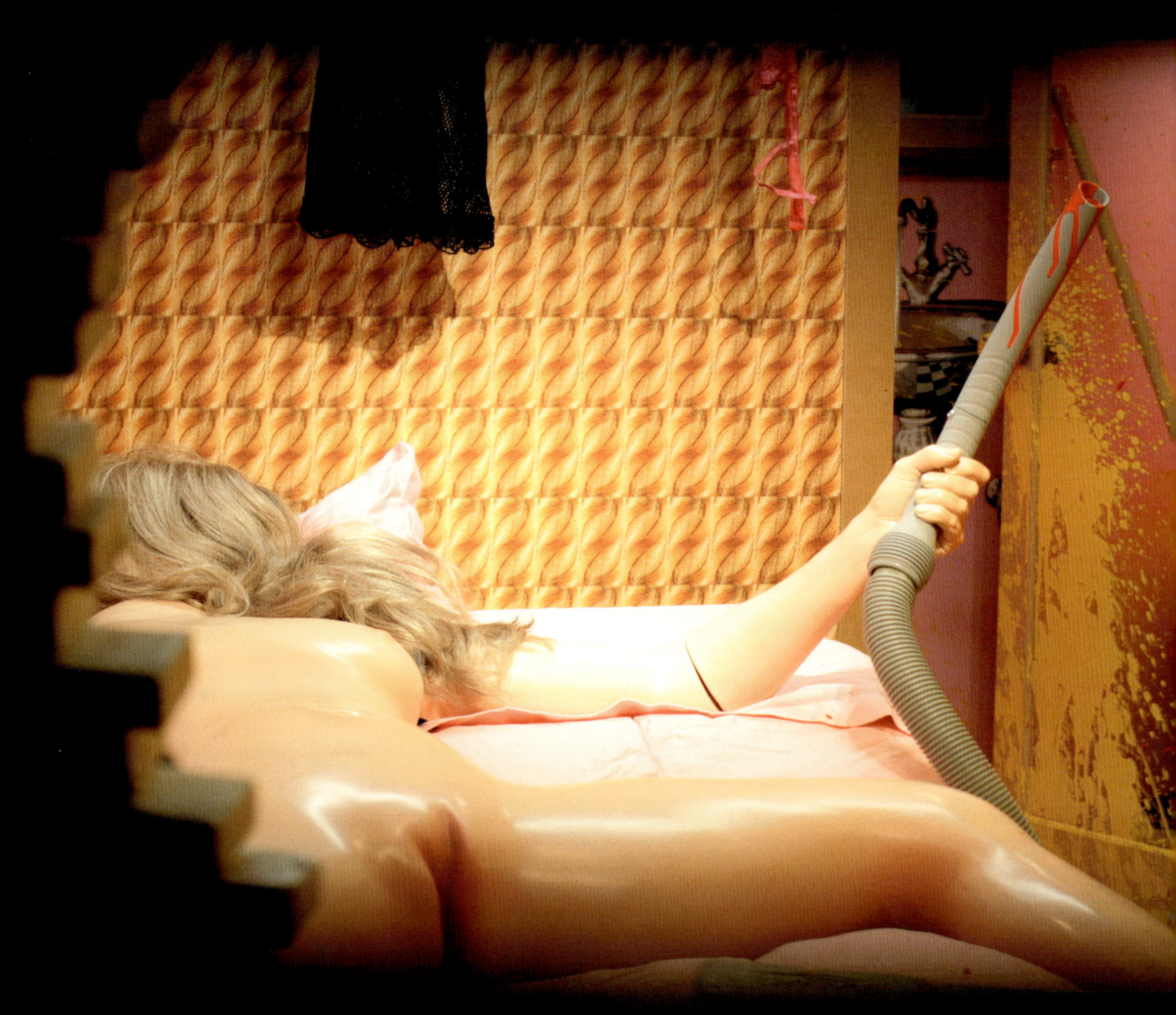

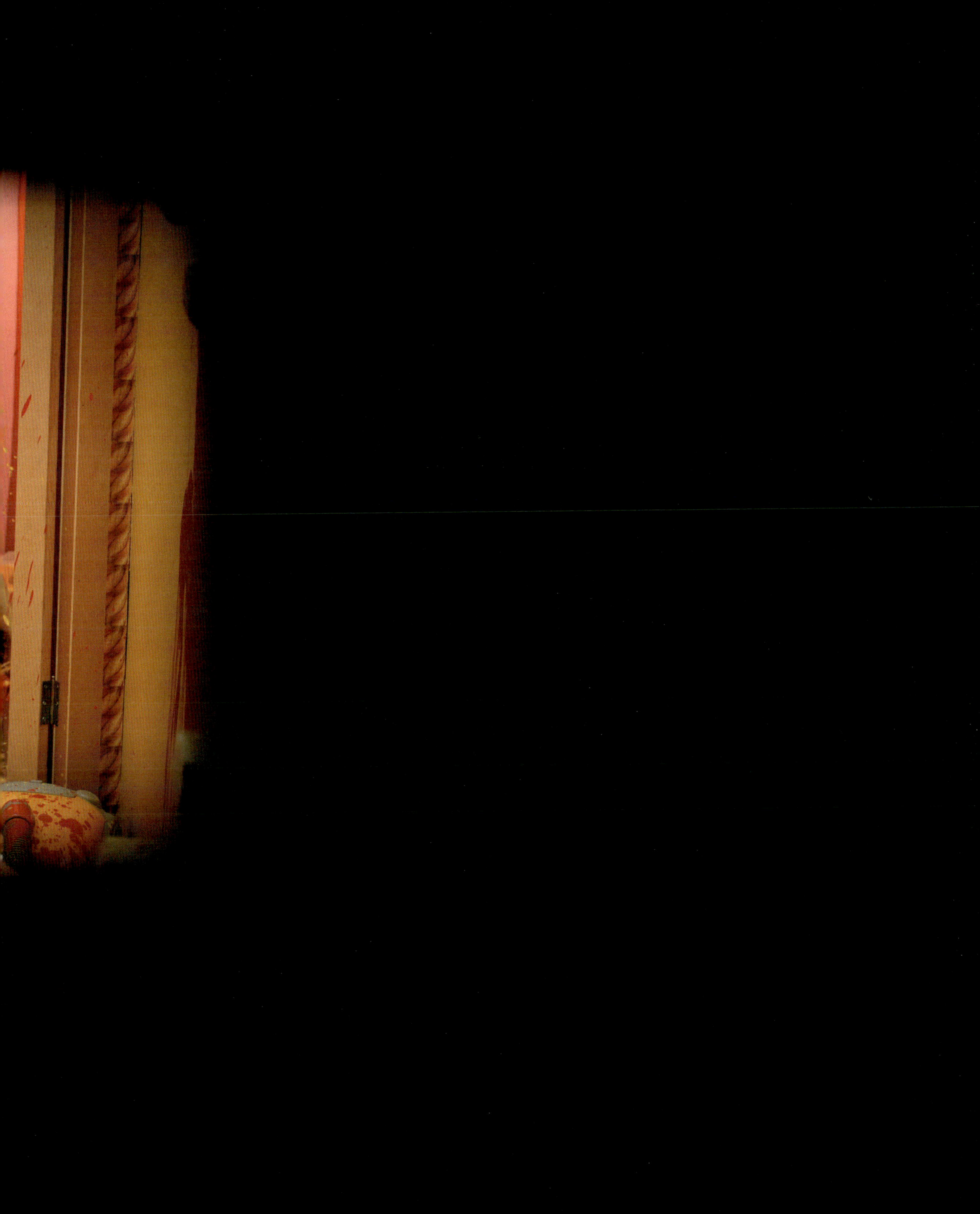

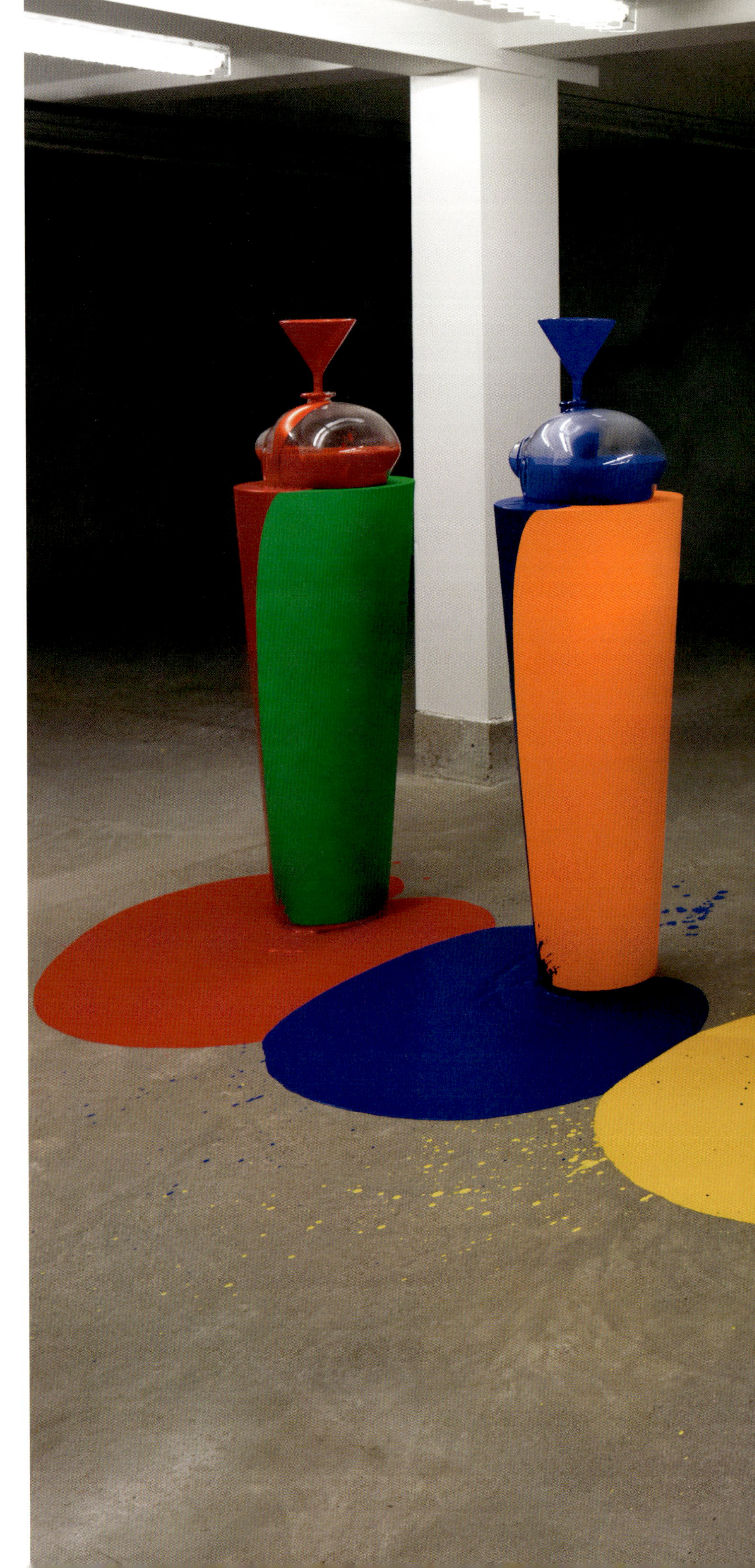

Five Glass Heads, 2006
PLATE 63

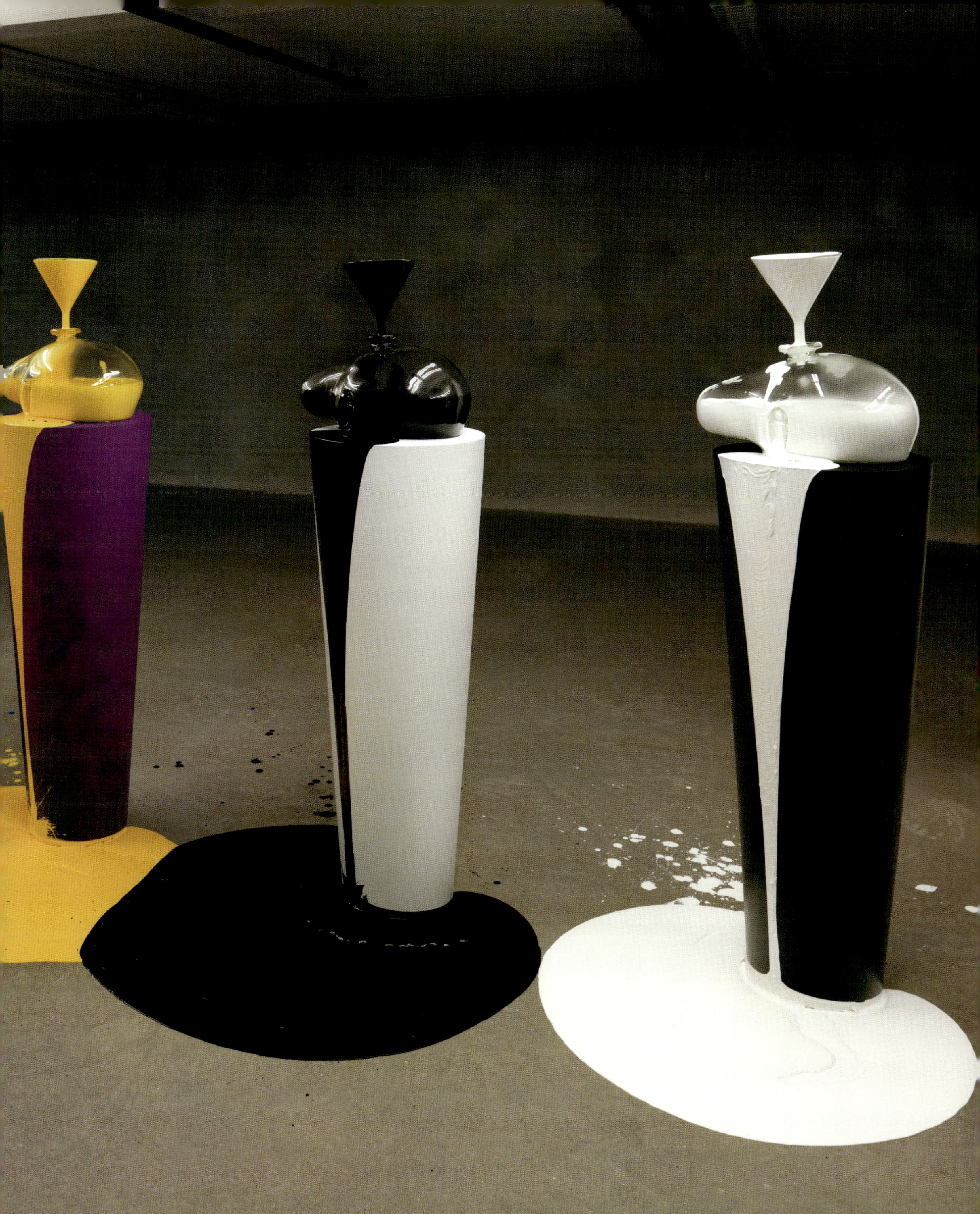

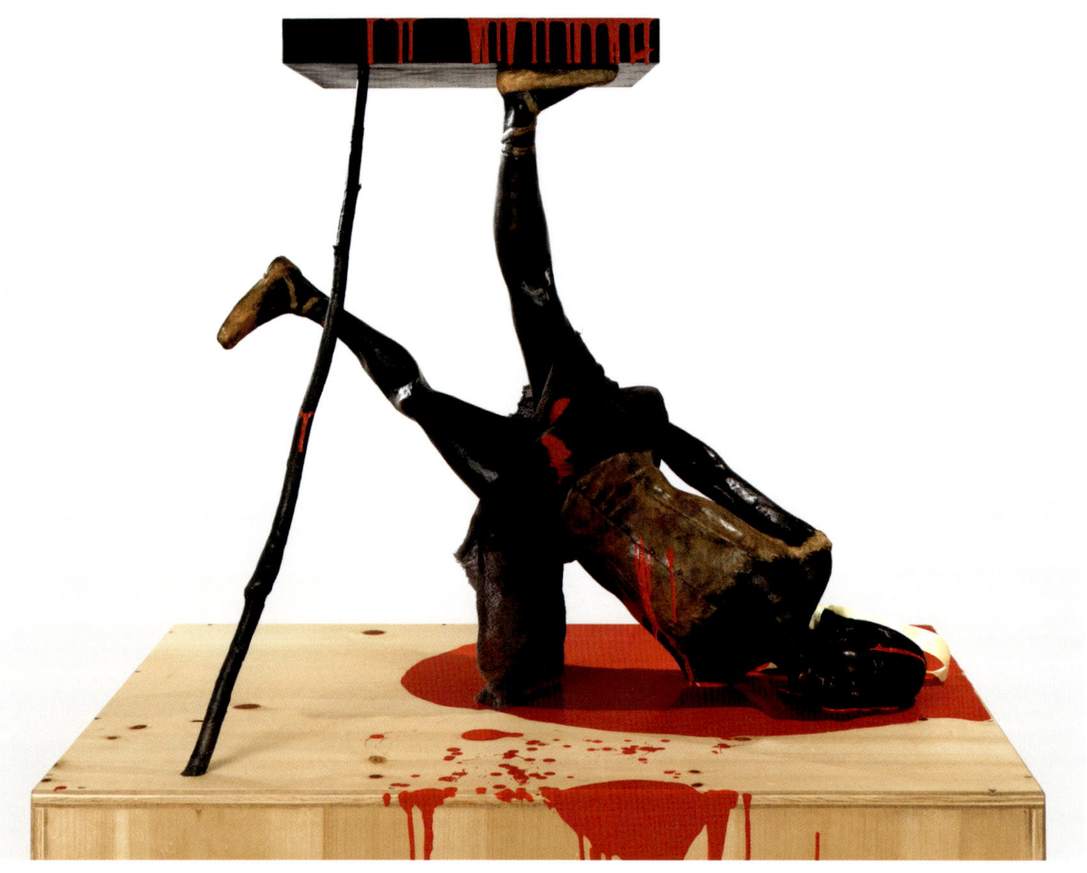

Ballerina, 2009
PLATE 64

(facing)
Ballerina, 2009
PLATE 65

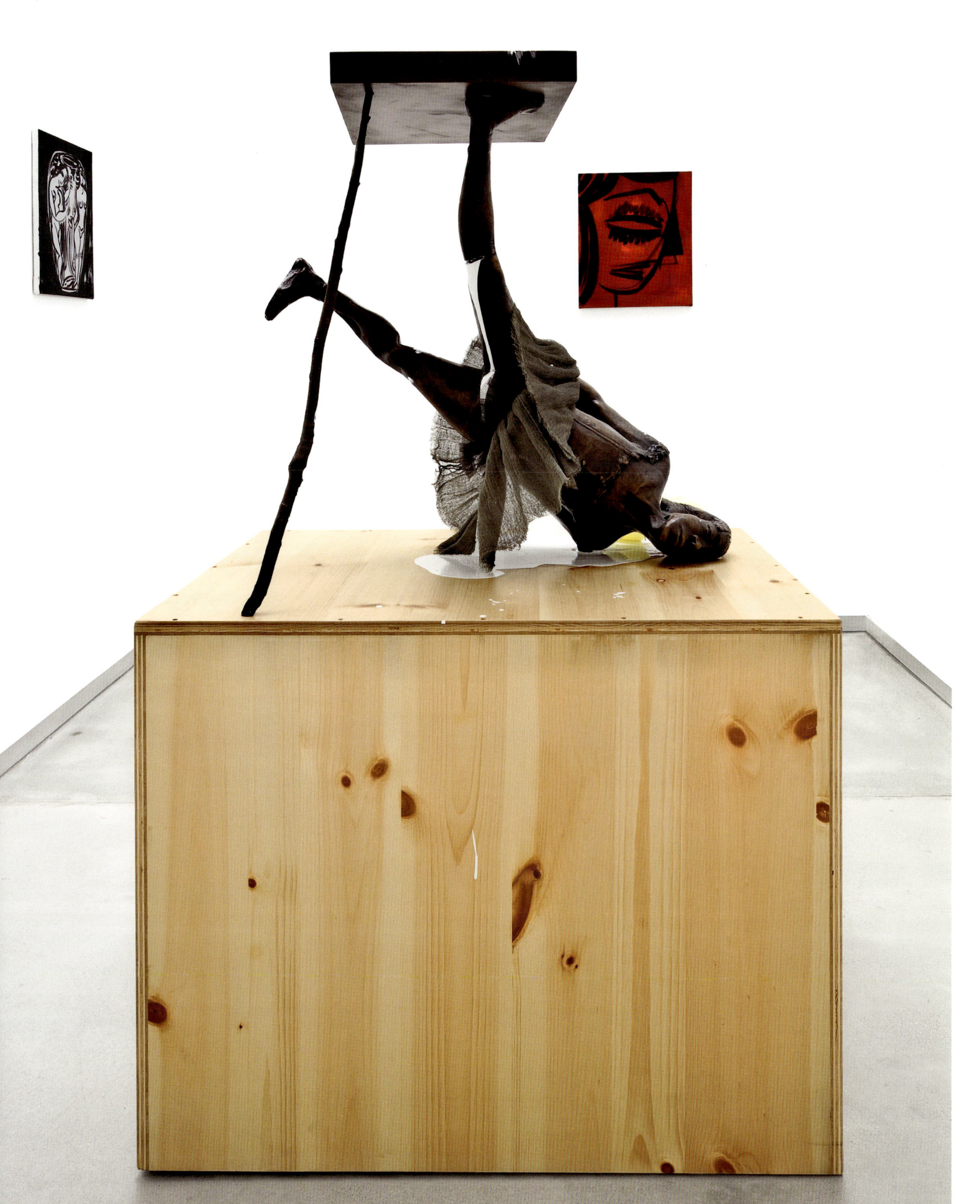

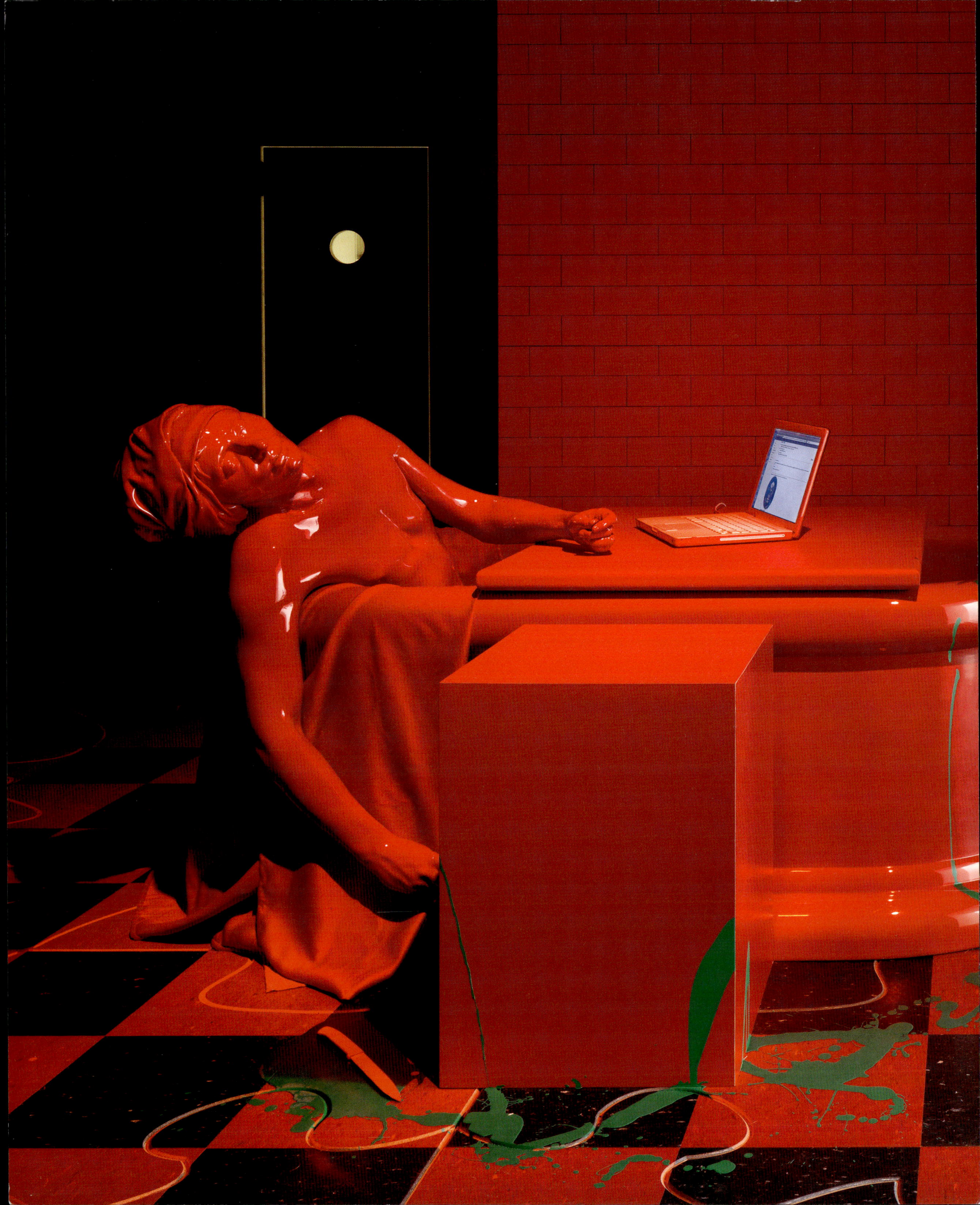

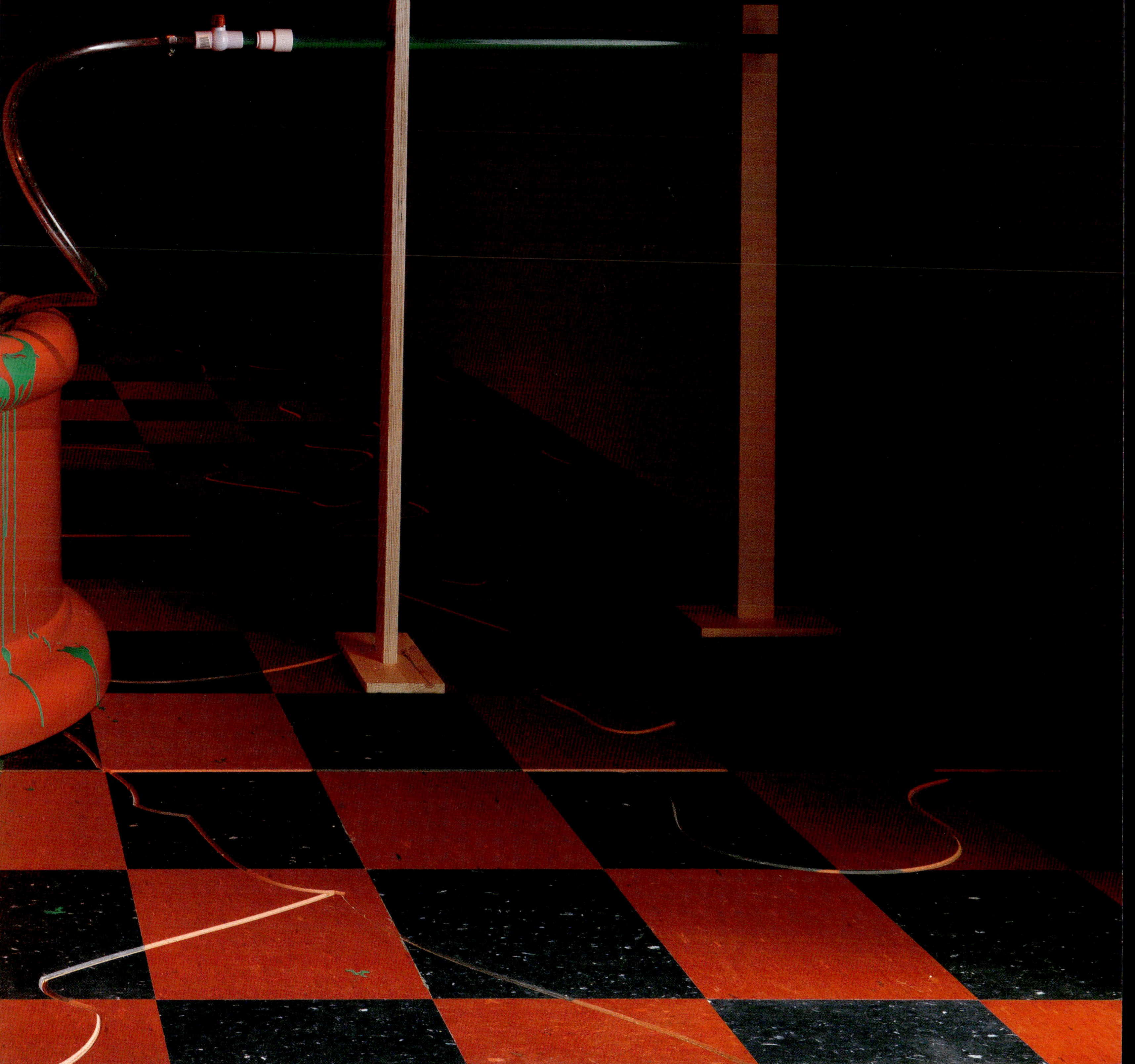

The Laundry Room (Death of Marat),
2009
PLATE 66

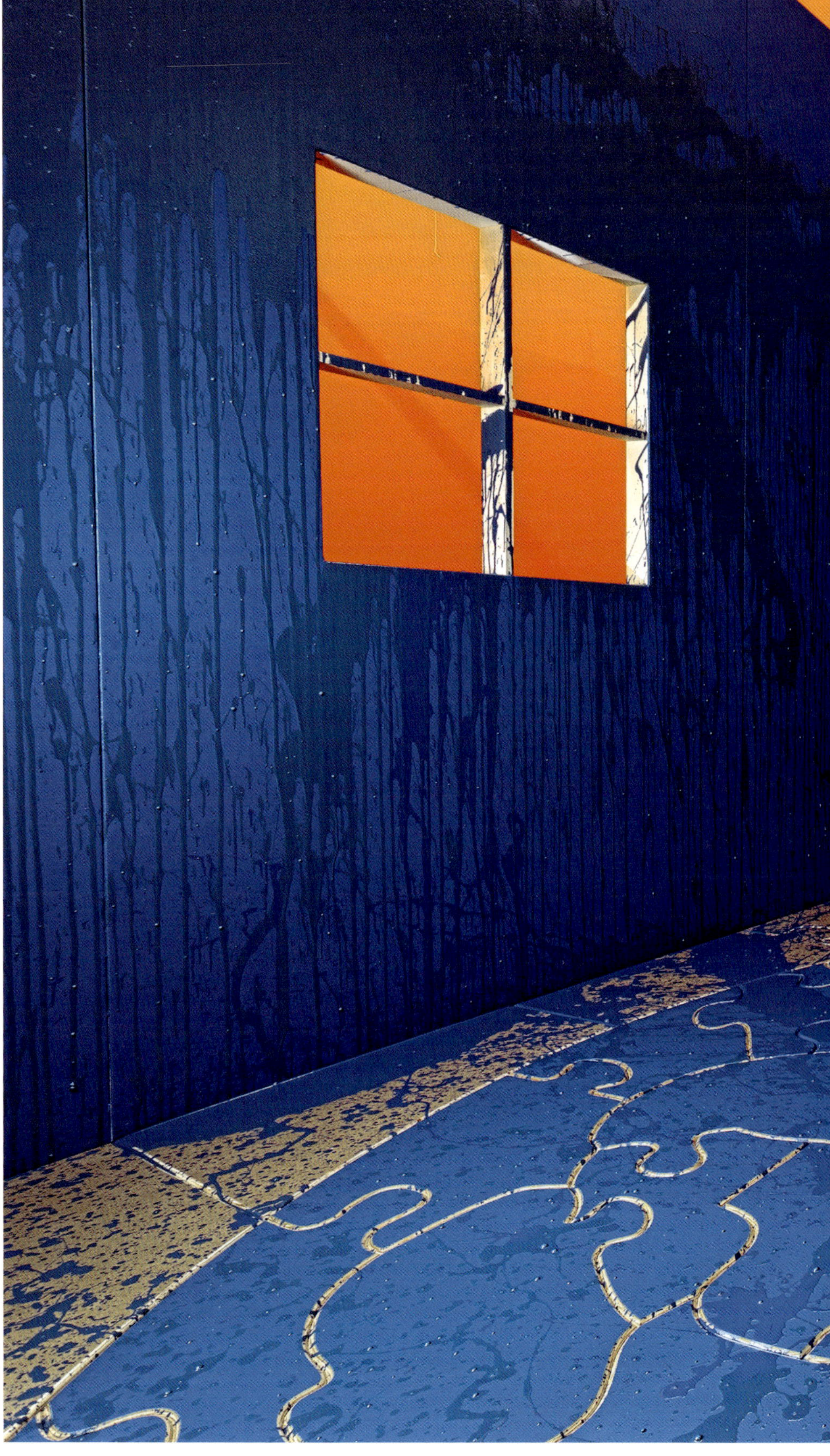

The Blue Room, 2011
PLATE 67

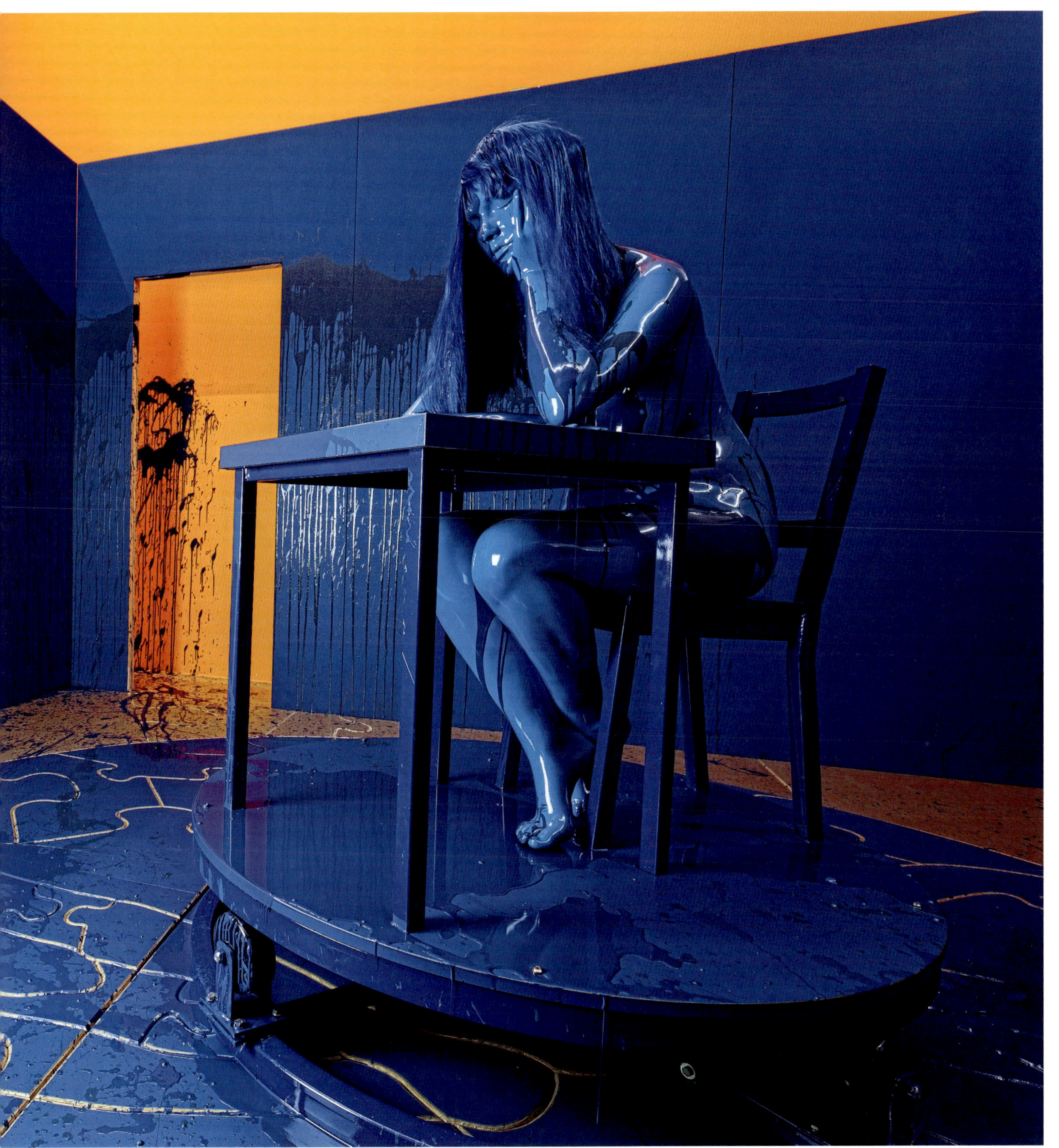

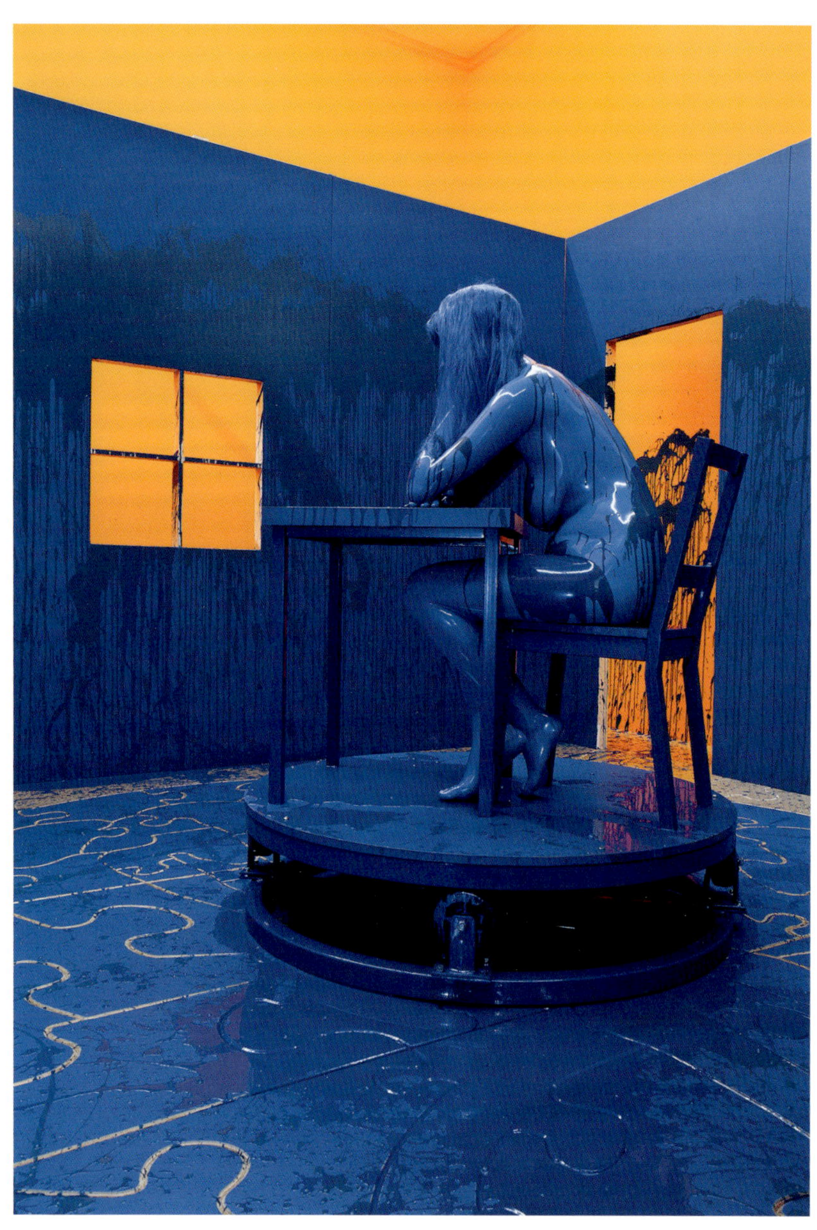

(above + facing)
The Blue Room, 2011

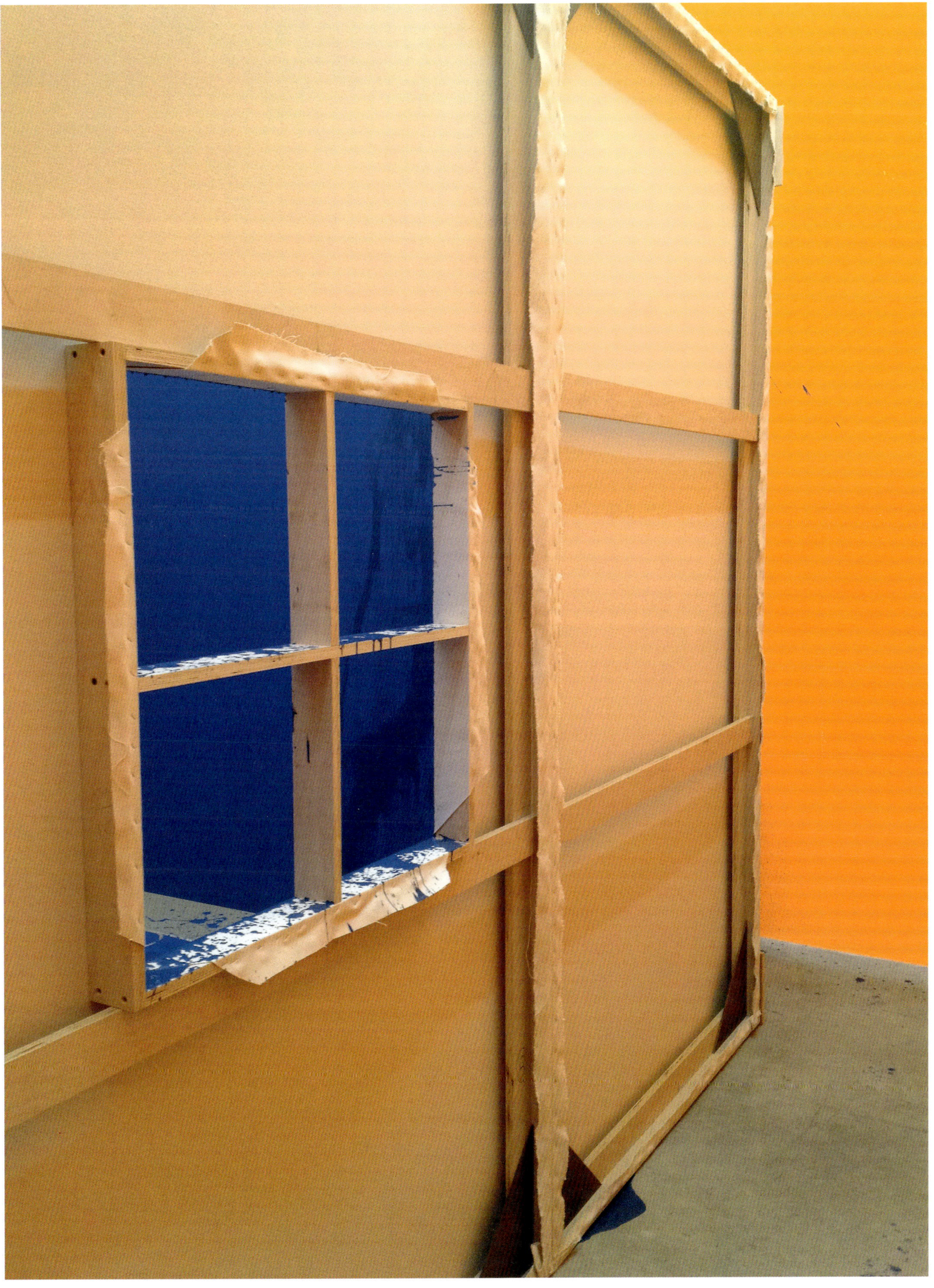

Complementary Colors Face-to-Face (Blue/Orange), 2011
PLATE 68

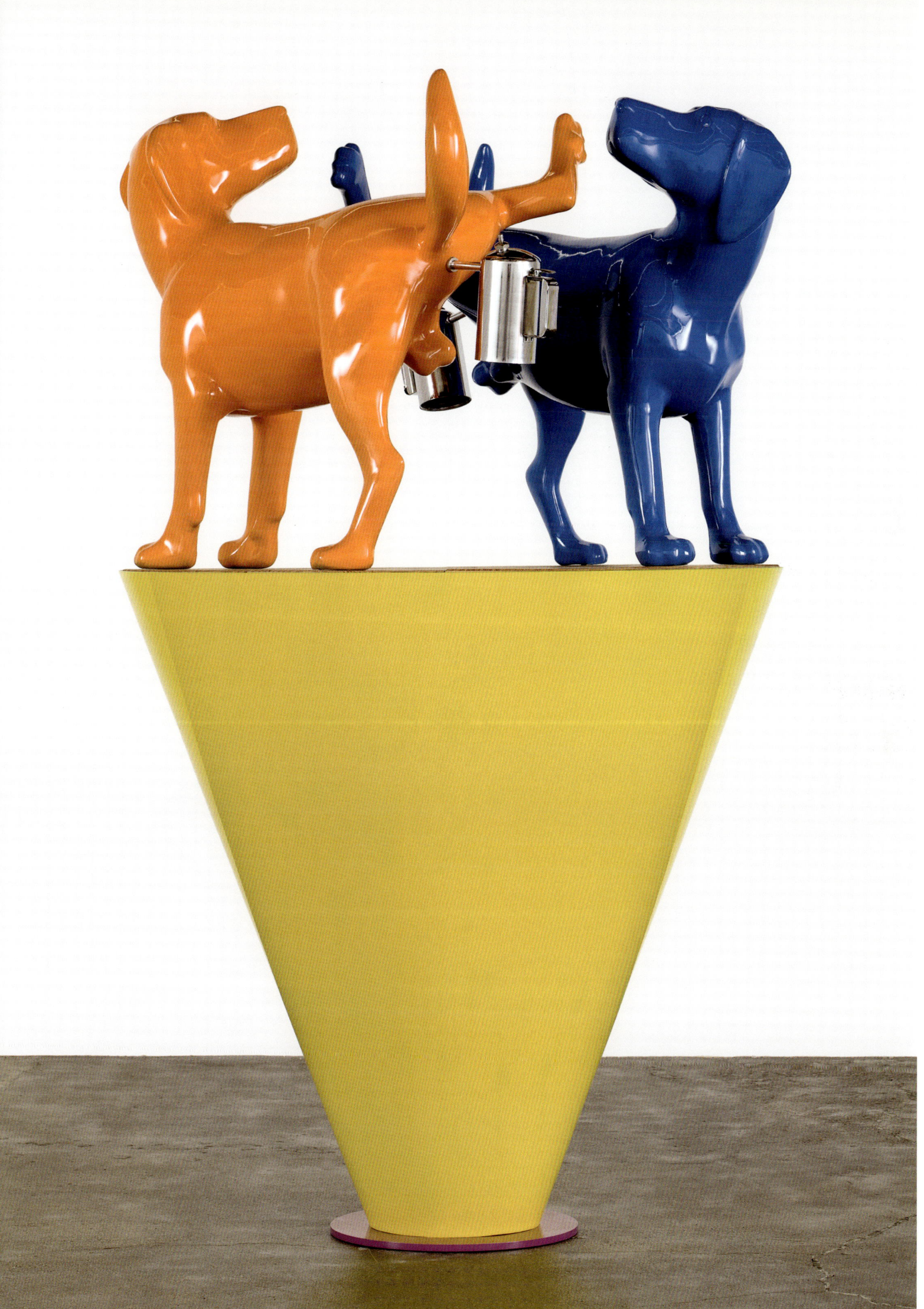

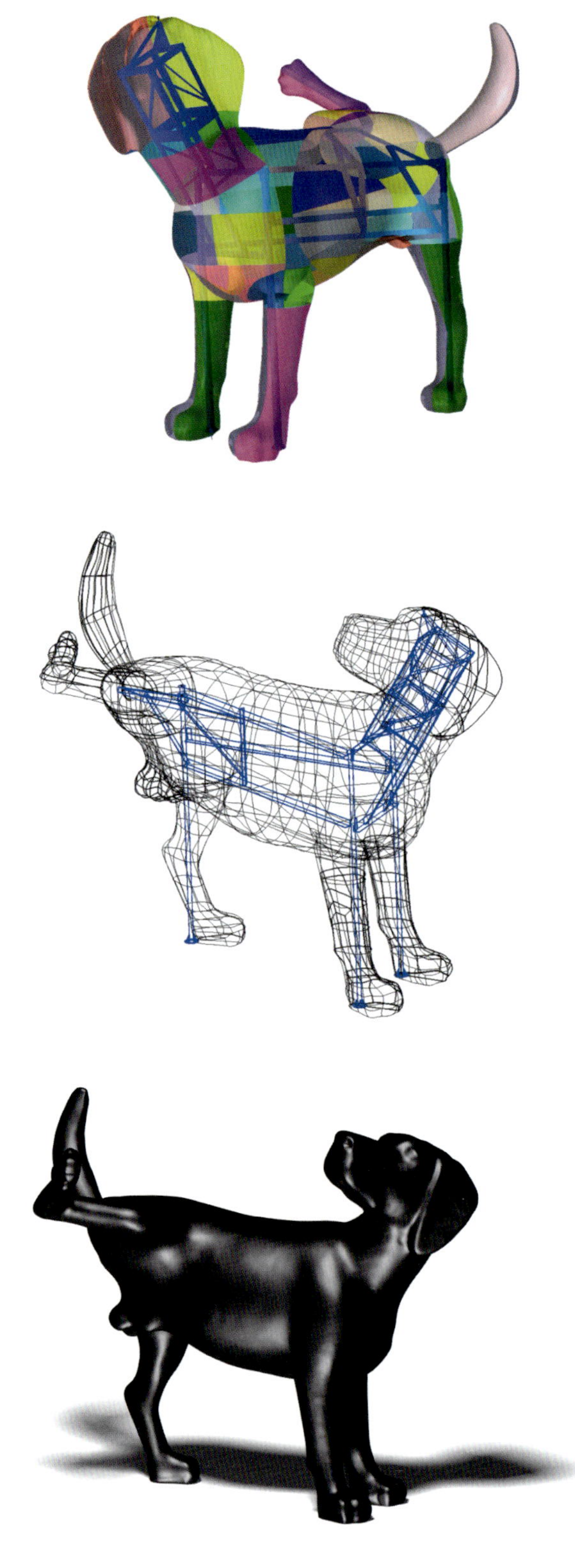

(all)
Bad Dog (computer renderings
and tail section in progress),
2013
PLATE 69

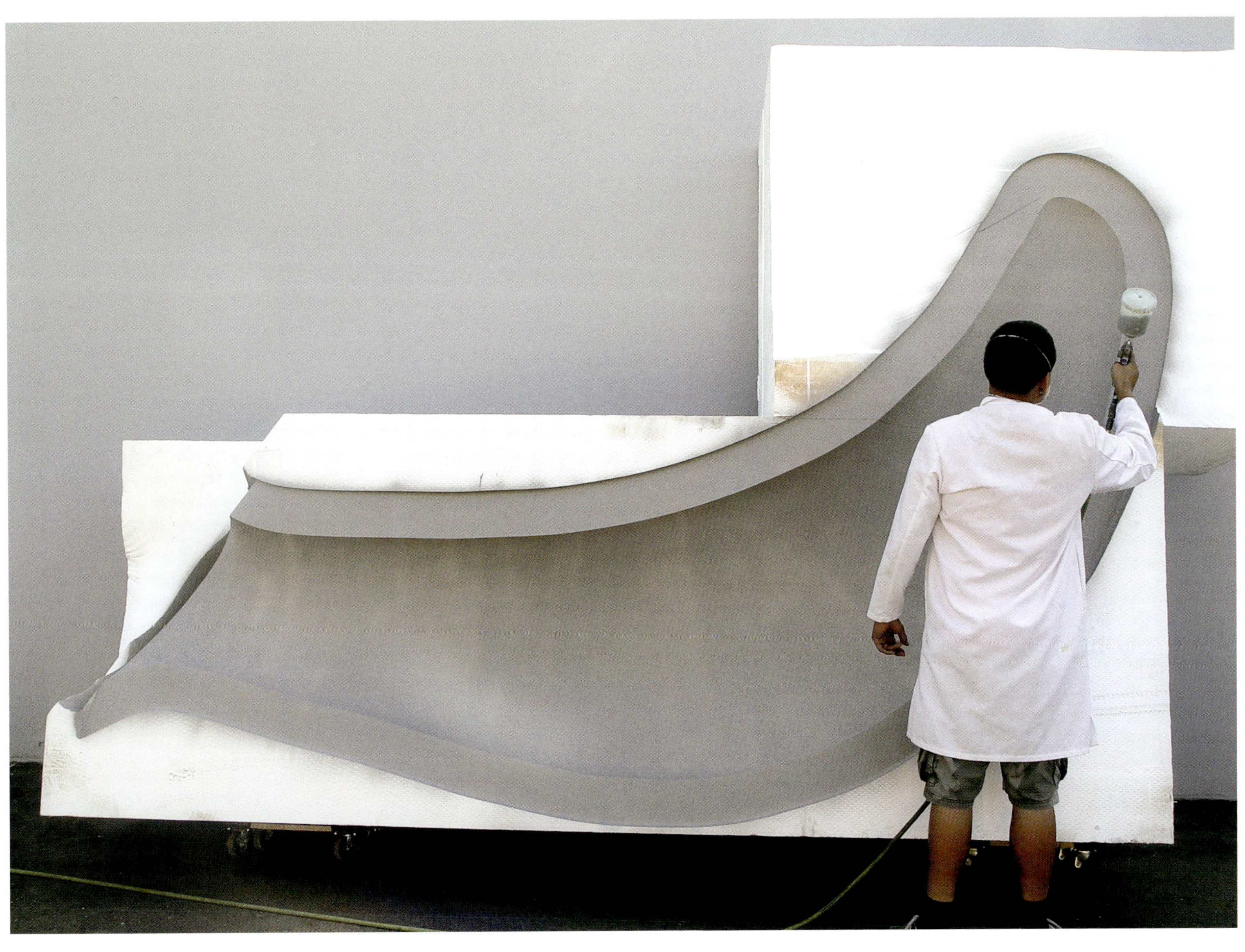

CHECKLIST OF THE EXHIBITION

Untitled (Drawing for "Painting Stuck to Wall of Room"), 1969. Graphite, oil paint, and masking tape on tracing paper. 33 ¾ × 41¾ in. (85.7 × 106 cm). The Menil Collection, Houston, gift of the artist
PLATE 4

Project Drawing (Maze for Eugenia Butler Gallery, Los Angeles), 1970. Oil and pencil on paper. 36 × 50 in. (91.4 × 127 cm). Collection of Alison Terbell Nikitopoulos and Dimitris E. Nikitopoulos
PLATE 3

Untitled (Model I for "Maze Eugenia Bulter Gallery, Los Angeles"), 1970. Glue, corrugated board. 2 ³⁄₁₆ × 4 ¾ × 4 ¾ in. (5.5 × 12.1 × 12.1 cm). Friedrich Christian Flick Collection, Hamburger Bahnhof
PLATE 1

Untitled ("Paint on the Rug"), 1970. Oil and acrylic on paper. 36 × 48 in. (91.4 × 121.9 cm). Kathryn Wortz, in memory of her parents, Ed and Melinda
PLATE 5

Untitled (plans for three-dimensional work), 1970. Oil and pencil on paper. 37 ¹⁄₁₆ × 44 ¹⁵⁄₁₆ in. (94.1 × 114.1 cm). Corcoran Gallery of Art, Washington, D.C., Museum Purchase 1971.31
PLATE 7

Project Drawing, 1972. Oil and pencil on paper. 37 × 42 in. (94 × 106.7 cm). Collection of Barbara Haskell
PLATE 6

Untitled, 1972. Pencil and oil on paper. 34 ½ × 40 ³⁄₈ in. (87.6 × 102.6 cm). Los Angeles County Museum of Art, Modern and Contemporary Art Council, New Talent Purchase Award (M.72.86.5)
PLATE 8

Cut the Rug, 1973. Oil and pencil on paper. 36 × 50 × 2 ½ in. (91.4 × 127 × 6.4 cm). Collection of Nancy Reddin Kienholz
PLATE 9

Project 1974, 1974. Acrylic paint, oil and pencil on mylar. 55 ½ × 43 ¼ in. (141 × 109.9 cm). Rennie Collection, Vancouver
PLATE 13

RIKOS, 1974. Oil and pencil on paper. 34 ½ × 45 in. (87.6 × 114.3 cm). Collection of Martin Seol Family Foundation
PLATE 10

Untitled (Drawing for a painting at Bykert Gallery), 1974. Pencil and oil on mylar. 55 ½ × 43 ¼ in. (141 × 109.9 cm). Rennie Collection, Vancouver
PLATE 11

Stedlijk [sic] Museum, 1975. Oil on tracing paper. 35 ½ × 45 ½ in. (90.2 × 115.6 cm). Courtesy of the artist
PLATE 16

Untitled ("3-3 Side by Side"), 1975. Oil on tracing paper. 35 ½ × 45 ½ in. (90.2 × 115.6 cm). Courtesy of the artist
PLATE 17

Untitled ("Paint every page…"), 1976. Graphite and oil on mylar. 49 × 48 in. (124.5 × 121.9 cm). Private collection
PLATE 33

Untitled (Study for "Untitled Free-standing Painting"), 1977. Pencil and colored pencil on mylar. 43 ¼ × 76 ¼ in. (109.9 × 193.7 cm). Rennie Collection, Vancouver
PLATE 12

100 Drawings, 1978. Mixed media/pencil on tracing paper. Approx. 12 × 9 in. (30.5 × 23 cm) each. Collection of Nancy Reddin Kienholz

Untitled, 1978. Pencil and acrylic on paper. 40 ¹⁄₈ × 51 ¹⁄₈ in. (102.1 × 130 cm). Private collection, Switzerland
PLATE 14

Untitled (Felsen Gallery), 1978. Oil and pencil on paper. 72 × 70 ½ in. (183 × 179 cm). Galerie Lelong Zurich
PLATE 15

Untitled (Study for "Untitled Wall Painting"), 1978. Pencil and oil on mylar. 43 × 47 in. (109.2 × 119.4 cm). Rennie Collection, Vancouver
PLATE 18

Big ball of small canvases stuck together with thick paint, 1979. Pencil and color pencil. 37 ¾ × 52 ¾ in. (96 × 134 cm). Collection Robert + Susy Rufli, Zurich-Switzerland
PLATE 34

Big Ideals, 1979. Oil and pencil on mylar. 47 ¼ × 37 ³⁄₈ in. (120 × 95 cm). Collection Robert + Susy Rufli, Zurich-Switzerland
PLATE 19

Planskizze für Installation (Sketch for Installation), 1979. Oil and pencil on mylar. 50 × 38 in. (127 × 96.5 cm). Private collection, Zurich
PLATE 20

Untitled, 1979. Pencil and acrylic on paper. 74 ¾ × 53 ¹⁄₈ in. (190 × 135 cm). Private collection, Switzerland
PLATE 21

Eight Projects for Filling a Room, ca. 1979. Pencil on transparent paper. 73 ¼ × 94 ⁷⁄₈ in. (186 × 241 cm). Galerie Lelong Zurich
PLATE 35

5050 Stacked Paintings, 1980–2013. Wood, canvas, acrylic paint. Approx. 120 × 360 × 180 in. (304.8 × 914.4 × 457.2 cm). Rennie Collection, Vancouver
PLATE 48

Project Drawing for "Big Ideas—1000 Pictures," 1980. Oil and pencil on mylar. 49 ³⁄₈ × 37 ¾ in. (125.4 × 95.9 cm). Collection of Elizabeth A. Greenberg
PLATE 36

Untitled, ca. 1980. Acrylic and graphite on vellum. 36 ¹⁄₈ × 53 in. (92 × 134.6 cm). Collection of Manny and Jackie Silverman
PLATE 37

Untitled, ca. 1980. Acrylic and graphite on mylar. 54 × 72 in. (137.2 × 183 cm). Jeff Kerns Collection, Los Angeles
PLATE 38

Untitled (Study I for "5050 Stacked Paintings"), ca. 1980–81. Pencil and oil on mylarfoil. 52 ¾ × 35 ²⁄₅ in. (134 × 90 cm). Friedrich Christian Flick Collection, Hamburger Bahnhof
PLATE 39

Fill a Room 1/2 Full III, 1981. Oil and pencil on mylar. 38 ½ × 61 in. (98 × 155 cm). Collection Robert + Susy Rufli, Zurich-Switzerland
PLATE 40

Untitled, 1983. Pencil and oil on acetate. 64 × 72 in. (on two sheets) (162.6 × 183 cm). Robert and Shaké Sarkis
PLATE 41

Untitled, 1984. Pencil and oil on acetate. 48 × 64 in. (122 × 162.6 cm). Robert and Shaké Sarkis
PLATE 42

P.S. 1.1.2., 1985. Oil and graphite on mylar. 23 ⅝ × 17 ⅝ in. (60 × 44.8 cm). Lenore and Bernard Greenberg
PLATE 22

Big Ordeals (Project Drawing 2), 1986. Oil and pencil on mylar. 18 × 24 in. (45.7 × 61 cm). The Menil Collection, Houston, gift of the artist
PLATE 25

Big Ordeals (Project Drawing 3), 1986. Oil and pencil on mylar. 18 × 24 in. (45.7 × 61 cm). The Menil Collection, Houston, gift of the artist
PLATE 26

Big Ordeals (Project Drawing 4), 1986. Oil and pencil on mylar. 18 × 24 in. (45.7 × 61 cm). The Menil Collection, Houston, gift of the artist
PLATE 27

Schloss Solitude, projects und plans, 1986. Acrylic paint, oil and pencil on mylar. 69 × 40 ½ in. (175.3 × 102.9 cm). Rennie Collection, Vancouver
PLATE 43

Untitled (Study for "Painting with Two Balls"), 1986. Pencil and oil on mylar. 73 ½ × 49 in. (186.7 × 124.5 cm). Rennie Collection, Vancouver
PLATE 24

Untitled (Study for Wall Painting), 1986. Pencil and oil on mylar. 56 × 41 ½ in. (142.2 × 105.4 cm). Rennie Collection, Vancouver
PLATE 23

Good Deal, 1987. Acrylic paint, steel. 106 × 288 × 288 in. (269.2 × 731.5 × 731.5 cm). Friedrich Christian Flick Collection, Hamburger Bahnhof
Ghent venue only
PLATE 51

Untitled, 1987. Pencil and acrylic on paper. 48 × 59 ⅞ in. (122 × 152 cm). Private collection, Switzerland
PLATE 28

Untitled (Study I for "Good Deal"), 1987. Pencil, oil on mylarfoil. 33 ½ × 33 ½ in. (85 × 85 cm). Friedrich Christian Flick Collection, Hamburger Bahnhof
Ghent venue only
PLATE 49

Untitled (Study II for "Good Deal"), 1987. Pencil, oil on mylarfoil. 33 ½ × 33 ½ in. (85 × 85 cm). Friedrich Christian Flick Collection, Hamburger Bahnhof
Ghent venue only
PLATE 50

1000 Clocks, 1987–92. Steel, aluminum, electric parts, fluorescent lights, oil paint, plastic. 141 ¾ × 432 ¼ × 360 ¼ in. (360 × 1098 × 915 cm). Hauser & Wirth Collection, Switzerland
Newport Beach and Ghent venues only
PLATE 54

3 Drawings for "1000 Clocks," 1987–92. Pencil and mixed media on paper. 35 ⅝ × 24 ⅛ in. (90.5 × 61.3 cm) each. Hauser & Wirth Collection, Switzerland
Newport Beach and Ghent venues only
PLATE 52

Clock Drawing, 1988. Ink and pencil on mylar. 38 × 54 in. (96.5 × 137.2 cm). Private collection
Newport Beach and Ghent venues only
PLATE 53

La Grande Jatte (after Georges Seurat), 1992–. Oil and graphite on canvas. 132 × 198 in. (335.3 × 502.9 cm). Rennie Collection, Vancouver
PLATE 61

Painting with Two Balls, 1997. Ford Pinto, metal, wood, canvas, acrylic paint. 240 ⅛ × 43 ¼ × 240 ⅛ in. (610 × 110 × 610 cm). Courtesy the artist and Hauser & Wirth
PLATE 55

Deer Beer, 1998. Mixed media. Dimensions variable. Friedrich Christian Flick Collection, Hamburger Bahnhof
Newport Beach and Ghent venues only
PLATE 56

Do It Yourself Painting (Still Life), 1998. Mixed media/assemblage/collage, MDO and MDF composition board, plastic decoy, cardboard, acrylic paint, steel cans, steel funnel, poultry fan, transformer, electronic wire, transformer, electronic wire, instruction silk screen. 42 × 42 × 84 in. (106.7 × 106.7 × 213.4 cm). Los Angeles County Museum of Art, Gift of the Modern and Contemporary Art Council (AC1999.72.1)
PLATE 57

Untitled (Model II for "5050 Stacked Paintings"), 1998. Plywood, corrugated board, adhesive, copper wire, pencil. 20 ¼ × 45 ⅗ × 51 ½ in. (51.4 × 116 × 131 cm). Friedrich Christian Flick Collection, Hamburger Bahnhof
PLATE 46

Untitled (Model III for "5050 Stacked Paintings"), 1998. Wood, plywood, corrugated board, crayon, pencil, cardboard, adhesive. 18 ⅕ × 30 ⅕ × 20 in. (46 × 76.5 × 51 cm). Friedrich Christian Flick Collection, Hamburger Bahnhof
PLATE 47

Untitled (Study II for "5050 Stacked Paintings"), 1999. Pencil on mylarfoil. 66 ⅖ × 42 ⅖ in. (168 × 107 cm). Friedrich Christian Flick Collection, Hamburger Bahnhof
PLATE 44

Untitled (Study III for "5050 Stacked Paintings"), 2000. Pencil, color pencil, marker, and printed letter on mylarfoil. 26 ½ × 42 in. (67.3 × 106.7 cm) Friedrich Christian Flick Collection, Hamburger Bahnhof
PLATE 45

Accidents in Abstract Painting, 2002. Cessna F150, aluminum aircraft model, crashed aircraft model; wood, mylar, electronic parts, plastic, rubber, cap, antenna, remote control, video (color, sound). 116 ⅞ × 431 ⅛ × 322 ⅞ in. (297 × 1095 × 820 cm). Courtesy the artist and Hauser & Wirth
Newport Beach and Ghent venues only
PLATE 58

Accidents in Abstract Painting No. 3, 2002. Oil and acrylic paint on mylar. 36 × 36 in. (91.4 × 91.4 cm). Private collection
Newport Beach and Ghent venues only

Upside Down Woman, 2005. Aquaresin. 59 × 46 ½ × 36 ¼ in. (150 × 118 × 92 cm). Rennie Collection, Vancouver
Munich and Ghent venues only
PLATE 59

Five Glass Heads, 2006. Glass, acrylic paint, aircraft plywood. 55 × 152 × 45 in. (139.7 × 386.1 × 114.3 cm). Rennie Collection, Vancouver
PLATE 63

The Maid's Room, 2006–07. Fiberglass, wood, motor, video, electric system, acrylic, paint and steel. 90 ½ × 200 ⅘ × 102 ½ in. (230.1 × 510 × 260.3 cm) Courtesy the artist, Galerie Georges-Philippe & Nathalie Vallois, and Hauser & Wirth
PLATE 62

Upside Down Man (Blue, Orange), 2008. Fiberglass, acrylic paint. 50 × 52 × 28 in. (127 × 132.1 × 71.1 cm). Courtesy the artist and David Kordansky Gallery, Los Angeles, CA
Munich and Ghent venues only
PLATE 60

Ballerina, 2009. Bronze, wood, acrylic paint, fabric. Edition 1 of 3. 60 × 30 × 40 in. (152.4 × 76.2 × 101.6 cm). Rennie Collection, Vancouver
PLATE 64

Ballerina, 2009. Bronze, wood, acrylic paint, fabric. Edition 2 of 3. 60 × 30 × 40 in. (152.4 × 76.2 × 101.6 cm). Beth Rudin DeWoody
PLATE 65

Ballerina, 2009. Bronze, wood, acrylic paint, fabric. 60 × 30 × 40 in. (152.4 × 76.2 × 101.6 cm). Courtesy Galerie Georges-Philippe & Nathalie Vallois, Private collection, Paris

The Laundry Room (Death of Marat), 2009. Acrylic paint, metal, wood, linoleum, aqua resin, plastic, fabric, computer, washing machine. 47 ¼ × 224 ⅜ × 224 ⅜ in. (120 × 570 × 570 cm). Courtesy the artist and Hauser & Wirth
PLATE 66

The Blue Room, 2011. Fiberglass, steel, wood, Formica, urethane paint, acrylic paint, canvas, wig, motor, rubber, and control panel. 175 × 175 × 108 in. (444.5 × 444.5 × 274.3 cm). Rubell Family Collection, Miami
Newport Beach venue only
PLATE 67

Complementary Colors Face-to-Face (Blue/Orange), 2011. Steel, wood, aluminum, paint. Edition 3 of 3. 86 × 56 × 56 in. (218.4 × 142.2 × 142.2 cm). Moira and Fred Kamgar
PLATE 68

Ain't Painting a Pain, 2012. Neon and acrylic paint. Approx. 72 × 120 in. (182.9 × 304.8 cm). Courtesy of the artist

Wall Painting, 2012. Oil paint, pencil on mylar. 43 ⅛ × 41 ⅞ in. (109.5 × 106.4 cm). Courtesy of the artist and Hauser & Wirth
PLATE 29

Untitled (Project for Orange County), 2012. Pencil and oil on mylar. 42 × 40 in. (106.7 × 101.6 cm). Courtesy of the artist
Newport Beach venue only
PLATE 30

Untitled (Project for Orange County), 2012. Pencil and oil on mylar. 42 × 41 in. (106.7 × 104.1 cm). Courtesy of the artist
Newport Beach venue only
PLATE 31

Untitled (Project for Orange County), 2012. Pencil and oil on mylar. 36 ¼ × 42 in. (92 × 106.7 cm). Courtesy of the artist
Newport Beach venue only
PLATE 32

Bad Dog, 2013. Fiber reinforced composite skin and steel. Approx. 336 × 384 in. (853.4 × 975.4 cm). Courtesy of the artist
Newport Beach venue only
PLATE 69

Reconstruction of **Untitled (Maze for Eugenia Butler Gallery, Los Angeles)**, 2013 Canvas, wood, acrylic paint 108 × 240 × 240 in. (274.3 × 609.6 × 609.6 cm). Collection of Alison Terbell Nikitopoulos and Dimitris E. Nikitopoulos, Courtesy of the artist
Newport Beach and Ghent venues only

CHRONOLOGY

Fatima Manalili with contributions
from David Mather, Andrew Berardini,
and Alberta Mayo

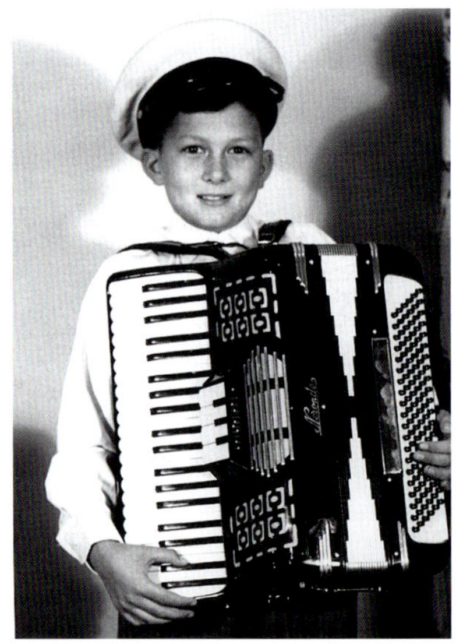

FIG. 1 (above)
Richard Jackson, age nine, 1948

FIG. 2 (right)
Sacramento Bee award
certificate, 1956

August 6, 1939

Richard Norris Jackson is born in Sacramento, California, to Rose and William Jackson. (FIG. 1)

1956

After two years of delivering the *Sacramento Bee* newspaper, Jackson receives a certificate of merit for his work. (FIG. 2)

1959–60

Jackson attends California State University, Sacramento, studying engineering for two years.

Travels to New York for two weeks and discovers the work of Jasper Johns.

In 1960 there was a county music station in Sacramento and the wife of the man who owned the station knew something about art. She took an interest in myself and a friend—thought we were interesting young

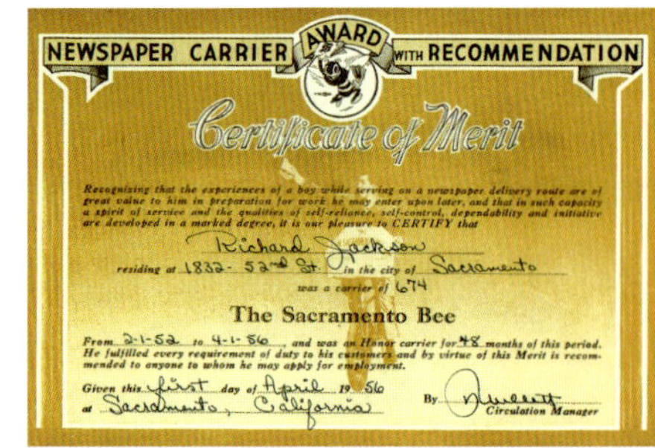

artists—so she paid for us to visit New York. I saw Jasper Johns' [work] and thought his Painting with Two Balls *was the greatest painting I had ever seen. I thought it was so strange, and I still do.*

—Richard Jackson[1]

1960

Serves in the Coast Guard out of San Francisco and Sacramento until 1966.

1. Richard Jackson, in Dennis Szakacs, "The Circus Is in Town" (interview with Jackson), *Mousse*, no. 25 (September 2010): 44.

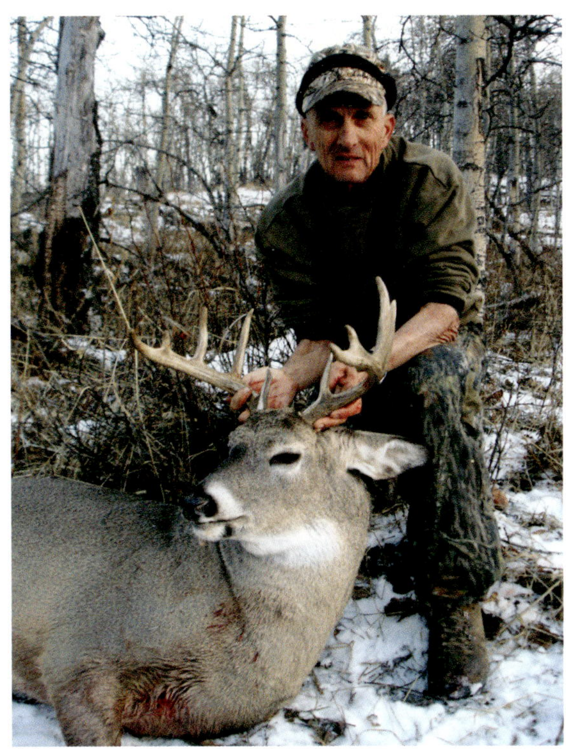

FIG. 3 (above)
Richard Jackson hunting in
Canada, 2009

FIG. 4 (below right)
Orange Grove studio, Pasadena,
California, 1970

Between 1960 and 1966 Jackson mines for
gold in Gold Lake, California, and he works as a
Christmas tree cutter each December.

1961

SOLO EXHIBITION
Crocker Art Museum, Sacramento

1963

The artist begins working as a distributor for the
New York Times, continuing to do so until 1965.

1964–65

Jackson meets Bruce Nauman in Sacramento.
Nauman later recalled hunting with Jackson:
"Richard hunted, took me once, and said, 'You've
got to have a good hunting knife.' His uncle or
father had given him the knife he'd been carrying
since he was young. But to buy one like it would
have cost too much, so we figured we'd make
it ourselves."[2] (FIG. 3)

1966

Runs the art gallery at California State University,
Sacramento. Organizes exhibitions by Bruce
Nauman and Peter Saul.

1968

Jackson invites Edward Kienholz to lecture in
Sacramento, and Kienholz accepts. During
that visit to Northern California, they go deer
hunting on Jackson's land in Colusa County,
California. Kienholz later said: "The best thing
about the trip was seeing Richard's work. His
canvases were stacked in a small shed behind his
house and I couldn't see too well, but I distinctly
remember the sense of movement as if
the images were compelled downward by a
reluctant gravity."[3]

Over the summer, Jackson goes to Idaho to stay
with Edward Kienholz.

Jackson relocates to Los Angeles, where he
works as a building contractor until 1995. Jackson
later recalled: "I was a slow learner. I didn't
have anything going before I got to Los Angeles.
There was no peer pressure in Sacramento.
It's a completely different situation when you
get in with people who are serious and ambitious,
aggressive and competitive."[4]

Jackson moves into Walter Hopps's house on
Orange Grove Boulevard in Pasadena, California.
He lives there for twenty-five years, sharing
the large house with Bruce Nauman for
several years. (FIG. 4)

SOLO EXHIBITION
Gallery 669, Los Angeles

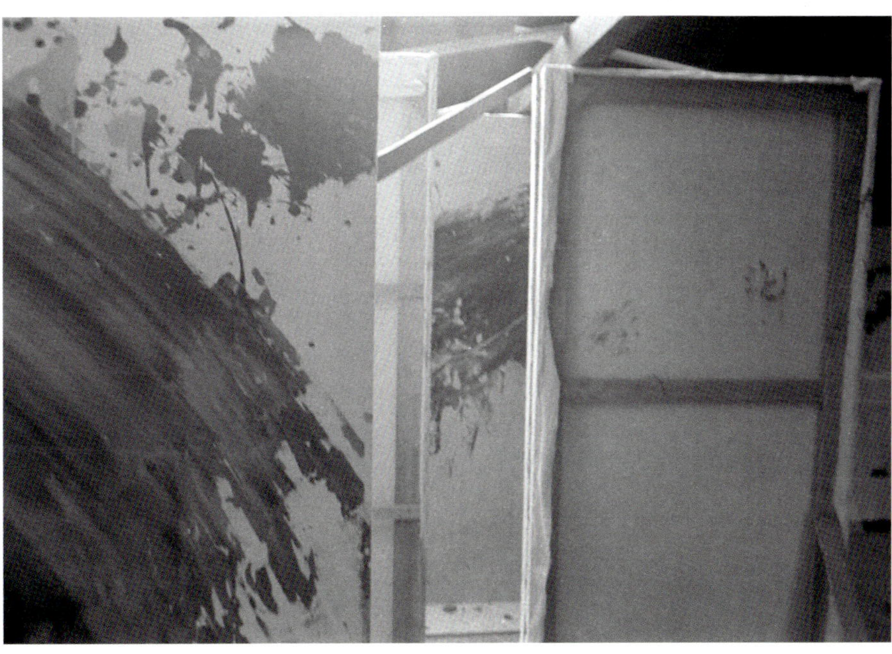

---

2. Bruce Nauman, quoted in Holland
Cotter, "At the Met: Susan Rothenberg
and Bruce Nauman," *New York Times*,
February 21, 1997.

3. Edward Kienholz, statement in
Richard Jackson, exh. cat. (Hope, ID:
Faith and Charity in Hope Gallery, 1978),
unpaged.

4. Jackson, in Szakacs, "Circus Is in
Town," 43.

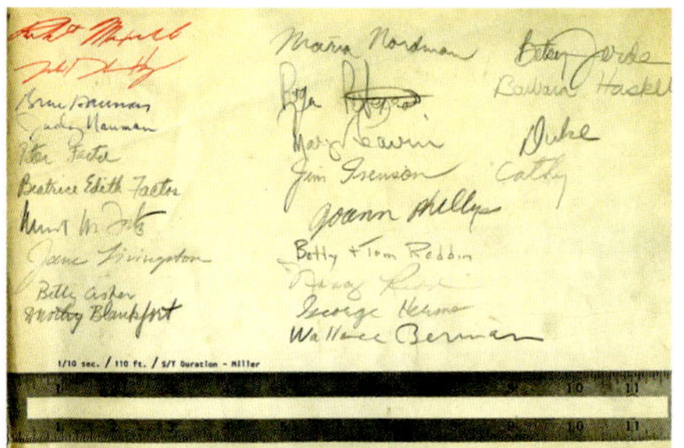

1969

Jackson works on the new building for the Pasadena Art Museum at its new location on Colorado Boulevard.

SOLO EXHIBITION
Eugenia Butler Gallery, Los Angeles

GROUP EXHIBITIONS
Indiana University Art Museum, Bloomington

Painting 1969, University of Nevada, Reno

Konzeption / Conception, Städtisches Museum Schloss Morsbroich, Leverkusen, Germany

1970

Jackson begins to apply paint directly to the wall using stretched canvas.

SOLO EXHIBITION
Eugenia Butler Gallery, Los Angeles. Creates *Untitled (Maze for Eugenia Butler Gallery)*.

A square maze is constructed of canvases. It has a single corridor that follows its inner perimeter. The corridor is two feet across, just wide enough for one person to pass through it. A single canvas, the same height as the maze walls and the width of the corridor, is pushed through the maze, dragging the paint across the inside walls.
—Peter Plagens[5]

Piece realized. Piece destroyed. Work purchased by Melinda Wortz. The original drawing was stolen from the exhibition. The drawing that the Wortz's have was re-done. Purchase price for the drawing and painting was $1,000.
—Richard Jackson[6]

Jackson's piece eludes easy categorization. Painted it certainly is, and a walk-in environment as well. Its particular combination of these two experiences is unique and accounts in part for the excitement it creates . . .

Following the paint-smeared corridor, along its concentric square maze, one anticipates a climatic painted enclosure in the center. The reverse is experienced as a central room re-duplicates the backstage feeling of the outermost surfaces one first encountered on entering the gallery. The sense of surprise and frustration are simultaneously evoked. Because one can never see all of the actual painting at once, the sense of mystery is maintained.

At the entrance of the painted corridor the hues are intense—oranges, greens, and blues. They then become subdued lavenders and aquas, and build in intensity again before the climax/anticlimax is reached. The painted surfaces are sensuously rich, a relatively rare quality recently, as oil painting seems to be relinquishing its favored status to process. Jackson's work successfully combines some of the best of both of these two possible worlds.
—Melinda Terbell[7]

Jackson re-creates this work in 2013 for *Richard Jackson: Ain't Painting a Pain*.

GROUP EXHIBITION
Photography into Sculpture, Museum of Modern Art, New York; reinstalled at Cherry and Martin, Los Angeles, in 2011

1971

GROUP EXHIBITIONS
Twenty-Four Young Los Angeles Artists, Los Angeles County Museum of Art

The Thirty-Second Biennial Exhibition of Contemporary American Art, Corcoran Gallery of Art, Washington, D.C.

The Corcoran exhibition, curated by Walter Hopps, includes works by twenty-two living American painters, eleven of whom were chosen by Hopps. Each of those artists in turn selects a colleague to be represented in the show. Hopps selects Jackson, who in turn chooses Franklin Owen, whom Jackson met while attending Sacramento State College.

Jackson's series of freestanding paintings were executed in the gallery space he had previously selected. Interested in useless or difficult spaces, he used a narrow hall as

---

FIG. 5 (above)
Exhibition announcement for
Cut the Rug, Los Angeles, 1973

FIG. 6 (right)
Exhibition sign-in sheet for
Cut the Rug, 1973

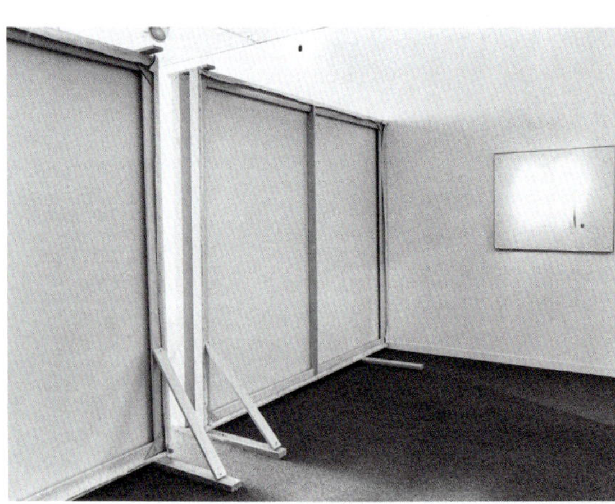

FIG. 7
Untitled, 1972. Paint, wood, canvas. 120 × 144 in. (304.8 × 365.8 cm). Los Angeles County Museum of Art, Gift of The Modern and Contemporary Art Council (M.72.9)

---

5. Peter Plagens, quoted in Iwan Wirth, ed., *Richard Jackson: Deer Beer*, exh. cat. (Cologne: Oktagon, 1998), 36.

6. Richard Jackson, in Wirth, *Deer Beer*, 36.

7. Melinda Terbell, "California, Los Angeles," *Arts Magazine* 45 (December 1970–January 1971): 49.

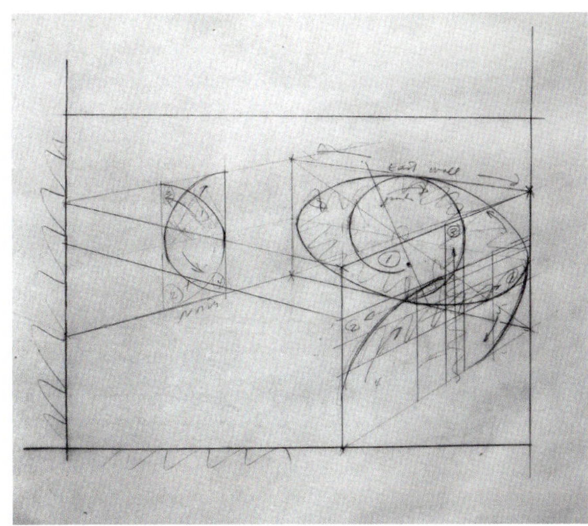

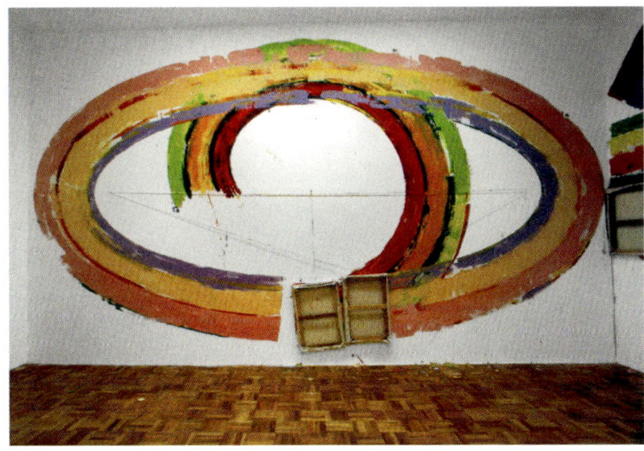

"container" for his enormous environmental action paintings done in Hofmannesque colors. One is certain to experience a different, more intimate dimension of the painting process when one enters his 40-foot-long environmental work, two free-standing canvases facing each other, through a 28-inch opening, or when one walks around the exposed backs of three paired off paintings, united by their fused surfaces, which act as free-standing objects. From their insides oozes pigment in complementary colors spilling over the floor and leaving colorful traces on the canvas backs. The painted surfaces removed from view constitute a hidden dimension, which certainly provides new aspects, at least for those interested in the process of environmental painting as a formalist statement.

—Viola Herms Drath[8]

1972

GROUP EXHIBITIONS
Los Angeles '72, Sidney Janis Gallery, New York

People had been telling me to design my work so it could be saved and re-used. This was my first attempt. I made the whole piece in sections that could be unscrewed so the work could be removed and reconstructed. I showed the gallery people how to take it apart. When they returned it, someone had trashed it with a hammer. The largest piece was about one foot long. They shipped the remains back. I gave up on that idea, it wasn't my idea, it wasn't a good idea.

—Richard Jackson[9]

John Baldessari / Francis Barth / Richard Jackson / Barbara Munger / Gary Stephan, Contemporary Arts Museum Houston

The surprise of Jackson's works is that their gesture and spontaneity is based on careful planning of composition and conceptual intent.

—Jay Belloli[10]

Fifteen Los Angeles Artists, Pasadena Art Museum, Pasadena, California

A lock-step system of nice (young?) artists working in clean, white rooms, making clean, rollable, elegant, ropy, dismountable, portable art to fit into the bed of a Ford Ranchero, to be driven to the clean, sunny parking lot of the clean new museum, where it's documented and fussed over by young curators, shown to other (young?) artists, young critics, nice, clean, elegant dealers, and older, richer collectors of artists and art, talked about at a series of nice, clean, beachy lawn parties and in nice, clean, lacquer-coated art magazine articles.

—Peter Plagens[11]

"*15 Artists*" was one of those local talent shows that don't register so forcefully in the era of international your city's name here biennials, but at the time it marked a coming-out for Pasadena's youngish troupe of artists—the "Williamsburg of its day," Plagens retrospectively describes the community, as opposed to Chelsea-ish Venice Beach. With comers like Allan McCollum, William Wegman, Karen Carson, and Richard Jackson showing, expectations ran high.

—Eric C. Banks[12]

1973

Jackson installs *Cut the Rug* in a former nightclub in an old building on Central Avenue in downtown Los Angeles. (FIGS. 5, 6)

SOLO EXHIBITION
Galerie Onnasch, Cologne

GROUP EXHIBITION
Drawings, Margo Leavin Gallery, Los Angeles

1974

Jackson installs his untitled work of 1972 in the permanent collection galleries of the Los Angeles County Museum of Art; it remains on view through 1975. (FIG. 7)

SOLO EXHIBITIONS
California State University, Sacramento

Painting, Mizuno Gallery, Los Angeles
(FIGS. 8, 9)

Though Jackson's configurations echo Stella's protractor or Johns' devices, and his style derives from Abstract Expressionism, his ultimate effects are individualistic. The sensation of being surrounded by enormous masses of paint is experienced as both powerful and seductive, or virile and beautiful. The paint itself luxuriates

8. Viola Herms Drath, "The Thirty-Second Corcoran Biennial, Art as a Visual Event," *Art International* 15 (May 1971): 43.

9. Jackson, in Wirth, *Deer Beer*, 42.

10. Jay Belloli, in *John Baldessari, Francis Barth, Richard Jackson, Barbara Munger, Gary Stephan*, exh. cat. (Houston: Contemporary Arts Museum Houston, 1972).

11. Peter Plagens, "The Decline and Rise of Younger Los Angeles Art," *Artforum* 10 (May 1972): 80.

12. Eric C. Banks, "10-20-30 Years Ago in *Artforum*: May 1972," *Artforum* 40 (May 2002): 48.

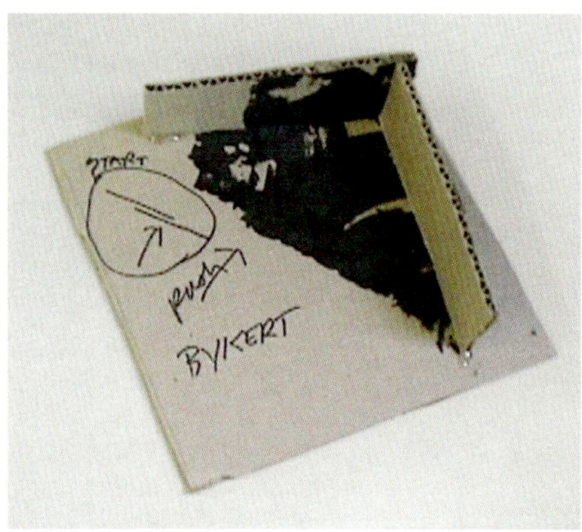

FIG. 10
Model for *Untitled*, 1974

FIG. 11 (right)
Richard Jackson, 1975

FIG. 12 (far right)
The Bedroom, 1976–82. Wood, acrylic
paint, furniture, clothing, books.
108 × 192 × 144 in. (274.3 × 487.7 ×
365.8 cm)

in the textural richness of spontaneous
drips and splatters, while maintaining a
solid hold on geometric structure. Instead
of the anguished struggles of Abstract
Expressionism, the emotional tone of
Jackson's piece is joyous and exhilarating
in terms of bodily response. It seems to
envelop the viewer with vibrant movements
of hedonistic color.

—Melinda Wortz[13]

Bykert Gallery, New York

*Two wall paintings, one free-standing work,
were all destroyed after exhibition. A
19-year-old art dealer. When he visited L.A.
I took him to Disneyland. He is still a friend.*
—Richard Jackson[14] (FIG. 10)

1975

SOLO EXHIBITION
Galleria Bocchi, Milan

GROUP EXHIBITIONS
*Fundamentele Schilderkunst / Fundamental
Painting*, Stedelijk Museum, Amsterdam

*My wall paintings were also temporary. They
were an experience rather than an object.
When they were done, they were done—they
were destroyed or disappeared afterwards.
When I run into people who saw those
paintings they always exaggerate how big
they were, how out of control they were, and*
what an experience they were. They don't
really exist physically. They exist in people's
minds. That's really important. I wanted
them to be like a circus. The circus comes to
town and is there for a while, and you go
see it or you don't, but then it's gone. And
you can tell your friends about it but it
doesn't exist in a storage rack. You can't
drag it out later and put it into a different
context compared to another picture. We
can't just keep stockpiling art. The best way
to preserve it is in people's memories.
Everything has a life and death so at some
point it's all gone.

—Richard Jackson[15]

Both Kinds: Contemporary Art from Los Angeles,
University Art Museum, University of California,
Berkeley

*Jackson includes time. It's a powerful
reconstructive force. When you look at the
thing, you don't see a thing, you see
what's been done. You say "Oh what's he
done to the wall?"*

—Peter Plagens[16]

Current Concerns, Part I, Los Angeles Institute
of Contemporary Art

(FIG. 11)

1976

Jackson begins *Bedroom*, a room-size
installation at his studio in Pasadena; the project

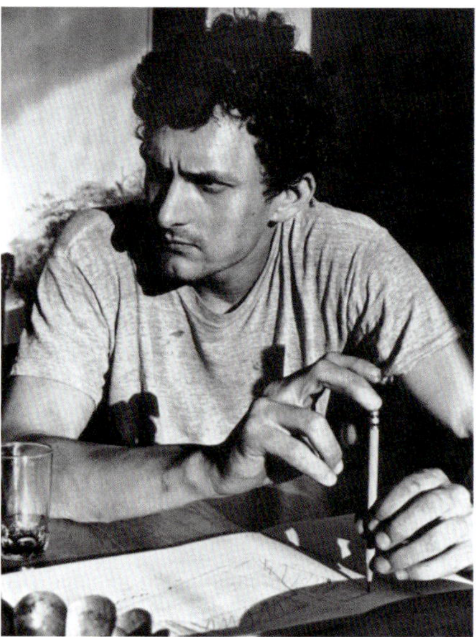

13. Melinda Wortz, "Richard Jackson
Installation," *Artweek* 5 (June 1, 1974): 16.

14. Jackson, in Wirth, *Deer Beer*, 55.

15. Jackson, in Szakacs, "Circus Is in
Town," 43.

16. Peter Plagens, *Both Kinds:
Contemporary Art from Los Angeles*
(Berkeley: University Art Museum,
University of California, 1975), unpaged.

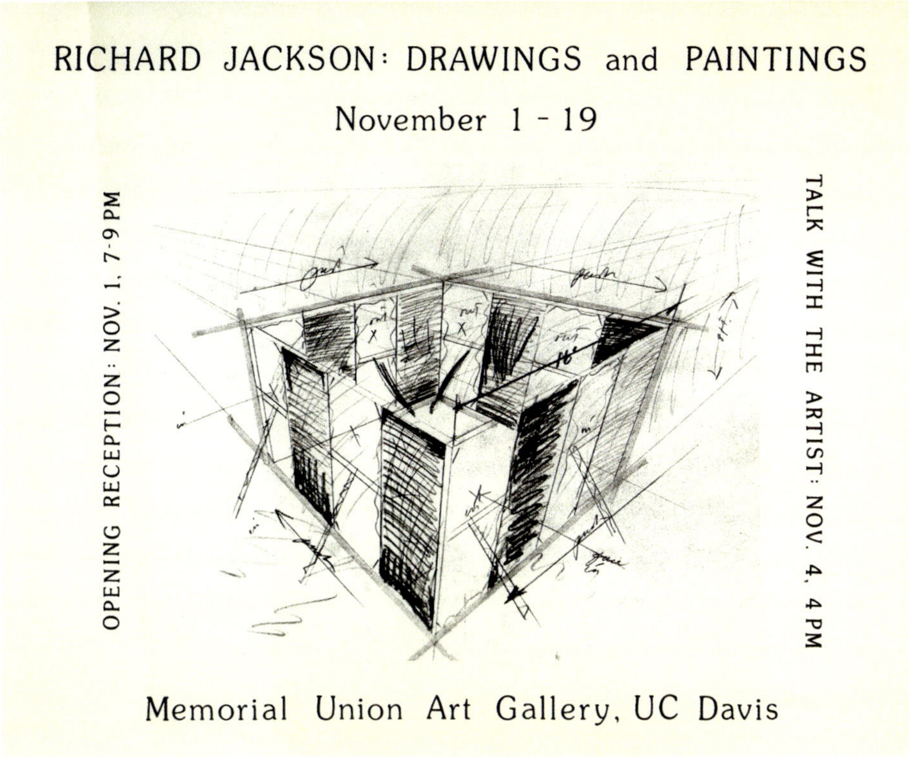

FIG. 13
Exhibition announcement for
Drawings and Paintings, Memorial
Union Art Gallery, University of
California, Davis, 1976

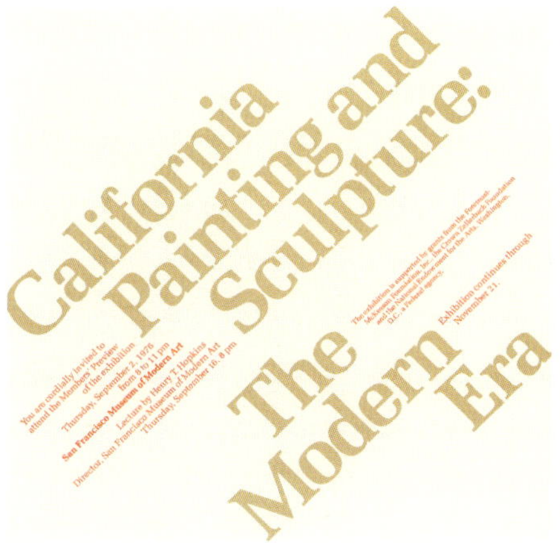

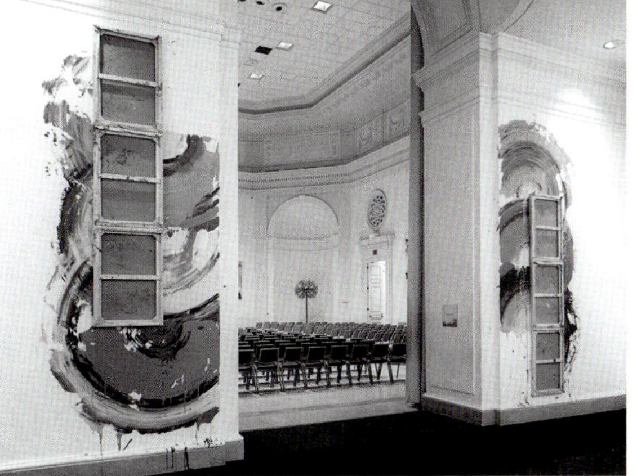

FIG. 14 (above)
Exhibition announcement for
*California Painting and Sculpture: The
Modern Era*, San Francisco Museum of
Modern Art, 1976

FIG. 15 (right)
Untitled, 1976. Canvas, wood, acrylic
paint. 166 × 103 in. each (421.6 ×
261.6 cm). Installation view, San
Francisco Museum of Modern Art

continues until 1982 and is eventually seen by only
two visitors before it is destroyed: Walter Hopps
and Count Giuseppe Panza di Biumo.

*Only two people ever saw it, one was Count
Panza. He said it was "very beautiful." I
think he lied to make me feel good. I told
him his collection was beautiful. I lied too.*
—Richard Jackson[17]

*Your bedroom installation (1976–1982), or
should it be called environment, blurs the
boundaries between the forms through
overspilling paint . . . even the pockets
of the clothes are filled with paint.
The installation was dismantled and not
preserved, ephemeral rather than
monumental. Could this be seen as a
reaction against the white cube?*
—Hans Ulrich Obrist[18] (FIG. 12)

SOLO EXHIBITIONS
Riko Mizuno Gallery, Los Angeles

Drawings and Paintings, Memorial Union Art
Gallery, University of California, Davis (FIG. 13)

*There is a difference between paint as the
source of color sensations and paint as
viscous substance in itself, and Jackson is
clearly more interested in the possibilities of
the latter. Sloppy mud or swirled icing, paint
as color on his canvases is unimportant, for
certainly yellow is as good as pink for
recording the movement of one canvas across
the surface of another. The purpose of the
paint is to record that movement.*

*That is why Jackson has made it clear
that the backs of these paintings are as
important as the fronts, for it is the entire
canvas that is the subject of his art. Sliding
into place as the room was enclosed, the
canvas as a whole is significant, for its
function as a wall demands the realization
that it is more than mere surface; it is
an object, front, back and sides. And as the
room was constructed, that idea was
built-in.*

—Christopher Brown[19]

Daniel Weinberg Gallery, San Francisco

GROUP EXHIBITIONS
California State University, Sacramento

De Anza College, Cupertino, California

*California Painting and Sculpture: The Modern
Era*, San Francisco Museum of Modern Art;
travels to National Collection of Fine Arts,
Smithsonian Institution, Washington, D.C.
(FIGS. 14, 15)

1977

SOLO EXHIBITIONS
Richard Jackson Paintings, Santa Ana College
Art Gallery, Santa Ana, California

Richard Jackson Installation, Fine Arts Gallery,
University of California, Irvine

17. Jackson, in Wirth, *Deer Beer*, 65.

18. Hans Ulrich Obrist, in Obrist and
Alberta Mayo, "Unusual Behavior: Ping
Pong" (interview with Jackson), in Wirth,
Deer Beer, 18.

19. Christopher Brown, "How to Paint a
Room," *California Aggie* (UC Davis),
Arts/Entertainment Supplement,
November 17–23, 1976, 3.

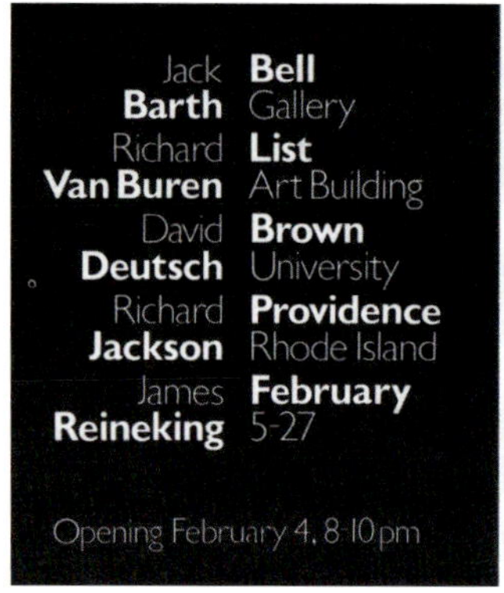

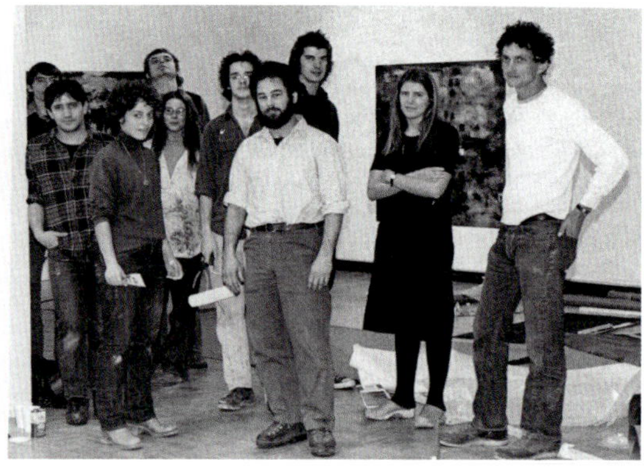

FIG. 17 (below)
Untitled, 1978. Oil and pencil on paper.
38 × 47½ in. (96.5 x 120.7 cm)

FIG. 18 (right)
Untitled, 1978. Canvas, wood, acrylic
paint. 192 × 321 × 229 in. (487.7 × 815.3 x
581.7 cm). Installation view, Rosamund
Felsen Gallery, Los Angeles

GROUP EXHIBITIONS
Jack Barth, Richard Van Buren, David Deutsch,
Richard Jackson, James Reineking, David
Winton Bell Gallery, Brown University, Providence,
Rhode Island (FIG. 16)

Rooms, Institute for Art and Urban Resources,
P.S. 1, Long Island City, New York

1978

SOLO EXHIBITIONS
Faith and Charity in Hope Gallery, Hope,
Idaho

For the exhibition, Jackson produces a series of
one hundred drawings for painting projects.
They are exhibited for the first time since 1978 in
Richard Jackson: Ain't Painting a Pain
(see pp. 81–112).

Richard Jackson, Rosamund Felsen Gallery,
Los Angeles

Jackson's new piece differed from most
process/environmental projects, for me, in
its generous complexity and almost poetic
evocativeness, particularly of the painter's
studio. The work is "about" painting, after
all, in an obvious way; and, responding to
the giant scale, one could almost fancy
oneself a mouse under a palette. In any case,
there was a definite sense of displacement,
imaginative as well as physical, and a quiet
exhilaration in the experience. Moreover,
the experience lingers, in my mind, at least,
more vividly, and certainly more pleasantly,
than that of the majority of such projects.
Jackson, who has been doing similar
work for a decade, commands a quality of
big lyricism that is extremely satisfying.
—Peter Schjeldahl[20]

In this installation, absurdity is accom-
panied by the grand gesture, the glory of
paint as material, the residue of physical
force, a sensitivity to architectural space

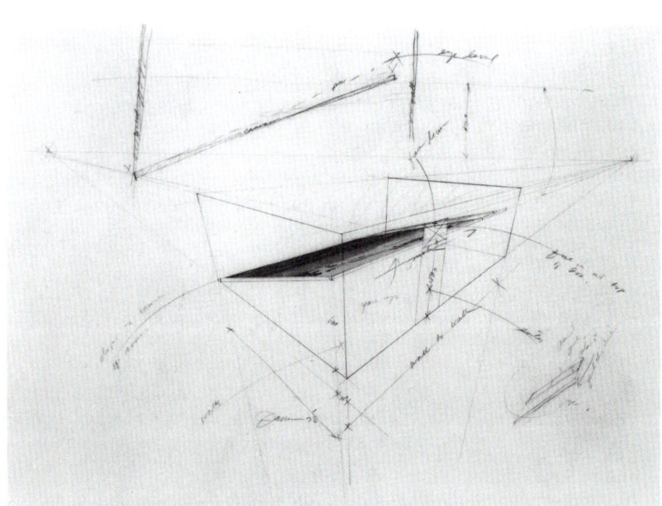

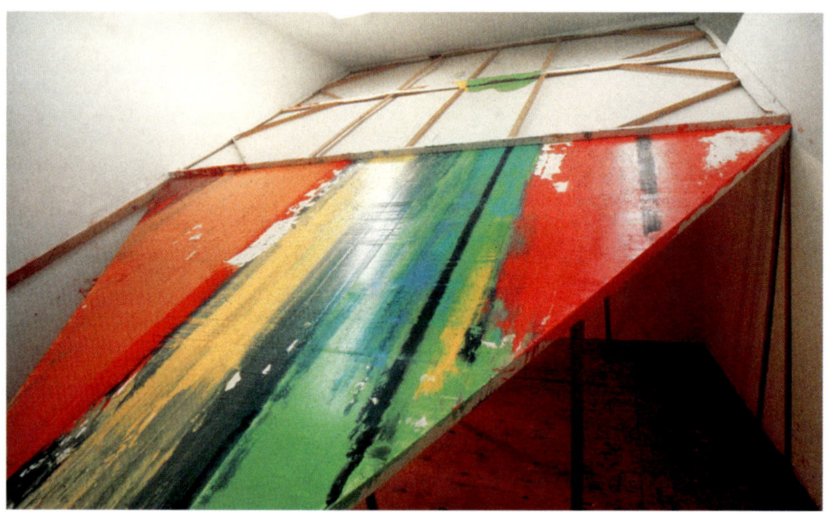

20. Peter Schjeldahl, "Richard Jackson
(Rosamund Felsen Gallery)," *Artforum* 17
(November 1978): 79–80.

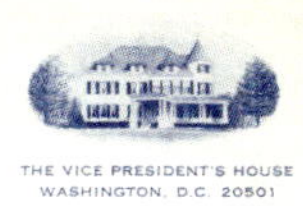

FIG. 19 (above)
Letter from Joan Mondale, wife of Vice President Walter Mondale, 1979

FIG. 20 (right)
Photograph from Joan Mondale, 1979

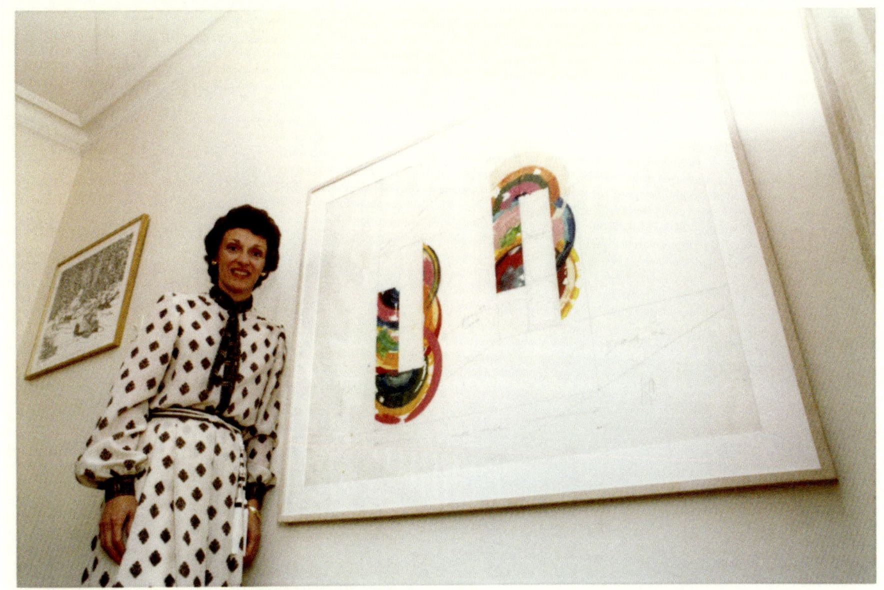

and to scale relations, and a tracing of the *immediate past (the process). It's no surprise that Jackson admires realist painters for their narrative content as well as their formal pursuits. His work has a sense of event, intrigue and disclosure that parallels good storytelling.*

—Barbara Noah[21] (FIGS. 17, 18)

GROUP EXHIBITION
Art about Art, Whitney Museum of American Art, New York; travels to North Carolina Museum of Art, Raleigh; Frederick S. Wight Art Gallery, University of California, Los Angeles; and Portland Art Museum, Portland, Oregon

The theme of art-about-art not only con-centrates on direct references to specific works of art, but also includes works that use the materials and techniques of art as their subject. . . . The actual support for a painting, the stretcher and canvas, is another recurring subject. The contemporary artist, working in his studio in constant contact with stretchers, has chosen this object to become an artwork in itself, or has utilized the back of the canvas as the main point of interest. Richard Jackson uses canvases as the instrument for making his wall instal-lations, leaving the stretchers facing

the wall to convey the sense of his process.

—Jean Lipman and Richard Marshall[22]

1979

Jackson participates in a residency program at Deutscher Akademischer Austausch Dienst (DAAD) in Berlin.

He receives a letter of acknowledgment and a photograph from Joan Mondale, the wife of the vice president of the United States, Walter Mondale. (FIG. 19 + FIG. 20)

SOLO EXHIBITIONS
Richard Jackson Installation, DAAD Galerie, Deutscher Akademischer Austausch Dienst (DAAD), Berlin

Wandbilder–Bildinstallationen, Galerie Maeght, Zurich

GROUP EXHIBITIONS
Wall Painting, Museum of Contemporary Art, Chicago

What interests me most about painting is the activity of making a work. What interests me most about art is—as embarrassing as it sounds—there are no rules.

—Richard Jackson[23]

New York Now, Phoenix Art Museum

21. Barbara Noah, "Richard Jackson at Rosamund Felsen," *Art in America* 66 (November–December 1978): 159.

22. Jean Lipman and Richard Marshall, *Art about Art*, exh. cat. (New York: Whitney Museum of American Art in association with E. P. Dutton, 1978), 33–34.

23. Richard Jackson, artist statement in *Wall Painting*, by Marcia Hafif et al., exh. cat. (Chicago: Museum of Contemporary Art, 1979), 12.

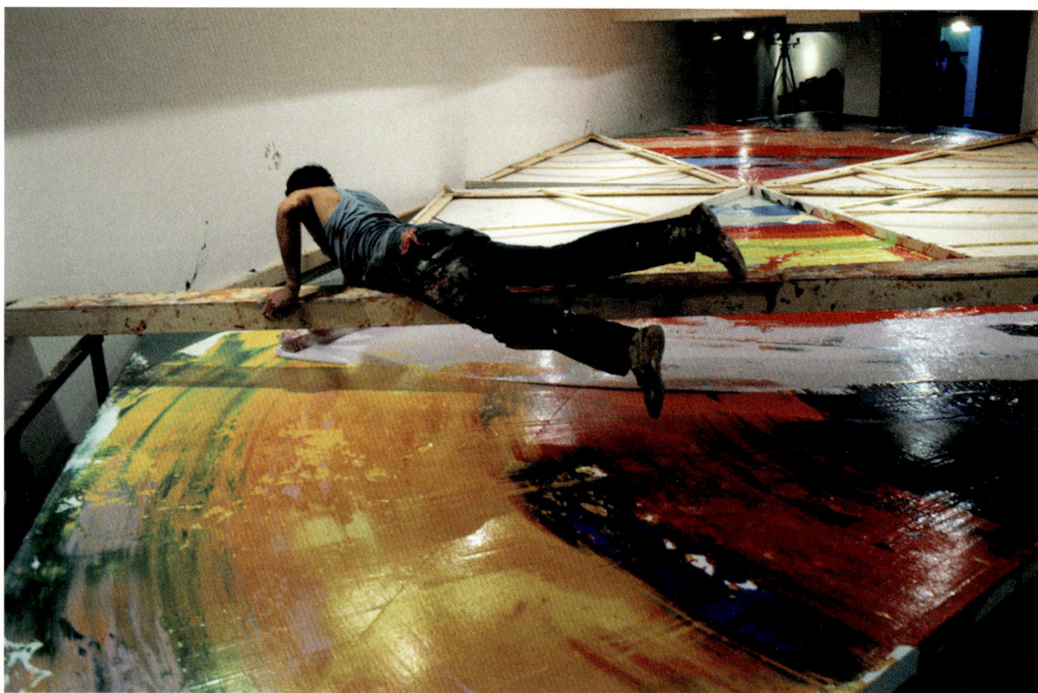

The absurdist humor in his undertaking is of a decidedly dadaist sort. Deliberate irrationality and negation of the canons of beauty, organizational logic and art are pressed into service to clear away the cobwebs of sedentary perceptions. . . . Jackson's wall is a tour de force of absurdity. The residue of the artist's activity suggests 1,000 meanings and confounds interpretation. The clarity and logic of its making is undone by the sheer pointlessness of its existence.

—Christopher Knight[25]

[Jackson] demonstrates a respect for classical methods but a disdain for their intellectual limitations; and 1000 Pictures succeeds precisely because it is able to implicate classical issues without accepting their established solutions.

—Michael Blaine[26] (FIG. 22)

1980

SOLO EXHIBITIONS

Richard Jackson: Big Ideas, Galerie Maeght, Paris (FIG. 21)

Richard Jackson: Installation, Forum Kunst Rottweil, Rottweil, Germany

Big Ideas—1000 Pictures, Rosamund Felsen Gallery, Los Angeles

Make a painting that fills a room. Then take small, perhaps 18 x 30 inch canvases. Use all colors. Put the paint on thickly. Pile the canvases on top of each other and from the floor to the ceiling. Start in one corner and work your way around to the door or the window. This project requires around 6,000 canvases and approx. 300 gallons of paint and needs a large room. If I simply pile up the canvases only in front of the doors and window openings it could look the same. Cheating is not a good idea but a bad idea.

—Richard Jackson[24]

It would be easy to dismiss 1,000 Pictures as a joke. Such dismissal, however, would be a mistake. This is not to say that a great deal of wit is not involved in Jackson's endeavor.

1981

SOLO EXHIBITIONS

Big Ideas—800 Pictures, Betsy Rosenfield Gallery, Chicago

Richard Jackson Projekte, Galerie Maeght, Zurich

One learns to foresee one's own needs—and to calculate them. . . . The powers of endurance are for the most part a matter of attitude. . . . If something has to be done, then do it. . . . Begin at the beginning and see it through to the end. . . . It is important to understand the absurd aspect of life from a lofty standpoint and, if possible, with humor. . . .

Above all I simply like Richard Jackson.

—Edward Kienholz[27]

GROUP EXHIBITIONS

Art in Los Angeles: The Museum as Site; Sixteen Projects, Los Angeles County Museum of Art

Jackson's work suggests a variety of concerns: that all artists make the same painting over and over again, that the museum is the ultimate warehouse, and that art is process. He affirms, too, the attraction the "grand machine" has traditionally held for artists. Jackson's colorful, painterly work is an accomplishment that totally disarms the viewer and provides a humorous and arresting counterpoint to the bland architectonics of the surrounding spaces.

—Stephanie Barron[28]

24. Jackson, in Wirth, *Deer Beer*, 87.

25. Christopher Knight, "The Great Wall of La Cienega," *Los Angeles Herald-Examiner*, September 18, 1980.

26. Michael Blaine, "Painting by Construction," *Artweek* 11 (September 27, 1980): 3.

27. Edward Kienholz, "For Richard Jackson," in *Richard Jackson: Projekte*, exh. cat. (Zurich: Galerie Maeght, 1981), unpaged.

28. Stephanie Barron, *Art in Los Angeles: The Museum as Site; Sixteen Projects*, exh. cat. (Los Angeles: Los Angeles County Museum of Art, 1981), 49.

Richard Jackson's The Big Idea *comprises an amazing 3,000 stretched and nominally painted canvases stacked upside-down in a vague, oozing, spheroid 16 feet wide. It looks like something left by a saucerful of aliens, whose laser radio has picked up garbled information about Sam Francis.*
—Peter Plagens[29]

"The Museum as Site" also included stunning individual works by each artist, but once again the exhibition did not live up to the title's promise. The premise of the show was, in the words of Curator Stephanie Barron, "the creation of works which depend upon or are related to particular sites." In fact, only two artists, Michael Asher and Terry Schoonhoven, took this challenge literally. . . .

Chris Burden's A Tale of Two Cities *and Richard Jackson's* The Big Idea *could all work equally well in any space of the appropriate dimensions and should not be jumbled together under the "site-specific" label. These terms need to be clarified for the public rather than confused.*
—Melinda Wortz[30]

What does the pervasiveness of the installational mean? Partly, the form may enable literal assertions of ego in a culture that is losing symbolic means for such assertions. This idea seems germane to Jackson's messy, magnificent 16-foot sphere of, count 'em, 3000 painted and stacked canvases in the museum's atrium.
—Peter Schjeldahl[31] (FIG. 23)

California: A Sense of Individualism, L.A. Louver Gallery, Venice, California

Abstraction in Los Angeles, 1950–1980: Selections from the Murray and Ruth Gribin Collection, CSUN Art Galleries, California State University, Northridge; travels to Fine Arts Gallery, University of California, Irvine

---

1982

GROUP EXHIBITIONS
Échange entre artistes: 1931–1982, Pologne–U.S.A.; Une expérience muséographique,

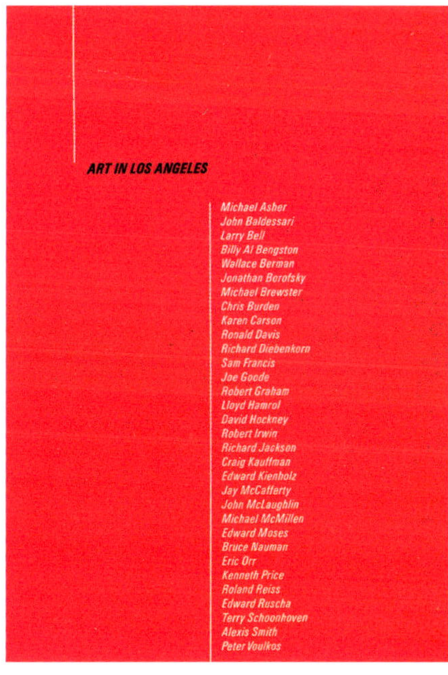

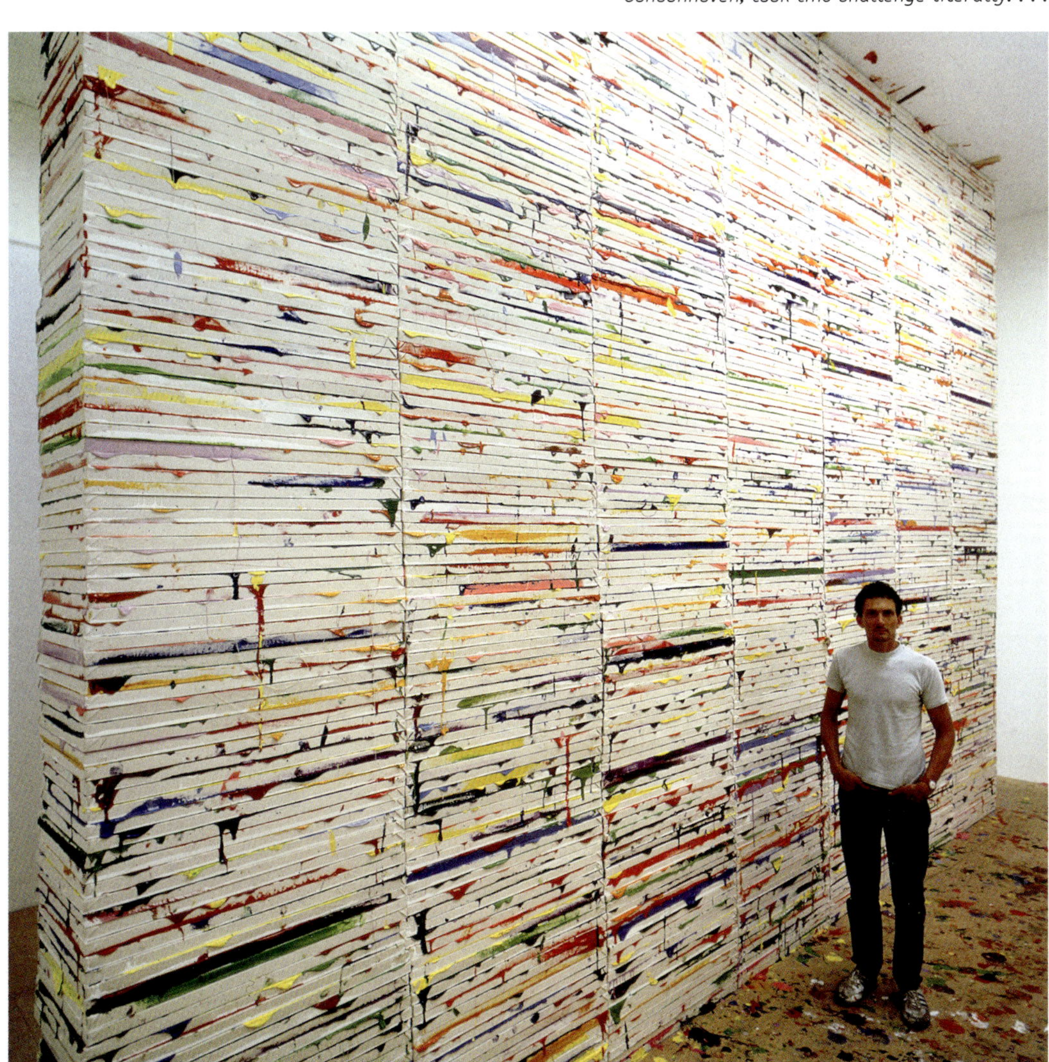

FIG. 22 (above)
Richard Jackson in front of *Big Ideas—1000 Pictures* at Rosamund Felsen Gallery, Los Angeles, 1980

FIG. 23 (right)
Exhibition announcement for *Art in Los Angeles: The Museum as Site; Sixteen Projects*, Los Angeles County Museum of Art, 1981

---

29. Peter Plagens, "Site Wars," *Art in America* 70 (January 1982): 92.

30. Melinda Wortz, "Art in Los Angeles: Seventeen Artists—Sixteen Projects," *Art News* 80 (November 1981): 165.

31. Peter Schjeldahl, "Spanning Time Zones," *Village Voice*, September 2–8, 1981, 70.

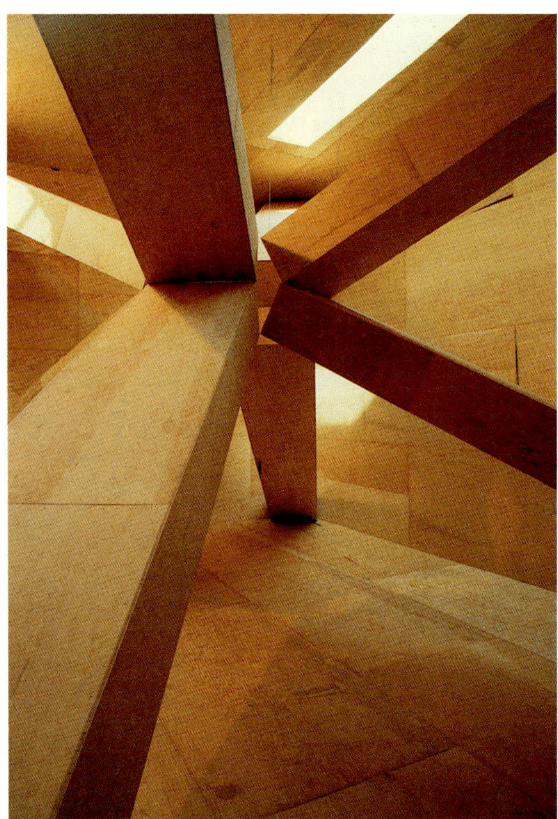

Big Ideals (detail), 1984. Canvas, wood, acrylic paint. 192 × 228 × 228 in. (487.7 × 581.7 × 581.7 cm). Installation view, Rosamund Felsen Gallery, Los Angeles

Animation-recherche-confrontation (ARC), Musée d'art moderne de la Ville de Paris

Drawings by Painters, Long Beach Museum of Art, Long Beach, California; travels to Mandeville Art Gallery, University of California, San Diego, and Oakland Museum

Drawings and notations are also to befound on the drawings of Richard Jackson and Tony DeLap. Both use their drawings as two-dimensional schemes for their more three-dimensional paintings: Jackson's constructions of painted canvases built in relation to an architectural context, and DeLap's shaped and fragmented low-relief wall paintings.

—Richard Armstrong[32]

1983

The artist self-publishes a spiral-bound limited-edition book of drawings titled *1/2 Full*.

SOLO EXHIBITION
Richard Jackson: 1000 Pictures; Installation and Drawings, Daniel Weinberg Gallery, San Francisco

GROUP EXHIBITION
Summer Show, Rosamund Felsen Gallery, Los Angeles

1984

SOLO EXHIBITIONS
Richard Jackson, Rosamund Felsen Gallery, Los Angeles

The content of my work has always been involved with Conceptualism and Minimalist attitudes about geometry, but I'm very political. I'd like to make art more public, less treasured. I'd like it to be more physical and more demanding. I'd like people to really think about it.

—Richard Jackson[33]

There is exuberant painterly energy on these canvases. Sweeps of thickly applied paint, layers of color upon color and lines moving every which way create an energetic optical field. However, [Jackson's] Expressionism is contained within an overarching analytic blueprint. Lurking within many of the canvases are diagrammatic structures; circles and lines mathematically subdivide the ceiling, and the centered, overhanging

stars are precisely aligned with the highest surface, which can be determined if one gets down on the floor. Big ideals are contained within Jackson's piece, but they are rational more than emotional. Yet if engineering takes precedence over expression during his composing process, the results speak convincingly of the power of abstraction to move us in unpredictable ways.

—Robert Pincus[34]

Untitled Construction, Rosamund Felsen Gallery, Los Angeles

Jackson's move into relatively simple sculpture from installations composed of thousands of paintings seems surprising until we realize that the controlling vision of the formal elements of his work has always been spare and geometric. Without the distraction of oozing pigment and implied messages about the futility and misuses of painting, he simply allows us to see organizational factors more clearly and to reflect on spaces and volumes instead of surfaces.

—Suzanne Muchnic[35] (FIG. 24)

1985

Jackson participates in the Visual Arts Program, Artpark, Lewiston, New York, and installs a permanent outdoor work. He described the project as follows: "A structure made of plywood that the viewer walks through, not realizing that it is a swastika. The picnic table is made of steel. The idea is: you need to look closely at things." (FIG. 25)

GROUP EXHIBITIONS
Cinquante ans de dessins américains, 1930–1980, École Nationale Supérieure des Beaux-Arts, Paris, organized by the Menil Collection, Houston; travels as *Amerikanische Zeichnungen, 1930–1980* to Städtische Galerie im Städelschen Kunstinstitut, Frankfurt, Germany

Buscaglia-Castellani Art Gallery, Niagara University, Niagara Falls, New York

1986

SOLO EXHIBITION
Richard Jackson: Large-Scale Installation and Drawings, Betsy Rosenfield Gallery, Chicago

32. Richard Armstrong, *Drawing by Painters* (Long Beach, CA: Long Beach Museum of Art, 1982), 13.

33. Jackson, quoted in Suzanne Muchnic, "Jackson Sculpture: Insights from Inside," *Los Angeles Times*, November 3, 1984.

34. Robert Pincus, "The Galleries: La Cienega Area," *Los Angeles Times*, July 27, 1984.

35. Suzanne Muchnic, "The Galleries: La Cienega Area," *Los Angeles Times*, November 9, 1984.

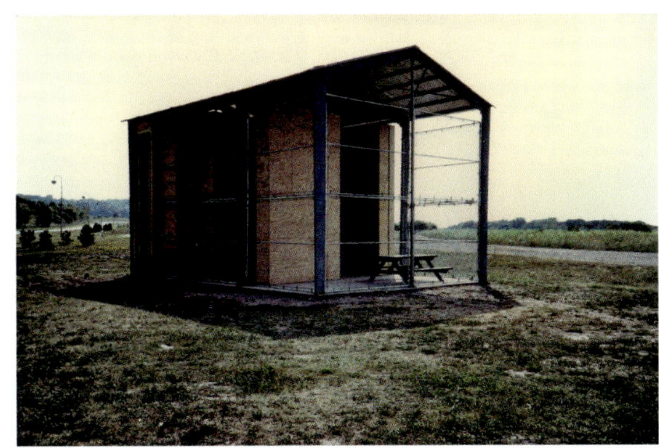

FIG. 25 (above)
Untitled, 1985. Plywood, steel, cinderblocks, chain-link fence, concrete 192 × 240 × 360 in. (487.7 × 609.6 × 914.4 cm). Installation at the Visual Arts Program, Artpark, Lewiston, New York

FIG. 26 (below)
Big Ordeals, 1986. Canvas, wood, acrylic paint. 116 × 175 × 175 in. (294.6 × 444.5 × 444.5 cm). Installation view, Betsy Rosenfield Gallery, Chicago

A painting made with a system much the same as in Big Ideals but more complicated. The piece was called "Big Ordeals" after it was made to gallery specifications with a 120 in. (304,8 cm) ceiling that turned out to be 116 in. (294,6 cm). In every case the artist makes things smaller than measurements given by galleries, realizing that they are too busy talking on telephones to confirm facts. 2 in. (5,1 cm) less was not enough. Big Ordeal.

—Richard Jackson[36] (FIG. 26)

GROUP EXHIBITIONS
Schloss Solitude—Pläne und Projekte, Schloss Solitude, Stuttgart, Germany

Point of View: Artworks from the Collection of Jeffrey Kerns, University Art Gallery, California State University, San Bernardino; travels to University Art Gallery, California State University, Sonoma, and Western Gallery, Western Washington University, Bellingham

1987

SOLO EXHIBITION
Richard Jackson Installation, Robert Else Gallery, California State University, Sacramento

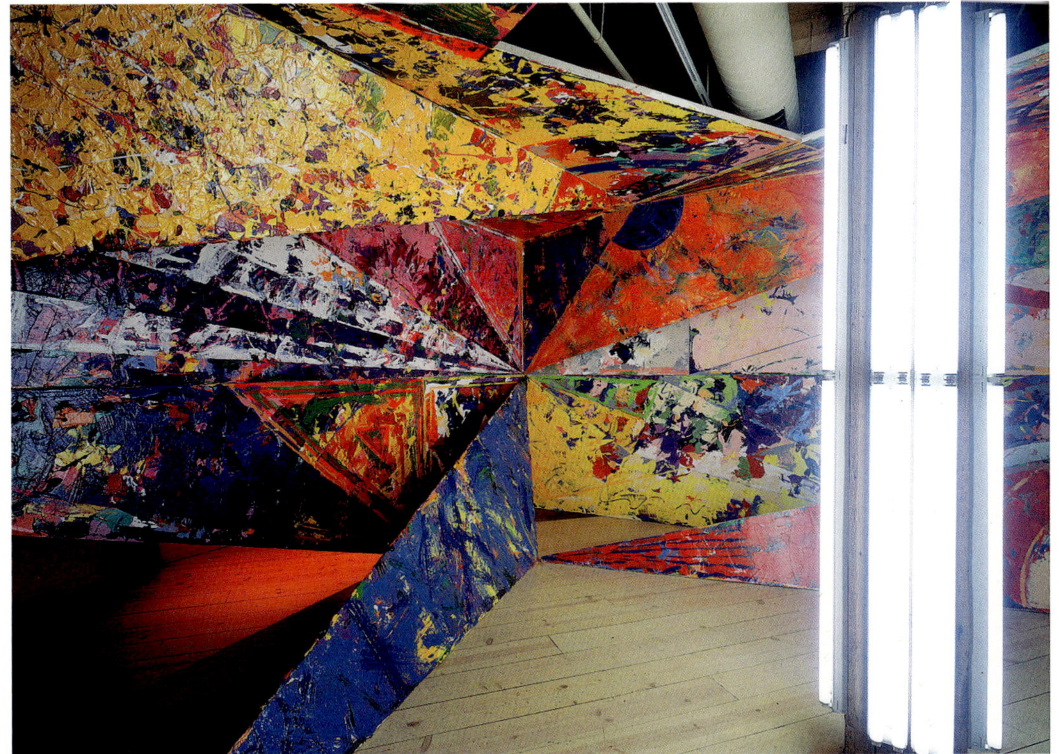

GROUP EXHIBITIONS
The Great Drawing Show, 1587–1987, Michael Kohn Gallery, Los Angeles

Betsy Rosenfield Gallery, Chicago

1988

Jackson receives a Pollock-Krasner Foundation Grant.

SOLO EXHIBITION
Richard Jackson: Installations, 1970–1988, Menil Collection, Houston

Richard Jackson from California explores the idea of interior painting in far more compelling ways. Jackson's long-term exhibition in the Menil Collection's annex (Richmond Hall) offers far more painterly and conceptually challenging solutions. Jackson's stacked canvases, his plywood rooms lushly painted inside only, and his wall compositions in which the faces of the canvases are placed against the wall make Knoebel's piece look tentative.

—Patricia C. Johnson[37]

But if [Jackson's] work begins with a gesture, he builds on it methodically, analyzing and plotting out complex operations with it like mathematical puzzles, creating mind-twisting patterns of complementary colors, positive and negative relationships and reversals. Standing in or in front of Jackson's work, one cannot help but be drawn into an attempt at figuring out the system of his maneuvers, for the logic of his tinkering ticks loudly through the seductive flow and exuberant splatter of his brightly colored paint.

—Susan Chadwick[38]

GROUP EXHIBITIONS
New Works on Paper, Rosamund Felsen Gallery, Los Angeles

Betsy Rosenfield Gallery, Chicago

Forty Years of Art: The California State University, Sacramento, William H. Cook Gallery, Rancho Cordova, California

One of a Kind: Contemporary Serial Imagery, Los Angeles Municipal Art Gallery

It is Jackson's project to similarly deconstruct, in series, the nature and

36. Jackson, in Wirth, *Deer Beer*, 101.

37. Patricia C. Johnson, "The 'Object-Makers,' Art by Young Germans on Exhibit," *Houston Chronicle*, November 26, 1989.

38. Susan Chadwick, "For Richard Jackson, the Point Is Painting," *Houston Post*, July 17, 1988.

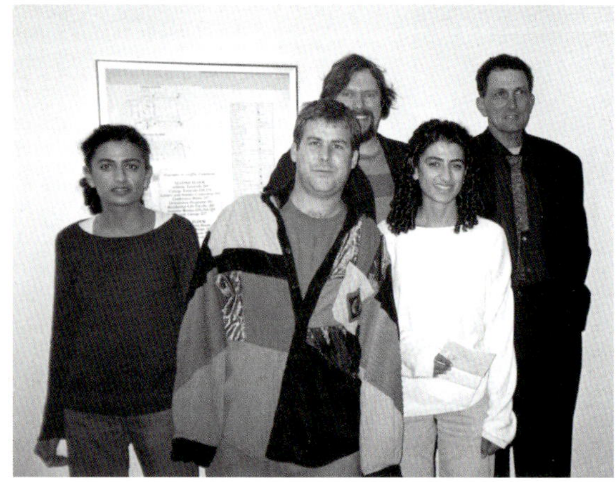

FIG. 27 (above)
L to R: Rachel Khedoori, Jason Rhoades, Steve Hurd, Toba Khedoori, Richard Jackson, University of California, Los Angeles, 1993

FIG. 28 (right)
Richard Jackson installing *Untitled* for *Richard Jackson Installationen und Bilder*, Galerie Tschudi, Glarus, Switzerland, 1989

utility of the production of painting. It is, perhaps, a subversive activity on the surface: Jackson begins with hundreds, even thousands, of stretched canvases, easel-sized in scale. He produces, on their surface, actual paintings. These paintings in turn become modular construction elements, like adobes, that he uses to build wall units and environmental surrounds, sometimes rectilinear, at other times, curved into spheres. These installations are, in a way, ephemeral. They are not in the usual sense art commodities, and exist more as concepts than as built installa-tions. Jackson, a skilled draftsman, has relied on his drawings to represent the conceptual nature of his projects. They are sophisticated studies in perspective, and underscore the serial nature of his work.
—Edward Leffingwell[39]

Balkon mit Fächer: 25 Jahre Berliner Künstlerprogramm des DAAD, Deutscher Akademischer Austausch Dienst (DAAD), Berlin; travels to DuMont Kunsthalle, Cologne, and Gemeentemuseum, the Hague, Netherlands

---

1989

Jackson begins teaching at the Department of Art, University of California, Los Angeles, and among his students are Julien Bismuth, Mike Bouchet, Rachel Khedoori, Toba Khedoori, Jennifer Pastor, and Jason Rhoades; Jackson remains on the faculty at UCLA until 1994. (FIG. 27)

SOLO EXHIBITION
Richard Jackson Installationen und Bilder, Galerie Tschudi, Glarus, Switzerland (FIG. 28)

GROUP EXHIBITION
Solitude Echos: Realisierte Projekte der Ausstellung Schloss Solitude—Pläne und Projekte, 1986, Kunstverein Ludwigsburg, Ludwigsburg, Germany

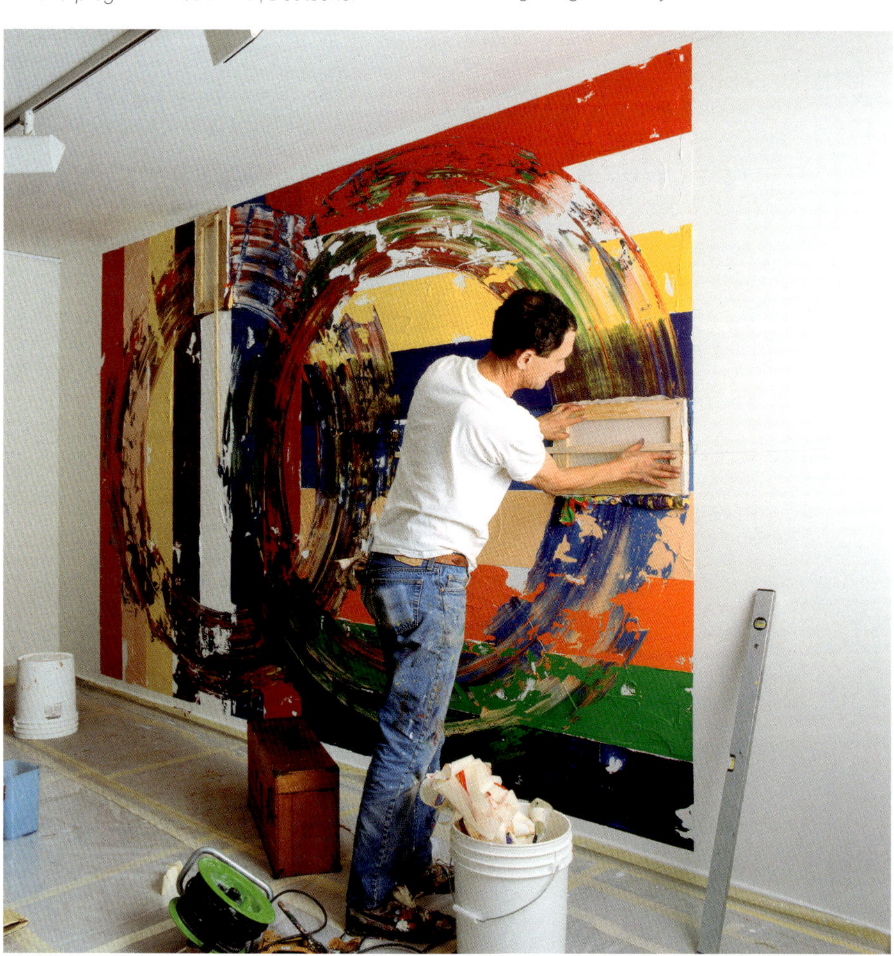

39. Edward Leffingwell, "Richard Jackson," in *One of a Kind: Contemporary Serial Imagery*, ed. Gail Barringer (Los Angeles: Los Angeles Municipal Art Gallery, 1989), 25.

1990

SOLO EXHIBITION
Richard Jackson: An Installation + Drawings,
Rosamund Felsen Gallery, Los Angeles

*"Commercialism doesn't interest me—it's
just too stupid," comments artist Richard
Jackson in explaining the extravagant
anti-materialism of his work. . . . Jackson
intends, he says, that his work read as a
protest against the commodification of art,
and his rap is peppered with populist ideas.
However, the set of art strategies he's
developed is rooted in a highly sophisticated grasp of the geometry of painting.
It takes a fair amount of background to get
the inferences in his work. On that score,
he's preaching the elitist art gospel
he claims to be disrupting.*
— Kristine McKenna[40]

*The centerpiece of Jackson's recent
installation was an untitled square maze
previously exhibited in Sacramento (1987)
and in Houston (1988). . . . Jackson's point is
that illusion, and by extension art, is always
performative—the result of the interaction
between the bodily senses and material
objects. The cell bars [of Untitled, 1987–90]
thus act as a physical paradigm for the
very mediation that makes art possible.*
— Colin Gardner[41]

GROUP EXHIBITIONS
*Past and Present: Selected Works by Gallery
Artists*, Rosamund Felsen Gallery, Los Angeles

California A–Z and Return, Butler Institute of
American Art, Youngstown, Ohio

1991

SOLO EXHIBITION
Confusing Ideas—Installationen / Zeichnung,
Brigitte March Galerie, Stuttgart, Germany

GROUP EXHIBITION
Quick Coagulation Forms the August Corpse,
Rosamund Felsen Gallery, Los Angeles

1992

SOLO EXHIBITION
Richard Jackson: Big Confusing Ideas, Santa
Monica Museum of Art, Santa Monica, California
(FIG. 29)

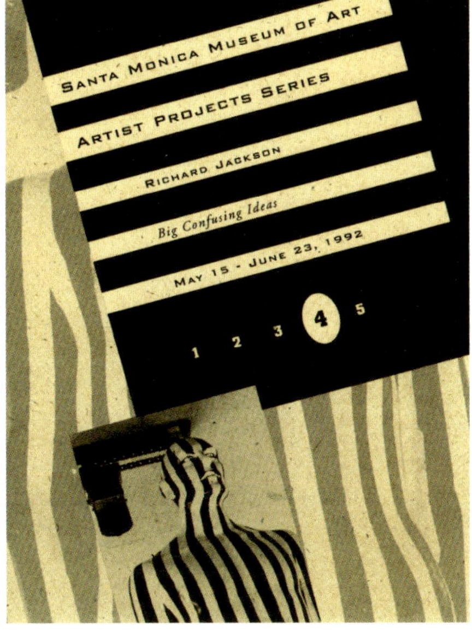

GROUP EXHIBITIONS
Helter Skelter: L.A. Art in the 1990s, Museum
of Contemporary Art, Los Angeles

*[1000 Clocks] was shown in "Helter Skelter:
L.A. Art in the 1990s," completely out of
context. It was the first and only time it
was assembled, therefore there were
no photographs in the catalog. Nothing was
written about this piece. The piece was
badly presented. The artist's fault.*
— Richard Jackson[42]

*And Richard Jackson condenses the crack
of time in a chamber built from scores
of synchronized clocks, which grabs you by
the mental lapels for but a split second.*
— Christopher Knight[43]

Force Sight, Schloss Presteneck, Stein am
Kocher, Germany

*Visiting Artist Program, Twentieth Anniversary
Show*, CU Art Galleries, University of Colorado
at Boulder

1993

The artist relocates to Sierra Madre, California.

SOLO EXHIBITION
*Richard Jackson: BIGOILIDEAS; Wandinstallation
und Zeichnungen*, Galerie Gudrun Spielvogel,
Munich

40. Kristine McKenna, "Richard
Jackson: Conceptual and Uncollectible,"
Los Angeles Times, November 27, 1990.

41. Colin Gardner, "Richard Jackson,"
Artforum 20 (February 1991): 131.

42. Jackson, in Wirth, *Deer Beer*, 112.

43. Christopher Knight, "An Art of
Darkness at MOCA," *Los Angeles
Times*, January 28, 1992.

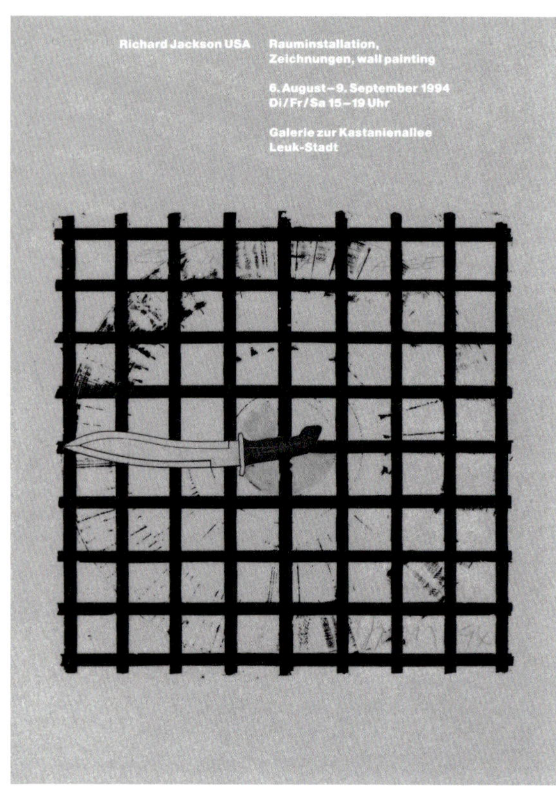

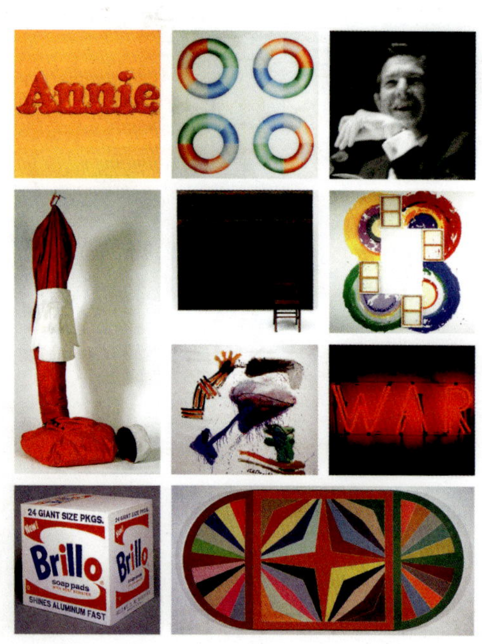

FIG. 30 (top)
Exhibition announcement for *Wall Painting/Room Installation*, Galerie zur Kastanienallee, Leuk-Stadt, Switzerland, 1994

FIG. 31 (bottom)
Exhibition announcement for *Radical Past: Contemporary Art and Music in Pasadena, 1960–1974*, 1999

GROUP EXHIBITION
Bright Light, Schloss Presteneck, Stein am Kocher, Germany

1994

SOLO EXHIBITION
Wall Painting/Room Installation, Galerie zur Kastanienallee, Leuk-Stadt, Switzerland (FIG. 30)

GROUP EXHIBITIONS
Virtual Reality Biennial of Contemporary Art, National Gallery of Australia, Canberra

Art as Healer, Weintraub Hunter Gallery, Sacramento

1995

Jackson attends the International Sculptors Symposium at Uludağ University in Bursa, Turkey. For this event, he also conceives and installs the work *Turkey Ball*.

1997

SOLO EXHIBITION
Richard Jackson: Paint Ball, David Zwirner, New York

The installation was less concerned with the esthetic qualities (or lack thereof) in these machine-made abstractions than with demystifying the artist's studio and what goes on there. . . . a witty parody of the dilemmas of contemporary creativity.

—Tom McDonough[44]

GROUP EXHIBITION
L'autre: 4e Biennale d'art contemporain de Lyon, Lyon, France

Along with Richard Jackson's Painting with Two Balls, *these enormous works could be seen as representing a new generation of Bachelor Machines, that class of objects Szeemann introduced 21 years ago at the Bern Kunsthalle in the exhibition of the same name. Described by Jean Clair on that occasion as delirious closed systems or organic-mechanical hybrids—the original group included Duchamp's* Large Glass, *works by James Lee Byars and Tinguely, and models based on projects by Leonardo da Vinci and Franz Kafka. . . . [They] are much like their predecessors: entirely self-justifying, enormously prodigal in their consumption of energy and grandly single-minded in carrying out their operations.*

—Sarah McFadden[45]

1998

Jackson receives Louis Comfort Tiffany Grant.

SOLO EXHIBITION
Richard Jackson: Deer Beer, Galerie Hauser & Wirth, Zurich

Richard Jackson acts. Not retrogressively ironically, not intellectualizingly, never cynically but absolutely directly. . . . A WORK of art is born and it dies like any other creature. The hunter's eyes sparkle.

—Harald Szeemann[46]

GROUP EXHIBITIONS
Kunstausstellung "Holderbank," 1995–2000, Holderbank Management and Consulting, Holderbank, Switzerland

Art Jonction 1998, Foire et festival d'art contemporain, Nice, France

1999

GROUP EXHIBITIONS
dAPERTutto, Italian Pavilion, Venice Biennale, Venice, Italy

Richard Jackson's 1000 Clocks *(1992), first seen in the L.A. MOCA exhibition* Helter Skelter: L.A. in the 1990s, *becomes a millennial work only as 1999 winds down. It consists of a chamber entirely surfaced with a grid of handmade, square-faced clocks which go "thunk" in adamant unison when the hands move. Perhaps more to the millenarian point is the artist's claim that he is considering making 2,000 of something to observe the new year.*

—Marcia Vetrocq[47]

Radical Past: Contemporary Art and Music in Pasadena, 1960–1974, Armory Center for the Arts, Pasadena, in collaboration with the Norton Simon Museum, Pasadena; Alyce de Roulet Williamson Gallery, Art Center College of Design, Pasadena; and New Pasadena Gallery, Pasadena. (FIG. 31)

44. Tom McDonough, "Richard Jackson at David Zwirner," *Art in America* 85 (December 1997): 89–90.

45. Sarah McFadden, "The 'Other' Biennial," *Art in America* 85 (November 1997): 88.

46. Harald Szeemann, "The Untiring Sparkle of the Hunter's Eyes," in Wirth, *Deer Beer*, 8.

47. Marcia Vetrocq, "The Venice Biennale Reformed, Renewed, Redeemed," *Art in America* 87 (September 1999): 89.

While Jackson's work appears to be a straightforward criticism of the banality of expressionist painting, it is not completely downward-looking and despairing. It offers an equally optimistic view of what painting could be, one that goes beyond the hope that painting can be only changed by an evolution in the materials used.

There is no reason why painting in Jackson's practice should not be conceptual, nor should it be restricted to a notional category of performance art. . . . For an artist as concerned with the dematerialization of the art object as Jackson, performance work is evidently more than simply another way of "staging" a picture.

—Andrew Gellatly[48]

Made in California: Art, Image, and Identity, 1900–2000, Los Angeles County Museum of Art (FIG. 32)

2001

GROUP EXHIBITION
Making the Making, Apexart, New York

2002

SOLO EXHIBITIONS
Richard Jackson: Paint Bear, Gabriele Senn Galerie, Vienna

Richard Jackson: Bank Job, BAWAG Foundation, Vienna

GROUP EXHIBITIONS
Project Room: Richard Jackson, Galerie Georges-Philippe & Nathalie Vallois, Paris

Plus Ultra, Kunstraum Innsbruck, Innsbruck, Austria (FIG. 33)

What About Hegel (and You)?, Brigitte March Galerie, Stuttgart, Germany

Iconoclash: Beyond the Image Wars in Science, Religion, and Art, ZKM Center for Art and Media, Karlsruhe, Germany

The House of Fiction: Sammlung (3), Sammlung Hauser & Wirth, Saint Gall, Switzerland

Ten Years, Galerie Hauser & Wirth, Zurich

FIG. 32 (below)
Who's Afraid of Red, Yellow, and Blue installation view, *Made in California: Art, Image, and Identity, 1900–2000*, Los Angeles County Museum of Art, 2000

FIG. 33 (right)
Cover for *Plus Ultra*, Kunstraum Innsbruck, Innsbruck, Austria, 2002

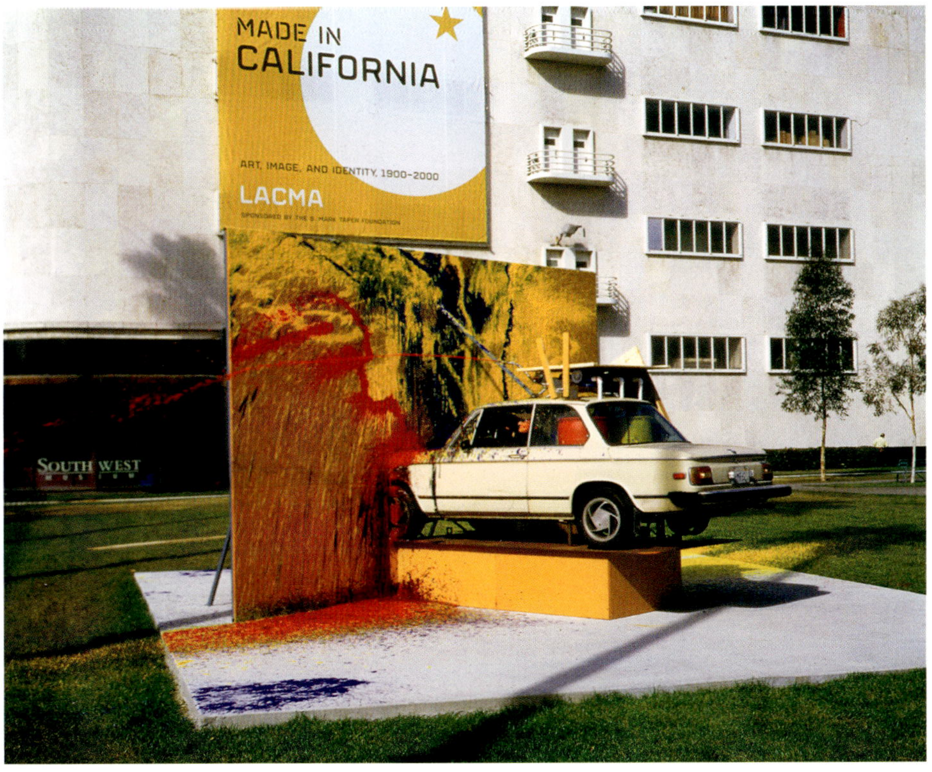

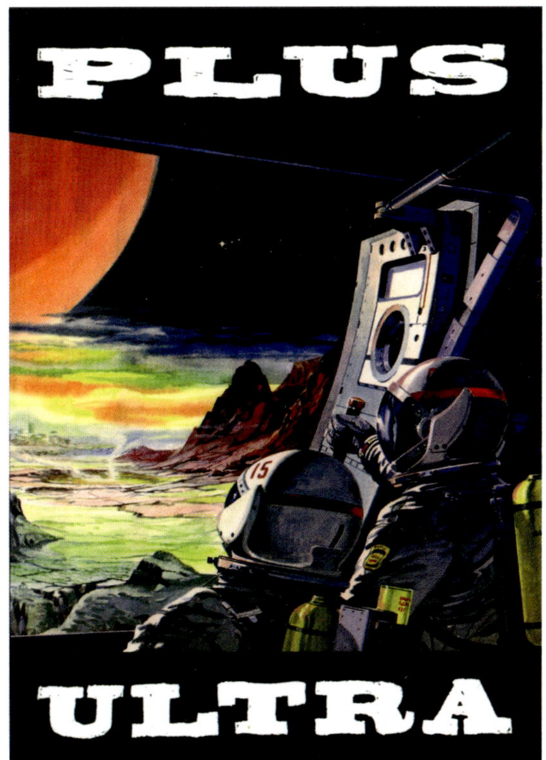

48. Andrew Gellatly, "Back in Los Angeles, We Missed Los Angeles," in *L.A.-ex Performances*, ed. Christa Häusler and Elisabeth Schweeger, exh. cat. (Ostfildern-Ruit, Germany: Hatje Cantz, 2001), 33–35.

GREAT EXPECTATIONS!

A CURA DI
CHARLOTTE LAUBARD
CHIARA PARISI
ALESSANDRO RABOTTINI
MARCELLO SMARRELLI

SAÂDANE AFIF
MICOL ASSAËL
ROBERTO CUOGHI
STÉPHANE DAFFLON
GINO DE DOMINICIS
DÉCOSTERD & RAHM
DIDIER FIUZA FAUSTINO
MASSIMO GRIMALDI
RICHARD JACKSON
JOHANNES KAHRS
JORGE PERIS
DIEGO PERRONE
PIETRO ROCCASALVA
MICHAEL SAILSTORFER
TINO SEHGAL
MARKUS SIXAY
JIM SHAW
PAUL THEK
BARTHÉLÉMY TOGUO

VERNISSAGE 29 NOVEMBRE
ore19,00
FERROTEL
c.so Vittorio Emanuele II, Pescara

30 NOVEMBRE ore19,00 FERROTEL
PERFORMANCE MUSICALE DEL DUO
MOU LIPS

IDEAZIONE CESARE MANZO
ORGANIZZAZIONE: MARCELLA RUSSO, SABINA DE DEO, MASSIMILIANO SCUDERI
ASSOCIAZIONE CULTURALE ARTENOVA
INFO: artenovaservizi@tin.it TEL. +39085297206-FAX. +390854221688
www.fuoriuso.it, email <info@fuoriuso.it>

FUORIUSO2003
XIV EDIZIONE
PESCARA 29 NOVEMBRE 03 – 9 GENNAIO 04
FERROTEL c.so Vittorio Emanuele II, Pescara

UNIVERSITÀ G. D'ANNUNZIO
CITTÀ DI PESCARA
PROVINCIA DI PESCARA
REGIONE ABRUZZO
FERROTEL PASSAGGIO CULTURALE

FIG. 34 (above)
Exhibition annoucement for *Great Expectations! Fuori Uso 2003*, Ferrotel, Castello di Rivoli, Pescara, Italy, 2003

FIG. 35 (below right)
Exhibition announcement for *Richard Jackson: BEER DEER BEAR*, Galerie Parisa Kind, Frankfurt, 2005

2003

SOLO EXHIBITION
Richard Jackson: Accidents in Abstract Painting, Galerie Hauser & Wirth, Zurich

GROUP EXHIBITIONS
Great Expectations! Fuori Uso 2003, Ferrotel, Castello di Rivoli, Pescara, Italy (FIG. 34)

Home, Galerie Georges-Philippe & Nathalie Vallois, Paris

2004

SOLO EXHIBITIONS
Richard Jackson: The Three Bears, Foundation 20 21, New York

> Meticulously constructed and deconstructed, Jackson's irreverent work has always been less about durable commercial objects than about the conceptual and mechanical efforts entailed in pushing painting out of its frame for good. Very cathartic.
> —Vivian Rehberg[49]

Richard Jackson: Unusual Behavior, Galerie Georges-Philippe & Nathalie Vallois, Paris

Richard Jackson: Dick's Pictures, Hasswellediger & Co. Gallery, New york

GROUP EXHIBITIONS
Lost Property, Domaine Pommery, Reims, France

Y a t'il un commissaire pour sauver l'exposition? Galerie Georges-Philippe & Nathalie Vallois, Paris

2005

Jackson begins teaching at the Mountain School of Arts, Los Angeles.

> Poring over photographs [of Jackson's work] in exhibition catalogues and art magazines, many of them from the 1970s, I perceived an intelligence that came through even in two-dimensional black and white.
> —Raphael Rubinstein[50]

SOLO EXHIBITIONS
Richard Jackson: BEER DEER BEAR, Galerie Parisa Kind, Frankfurt (FIG. 35)

Richard Jackson: The Pink Empire, Galerie Hauser & Wirth, London

> Sometimes an artist comes along who has such absurd and preposterous ideas you can only applaud. In Richard Jackson, we have such an artist.
> —Jessica Lack[51]

GROUP EXHIBITIONS
Dionysiac: L'art en flux, Centre Georges Pompidou, Musée National d'Art Moderne, Paris

> Since the show features McCarthy's own avowed influence, Richard Jackson (whose punning Pump Pee Doo, 2005, is a line-up of plastic bears in Pompidou-style primary colours urinating into urinals modelled on the famous readymade by Duchamp in the institution's collection) it also functions as a timeline tracing the excessive impulse through recent art.
> —Martin Herbert[52] (FIG. 36)

Été urbain, Gabriele Senn Galerie, Vienna
De l'idiotie aux burlesques contemporains, Galerie Nationale du Jeu de Paume, Paris, and Domaine Pommery, Reims, France

Californian Artists in Greek Collections, Art Athina 2005, Athens, Greece

Richard Jackson
BEER DEER BEAR

Eröffnung: Freitag, 21. Oktober, 19 bis 21 Uhr
Ausstellungsdauer: 22. Oktober bis 28. November 2005
Di - Fr 13 - 18 Uhr, Sa 12 - 16 Uhr

Galerie Parisa Kind
Fahrgasse 7
Tel.: 069 - 29 72 88 40
www.parisakind.de

60311 Frankfurt am Main
Fax: 069 - 96 37 48 85
info@parisakind.de

ART COLOGNE: Halle 10.1 / Stand B 74

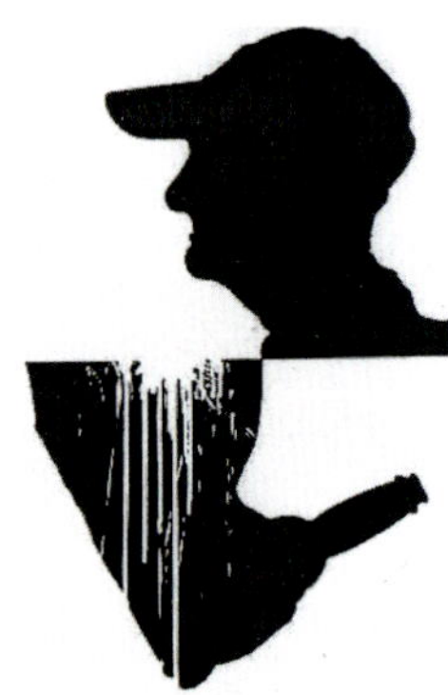

49. Vivian Rehberg, "Critic's Pick: Richard Jackson," Artforum.com, March 10, 2004, http://www.artforum.com/archive/id=6490.

50. Raphael Rubenstein, "In a Liquid Medium," *Art in America* 8 (September 2005): 132.

51. Jessica Lack, "Preview: Richard Jackson," *Guardian*, June 3, 2005.

52. Martin Herbert, "Dionysiac: Pompidou Centre, Paris," *Art Monthly*, no. 286 (May 2005): 25.

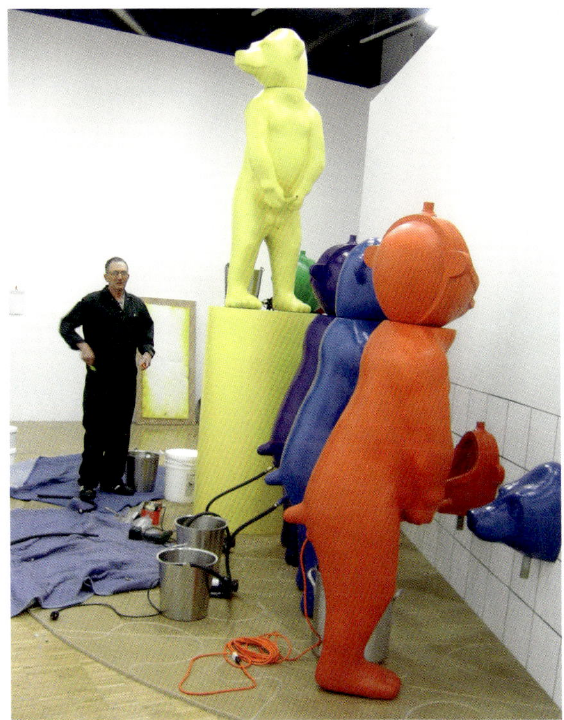

FIG. 36
Jackson installing *Pump Pee Doo* for
Dionysac: L'art en flux, Centre Georges
Pompidou, Musée National d'Art Moderne,
Paris, 2005

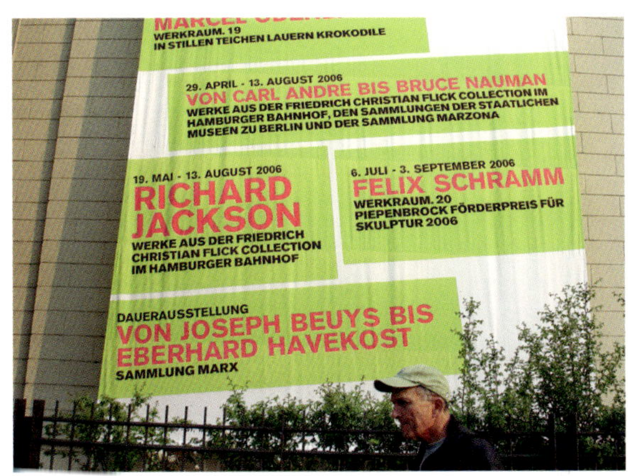

FIG. 37 (above)
*Richard Jackson: Werke aus der Friedrich
Christian Flick Collection im Hamburger
Bahnhof*, Hamburger Bahnhof Museum für
Gegenwart, Berlin, 2006

FIG. 38 (right)
Jackson installing *The Maid's Room* at
Galerie Georges-Philippe & Nathalie
Vallois, Paris, 2007

2006

SOLO EXHIBITION
*Richard Jackson: Werke aus der Friedrich
Christian Flick Collection im Hamburger Bahnhof*,
Hamburger Bahnhof Museum für Gegenwart,
Berlin

*The ultimate scale of the works, when
eventually realized in site-specific
installations, is given by Jackson's estimate
of the limits of human capability and
spatio-temporal constraints. Unabashedly
conceding the difficulty of generating new
ideas, he is content to spend extended
periods of time experimenting, refining and
building components whereby the time
and labor invested embody the work.*

—Catherine Nichols[53] (FIG. 37)

GROUP EXHIBITIONS
Metro Pictures: Part 1, Moore Space, Miami

*Ballerina in a Whirlpool: Works by Isa Genzken,
Richard Jackson, Roman Signer, and Diana
Thater from the Hauser & Wirth Collection*,
Staatliche Kunsthalle Baden-Baden, Baden-
Baden, Germany

Accidents, Galerie Georges-Philippe & Nathalie
Vallois, Paris

Le noir est une couleur, Marguerite and Aimé
Maeght Foundation, Saint-Paul-de-Vence,
France

Los Angeles–Paris, Centre Georges Pompidou,
Musée National d'Art Moderne, Paris

Los Angeles, 1955–1985: Birth of an Art Capital,
Centre Georges Pompidou, Musée National d'Art
Moderne, Paris

2007

SOLO EXHIBITIONS
*Richard Jackson: The Maid's Room / The Dining
Room*, Galerie Georges-Philippe & Nathalie
Vallois, Paris (FIG. 38)

Richard Jackson: New Works, 2006–2007, Yvon
Lambert Gallery, New York

*In its plenitude and sheer excess, Richard
Jackson's painting shares the openness
and quixotic nature of the libido described
by Lyotard. But even while it appears to
celebrate aspects of the human, his
painting is being extended to mannequins
and machines that betoken its potential
post-human role, thus continuing
Jackson's professed goal to extend
painting's limits.*

—Robert Hobbs[54]

*Venerable California artist Richard Jackson
might be thought of as a missing link
between the Viennese actionists and
contemporaries such as Paul McCarthy,
Bruce Nauman, or even the late Jason
Rhoades. . . . As much exorcism as
excoriation, Jackson's works also touch on
the prophetic. Fiercely mocking, even
profane provocations that strike at any
number of still-cherished cultural tropes
(whether childbirth or the image of the
noble soldier), they are expressive of a
timely, impolitic, and protean outrage, what
Wallace Stevens called nobility, "a violence
from within that protects us from a
violence without."*

—Tom Breidenbach[55]

GROUP EXHIBITIONS
Oeuvres encombrantes, Galerie Georges-
Philippe & Nathalie Vallois, Paris

Bodycheck: 10. Kleinplastik Fellbach Triennial,
Fellbach, Germany

Size Matters: XXL, Recent Large-Scale Paintings,
Hudson Valley Center for Contemporary Art,
Peekskill, New York

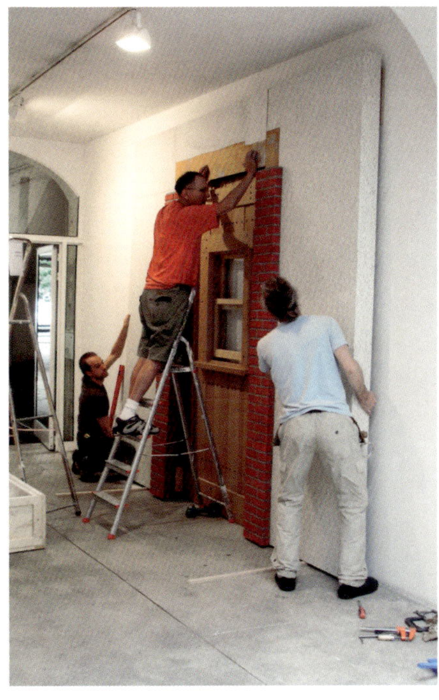

53. Catherine Nichols, "Richard Jackson
and the Domain of the Great Bear," in
*Richard Jackson: Werke aus der
Friedrich Christian Flick Collection im
Hamburger Bahnhof* (Berlin: Hamburger
Bahnhof—Museum für Gegenwart,
2006), 26.

54. Robert Hobbs, "Expanding
Painting's Limits," in *Richard Jackson:
New Works, 2006–2007* (Paris: Yvon
Lambert, 2007), unpaged.

55. Tom Breidenbach, "Richard
Jackson," *Artforum* 45 (Summer 2007):
498–99.

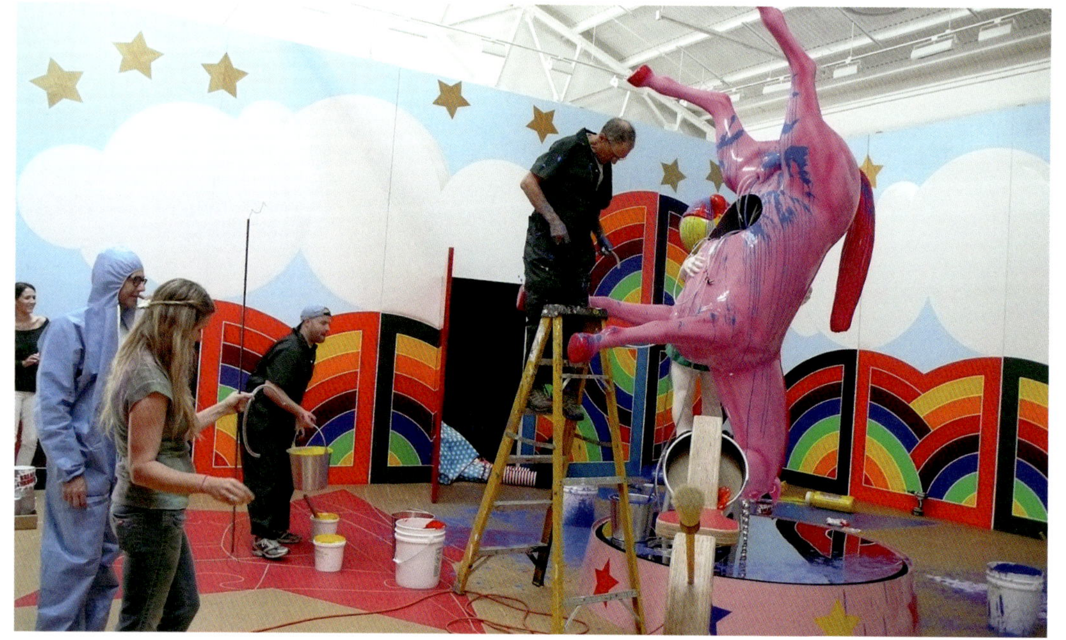

2008

GROUP EXHIBITIONS

Trahison: Collection du CAPC, CAPC, Musée
d'art contemporain de Bordeaux, Bordeaux,
France

The Stranger, Yvon Lambert Gallery, New York

Ne pas jouer avec des choses mortes, Villa Arson,
Nice, France

Hotel California, Galerie Georges-Philippe &
Nathalie Vallois, Paris

Comme des bêtes: Ours, chat, cochon & cie,
Musée Cantonal des Beaux-Arts de Lausanne,
Lausanne, Switzerland

*Cult of the Artist: "I can't just slice off an ear
every day"; Deconstructing the Myth of the Artist*,
Nationalgalerie im Hamburger Bahnhof and
Staatliche Museen zu Berlin

2009

SOLO EXHIBITION

Richard Jackson: The Laundry Room, Galerie
Hauser & Wirth, Zurich

GROUP EXHIBITIONS

*Vraoum! Trésors de la bande dessinée et art
contemporain*, Maison Rouge, Paris

*Quand la première ivresse des succès bruyants
aura fait son effet . . .* , Château Guiraud,
Sauternes, France

Under a Vanishing Night: New Work from L.A.,
Fourteen30 Contemporary, Portland, Oregon

Franz Ackermann, Richard Jackson, Otero
Plassart Gallery, Los Angeles

*Jackson, who hasn't had a hometown solo
exhibition in seventeen years, uses paint in
a way that recalls blood and guts or the
slippery leavings of an abattoir. While art
critics have quibbled over the supposed
death of painting for years, Jackson has
had its blood on his hands—or, metaphorically, at least, on the instruments he uses
to pump and squeeze paint all over the
gallery. . . . For Jackson painting is a messy
endgame, a means to reveal its multifarious
possibilities.*

—Andrew Berardini[56]

*The gallery that contains the Baldessari and
the Baxter is the glowing, prismatic heart*

56. Andrew Berardini, "Critic's Pick:
Richard Jackson, Franz Ackermann,"
Artforum.com, March 28, 2009, http://
www.artforum.com/archive/id=22362.

*of the show, the place where painting most
powerfully reasserts itself under duress.
A multicolored fluorescent square—an
empty-centered "painting" by Dan Flavin—
bleeds red, yellow and green toward a giant
wall slathered with juicy, layered paint in
all colors by the California artist Richard
Jackson, who has recreated an earlier work
here and re-titled it SAM. Jackson's work
is made by applying paint thickly to
canvases, then turning the canvases toward
the wall and smearing the paint onto the
wall in (Johnsian) arcs, finally leaving the
backward-facing canvases hanging in the
midst of the glorious, swooping goop.*

*Darling has taken this backward-facing
trope as the theme of this entire room.*

—Jen Graves[57]

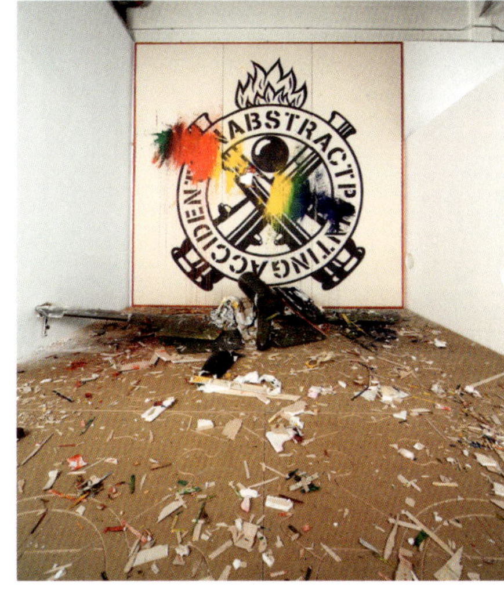

2010

SOLO EXHIBITIONS
Richard Jackson, Rennie Collection, Wing Sang
Building, Vancouver

Richard Jackson BIG PIG, Kunststiftung Erich
Hauser, Rottweil, Germany (FIG. 39)

*Another sculpture, by Richard Jackson,
represents a dog lifting its leg in satiny
cast aluminum. . . . The idea is that when a
collector buys it and installs it in his home,
the dog will, by means of attached plumbing,
spray red paint on the proud new owner's
wall. This calls to mind that chestnut of
modernist lore, Jackson Pollock drunkenly
urinating in his patron Peggy Guggenheim's
fireplace. The moral of the story being:
artists are wild, and collectors are tame,
but not above vicariously enjoying the
wildness of artists.*

—Ken Johnson[58]

GROUP EXHIBITIONS
Promenades, Le Magasin, Centre National d'Art
Contemporain, Grenoble, France

The Artists' Museum, Museum of Contemporary
Art, Los Angeles

2011

SOLO EXHIBITION
David Kordansky Gallery, Los Angeles

*Richard Jackson breaks a 20-year fast from
solo gallery exhibitions in Los Angeles with*

*an invigorating, over-the-top painting
installation. Painting is asserted as
delirious madness, as worthwhile for its
irrational folly as for any more ostensibly
sober reason.*

—Christopher Knight[59] (FIG. 40)

GROUP EXHIBITIONS
American Exuberance, Rubell Family Collection,
Miami

Under the Big Black Sun: California Art, 1974–1981,
Museum of Contemporary Art, Los Angeles

State of Mind: New California Art circa 1970,
Orange County Museum of Art, Newport Beach,
California

2012

SOLO EXHIBITION
*Richard Jackson: Accidents in Abstract Painting,
the Armory*, Armory Center for the Arts,
Pasadena, California (FIG. 41)

Richard Jackson Blue Prints, Galerie Parisa Kind,
Frankfurt

GROUP EXHIBITION
Y...as in Yet, Shanaynay, Paris

Hotel California II, Mitterand + Cramer, Geneva

2013

SOLO EXHIBITION
Richard Jackson: Ain't Painting a Pain, Orange
County Museum of Art, Newport Beach,
California

---

57. Jen Graves, "Exquisite Pain: The
Torture of Painting after World War II at
SAM," The Stranger Online, July 7, 2009,
http://www.thestranger.com/seattle/
exquisite-pain/Content?oid=1808230.

58. Ken Johnson, "Ahoy from Nudes, a
Pirate, and Scrooge McDuck," *New York
Times*, March 5, 2010.

59. Christopher Knight, "Art Review:
'Richard Jackson' at David Kordansky
Gallery," *Los Angeles Times*, September
15, 2011.

BIBLIOGRAPHY

Monographs

Kotinkaduwa, Angela, Jennifer Liese, and Samantha Tsao, eds. *Richard Jackson*. Exh. cat. Galerie Georges-Philippe & Nathalie Vallois, Paris; Hauser & Wirth, Zurich and London; Haswellediger & Co., New York; and Nyehaus, New York. Contributions by Bozidar Brazda, Julien Bismuth, Carissa Rodriguez, and Paul McCarthy. New York: Haswellediger, 2005.

Richard Jackson. Exh. cat. Essay by Edward Kienholz. Hope, ID: Faith and Charity in Hope Gallery, 1978.

Richard Jackson. Exh. cat. Essay by Jörn Merkert. Paris: Galerie Maeght, 1980.

Richard Jackson. Text by Andrew Berardini. Montreal: ABC Art Books Canada, 2010.

Richard Jackson: Bank Job. Exh. cat. Interview by Christine Kintisch. Vienna: BAWAG Foundation; Zurich: Galerie Hauser & Wirth, 2002.

Richard Jackson: Entstehung eines Wandbildes. Exh. cat. Essay by Gottfried Boehm. Trans. by Isabel Feder. Zurich: Rolf Schroeter, 1988.

Richard Jackson: Installation. Exh. cat. Essay by Melinda Wortz. Irvine: Fine Arts Gallery, University of California, 1977.

Richard Jackson: Installations. Exh. brochure. Essays by Edward Kienholz and Toni Stoos. Trans. by Barbara Richter and Philippa Mann. Berlin: Berliner Künstlerprogramm des Deutschen Akademischen Austausch Dienstes (DAAD), 1979.

Richard Jackson: New Works, 2006–2007. Exh. cat. Essay by Robert Hobbs. New York: Yvon Lambert, 2007.

Richard Jackson: Projekte. Exh. cat. Essay by Edward Kienholz. Zurich: Galerie Maeght, 1981.

Richard Jackson: Werke aus der Friedrich Christian Flick Collection im Hamburger Bahnhof. Exh. cat. Essays by Gabriele Knapstein, Eugen Blume, and Catherine Nichols. Trans. by Catherine Nichols and Nikolaus G. Schneider. Berlin: Nationalgalerie im Hamburger Bahnhof, in association with Staatliche Museen zu Berlin, 2006.

Richter, Barbara, ed. *Richard Jackson*. Exh. cat. Essays by Thomas Deecke and Edward Kienholz. Trans. by Keto von Waberer and Barbara Richter. Zurich: Galerie Maeght, 1979.

Seinsoth, Karin, ed. *Richard Jackson: Big Pig*. Exh. cat. Rottweil, Germany: Kunststiftung Erich Hauser, 2010.

Wirth, Iwan, ed. *Richard Jackson: Deer Beer*. Exh. cat. Texts by Walter Hopps, Hans Ulrich Obrist, and Harald Szeemann. Trans. by Ann Thursfield-Stinglwagner and Brigitte Kalthoff. Cologne: Oktagon, 1998.

Books and Catalogs

Abstraction in Los Angeles, 1950–1980: Selections from the Murray and Ruth Gribin Collection. Exh. cat. Essays by Jean-Luc Bordeaux, Melinda Wortz, and William Hemmerdinger. Northridge: Fine Arts Gallery, California State University, 1981.

Amerikanische Zeichnungen, 1930–1980. Exh. cat. Essays by Walter Hopps, Neil Printz, and Klaus Gallwitz. Frankfurt am Main, Germany: Städelsche Kunstinstitut and Städtische Galerie Frankfurt, 1985.

Annual Report, 1977–1978. Buffalo, NY: Buffalo Fine Arts Academy, Albright-Knox Art Gallery, 1978.

Art about Art. Exh. cat. Essays by Jean Lipman, Richard Marshall, and Leo Steinberg. New York: Whitney Museum of American Art and Dutton, 1978.

Art as Healer. Exh. cat. Essay by Victoria Dalkey. Sacramento: Weintraub Hunter Gallery, in association with the School of Medicine, University of California, Davis, 1994.

Art in Los Angeles: The Museum as Site; Sixteen Projects. Exh. cat. Essay by Stephanie Barron. Los Angeles: Los Angeles County Museum of Art, 1981.

Awards in Painting, Sculpture, Printmaking, Photography, and Craft Media. New York: Louis Comfort Tiffany Foundation, 1997.

Balkon mit Fächer: 25 Jahre Berliner Künstlerprogram des DAAD. Exh. cat. Essays by René Block, Joachim Sartorius, and Wolfgang Siano. Berlin: Deutsche Akademische Austausch Dienst (DAAD), 1988.

Barron, Stephanie, Sheri Bernstein, and Ilene Susan Fort. *Made in California: Art, Image, and Identity, 1900–2000*. Exh. cat. Los Angeles: Los Angeles County Museum of Art; Berkeley and Los Angeles: University of California Press, 2000.

Belloli, Jay. *Radical Past: Contemporary Art and Music in Pasadena, 1960–1974*. Exh. cat. Essays by Jay Belloli, Linda Centell, Michelle Deziel, Suzanne Muchnic, Peter Plagens, and Jeff von der Schmidt. Pasadena, CA: Armory Center for the Arts and Art Center College of Design, 1999.

Bericht über das Geschäftsjahr 1993/94. Zurich: Daimler-Benz Finanz, 1994.

Both Kinds: Contemporary Art from Los Angeles. Exh. cat. Essay by Peter Plagens. Berkeley: University Art Museum, University of California, 1975.

Bright Light. Exh. cat. Essay by Manfred Schneckenburger. Stuttgart, Germany: Brigitte March Galerie, 1993.

Bunnell, Peter C. "Remembering L.A." In *The Collectible Moment: Catalogue of Photographs in the Norton Simon Museum*, edited by Gloria Williams Sander. New Haven, CT: Yale University Press for the Norton Simon Art Foundation, 2006.

California A–Z and Return. Exh. cat. Essay by John Fitzgibbon. Youngstown, OH: Butler Institute of American Art, 1990.

Cinquante ans de dessins américains, 1930–1980. Exh. cat. Essays by Walter Hopps and Neil Printz. Paris: École Nationale Supérieure des Beaux-Arts; Houston: Menil Collection, 1985.

Darling, Michael, ed. *Target Practice: Painting under Attack, 1949–78*. Exh. cat. Essays by Michael Darling, Elizabeth Magnini, Mika Yoshitake, and Graham Bader. Seattle: Seattle Art Museum, 2009.

Drawings by Painters. Exh. cat. Essay by Richard Armstrong. Long Beach, CA: Long Beach Museum of Art, 1982.

Eagle, Mary, and Christopher Chapman. *Virtual Reality*. Exh. cat. Text on Jackson by Michael Desmond. Canberra: National Gallery of Australia; London: Thames & Hudson, 1995.

Échange entre artistes, 1931–1982: Pologne–USA; Une expérience muséographique. Exh. cat. Essay by Pontus Hultén. Paris: Musée d'Art Moderne de la Ville de Paris and Animation-recherche-confrontation (ARC), 1982.

Emslander, Fritz, and Michaela Unterdörfer, eds. *Ballerina in a Whirlpool: Werke von Isa Genzken, Richard Jackson, Roman Signer, Diana Thater, aus der Hauser & Wirth Collection*. Exh. cat. Staatliche Kunsthalle, Baden-Baden, Germany. Essays by Michaela Unterdörfer and Sabine Sarwa. Cologne: Snoeck, 2006.

Fibicher, Bernard, ed. *Comme des bêtes: Ours, chat, cochon & cie*. Exh. cat. Essays by Marie Alamir, Bernard Fibicher, Magali Moulinier, Groupe de la Riponne, Michel Sartori, and Anne Sauvagnargues. Lausanne, Switzerland: Musée Cantonal des Beaux-Arts de Lausanne, in association with Editions 5 Continents, Milan, 2008.

Fricke, Marion, and Roswitha Fricke, eds. *The Context of Art / The Art of Context*. Essay by Seth Siegelaub. Trans. by Daniel Marzona. Trieste, Italy: Navado Press, 2004.

Good Deal. Exh. cat. Sacramento: Robert Else Gallery, California State University, 1987.

Great Expectations! Fuori Uso 2003. Exh. cat. Texts by Giacinto di Pietrantonio and Marco Tagliafierro. Trans. by Angelamaria Fiore. Pescara, Italy: Fuori Uso and Associazione culturale Arte Nova, 2003.

Grenier, Catherine, ed. *Los Angeles, 1955–1985: Birth of an Art Capital*. Exh. cat. Essays by Howard N. Fox, David E. James, Catherine Grenier, Alfred Pacquement, and Bruno Racine. Paris: Centre Georges Pompidou and Panama Musées, 2006.

Grieger, Susan. *Friends / Artists*. Pasadena, CA: Susan Grieger, 1975.

Haskell, Barbara. *Fifteen Los Angeles Artists*. Exh. cat. Pasadena, CA: Pasadena Art Museum, 1972.

Hopkins, Henry T. *California Painters: New Work*. San Francisco: Chronicle, 1989.

———. *Painting and Sculpture in California: The Modern Era*. Exh. cat. San Francisco: San Francisco Museum of Modern Art, 1977.

Howard, William V. *Painting 1969: Arts 1969 Festival; Painting Invitational*. Exh. cat. Reno: University of Nevada, 1969.

"Ich kann mir nicht jeden Tag ein Ohr abschneiden": Dekonstruktionen des Künstlermythos. Exh. cat. Essays by Gabriele Knapstein and Peter-Klaus Schuster et al. Berlin: Nationalgalerie, Staatliche Museen zu Berlin; Cologne: DuMont, 2008.

Jack Barth, Richard Van Buren, David Deutsch, Richard Jackson, James Reineking. Exh. brochure. Providence, RI: David Winton Bell Gallery, List Art Building, Brown University, 1977.

John Baldessari, Francis Barth, Richard Jackson, Barbara Munger, Gary Stephan. Exh. cat. Text by Jay Belloli. Houston: Contemporary Arts Museum Houston, 1972.

Knubben, Claudia, and Jürgen Knubben. *Aus der Küche der Künste: 25 Jahre Forum Kunst Rottweil*. Rottweil, Germany: Forum Kunst Rottweil, 1994.

L.A.-ex Performances. Exh. cat. Christa Häusler and Elisabeth Schweeger, eds. Essays by Andrew Gellatly, Meg Cranston, Richard Jackson, Diana Thater and T. Kelly Mason, Raymond Pettibon, Jonathan Meese, Hans

Weigand, and Peter Kroher. Ostfildern-Ruit, Germany: Hatje Cantz, 2001.

Latour, Bruno, and Peter Weibel, eds. *Iconoclash: Beyond the Image Wars in Science, Religion, and Art.* Exh. cat. Karlsruhe, Germany: ZKM; London: MIT Press, 2002.

Linsenmaier-Wolf, Christa, ed. *Bodycheck: 10. Triennale Kleinplastik Fellbach.* Exh. cat. Essays by Nicole Fritz, Barbara Wagner, Harriet Zillich, Fritz Emslander, Murkus Bulling, and Matthias Winzen. Cologne: Snoeck, 2007.

Los Angeles '72. Exh. brochure. Essay by Maurice Tuchman and Jane Livingston. New York: Sidney Janis Gallery, 1972.

Macel, Christine. *Dionysiac.* Exh. cat. Essays by Christine Macel, Barbara Stiegler, and Jean-Pierre Criqui. Paris: Centre Pompidou, 2005.

Making the Making. Exh. pamphlet. Text by Charles Goldman. New York: Apex Art Curatorial Program, 2001.

Mangion, Éric, and Marie de Brugerolle, eds. *Ne pas jouer avec des choses mortes.* Exh. cat. Villa Arson, Nice, France. Interviews with Paul McCarthy and Richard Jackson. Texts by Éric Mangion, Marie de Brugerolle, Arnaud Labelle-Rojoux, Patricia Brignone, Gérard Wajcman, Catherine Wood, and Julien Bismuth. Dijon, France: Presses du Réel; Zurich: JRP|Ringier, 2008.

March, Brigitte, ed. *Force Sight.* Exh. cat. Schloss Presteneck, Neuenstadt, Germany. Essay by Yves Michel Bernard. Böblingen, Germany: Art Publishing, 1992.

Morel, Frédéric, and Fabrice Bousteau, eds. *De l'idiotie aux burlesques contemporains.* Exh. cat. Paris: Beaux Arts, in association with Galerie Nationale du Jeu de Paume, Paris, and Domaine Pommery, Reims, 2005.

Nègre, Louis. *Quand la première ivresse des succès bruyants aura fait son effet. . . .* Exh. cat. Château Guiraud, Sauternes, France, and CAPC, Musée d'Art Contemporain Bordeaux. Bordeaux, France: Féret, 2009.

New York Now. Exh. cat. Essay by Robert H. Frankel. Phoenix: Phoenix Art Museum, 1979.

1985 Artpark Visual Arts Program. Essay by Christopher Knight. Lewiston, NY: Artpark, 1985.

One of a Kind: Contemporary Serial Imagery. Exh. cat. Edited by Gail Barringer. Texts by John Coplans and Edward Leffingwell. Los Angeles: Los Angeles Municipal Art Gallery, 1989.

Plus Ultra: Jenseits der Moderne? / Beyond Modernity? Exh. cat. Essays by Stefan Bidner, Thomas Feuerstein, F. E. Rakuschan, Helmut Willke, Roberto Ohrt, Markus Neuwirth, and Thomas Rainer. Frankfurt, Germany: Revolver, 2005.

Point of View: Artworks from the Collection of Jeffrey Kerns. Exh. cat. Essay by Michael Kohn. San Bernardino: University Art Gallery, California State University, 1986.

4e Biennale d'art contemporain de Lyon: L'autre. Exh. cat. Essay by Harald Szeemann. Lyon, France: Réunion des Musées Nationaux, 1997.

Rona, Zeynep, ed. *International Sculptors Symposium.* Participants: Richard Jackson, Les Levine, Yutaka Matsuzawa, Füsun Onur, Patrick Raynaud, Mike Rodemer, Yildiz Tüzün, and Günther Uecker. Translated by Angela Roome. Bursa, Turkey: Uludag University, 1995.

Rosenberg, David, and Pierre Sterckx, eds. *Vraoum! Trésors de la bande dessinée et art contemporain.* Exh. cat. Maison Rouge—Fondation Antoine Galbert. Lyon, France: Fage, 2009.

Schimmel, Paul. *Helter Skelter: L.A. Art in the 1990s.* Exh. cat. Essays by Norman M. Klein and Lane Relyea. Los Angeles: Museum of Contemporary Art, 1992.

Schloss Solitude–Pläne und Projekte. Exh. cat. Stuttgart, Germany: Brigitte March, 1986.

Spielvogel, Gudrun. *1991–1996, Galerie & Edition.* Munich: Galerie Gudrun Spielvogel, 1996.

Szeemann, Harald, and Cecilia Liveriero Lavelli, eds. *dAPERTutto: 48a Esposizione Internazionale d'Arte; La Biennale di Venezia.* Exh. cat. Venice, Italy: Edizioni La Biennale di Venezia and Marsilio, 1999.

2006 Program of the Mountain School of the Arts. Los Angeles: Mountain School of the Arts, 2006.

Unterdörfer, Michaela, ed. *The House of Fiction.* Exh. cat. Sammlung Hauser & Wirth. Nuremberg, Germany: Verlag für moderne Kunst.

Wall Painting. Exh. cat. Essays by Judith Russi Kirshner and John Hallmark Neff. Chicago: Museum of Contemporary Art, 1979.

Widmer, Derrick, ed. *Kunstausstellung "Holderbank," 1995–2000.* Texts by Derrick Widmer and André Kamber. Holderbank, Switzerland: Holderbank Management and Consulting, 1998.

Wilde, Eliane de, ed. *Fundamentele schilderkunst / Fundamental Painting.* Exh. cat. Essay by Rini Dippel. Amsterdam: Stedelijk Museum, 1975.

Writings by the Artist

"Ab Isms Expressionism Expansionism Optimism." *Artforum* 10 (Summer 2011): 335.

"Constructed Reality." *Artforum* 45 (October 2006): 62.

"A Few Words about Ed Kienholz." In *Kienholz: A Retrospective,* by Walter Hopps, 283. Exh. cat. New York: Whitney Museum of American Art, 1996.

1/2 Full. Privately printed, 1983.

"Letter." In *Statements on Art,* ed. by Donald Sultan and Nancy Davidson. Chicago: N.A.M.E. Gallery, 1977.

Richard Jackson: Manual of Instructions for "The Maid's Room." Paris: Galerie Georges-Philippe & Nathalie Vallois; Zurich: Hauser & Wirth, 2007.

Untitled broadside. Los Angeles: Eugenia Butler Gallery, 1969.

Articles

"Abstrakter Expressionismus—Werke des amerikanischen Konzeptkünstlers Richard Jackson in der BAWAG Foundation." *Der Standard,* May 7, 2002.

Albright, Thomas. "How an Artist Stacks Up These Days." *San Francisco Chronicle,* June 14, 1983.

Allman, Paul. "Art Who?" *Independent and Gazette,* April 12, 1975.

Allsop, Laura. "On with the New: Yvon Lambert." *Art Review,* no. 9 (March 2007): 34.

"American Art Maverick Unveils Latest Work." *Durrants,* June 3, 2005, 5.

Arlitt, Sabine. "Malerei unter Schock." *Züritipp,* April 17, 2003, 48.

Azimi, Roxana. "Californie: Des affreux jojos aux radicaux." *L'Oeil,* no. 571 (July–August 2005): 108–11.

———. "Les turbulents californiens ne font plus peur." *Le Monde,* October 2–3, 2005.

Bader, Jörg. "Zürcher Geschnetzeltes: Rockenschaub und Jackson bei Hauser und Wirth im Löwenbräu." *Frankfurter Allgemeine,* November 28, 1998.

"Bank Job—Die BAWAG Foundation, 1010 Wien, präsentiert vom 8. Mai bis 30. Juni zum ersten Mal in Österreich mit einer Einzelausstellung

Arbeiten des kalifornischen Künstlers Richard Jackson." *Vernissage*, June 2002, 16–19.

Banks, Eric C. "10·20·30 Years Ago in *Artforum*: May 1972." *Artforum* 40 (May 2002): 48.

Bannon, Anthony. "Artpark's Assertive New Installations." *Buffalo News*, July 19, 1985.

"Bärenjagd." *Die Presse* (Vienna), June 17 / July 1 / August 30, 2002.

Baun, Adrienne, and Petra Bosetti. "Entdeck-ungsreise statt Blockbuster." *ART: Das Kunstmagazin*, no. 7 (July 2007): 100.

Becker, Maria. "Unterhaltsam, hybrid, wohnzimmertauglich." *Bazartmagazin*, *Basler Zeitung*, June 18, 2005, 6.

Bellet, Harry. "Richard Jackson." *Le Monde*, September 15, 2007.

Bellet, Harry, and Benjamin Roure. "Les vedettes de l'art trash au Centre Pompidou." *Le Monde*, February 20–21, 2005.

Bellini, Andrea. "Cautious Alternatives." *Flash Art* 39 (July–September 2006): 106–10.

Berardini, Andrew. "Critic's Pick: Richard Jackson, Franz Ackermann." *Artforum* online, March 28, 2009, http://artforum.com/archive/id=22362.

Bergez, Wladimir. "Richard Jackson." *Art présence*, no. 52 (October–December 2004): 3–11.

"Die Bier-Bären." *Wiener Bezirksblatt*, June 10, 2002.

Bismuth, Léa. "Expos-Critiques: Richard Jackson." *Paris Art*, June 2007.

Blaine, Michael. "Painting by Construction." *Artweek* 11 (September 27, 1980): 3.

Blase, Christopher. "'L'autre,' 4e Biennale d'art contemporain de Lyon." *Artforum* 36 (October 1997): 94–95.

Blouin, Patrice. "Burlesque et idiotie, frères amis." *Beaux Arts Magazine*, June 2005, 71–90.

Bonnet, Frédéric. "Centre Pompidou 'Dionysiac,' son flux et ses reflux." *Journal des arts*, no. 213 (April 15–28, 2005): 11.

Borchhardt-Birbaumer, Brigitte. "Der anarchistische Bildjäger." *Wiener Zeitung*, June 12, 2002.

Breerette, Geneviève. "Des figures de l'excès, plus désagréables que dérangeantes." *Le Monde*, February 20–21, 2005.

Breidenbach, Tom. "Richard Jackson." *Artforum* 45 (Summer 2007): 498–99.

Brown, Christopher. "How to Paint a Room." *California Aggie* (UC Davis), Arts/Entertainment Supplement, November 17–23, 1976, 3.

Browning, Jeffrey. "An Architecture of Paint." *Arts + Architecture* 3, no. 4 (1985): 44–49.

Buchhart, Dieter. "Richard Jackson: Ich bin ein Kunstterrorist" (interview). *Kunstforum International*, no. 165 (June–July 2003): 216–29.

Bulmer, Marge. "A Sculpture to Enter." *Artweek* 15 (December 15, 1984): 4.

Bunnell, Peter C. "Photography into Sculpture." *Arts in Virginia* 11 (Spring 1971): 18–25.

Burnham, Jack. "Painting up against the Wall." *New Art Examiner* 6 (May 1979): 4.

Busse, Gundel-Maria. "Etwas sehr einfaches." *Main-Echo*, November 16, 2005.

Chadwick, Susan. "Critic's Choice." *Houston Post*, January 6, 1989.

———. "For Richard Jackson, the Point Is Painting." *Houston Post*, July 17, 1988.

Chateigné, Yann. "Cra-Z-Boy: Richard Jackson." *Cahiers du Fonds national d'art contemporain*, no. 8 (2007): 12.

Chlan, Ilse. "Richard Jackson: Kunst ist etwas sehr einfaches." *Pharma-Time*, June 2002.

Colard, Jean-Max. "Sexorama." *Les inrockuptibles*, no. 609/611 (July 31–August 20, 2007): 96–97.

Cotter, Holland. "At the Met: Susan Rothenberg and Bruce Nauman." *New York Times*, February 21, 1997.

Cernetig, Miro. "Creative Genius Meets Big Money." *Vancouver Sun*, April 23, 2010.

———. "Painting Goes off the Wall." *Vancouver Sun*, April 24, 2010.

Cohen, Rachel. "It Only Happens Once." *Modern Painters* 16 (Spring 2003): 26–29.

Coomer, Martin. "Richard Jackson." *Time Out London*, July 13–20, 2005, 65.

Curtis, Cathy. "Assessing the Current Vitality of Repetition." *Los Angeles Times*, December 30, 1988.

Dalkey, Victoria. "Major and Minor Scales–Sizing Up Two Exhibits That Push at the Boundaries of Modern Art." *Sacramento Bee*, November 15, 1987.

Danby, Charles. "'Dionysiac.'" *Art Review*, April 2005, 104.

Danicke, Sandra. "Die Farben der Hirsche." *Frankfurter Rundschau*, November 22, 2005.

Danilowicz, Nathan. "Ackermann / Jackson." *ArtUS*, no. 26 (2009): 6–7.

Davidow, Joie. "Pick of the Week." *LA Weekly*, July 24–30, 1981.

Denet, Muriel. "Dionysiac." *Paris Art*, March 2005.

Dick, Leslie. "Dionysiac." *Modern Painters* 17 (June 2005): 112–13.

Dörfert, Petra. "Befremdliche Objektewelt." *Kunstzeitung*, no. 133 (September 2007): 19.

Douroux, Xavier, and Yves Aupetitallot. "A propos de Harald Szeemann tentative d'épuisement de L'autre the Other, Every Which Way." *Art Press*, no. 226 (July–August 1997).

Drath, Viola Herms. "The Thirty-Second Corcoran Biennial, Art as a Visual Event." *Art International* 15 (May 1971): 40–45.

Drohojowska, Hunter. "He's the Master of the 'Painting-Event,'" *Los Angeles Herald-Examiner*, August 17, 1984.

———. "Richard Jackson at the Rosamund Felsen Gallery." *LA Weekly*, August 2–9, 1984, 51.

Duault, Nicole. "Rires, sexe, déjections et congélation." *Journal du dimanche*, February 13, 2005.

Dunham, Judith L. "'Both Kinds': Contemporary L.A. Art." *Artweek* 6 (May 3, 1975): 1, 20.

———. "Evidence of Process—Richard Jackson, Chris Darton." *Artweek* 7 (November 27, 1976): 1, 16.

Duponchelle, Valérie, and Béatrice De Rochebouët. "A la conquête du contemporain." *Le Figaro*, October 7, 2005.

Dusini, Matthias. "Bär im Öl." *Falter*, no. 21 (May 2002): 60.

Eagle, Joanna. "The Corcoran Biennial: Hopps, Skips, and Jumps." *Art Gallery Magazine* 14 (March 1971): 37–40.

"Eruption und Planung." *Neue Zürcher Zeitung*, December 12, 1998.

Feeser, Sigrid. "Bodycheck 10. Triennale Kleinplastik Fellbach: Alte Kelter Fellbach, 23.6–23.9.2007." *Kunstforum International*, no. 188 (October–November 2007): 432–34.

Filipovic, Elena. "Dionysiac." *Frieze*, no. 93 (September 2005): 140.

Fineman, Mia. "Looks Brilliant on Paper, but Who, Exactly, Is Going to Make It?" *New York Times*, May 7, 2006.

Fronz, Hans-Dieter. "Alles dreht sich um den Kreis." *Badische Zeitung*, October 4, 2006.

——. "Ballerina in a Whirlpool." *Kunstforum International*, no. 183 (December 2006–February 2007): 357–58.

——. "Comme des bêtes." *Kunstforum International*, no. 191 (May–July 2008): 372.

——. "Einlass für Dinos und Mäuse." *Badische Zeitung*, July 13, 2007.

——. "Galerie Hauser and Wirth, Zurich." *Handelszeitung* (Zurich), November 11, 1998.

Gardner, Belinda Grace. "Leinwand von innen." *Artnet*, www.artnet.de, July 31, 2006.

Gardner, Colin. "Richard Jackson." *Artforum* 29 (February 1991): 134–35.

Gauthier, Michel. "Dionysiac." Translated by C. Penwarden. *Art Press*, no. 312 (May 2005): 78–79.

Gauville, Hervé. "'Dionysiac' sans plaisir." *Libération*, February 26–27, 2005.

Glover, Michael. "Anarchy Rules at the Pompidou in a Celebration of Dionysus." *Times of London*, March 30, 2005.

Graves, Jen. "Exquisite Pain: The Torture of Painting after World War II at SAM." *The Stranger Online*, July 7, 2009, http://www.thestranger.com/seattle/exquisite-pain/Content?oid=1808230.

Haase, Amine. "48. Biennale von Venedig: Versöhnung der Gegensätze." *Kunstforum International* 147 (September–November 1999): 150–60.

Hammond, Pamela. "1,000 Pictures, Richard Jackson at Rosamund Felsen." *Images and Issues* 1 (Winter 1980–81): 45–46.

Hemmerdinger, William. "The Murray and Ruth Gribin Collection: A Critical View." *Journal of the Los Angeles Institute of Contemporary Art*, no. 30 (September–October 1981): 25.

Herbert, Martin. "Dionysiac: Pompidou Centre, Paris." *Art Monthly*, no. 286 (May 2005): 24–26.

Horny, Henriette. "Kunst ist nie wirklich fertig." *Kurier*, May 8, 2002.

Hughes, Jeffrey. "Vienna: Richard Jackson, BAWAG Foundation." *Sculpture* 22 (May 2003): 83–84.

Hultén, Pontus. "Installationen und Bilder von Richard Jackson." *Glarner Nachrichten*, April 20, 1989.

James, Bruce. "User-friendly Artworks Are a Virtual Reality." *The Age*, December 1994.

——. "With a Slip of the Eye." *Sydney Morning Herald*, December 21, 1994.

Johnson, Ken. "Ahoy from Nudes, a Pirate and Scrooge McDuck." *New York Times*, March 5, 2010.

——. "Richard Jackson." *New York Times*, September 19, 1997.

——. "Richard Jackson, 'Dick's Pictures.'" *New York Times*, January 7, 2005.

——. "Some Shows for Escape, Some for Introspection." *New York Times*, July 4, 2008.

Johnson, Patricia C. "Jackson's Menil Exhibit: Art to Be Experienced." *Houston Chronicle*, July 24, 1988.

——. "The Menil . . . One Year Later." *Houston Chronicle*, June 19, 1988.

——. "The 'Object-Makers,' Art by Young Germans on Exhibit." *Houston Chronicle*, November 26, 1989.

Kandel, Susan. "L.A. in Review." *Arts Magazine*, no. 66 (April 1992): 98–99.

——. "Trapped behind Bars: Richard Jackson at the Santa Monica Museum of Art." *Los Angeles Times*, May 23, 1992.

Kern, Ingolf. "Zbigniew Libera." *Monopol*, no. 11 (November 2007): 31.

Kihm, Christophe. "Richard Jackson: Galerie G-P et N. Vallois." *Art Press*, no. 302 (June 2004): 79–80.

——. "Richard Jackson: La pensée et l'accident / Thought and Accident." Translated by L.-S. Torgoff. *Art Press*, no. 318 (December 2005): 36–41.

Knight, Christopher. "An Art of Darkness at MOCA." *Los Angeles Times*, January 28, 1992.

——. "The Great Wall of La Cienega." *Los Angeles Herald-Examiner*, September 18, 1980.

——. "PST: Richard Jackson Makes a Painting with a Drone Airplane Crash." *Los Angeles Times*, January 23, 2012.

——. "'Richard Jackson' at David Kordansky Gallery." *Los Angeles Times*, September 15, 2011.

Krauss, Rosalind E. "Washington." *Artforum* 9 (May 1971): 83–85.

Kreis, Elfi. "Den Kinderschuhen entwachsen." *Kunstzeitung*, no. 130 (June 2007): 27.

——. "Richard Jackson im Hamburger Bahnhof." *Kunstzeitung*, no. 119 (July 2006): 9.

"Kreisen und Umkreisen." *Neue Zürcher Zeitung*, November 4, 2006.

Kuhn, Nicola. "Malen, jagen und ein Bier dazu." *Der Tagesspiegel*, May 19, 2006.

Kunitz, Daniel. "Rare Breed." *Art Review*, May–June 2005, 92–97.

"Kunst feiert Kunst: Hauser and Wirth eröffnet Jubiläumsaustellung." *Metropol*, January 18, 2002.

"Kunst/Werk des Monats Mai: Richard Jackson und seine Skulptur *Two Heads*." www.magazine.orf.at/treff.kultur, May 4, 2002.

Lack, Jessica. "Preview: Richard Jackson." *Guardian*, June 3, 2005.

Laubard, Charlotte. "Qui a peur de Richard Jackson?" *o2*, no. 29 (Spring 2004).

Lavelli, Cecilia Liveriero, and Franklin Sirmans. "Harald Szeemann." *Flash Art* 30 (Summer 1997): 89.

Lavrador, Judicaël. "Californicréation." *Les Inrockuptibles*, no. 482 (February 23–March 1, 2005): 82–83.

——. "Paintball." *Les Inrockuptibles*, no. 433 (March 17–23, 2004): 105.

——. "Quelle place pour la peinture aujourd'hui? Famille 5: Sur le mur (du fond)." *Beaux Arts Magazine*, no. 285 (March 2008): 52–63.

——. "Richard Jackson: Mr. Dynamite." *Beaux Arts Magazine*, no. 277 (July 2007): 86–89.

Lenhardt, Christiane. "Spielerisch die Welt umkreisen und erklären." *Badisches Tagblatt*, September 30, 2006.

Lewis, Louise. "Richard Jackson's Painting–Unexpected Echoes of Art History." *Artweek* 8 (October 22, 1977): 7.

Linsenmann, Andreas. "Kantige Konfrontation." *NRWZ zum Wochenende* (Rottweil, Germany), July 24, 2004.

Louvel, Henri. "Art Jonction 98, une grande année pour un Grand Crue niçois." *Art Jonction: Le Journal*, no. 12 (Spring 1998): 1, 3.

Mack, Gerhard. "Richard Jackson in der Galerie Hauser und Wirth 1." *Kunst-Bulletin*, no. 12 (December 1998): 43.

"Malende Maschinen." *FSG–Direkt* (Vienna), May 28, 2002.

Malherbe, Anne. "Richard Jackson." Translated by L.-S. Torgoff. *Art Press*, no. 334 (April 2007): 71–72.

Marboe, Isabella. "Bärig, witzig–Richard Jackson 'Bank Job' in der BAWAG-Foundation." *Die Furche*, May 16, 2002.

Marsala, Helga. "Dionysiac." *Exibart*, March–April 2005.

Marti, Petsch. "Das Bild als Bild in Frage gestellt." *Glarner Nachrichten*, April 25, 1989.

Matthias, Rosemary. "'Los Angeles '72': Sidney Janis Gallery, N.Y." *Arts Magazine* 47 (September–October 1972): 58.

Maulmin, Valérie de. "Décapant Richard Jackson." *Connaissance des arts*, no. 650 (June 2007): 154.

Maurer, Simon. "Künstler und Jäger." *Züritip*, October 30, 1998, 67.

Mayer, Rosemary. "Richard Jackson, Bykert Gallery." *Arts Magazine* 47 (March 1973): 72–73.

Mayo, Alberta. "The bear went over the mountain to see what he could see." Unpublished text, 2002.

Mays, John Bentley. "Worthwhile Artpark Exhibit Shows Sculpture's in a Rut." *Toronto Globe and Mail*, July 17, 1985.

McDonough, Tom. "Richard Jackson at David Zwirner." *Art in America* 85 (December 1997): 89–90.

McFadden, Sarah. "The 'Other' Biennial." *Art in America* 85 (November 1997): 84–91.

McKenna, Christine. "Richard Jackson: Conceptual and Uncollectible." *Los Angeles Times*, November 27, 1990.

Melchart, Erwin. "Der Bär ist los!" *Neue Kronen Zeitung*, May 11, 2002.

Metzger, Rainer. "Plumeau bis Plafond." *Art Magazine*, May 10, 2002, http://www.artmagazine.cc/content3952.html.

Miller, Donald. "Washington." *Arts Magazine* 45 (April 1971): 77.

Millet, Catherine, ed. "69/96, Avant-gardes et fin de siècle: 75 artistes racontent leur parcours." Special issue, *Art Press*, no. 17 (1996).

Mittringer, Markus. "Lernen, allein zu leben." *Der Standard*, May 8, 2002.

Moss, Jennifer. "The 'Cowboy' of Modern Art." *Vancouver Sun*, May 10, 2010.

Muchnic, Suzanne. "Art in the City of Angels and Demons." *Los Angeles Times*, January 26, 1992.

———. "Drawings by California Painters." *Los Angeles Times*, February 16, 1982.

———. "The Galleries, La Cienega Area." *Los Angeles Times*, November 9, 1984.

———. "Jackson Sculpture: Insights from Inside." *Los Angeles Times*, November 3, 1984.

———. "Painting with Painting." *Artweek* 9 (September 9, 1978): 1, 20.

Noah, Barbara. "Richard Jackson at Rosamund Felsen." *Art in America* 66 (November–December 1978): 159.

Ollman, Leah. "Richard Jackson at Otero Plassart." *Los Angeles Times*, March 27, 2009.

Pagel, David. "Delincuencia juvenil y falsa adolescencia." *Lapiz* 10 (April–May 1992): 28–35.

———. "The Present as Future History." *Artweek* 20 (January 7, 1989).

Pilven, Marguerite. "Richard Jackson, Unusual Behavior." *Paris Art* online, May 2004.

Pincus, Robert. "The Galleries: La Cienega Area." *Los Angeles Times*, July 27, 1984.

Plagens, Peter. "The Decline and Rise of Younger Los Angeles Art." *Artforum* 10 (May 1972): 80.

———. "Los Angeles: Richard Jackson, Charles Garabedian, Eugenia Butler Gallery." *Artforum* 9 (January 1971): 90–91.

———. "Site Wars." *Art in America* 70 (January 1982): 91–98.

"Plastikbären tanzen kaum." *Die Presse* (Vienna), August 6, 2002.

Pricco, Evan. "Showstoppers: Richard Jackson." *Juxtapoz*, no. 82 (November 2007).

Prodhon, Françoise-Claire. "Art contemporaine, une entrée en matière." *Architectural Design* (French ed.), no. 78 (October 2008).

"Der Prozess vor dem Objekt." *Wiener Zeitung*, May 2, 2002.

Raap, Jürgen. "My Home Is My Castle: Künstlerische 'Wohnwelten,'" *Kunstforum International*, no. 184 (March–April 2007): 70–85.

Reber, Simone. "Hamburger Bahnhof: Richard Jackson." *Kultur Radio*, Rundfunk Berlin-Brandenburg, May 23, 2006.

Rehberg, Vivian. "Critic's Pick: Richard Jackson." *Artforum* online, March 2004. http://artforum.com/picks/id=29154&view=print

———. "Paris: Richard Jackson." *Modern Painters* 19 (October 2007): 99.

Renner, Sascha. "Im Schleudergang." *Tagesanzeiger*, April 9–15, 2009.

Reichart, Helga. "Mit Vollgas durch die Wand." *Dolomiten*, December 10, 2002.

———. "Mit Vollgas durch die Wand und weiter." *Salzburger Nachrichten*, December 5, 2002.

Richard, Paul. "Corcoran's Suggestive Thought Fields." *Washington Post*, February 27, 1971.

"Richard Jackson." *Beaux Arts Magazine* (November 2008): 108–11.

"Richard Jackson–Bank Job." *Die Universität*, May 7, 2002.

"Richard Jackson in der BAWAG Foundation." *Diskurs*, May–June 2002, 39–41.

Rubenstein, Raphael. "Into a Liquid Medium." *Art in America* 8 (September 2005): 132–37.

Salazar, Gregorio. "Richard Jackson's Museum of the Mind." *Public News*, no. 327 (July 20, 1988): 12.

Sax, George. "*In Addition* Is an Amusing Tie-in to Artpark but Leaves Loose Ends." *Buffalo News*, July 9, 1985.

Schjeldahl, Peter. "L.A. Demystified!" *Village Voice*, June 3–9, 1981, cover, 32–37.

———. "Richard Jackson (Rosamund Felsen Gallery)." *Artforum* 17 (November 1978): 78–80.

———. "Spanning Time Zones." *Village Voice*, September 2–8, 1981, 70.

Schindler, Anna. "Fliegende Malmaschine." *Kunstzeitung*, no. 81 (May 2003): 20.

Schlesser, Thomas. "Dionysiac." *Art 21* (March–April 2005).

Schlocker, Edith. "Ironische Grenzüberschreitungen." *Tiroler Tageszeitung*, October 11, 2002.

Schütte, Christoph. "Pollock mit Jagdschein." *Frankfurter Allgemeine Zeitung*, November 9, 2005.

Schwerfel, Heinz Peter. "Biennale 99: Grosse Oper." *Art: Das Kunstmagazin*, no. 8 (August 1999): 12–23.

Schwerzmann, Jörg. "Farbige Bruchlandung." *Bolero*, May 2003, 48.

Sennewald, Jens E. "Nietzsche mit *Luftgitarre*." *Die Presse* (Vienna), February 17, 2005.

Sharp, Willoughby. "Outsiders: Baldessari, Jackson, O'Shea, Ruppersberg: Outdoor Sculpture Projects." *Arts Magazine* 45 (Summer 1970): 42–45.

Shere, Charles. "'Both Kinds' at U.C. Art Museum Views L.A. Art." *Oakland Tribune*, April 6, 1975.

Singerman, Howard. "Art in Los Angeles." *Artforum* 20 (March 1982): 75–77.

Sourgins, Christine. "Dionysos contre Dionysiac." *L'Humanité*, June 28, 2005.

Spiegler, Almuth, "Bären spritzen Farbe und wollen ins Bett gejagt werden." *Die Presse* (Vienna), May 8, 2002.

Stech, Fabian. "Sex and Drugs and Rock'n Roll." *Kunstforum International*, no. 176 (June–August 2005): 380–82.

Steinberger, Petra. "Krieg den Palästen, Friede den Surfern; Visionen einer stadt, die keine ist: Die Ausstellung 'L.A.-ex' in der Villa Stuck in München." *Süddeutsche Zeitung*, April 13, 2000.

Still, Gertrude Grace. "The Reversed Canvas." *Portfolio*, no. 3 (January–February 1981): 48–51.

Stoesz, David. "The Slutty Eye: Soft Target." *Seattle Weekly*, July 14, 2009.

Szakacs, Dennis. "The Circus Is in Town" (interview). *Mousse*, no. 25 (September 2010): 42–53.

Terbell, Melinda. "California: Los Angeles." *Arts Magazine* 45 (December 1970–January 1971): 49.

Thiele, Carmela. "Wanderung in die Tiefe." *Badische Neueste Nachrichten*, September 30, 2006.

Tholl, Egbert. "Der Mensch und seine Maschine—Richard Jacksons Malperformance 'De Nada/Circle Jerk,'" *Süddeutsche Zeitung*, May 30, 2000.

Thum, Alfred. "Art Joncton 1998 in Nizza." *Riviera-Côte d'Azur Zeitung*, no. 5 (May 1998).

Träger, Wolfgang. "Biennale Venedig: 'dAPERTutto.'" *Kunstforum International*, no. 147 (September–November 1999): 174–266.

Turner, Grady T. "Richard Jackson—David Zwirner." *Flash Art* 30 (November–December 1997): 112.

Van Proyen, Mark. "Grand Gesture." *Artweek* 14 (July 2, 1983): 4.

Vasquez, Mario. "Franz Ackermann and Richard Jackson at Otero-Plassart." *Super Mario's Art Blog*, February 2009. http://mariosartworld. blogspot.com/2009/02/franz-ackerman-and-richard-jackson-at.html.

Ventrocq, Marcia. "The Venice Biennale Reformed, Renewed, Redeemed." *Art in America* 87 (September 1999): 89.

Viladas, Pilar. "Art + Commerce." *New York Times*, October 8, 2006.

Vogel, Carol. "At Venice Biennale, Art Is Turning into an Interactive Sport." *New York Times*, June 14, 1999.

Walde, Gabriela. "Chance verpasst: Richard Jackson in Berlin." *Die Welt*, July 14, 2006.

———. "Wenn Wände fröhlich Farbe spucken." *Die Morgenpost*, May 19, 2006.

Wendorf, Alexandra. "Bodycheck: Ein neuer Blick auf die Skulptur abseits der Grand Tour überzeugt die 10. Triennale Kleinplastik in Fellbach." *Junge Kunst*, no. 72 (2007): 9–14.

Werneburg, Brigitte. "Rad schlagende Farbräusche." *Die Tageszeitung*, July 7, 2006.

Wesley, Eric. "Place Matters: Los Angeles Sculpture Today." *Art in America* 94 (November 2006).

Wortz, Melinda. "Art in Los Angeles: 17 Artists—16 Projects." *ARTnews* 80 (November 1981): 161–65.

———. "Richard Jackson Installation." *Artweek* 5 (June 1, 1974): 15–16.

"Die Zeit wird bei 1000 Uhren zur physischen Erfahrung." *Badisches Tagblatt*, September 28, 2006.

Zwerger, Isolde. "Aufbrechen in ein neues Universum." *Kurier*, October 11, 2002.

Videos

"Accidents in Abstract Painting." Recorded by Damon McCarthy. 2002. DVD, NTSC loop, 30:32 min.

"Airplane/Accidents." Documentation of installation, Hauser & Wirth, Zurich; recorded by Videocompany.ch. 2003. DVD loop, 00:32 min.

"Airplane Fan (Jeu de Paume)." Documentation of activation; recorded by Alberta Mayo. 2005. DVD, 2:27 min.

"Airplane Fan 3 (Vallois)." Documentation of activation; recorded by Alberta Mayo. 2005. DVD, 6:53 min.

"Bear Bottle." Documentation of activation in the artist's studio; recorded by Alberta Mayo. 2005. DVD, 10:00 min. (re-edited to 7:58). http://youtu. be/3U9LynfUEak

"Black Head (White Paint)." Documentation of work in the artist's studio; recorded by Alberta Mayo. 2005. DVD, 4:22 min.

"Blue Head (Orange Paint)." Documentation of work in the artist's studio; recorded by Alberta Mayo. DVD, 5:40 min.

"Bob's Duck (Vallois)." Documentation of activation; recorded by Alberta Mayo. 2006. DVD/PAL, 7:34 min.

"Confusion in the Vault." Documentation of activation at Hauser & Wirth, London; recorded by Alberta Mayo. 2005. DVD, 6:22 min.

"Cra-Z-Boy (Vallois)." Documentation of activation; recorded by Alberta Mayo. 2004. DVD, 19:14 min. http://www.myspace.com/manitobamuseum/videos/video/64133150

"dAPERTutto 48a." Venice Biennale. 1999. PAL, home video A.S.A.C. 60:00 min.

"Deer Beer." Documentation of activation at Hamburger Bahnhof, Germany; recorded by Alberta Mayo. 2008. DVD, 6:23 min. http://www.myspace.com/manitobamuseum/videos/deer-beer/44999231

"DEER BEER BEAR." Documentation of installation at Gallery Parisa Kind, Frankfurt am Main, Germany; recorded by Isabelle Fein. 2005. DVD, 42:15 min.

"DeNada/Circle Jerk." Documentation of *L.A.-ex Performances*, Marstall, Munich. May 24–25, 2000. VHS/NTSC, 1:33:50 min

"The Delivery Room." Documentation of installation at Yvon Lambert, New York; recorded by Alberta Mayo. 2007. DVD, 31:07 min. http://www.myspace.com/manitobamuseum/videos/the-delivery-room/56748725

"Dick's Buck Buck's Dick." Documentation of installation in the artist's studio; recorded by Alberta Mayo. 2004. DVD, 00:14 min.

"The Dining Room." Documentation of installation at Galerie Georges-Philippe & Nathalie Vallois, Paris; recorded by Alberta Mayo. 2007. DVD, 39:32 min. http://www.myspace.com/manitobamuseum/videos/richard-jackson-the-dining-room/56983289

"Dionysiac Documentary." Documentation of installation of exhibition at Centre Pompidou, Paris; recorded by Natsu Koushino. 2005. DVD, 41:33 min.

"Documenta '92 West Coast Artists, 1992." Produced and directed by Alexander von Wechmar, broadcast on German Public Television ARD and the European Cultural Channel, ARTE. 1992.

"Ducks in the Men's Room." Documentation of installation, Art Basel, Miami Beach; recorded by Alberta Mayo. 2006. DVD, 41:05 min.

"5 Clock Room." 1994. VHS/NTSC, 5:00 min.

"Five Heads." Compilation of footage documenting various activations in the artist's studio; recorded by Alberta Mayo. 2005. DVD, 27:01 min.

"46 N. Los Robles – A History of the Pasadena Art Museum." Peggy Phelps, Eudorah Moore, Larry Bell, Tom Terbell, Richard Jackson. Pacific Asia Museum and Mosaic Films, 2011. 42:59 min.

"Four Videos: Black Head (white paint), Red/Green and Black/White Bears, White Head (black paint), Bear Bottle." Documentation of activations in the artist's studio; recorded by Alberta Mayo. 2005. DVD, 37:44 min.

"Glass Baby in Zurich." Documentation of fabrication at Hauser & Wirth; recorded by Alberta Mayo. 2009. Mini DV, 7:07 min. http://www.myspace.com/manitobamuseum/videos/glass-baby-in-zurich/55015607

"Here and There: California Artists in Germany during the 1970s featuring Eleanor Antin, John Baldessari, Joe Goode, Richard Jackson, Nancy Reddin Kienholz, David Lamelas and Ed Ruscha." Produced and directed by Doris Berger. 2012. HD video, 29:51 min.

"The Laundry Room." Documentation of installation at Hauser & Wirth, Zurich; recorded by Alberta Mayo. 2009. DVD, 56:36 min. http://www.myspace.com/manitobamuseum/videos/video/57463048

"La-Z-Boy (Vallois)." Documentation of installation; recorded by Alberta Mayo. 2004. DVD, 27:54 min. http://www.myspace.com/manitobamuseum/videos/video/64134714

"The Little Girl's Room." Documentation of activation at David Kordansky Gallery, Culver City, CA; recorded by Alberta Mayo. 2011. DVD, 31:45 min. http://youtu.be/Gvb78Fx-7Z0

"The Kid's Table." Documentation of installation at Otero Plassart, Los Angeles; recorded by Alberta Mayo. 2009. DVD, 20:36 min. http://www.myspace.com/manitobamuseum/videos/video/53165704

"Kunstausstellung in Holderbank." bild, schnitt & ton, Christian Fricker, PAL. September 1998. c. 55 min.

"Paint Ball." Documentation by Mike Ballou of a performative event by Richard Jackson at David Zwirner Gallery, New York. September 9, 1997. 8mm film, b&w, sound, 15:00 min.

"Paint Bear, 2000." Galerie Senn, Vienna. 2000. Mini DV.

"Painting (Haswellediger & Co. and Foundation 20 21)." Documentation of installations; recorded by Alberta Mayo. 2004. DVD, 18:14 min.

"Pig Hunt." Documentation recorded by Videocompany.ch. 2000–01. Demo DVD PAL, 6:06 min.

"Pig Hunt:" http://youtu.be/YPkZxZvpksQ; "The Delivery Room:" http://youtu.be/hrMDGMoxi6o; "Big Pig:" http://youtu.be/PJCnPE4BS2c

"The Pink Empire, Hauser & Wirth London." Documentation of installation; recorded by Alberta Mayo. 2005. DVD, 41:46 min.

"Pink Head (Pink Paint), Artist's Proof." Activation of work in the artist's studio; recorded by Alberta Mayo. 2005. DVD, 7:00 min.

"Pinto Ball Part I." Richard Jackson in the studio. 1996. NTSC, 8:50 min. http://www.myspace.com/manitobamuseum/videos/video/103851896

"Red Head (for Marc & Susan)." Activation of work at Hauser & Wirth workshop; recorded by Alberta Mayo. 2005. DVD, 2:13 min.

"Red/Green and Black/White Bears." Activation of work in the artist's studio; recorded by Alberta Mayo. 2005. DVD, 15:00 min.

"Richard and Ron Skin a Buck." Artist and Ron LaGrande skin deer on Jackson Ranch; recorded by Alberta Mayo. 2010. DVD, 20:20 min. http://www.myspace.com/manitobamuseum/videos/richard-and-ron-skin-a-buck/106389887

"Richard Jackson Accidents in Abstract Painting." Video by Wyatt Sadler, Byron Price, Greg Fogel, Karl Klingebeil, Mujahid Abdulrahim Naotaka Hiro, and Rachel Khedoori. Edited by Wyatt Sadler. Edited footage from *Accidents in Abstract Painting* performance near the Rose Bowl in Pasadena. January 22, 2012. DVD, 6:23 min.

"Richard Jackson Installations 1970–1988." Interview by Deborah Velders, sound by A. C. Conrad. Houston: The Menil Collection, 1988. VHS, 39:46 min.

"Richard Jackson." Interview with the artist. Chicago: Museum of Contemporary Art Chicago, 1979. Three ¾-inch U-matic tapes. Part of the collection of videotapes of artists' interviews, titled "Museum of Contemporary Art interviews, 1979–1983," housed at Archives of American Art, Smithsonian Institution, Washington, D.C. (donated in 1986).

"Richard Jackson: Pig Hunt, The Delivery Room, Big Pig-Erich-Hauser-Preisträger 2010." Documentation of installation in Rottweil, Germany; recorded by Alberta Mayo. 2010. DVD, 12:00 min.

"Richard Jackson." Interview with the artist on behalf of opening of exhibition. London: Hauser & Wirth London; documented by Alberta Mayo. June 2, 2005. DVD, 29:23 min.

"Turkey Ball." Bursa, Turkey. 1995. VHS/NTSC, 9:16 min.

"Two mazes:" http://youtu.be/E5jJVmehhTI; "Big Ordeals:" http://youtu.be/9vHOkVqztqY

"Untitled Wall Painting (40 Canvases):" http://youtu.be/u5FcNFAHo2o

"Untitled (Wall Painting), Galerie Georges-Philippe & Nathalie Vallois." Documentation of installation; recorded by Alberta Mayo. 2004. DVD, 47:23 min.

"Untitled (Wall Painting), Hamburger Bahnhof." Documentation of installation; recorded by Alberta Mayo. 2006. DVD, 55:42 min.

"Upside Down Room." Documentation of the work in the artist's studio; video by Richard Jackson. 1996. VHS/NTSC, 1:52 min.

"Wall Painting:" http://youtu.be/qbLrkGx3BFY; "Big Ideas—1,000 Canvases:" http://youtu.be/mGxywSifg38; "Painting with Two Balls:" http://youtu.be/N6Ylssgcu5g;

"The War Room (Assembling the Globe)." Documentation of installation; recorded by Alberta Mayo. 2007. DVD, 24:07 min. http://www.myspace.com/manitobamuseum/videos/richard-jackson-the-war-room/56982625

"The War Room (Painting)." Documentation of activation; recorded by Alberta Mayo. 2007. DVD, 29:58 min. http://www.myspace.com/manitobamuseum/videos/video/60806913

"White Head (Black Paint)." Documentation of work in the artist's studio; recorded by Alberta Mayo. 2005. DVD, 8:38 min.

"Who's Afraid of Red, Yellow, and Blue?" Documentation of installation; recorded by Damon McCarthy. Los Angeles: Los Angeles County Museum of Art, 2000. 10:57 min. http://www.myspace.com/manitobamuseum/videos/video/56074308

"Who's Afraid of Red, Yellow, and Blue?" Interview with Jackson and documentation of installation at Kunstraum Innsbruck, Austria; recorded by dejavu Film, 2002. DVD NTSC, 23:42 min.

"Yellow Head (Purple Paint)." Documentation of work in the artist's studio; recorded by Alberta Mayo. 2005. DVD, 6:35 min.

CONTRIBUTORS

Michael Darling is the James W. Alsdorf Chief Curator at the Museum of Contemporary Art Chicago. From 2007 to 2010 he was curator of modern and contemporary art at the Seattle Art Museum, where he organized *Target Practice: Painting under Attack, 1949–78* (2009). Prior to joining the Seattle Art Museum, Darling was associate curator at the Museum of Contemporary Art, Los Angeles, where his exhibitions included *Sam Durant* (2002), *Painting in Tongues* (2006), and *Superflat* (2001).

Fatima Manalili is a curatorial associate at the Orange County Museum of Art. She received her MA in cultural studies from Claremont Graduate University and completed her BA in art history from the University of California, Los Angeles.

Hans Ulrich Obrist is codirector of exhibitions and programs and director of international projects at the Serpentine Gallery. He was curator of the Musée d'Art Moderne de la Ville de Paris from 2000 to 2006 and was curator of museum in progress, Vienna, from 1993 to 2000. His exhibitions include *Take Me, I'm Yours*, *Cities on the Move*, the first Berlin Biennale, Manifesta 1, *Uncertain States of America*, and the second Guangzhou Biennale. In 2007, Obrist co-curated *Il tempo del postino* with Philippe Parreno for the Manchester International Festival. He is the editor of the book series *Hans Ulrich Obrist: Interviews*.

Dennis Szakacs, curator of *Richard Jackson: Ain't Painting a Pain*, is director of the Orange County Museum of Art where he has overseen the development and presentation of over twenty-five exhibitions of modern and contemporary art since 2003, including the first retrospectives of Mary Heilmann, Peter Saul, and Jack Goldstein. He was deputy director of the New Museum in New York from 1996 to 2002 and managing director of MOMA P.S. 1 from 1994 to 1996. He began his career at the Southeastern Center for Contemporary Art in North Carolina, where he was editor of *Next Generation: Southern Black Aesthetic* (1990).

Jeffrey Weiss is curator of the Panza Collection at the Solomon R. Guggenheim Museum, New York. He was curator and head of modern and contemporary art at the National Gallery of Art in Washington, D.C. from 2000 to 2007 and director of the Dia Art Foundation, New York, from 2007 to 2008. Weiss has organized exhibitions on Jasper Johns, Pablo Picasso, and Mark Rothko. He was the editor of *Dan Flavin: New Light* (2006) and is currently at work on a complete catalog of the early object sculptures of Robert Morris and on *Material Uncanny*, a book concerning topics in minimalist and postminimalist art.

Philippe Van Cauteren is artistic director of S.M.A.K. Museum for Contemporary Art, Ghent, Belgium. Under his guidance the museum's exhibition program has concentrated on major monographical exhibitions, including Lois and Franziska Weinberger, Kendell Geers, Paul Mc Carthy, Mark Manders, Dara Birnbaum, Jorge Macchi, Nedko Solakov, and Richard Jackson. He previously worked as a freelance curator and publicist in Germany, Mexico, Chile, and Brazil. In 2002, he was curator of the first Biennal Ceara America in Fortaleza (Brazil). In 2012, he curated the exhibition TRACK (Ghent).

John C. Welchman is professor of art history at the University of California, San Diego. His books include *Art after Appropriation: Essays on Art in the 1990s* (2001), *The Dada and Surrealist Word-Image* (1989), and *Mike Kelley* (1999). Forthcoming publications include *XX to XXI: Essays on European Art, Essays on Contemporary European Art*, and a monograph on Mike Kelley. He has contributed essays to numerous museum exhibition catalogs.

Corcoran Gallery of Art, Washington, D.C.

Beth Rudin DeWoody

Friedrich Christian Flick Collection,
Hamburger Bahnhof

Galerie Georges-Philippe &
Nathalie Vallois

Galerie Lelong Zurich

Elizabeth A. Greenberg

Lenore and Bernard Greenberg

Barbara Haskell

Hauser & Wirth

Hauser & Wirth Collection, Switzerland

Moira and Fred Kamgar

Jeff Kerns Collection, Los Angeles

Nancy Reddin Kienholz

David Kordansky Gallery, Los Angeles, CA

Los Angeles County Museum of Art

The Menil Collection, Houston

Alison Terbell Nikitopoulos and
Dimitris E. Nikitopoulos

Private collections

Private collection, Paris

Private collection, Switzerland

Private collection, Zurich

Rennie Collection, Vancouver

Rubell Family Collection, Miami

Robert + Susy Rufli, Zurich-Switzerland

Robert and Shaké Sarkis

Manny and Jackie Silverman

Martin Seol Family Foundation

Kathryn Wortz, in memory of her parents
Ed and Melinda

CREDITS

All Richard Jackson works reproduced in this catalog are ©Richard Jackson and, unless otherwise noted, have been provided by the artist.

Photo by Stephan Altenburger Photography Zurich, Courtesy of the artist and Hauser & Wirth: cover, 2–3, 30, 38 (right), 43, 67, 177, 179, 185, 186, 195, 197, 205, 206–07, 213, 232–33, 235, 236–37, 239, 244, 245, 260–61; Photo by Alberta Mayo: frontispiece, 14, 20 (left), 21(left), 72, 77, 132, 148, 151, 224–25, 241 (top, middle), 289 (bottom, right), 290 (bottom), 304; Photo by SITE Photography, Vancouver, Courtesy of Rennie Collection, Vancouver: 11, 16–17, 27, 42, 51, 157, 188, 189, 247, 248–49, 256–57, 258, back cover; Image courtesy Rubell Family Collection, Miami: 12, 40 (right), 262–63, 264; ©Kienholz, Courtesy of L.A. Louver, Venice, CA: 15 (left); Digital Image ©2012 Museum Associates/ LACMA, Licensed by Art Resource, NY ©Kienholz, Courtesy of L.A. Louver, Venice, CA: 15 (right); Licensed by Harold Lloyd Entertainment, Inc.: 18 (left); Photo by Chris Bliss: 18 (right), 82–112, 114, 124 (left, right), 126–27 (bottom), 198, 199, 201; Digital Image ©2012 Museum Associates/ LACMA, Licensed by Art Resource, NY: 19, 139, 169, 274 (bottom); ©2012 Bruce Nauman / Artists Rights Society (ARS), New York: 20 (right); Archive Hauser & Wirth Collection, Switzerland: 21 (right), 47, 235; Image courtesy Rosamund Felsen Gallery, Santa Monica, Photo by Douglas M. Parker Studio: 23, 210, 282; Art ©Jasper Johns / Licensed by VAGA, New York, NY: 24, 125 (bottom); Photo by Paul Hester: 25, 136, 163, 180, 181, 190–91; Photography ©The Art Institute of Chicago: 26 (top); Licensed by Warner Bros. Entertainment Inc. All Rights Reserved: 28; Photo by Jason Wierzbicki ©2012 Artists Rights Society (ARS), New York / ADAGP, Paris / Succession Marcel Duchamp: 32 (top); Photo by Graydon Wood ©2012 Artists Rights Society (ARS), New York / ADAGP, Paris / Succession Marcel Duchamp: 32 (bottom); Photo by J. Geleyns/ www. roscan.be ©Royal Museum of Fine Arts of Belgium, Brussels: 35; Image courtesy Armory Center for the Arts, Pasadena, California, Photo by Joshua White: 37; Photo by Asghar Achakzai AFP/Getty Images: 38 (left); Photo by Rene-Gabriel Ojeda, Réunion des Musées Nationaux / Art Resource, NY: 39 (top); ©2012 Estate of Pablo Picasso / Artists Rights Society (ARS), New York: 39 (top, bottom); ©1963 Julian Wasser, Courtesy of Craig Krull Gallery, Santa Monica: 40 (left); ©2012 Alice Aycock: 44; ©2012 Artists Rights Society (ARS), New York/SABAM Brussels: 50; Photo by William Nettles, Los Angeles ©Jeff Koons: 53; Photo by Lee Stalsworth ©2012 Artists Rights Society (ARS), New York / ADAGP, Paris / Succession Marcel Duchamp: 58 (top); Photo by Charles Wilp; bpk, Berlin/Art Resource, NY ©2012 Artists Rights Society (ARS), New York / ADAGP, Paris: 59 (left); ©Alfons Schilling: 59 (right); Photo by Nathaniel Wilson, Seattle Art Museum: 60; Image courtesy Statens Museum for Kunst/National Gallery of Denmark, www.smk.dk: 61; Photo by

Grant Taylor: 62 (top), 278 (bottom right); Photo by Bernadette Mayer, Courtesy Acconci Studio ©2012 Vitto Acconci / Artists Rights Society (ARS), New York: 62 (bottom); Photo by Douglas M. Parker Studio: 68, 165, 235, 283 (bottom); Photo by Leonard Davidson: 73; ©Chris Burden, Courtesy of the artist and Gagosian Gallery: 74; © Estate of Mike Kelley: 76; Image courtesy Rosamund Felsen Gallery, Santa Monica: 116; Digital Image ©The Museum of Modern Art/ Licensed by SCALA / Art Resource, NY, Art © Robert Rauschenberg Foundation / Licensed by VAGA, New York, NY: 119; Image courtesy Hauser & Wirth, Photo by Al Payne: 120; Photo by Mitro Hood, Art ©Jasper Johns / Licensed by VAGA, New York, NY: 121; Photo by Robert McKeever, New York, Art ©Jasper Johns / Licensed by VAGA, New York, NY: 122; ©2012 Frank Stella / Artists Rights Society (ARS), New York: 126 (top); Photo by Robert Shankar, Courtesy Daniel Weinberg Gallery: 128; ©Hans Namuth Ltd.: 129; ©William Klein, Courtesy of Howard Greenberg Gallery, New York: 134 (left); Photo by Shunk-Kender ©Roy Lichenstein Foundation, ©2012 NIKI CHARITABLE ART FOUNDATION, All Rights Reserved: 134 (right); Courtesy Estate of Eugenia P. Butler: 135; Photo by Pablo Mason, Image courtesy The Museum of Contemporary Art, San Diego ©2012 Bruce Nauman / Artists Rights Society (ARS), New York:137; Image courtesy Jason Rhoades Archives: 142, 284 (left); Digital Image ©The Museum of Modern Art/ Licensed by SCALA / Art Resource, NY, Art © James Rosenquist / Licensed by VAGA, New York, NY: 144–45 (bottom); ©2012 The Pollock-Krasner Foundation / Artists Rights Society (ARS), New York: 146; Courtesy Galerie Georges-Philippe & Nathalie Vallois: 152; Photo by Gérard Blot/Hervé Lewandowski, Réunion des Musées Nationaux / Art Resource, NY: 155; ©Andrew Dadson, Image courtesy Andrew Dadson: 159; Photo by Stefan Rötheli, Zurich, Courtesy of Friedrich Christian Flick Collection, Hamburger Bahnhof: 162, 222, 223, 228, 229, 240–41;Photo by Frank J. Thomas, Courtesy of the Frank J. Thomas Archives: 167, 169, 183, 185, 204, 273 (bottom), 275; Photo by Jon Gordon: 172–73; Image courtesy Rennie Collection, Vancouver: 174, 175, 182, 218; Photo by Joshua White: 187, 234; Photo by Grant Mudford: 208, 284, 291; Photo by Rita Palanikumar, Courtesy of Friedrich Christian Flick Collection, Hamburger Bahnhof: 211; Photo by Eduardo Calderón: 214–15, 216–17; Photo by Christian Schwager, Winterhus, Courtesy of Friedrich Christian Flick Collection, Hamburger Bahnhof: 219, 220–21; Photo by Roman März, Berlin, Courtesy of Friedrich Christian Flick Collection, Hamburger Bahnhof: 230–231; Courtesy of Hauser & Wirth: 243; Photo by Fredrik Nilsen, Courtesy of David Kordansky Gallery, Los Angeles and Hauser & Wirth: 259, 267; Photo by Beverly Joel: 265; Image courtesy ADM-Works: 268–69; Photo by Jason Wilson: 273; Image courtesy San Francisco Museum of Modern Art Archives: 277 (bottom, right);

Photo by Niklaus Stauss, Zurich: 280; Photo by Rolf Schroeter. ©Pro Litteris, 8033 Zurich: 284 (right); Photo by Jason Rhoades: 287 (left).

Errors or omissions in credit citations or failure to obtain permission if required by copyright law have been either unavoidable or unintentional. The authors and publishers welcome any information that would allow them to correct future reprints.

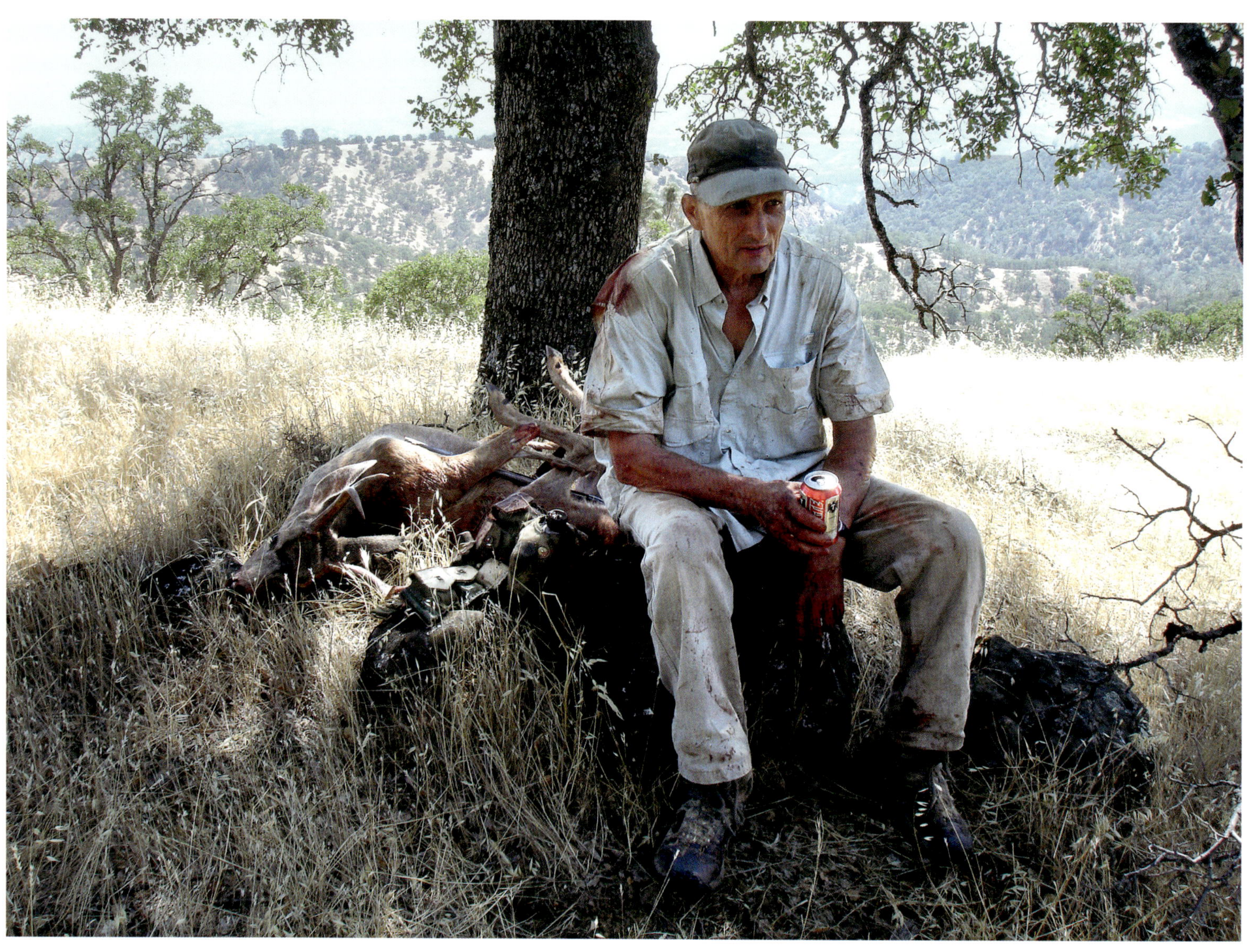

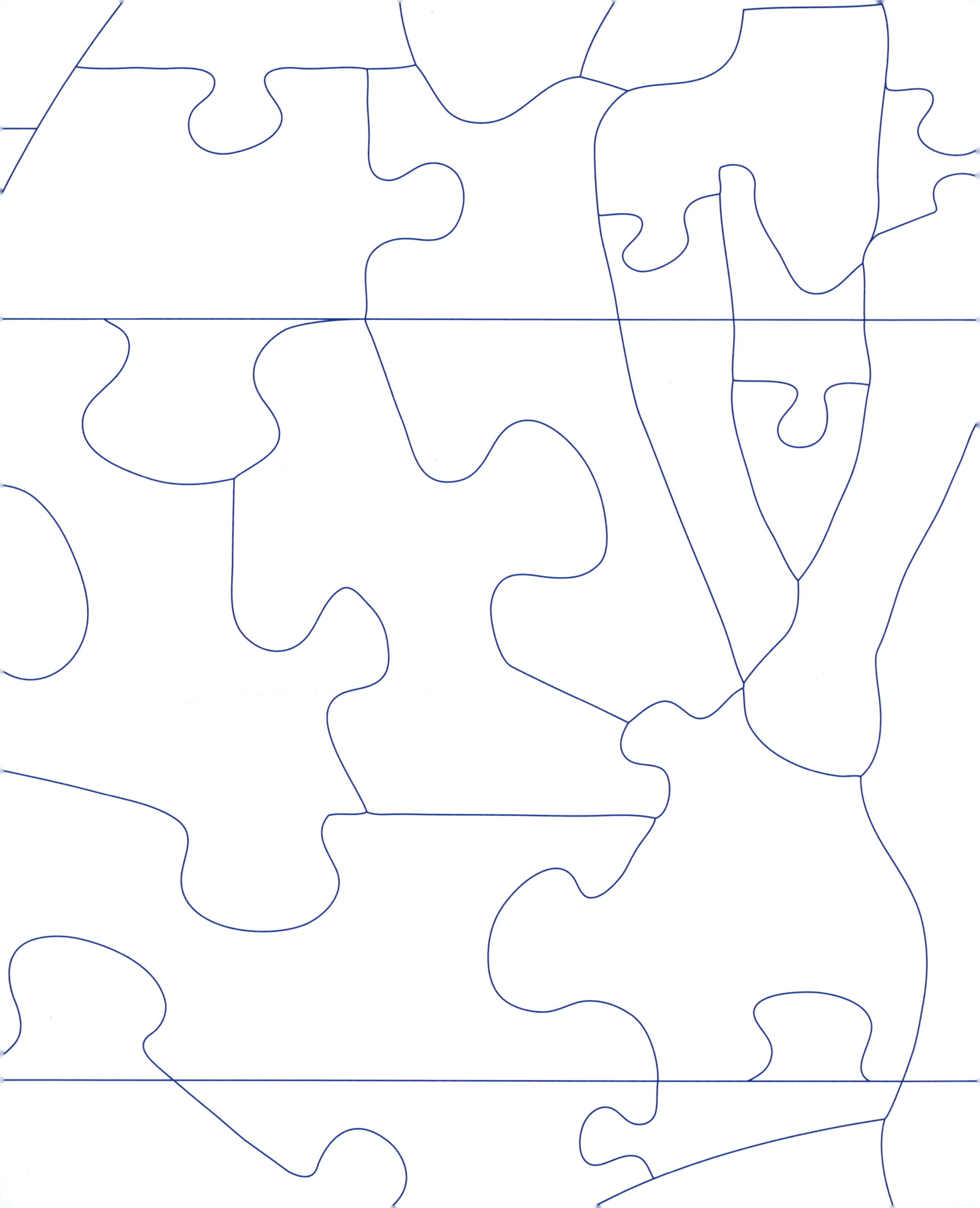